Lecture Notes in Artificial Intelligence 5239

Edited by R. Goebel, J. Siekmann, and W. Wahlster

Subseries of Lecture Notes in Computer Science

Klaus-Dieter Althoff   Ralph Bergmann
Mirjam Minor   Alexandre Hanft (Eds.)

Advances in
Case-Based Reasoning

9th European Conference, ECCBR 2008
Trier, Germany, September 1-4, 2008
Proceedings

 Springer

Series Editors

Randy Goebel, University of Alberta, Edmonton, Canada
Jörg Siekmann, University of Saarland, Saarbrücken, Germany
Wolfgang Wahlster, DFKI and University of Saarland, Saarbrücken, Germany

Volume Editors

Klaus-Dieter Althoff
Mirjam Minor
University of Hildesheim
Institute of Computer Science
31141 Hildesheim, Germany
E-mail: {althoff, minor}@iis.uni-hildesheim.de

Ralph Bergmann
Alexandre Hanft
University of Trier
Department of Business Information Systems II 54286 Trier, Germany
E-mail: {bergmann, hanft}@uni-trier.de

Library of Congress Control Number: Applied for

CR Subject Classification (1998): I.2, J.4, J.1, J.3, F.4.1

LNCS Sublibrary: SL 7 – Artificial Intelligence

ISSN   0302-9743
ISBN-10   3-540-85501-7 Springer Berlin Heidelberg New York
ISBN-13   978-3-540-85501-9 Springer Berlin Heidelberg New York

Springer is a part of Springer Science+Business Media

springer.com

© Springer-Verlag Berlin Heidelberg 2008
Printed in Germany

Typesetting: Camera-ready by author, data conversion by Scientific Publishing Services, Chennai, India
Printed on acid-free paper   SPIN: 12514021   06/3180   5 4 3 2 1 0

Preface

This volume contains the papers presented at the 9th European Conference on Case-Based Reasoning (ECCBR 2008).

Case-based reasoning (CBR) is an artificial intelligence approach whereby new problems are solved by remembering, adapting and reusing solutions to a previously solved, similar problem. The collection of previously solved problems and their associated solutions is stored in the case base. New or adapted solutions are learned and updated in the case base as needed.

In remembrance of the First European Workshop on Case-Based Reasoning, which took place 15 years ago at the European Academy Otzenhausen, not far from Trier, this year's conference was especially devoted to the past, present, and future of case-based reasoning.

ECCBR and the International Conference on Case-Based Reasoning (IC-CBR) alternate every year. ECCBR 2008 followed a series of seven successful European workshops previously held in Otzenhausen, Germany (1993), Chantilly, France (1994), Lausanne, Switzerland (1996), Dublin, Ireland (1998), and Trento, Italy (2000), and three European conferences in Aberdeen, UK (2002), Madrid, Spain (2004), and Ölüdeniz/Fethiye, Turkey (2006). The International Conferences on Case-Based Reasoning (ICCBR) were previously held in Sesimbra, Portugal (1995), Providence, Rhode Island, USA (1997), Seeon, Germany (1999), Vancouver, Canada (2001), Trondheim, Norway (2003), Chicago, USA (2005), and Belfast, Northern Ireland (2007). These meetings have a history of attracting first-class European and international researchers and practitioners. The proceedings of the ECCBR and ICCBR conferences are published by Springer in their LNAI series.

The ECCBR 2008 conference was held at the University of Trier, Germany and offered a number of new program elements. This included the first *Computer Cooking Contest* (CCC), a CBR system competition demonstrating the application of case retrieval, adaptation, and combination methods for cooking recipes. CCC was co-organized by Mirjam Minor (University of Trier), Armin Stahl (DFKI), and Ralph Traphöner (empolis), and a professional cook was responsible for evaluating the computer generated recipes.

Furthermore, ECCBR 2008 focused on two special areas with high relevance to CBR: *The Role of CBR in the Future Internet* (chaired by Enric Plaza) and *CBR in Healthcare* (chaired by Isabelle Bichindaritz and Stefania Montani). When submitting a paper, the authors could relate their paper to one of these areas. In each focus area, the area chairs selected three papers for oral presentation.

The workshops, which took place on the first day of the conference, covered various topics of specific interest to the CBR community such as Knowledge Discovery, Similarity, Context-Awareness, Uncertainty, Health Sciences, and the

Computer Cooking Contest Workshop. The second day was the traditional Industry Day, giving insight into fielded CBR applications. It also included the Poster Session with its lively discussions. The remaining two days were devoted to invited talks and technical presentations on both theoretical and applied research in CBR as well as to the presentations related to the two special areas.

A total of 71 papers were submitted by authors from 19 different countries, not only from Europe, but also from America, Asia, and Africa. The accepted 39 papers (18 oral presentations and 21 poster presentations) were chosen based on a thorough and highly selective review process. Each paper was reviewed and discussed by at least three Program Committee members and revised according to their comments. We believe that the papers in this volume give a representative snapshot of current research and contribute to both theoretical and applied aspects of CBR research. The proceedings have been organized into three sections: invited talks (3 papers), research papers (34), and application papers (5).

The chairs would like to thank the invited speakers Isabelle Bichindaritz, Enric Plaza, Pádraig Cunningham, and Barry Smyth for their contribution to the success of this conference. While the talk of Cunningham and Smyth was explicitly devoted to the past of ECCBR, the talks of Bichindaritz and Plaza represented the respective focus areas they were chairing. Particular thanks go to the Program Committee and additional reviewers for their efforts and hard work during the reviewing and selection process.

We are also grateful for the work of the Industry Chair Ralph Traphöner, the Workshops Coordinator Martin Schaaf as well as the chairs of the respective workshops and their various committee members for their preparations for Industry Day and the workshops. We thank all the authors who submitted papers to the conference and gratefully acknowledge the generous support of the sponsors of ECCBR 2008 and their, partly long-time, sponsorship of ECCBR and ICCBR.

This volume has been produced using the EasyChair system[1]. We would like to express our gratitude to its author Andrei Voronkov. Finally, we thank Springer for its continuing support in publishing this series of conference proceedings.

June 2008

Klaus-Dieter Althoff
Ralph Bergmann
Mirjam Minor
Alexandre Hanft

---

[1] http://www.easychair.org

Conference Organization

Program Chairs

Klaus-Dieter Althoff   University of Hildesheim, Germany
Ralph Bergmann   University of Trier, Germany

Local Organization

Mirjam Minor   University of Trier, Germany

Proceedings and Conference Management System

Alexandre Hanft   University of Hildesheim, Germany

Industry Day Coordination

Ralph Traphöner   empolis GmbH, Germany

Workshop Coordination

Martin Schaaf   University of Hildesheim, Germany

Program Committee

Agnar Aamodt	Norwegian University of Science and Technology, Norway
David W. Aha	Naval Research Laboratory, USA
Esma Aimeur	University of Montreal, Canada
Klaus-Dieter Althoff	University of Hildesheim, Germany
Josep-Lluís Arcos	IIIA-CSIC, Spain
Kevin Ashley	University of Pittsburgh, USA
Brigitte Bartsch-Spörl	BSR Consulting, Germany
Ralph Bergmann	University of Trier, Germany
Isabelle Bichindaritz	University of Washington, USA
Enrico Blanzieri	University of Trento, Italy
Derek Bridge	University College Cork, Ireland
Robin Burke	DePaul University, USA
Hans-Dieter Burkhard	Humboldt University Berlin, Germany
William Cheetham	General Electric Co. NY, USA

VIII Organization

Susan Craw	Robert Gordon University, UK
Pádraig Cunningham	Trinity College Dublin, Ireland
Belén Díaz-Agudo	Univ. Complutense de Madrid, Spain
Peter Funk	Malardalens University, Sweden
Ashok Goel	Georgia Institute of Technology, USA
Andrew Golding	Lycos Inc., USA
Pedro A. González-Calero	Univ. Complutense de Madrid, Spain
Mehmet Göker	PricewaterhouseCoopers, USA
Eyke Hüllermeier	University of Marburg, Germany
Igor Jurisica	Ontario Cancer Institute, Canada
David Leake	Indiana University, USA
Ramon López de Mántaras	IIIA-CSIC, Spain
Michel Manago	empolis, France
Cindy Marling	Ohio University, USA
Lorraine McGinty	University College Dublin, Ireland
David McSherry	University of Ulster, UK
Erica Melis	Saarland University, Germany
Mirjam Minor	University of Trier, Germany
Stefania Montani	University of Eastern Piedmont, Italy
Héctor Muñoz-Avila	Lehigh University, USA
David Patterson	University of Ulster, UK
Petra Perner	Institute of Computer Vision and Applied CS, Germany
Enric Plaza	IIIA-CSIC, Spain
Luigi Portinale	University of Eastern Piedmont, Italy
Lisa S. Purvis	Xerox Corporation, NY, USA
Francesco Ricci	ITC-irst, Italy
Michael M. Richter	University of Calgary, Canada
Thomas Roth-Berghofer	DFKI, Germany
Martin Schaaf	University of Hildesheim, Germany
Rainer Schmidt	University of Rostock, Germany
Barry Smyth	University College Dublin, Ireland
Raja Sooriamurthi	Indiana University, USA
Armin Stahl	DFKI Germany
Jerzy Surma	Warsaw School of Economics, Poland
Henry Tirri	University of Helsinki, Finland
Brigitte Trousse	INRIA Sophia Antipolis, France
Ian Watson	University of Auckland, New Zealand
Rosina Weber	Drexel University, USA
Stefan Wess	empolis, Germany
David C. Wilson	University of North Carolina, Charlotte, USA
Nirmalie Wiratunga	Robert Gordon University, UK
Qiang Yang	University of Science and Technology, Hong Kong

Additional Reviewers

Ibrahim Adeyanju	Eva Armengol	Riccardo Bellazzi
Ralf Berger	Steven Bogaerts	Ann Bui
Edwin Costello	Sarah Jane Delany	Sidath Gunawardena
Marco A. Gómez-Martín	Manfred Hild	Chad Hogg
Stephen Lee-Urban	Giorgio Leonardi	Gabriela Lindemann
Craig MacDonald	Diego Magro	Tariq Mahmood
Erik Olsson	Amandine Orecchioni	Belén Prados Suárez
Juan A. Recio-García	Niall Rooney	Raquel Ros
Antonio A. Sánchez-Ruiz	Ning Xiong	
Bassant Mohamed Aly	El Bagoury	

Conference Sponsors

empolis GmbH, Germany
DFKI GmbH, Germany
Daimler AG, Germany

Table of Contents

Invited Talks

Research Papers

Application Papers

Case-Based Reasoning in the Health Sciences: Why It Matters for the Health Sciences and for CBR

Isabelle Bichindaritz

University of Washington, Tacoma, Institute of Technology
1900 Commerce Street, Box 358426,
Tacoma, WA 98402, USA
ibichind@u.washington.edu

Abstract. Biomedical domains have been an application domain of choice for artificial intelligence (AI) since its pioneering years in expert systems. Some simple explanations to this phenomenon are the intellectual complexity presented by this domain, as well as the dominant industry market share of healthcare. Following in AI's tracks, case-based reasoning (CBR) has been abundantly applied to the health sciences domain and has produced an excellent as well as varied set of publications, which has fostered CBR research innovation to answer some of the research issues associated with this intricate domain. Some notable examples are synergies with other AI methodologies, and in particular with ontologies [8] and with data mining, the study of the temporal dimension in CBR, the processing of multimedia cases, and novel tasks for CBR such as parameter setting. However CBR has a major endeavor to take on in the health sciences: how to position itself with regard to statistics for studying data? Some claim that CBR proposes an alternative viewpoint on the concept of evidence in biomedicine; others that CBR and statistics complement one another in this domain. In any case, an interesting question to study is whether CBR could become one day as fundamental to the health sciences as statistics is today? This question in particular broadens the health sciences challenge to a universal scope.

1 Introduction

Case-based reasoning (CBR) in the health sciences (CBR-HS) has developed as a specialized area within case-based reasoning research and applications. This paper presents a survey of the accomplishments of CBR in the health sciences for CBR, more generally AI, and for the health sciences.

CBR is a valued knowledge management and reasoning methodology in biomedical domains because it founds its recommendations on contextual knowledge by capturing unique clinical experience. This type of knowledge is much more detailed and to the point for solving clinical problems, and allows to account for some of the complexity inherent to working in clinical domains [31]. As a matter of fact, cases play an essential role in medical training and medical expertise acquisition, and a comprehensive set of CBR systems in medicine now has been built and evaluated successfully [31]. Their usefulness in clinical settings has been shown for decision-support, explanation, and quality control [31]. If the value of contextual, instance-based knowledge,

K.-D. Althoff et al. (Eds.): ECCBR 2008, LNAI 5239, pp. 1–17, 2008.

is not in question, however main accomplishments remain to be reached, for which practical endeavors are underway to validate the methodology in health domains.

The choice of health sciences domains to show case CBR usefulness in and impact on science and society is neither novel nor fortuitous. These domains have been a major application area for artificial intelligence (AI) from its beginnings. Moreover the healthcare domain is one of the leading industrial domains in which computer science is applied. Its importance in computer science research is second to none. This preeminence of health sciences domains for computer science, artificial intelligence, and CBR is discussed in the second section. Artificial intelligence has researched applications in the health sciences from its inception. The third section reviews progress in artificial intelligence in biology and medicine, and explains its contributions to the field of AI as well as to the health sciences. Similarly, CBR has invested itself in applications to the health sciences from its pioneering years. The fourth section reviews progress in case-based reasoning in biology and medicine, and highlights its contributions to the field of CBR as well as to the health sciences. The following sections highlight main research topics in CBR in the health sciences, such as complementarity and synergies with other artificial intelligence methodologies, and complementarity and synergies with statistics. They are followed by the conclusion.

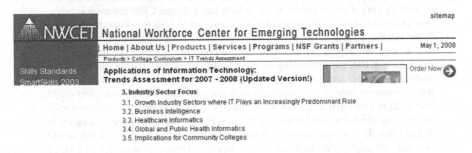

Fig. 1. Forecasts for the evolution of computer science to be "more and more infused by application areas"

2 Health Sciences Domains

Health Sciences domains encompass healthcare and health research, with in particular human biology, genetics, proteomics, and phylogenetics aspects. In terms of computer science, forecasts for the development of the profession confirm a general trend to be "more and more infused by application areas". The emblematic application infused areas are health informatics and bioinformatics. For example the National Workforce Center for Emerging Technologies (NWCET) lists among such application areas healthcare informatics and global and public health informatics (see Fig. 1). The predominant role plaid by the health sciences sectors is confirmed by statistics from the Department of Labor, which predicts among the highest increases in wage and salary employment growth between 2006 and 2016 the offices of healthcare practitioners (close 2nd overall rank), private hospitals (6th overall rank), residential care facilities (9th overall), and home healthcare services (12th overall). By comparison, amusement, gambling, and recreational services rank only 13th. The strength of health related industries answers a need for increased access to healthcare. This social need also fosters research funding and endeavors. It is notable that the Science Citation Index (Institute for Scientific Information – ISI – Web of Knowledge) lists among computer science a specialty called "Computer science, Interdisciplinary applications". Moreover this area of computer science ranks the highest within the computer science discipline in terms of number of articles produced as well as in terms of total cites (see Fig. 2). These figures confirm the other data pointing toward the importance of applications in computer science. Among the journals within this category, many relate to bioinformatics or medical informatics journals. It is also notable that some health informatics or bioinformatics journals are also classified in other areas of computer science. In addition, the most cited new papers in computer science are frequently bioinformatics papers. For example, all the papers referenced as "new hot papers" in computer science in 2008 until June included have been bioinformatics papers.

Rank	Category (linked to category information)	Total Cites	Median Impact Factor	Aggregate Impact Factor	Aggregate Immediacy Index	Aggregate Cited Half-Life	# Journals	Articles
1	COMPUTER SCIENCE, ARTIFICIAL INTELLIGENCE	110705	0.930	1.511	0.206	7.0	85	5298
2	COMPUTER SCIENCE, CYBERNETICS	12031	0.859	0.835	0.129	7.1	18	894
3	COMPUTER SCIENCE, HARDWARE & ARCHITECTURE	52929	0.694	0.909	0.121	8.7	44	3245
4	COMPUTER SCIENCE, INFORMATION SYSTEMS	78203	0.830	1.177	0.178	6.8	87	6379
5	COMPUTER SCIENCE, INTERDISCIPLINARY APPLICATIONS	121793	0.862	1.609	0.243	6.0	87	7531
6	COMPUTER SCIENCE, SOFTWARE ENGINEERING	63797	0.782	0.874	0.120	8.2	82	4936
7	COMPUTER SCIENCE, THEORY & METHODS	76451	0.840	0.952	0.151	8.5	75	4372

Fig. 2. Interdisciplinary applications of computer science represent the most cited literature within computer science in the Journal Citation Reports in the ISI Web of Knowledge

Therefore it is understandable that health sciences applications of computer science represent a major specialization area in computer science, based on complex interdisciplinary research.

3 Artificial Intelligence in the Health Sciences

The health sciences have motivated an abundance of applied AI research both to take on the challenge of its complexity – similarly to the chess playing challenge – and for its particular influential role on society.

3.1 History

Since the early days of artificial intelligence, health sciences have been a favorite application area. First were developed decision-support systems such as INTERNIST in 1970 [41] and MYCIN [54] in 1976. INTERNIST is classified as a rule-based expert system focused on the diagnosis of complex diseases [41]. It has been commercialized later on as Quick Medical Reference (QMR) to support internists' diagnosis. MYCIN was also a rule-based expert system, but applied to the diagnosis and treatment of blood infections [54]. Created by Ted Shortliffe, this knowledge-based system mapped symptoms to diseases, led to clinical evaluation of its effectiveness, and to the development of an expert system shell EMYCIN. The evolution of artificial intelligence engendered new generations of artificial intelligence systems in medicine, expanding the range of AI methodologies in biomedical informatics, such as implementation of clinical practice guidelines in expert systems, data mining to establish trends and associations between symptoms, genetic information, and diagnoses, and medical image interpretation, to name a few. Researchers stressed the value of early systems for testing artificial intelligence methodologies.

3.2 Impact on Artificial Intelligence

These systems provided a very valuable feedback to AI researchers regarding the validity of their approach, as reported by Ted Shortliffe: "Artificial intelligence, or AI, is largely an experimental science—at least as much progress has been made by building and analyzing programs as by examining theoretical questions. MYCIN is one of several well-known programs that embody some intelligence and provide data on the extent to which intelligent behavior can be programmed. ... We believe that the whole field of AI will benefit from such attempts to take a detailed retrospective look at experiments, for in this way the scientific foundations of the field will gradually be defined." [49] When evaluating the advances of artificial intelligence systems in medicine, several levels of evaluation can be proposed, which can be roughly differentiated as computer system, user satisfaction, process variables, and domain outcomes levels:

1. The computer system level is how effectively the program is performing its task. Measures include diagnosis accuracy for a decision-support system providing diagnostic recommendations, or precision and recall in an intelligent retrieval system for medical information. Measures can be integrated in the system programming.
2. The user satisfaction level involves assessing the user satisfaction with the system – the user can be either the physician or the patient, whether the patient uses the system or not. A questionnaire can be administered to the patients or physicians.
3. The process variables level works by measuring some variable connected in the clinical process, such as confidence in decision, pattern of care, adherence to protocol, cost of care, and adverse effects [56].
4. The domain outcomes level aims at measuring clinical outcomes of the system. This requires conducting a randomized clinical trial to measure improvements in patient health or quality of life. For example one such measure may involve the number of complications, or the cost of care, or even the survival duration.

3.3 Impact on Health Sciences

Notably, critics of artificial intelligence expressed concerns that the field had not been able to demonstrate actual clinical outcomes. AI researchers mostly showed satisfaction with computer system level evaluation results, some user satisfaction level results and little process variables results. One major step was to include AI systems in clinical practice. AI systems in use today are numerous. One of the first one was NéoGanesh, developed to regulate the automatic ventilation system in the Intensive

Care Unit (ICU), in use since 1995 [22]. Another example is Dxplain, a general expert system for the medical field, associating 4,500 clinical findings, including laboratory test results, with more than 2,000 diseases [4]. Some of these systems are available for routine purchase in medical supplies catalogues.

Even though clinical outcomes have been rare, there have been several studies showing the effectiveness of these systems in clinical practice in terms of improving the quality of care, the safety, and the efficiency [56]. One such example is a 1998 computer-based clinical reminder system showing evidence that a particular clinical act – discussing advance directives with a patient – was significantly better performed with the clinical reminders under evaluation than without them [20]. More generally prescription decision-support systems (PDSS) and clinical reminder systems, often based on clinical guidelines implementation, have consistently shown clinical outcomes in several studies [16]. However clinical outcomes are rarely measured, while process variables and user satisfaction are often measured. Obviously computer system intrinsic measures are always reported.

The success of AI in the health sciences is explained by the shift of focus from centering the system success on the computational performance versus the application domain performance. Indeed successful systems provide a practical solution to a specific healthcare or health research problem. The systems presenting the largest impact, such as the clinical reminders, do not have to represent a challenging AI difficulty, but they have to fit perfectly well the clinical domain in which they are embedded – they are application domain driven – versus AI driven.

4 Case-Based Reasoning in the Health Sciences

Case-based reasoning (CBR) [1] in the health sciences is a particularly active area of research, as attest in particular several recent workshops conducted at ICCBR-03, ECCBR-04, ICCBR-05, ECCBR-06, and ICCBR-07. Additionally journals special issues on CBR in the Health Sciences have been published in Artificial Intelligence in Medicine, Computational Intelligence, and Applied Intelligence. As the health sector is continuing to expand due to population lifespan increase, advanced decision-support systems become more and more sought after in the evolution of medicine towards a more standardized and computerized science. CBR systems are notable examples of decision-support systems as they base their recommendations on the subset of the most similar or most reusable experiences previously encountered. It is thus a method of choice for such experimental sciences as the natural and life sciences and in particular for biology and medicine.

4.1 History

Early CBR systems in biomedicine have been Kolodner & Kolodner (1987) [34], Bareiss & Porter (1987) [4], Koton (1988) [35], and Turner (1989) [58]. They focused on diagnosis and were not yet systems developed in clinical settings. In that sense, CBR followed the early goals of AI to represent experts reasoning. All the first systems developed in CBR in the health sciences have been devoted to modeling medical expertise along the main medical tasks: diagnosis, treatment planning, and follow-up.

The main pioneering systems in CBR in the health sciences, with their application domain and type of task, are, ranked by date:

- SHRINK, psychiatry, diagnosis (1987) [34];
- PROTOS, audiology disorders, diagnosis (1987) [3];
- CASEY, heart failure, diagnosis (1988) [35];
- MEDIC, dyspnoea, diagnosis (1988) [58];
- ALEXIA, hypertension, assessment tests planning (1992) [14];
- ICONS, intensive care, antibiotics therapy (1993) [28];
- BOLERO, pneumonia, diagnosis (1993) [36];
- FLORENCE, health care planning (1993) [15];
- MNAOMIA, psychiatry, diagnosis, treatment planning, clinical research assistance (1994) [6];
- ROENTGEN, oncology, radiation therapy (1994) [5];
- MACRAD, image analysis (1994) [37].

Later, CBR has been applied to a variety of tasks, among which we can cite diagnosis (and more generally classification tasks) (SCINA 1997 [30], CARE PARTNER 1998 [14], AUGUSTE 2001 [39]), treatment planning (and similar tasks such as assessment tests planning) (CARE PARTNER 1998 [14], CAMP 1999 [38], AUGUSTE 2001 [39], T-IDDM 2000 [44]), image analysis (Imagecreek 1996 [29]), long-term follow-up [14], quality control, tutoring (CADI 1996 [26]), and research assistance (in conjunction with data mining). We count today more than 300 papers published in specialized CBR conferences and workshops, AI journals, books, but also medical informatics and bioinformatics conferences and journals. We also note a regular increase in the number of papers published in CBR in biomedicine. Several reviews on CBR in medicine have been published. We can list Schmidt et al. (2001) [50], Nilsson & Sollenborn (2004) [46], Holt et al. [36], Bichindaritz (2006) [9], and Bichindaritz and Marling (2006) [13].

4.2 Impact on CBR

CBR has found in biomedicine one if its most fruitful application areas, but also one of its most complex ones. The main reason for these achievements and interest from the biomedical community is that case-based reasoning capitalizes on the reuse of existing cases, or experiences. These abound in biology and medicine, since they belong to the family of descriptive experimental sciences, where knowledge stems from the study of natural phenomena, patient problem situations, or other living beings and their sets of problems. In particular, the important variability in the natural and life sciences plays an active role in fostering the development of case-based approaches in these sciences where complete, causal models fully explaining occurring phenomena are not available. One consequence of this fact is that biomedicine is a domain where expertise beyond the novice level comes from learning by solving real and/or practice cases, which is precisely what case-based reasoning is accomplishing. Prototypical models are often more adapted to the description of biomedical knowledge [14] than other types of models, which also argues in favor of case-based reasoning.

Among the complexities of biomedicine, we can list the high-dimensionality of cases, as is noted in particular in bioinformatics [17, 18, 21], but also in long-term follow-up [12]. Multimedia case representation and the development of suitable CBR methods for handling these represent another complexity, for example in medical image interpretation [24, 29, 32, 49], in sensor data interpretation [27], or in time series case features [49]. Other factors are the co-occurrence of several diseases, not clearly bounded diagnostic categories, the need to mine for features that can be abstracted from time series representing temporal history [49], sensor signals [27], or other continuous input data, and the use of data mining techniques in addition to case-based reasoning [11, 32]. Other aspects deal with specificity of the medical domain, such as dealing with safety critical constraints, assisting the Elderly and the Disabled [19], or the usefulness of explanations [23].

Recently, a major trend seems to be the widening of applications of CBR beyond the traditional diagnosis, treatment, or quality control types toward the *applicability of CBR to novel reasoning tasks*. An interesting example of system studies how cases can represent non-compliance instances of clinical guidelines, and eventually lead to expert refinement of these guidelines [43]. Another paper demonstrates the usefulness of CBR to configure parameters for the task of temporal abstraction [53] in haemodyalisis [42]. All these papers open new fields of application for CBR, which will foster the spread of CBR in biomedical domains.

CBR-HS papers address all aspects of the CBR methodology, and attempt to advance basic research in CBR. For example, some research addresses retrieval questions [10], while others address adaptation [2, 59]. Bichindaritz [10] shows how memory organization for CBR can bridge the gap between CBR and information retrieval systems. The article surveys the different memory organizations implemented in CBR systems, and the different approaches used by these systems to tackle the problem of efficient reasoning with large case bases. The author then proposes a memory organization to support case-based retrieval similar to the memory organization of information retrieval systems and particularly Internet search engines. This memory organization is based on an inverted index mapping case features with the cases in memory. D'Aquin et al. provide principles and examples of adaptation knowledge acquisition in the context of their KASIMIR system for breast cancer decision support [2]. These authors have identified some key adaptation patterns, such as adaptation of an inapplicable decision, and adaptation based on the consequences of a decision. In addition, KASIMIR has also acquired retrieval knowledge to take into account missing data and the threshold effect. The paper broadens the discussion by proposing a sketch of a methodology for adaptation knowledge acquisition from experts.

Several authors have focused on the importance of prototype-based knowledge representation in CBR-HS [7, 52], which encourages further research in this direction.

CBR-HS main impact on CBR can be further developed as the multimodal reasoning and synergies aspects with other AI methodologies. Since AI in the health sciences has been much more studied than CBR-HS, CBR-HS very often relies on complementarity with AI to be fully applicable to this domain. This aspect is therefore developed in section 5.

4.3 Impact on the Health Sciences

Several CBR-HS systems have been tested successfully in clinical settings. However, none has been placed in routine use in a clinical setting. It is important to note that this might not be the goal of such systems to be placed in permanent clinical use. For example bioinformatics systems often aim at analyzing data, just like data mining systems, which is more of value to biomedical researchers. There is often a misperception that only clinical applications are pertinent to biomedical domains. Biomedical research support lies also within the range of activities of AI or CBR in the health sciences. The fate of clinical CBR systems is often more within the realm of the pilot testing or clinical trial than the daily clinical use, in part because its researchers are generally not medical doctors. It is notable that most AI system in clinical use have been developed by medical doctors.

However just like for AI in the health sciences, the shift from CBR driven systems to application domain driven systems is currently occurring. Several systems under development aim at being placed in routine clinical use [43].

One of the most interesting impacts of CBR-HS on the health sciences lies in the place CBR has to find with regard to statistics, which is the data analysis and processing method of reference in experimental sciences. This is a major trend in CBR-HS research, to which section 6 is dedicated.

5 CBR Versus AI in the Health Sciences

CBR systems often resort to other AI methodologies either to complement CBR, or to partake in larger AI systems. The main forms encountered relate to data mining, although other multimodal reasoning schemes are also frequent.

5.1 Synergies with Data Mining and Knowledge Discovery

These synergies involve either proposing data mining as a separate process in preparation for CBR, for example as pre-processing for feature mining from time series [27] or for prototype mining [11], or during the CBR reasoning cycle, such as for retrieval of cases involving temporal features [45] or for memory organization [32].

In the *decoupled synergy between knowledge discovery, data mining, and CBR*, Funk and Xiong present a case-based decision-support system for diagnosing stress related disorders [27]. This system deals with signal measurements such as breathing and heart rate expressed as physiological time series. The main components of the system are a signal-classifier and a pattern identifier. HR3Modul, the signal-classifier, uses a feature mining technique called wavelet extraction to learn features from the continuous signals. Being a case-based reasoning system, HR3Modul classifies the signals based on retrieving similar patterns to determine whether a patient may be suffering from a stress related disorder as well as the nature of the disorder [27]. Advancing this research, Funk and Xiong [27] argue that medical CBR systems incorporating time series data and patterns of events are fertile ground for knowledge discovery. While CBR systems have traditionally learned from newly acquired individual cases, case bases as a whole are infrequently mined to discover more general knowledge.

Such knowledge mining would not only improve the performance of CBR systems, but could turn case bases into valuable assets for clinical research.

The *integrated synergy between knowledge discovery, data mining, and CBR* is exemplified by Jänichen and Perner [32] who present a memory organization for efficient retrieval of images based on incremental conceptual clustering for case-based object recognition. These authors explain that case-based image interpretation in a biological domain, such as fungi spore detection, requires storing a series of cases corresponding to different variants of the object to be recognized in the case base. The conceptual clustering approach provides an answer to the question of how to group similar object shapes together and how to speed up the search through memory. Their system learns a hierarchy of prototypical cases representing structural shapes and measures the degree of generalization of each prototype [32].

Bichindaritz [11] explores automatically learning prototypical cases from biomedical literature. The topic of case mining is an important recent trend in CBR to enable CBR to capitalize on clinical databases, electronic patient records, and biomedical literature databases. Following, this author studies how mined prototypical cases can guide the case-based reasoning of case-based decision-support systems as well as the different roles of prototypical cases for guiding the case-based reasoning, to make it more compliant with recent biomedical findings in particular [11].

5.2 Multimodal Architectures

Many papers focus on how CBR can be used in conjunction or in complement of yet other AI methodologies or principles [8, 24, 25, 43].

Dìaz et al. demonstrate the applicability of CBR to the classification of DNA microarray data and show that CBR can be applied successfully to domains struck by the 'curse of dimensionality' [21]. This 'curse,' a well-known issue in bioinformatics, refers to the availability of a relatively small number of cases, each having thousands of features. In their Gene-CBR system, for cancer diagnosis, a case has 22,283 features, corresponding to genes. The authors have designed a hybrid architecture for Gene-CBR, which combines fuzzy case representation, a neural network to cluster the cases for genetically similar patients, and a set of if-then rules extracted from the case base to explain the classification results [21].

To explore further this synergy, Montani explains how CBR can be used to configure the parameters upon which other AI methodologies rely [42]. This paper also provides a detailed analysis of the reasons why CBR is not more integrated today in mainstream clinical practice, such as the complexity of the medical domain, and some advances still required in the CBR methodology.

Yet another paper in this category is a case-based diagnostic system presenting a novel hypothetico-deductive CBR approach to minimize the number of tests required to confirm a diagnostic hypothesis [40]. A very interesting paper studies how cases can represent non-compliance instances of clinical guidelines, and eventually lead to expert refinement of these guidelines [43]. Other work capitalizes on the complementarity between knowledge-bases, ontologies, and CBR [8].

6   CBR Versus Statistics in the Health Sciences

In health sciences domains, statistics is considered as the scientific method of choice for collecting and analyzing data. Therefore CBR-HS systems have studied how to position CBR in these domains in comparison with it.

6.1   The Role of Statistics in the Health Sciences

Biometry is "the application of statistical methods to the solution of biological problems" [65]. Statistics has several meanings. A classical definition of statistics is "the scientific study of data describing natural variation." [65] Statistics generally studies populations or groups of individuals: "it deals with quantities of information, not with a single datum". Thus the measurement of a single animal or the response from a single biochemical test will generally not be of interest; unless a sample of animals is measured or several such tests are performed, statistics ordinarily can play no role [65]. Another main feature of statistics is that the data are generally numeric or quantifiable in some way. Statistics also refers to any computed or estimated statistical quantities such as the mean, mode, or standard deviation [65].

The origin of statistics can be traced back to the seventeenth century, and derives from two sources. One is related to political science and was created to quantitatively describe the various affairs of a government or state, from which the term statistics was coined. In order to deal with taxes and insurance data, problems of censuses, longevity, and mortality were studied in a quantitative manner [65]. The second source of statistics is the theory of probabilities developed also in the seventeenth century around the popular interest in games of chance among upper society (Pascal, de Fermat, Bernouilli, de Moivre) [65]. The science of astronomy also fostered the development of statistics as a mathematical tool to build a coherent theory from individual observations (Laplace, Gauss) [65]. Applications of statistics to the life sciences emerged in the nineteenth century, when the concept of the "average man" was developed (Quetelet) and those of statistical distribution and variation [65].

Statistics researchers focus on summarizing data: "All these facts have been processed by that remarkable computer, the human brain, which furnishes an abstract" [65]. Statistics involves reducing, synthesizing data into figures representing trends or central tendencies [65].

There are actually two approaches in statistics:

– The experimental approach, at the basis of any theory formation in experimental sciences, and in particular in the life sciences, refers to a method aiming at identifying relations of cause to effect. A statistical experiment needs to follow a precise and controlled plan with the goal of observing the effect of the variation of one or more variables on the phenomenon under study, while eliminating any potential hidden effects. The statistician is responsible for the complete conduct of the experiment from the onset, and his role is to ensure that the data collected will be able to derive the stated research hypothesis while all laws of the theory of probabilities are followed. Researchers gather data in very strict contexts such as randomized clinical trials in medicine. The subsequent statistical data analysis of collected data represents only a small part of the statistician's work,

– The descriptive approach deals with a set of data and how to summarize or represent it in a meaningful way through mainly quantitative features, although qualitative variables are also considered.

Statistical data analysis is derived from the statistical descriptive approach, but deals only with the data analysis part. It is this part of statistics that relates to data mining, in particular so called inferential statistics, interested in building a model from data before applying it to new data to produce inferences. Data analysis has freed itself from the constraints of the theory of probabilities to analyze data a posteriori.

6.2 The Role of CBR in the Health Sciences

CBR brings to the life sciences a method for processing and reusing datum, which statistics clearly considers outside of its scope. However, CBR partakes in the definition cited above of statistics as "the scientific study of data describing natural variation." Indeed CBR does participate in the study of data, but particularly of datum. It deals with natural variation in a novel manner, though analogical inference and similarity reasoning. The rise of computers and their current ubiquity has made practically possible the study of the datum because case bases can handle large numbers of cases and still process each of them individually efficiently without having to summarize the data. Therefore CBR can be seen as an advance in the scientific study of data made possible by progress in computer science.

This study of how CBR can complement statistics has been a main focus of CBR-HS research. This is also one of the most salient contributions CBR-HS can make to CBR in general. Advances in this articulation will be applicable to any application of CBR to experimental sciences.

Many of the tasks performed by CBR-HS systems compete with corresponding statistical methods, particularly those of inferential statistics. For example, Schmidt et al. [51] present a CBR system for the prediction of influenza waves for influenza surveillance. The authors compare their method with classical prediction methods, which are statistical, and argue that CBR is more appropriate in this domain due to the irregular cyclicality of the spread of influenza. The rationale behind this is that statistical methods rely on laws of the theory of probabilities which are often not met in practice. In these circumstances, methods like CBR can be advantageous because they do not rely on these laws. Another interesting example demonstrates how CBR can be used to explain exceptions to statistical analysis and particularly data summaries [60].

Some of the most interesting research in this domain is the role of CBR as an evidence gathering mechanism for medicine [12]. CBR can detect and represent how cases can illustrate contextual applications of guidelines [12], spark the generation of new research hypotheses [12], such as how repeated exceptions to clinical guidelines can lead to modifications of the clinical guidelines [43].

More generally, one of the main motivations for the development of case-based reasoning systems in biomedicine is that cases, as traces of the clinical experience of the experts, play a unique and irreplaceable role for representing knowledge in these domains [48]. Recent studies have worked at better formalizing this specific role. These studies explain that the gold standard for evaluating the quality of biomedical knowledge relies on the concept of evidence [48]. Pantazi et al. propose an extension of the definition of *biomedical evidence* to include knowledge in individual cases,

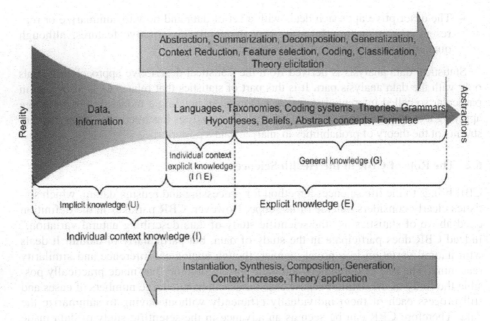

Fig. 3. The knowledge spectrum in biomedical informatics [47]

suggesting that the mere collection of individual case facts should be regarded as evidence gathering [48]. To support their proposal, they argue that the traditional, highly abstracted, hypothesis centric type of evidence that removes factual evidence present in individual cases, implies a strong *ontological commitment* to methodological and theoretical approaches, which is the source of the never-ending need for *current* and *best* evidence, while, at the same time, offering little provision for the reuse of knowledge disposed of as obsolete [48] (see Fig. 3). By contrast, the incremental factual evidence about individuals creates, once appropriately collected, a growing body of context-dependent evidence that can be reinterpreted and reused as many times as possible.

Currently, the concept of evidence most often refers to an abstract proposition derived from multiple, typically thousands of cases, in the context of what is known as a *randomized controlled trial* [48]. Hypothesis forming is the cornerstone of this kind of biomedical research. Hypotheses that pass an appropriately selected statistical test become evidence [48]. However, the process of hypothesis forming also implies a commitment to certain purposes (e.g., research, teaching, etc.), and inherently postulates ontological and conceptual reductions, orderings and relationships [48]. All these are direct results of the particular conceptualizations of a researcher who is influenced by experience, native language, background, etc. This reduction process will always be prone to errors as long as uncertainties are present in our reality. In addition, even though a hypothesis may be successfully verified statistically and may become evidence subsequently, its applicability will always be hindered by our inability to fully construe its complete meaning [48]. This meaning is defined by the complete context where the hypothesis was formed and which includes the data sources as well as the context of the researcher who formed the hypothesis [48].

The discussion about commitment to research designs, methodological choices, and research hypotheses led Pantazi et al. to propose to extend the definition and the understanding of the concept of evidence in biomedicine and align it with an intuitively appealing direction of research: *case-based reasoning* (CBR) [48]. From this perspective, the concept of evidence, traditionally construed on the basis of knowledge applicable to populations, is evolved to a more complete, albeit more complex construct which emerges naturally from the attempt to understand, explain and manage unique, individual cases. This new perspective of the concept of evidence is surprisingly congruent with the current acceptation of the notion of evidence in forensic science for instance [48]. Here, by evidence, one also means, besides general patterns that apply generally to populations, the recognition of any spatio-temporal form (i.e., pattern, regularity) in the context of a case (e.g., a hair, a fiber, a piece of clothing, a sign of struggle, ...) which may be relevant to the solution to that case. This new view where a body of evidence is incremental in nature and accumulates dynamically in form of facts about individual cases is a striking contrast with traditional definitions of biomedical evidence. Case evidence, once appropriately collected, represents a history that can be reinterpreted and reused as many times as necessary. But most importantly, the kind of knowledge where the "what is", i.e., case data, is regarded as evidence can be easily proven to be less sensitive to the issues of *recency* (i.e., current evidence) and *validity* (i.e., best evidence) [48].

The evidence gathering mechanism allowed by CBR can lead to the design of new research hypotheses, and engender statistical experiments aiming at integrating the new knowledge in the theory, traditionally built through the statistical approach. Therefore the evidence gathering role of CBR complements particularly well the statistical approach. As a matter of fact, CBR, by allowing the scientific study of the datum, feels a gap in the statistics purpose, which is the scientific study of data.

7 Conclusion

CBR has found in the health sciences an exceptional rich field of experiment from which it has expanded its methodology in many important directions. CBR-HS has also contributed to the health sciences through pilot studies and in synergy with other successfully deployed AI in the health sciences applications. However CBR is called to fit even more closely the needs of the health sciences domain by providing a computational methodology for processing contextual knowledge, in the form of cases – the datum, now made possible by the advancement of computer science. CBR should rise to this challenge to define itself as a scientific approach in a manner similar, though complementary - to the statistics approach in experimental sciences, the influence of which has shaped the advancement of science for centuries in these application domains.

References

1. Aamodt, A., Plaza, E.: Case-Based Reasoning: Foundational Issues, Methodologies Variations, and Systems Approaches. AI Communications 7(1), 39–59 (1994)
2. d'Aquin, M., Lieber, J., Napoli, A.: Adaptation Knowledge Acquisition: A Case Study for Case-Based Decision Support in Oncology. Computational Intelligence, 161–176 (2006)

3. Bareiss, E.R., Porter, B.W., Wier, C.C.: Protos: an exemplar-based learning apprentice. In: Proceedings of the Fourth International Workshop on Machine Learning, pp. 12–23. Morgan Kaufmann, Los Altos (1987)
4. Barnett, G.O., Cimino, J.J., Huppa, J.A.: Dxplain: an evolving diagnostic decision-support system. JAMA 258, 69–76 (1987)
5. Berger, J.: Roentgen: Radiation Therapy and Case-based Reasoning. In: O'Leary, D., Selfridge, P. (eds.) Proceedings of the Conference on Artificial Intelligence Applications, pp. 171–177. IEEE Press, Los Alamitos (1994)
6. Bichindaritz, I.: A case based reasoner adaptive to several cognitive tasks. In: Veloso, M., Aamodt, A. (eds.) ICCBR 1995. LNCS, vol. 1010, pp. 391–400. Springer, Heidelberg (1995)
7. Bichindaritz, I.: Prototypical Cases for Knowledge Maintenance for Biomedical CBR. In: Weber, R., Richter, M. (eds.) International Conference in Case-based Reasoning. LNCS (LNAI), pp. 492–506. Springer, Heidelberg (2007)
8. Bichindaritz, I.: Mémoire: Case-based Reasoning Meets the Semantic Web in Biology and Medicine. In: Funk, P., González Calero, P.A. (eds.) ECCBR 2004. LNCS (LNAI), vol. 3155, pp. 47–61. Springer, Heidelberg (2004)
9. Bichindaritz, I.: Case-Based Reasoning in the Health Sciences. Artificial Intelligence in Medicine 36(2), 121–125 (2006)
10. Bichindaritz, I.: Memory Organization as the Missing Link between Case-Based Reasoning and Information Retrieval in Biomedicine. Computational Intelligence, 148–160 (2006)
11. Bichindaritz, I.: Prototypical Case Mining from Biomedical Literature. Applied Intelligence 28(3), 222–237 (2007)
12. Bichindaritz, I., Kansu, E., Sullivan, K.M.: Case-based reasoning in care-partner: gathering evidence for evidence-based medical practice. In: Smyth, B., Cunningham, P. (eds.) Proceedings of the 4th European Workshop on CBR, pp. 334–345. Springer, Berlin (1998)
13. Bichindaritz, I., Marling, C.: Case-Based Reasoning in the Health Sciences: What's Next? Artificial Intelligence in Medicine 36(2), 127–135 (2006)
14. Bichindaritz, I., Seroussi, B.: Contraindre l'analogie par la causalite. Technique et Sciences Informatiques 11(4), 69–98 (1992)
15. Bradburn, C., Zeleznikow, J.: The application of case-based reasoning to the tasks of health care planning. In: Proceedings of the First European Workshop on CBR, pp. 365–378. Springer, Berlin (1993)
16. Coiera, E.: Guide to Health Informatics. Arnold Publications (2003)
17. Costello, E., Wilson, D.C.: A Case-Based Approach to Gene Finding. In: McGinty, L. (ed.) Workshop Proceedings of the Fifth International Conference on Case-Based Reasoning, NTNU, Trondheim, Norway, pp. 19–28 (2003)
18. Davies, J., Glasgow, J., Kuo, T.: Visio-Spatial Case-Based Reasoning: A Case Study in Prediction of Protein Structure. Computational Intelligence, 194–207 (2006)
19. Davis, G., Wiratunga, N., Taylor, B., Craw, S.: Matching SMARTHOUSE Technology to Needs of the Elderly and Disabled. In: McGinty, L. (ed.) Workshop Proceedings of the Fifth International Conference on Case-Based Reasoning, NTNU, Trondheim, Norway, pp. 29–36 (2003)
20. Dexter, P.R., Wolinsky, F.D., Gramelspacher, G.P.: Effectiveness of Computer-Generated Reminders for Increasing Discussions about Advance Directives and Completion of Advance Directive Forms. Annals of Internal Medicine 128, 102–110 (1998)

21. Dìaz, F., Fdze-Riverola, F., Corchado, J.M.: Gene-CBR: A Case-Based Reasoning Tool for Cancer Diagnosis using Microarray Datasets. Computational Intelligence, 254–268 (2006)
22. Dojat, M., Brochard, L., Lemaire, F., Harf, A.: A knowledge-based system for assisted ventilation of patients in intensive care units. International Journal of Clinical Monitoring and Computing 9, 239–250 (1992)
23. Doyle, D., Cunningham, P., Walsh, P.: An Evaluation of the Usefulness of Explanation in a CBR System for Decision Support in Bronchiolitis Treatment. Computational Intelligence, 269–281 (2006)
24. El Balaa, Z., Strauss, A., Uziel, P., Maximini, K., Traphoner, R.: FM-Ultranet: A Decision Support System Using Case-Based Reasoning Applied to Ultrasonography. In: McGinty, L. (ed.) Workshop Proceedings of the Fifth International Conference on Case-Based Reasoning, NTNU, Trondheim, Norway, pp. 37–44 (2003)
25. Evans-Romaine, K., Marling, C.: Prescribing Exercise Regimens for Cardiac and Pulmonary Disease Patients with CBR. In: McGinty, L. (ed.) Workshop Proceedings of the Fifth International Conference on Case-Based Reasoning, NTNU, Trondheim, Norway, pp. 45–52 (2003)
26. Fenstermacher, K.D.: An application of case-based instruction in medical domains. In: Proceedings of the Spring Symposium on Artificial Intelligence in Medicine, pp. 50–54. AAAI Press/The MIT Press, Cambridge (1996)
27. Funk, P., Xiong, N.: Case-Based Reasoning and Knowledge Discovery in Medical Applications with Time Series. Computational Intelligence, 238–253 (2006)
28. Gierl, L.: Icons: cognitive basic functions in a case-based consultation system for intensive care. In: Andreassen, S., et al. (eds.) Proceedings of the 4th Conference on Artificial Intelligence in Medicine Europe, pp. 230–236. Elsevier Science Publishers, Amsterdam (1993)
29. Grimnes, M., Aamodt, A.: A two layer case-based reasoning architecture for medical image understanding. In: Smith, I., Faltings, B.V. (eds.) EWCBR 1996. LNCS, vol. 1168, pp. 164–178. Springer, Heidelberg (1996)
30. Haddad, M., Adlassnig, K.P., Porenta, G.: Feasibility analysis of a case-based reasoning system for automated detection of coronary heart disease from myocardial scintigrams. Artificial Intelligence in Medicine 9(1), 61–78 (1997)
31. Holt, A., Bichindaritz, I., Schmidt, R.: Medical Applications in Case-based Reasoning. The Knowledge Engineering Review 20(03), 289–292 (2005)
32. Jänichen, S., Perner, P.: Conceptual Clustering and Case Generalization of 2-dimensional Forms. Computational Intelligence, 177–193 (2006)
33. Jurisica, I., Glasgow, J.: Applications of Case-Based Reasoning in Molecular Biology. AI Magazine 25(1), 85–95 (2004)
34. Kolodner, J.L., Kolodner, R.M.: Using Experience in Clinical Problem Solving: Introduction and Framework. IEEE Transactions on Systems, Man, and Cybernetics SMC-17(3), 420–431 (1987)
35. Koton, P.: Reasoning about evidence in causal explanations. In: Proceedings of AAAI 1988. Seventh National Conference on Artificial Intelligence, pp. 256–261. Morgan Kaufmann, Palo Alto (1988)
36. Lopez, B., Plaza, E.: Case-Base Planning for medical diagnosis. In: Komorowski, J., Raś, Z.W. (eds.) ISMIS 1993. LNCS, vol. 689, pp. 96–105. Springer, Heidelberg (1993)
37. Macura, R.T., Macura, K.J., Toro, V.E., Binet, E.F., Trueblood, J.H., Ji, K.: Computerized case-based instructional system for computed tomography and magnetic resonance imaging of brain tumors. Investigative Radiology 29(4), 497–506 (1994)

38. Marling, C.R., Petot, G.J., Sterling, L.S.: Integrating Case-Based and Rule-Based Reasoning to Meet Multiple Design Constraints. Computational Intelligence 15(3), 308–332 (1999)
39. Marling, C.R., Whitehouse, P.J.: Case-based reasoning in the care of alzheimer's disease patients. In: Aha, D.W., Watson, I. (eds.) ICCBR 2001. LNCS (LNAI), vol. 2080, pp. 702–715. Springer, Heidelberg (2001)
40. McSherry, D.: Hypothetico-Deductive Case-based Reasoning. In: Wilson, D.C., Khemani, D. (eds.) Proceedings of Case-based Reasoning in the Health Sciences Workshop. International Conference on Case-based Reasoning (ICCBR), Belfast, pp. 315–326 (2007)
41. Miller, R.A., Pople Jr., H.E., Myers, J.D.: Internist-1, an experimental computer-based diagnostic consultant for general internal medicine. N. Engl. J. Med. 307(8), 468–476 (1982)
42. Montani, S.: Exploring new roles for case-based reasoning in heterogeneous AI systems for medical decision support. Applied Intelligence, 275–285 (2007)
43. Montani, S.: Case-based Reasoning for Managing Non-compliance with Clinical Guidelines. In: Wilson, D.C., Khemani, D. (eds.) Proceedings of Case-based Reasoning in the Health Sciences Workshop. International Conference on Case-based Reasoning (ICCBR), Belfast, pp. 325–336 (2007)
44. Montani, S., Bellazzi, R., Portinale, L., Stefanelli, M.: A multi-modal reasoning methodology for managing iddm patients. International Journal of Medical Informatics 256, 58–59, 243–256 (2000)
45. Montani, S., Portinale, L.: Accounting for the Temporal Dimension in Case-Based Retrieval: a Framework for Medical Applications. Computational Intelligence 22(3-4), 208–223 (2006)
46. Nilsson, M., Sollenborn, M.: Advancements and Trends in Medical Case-Based Reasoning: An Overview of Systems and System Development. In: Barr, V., Markov, Z. (eds.) Proceedings of the Seventeenth International Florida Artificial Intelligence Research Society Conference – Special Track on Case-Based Reasoning, pp. 178–183. AAAI Press, Menlo Park (2004)
47. Pantazi, S.V., Arocha, J.F.: Case-based Medical Informatics. BMC Journal of Medical Informatics and Decision Making 4(1), 19–39 (2004)
48. Pantazi, S.V., Bichindaritz, I., Moehr, J.R.: The Case for Context-Dependent Dynamic Hierarchical Representations of Knowledge in Medical Informatics. In: Proceedings of ITCH 2007, pp. 123–134 (2007)
49. Perner, P.: Different Learning Strategies in a Case-Based Reasoning System for Image Interpretation. In: Smyth, B., Cunningham, P. (eds.) EWCBR 1998. LNCS (LNAI), vol. 1488, pp. 251–261. Springer, Heidelberg (1995)
50. Schmidt, R., Montani, S., Bellazzi, R., Portinale, L., Gierl, L.: Case-Based Reasoning for Medical Knowledge-based Systems. International Journal of Medical Informatics 64(2-3), 355–367 (2001)
51. Schmidt, R., Waligora, T., Gierl, L.: Predicting Influenza Waves with Health Insurance Data. Computational Intelligence, 224–237 (2006)
52. Schmidt, R., Waligora, T., Vorobieva, O.: Prototypes for Medical Case-Based Applications. In: Industrial conference on Data Mining. LNCS (LNAI). Springer, Heidelberg (in press, 2008)
53. Shahar, Y., Miksch, S., Johnson, P.: The Asgaard project: A task-specific framework for the application and critiquing of time-oriented clinical guidelines. Artificial Intelligence in Medicine 14, 29–51 (1998)
54. Shortliffe, E.H.: Computer-Based Medical Consultations: MYCIN. Elsevier/North Holland, New York (1976)

55. Shortliffe, E.H., Buchanan, B.G.: Rule-Based Expert Systems: The MYCIN Experiments of the Stanford Heuristic Programming Project. Addison-Wesley, Reading (1984)
56. Sinchenko, V., Westbrook, J., Tipper, S., Mathie, M., Coiera, E.: Electronic Decision Support Activities in different healthcare settings in Australia. In: Electronic Decision Support for Australia's Health Sector, National Electronic Decision Support Taskforce, Commonwealth of Australia, (2003),
    http://www.health.gov.au/healthonline/nedst.htm
57. Sokal, R.R., Rohlf, F.J.: Biometry. The Principles and Practice of Statistics in Biological Research. W.H. Freeman and Company, New York (2001)
58. Turner, R.M.: Organizing and using schematic knowledge for medical diagnosis. In: Proceedings of the First Workshop on CBR, pp. 435–446. Morgan Kaufmann, San Mateo (1988)
59. Vorobieva, O., Gierl, L., Schmidt, R.: Adaptation Methods in an Endocrine Therapy Support System. In: McGinty, L. (ed.) Workshop Proceedings of the Fifth International Conference on Case-Based Reasoning, NTNU, Trondheim, Norway, pp. 80–88 (2003)
60. Vorobieva, O., Rumyantsev, A., Schmidt, R.: ISOR-2: A Case-Based Reasoning System to Explain Exceptional Dialysis Patients. In: Industrial conference on Data Mining. LNCS (LNAI), pp. 173–183. Springer, Heidelberg (2007)

An Analysis of Research Themes in the CBR Conference Literature*

Derek Greene, Jill Freyne, Barry Smyth, and Pádraig Cunningham

University College Dublin
{Derek.Greene,Jill.Freyne,Barry.Smyth,Padraig.Cunningham}@ucd.ie

Abstract. After fifteen years of CBR conferences, this paper sets out to examine the themes that have evolved in CBR research as revealed by the implicit and explicit relationships between the conference papers. We have examined a number of metrics for demonstrating connections between papers and between authors and have found that a clustering based on co-citation of papers appears to produce the most meaningful organisation. We have employed an Ensemble Non-negative Matrix Factorisation (NMF) approach that produces a "soft" hierarchical clustering, where papers can belong to more than one cluster. This is useful as papers can naturally relate to more than one research area. We have produced timelines for each of these clusters that highlight influential papers and illustrate the life-cycle of research themes over the last fifteen years. The insights afforded by this analysis are presented in detail. In addition to the analysis of the sub-structure of CBR research, this paper also presents some global statistics on the CBR conference literature.

1 Introduction

To mark fifteen years of international conferences on case-based reasoning (CBR), we have set out to explore what can be learned about the internal organisation of CBR research by analysing the relationships that can be discerned from the literature. The objective is to discover the underlying themes within the literature, and to examine how these themes have evolved over the course of the conference series. A common way to perform this type of task is to apply unsupervised learning techniques to identify clusters of associated papers or authors, which correspond to thematic groups [1]. In this paper, we propose a new ensemble approach to Non-negative Matrix Factorisation (NMF) [2] for identifying such groups. We describe the application of this algorithm to the network constructed from the bibliography of the CBR conference series. From the resulting clustering, we highlight ten important research themes for discussion. We identify the influential papers within these clusters, and we also highlight those papers that have played a central role in the body of CBR literature as a whole. We hope that the results of our investigation will be of broad interest to the CBR community, as well as assisting new researchers to identify the current key themes within CBR and the seminal research papers supporting these themes.

---

* This research was supported by Science Foundation Ireland Grant No. 05/IN.1/I24.

K.-D. Althoff et al. (Eds.): ECCBR 2008, LNAI 5239, pp. 18–43, 2008.

Given the objective of discovering the inherent organisation of the CBR research literature, there are three issues to be considered:

1. Should the organisation be based upon authors or papers?
2. What is the best measure of similarity to use in organising things?
3. What technique (algorithm) should be used to perform the organisation?

In large bibliometric analysis tasks, it is perhaps more conventional to use authors rather than papers as the basic unit of organisation. However, we have found that an analysis based on papers produces a clearer picture when working with a relatively small set of papers. We suggest that this is because we are partitioning a specific discipline into sub-topics, and because individual authors in the CBR area have frequently contributed to a range of different sub-topics, making an analysis based on authors more convoluted.

A variety of different measures can be used to identify relationships between papers and between authors in a collection of publications. A simple approach is to examine co-authorship relations between authors. However, in the CBR literature this approach appears to tell us more about geography than research themes. Citation links between papers are another important source of information, as they allows us to construct a network of scientific communication [3]. A related source of information, paper and author *co-citations*, has been frequently shown in bibliometric research to uncover more significant relationships than those identified using raw citation counts [4]. Text similarity, based on a "bag-of-words" representation of a corpus of papers, is yet another useful measure of similarity between research papers.

Among these different measures, we have found paper-paper co-citations to be particularly informative in the task of analysing the network formed from the publications of the CBR conference series (see Section 4). Taking co-citation as a useful means of assessing connectedness amongst research papers, it is interesting to look at the *eigenvector centrality* of overall network of papers covered in this study. The top ranked list of papers based on this criterion is presented in Section 4.1. It is interesting to compare this ranking with the list of papers as ordered by raw citation frequencies – this list is also presented in that section.

One of the objectives of this work was to checkpoint the progress of case-based reasoning research, after these last fifteen years of European and International conferences. We were particularly interested in understanding the thematic relationship between "modern case-based reasoning" and the more traditional view of case-based reasoning that dominated research prior to the commencement of the ECCBR/ICCBR series. To what extent have important new research themes emerged in the last fifteen years, for example? Is there evidence to suggest that more traditional lines of enquiry have reached a natural conclusion within the research space? With this in mind our cluster-based analysis has revealed a number of interesting results.

The good health of CBR research is supported by the frequent emergence of novel research ideas that have a history of developing into significant themes in their own right. As we explore the research groupings that have emerged in our analysis (see Section 4.2), we will highlight examples of important research themes that have developed and matured over the past fifteen years. For example, since the early work of [5], *conversational case-based reasoning* has emerged as an important area of research that continues to attract a significant contribution at modern CBR conferences. And more recently we have seen new work in the area of *explanation* in CBR, focusing on the role that cases play when it comes to justifying decisions or recommendations to end-users; see for example [6,7,8]. Although the earliest paper in this theme is the paper by Aamodt from 1993 [9] this is still a new area of activity that has captured the attention of CBR researchers and is likely to grow in maturity over the coming years.

Of course, research themes naturally come and go with some research activities maturing to merge with the mainstream of CBR, while others appear to be more short-lived as their activity levels are seen to decline. Perhaps one of the most significant themes that has emerged in recent times has centred on the idea of *case base maintenance* – the need to actively maintain the quality of live case bases – and developed from the early work of [5,10,11,12,13]. This is a good example of a research area whose activity has now begun to reduce as maintenance techniques become well established within CBR systems; indeed this line of research has had a lasting influence on the CBR process model with a maintenance component now seen as a standard part of the CBR process [14]. More recent research in the area *diversity* — challenging the traditional similarity assumption in CBR and arguing the need for diversity among retrieved cases — seems to be heading in a similar direction: a critical mass of research from 2001 - 2004 (e.g., [15,16,17,18]) looks to be reaching a natural conclusion as the basic trade-off between similarity and diversity comes to be accepted by practitioners.

This paper begins in Section 2, with a description of the data that has been gathered for this work. The cluster analysis technique used in our work is described in Section 3. A discussion of the findings of our analysis task is presented in Section 4, and the paper finishes with some conclusions in Section 5.

2 Data Representation

Since the conception of the CBR conference series (ECCBR/ICCBR/EWCBR) in 1993, a total of 672 papers have been published by 828 individual authors. Data on these papers was gathered from the Springer online bibliographies[1] for each of the annual conference proceedings. These bibliographies are available in the form of RIS files, a tagged file format for expressing citation information, including details such as the issue title, paper titles, author lists, and abstracts for each publication in the conference series.

To determine the connections within the network of CBR publications, we submitted queries to Google Scholar[2] to retrieve the list of papers referencing each of the 672 "seed" papers. Each list contains all of the Google verified citations that a given paper had received at query submission time (December

[1] Downloaded from http://www.springer.com
[2] See http://scholar.google.com

2007). In total 7078 relevant citation links were recorded. Note that, while citation information from the supplementary (*i.e.* non-seed) set of papers was used to provide additional information regarding co-citations, only the 672 seed papers and their associated authors were considered as data objects in our analysis.

In addition to the information provided by citation links, the availability of paper titles and abstracts in the RIS format allowed us to construct an alternative view of the seed papers, in the form of a "bag-of-words" text representation. After applying standard stemming, stop-word removal and TF-IDF pre-processing techniques, the 672 conference papers were represented by feature vectors corresponding to 1487 unique terms. Similarity values between pairs of papers were computed by finding the cosine of the angle between their respective term vectors.

2.1 Co-citation Analysis

The most fundamental representation used to model scientific literature in bibliometrics is the unweighted directed citation graph, where an edge exists between the paper P_i and the paper P_j if P_i cites P_j. This graph can be represented by its asymmetric adjacency matrix $\mathbf{A}$. However, it has been established in bibliometrics research that co-citation information can be more effective in revealing the true associations between papers than citations alone [4].

The concept of co-citation analysis is illustrated in Figure 1. A direct analysis of citation shows for instance that P_1 is related to P_2. However, the fact that P_3 and P_4 are both cited by P_1 and P_2 indicates a strong relationship between these papers. In this simple example co-citation analysis suggests a weaker relationship between P_3 and P_5 and P_4 and P_5 based on co-citation in P_2. Thus co-citation has the potential to reveal indirect associations that are not explicit in the citation graph.

Consequently, a network of publications is often represented by its weighted undirected co-citation graph. This graph has a symmetric adjacency matrix defined by $\mathbf{C} = \mathbf{A}^\mathsf{T}\mathbf{A}$, where the off-diagonal entry C_{ij} indicates the number of papers jointly citing both P_i and P_j. Note that the entry C_{ii} on the main diagonal correspond to the total number of citations for the paper P_i.

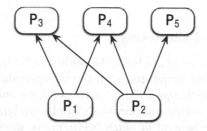

Fig. 1. Co-citation information can be more effective in revealing relationships between papers that direct citations. In this example, the fact that papers P_3 and P_4 are both cited by papers P_1 and P_2 is indicative of a relationship between them. (Note that an arrow from P_i to P_j indicates that paper P_i cites paper P_j.)

Rather than using raw co-citation values in $\mathbf{C}$ as a basis for measuring the similarity between papers, a variety of normalisation strategies have been proposed in the area of bibliometrics [19]. The *CoCit-Score*, proposed by Gmür [3], has been shown to be a particularly effective choice for clustering co-citation data. This measure allows us to compute a pairwise similarity matrix $\mathbf{S}$, such that the similarity between a pair of papers (P_i, P_j) is given by normalising their co-citation frequency with respect to the minimum and mean of the pair's respective citation counts:

$$S_{ij} = \frac{C_{ij}{}^2}{min(C_{ii}, C_{jj}) \times mean(C_{ii}, C_{jj})} \tag{1}$$

Each entry S_{ij} is in the range $[0, 1]$, where a larger value is indicative of a stronger association between a pair of papers.

3   Cluster Analysis Techniques

A natural approach to identifying the thematic subgroups in a bibliographic network, such as the CBR conference series dataset, is to apply cluster analysis techniques. Traditional methods such as hierarchical agglomerative clustering have previously been used for this task [19]. However, a distinct drawback of these methods lies in the fact that each paper can only reside in a single branch of the tree at a given level, and can only belong to a single leaf node.

As an alternative, matrix decomposition techniques such as Non-negative Matrix Factorization (NMF) have been recently employed in the analysis of data where overlapping structures may exist [2]. Unlike other hierarchical or partitional clustering algorithms that produce disjoint (*i.e.* non-overlapping) clusters, an NMF factorisation allows each data object to potentially belong to multiple clusters to different degrees, supporting the identification of overlapping subgroups. However, there are a number of drawbacks apparent when applying NMF in practical applications, notably its sensitivity to the choice of parameter k, and the difficulty in interpreting the factors produced by the decomposition procedure.

3.1   Soft Hierarchical Clustering

We would ideally like to combine both the ability of NMF techniques to accurately identify overlapping structures, with the interpretability and visualization benefits of hierarchical techniques. Towards this end, we make use of the *Ensemble NMF* algorithm [20], which was previously applied to large protein interaction networks to address the issue of proteins belonging to more that one functional group. In the context of the CBR bibliographic network, we apply it to identify overlapping subgroups corresponding to specific areas of research within the CBR community, and to investigate how these areas have developed over the course of the conference series. The Ensemble NMF algorithm is motivated by existing unsupervised ensemble methods that have been proposed to improve the accuracy and robustness of cluster analysis procedures by aggregating a diverse collection of different clusterings [21]. However, rather than combining hard clusterings (*i.e.* sets of disjoint, non-overlapping clusters), the algorithm involves aggregating multiple NMF factorisations. We refer to the output of this procedure as a *soft hierarchical clustering* of the data, as data objects (*e.g.* research papers) are organised into a binary tree such that they can be associated with multiple nodes in the tree to different degrees. A complete description of the Ensemble NMF algorithm is provided in Appendix A.

3.2 Assessing Paper Importance

When seeking to identify groups of related papers, the use of Ensemble NMF in conjunction with a similarity matrix constructed using a co-citation similarity function (such as Eqn. 1) is appropriate. However, the values in the resulting membership vectors will measure the level of *association* between each paper and a given cluster, rather than indicating the *importance* of the paper within that cluster. For instance, a paper may receive a high membership weight for a cluster as it is strongly related to the specific theme represented by the cluster, when in fact it has received relatively few citations in the literature.

To produce a meaningful ranking of the importance of the papers occurring in each cluster, we apply a re-weighting scheme based on the concept of centrality. In graph theory, the *degree* of a vertex in a graph refers to the number of edges incident to that vertex. A related measure, *degree centrality*, is commonly used as a means of assessing importance in social network analysis [22]. The rationale behind this measure is that the greater the degree of a vertex, the more potential influence it will exert in a network. For a weighted graph, we can compute a centrality score for a given vertex based on the sum of the edge weights on the edges incident to that vertex. For the co-citation graph with adjacency matrix C, this will represent the sum of the number of co-citations for each paper.

Since our focus was on the identification of influential papers within each subgroup, we consider a measure of *local degree centrality* based on co-citation counts. Firstly, for each cluster node in the soft hierarchy, we assign papers to the cluster if their previous membership weight for that cluster exceeds a given threshold. We found experimentally that a threshold of 0.1 proved suitable in this context. Subsequently, for each paper deemed to belong to a given cluster, we calculate the number of co-citations between the paper and all other papers deemed to be in that cluster. To make scores comparable across different clusters, these values can be normalised with respect to the total number of unique pairs of articles in a given cluster. This yields new membership weights in the range $[0, 1]$, where a higher score indicates that a paper is more influential in the area of research covered by a specific cluster.

3.3 Back-Fitting Recent Papers

One drawback of citation analysis is that we must wait for a sufficient amount of time to pass for citations to accrue in order to identify the associations between a paper and previously published work. As a result, most recent papers in the CBR conferences series (from 2005 onwards) did not feature strongly in the clusters generated on co-citation data. To address this issue, we propose a simple approach to "back-fit" these papers to the clusters generated with Ensemble NMF. Using the disjoint cluster memberships derived in Section 3.2, we associate each unassigned recent paper to a cluster if that paper cites three or more of the papers within the cluster. This stringent threshold led to relatively few assignments, which is desirable as we only wished to identify new papers that were strongly related to the groups discovered during the clustering process.

3.4 Labelling Clusters

The text representation described in Section 2 proved valuable as a means of summarising the content of the clusters in the soft hierarchy prior to human inspection. Cluster keywords were automatically identified by ranking the terms for each cluster based on their Information Gain [23]. Given a cluster of papers, the ranking of terms for the cluster is performed as follows: firstly the centroid vector of the cluster is computed; subsequently, we compute the Information Gain between the cluster centroid vector and the centroid vector for the entire set of papers. Terms that are more indicative of a cluster will receive a higher score, thereby achieving a higher ranking in the list of keywords for the cluster.

4 Analysis

In this section, we discuss the analysis of the CBR dataset described in Section 2 based on the application of the Ensemble NMF algorithm. As noted previously, a variety of different measures can be used to identify groupings in a collection of publications. In our initial experiments, we applied the algorithm to four different representations of the CBR network: the raw author-author co-citation matrix, the raw paper-paper co-citation matrix, the paper-paper CoCit-score matrix, and the Cosine similarity matrix constructed from the text data. Note that co-citation links from the supplementary papers retrieved from Google Scholar (as described in Section 2) was used in the construction of the co-citation matrices.

For each data representation, 1000 ensemble members were generated using symmetric NMF, with a range $k \in [15, 20]$ used for the number of basis vectors in each factorisation. This range was chosen by inspecting the gaps between the ordered set of eigenvalues in the eigenvalue decomposition of the individual similarity matrices, as frequently applied in spectral analysis [24]. These evaluations showed that clusterings generated on the CoCit-score matrix yielded clusters that were far more informative in terms of producing meaningful thematic groupings, without containing an undue bias toward the geographical co-location of authors. Consequently, in the remainder of this paper we focus on the output of the Ensemble NMF algorithm on this particular representation.

To examine these results in detail, we developed the "NMF Tree Browser" tool, a cross-platform Java application for visually inspecting a soft hierarchy

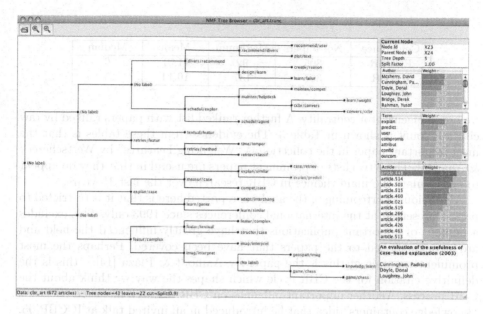

Fig. 2. Screenshot of the *NMF Tree Browser* application displaying the output of the Ensemble NMF procedure when applied to the CBR network dataset.

as produced by the Ensemble NMF algorithm. The clustering is graphically arranged in a tree view, where the user can click on any node to reveal its contents, in terms of relevant papers, authors and descriptive terms. A screenshot of the main window of the application is shown in Figure 2. The application is freely available online[3], together with the data files used in our experiments.

4.1 Global Picture

In this section we look at the salient global statistics for the complete set of papers presented at the conference series since 1993. Some statistics on citations are provided in Table 1. It is interesting to note that ICCBR papers are no more significant (in terms of citations) than ECCBR papers. In fact the mean and median number of citations per paper is marginally higher for ECCBR than for ICCBR. We feel this validates our strategy of treating these as a homogenous set of papers.

Given that the main findings in this paper entail a clustering of the papers based on co-citation links, it is interesting to see which papers are most 'central' to the overall collection based on these co-citation links. Following the literature on centrality in social network analysis, we selected eigenvector centrality and degree centrality as appropriate measures for this exercise [22]. Table 2 shows the top 10 papers ranked by eigenvector centrality. This table also shows a count of co-citations for these papers – this corresponds to degree centrality and correlates

---

[3] The browser tool and data files can be downloaded from http://mlg.ucd.ie/cbr

Table 1. A comparison of overall citation statistics between ECCBR and ICCBR

Conference	No. Papers	Maximum	Mean	Median
ECCBR	305	92	11.01	6
ICCBR	367	137	10.14	5

well with eigenvector centrality. A further ranked list with papers ranked by raw citation count is shown in Table 3. The evidence from these tables is that the most important paper in the collection is "Weighting Features" by Wettschereck & Aha [25]. These two lists of prominent papers are useful in that they do appear to encapsulate the main themes in CBR research over the last 15 years.

An obvious shortcoming of the analysis reported here is that it is restricted to papers presented at the international conferences since 1993 only. This excludes a number of important publications that have greatly influenced the field and are strongly linked to the papers that have been covered. Perhaps the most prominent example of this is the paper by Aamodt & Plaza [14] – this is the definitive citation for the CBR cycle which shapes the way we think about the CBR process. Another important influence on CBR research has been Richter's "knowledge containers" idea that he introduced in an invited talk at ICCBR'95. Unfortunately this work is not included in the CBR conference proceedings, but is described elsewhere [26].

4.2 Analysis of Subgroups

As a result of this analysis we have been able to identify a number of important research themes within the CBR literature, corresponding to cohesive clusters in the soft hierarchy produced by Ensemble NMF. We refer to these as the *modern* CBR themes, since they reflect how research focus has shifted over the past fifteen years, and they clearly differ from more traditional CBR themes such as representation and indexing, retrieval and similarity, adaptation, learning, analogy, planning and design etc. In this section we briefly review and discuss these *modern* CBR themes.

In addition, Figures 3 and 4 provide timelines which profile each theme in terms of its core papers, and their relative centrality and impact for the duration of the conference series. Each timeline shows the papers in a selected cluster (*i.e.* modern research theme) in three dimensions: the year of the conference (x-axis), the centrality of the paper in the cluster (y-axis), and the number of citations for that paper (depicted by the size of the disc representing the paper). For reasons of scale, papers with more than 50 citations are represented by a disc of size 50 – this only happens for 3% of papers. Since eigenvector centrality can be unreliable for small clusters, paper importance is measured by [0-1]-normalised local degree centrality, as previously defined in Section 3.2. It can be seen from the figures that different clusters have different importance profiles. This can be interpreted to mean than clusters such as Case-Base Maintenance are more compact and cohesive than clusters such as Case Retrieval. The timelines also show papers that have been back-fitted to the clusters as described in Section 3.3.

Table 2. A ranked list of the top 10 papers in the overall collection based on eigenvector centrality. The total number of citations and the number of co-citations for these papers is also shown.

#	Paper	Year	Citations	Co-cites
1	*Weighting features* Wettschereck & Aha	1995	137	522
2	*Modelling the competence of case-bases* Smyth & McKenna	1998	92	525
3	*Refining conversational case libraries* Aha & Breslow	1997	117	518
4	*Maintaining unstructured case bases* Racine & Yang	1997	72	469
5	*Using introspective learning to improve retrieval in CBR: A case study in air traffic control* Bonzano et al.	1997	74	473
6	*Similarity vs. diversity* Smyth & McClave	2001	72	452
7	*Building compact competent case-bases* Smyth & McKenna	1999	64	399
8	*Categorizing case-base maintenance: dimensions and directions* Leake & Wilson	1998	82	322
9	*Diversity-conscious retrieval* McSherry	2002	44	362
10	*Similarity measures for object-oriented case representations* Bergmann & Stahl	1998	66	403

These papers are represented by blue discs. Note that all papers mentioned in this section are labelled with their corresponding reference number.

Recommender Systems and Diversity: Recent research interest in recommender systems has provided the impetus for a new take on one of the long-held assumptions that has underpinned case-based reasoners, namely the *similarity assumption*. The similarity assumption states that the similarity between the target specification (query) and cases in the case base is the primary retrieval constraint in CBR systems; in other words, that cases should be selected and ranked for retrieval in terms of their similarity to the target specification. The idea that this assumption does not always hold is an important theme within the area of recommender systems (both single-shot and conversational). The work of [15] argued that an exclusive focus on similar cases can lead to the retrieval of a homogeneous set of case that fail to offer the user a diverse set of alternatives, which is often an important consideration in many recommendation scenarios. In addition [15] first introduced the notion of a diversity conscious approach to case retrieval, with a view to producing more diverse retrieval-sets that provide a better set of alternatives to a user. This work captured the interest on a

Table 3. A ranked list of the top 10 papers in the overall collection based on total citation count

#	Paper	Year	Citations
1	*Weighting features* Aha & Wettschereck	1995	137
2	*Refining conversational case libraries* Aha & Breslow	1997	117
3	*Modelling the competence of case-bases* Smyth & McKenna	1998	92
4	*Categorizing case-base maintenance: dimensions and directions* Leake & Wilson	1998	82
5	*Using k-d trees to improve the retrieval step in case-based reasoning* Althoff et al.	1993	76
6	*Using introspective learning to improve retrieval in CBR: a case study in air traffic control* Bonzano et al.	1997	74
7	*Explanation-driven case-based reasoning* Aamodt	1993	72
8	*Maintaining unstructured case bases* Racine & Yang	1997	72
9	*Similarity vs. diversity* Smyth & McClave	2001	72
10	*Cases as terms: A feature term approach to the structured representation of cases* Plaza	1995	70

number of CBR researchers with the work of [17,18,27,28] providing a number of extensions to this original diversity work.

This particular theme is notable because of the relatively large number of highly cited, very central papers over a short and recent time period as shown in Figure 3. The first two papers in this cluster [29,30] are early papers on recommender systems that are also prominent in the Conversational CBR cluster described later. This shows the benefit of a clustering strategy that allows objects to belong to more than one cluster.

Case-Base Maintenance: One cluster of research that stands out particularly well in our co-citation analysis concerns the area of *case base maintenance*. In fact, this line of research has had a lasting impact on the landscape of case-based reasoning, with maintenance now viewed an a standard component of modern CBR systems. At the heart of case-base maintenance is the idea that the quality of the case base as a whole needs to be actively managed, to ensure that erroneous cases can be identified, if not removed, and so that redundancy may be reduced as a way to stave of the impact of the utility problem. A key publication in this area of research is the work of Leake & Wilson [10] which attempted, for the first time, to categorise the various factors that influence case base maintenance as well as laying out the challenges and opportunities for future research.

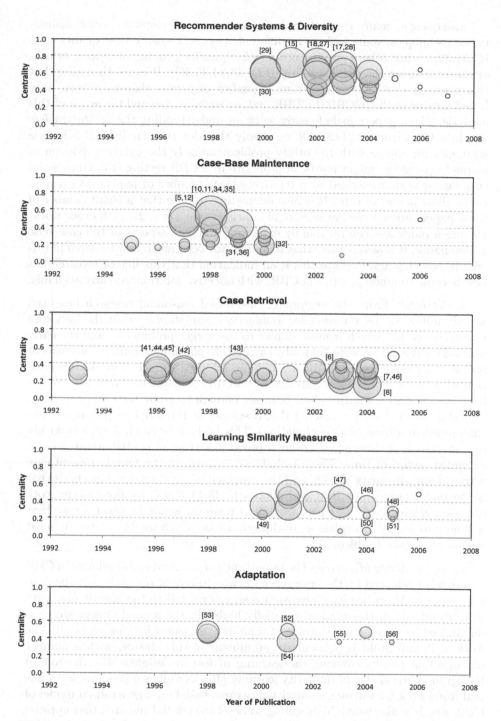

Fig. 3. Timeline plots for selected leaf node clusters. The size of the disc for each paper indicates its number of citations, and the position on the y-axis indicates its centrality.

Subsequently, many researchers have focused on developing specific maintenance techniques, some looking at different ways to measure case quality (e.g.
[11,31,32]), while others propose novel techniques for pruning or editing or otherwise optimising the case base (e.g. [12,5,33,34,35,36]). It is worth noting that
this research area has evolved from a number of papers that have been published outside of the ICCBR/ECCBR and, as such, are beyond the scope of this
analysis. These papers include early work on understanding the *utility problem*
[37] in a CBR context [38,39,40], especially the idea that traditional ML-style
strategies for coping with the utility problem, namely the outright deletion of
learned knowledge, might not be appropriate in a CBR setting [13]. Once again
this cluster is characterised by a relatively large number of papers over a relatively short period of time. It is also interesting to note that a small number of
these papers attract the lion's share of citations (see Table 2), with other works
playing a much less central role by exploring different aspects of the case base
maintenance. It is also notable that there has not been much new research in this
area in recent years. Perhaps this is an indication that this line of research has
now become common practice in CBR, with effective solutions already available.

Case Retrieval: From the beginning, case-based reasoning research has been
heavily influenced by the so-called *similarity assumption* — that the best case
to retrieve is that which is most similar to the target problem — and the early
years of CBR research were guided by cognitively-plausible similarity assessment
techniques. Contemporary CBR research has adopted a much more flexible position when it comes to case retrieval and similarity assessment. Many researchers
have argued that similarity alone is rarely enough to guide retrieval, for example, while others have pointed out that cases can be retrieved for purposes other
than problem solving (e.g., explanation). This body of research is evident within
our analysis as a cluster that covers a broad spectrum of contributions over an
extended period of time. These include early work on the foundations of case
retrieval and similarity [41,42], and the proposal of novel retrieval methods that
go beyond a pure similarity-based approach [43,44,45,46], to more recent work
on case explanation [7,8], where the job of retrieval is not to select a case that
will help to justify or explain a conclusion, a case which might not be the most
similar to a given problem [6].

Learning Similarity Measures: The importance of retrieval and similarity in CBR
research is evidenced by the emergence of two clusters of research that speak to
these topics. Above we have discussed research related to the role of similarity
in retrieval and in this section we briefly highlight the second cluster which is
dominated by work on the learning of similarity measures for case retrieval. The
work of Armin Stahl is particularly prominent in this cluster, with a number
of important papers covering the learning of feature weights [47], the role of
background knowledge in similarity learning [46], as well as a proposal for a formal framework for learning similarity measures based on a generalised model of
CBR [48]. It is also worth highlighting some of the related research that appears
in this cluster, which focuses on the role of user preferences in similarity with

research by [49,50,51], for example, looking at different approaches to harnessing user profiles and user preferences in similarity-based retrieval.

Adaptation: One of the smaller clusters of research activity that has emerged from our analysis is in the area of *case adaptation*. Despite a strong showing in the early years of CBR, work in the area of adaptation is now far less prominent, at least within the ECCBR/ICCBR series. And while the level of activity on this topic has promoted some to proclaim the death of case adaptation there are clear signs that researchers have not given up on this most challenging of CBR tasks. This cluster, for example, reflects recent work in the area of case adaptation and includes practical work on domain specific adaptation techniques [52] and more general approaches to case adaptation such as the work of [53,54,55,56]

Image Analysis: CBR researchers will not be surprised to see that image analysis (particularly medical image analysis) has been identified as a distinct research theme in the CBR literature. The earliest paper in the cluster that has been identified is from ICCBR'95 by Macura & Macura [57], which describes the application of CBR in the area of radiology imaging. Two other central papers in this cluster are the paper on using CBR for image segmentation by Perner [58] and a paper describing a CBR architecture for medical image understanding by Grimes & Aamodt [59]. This cluster also includes two papers on geospatial image analysis, although the dominant theme in this area of CBR has been medical image analysis. Given that significant research challenges still exist in image analysis it is interesting that the clustering has attached few very recent papers to this theme. The process of back-fitting recent papers as described in Section 3.3 has added only one paper. Part of the explanation for this is that some of the research activity in this area is reported outside the CBR conferences. Surely this is an area of research that warrants more attention from the CBR community.

Textual CBR: Ensemble NMF co-citation clustering identifies a theme that is characterised by terms such as *textual, CCBR, text, question* and *taxonomy*. An examination of the papers in this cluster shows that it covers Textual CBR. While the earliest paper in this theme is from Brüninghaus & Ashley in 1997 [60] most of the material is from recent years. So this is a new but still well established theme in CBR research. Some key papers in this cluster are the 2002 paper by Gupta *et al.* [61] and the 2004 paper by Wiratunga *et al.* [62]. It is interesting that if the clustering is allowed to further divide the corpus then this cluster splits into two distinct sub-groups: one pertaining to textual CBR [60,63,64,62], and another pertaining to conversational CBR [61,65].

Conversational CBR: The cluster analysis reveals some interesting insights into research on conversational CBR (CCBR). In fact CCBR papers are divided into two sub-groups: one is associated with textual CBR in the overall cluster hierarchy and the other is linked to learning and induction. The key papers in the *textual* side of conversational CBR have been described already in the previous section. Some central papers from the *learning* side of CCBR are the

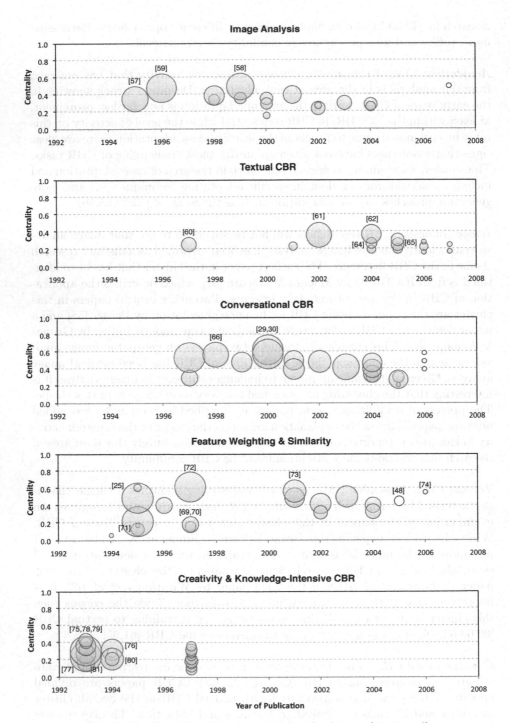

Fig. 4. Timeline plots for selected leaf node clusters (continued)

2000 paper by Doyle & Cunningham [29], the 2000 paper by Göker & Thompson [30] and the 1998 paper by Aha *et al.* [66]. This is a significant cluster that contains seventeen papers, most of which have attracted an impressive number of citations. In addition to this link to conversational CBR, this cluster also links to the Recommender Systems and Diversity theme where the papers [29,30] are also prominent. The back-fitting process has attached another three papers to this cluster. It is clear from the timelines in Figure 4 that this research area is in rude good health with considerable activity in the area.

Feature Weighting and Similarity: In fact, the clustering further divides this cluster into two sub-groups, one on fault diagnosis and another on feature weight learning. The former is unusual in that it contains no recent papers; there is one paper from 2000 [67], and before that the most recent papers are from 1997 [68,69,70]. There have continued to be papers on diagnosis in the research literature but it does not seem to connect with this literature through co-citation. Instead the clustering process has connected more recent papers on diagnosis with research on textual CBR or with work on similarity for structured representations. Two representative papers that describe the work on fault diagnosis in this cluster are the work of Netten & Vingerhoeds [71], and Jarmulak *et al.* [69].

The other part of this cluster comprises papers on feature weight learning. The seminal paper in this collection is the paper by Wettschereck & Aha from 1995 on "Weighting Features" [25]. This is also the most central and significant paper is the whole 15 year collection (see Section 4.1). Other central papers in this cluster are the paper on using introspective learning to learn feature weights by Bonzano *et al.* [72] and the work by Stahl on learning feature weights from case order feedback [73]. While activity in this area may be slowing down, there appears to be ongoing work as the process of back-fitting papers has linked two papers from 2004 and 2005 to this cluster [48,74].

Creativity & Knowledge-Intensive CBR: One of the more remarkable groupings revealed by the clustering process is the one we have called "Creativity & Knowledge Intensive CBR". The keywords associated with this cluster are *creative, reason, design, rule, interpolation, tune, represent, model, integrate* and *adapt* and the influential papers include [75,76,77,78,79,80]. This cluster is unusual in that the most recent papers are from 1997. Thus, it represents a body of research that has either waned or been taken up in other areas. An analysis of the prominent papers in this cluster supports the impression created by the list of terms above that this cluster covers research on knowledge intensive CBR and links with earlier work on analogy and model-based reasoning. This cluster includes papers on CBR as a creative problem solving process; the first paper in this sequence is the invited paper from the 1993 conference by Kolodner on "Understanding Creativity: A Case-Based Approach" [81].

It would be wrong to think of this as a strand of CBR research that did not 'work out'. Rather, some of the papers in this cluster have proved influential in other areas within CBR. For instance, the paper by Bunke and Messmer, on "Similarity Measures for Structured Representations" [77] is a very influential paper in work on similarity and is still cited today. Furthermore the connection between CBR and induction that went on to be a major theme in CBR in the late 1990s is a prominent theme in some of the papers in this cluster [76,82]. The paper by Smyth and Keane on retrieving adaptable cases [78] marked the beginning of a strand of research that offered a new perspective on case retrieval. On the other hand, the view of CBR as a model of creativity does seem to have waned. Perhaps this is no surprise as, to a large extent, the modern view of CBR is one the emphasises retrieval rather than adaptation and, arguably, creativity demands a significant measure of adaptation by definition. The early work of creativity [81] stems from a time when there was a more optimistic view of the potential for automated adaptation, and the lack of significant research activity in the area of adaptation (as discussed above) suggests that this view is no longer held.

5   Conclusion

In this work, we have set out to review the last fifteen years of CBR research with a view to understanding how major research themes have developed and evolved over this extended period of time. Unlike many more traditional research reviews, which tend to adopt a top-down style of analysis based on long-accepted thematic norms, we have instead opted for a bottom-up style of analysis. Our intuition has always been that CBR research tends to be dynamic, with new research themes emerging on a reasonably regular basis, and as such a pre-canned top-down analysis would run the risk of missing important developments that fall outside of the traditional themes.

Our bottom-up analysis has focused on mining the relationships between papers and authors from the fifteen years of international CBR conferences. The results confirm that modern CBR research is characterised by a set of research themes that are significantly different from those that would have characterised the early years of the field. We have identified strong clusters of activity in areas such as Recommender Systems & Diversity, Textual CBR, Case-Base Maintenance and Conversational CBR, which we believe to be characteristic of modern CBR research. Interestingly, many of the more traditional research themes do not feature prominently in the clusters of research that have emerged from our analysis. For example, the traditional themes of *representation and indexing*, *analogy*, *architectures*, and *design and planning* are conspicuous by their absence and even critical areas of research such as *adaptation* or *similarity and retrieval* have either become less active or have fundamentally changed their emphasis.

It is also pleasing to note from Figures 3 and 4 that new themes can emerge (e.g. Recommender Systems & Diversity), and that research activity in an area can come to a close (e.g. Case-Base Maintenance), as it matures to deliver effective solutions to the community. This can be considered a sign of a healthy research area.

The choice of a clustering algorithm that produces a "soft" hierarchical organisation, allowing the identification of localised groupings where papers may belong to more than one cluster, has proved effective. This has revealed some interesting links and overlaps between areas. For instance, overlaps between the areas of Textual CBR and Conversational CBR, and between Conversational CBR and Recommender Systems. It has also revealed the two aspects of Conversational CBR, the textual side and the learning side.

In this paper we have limited our discussion to the ten most prominent research themes, largely based on the size of the cluster (in terms of papers published). It is worth highlighting that a number of more minor clusters have also been identified, including:

- CBR on temporal problems: *time, temporal, prediction, series.*
- Games and chess: *game, chess, automatic, sequential.*
- Scheduling and agents: *schedule, agent, exploration.*
- Structural cases: *structural, case, induction, logic.*

Clearly these clusters also represent important and interesting lines of research. Work in the area of games and chess, while something of a *niche* area, has been part of CBR research since 1995 [83], and continues to attract research interest. Others clusters such as *CBR on temporal problems* cover a broad spectrum of work dealing with a range of issues, such as using CBR to predict time-series [84] and the representation of temporal knowledge in case-based prediction [85] to more recent work on so-called historical case-based reasoning [86]. There is no doubt that these themes are worthy of additional research, and a further exploration of the papers in these clusters will no doubt lead to further fruitful insights into the ever-changing landscape of CBR research.

References

1. Greene, D., Cunningham, P., Mayer, R.: Unsupervised learning and clustering. In: Cord, M., Cunningham, P. (eds.) Machine Learning Techniques for Multimedia: Case Studies on Organization and Retrieval, pp. 51–90. Springer, Heidelberg (2008)
2. Lee, D.D., Seung, H.S.: Learning the parts of objects by non-negative matrix factorization. Nature 401, 788–791 (1999)
3. Gmür, M.: Co-citation analysis and the search for invisible colleges: A methodological evaluation. Scientometrics 57, 27–57 (2003)
4. White, H., Griffith, C.: Author Cocitation: A Literature Measure of Intellectual Structure. J. ASIS 32, 163–171 (1981)
5. Aha, D., Breslow, L.: Refining conversational case libraries. Case-Based Reasoning Research and Development, 267–278 (1997)
6. Cunningham, P., Doyle, D., Loughrey, J.: An evaluation of the usefulness of case-based explanation. Case-Based Reasoning Research and Development, 1065 (2003)
7. McSherry, D.: Explaining the pros and cons of conclusions in cbr. Advances in Case-Based Reasoning, 317–330 (2004)
8. Doyle, D., Cunningham, P., Bridge, D., Rahman, Y.: Explanation oriented retrieval. Advances in Case-Based Reasoning, 157–168 (2004)
9. Aamodt, A.: Explanation-driven case-based reasoning. Advances in Case-Based Reasoning (1993)

10. Leake, D.B., Wilson, D.C.: Categorizing case-base maintenance: Dimensions and directions. Advances in Case-Based Reasoning, 196 (1998)
11. Smyth, B., McKenna, E.: Modelling the competence of case-bases. Advances in Case-Based Reasoning, 208 (1998)
12. Racine, K., Yang, Q.: Maintaining unstructured case bases. Case-Based Reasoning Research and Development, 553–564 (1997)
13. Smyth, B., Keane, M.T.: Remembering to forget: A competence-preserving case deletion policy for case-based reasoning systems. In: IJCAI, pp. 377–383 (1995)
14. Aamodt, A., Plaza, E.: Case-based reasoning: Foundational issues, methodological variations, and system approaches. AI Communications 7, 39–59 (1994)
15. Smyth, B., McClave, P.: Similarity vs. diversity. In: Aha, D.W., Watson, I. (eds.) ICCBR 2001. LNCS (LNAI), vol. 2080, p. 347. Springer, Heidelberg (2001)
16. McSherry, D.: Diversity-conscious retrieval. In: Craw, S., Preece, A.D. (eds.) ECCBR 2002. LNCS (LNAI), vol. 2416, pp. 27–53. Springer, Heidelberg (2002)
17. McGinty, L., Smyth, B.: On the role of diversity in conversational recommender systems. Case-Based Reasoning Research and Development, 1065 (2003)
18. Bridge, D., Ferguson, A.: Diverse product recommendations using an expressive language for case retrieval. In: Craw, S., Preece, A.D. (eds.) ECCBR 2002. LNCS (LNAI), vol. 2416, pp. 291–298. Springer, Heidelberg (2002)
19. He, Y., Cheung Hui, S.: Mining a Web Citation Database for author co-citation analysis. Information Processing and Management 38, 491–508 (2002)
20. Greene, D., Cagney, G., Krogan, N., Cunningham, P.: Ensemble Non-negative Matrix Factorization Methods for Clustering Protein-Protein Interactions. Bioinformatics (2008)
21. Strehl, A., Ghosh, J.: Cluster ensembles - a knowledge reuse framework for combining partitionings. In: Proc. Conference on Artificial Intelligence (AAAI 2002), pp. 93–98. AAAI/MIT Press (2002)
22. Wasserman, S., Faust, K.: Social Network Analysis: Methods and Applications. Cambridge University Press, Cambridge (1994)
23. Yang, Y., Pedersen, J.O.: A comparative study on feature selection in text categorization. In: Fisher, D.H. (ed.) Proc. 14th International Conference on Machine Learning (ICML 1997), Nashville, US, pp. 412–420. Morgan Kaufmann Publishers, San Francisco (1997)
24. Ng, A., Jordan, M., Weiss, Y.: On Spectral Clustering: Analysis and an Algorithm. Advances in Neural Information Processing 14, 849–856 (2001)
25. Wettschereck, D., Aha, D.: Weighting features. Case-Based Reasoning Research and Development, 347–358 (1995)
26. Richter, M.M.: Introduction. In: Lenz, M., Bartsch-Spörl, B., Burkhard, H.-D., Wess, S. (eds.) Case-Based Reasoning Technology. LNCS (LNAI), vol. 1400, pp. 1–16. Springer, Heidelberg (1998)
27. Mougouie, B., Richter, M.M., Bergmann, R.: Diversity-conscious retrieval from generalized cases: A branch and bound algorithm. Case-Based Reasoning Research and Development, 1064 (2003)
28. McSherry, D.: Similarity and compromise. Case-Based Reasoning Research and Development, 1067 (2003)
29. Doyle, M., Cunningham, P.: A dynamic approach to reducing dialog in on-line decision guides. In: Blanzieri, E., Portinale, L. (eds.) EWCBR 2000. LNCS (LNAI), vol. 1898, pp. 323–350. Springer, Heidelberg (2000)
30. Goker, M., Thompson, C.: Personalized conversational case-based recommendation. In: Blanzieri, E., Portinale, L. (eds.) EWCBR 2000. LNCS (LNAI), vol. 1898, pp. 29–82. Springer, Heidelberg (2000)

31. Portinale, L., Torasso, P., Tavano, P.: Speed-up, quality and competence in multi-modal case-based reasoning. In: Althoff, K.-D., Bergmann, R., Branting, L.K. (eds.) ICCBR 1999. LNCS (LNAI), vol. 1650, p. 718. Springer, Heidelberg (1999)
32. Reinartz, T., Iglezakis, I., Roth-Berghofer, T.: On quality measures for case base maintenance. In: Blanzieri, E., Portinale, L. (eds.) EWCBR 2000. LNCS (LNAI), vol. 1898, pp. 247–259. Springer, Heidelberg (2000)
33. Smyth, B.: Competence models and their applications. In: Blanzieri, E., Portinale, L. (eds.) EWCBR 2000. LNCS (LNAI), vol. 1898, pp. 1–2. Springer, Heidelberg (2000)
34. Heister, F., Wilke, W.: An architecture for maintaining case-based reasoning systems. Advances in Case-Based Reasoning, 221 (1998)
35. Surma, J., Tyburcy, J.: A study on competence-preserving case replacing strategies in case-based reasoning. Advances in Case-Based Reasoning, 233 (1998)
36. Munoz-Avila, H.: A case retention policy based on detrimental retrieval. In: Althoff, K.-D., Bergmann, R., Branting, L.K. (eds.) ICCBR 1999. LNCS (LNAI), vol. 1650, p. 721. Springer, Heidelberg (1999)
37. Minton, S.: Quantitative results concerning the utility of explanation-based learning. Artif. Intell. 42, 363–391 (1990)
38. Ram Jr., A., Francis, A.G.: The utility problem in case-based reasoning. In: Proceedings AAAI 1993 Case-Based Reasoning Workshop (1993)
39. Smyth, B., Cunningham, P.: The utility problem analysed. Advances in Case-Based Reasoning, 392–399 (1996)
40. Ram Jr., A., Francis, A.G.: A comparitive utility analysis of case-based reasoning and control-rule learning systems. In: Lavrač, N., Wrobel, S. (eds.) ECML 1995. LNCS, vol. 912, pp. 138–150. Springer, Heidelberg (1995)
41. Osborne, H., Bridge, D.: A case base similarity framework. Advances in Case-Based Reasoning, 309–323 (1996)
42. Osborne, H., Bridge, D.: Similarity metrics: A formal unification of cardinal and non-cardinal similarity measures. Case-Based Reasoning Research and Development, 235–244 (1997)
43. Smyth, B., McKenna, E.: Footprint-based retrieval. In: Althoff, K.-D., Bergmann, R., Branting, L.K. (eds.) ICCBR 1999. LNCS (LNAI), vol. 1650, p. 719. Springer, Heidelberg (1999)
44. Schaaf, J.: Fish and shrink. a next step towards efficient case retrieval in large scaled case bases. Advances in Case-Based Reasoning, 362–376 (1996)
45. Lenz, M., Burkhard, H., Bruckner, S.: Applying case retrieval nets to diagnostic tasks in technical domains. Advances in Case-Based Reasoning, 219–233 (1996)
46. Gabel, T., Stahl, A.: Exploiting background knowledge when learning similarity measures. Advances in Case-Based Reasoning, 169–183 (2004)
47. Stahl, A., Gabel, T.: Using evolution programs to learn local similarity measures. Case-Based Reasoning Research and Development, 1064 (2003)
48. Stahl, A.: Learning similarity measures: A formal view based on a generalized cbr model. Case-Based Reasoning Research and Development, 507–521 (2005)
49. Gomes, P., Bento, C.: Learning user preferences in case-based software reuse. In: Blanzieri, E., Portinale, L. (eds.) EWCBR 2000. LNCS (LNAI), vol. 1898, pp. 112–123. Springer, Heidelberg (2000)
50. Bradley, K., Smyth, B.: An architecture for case-based personalised search. Advances in Case-Based Reasoning, 518–532 (2004)
51. Hayes, C., Avesani, P., Baldo, E., Cunningham, P.: Re-using implicit knowledge in short-term information profiles for context-sensitive tasks. Case-Based Reasoning Research and Development, 312–326 (2005)

52. Bandini, S., Manzoni, S.: Cbr adaptation for chemical formulation. In: Aha, D.W., Watson, I. (eds.) ICCBR 2001. LNCS (LNAI), vol. 2080, p. 634. Springer, Heidelberg (2001)
53. McSherry, D.: An adaptation heuristic for case-based estimation. Advances in Case-Based Reasoning, 184 (1998)
54. Neagu, N., Faltings, B.: Exploiting interchangeabilities for case adaptation. In: Aha, D.W., Watson, I. (eds.) ICCBR 2001. LNCS (LNAI), vol. 2080, p. 422. Springer, Heidelberg (2001)
55. Neagu, N., Faltings, B.: Soft interchangeability for case adaptation. Case-Based Reasoning Research and Development, 1066 (2003)
56. Tonidandel, F., Rillo, M.: Case adaptation by segment replanning for case-based planning systems. Case-Based Reasoning Research and Development, 579–594 (2005)
57. Macura, R., Macura, K.: Macrad: Radiology image resource with a case-based retrieval system. Case-Based Reasoning Research and Development, 43–54 (1995)
58. Perner, P.: An architecture for a cbr image segmentation system. In: Althoff, K.-D., Bergmann, R., Branting, L.K. (eds.) ICCBR 1999. LNCS (LNAI), vol. 1650, p. 724. Springer, Heidelberg (1999)
59. Grimnes, M., Aamodt, A.: A two layer case-based reasoning architecture for medical image understanding. Advances in Case-Based Reasoning, 164–178 (1996)
60. Bruninghaus, S., Ashley, K.D.: Using machine learning for assigning indices to textual cases. Case-Based Reasoning Research and Development, 303–314 (1997)
61. Gupta, K.M., Aha, D.W., Sandhu, N.: Exploiting taxonomic and causal relations in conversational case retrieval. In: Craw, S., Preece, A.D. (eds.) ECCBR 2002. LNCS (LNAI), vol. 2416, pp. 175–182. Springer, Heidelberg (2002)
62. Wiratunga, N., Koychev, I., Massie, S.: Feature selection and generalisation for retrieval of textual cases. Advances in Case-Based Reasoning, 806–820 (2004)
63. Bruninghaus, S., Ashley, K.D.: The role of information extraction for textual cbr. In: Aha, D.W., Watson, I. (eds.) ICCBR 2001. LNCS (LNAI), vol. 2080, p. 74. Springer, Heidelberg (2001)
64. Lamontagne, L., Lapalme, G.: Textual reuse for email response. Advances in Case-Based Reasoning, 242–256 (2004)
65. Gu, M., Aamodt, A.: A knowledge-intensive method for conversational cbr. Case-Based Reasoning Research and Development, 296–311 (2005)
66. Aha, D.W., Maney, T., Breslow, L.A.: Supporting dialogue inferencing in conversational case-based reasoning. Advances in Case-Based Reasoning, 262 (1998)
67. Vollrath, I.: Handling vague and qualitative criteria in case-based reasoning applications. In: Blanzieri, E., Portinale, L. (eds.) EWCBR 2000. LNCS (LNAI), vol. 1898, pp. 403–444. Springer, Heidelberg (2000)
68. Faltings, B.: Probabilistic indexing for case-based prediction. Case-Based Reasoning Research and Development, 611–622 (1997)
69. Jarmulak, J., Kerckhoffs, E., van't Veen, P.: Case-based reasoning in an ultrasonic rail-inspection system. In: Case-Based Reasoning Research and Development, pp. 43–52 (1997)
70. Trott, J., Leng, B.: An engineering approach for troubleshooting case bases. Case-Based Reasoning Research and Development, 178–189 (1997)
71. Netten, B., Vingerhoeds, R.: Large-scale fault diagnosis for on-board train systems. Case-Based Reasoning Research and Development, 67–76 (1995)
72. Bonzano, A., Cunningham, P., Smyth, B.: Using introspective learning to improve retrieval in cbr: A case study in air traffic control. Case-Based Reasoning Research and Development, 291–302 (1997)

73. Stahl, A.: Learning feature weights from case order feedback. In: Aha, D.W., Watson, I. (eds.) ICCBR 2001. LNCS (LNAI), vol. 2080, p. 502. Springer, Heidelberg (2001)
74. Stahl, A.: Combining case-based and similarity-based product recommendation. Advances in Case-Based Reasoning, 355–369 (2006)
75. Arcos, J.L., Plaza, E.: A reflective architecture for integrated memory-based learning and reasoning. Advances in Case-Based Reasoning (1993)
76. Armengol, E., Plaza, E.: Integrating induction in a case-based reasoner. Advances in Case-Based Reasoning, 2–17 (1994)
77. Bunke, H., Messmer, B.: Similarity measures for structured representations. Advances in Case-Based Reasoning (1993)
78. Smyth, B., Keane, M.: Retrieving adaptable cases: The role of adaptation knowledge in case retrieval. Advances in Case-Based Reasoning (1993)
79. Nakatani, Y., Israel, D.: Tuning rules by cases. Advances in Case-Based Reasoning (1993)
80. Richards, B.: Qualitative models as a basis for case indices. Advances in Case-Based Reasoning, 126–135 (1994)
81. Kolodner, J.: Understanding creativity: A case-based approach. Advances in Case-Based Reasoning (1993)
82. Sebag, M., Schoenauer, M.: A rule-based similarity measure. Advances in Case-Based Reasoning (1993)
83. Flinter, S., Keane, M.: On the automatic generation of case libraries by chunking chess games. Case-Based Reasoning Research and Development, 421–430 (1995)
84. Nakhaeizadeh, G.: Learning prediction of time series - a theoretical and empirical comparison of cbr with some other approaches. Advances in Case-Based Reasoning (1993)
85. Jære, M.D., Aamodt, A., Skalle, P.: Representing temporal knowledge for case-based prediction. In: Craw, S., Preece, A.D. (eds.) ECCBR 2002. LNCS (LNAI), vol. 2416, pp. 225–234. Springer, Heidelberg (2002)
86. Ma, J., Knight, B.: A framework for historical case-based reasoning. Case-Based Reasoning Research and Development, 1067 (2003)
87. Ding, C., He, X.: On the Equivalence of Non-negative Matrix Factorization and Spectral Clustering. In: Jonker, W., Petković, M. (eds.) SDM 2005. LNCS, vol. 3674. Springer, Heidelberg (2005)
88. Opitz, D.W., Shavlik, J.W.: Generating accurate and diverse members of a neural-network ensemble. Advances in Neural Information Processing Systems 8, 535–541 (1996)
89. Schölkopf, B., Smola, A., Müller, K.R.: Nonlinear component analysis as a kernel eigenvalue problem. Neural Computation 10, 1299–1319 (1998)
90. Ding, C., He, X.: Cluster merging and splitting in hierarchical clustering algorithms. In: Proc. IEEE International Conference on Data Mining (ICDM 2002), p. 139 (2002)
91. Giurcaneanu, C.D., Tabus, I.: Cluster structure inference based on clustering stability with applications to microarray data analysis. EURASIP Journal on Applied Signal Processing 1, 64–80 (2004)

Appendix A: Ensemble NMF Algorithm

This appendix describes the operation of the Ensemble NMF clustering algorithm that was used in the analysis described in Section 4. The approach is suitable for the identification of localised structures in sparse data, represented in the form of a non-negative pairwise similarity matrix, such as the co-citation matrix of the CBR network defined by Eqn. 1. The algorithm consists of two distinct phases: a *generation phase* in which a collection of NMF factorisations is produced (*i.e.* the members of the ensemble), and an *integration phase* where these factorisations are aggregated to produce a final soft hierarchical clustering of the data.

A.1   Ensemble Generation Phase

Given a dataset consisting of n data objects (*e.g.* research papers), the generation phase of the ensemble process involves the production of a collection of τ "base" clusterings. These clusterings represent the individual members of the ensemble. Since we are interested in combining the output of multiple matrix factorisations, each member will take the form of a non-negative $n \times k_i$ matrix factor $\mathbf{V}_i$, such that k_i is the number of basis vectors (*i.e.* clusters) specified for the i-th factorisation procedure.

To generate the collection of base clusterings, we employ the symmetric NMF algorithm proposed by Ding *et al.* [87]. This algorithm decomposes a non-negative pairwise similarity matrix $\mathbf{S} \in \mathbb{R}^{n \times n}$ to produce a factor $\mathbf{V}$ by minimising the objective function given by the Frobenius norm:

$$\min_{\mathbf{V}>0} \left\| \mathbf{S} - \mathbf{V}\mathbf{V}^\mathsf{T} \right\|_F^2 \tag{2}$$

The optimal factor can be approximated by starting with an initial randomly-generated factor and repeatedly applying a single update rule until convergence:

$$V_{cj} \leftarrow V_{cj} \left(1 - \beta + \beta \frac{(\mathbf{SV})_{cj}}{(\mathbf{V}\mathbf{V}^\mathsf{T}\mathbf{V})_{cj}} \right) \tag{3}$$

where $0 < \beta \leq 1$ is a user-defined parameter which controls the rate of convergence. We have observed that, not only is the algorithm efficient in comparison to other NMF algorithms, but it also has a tendency to produce relatively sparse factors representing localised clusters.

It has been demonstrated that supervised ensembles are most successful when constructed from a set of accurate classifiers whose errors lie in different parts of the data space [88]. Similarly, unsupervised ensemble procedures typically seek to encourage diversity with a view to improving the quality of the information available in the integration phase. A simple but effective strategy is to rely on the inherent instability of randomly-initialised factorisation algorithms. By employing a stochastic initialisation scheme, symmetric NMF will generally converge to a variety of different local solutions when applied multiple times to the same matrix $\mathbf{S}$. The level of diversity among the ensemble members can be increased by varying the number of clusters in each base clustering, such as by randomly selecting a value k_i from a predefined range $[k_{min}, k_{max}]$. An important benefit of this strategy is that it ameliorates a model selection problem with NMF which is highly sensitive to the choice of the number of basis vectors k_i.

Further improvements in performance and accuracy can be achieved by seeding each NMF factorisation using the output of the less computationally expensive kernel k-means algorithm [89]. Specifically, to seed the i-th base clustering, we randomly assign data objects to k_i clusters and apply kernel k-means to the matrix $\mathbf{S}$. The resulting disjoint clustering can be represented as an $n \times k_i$ partition matrix, where the j-th column is a binary membership indicator for the j-th cluster. This partition matrix is subsequently used as the initial factor for symmetric NMF. The use of random cluster assignment and the tendency of kernel k-means to converge to a local solution ensures that sufficient diversity in the ensemble is maintained.

A.2   Ensemble Integration Phase

We now propose an approach for combining the factors produced during the generation phase to construct a soft hierarchical clustering of the original dataset.

Graph Construction. From the generation phase, we have a collection of τ factors, giving a total of $l = (k_1 + k_2 + \cdots + k_\tau)$ individual basis vectors across all factors. We denote these vectors as the set $\mathbb{V} = \{v_1, \ldots, v_l\}$. This set can be modelled as a complete weighted graph consisting of l vertices, where each vertex represents a basis vector v_i. The weight on each edge indicates the similarity between the pair of vectors associated with the two vertices. The value of the edge weight is computed as the $[0, 1]$-normalised Pearson correlation between a pair of vectors (v_i, v_j):

$$ncor(v_i, v_j) = \frac{1}{2} \left(\frac{(v_i - \bar{v}_i)^\mathsf{T} (v_j - \bar{v}_j)}{||(v_i - \bar{v}_i)|| \cdot ||(v_j - \bar{v}_j)||} + 1 \right) \tag{4}$$

The entire graph can be represented by its adjacency matrix $\mathbf{L}$, where $L_{ij} = ncor(v_i, v_j)$.

Meta-Clustering. Following the lead of the MCLA approach described by Strehl & Ghosh [21], we produce a "meta-clustering" (*i.e.* a clustering of clusters) of the graph formed from the basis vectors in $\mathbb{V}$. This is achieved by applying an agglomerative clustering algorithm to $\mathbf{L}$, resulting in a disjoint hierarchy of "meta-clusters" (*i.e.* tree nodes containing basis vectors from $\mathbb{V}$). Rather than using a traditional linkage function such as average linkage during the agglomeration process, we compute the similarity between pairs of meta-clusters based on the *min-max* graph partitioning objective [90]. This linkage function has a tendency to produce clusters which are relatively balanced in size. Formally, given the matrix $\mathbf{L}$, the min-max inter-cluster similarity between a pair of meta-clusters (M_a, M_b) is defined as:

$$sim(M_a, M_b) = \frac{s(M_a, M_b)}{s(M_a, M_a) \, s(M_b, M_b)} \tag{5}$$

such that

$$s(M_a, M_b) = \sum_{v_i \in M_a} \sum_{v_j \in M_b} L_{ij}$$

Soft Hierarchy Construction. The output of the meta-clustering procedure is a clustering of the basis vectors in $\mathbb{V}$, in the form of a traditional disjoint hierarchical tree. We wish to transform this into a *soft hierarchical clustering* of the original dataset. That is, a binary tree structure, where each node M_a in the hierarchy is associated with an n-dimensional vector y_a containing non-negative real values indicating the degree of membership for all n data objects. In practice, these node membership vectors will become increasingly sparse as we proceed further down the tree, representing more localised sub-structures.

To transform the meta-clustering into a soft hierarchy, we process each node M_a in the meta-clustering tree, computing the membership vector y_a as the mean of all the basis vectors contained in M_a:

$$y_a = \frac{1}{|M_a|} \sum_{v_i \in M_a} v_i \qquad (6)$$

We associate the vector y_a with the position held by the node M_a in the original meta-clustering tree. By preserving the parent-child relations from that tree, these vectors can be linked together to form a soft hierarchy as defined above.

Final Model Selection. A hierarchical meta-clustering of the l basis vectors in $\mathbb{V}$ will yield a corresponding soft hierarchy containing l leaf nodes. However, a certain proportion of these nodes will be redundant, where the membership vectors of a pair of sibling nodes may be nearly identical to the membership vector of their parent node. This situation will arise when a tree node in the meta-clustering of $\mathbb{V}$ contains basis vectors that are highly similar to one another. Ideally we would like to prune the soft hierarchy to remove all redundant leaf and internal nodes, thereby facilitating visualisation and human interpretation.

The concept of ensemble *stability* has previously been considered as a means of identifying an appropriate cut-off point in a disjoint hierarchy [91]. Here we propose a stability-based approach to identifying an appropriate cut-off level, which is applicable to a soft hierarchy. Specifically, we consider a tree node to be *stable* if the basis vectors in the corresponding meta-cluster are highly similar, while an *unstable* node has a corresponding meta-cluster consisting of basis vector that are dissimilar to one another. To numerically assess stability, we measure the extent to which an internal node can be split into diverse sub-nodes. Given a node M_a with child nodes (M_b, M_c), this can be quantified in terms of the weighted similarity between the membership vector y_a and the pair of vectors (y_b, y_c) associated with the child nodes:

$$split(M_a) = \frac{|M_b|}{|M_a|} ncor(y_a, y_b) + \frac{|M_c|}{|M_a|} ncor(y_a, y_c) \qquad (7)$$

From this, we define the *splitting factor* of an internal node M_a as the minimum value for Eqn. 7 among M_a and all child nodes below M_a in the hierarchy. A lower value indicates a lower degree of stability for the branch beginning at M_a. Using this criterion, we can prune a soft hierarchy by processing each internal node M_a in the tree, starting at the root node. The child nodes of M_a (together

---

Inputs:
- **S**: Non-negative pairwise similarity matrix.
- τ: Number of factorisations to generate.
- $[k_{min}, k_{max}]$: Range for selecting number of clusters in each factorisation.

Generation Phase:
1. For $i = 1$ to τ
   - Randomly select $k_i \in [k_{min}, k_{max}]$.
   - Apply kernel k-means to **S** to initialise $\mathbf{V}_i \in \mathbb{R}^{n \times k_i}$.
   - Apply symmetric NMF to **S** and $\mathbf{V}_i$.
   - Add each column vector of $\mathbf{V}_i$ to the set $\mathbb{V}$.

Integration Phase:
1. Construct the adjacency matrix **L** from the set $\mathbb{V}$ according to Eqn. 4.
2. Apply min-max hierarchical clustering to **L** to produce a meta-clustering of the basis vectors.
3. Build a soft hierarchy by computing the mean vector for each tree node in the meta-clustering.
4. If required, recursively remove redundant tree nodes based on the *splitting factor* criterion.

Fig. 5. Summary of Ensemble NMF clustering algorithm

with all the nodes below them) are removed from the tree if the splitting factor of M_a is greater than or equal to a user-defined threshold λ. In practice we have observed that a threshold value of $\lambda = 0.9$ frequently leads to the elimination of redundant nodes without removing those containing informative structures.

The pruning procedure outlined above allows us to construct a tree with k leaf nodes, where the value k does not need to be specified *a priori*. As with cut-off techniques used to convert a disjoint hierarchy to a flat partition, we can produce a flat soft clustering from the leaf nodes in the tree. Specifically, we construct a $n \times k$ matrix whose columns correspond to the vectors of the k non-redundant leaf nodes in the soft hierarchy. Unlike spectral dimension reduction procedures such as PCA, standard NMF techniques do not produce an ordering of the new dimensions in terms of importance. To produce an ordering of the columns in the flat soft clustering, the related k leaf nodes may be ranked based on their *splitting factor*, with the first column corresponding to the most stable node. The complete Ensemble NMF algorithm is summarised in Figure 5.

Semantics and Experience in the Future Web

Enric Plaza

IIIA, Artificial Intelligence Research Institute
CSIC, Spanish Council for Scientific Research
Campus UAB, Bellaterra, Catalonia (Spain)
enric@iiia.csic.es

Abstract. The Web is a vibrant environment for innovation in computer science, AI, and social interaction; these innovations come in such great number and speed that it is unlikely to follow them. This paper will focus on some emerging aspects on the web that are an opportunity and challenge for Case-based Reasoning, specifically the large amount of *experiences* that individual people share in the Web. The talk will try to characterize this experiences, these bits of practical knowledge that go from simple but practical facts to complex problem solving descriptions. Then, I'll focus on how CBR ideas could be brought to bear in sharing and reusing this experiential knowledge, and finally on the challenging issues that have to be addressed for that purpose.

1 Introduction

The Web is a vibrant environment for innovation in computer science, AI, and social interaction; these innovations come in such great number and speed that it is unlikely to follow them. This paper will focus on some emerging aspects on the web that are an opportunity and challenge for Case-based Reasoning, specifically the large amount of *experiences* that individual people share in the Web. These experiences, ranging from client reports on hotels they have visited to small explanations on how to do certain things, are searched for and reused by thousands of people. These experiences can be found in forums and blogs, in normal web pages and in specialized services like Question-Answer websites.

However, they are treated *documents*, not as experiences. That is to say, they are represented, organized, analyzed, and retrieved as any other document. The main purpose of this paper is to argue that there is a special kind of content, namely experiences, that provides a specific form of knowledge, experiential knowledge, and they should be represented, organized, analyzed, and retrieved in accordance to this nature. Moreover, the paper will provide some food for thought by proposing some ideas on the conditions required and the techniques suitable to build systems capable of reusing experiential knowledge provided by other people in specific domains.

The structure of this paper is as follows. Sections 2 and 3 discuss two of the most noteworthy components of current debate on the web, namely adding a semantic substrate to the web (e.g. the semantic web, folksonomies) and the

K.-D. Althoff et al. (Eds.): ECCBR 2008, LNAI 5239, pp. 44–58, 2008.

phenomenon of social networking. Then Section 4 discusses the nature of experiential knowledge, while Section 5 elaborates the conditions for reusing other people's experiences.Next Section 6 discusses the relationship of semantics and experience, Section 7 presents several forms of experience and discusses their properties, and Section 8 proposes a process model for systems reusing experiential knowledge on the web.

2   Semantics, Up and Down

In this section, I want to examine two approaches to imbue semantics in the web content: the top-down approach of the semantic web and the bottom-up approach of social networks. The Semantic Web (SW) [1] was proposed with the purpose of allowing the human-produced web content to be understood by automatic systems: ontologies define the terminology that "agents" use while roaming the web pages entered by humans using SW-enabled tools. This proposal is a top-down approach to semantics, in the sense that someone designs and maintains the definition of an ontology for a given domain. In a new paper revisiting the SW [2] this vision is refined: ontologies "must be developed, managed aged, and endorsed by committed practice communities." I think the conditions are even more restrictive: an ontology only makes sense for a domain if used by a *community of practice* — not just any community that endorses a particular ontology specification. A community of practice (CoP) is developed by a process of social learning of a group of people with common goals, while they interact with the purpose of achieving those same goals. Knowledge Management (KM), initially focused on *explicit knowledge*, has used the concept of CoP to address *tacit knowledge* which cannot easily be captured, codified and stored. From this perspective on semantics, SW and KM share a great deal of challenging issues.

Folksonomies, the bottom-up approach to web semantics, originates from the tagging processes in software platforms for social networks, sometimes called "Web 2.0". Folksonomies are lightweight shallow ontologies that emerge in specific community of practice where users "tag" some content objects (like photos in Flickr.com) with whatever keyword they deem more appropriate. Folksonomies are interesting in that they emerge from the social learning process of a community of practice: people learn to use other people's tags and introduce their own that, if found useful, will be used by the community at large. For this reason, folksonomies are a way to capture part of the elusive *tacit knowledge* in a network of practice (the name given to a community of practice in a social network software platform).

Some people would object considering a bag of keywords or tags an ontology, insisting it is merely a type of meta-data, but so are ontologies. The argument usually focus on the fact that ontologies are structured and folksonomies unstructured, but the main difference is in the way semantics are assigned: while ontologies are based on explicit specification of terms, folksonomies rely on a statistical analysis of the usage of terms in the context of a network of practice. From the standpoint of the philosophy of language, ontologies purport a *logicist* approach to the meaning of terms: a term is an instance of a concept if and only if it satisfies the concept's definition. On the other hand, folksonomies seem closer to Wittgenstein's notion of *language-game*: a term has a specific meaning by the way it is used in a particular context [3].

Some researchers will inevitably try an hybrid approach combining a top-down ontological approach with a bottom-up user-driven open-ended folksonomy: an ontology may define the explicit preexisting knowledge in a domain while the folksonomy captures part of the explicit and tacit knowledge of a network of practice. Although bridging the gap between both approaches is an interesting research issue, this is beyond the scope of this paper. For the purposes of this paper, the important point is that ontologies, the SW, and web semantics in general, are a *enabling technologies*: a substrate that provides some service required by more complex tasks — not a way to do more complex tasks. Specially the SW seems now to be a platform to develop a specific type of applications called ontology-based systems [4]. At the end of the day, the developers of a new web-based system will have to decide what kind of semantic model is suited for the specific web content they have to work with. The suitability of semantic models to different application domains and type of content is an empirical one, and the future web-based systems will explore and ascertain their advantages and shortcomings.

Let us now examine the existing, most burgeoning new systems in the web: social networking software.

3   The Network Is the Content (or Vice Versa)

"The network is the computer" claimed J. B. Gage of Sun Microsystems to emphasize the importance of network access for modern computing systems; nevertheless, Oracle's "network computer" (a diskless desktop computer promoted by Sun and Oracle) was not a successful answer to that claim. The myriad new software platforms for social networking seem to make a similar claim: the social network is the most important part of the so called Web 2.0. Indeed, the network effect in the web has impressing performance, from Google's page ranking based on hyperlink connectivity to Facebook or MySpace social networking websites. However, social networking is part of the picture but it is not the whole picture: some systems like LinkedIn focus the network of social relationships, while others like Flickr the (photographic) content is the most important part and the social network (as such) plays a lesser role.

From my point of view, what is most relevant is the *user-contributed content*, be it photographs or links to other people: the personal relationships that constitute social networks are part of the content contributed by users. This does not deny that the social networking plays an important role in facilitating the contribution of content by the users, quite the contrary: social networks create wealth and can originate a "social production mode" (see for instance Yochai Benkler's *The Wealth of Networks* [5], that presents a comprehensive social theory of the Internet and the networked information economy). Thus, networking facilitates the creation/contribution of content, and it is indispensable; but as a social mode of production[1] is a means to an end, namely what is produced: the *user-contributed content.*

Be that as it may, the bootstrapping of social networks and social production of content is outstanding. In this paper I want to focus on a particular kind of content that can easily be contributed by people: their own experience in some domain or other.

4   The Case for Experience

Before proceeding on to discuss user-contributed experiential knowledge on the web we need first to elucidate what the term *experience* means. Case-based reasoning (CBR) may be understood, first and foremost, as learning to solve problems (or take decisions) from past experience. More specifically, past experience is represented in the form of a collection of *cases*, where a case (*situation1, outcome1*) is to be understood as knowing that in the past, when what is described in *situation1* held, then the *outcome1* (that may be a consequence or a decision) also happened. Thus, a case is a statement (at some level of description) of a fact observed or experienced in the world. Additionally, CBR systems use case-based inference (also called analogy and similarity-based inference) based on the assumption that when a new *situation2* is similar to an old *situation1* then we can plausibly predict an *outcome2* similar to *outcome1* is correct.

The representation of cases, situations and outcomes may be very different across domains (from k-NN classification to case-based planning); but they have in common that they present the knowledge of an observed factual situation: e.g. "this is a good hotel because my stay was very agreeable", or "I did this sequence of actions (this plan), in this situation, and I achieved that goal". Although there are no "cases" as such on the web there is a huge amount of this kind of *practical knowledge* present today in the web. This kind of practical knowledge coming from the direct observation or experiences of people is what we will call *experience.*

In all likelihood, experiential content in the web is one of the most valuable web resources: people constantly use these resources to decide issues (e.g. booking a hotel, visiting or not some tourist spot) or solving problems (e.g. browsing through a forum on digital photography to learn how to solve some issue they encountered in a photo they made). In economic terms, experiential content is one of the most added-value resources on the web today, and if properly marshaled could provide attractive added-value services.

The technological challenge is how to represent, organize, and reuse experiential content. I surmise that the first step to address this challenge is to recognize that there is such a thing as "experiential content," and not merely hyperlinked texts. The way content is organized nowadays is a network of documents, and

---

[1] *Social Production* is production of information, knowledge and culture that is not based on price signals or on command structures [5]. Computers are the main means of production and networks those of distribution.

possibly in the next future, *annotated documents* (using ontology-defined concepts or folksonomy-based tags).

Moreover, the way users work with web content is what I'll call *Search & Browse* (S&B). The web users typically need to *first* use a search engine to find a "resource," this may be an external search engine (e.g. Google or Yahoo to find a website or a page) or an internal search engine (e.g. search inside a forum for the posts that may talk about the topic of interest). *Next*, the users need to browse a (sometimes disturbingly) large collection of "found items," perform a cursory read of them to filter out those blatantly irrelevant, then read carefully the rest (while eliminating those subtly irrelevant) to isolate the relevant content. Finally, the users have to *reuse* the relevant content, that may be dispersed in a dozens of pages in different websites; notice that there is no support for the users' task and they simply use "copy & paste" to aggregate the information found or print all those pages and then aggregate that information.

4.1   Found and Lost

A specific example may be useful to illustrate this scenario. Let us consider the task of deciding which hotel to book and consider the existing experiential content of previous hotel clients that describe their good and bad experiences in those hotels. Let us say there are H hotels in the intended destination, W websites with hotel-related experiential content, and each hotel in each websites has on average C client reports: a user to be well informed would need to search & browse $H \times W \times C$ user-contributed experience items. This is a huge amount of valuable information but ineffective if it is to be manually processed, as is the case now in the S&B paradigm where there is no support for the task the users want to carry out, and for which reason they have performed a search in the first place.

Certainly, the users are capable of cutting down the work by filtering out information: by selecting a few websites (equivalent to performing a sampling operation $w = sample(W)$), the reducing the eligible hotels by some hard constraints like "3- or 4-star hotels only" (a filtering operation $h = filter(H)$), and finally accessing a subset of all client reports (a sampling operation $c = sample(C)$), the workload is reduced to examining $h \times w \times c$ client reports. Notice that there is no computer support to perform a good sampling of websites or client reports: the users have no way to know if the acquire a *good sample* of the population — simply having this kind of support automated would improve both user workload and output quality.

Moreover, the real task for the users starts now and is also unsupported: they have to aggregate for each hotel in h a number of around $w \times c$ client reports, e.g. determining pros and cons for each hotel according to the majority opinion of those reports, and finally deciding on the hotel that better fit their interests. Clearly, the S&B paradigm does not support this process and the users end up making a less informed decision. However, AI techniques could be used to support this decision, and I'm not referring to data mining or recommender systems, but to a reinterpretation of Case-based Reasoning that would allow us to support users in using experiential knowledge provided by a community of practice.

5   Reusing Other People's Experiences

Considering again the hotel selection example, we can easily substitute the *Search & Browse* process by *Retrieve & Reuse* processes of CBR:

1. the Retrieve process searches for client reports of hotels close to the declared interests of a user and selects a subset of them; then
2. the Reuse process analyzes the retrieved client reports in order to aggregate the information about pros and cons of each hotel and finally produces a ranking of hotels taking into account both the user's interests and the pros and cons of each hotel.

This mapping is sound, in the sense that both Retrieve and Reuse processes follow the ideas in [6]:

1. given a problem (a specific task to be achieved) the Retrieve process selects the subset of cases (experiential knowledge) most similar (or relevant) to that problem, while
2. the Reuse process combines, in some specific way, the (experiential) content of those retrieved cases (and possibly using some domain-specific knowledge as well) in order to achieve a solution for that problem (that specific task to be achieved).

   This rather abstract mapping allows us to determine in what a CBR approach to support experiential reuse in the web add to the S&B paradigm: the definition of a user-defined task to be achieved. Indeed, only when a problem (a specific task to be achieved) is posited then a *Retrieve & Reuse* approach can be used. Let us return to the hotel selection example again. Clearly the kind of hotel the user is interested in depends on the type of travel. For instance, whether it's in a one-night business trip or a week of leisure, the pro and con factors that are important may vary for one kind of travel to another. For instance, the factor of whether the hotel staff is categorized as friendly (in pros) or unfriendly (in cons) depends on the trip: a friendly/unfriendly staff is not important in a a one-night business trip while is quite important on a leisure week travel. This correspondence between the hotel client reports and the user interests would be performed inside the Reuse process, e.g. preferring those hotels with a clear majority of client reports stating a friendly stuff and the other factors important for the user. Notice that this is precisely the work the human user has to do, without any support, while examining $h \times w \times c$ client reports.

   Nevertheless, there are differences from the traditional CBR approach with respect to a *Retrieve & Reuse* approach to use the experiential knowledge of other people. These differences stem from tacit hypotheses used in CBR or implicit assumptions built from practice in building CBR systems. A first implicit assumption is that the Retrieve process will select one case (or a small number of cases) on which the Reuse process will work upon. As the hotel scenario shows, this is not the best option when dealing with experiential knowledge coming from a (potentially large) number of people. In the hotel scenario the role of the Reuse process is to select, among a huge number of client reports, a sufficient number of reports about hotels that are relevant for the specific request of a user (here seems more appropriate to call a user-defined query a *task* or a *request* than a *problem*).

Since the Reuse process needs to aggregate information from disparate sources in order to avoid noisy data, the sample of data has to be large enough so that aggregation methods like averages or weighted averages are meaningful. That is to say, in the hotel scenario the role of the Retrieve process may be to select the hotels relevant for the task at hand within some given ranges, for instance, of price and location, and then gathering all their relevant client reports. Additionally, the Retrieve process could perform an additional filtering or client reports based on their age, client reputation, etc. Then, given this sizeable sample of people's reports on their experiences, the Reuse process may be able to aggregate, from the evidence of disparate sources, the likelihood that one or a few hotels are the most adequate for the particular interests of a user travel.

The robustness of using experiential knowledge originating from multiple sources has been studied in several scientific fields. In Machine Learning, the "ensemble effect" states that using an ensemble of learning systems reduces always the error when compared to any single learning system. The only requirements for the "ensemble effect" to take place is that the prediction of individual learning systems is better than random and that their errors are not correlated with one another [7]. Similar properties have been characterized in Social Choice Theory, where the Condorcet Jury Theorem provides a similar property for taking average measures like voting in a jury [8]. Communities of practice on the web have been known to show a similar effect, a fact popularized in James Surowiecki's book *The Wisdom of the Crowds* — where similar conditions are prescribed in order to insure the emerging effect of wise decision or prediction by aggregating information from a crowd of people.

Therefore, a challenge for applying an approach like the *Retrieve & Reuse* one sketched here is to enlarge the core ideas of CBR, namely reasoning and learning from past experience, to a scenario where experiential knowledge originates from multiple individual sources; this multiplicity would require that we incorporate aggregation measures that obtain the desired "ensemble effect" into the Retrieve & Reuse processes. There are other CBR assumptions that need to be challenged to develop systems that reuse experiential knowledge on the web, and we will summarily address them in the next sections.

6   Semantics and Experience

In this section I will address to more challenging issues that need to be addressed in order to reuse experiential knowledge on the web, namely the semantics and structure of experiential knowledge. Concerning semantics, we have already discussed in section 2 the top-down approach of the semantic web and the bottom-up approach of folksonomies. Both approaches are suitable to be used in a CBR-like approach to reasoning from experiential knowledge on the web:

1. the semantic web uses ontologies expressed in description logics (specifically the OWL language[2]), which is compatible with the research line on knowledge-intensive CBR systems development using description logics;
2. Textual CBR [9] has been working on a bottom-up and hybrid approaches to semantics in cases expressed as text, which is compatible with the current research goals of folksonomies and web text mining — I think that the natural extension of Textual CBR is to address the challenges of textual experiential knowledge on the web.

Since both semantic approaches, or a combination of top-down and bottom-up approaches, are suitable for a CBR-like approach to reuse web experiential knowledge, the challenges are simply the same of any other web-based system developed using Artificial Intelligence techniques. Moreover, since the applicability and utility of either semantic approach may vary for different application domains, it is an empirical issue to determine when and how these semantic approaches will be useful. In this sense, the approach to reuse web experiential knowledge I'm sketching here would be neutral on these semantic debates, trying to find a suitable trade-off for a particular application domain and to keep up with the new developments in web semantics.

Nevertheless, the focus on user-contributed experiential knowledge poses some practical constraints. The first one is that the form in which experiential knowledge is expressed has to be an easy and natural form to the people integrating a community of practice; otherwise, very few content will be contributed, in practice, by this people. This constraint seems to bias experience representation towards text-based content, but this again depends on the specific community of practice we are dealing with in a particular application domain. Ontology-based approaches require a highly structured representation of content, but technical communities of practice (e.g. medicine, engineering) may accept this approach if they find provided services useful.

For other users in general a text-based approach seems more suitable, but it need not be completely free text, we should be able to provide semi-structured cases where the users can textually enter their experiences. This idea leads us to the second challenging issue I'd like to discuss: the structure of experiential knowledge.

7 Forms of Experience

An important issue about experiential knowledge on the web, as mentioned before in section 4, is that *cases* as such are not already present on the web. Recalling the hotel selection example we can see there is no collection of cases of the form (*situation, outcome*); instead we had *records of individual experiences*

---

[2] An overview of OWL is available at http://www.w3.org/TR/owl-features.

in the form of client reports. That is to say, we have a collection of *situations* without the *outcome*. For the task at hand, selecting a hotel, it is tempting to conceive of the *outcome* as the selected hotel: this is true for the system outputting a recommended hotel but it is not applicable to the client reports. A case in the standard sense would be a pair where a *situation* would describe the interests, preferences and constraints of a user and an *outcome* would be a hotel satisfying (most of) them. However, the client reports do not directly specify the persons interests, preferences and constraints; it is an *account* of an experience that may have been positive or negative (or something in between). Nevertheless, as I tried to show in the hotel scenario, some of this information is implicit and can be extracted: the analysis of the client records in terms of pro and con factors is a way to uncover the tacit interests and preferences of the users giving an account of their experiences.

There may be other ways to uncover the important factors in experiential accounts, since this pro and cons analysis is just an example. This leads us to the core issue in this approach: How many different *forms of experience* are there? Do we need to develop a new form or structure of experience for every new application domain? This circumstance could make impractical to apply this approach on the web at large. If not, are there a small collections of *forms of experience* that could be characterized and reused? Which are they and how to find them? I really have no answer in advance, since it is essentially an empirical matter to be settled only after trying to develop systems that reuse experiential knowledge on the web. I have some suggestions, though, as to how to proceed for developing systems that reuse experiential knowledge on the web.

The first one is trying to characterize a *form of experience* for each class of task commonly known in CBR systems: e.g. classification, regression, planning and configuration[3]. These tasks are classically differentiated by the form of the solution:

- *Classification* is a task that selects one solution from an enumerated collection of known solutions; the hotel selection scenario is thus a classification task. Variations of classification included here are: multilevel hierarchical classification and ranking of alternatives numerically or by partial ordering.
- *Regression* is a task where the numerical value of an attribute is predicted; case-base interpolation is the method of choice.
- *Planning* is a task that builds a solution composed by a sequence of actions or a partially ordered collection of actions; case-based planning has been extensively researched to deal with this kind of tasks.
- *Configuration* is a task that builds a solution composed by a network of interconnected solution elements; case-based configuration and design systems have developed techniques for this kind of task.

It seems reasonable to assume that the differences on the solution structures of these tasks imply that the corresponding experiential knowledge would also be

---

[3] This list does not intend to be closed or exhaustive, other tasks like scheduling etc., could be included and should be taken in to account in the long run.

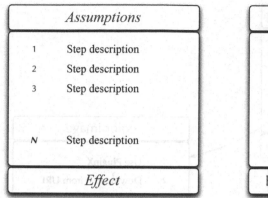

Fig. 1. Semi-structured form of experience for *How-To* tasks

structurally different. However, each class of task may have a sufficient degree of internal coherence to allow the development of experience-reuse systems applicable inside a class of tasks. For instance, the method of analyzing pros and cons in hotel client reports could be used, in principle, to other application domains whose task is a form of classification: e.g. selecting a digital camera, or selecting a B/W plugin for Photoshop. Moreover, other different techniques to reuse experiential knowledge for classification tasks could be developed. Again, only empirical evidence will determine whether the hypothesis suggested here is correct or not.

As a further example, let us consider *planning* in the context of experiential knowledge on the web. Since a plan is just a way to achieve some effect or goal performing a series of steps, it is easy to see that they are pervasive on the web, although they are not called "plans": sometimes they are called *How-Tos*, but most times they are just descriptions of how to do something in few steps. Forums are websites where a large number of *How-Tos* can be found. For instance, forums store numerous records of "question and answer" pairs that may be interpreted as problems and their solution-plan. A specific forum like one devoted to digital photography has both a community of practice and a shared vocabulary of terms (e.g. B/W image), verbs (actions) and proper nouns (e.g. "Photoshop"). A typical scenario is when a user asks how to perform some effect on an image and the answer is a plan of the form *"assuming you have Photoshop, you should download this PluginX from this URL, install it and then set it up in the beginner mode, you'll already have a good quality B/W image."* Forums organize this content in a structure based on questions and answers, and thus we are expected to use Search & Browse to find and reuse this experience. Capturing this experiential knowledge from free text using NLP techniques is certainly an option, but a computationally costly one.

Another option is to design some semi-structured representation for this form of experience that, if stored on a website (substituting the questions and

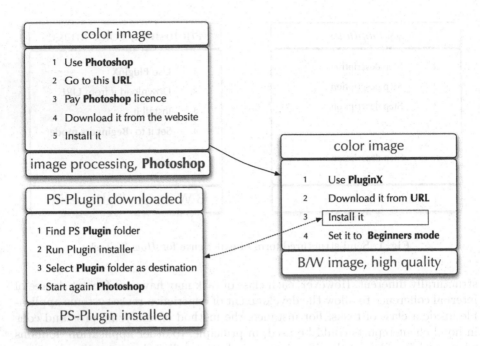

Fig. 2. Reusing experiential knowledge by combining *How-To*s

answers structure), would facilitate the analysis, retrieval and reuse of *How-To* knowledge. As a further elaboration of this scenario, consider a possible semi-structured template for *How-To* experiential knowledge as that show in Figure 1. The semi-structured template clearly separates plan preconditions (*Assumptions*), plan goals (*Effects*) and each one of the *Steps* or actions of the plan. Albeit text processing is still necessary, the previous example on *PluginX* shown at the right hand side of Fig. 1 is now more easily analyzed for the purposes of its reuse. Recall that the final user will be able to understand and perform this *How-To*, we need only enough structure to (1) allow a user to express the problem she wants to solve, e.g. "I have Photoshop and I want to transform a color image into B/W image a high quality," and (2) *recognize* that the *How-To* in Fig. 1 is a way to solve that problem.

Moreover, accessing a large repository of *How-To*s would also enable forms of *case-based plan adaptation*. Consider the situation where the user has the same goal but she does not have Photoshop. Figure 2 shows how a new plan can be generated by concatenating two *How-To*s: the first plan is one for acquiring Photoshop, while then second plan is that of Fig. 1 that uses a Plugin to achieve B/W image. Since the effect of the first *How-To* is having Photoshop, now the second plan can be safely used since the Photoshop assumption is now satisfied. Another form of adaptation is expanding a step, that is in fact a sup-plan, into its component sub-steps. Fig. 2 shows that Step 3 "Install Plugin" is not an atomic action, but can expanded into 4 steps because there is a *How-To* in the repository whose goal is to install Photoshop plugins. This form of plan adaptation should be feasible whenever we have a large repository of plan-like *How-Tos*, and it is in fact very akin to the currently fashionable idea of "mash-ups"[4] on the web.

Planning by reusing, adapting and combining user-contributed plans can be applied to a large number domains, from *How-Tos* and methods to itineraries and route sheets, as long as a large repository of "action sequences" is available. The fact that these plans have been already tried by someone and were successful gives us a further advantage. The *ensemble effect* can be used on a large repository: when several methods or plans are found to achieve the same result then aggregation techniques like voting can be used to determine the one that is considered more reliable (at least inside a community of practice).

Therefore, the hypothesis put forward in this section is that several forms of experience could be defined with sufficient internal coherence so that is possible and practical to build systems for reusing experiential knowledge. The next section discusses the overall organization of such systems.

8   The EDIR Cycle

These ideas can be integrated into a process model called the EDIR cycle, shown in Fig. 3; the EDIR cycle consists of four processes: *Express, Discover, Interpret,* and *Reuse.* They should be understood as interrelated processes, not as sequential or causally dependent steps: the state of the reuse process may require changes of bias or revisions of state in the interpret or discover processes as well as the other way around.

Express. This process addresses the different ways in which experience can be expressed by a contributing user inside a community of practice. Free, semi-structured and ontology-based templates for specific forms of experience and application domains need to be developed and tested; the research goal is finding a trade-off that (a) allows sufficient structuring of the expressed experiences for automated analysis and (b) feels as a natural and unobtrusive way to express experiences for the users in a community of practice.

Discovery. This process addresses the different ways in which specific experiential content is recognised and retrieved as possibly relevant to a given query posed by a system user. The research goal is determining how to extend CBR retrieval techniques to work on experiential content integrating semantic web and/or bottom-up semantic analysis. The conditions under which the Discovery process has to work requires a fast and possibly shallow analysis of large quantities of experiential reports; the expected output is a moderately-sized collection of experiences that are (likely) relevant to the current query.

Interpret. This process addresses the different ways to build semantic interpretations of the discovered experiences. The semantics are only assumed to hold inside a community of practice. These interpretations can be understood

---

[4] A *mash-up* refers to a web application that combines data from more than one source into a new integrated service.

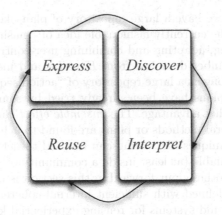

Fig. 3. The EDIR cycle for systems reusing experiential knowledge on the web

as a more in-depth analysis of the experiences selected by the Discovery process using the semantic model of the community of practice and the available domain knowledge. Several transformations are envisioned in the Interpret process: (a) eliminating a subset of discovered experiences as non-relevant; (b) transforming discovered experiences into a new canonical representation; (c) translating discovered experiences into a canonical vocabulary coherent with the one used to build the final users queries. One or several of these transformations will be used in a particular system, but the final outcome is a collection of canonical experience descriptions to be used by the Reuse process.

Reuse. This process addresses the different ways in which the experiential content provided by the Interpret process is used to achieve the goals of a user as described in a particular query. Reuse techniques from CBR may need to be revised or extended in order to be applicable in this context (e.g. case-based adaptation) but also new methods that rely on the nature of large repositories of human experience should be developed (e.g. methods based on the *ensemble effect*). Moreover there may be different modalities of experience reuse: from automated experience reuse (yielding to the user the complete solution provided by reusing experiential knowledge) to the opposite extreme where the user receives directly a small selection of relevant and reliable experiences. Intermediate modalities may perform part of the reuse process automatically while supporting the user in reuse finalization.

The EDIR cycle is a process model, so the relationship of the four processes is not sequential in an implementation of the model. Clearly, during an interaction with the final user to elucidate the requirements of her enquiry several discovery and interpretation processes may be launched and their results used to help the user narrow her options or change her preferences.

Finally, let's compare this EDIR approach with the current Search & Browse approach. The main difference is that the EDIR approach requires a *query*: a description of the kind of result needed by the system —a definition of the *problem to be solved.* Only with a query it is possible to *reuse* experiences, since the Reuse process employs methods that try to satisfy the requirements of the current query using a collection of selected experiences. A second but important difference concerns the form and organization of content. The Search & Browse approach assumes the existence of just hyperlinked documents: even when some structure is present (e.g. question-answer structures in forums), this structure is not exploited to improve the results. The EDIR approach intends to characterize a particular kind of content, experiential knowledge, and it is thus concerned on how to adequately express, represent, organize, analyze, and retrieve this content.

9   Discussion

This paper is about current and future challenges on reasoning from experience. As such, I've dispensed with some formalities of the typical structure and content of scientific papers. There is not proper state of the art section, albeit sections 2 and 3 deal with the main issues on the state of the art for the purposes of this paper. There is no state of the art on natural language processing and text mining applied to the web, but this is because they are orthogonal to the purposes of this paper: they can be applied, and they mostly are applied inside the S&B approach; but they could also be used in an EDIR approach to experiential knowledge reuse.

The purpose of the paper is not presenting a specific contribution but a series of ideas that open a discussion on how to apply AI techniques, in general, and CBR techniques in particular, to the ever-growing World-Wide Web. The main idea to be opened to debate is whether there is, or is useful to conceive of, experiential knowledge on the web. I've not given a formal definition of *experience*, but my use of the term is close to the common sense meaning, and the examples presented, should be enough for a Wittgenstein-like grasp of its meaning. I found worthy of attention that trying to apply CBR ideas like reuse of past experience to the web, I've had had to abandon a straightforward notion of *case*. CBR cannot be directly applied to the web, since there are no ready-made cases preexisting on the web. However, if we understand CBR as ways of reusing past experience, we can generalize these core ideas in CBR and investigate how could we possibly reuse the experiences that people are already providing on the web.

The EDIR cycle is simply a way to organize the different issues and challenges to be addressed in developing systems for reusing experiential knowledge on the web. As such, is a tool for helping to start thinking and debating about how to build systems that reuse experience, and should be left aside when enough progress is made that shows how to proceed. I cannot claim that I can show some example system that follows the EDIR cycle, and nevertheless I can point you to the Poolcasting system, developed by Claudio Baccigalupo under my supervision as part of his Ph. D. Indeed, the Poolcasting system does not follow the EDIR cycle, since it was being developed in parallel with this proposal, and yet it shows an example of how extending some core CBR ideas we can develop a system that reuse experiential knowledge from a web community of practice.

Poolcasting generates a stream of songs that is customized for a group of listeners [10]. We needed to perform data mining processes over web communities of practice to acquire the semantics of the vocabulary of terms the systems uses. Several web-enabled information resources on the web needed to be accessed and integrated with Poolcasting to acquire a domain model. The experiential knowledge we used did not have the form of *cases*, but it is nevertheless a form of content that expresses the listening experience of the users as recorded by the music player devices. Because of this, Poolcasting is able to build, from the listening experience of a user, a model of user's musical interests that is exploited by a Reuse process.

Thus, while I cannot claim that Poolcasting is a result of the EDIR approach, it stems from the same core ideas, and as such worthy of being considered a proof of concept. The bottom-line is that I think experience reuse can be brought to the web, and the core ideas of CBR may be very useful in this endeavor.

Acknowledgements. This paper has benefited from long, engaging discussions of the author with many people, specially Agnar Aamodt, Josep-Lluís Arcos, Paolo Avesani, Klaus-Dieter Althoff, Ralph Bergmann, Susan Craw, and Nirmalie Wiratunga; all errors or misconceptions, however, are the author's responsibility. *This research has been partially supported by the Project MID-CBR (TIN2006-15140-C03-01).*

References

1. Berners-Lee, T., Hendler, J., Lassila, O.: The semantic web. Scientific American Magazine (2001)
2. Shadbolt, N., Wendy Hall, T.B.L.: The semantic web revisited. IEEE Intelligent Systems 21(3), 96–101 (2006)
3. Wittgenstein, L.: Investigacions filosòfiques (Philosophische Bemerkungen). Ed. Laia, Barcelona (1983) (1953)
4. Davies, J.: Semantic Web Technologies: Trends and Research in Ontology-based Systems. Wiley, Chichester (2006)
5. Benkler, Y.: The Wealth of Networks. How Social Production Transforms Markets and Freedom. Yale University Press (2006)
6. Aamodt, A., Plaza, E.: Case-based Reasoning: Foundational issues, methodological variations, and system approaches. Artificial Intelligence Communications 7(1), 39–59 (1994), http://www.iiia.csic.es/People/enric/AICom_ToC.html
7. Perrone, M.P., Cooper, L.N.: When networks disagree: Ensemble methods for hydrid neural networks. In: Artificial Neural Networks for Speech and Vision. Chapman-Hall, Boca Raton (1993)
8. Sunstein, C.R.: Group judgments: Deliberation, statistical means, and information markets. New York University Law Review 80, 962–1049 (2005)
9. Weber, R.O., Ashley, K.D., Brninghaus, S.: Textual case-based reasoning. The Knowledge Engineering Review 20, 255–260 (2005)
10. Baccigalupo, C., Plaza, E.: A case-based song scheduler for group customised radio. In: Weber, R.O., Richter, M.M. (eds.) ICCBR 2007. LNCS (LNAI), vol. 4626, pp. 433–448. Springer, Heidelberg (2007)

Recognizing the Enemy: Combining Reinforcement Learning with Strategy Selection Using Case-Based Reasoning

Bryan Auslander, Stephen Lee-Urban, Chad Hogg, and Héctor Muñoz-Avila

Dept. of Computer Science & Engineering
Lehigh University
Bethlehem, PA, USA

Abstract. This paper presents CBRetaliate, an agent that combines Case-Based Reasoning (CBR) and Reinforcement Learning (RL) algorithms. Unlike most previous work where RL is used to improve accuracy in the action selection process, CBRetaliate uses CBR to allow RL to respond more quickly to changing conditions. CBRetaliate combines two key features: it uses a time window to compute similarity and stores and reuses complete Q-tables for continuous problem solving. We demonstrate CBRetaliate on a team-based first-person shooter game, where our combined CBR+RL approach adapts quicker to changing tactics by an opponent than standalone RL.

1 Introduction

Reinforcement Learning (RL) has been successfully applied to a variety of domains including game theoretic decision processes [1] and RoboCup soccer [2]. It has also been applied successfully for a number of computer gaming applications including real-time strategy games [3], backgammon [4], and more recently for first-person shooter (FPS) games [5].

Despite these successes, it may take a while before an agent using RL adapts to changes in the environment. This is the result of the exploration process, in which the agent must try new actions with unknown utility to develop a policy maximizing its expected future rewards. This can be problematic in some applications. For example, we observed this when applying RL techniques to team-based first-person shooters (TFPS). TFPS is a very popular game genre where teams of two or more players compete to achieve some winning conditions. In TFPS games, individual players must have good reflexes to ensure short-term survival by shooting the enemy and avoiding enemy fire while working together to achieve the winning conditions of the game. In recent work we constructed an agent, Retaliate, which uses an online RL algorithm for developing winning policies in TFPS games [5]. Specifically, Retaliate uses the Q-learning variant of RL, in which a policy is encoded in a table of expected rewards for each state-action pair, called a Q-table. Retaliate demonstrated that it was capable of developing a winning policy very quickly within the first game against an opponent that

K.-D. Althoff et al. (Eds.): ECCBR 2008, LNAI 5239, pp. 59–73, 2008.

used a fixed strategy. We also observed that it took Retaliate a number of iterations before it adapted when the opponent changed its strategy. Thus, we began considering techniques that would allow us to speed up the adaptation process in such situations where the strategy employed by an opponent changes.

In this paper we present CBRetaliate, an agent that uses Case-Based Reasoning (CBR) techniques to enhance the Retaliate RL agent. Unlike most previous work where RL is used to improve accuracy in the case selection process, CBRetaliate uses CBR to jump quickly to previously stored policies rather than slowly adapting to changing conditions. Cases in CBRetaliate contain features indicating sensory readings from the game world when the case was created. They also store the complete Q-table that is maintained by CBRetaliate when the case was created. CBRetaliate stores a case when it has been accumulating points at a faster rate than its opponent during a time window. When it is accumulating points more slowly than its opponent, it attempts to retrieve a similar case. CBRetaliate uses an aggregated similarity metric that combines local similarity metrics for each feature. This similarity metric is computed by matching sensory readings from the current gaming world and those of the case over the time window. When a case is retrieved, its associated Q-table is adapted by Retaliate by using standard RL punishment/reward action selection.

Our working hypothesis is as follows. The use of CBR will allow CBRetaliate to recognize strategies similar to ones it has faced previously but different from the one it has most recently fought, and thus to outperform Retaliate when such a strategy change occurs. We tested our hypothesis with an ablation study comparing the performance of Retaliate and CBRetaliate in games against a number of opponents each using a different strategy. Each of these tests consisted of a tournament of several consecutive games with the Q-table saved between games. Within a tournament, CBRetaliate was able to more soundly beat an opponent similar to one it had previously faced by loading a case learned from the previous opponent. The nature of its opponent was not defined for CBRetaliate, but needed to be inferred from sensory readings describing the behavior it observed over time.

The paper continues as follows: the next section describes the TFPS game and the Retaliate algorithm. Next, in Section 3, we describe CBRetaliate by discussing how it uses the phases of the CBR problem-solving cycle. The next section describes the empirical evaluation. Section 5 presents related work. We conclude this paper with some final remarks.

2   Background

The CBRetaliate agent is an extension of an existing Reinforcement Learning agent, Retaliate, to use techniques from Case-Based Reasoning. As a testbed for this agent, we use a configuration of a first-person shooter game in which individual computer-controlled players (bots) act independently but follow a team-level strategy to achieve their objectives.

2.1 Domination Game Domain

Unreal Tournament (UT) is a first-person shooter game in which the usual objective is to shoot and kill opposing players. Players track their health and their weapon's ammunition, as well as attempt to pick up various items strewn about the map while amassing kills and preserving their own life. Opponents may be other human players via online multiplayer action or computer-controlled bots. An interesting feature of UT is the ability to play several different game variants. One of these variants is a domination game, a feature offered by many team-based multiplayer game.

In a domination game, the player's objective is not to earn kills, although this is usually necessary. Rather, the goal is to accumulate points for a player's team by controlling certain locations in the game world known as domination locations. A domination point is controlled by the team of the player who was last in the location, and lost when a player from the opposing team reaches it. Each domination point produces points over time for the team that controls it, and the game ends when one team's score reaches some threshold.

Domination games are ideal test domains for cooperative artificial intelligence agents because they require both tactics to succeed in individual firefights and strategy to decide how and where individual bots should be deployed. We have chosen to focus exclusively on strategy, using an abstract model described in Section 2.4.

2.2 HTNbots

One of the first successful agents developed for controlling teams of bots in UT domination games was HTNbots [6]. HTNbots uses Hierarchical Task Network (HTN) planning to generate plans during the game. The preconditions of HTN methods used by HTNbots map to state information about the game world, and the operators correspond to commands telling each individual bot where it should attack or patrol. We now use HTNbots as a known difficult opponent against which Retaliate and CBRetaliate can be compared.

2.3 Retaliate

Retaliate is an online RL algorithm for developing winning policies in team-based first-person shooter games. Retaliate has three crucial characteristics: (1) individual bot behavior is fixed although not known in advance, therefore individual bots work as plugins, (2) Retaliate models the problem of learning team tactics through a simple state formulation, (3) discount rates commonly used in Q-learning are not used. As a result of these characteristics, the application of the Q-learning algorithm results in the rapid exploration towards a winning policy against an opponent team. In our empirical evaluation we demonstrate that Retaliate adapts well when the environment changes.

Retaliate is controlled by two parameters: ε, which is known as the "epsilon-greedy" parameter and controls the trade-off between exploration and exploitation by setting the rate at which the algorithm selects a random action rather

---

Algorithm 1. RetaliateTick(Q_t)

1: **Input**: Q-Table Q_t
2: **Output**: updated Q-table
3: ε is .10, and $State_{prev}$ is maintained internally
4: **if** rand(0, 1) $> \varepsilon$ **then** {epsilon greedy selection}
5:     $Act \leftarrow$ applicable action with max value in Q-table
6: **else**
7:     $Act \leftarrow$ random applicable action from Q-table
8: $State_{now} \leftarrow$ Execute(Act)
9: $Reward \leftarrow$ Utility($State_{now}$) − Utility($State_{prev}$)
10: $Q_t \leftarrow$ update Q-table
11: $State_{prev} \leftarrow State_{now}$
12: return Q_t

---

than the one that is expected to perform best, and α, which is referred to as the "step-size" parameter and influences the rate of learning. For our case study, we found that setting ε to 0.1 and α to 0.2 worked well.

The following computations are iterated through until the game is over. First, the next team action to execute, Act, is selected using the epsilon-greedy parameter. The selected action Act is then executed.

On the next domination ownership update from the server, which occurs rougly every four seconds, the current state $State_{now}$ is observed and the Q values for the previous state $State_{prev}$ and previously selected actions are updated based on whether or not $State_{now}$ is more favorable than $State_{prev}$. New actions are selected from the new current state, and the process continues.

The reward for the new state $State_{now}$ is computed as the difference between the utilities in the new state, and the previous state $State_{prev}$. Specifically, the utility of a state s is defined by the function $U(s) = F(s) - E(s)$, where $F(s)$ is the number of friendly domination locations and $E(s)$ is the number that are controlled by the enemy. This has the effect that, relative to team A, a state in which team A owns two domination locations and team B owns one has a higher utility than a state in which team A owns only one domination location and team B owns two. The reward function, which determines the scale of the reward, is computed as $R = U(State_{now}) - U(State_{prev})$.

The calculated reward R is used to perform an update on the Q-table entry $Q(s, a)$ for the previous state s in which the last set of actions a were ordered. This calculation is performed according to the following formula, which is standard for computing Q-table entries in temporal difference learning [7]:

$$Q(s, a) \leftarrow Q(s, a) + \alpha(R + \gamma \times max_{a'}Q(s', a') - Q(s, a))$$

In this computation, the entry in the Q-table for the action a that was just taken in state s,$Q(s, a)$, is updated. The function $max_{a'}$ returns the value from the Q-table of the best team action that can be performed in the new state s' which is simply the highest value associated with s' in the table for any a'. The value of γ ($\gamma = 1$ in Retaliate), the 'discount rate parameter', adjusts the relative influences of current and future rewards in the decision making process.

2.4 Game Model

The Q-learning algorithm on which Retaliate is based stores the expected future reward of each potential action in each state. There are many potential features that could be used to define the state of the game and numerous actions a bot may take at various levels of granularity. In Retaliate, we chose to use a very simple, abstract model of the game world. Specifically, each state is defined by the current ownership of each domination point. For a game containing three domination points and two teams, as in our experiments, each state is a 3-tuple where each value is either "Friendly", "Enemy" or "Unowned" (the default before any bot has entered the location). Thus, such a game has 27 possible states.

Because we are focusing on grand team strategy rather than tactics, our action model is similarly simple. Each action consists of the assignments of each bot on the team to one of the domination points. Thus, a game with three domination points and teams of three bots will similarly have 27 possible actions.

This model of the world is quite simple, but surprisingly effective. Enough information is provided to allow the representation of a robust strategy and the Q-table is small enough that the algorithm is able to converge to a reasonably complete table within the space of only a few games.

3 Algorithm

When the situation changes so dramatically that the policy encoded by Retaliate is no longer valid, such as by changing the opponent, the Q-learning algorithm must slowly explore the policy space again, trying actions and updating the rewards until it finds a new good policy. We developed CBRetaliate to solve this problem by storing winning policies and retrieving them later based on other types of features from the game state. In this section we present the contents of cases, how similarity is computed, and finally the psuedocode for CBRetaliate.

3.1 Case Features and Similarity Functions

As stated previously, CBRetaliate uses an aggregated similarity metric that combines the local similarity metrics for each case feature. Local similarities are valued between zero and one, and are computed by matching sensory readings from a time window within the current game world with those stored in the case. The value of the aggregate is simply the sum of the local similarity for each feature, divided by the number of features. We found CBRetaliate to be effective with this naive aggregate function and feature weights, but expect that much better performance would be possible if these parameters were carefully tuned.

Each case contains a Q-table along with a set of features that are summarized in Table 1. The first two categories of features, *Team Size* and *Team Score* are notable because they do not involve the navigation task. Whereas our RL problem model is limited to domination location ownership in order to reduce the state space, the CBR component does not share this restriction. Consequently,

Table 1. Description of feature categories and their local similarity function name

Category	Description	Local Sim. Function
Team Size	The number of bots on a team.	Sim_{TSize}
Team Score	The score of each team	Sim_{TScore}
Bot/Dom Dist.	Distance of each bot to each dom. loc.	Sim_{Dist}
Dom Ownership	Which team owns each of the dom. locs	Sim_{Own}

the name of each team as well as the map name could have been used as features, however, we wished to demonstrate the ability of CBRetaliate to recognize strategies and situations based on behavior and observations.

The *Team Size* category is currently a single feature that records the number of bots on a team. Teams are assumed to be of equal size, however this assumption could be easily dropped by adding a feature for each team. If x is the size of the team in the current game and y is the team size from a case, $Sim_{Tsize}(x, y)$ is equal to one when $x = y$ and zero otherwise.

The *Team Score* category consists of two features, namely the score of each team. So, if x is the score of team A in the current game and y is the score of team B from a case, then the similarity is computed by $Sim_{TScore}(x, y) = 1 - (|x - y|/SCORE\_LIMIT)$. The constant $SCORE\_LIMIT$ is the score to which games are played and is 100 in our experiments. In our case-base, team A is always CBRetaliate and team B is the opponent.

The next category of features, *Bot/Dom Dist.*, uses the Euclidian distance of each bot to each domination location to compute similarity. That is, each case contains, for each opponent bot b and for each domination location l, the absolute value of the Euclidian distance from b to l. Specifically, if x is the Euclidian distance of b to l in the current game and y the analogous distance from the case, then $Sim_{Dist}(x, y) = 1 - (|x - y|/MAX\_DIST)$. The constant MAX_DIST is the maximum Euclidian distance any two points can be in an Unreal Tournament map. With an opposing teams of size 3 and a map with 3 domination locations, this category has a total of $3 * 3 = 9$ features.

The final category of features, *Dom Ownership*, uses the fraction of time each team t has owned each domination location l during the time window δ (elaborated upon in the next subsection) to compute similarity. So, if x is the fraction of time t has controlled l in the current game and y is the analogous fraction from the case, then $Sim_{Own}(x, y) = 1 - |x - y|$. Intuitively, with 2 teams and 3 domination locations, this category has a total of 6 features.

3.2   The CBRetaliate Algorithm

Algorithm 2 shows at a high-level how CBRetaliate operates during a single game. However, before explaining the algorithm, we must first define four constants that control its behavior.

The first constant, U^l, defines the minimum number of game cycles that must occur, since the last case was retrieved or retained, before the load of a case is considered. During retrieval the best case is returned and is used only if its similarity is above the second constant, $THRESH$. The third constant, U^s, has the same meaning as U^l except controls when saving can occur. For our empirical evaluation we used $U^l = 22$, $U^s = 30$, and 0.75 for $THRESH$.

The fourth and final constant, δ, is used in two important ways. On the one hand, δ is used to determine whether or not CBRetaliate is accumulating points faster than its opponent by computing the current difference in score at game cycle t and subtracting from that the score difference at cycle $t - \delta$. On the other hand, δ is also used to compute the so-called "sliding average" of domination location ownership. This average tracks, for each domination location l, the fraction of time that each team has owned l within the window defined between the current game cycle t and $t - \delta$ (this value is used in Sim_{Own}). For our empirical evaluation, we set δ to 15.

Algorithm 2. CBRetaliate(CB, Q_t)

1: **Input**: case-base CB, Q-table Q_t
2: **Output**: The updated CB, and the Q-table last loaded Q_t
3:    $num\_updates \leftarrow 0$
4: **while** game is not over **do**
5:    $num\_updates$++
6:    $Q_t \leftarrow$ RetaliateTick(Q_t) {Revise}
7:    $S_{now} \leftarrow$ GetCurrentState
8:    **if** $num\_updates >= \delta$ **then** {wait for window}
9:      **if** $(ScoreDiff_{now} - ScoreDiff_{now-\delta}) > 0$ **then**
10:        **if** $num\_updates >= U^s$ **then** {enough Q-table updates}
11:          $CB \leftarrow$ SaveCase(Q_t, CB, S_{now}) {Retain}
12:          $num\_updates \leftarrow 0$
13:      **else**
14:        **if** $num\_updates >= U^l$ **then** {enough Q-table updates}
15:          $SimCase \leftarrow$ OnePassRetreive(S_{now}) {find most sim case}
16:          **if** similarity($S_{now}, SimCase$) $> THRESH$ **then** {similar enough}
17:            $Q_t \leftarrow$ getQTable($SimCase$) {Reuse}
18:            $num\_updates \leftarrow 0$
19: **return** (CB, Q_t)

Algorithm 2 works as follows. When started for the first time, the case-base CB is empty, and every entry in the Q-table is initialized to the same default value. During a game, the number of game cycles that have passed since the last case load or save is tracked with the variable $num\_updates$. In line 6, algorithm 1 is used to update the Q-table on every game cycle, as explained in Section 2.3. Line 8 ensures that there have been at least δ game cycles since the last case was loaded or saved before allowing the algorithm to proceed. As a consequence of waiting at least δ game cycles, the Retaliate algorithm is able to perform at least a few Q-table updates before an alternate table is considered. This helps avoid reloading tables when losing, and also gives Retaliate a chance to learn a better strategy.

If enough cycles have occurred, line 9 computes whether or not CBRetaliate has increased its winning margin in the last δ updates. If the winning margin has increased, and there have been a sufficient number of game cycles (U^s), the current Q-table is added to the case-base, along with all features describing the current game state (S_{now}), and *num_updates* is reset. A save when the winning margin has increase is sensible because the Q-table in use is clearly working well against the opponent. Otherwise, if the winning margin has decreased and there have been a sufficient number of game cycles (U^l), the case in the case base most similar to the current game features is retrieved. If the similarity of the retrieved case is above $THRESH$, the Q-table from that case is used to replace the Q-table currently-in-use and *num_updates* is reset.

4   Evaluation

To evaluate the effectiveness of combining Case-Based Reasoning with Reinforcement Learning in this way, we have performed several experiments using the technique to control teams of bots in domination games. It should be noted that we found a bug that gives the learning teams an advantage over non-learning teams. However, this glitch does not effect our claims of using CBR with RL, because both CBRetaliate and Retaliate are learning teams.

4.1   Evaluation against CompositeBot

In order to easily test our hypothesis about an opponent that changes strategies, we developed a simple configurable agent called CompositeBot. CompositeBot does not use any information about the game state, but simply provides static assignments of each team member to a domination point. Rather than changing strategies within a single game, we ran a series of seven games consecutively, changing the configuration of CompositeBot (its static assignments) between each game. The map on which these games were played contains three domination points that we will call "A", "J", and "R".

In the first three games, we configured CompositeBot to use a strategy of stationing two bots at one of the domination points and one at another, changing the points selected between games. The next three games are repeats of the first three. In the last game, the opponent sends one bot to each domination point. The specific strategies used in each game are shown in Table 2.

We ran 15 trials each of both Retaliate and CBRetaliate against this series of opponents. Each trial begins with an empty Q-table and (for CBRetaliate) an empty case base. Both the Q-table and case base are updated and enhanced throughout the course of the 7 games.

The results of this experiment are summarized in Table 3. Each game ends when one of the team reaches 100 points. All results are an average over the 15 trials. The values in this table are the difference in score between the algorithm being tested and its opponent when the game is 25% finished and when it is complete. Differences that are statistically significant with a 90% confidence level are bolded.

One of the motivations for this work was an expectation that CBRetaliate would have much better early performance than Retaliate when facing an

Table 2. CompositeBot configurations

Game	1	2	3	4	5	6	7
Strategy	AAJ	RRA	JJA	AAJ	RRA	JJA	AJR

Table 3. CompositeBot results

		Difference At 25%	Different At 100%
Game 1	Retaliate	7.72	53.57
	CBRetaliate	8.10	52.93
Game 2	Retaliate	**9.7**	48.35
	CBRetaliate	**6.01**	46.49
Game 3	Retaliate	**6.96**	**47.75**
	CBRetaliate	**11.18**	**68.49**
Game 4	Retaliate	**6.02**	**57.8**
	CBRetaliate	**10.05**	**65.84**
Game 5	Retaliate	8.37	37.54
	CBRetaliate	7.5	49.11
Game 6	Retaliate	6.53	58.66
	CBRetaliate	7.92	62.98
Game 7	Retaliate	**3.40**	53.01
	CBRetaliate	**10.1**	58.35

opponent from which it had already stored cases, because it would be able to immediately jump to a Q-table that had been effective against the opponent in the past. Thus, we would expect CBRetaliate to perform significantly better than Retaliate in the first 25% of games 4, 5, and 6. Although this is the case in games 3, 4, and 7, it is not true of 5 or 6. Furthermore, Retaliate has an early advantage in the second game. There are two reasons why we have not consistently seen this expectation met. First, the features used for case retrieval require trend information about the game. Thus, it is difficult to reliably select a good case until enough of the game has been played to recognize the opponent's strategy. The other contributing factor is that the locations of the domination points are not known at the beginning of the game, and strategies cannot be used until the bots have discovered them by exploring the map. We do not explicitly count the exploration phase as a team action, but rather treat it as an initialization phase because all teams use the same search algorithm for the same length of time. Work is underway to remove the need for finding locations. All domination points are found, on average, when 13% of the game is finished, but in rare cases there have been games that end before all have been found.

In game 1, Retaliate and CBRetaliate perform nearly identically by the end of the game. This is expected, because when CBRetaliate has no cases stored it works exactly like Retaliate (except that it stores new cases). Figure 1 shows the comparative performance of Retaliate and CBRetaliate in the first game. This and all future graphs show the difference between the scores of each algorithm and its opponent over time, which is scaled to the percentage of game finished to facilitate averaging over several trials.

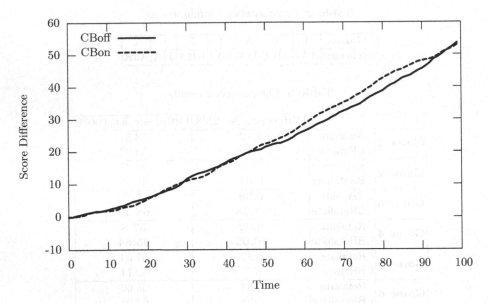

Fig. 1. Averaged score differential in game 1

Retaliate gains a small advantage in the second game, but is beaten soundly in the third. At the start of game 3, Retaliate will have a mature Q-table built to counter a strategy that heavily defends domination point "R", lightly defends point "A", and ignores "J". Such a Q-table will be poorly suited to fighting an opponent who heavily defends "J", lightly defends "A", and ignores "R". Retaliate is able to win in spite of its poor initial strategy by adapting and favoring those decisions that have positive outcomes. CBRetaliate, however, loads a Q-table from the end of the first game. The strategies of the opponents in the first and third games are not identical, but they are similar enough that a strategy effective against one will be somewhat effective against the other.

CBRetaliate wins by a smaller but still significant margin in game 4, where it faces an opponent identical to the one from game 1. The score differentials from this game are shown in Figure 2. In this case Retaliate should have a reasonable strategy from the previous game, but CBRetaliate is able to load an excellent strategy from the first game. On average, CBRetaliate wins by a similar margin in games 5 and 6, but these results are not statistically significant due to higher variance. CBRetaliate also does well against the balanced strategy of game 7, even though it has not previously faced that strategy. This is because it returns to a less mature Q-table from the early parts of a previous game that is more suited to combating a balanced strategy than the specialized Q-table that Retaliate starts with.

4.2 Evaluation against HTNbots

We also performed a second experiment in which CBRetaliate and Retaliate were matched against HTNbots. For this experiment, we used a sequence of 10 games.

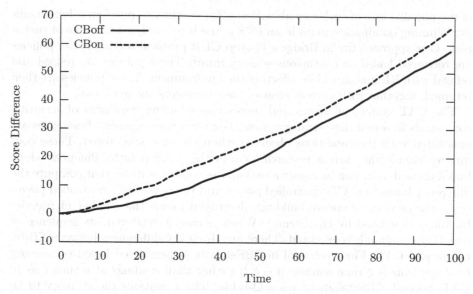

Fig. 2. Averaged score differential in game 4

We did not alter HTNbots between games, but expected that its natural ability to choose different strategies would allow it to perform better against Retaliate than against CBRetaliate.

Surprisingly, this was not the case. The only stastically significant difference between the performance of Retaliate and CBRetaliate against HTNbots was in game 8, where Retaliate won by a higher margin. Across all 10 games, Retaliate beat HTNbots by an average of 22.73 points while CBRetaliate's margin of victory was 23.86 points, a nearly indistinguishable difference.

The reason for these results is a design flaw with the knowledge base encoded in HTNbots that was only revealed through these experiments. HTNbots has one strategy used when not all domination points have been found and one strategy for each number of domination points it controls when the locations of all are known. Ownership of domination points can change quite rapidly during a competitive game, causing HTNbots to quickly oscillate between strategies as it loses and retakes domination points. CBRetaliate is designed to respond to significant, long-lasting changes in strategy. Thus, it retrieves cases based on observed behavior over a time interval. If the opponent is frequently changing strategies such that throughout most of the game it is using its control-one strategy 60% of the time and its control-two strategy 40% of the time, then this combination is effectively a single static strategy, and CBRetaliate will have no significant advantage over Retaliate.

5   Related Work

There are a number of works combining Case-Based Reasoning and Reinforcement Learning. In his ICCBR-05 invited talk, Derek Bridge pointed out that one of the possible uses of such a combination is for continuous problem solving tasks [8]. Winning domination maps in an FPS game is precisely an example of such a task. Our approach fits in Bridge's 11-step CBR problem solving cycle; policies are retrieved based on continuous sensory input. These policies are reused and refined with RL updates while affecting the environment. These policies are then retained, together with current sensory measurements, as new cases.

The CAT system [9] stores and reuses cases having sequences of scripting commands in a real-time strategy game. For retrieval purposes, these cases are annotated with the conditions observed when the case was stored. These conditions include the current research level in the game (which influences which buildings and units can be constructed) and several conditions that compute the difference between CAT's controlled player and the opponent's controlled player (e.g., the number of enemy buildings destroyed minus the number of friendly buildings destroyed by the enemy). When a case it retrieved, its sequence of scripting commands is executed. There are three key differences between CBRe-taliate and CAT. First, retrieval in CBRetaliate is performed based on sensory readings from a δ-time window $[t - \delta, t]$ rather than readings at a time t as in CAT. Second, CBRetaliate stores a Q-table, which contains the strategy to be followed and alternative strategies, rather than a sequence of scripted actions. A policy can be seen as representing multiple sequences of scripted actions. Third, in CAT, the case's scripted actions are not adapted. In CBRetaliate, the retrieved Q-table is adapted with the standard reward and punishment operations of RL.

In [10], a CBR system capable of playing real-time strategy games is presented. The system learns cases by observing users' actions. It reuses cases by combining them into strategies that consists of the combination of individual cases. In contrast, CBRetaliate stores Q-tables as cases, which contain the winning strategy together with alternative strategies.

The CARL architecture combines CBR and RL to create agents capable of playing real-time strategy games [11]. CARL is a multi-level architecture similar in spirit to hierarchical task network representations [12] where the higher levels of the hierarchy represents strategies and the low level concrete actions. At the highest level a hand-coded planner is used. At the intermediate level, CBR and RL are used to select the specific tactic (e.g., to attack, to defend), and at the concrete level a plan executor module controls the actions being executed. As a comparison, CBRetaliate can be seen as a two-level architecture. At the top level CBR and RL are used to learn and reuse the strategy to follow. At the bottom level, bots follow these strategies using hard-coded programs. This difference is not arbitrary but almost certainly a design decision that reflects the difference between the two game genres that each system is targeting. In first-person shooters, targeted by CBRetaliate, fast reflexes are needed from individual bots, as players need to respond in fractions of a second to attacks from an opponent or make quick decisions to grab a nearby weapon or follow an opponent. Therefore, in CBRetaliate individual bot behavior is hard-coded. In real-time strategy games, players have more time (seconds at least) to decide if they are going to attack or defend. Like in CBRetaliate, cases in CARL stored what amounts to a

Q-table, annotated with the applicability conditions. But unlike CBRtaliate but as with CAT, case retrieval in CARL is based on mapping of current readings at time t rather than in a time window $[t - \delta, t]$ as in CBRetaliate.

CBRetaliate is closely related to *Continuous Case-Based Reasoning*, which was implemented in the SINS system for robot navigation tasks [13]. Continuous CBR advocates that in domains involving real time execution, a time window or *time-history*, as originally called, should be considered during retrieval. All features in SINS are numerical, reflecting the navigation domain targeted. Thus, the difference in trajectories is reflected in the computation of similarity. CBRetaliate also uses features that reflect geometrical relations in the map (e.g., distance between a bot and a domination location). However, CBRetaliate also uses features that are not geometrical relations (e.g., the current score in the game). As a result, we needed to use an aggregate similarity metric to combine these distinctive local similarity metrics. Another difference is that SINS did not use RL for adapting the navigation path. This is possibly due to the fact that a direct application of RL would have resulted in a large search space. More recent work on robotics have found ways to work around that problem (e.g., [14]).

Researchers have proposed to use domain knowledge encoded as HTNs or similar representations in the context of RL and more generally MDPs [15,16]. One of the results of combining HTN-like knowledge and RL/MDPs is a significant reduction in the search space compared to standalone RL/MDPs. The reason for this is that knowledge encoded in the HTN eliminates unneccesary parts of the search space, parts which *pure* RL/MDPs approaches would otherwise need to explore. In CBRetaliate we do not provide such knowledge in advance, so it is conceivable that CBRetaliate could also benefit from search reduction, albeit with the tradeoff of extra effort required to encode the domain knowledge.

6   Conclusions

It is possible to enhance the states as defined currently in Retaliate by adding the 18 features currently used in CBRetaliate to compute case similarity to the 3 features already used by Retaliate. This would require discretizing the real-valued attributes and vastly increasing the number of states in the Q-table. Rather than using such an expanded table, which would pose technical challenges and require far more time to become mature, CBRetaliate can be seen as partitioning the space of possibilities into regions, each with a suitable Q-table associated with it, and using CBR to "jump" to the appropriate region of the space by selecting a suitable 27-cell table for that region. In our experiments, this capability of CBRetaliate to jump between regions demonstrated speed-up in the elicitation of a winning policy when the opponent was changed.

Another point to be made is that we applied in our experiments a naive approach when computing the local similarities. For each feature, local similarity is basically defined as a linear interpolation between the lowest and the highest possible distance between pairs of values for that feature. Furthermore, no weights were used when aggregating these local similarities to compute a global similarity metric. Significant gains in accuracy of the retrieval process can be made if we use feature weighting, which could be computed by using statistical sampling. The same can be said with the retrieval threshold. It was set to 75% in our experiments and this value was selected arbitrarily. Retrieval accuracy could be improved by tuning the threshold. The reason for not doing any of these possible improvements is that we wanted to test our working hypothesis without tweaking these parameters, so that we could confidently attribute the results to the CBR approach rather than to some tweaking of these parameters.

In this paper we presented CBRetaliate, a CBR + RL system that is intended to enhance RL capabilities for situations in which the environment suddenly changes. CBRetaliate uses time windows during case retrieval and retention. It stores and retrieves Q-tables to allow the RL algorithm to rapidly react to changes in the environment. We demonstrated our approach in a TFPS game, which is characterized by the speed in the decision making by individual bots and in the overall strategy. Our results demonstrate that CBR can effectively speed-up the RL adaptation process in dynamic environments.

As future work, we want to study case-base maintenance issues in the context of CBRetaliate. In the experiments reported in this paper, we reset the case base at the beginning of each tournament. As a result, the retrieval times were very low and did not have any effect on the overall performance of the agent. Clearly this will change in situations when the case base becomes permanent, and a mechanism to refine the case base will be necessary. This poses some interesting research questions: (1) Because cases contain Q-tables, how can we tell if a case is covered by another case? (2) As the Q-table of a retrieved case is updated with RL, can we identify situations where the updated Q-table should replace one of the retrieved cases instead of being stored as a new case as currently done by CBRetaliate? We intend to address these and other questions in the future.

Acknowledgments

This research was in part supported by the National Science Foundation (NSF 0642882).

References

1. Bowling, M.H., Veloso, M.M.: Multiagent learning using a variable learning rate. Artificial Intelligence 136(2) (2002)
2. Salustowicz, R.P., Wiering, M.A., Schmidhuber, J.: Learning team strategies: Soccer case studies. Mach. Learn. 33(2-3) (1998)
3. Ponsen, M., Spronck, P.: Improving adaptive game AI with evolutionary learning. In: Proceedings of Computer Games: Artificial Intelligence, Design and Education (CGAIDE 2004) (2004)
4. Tesauro, G.: Temporal dierence learning and TD-Gammon. Communications ofthe ACM 38(3) (1995)

5. Smith, M., Lee-Urban, S., Muñoz-Avila, H.: RETALIATE: Learning winning policiesin rst-person shooter games. In: Proceedings of the Seventeenth Innovative Applications of Articial Intelligence Conference (IAAI 2007), AAAI Press, Menlo Park (2007)
6. Hoang, H., Lee-Urban, S., Muñoz-Avila, H.: Hierarchical plan representations for encoding strategic game AI. In: Proceedings of the rst Arti cial Intelligence and-Interactive Digital Entertainment Conference (AIIDE 2005). AAAI Press, Menlo Park (2005)
7. Sutton, R.S., Barto, A.G.: Reinforcement Learning: An Introduction. MIT Press, Cambridge (1998)
8. Bridge, D.: The virtue of reward: Performance, reinforcement and discovery in case-based reasoning. In: Invited Talk at the 6th International Conference on Case-Based Reasoning (ICCBR 2005) (2005)
9. Aha, D.W., Molineaux, M., Ponsen, M.J.V.: Learning to win: Case-based plan selection in a real-time strategy game. In: Proceedings of the 6th International Conference on Case-Based Reasoning (ICCBR 2005) (2005)
10. Ortañón, S., Mishra, K., Sugandh, N., Ram, A.: Case-based planning and execution for real-time strategy games. In: Proceedings of the 7th International Conference on Case-Based Reasoning Research and Development (ICCBR 2007) (2007)
11. Sharma, M., Holmes, M., Santamaría, J.C., Irani, J.A., Isbell, C., Ram, A.: Transferlearning in real-time strategy games using hybrid CBR/RL. In: Proceedings of the20th International Joint Conference on Articial Intelligence (IJCAI 2007) (2007)
12. Erol, K., Hendler, J., Nau, D.S.: HTN planning: complexity and expressivity. In: Proceedings of the Twelfth National Conference on Artificial Intelligence (AAAI 1994) (1994)
13. Ram, A., Santamaria, J.C.: Continuous case-based reasoning. Artificial Intelligence 90(1-2) (1997)
14. Ros, R., Veloso, M.M., de Mántares, R.L., Sierra, C., Arcos, J.L.: Retrievingand reusing game plays for robot soccer. In: Proceedings of the 8th European Conference on Advances in Case-Based Reasoning (ECCBR 2006) (2006)
15. Kuter, U., Nau, D.: Using domain-congurable search control in probabilistic planners. In: Proceedings of the The Twentieth National Conference on Artificial Intelligence (AAAI 2005) (2005)
16. Ulam, P., Goel, A., Jones, J., Murdock, J.W.: Using model-based re ection toguide reinforcement learning. In: Proceedings of the Nineteenth International JointConference on Articial Intelligence (IJCAI 2005) Workshop on Reasoning, Representation and Learning in Computer Games (2005)

Formal and Experimental Foundations of a New Rank Quality Measure

Steven Bogaerts[1] and David Leake[2]

[1] Mathematics and Computer Science Department, Wittenberg University, P.O. Box 720
Springfield, OH 45501, U.S.A.
sbogaerts@wittenberg.edu
[2] Computer Science Department, Indiana University, Lindley Hall 215
Bloomington, IN 47405, U.S.A.
leake@cs.indiana.edu

Abstract. In previous work, Bogaerts and Leake [1,2] introduced the *rank quality* measure for the evaluation of conversational case-based reasoning (CCBR) systems. Rank quality assesses how well a system copes with the limited problem information available in an ongoing dialog, giving useful evaluation information not readily available from standard precision and efficiency measures. However, that work also revealed surprising challenges for developing rank quality measures, restricting the proposed measures' applicability. This paper explores two open questions from that work: 1) *how to define a rank quality measure immune to the previous pitfalls*, and 2) *how to assess the meaningfulness of any proposed rank quality measure*. The paper establishes formal requirements for a rank quality measure, presents a new formulation of the measure, and provides a formal proof and empirical evidence to support that the new measure avoids previous pitfalls and meets the formal requirements.

1 Introduction

Influential work by Aha and Breslow [3] proposed evaluating conversational case-based reasoning (CCBR) systems by two criteria: *precision*, which measures whether the solution of the selected case solves the target problem, and *efficiency*, which measures the number of questions that are asked before a candidate case is selected. These measures[1] focus on judging the system at the close of the conversation, when a case has been selected. In practice, automated system evaluations based on these measures typically depend on a simulated user to perform case selection. The simulated user proceeds through the conversation and eventually selects a case according to given criteria, commonly when the top case or cases exceed a pre-set similarity threshold.

Evaluations of precision and efficiency can provide valuable information, especially in the concrete context of a fielded system, for which a holistic evaluation may be appropriate. However, it may be difficult to use their results to assess specific core system capabilities (e.g., the quality of similarity assessment), because the results of such measures depend on multiple factors whose effects may interact, making more difficult the task of credit/blame assignment for system performance [1,2]:

---

[1] We use "measure" informally, rather than referring to "measure" in the mathematical sense.

K.-D. Althoff et al. (Eds.): ECCBR 2008, LNAI 5239, pp. 74–88, 2008.

- Precision and efficiency measures depend on *case selection* by the simulated user. If the experiment is aimed at systematically studying the CCBR system's performance for given user populations, and can reliably model those populations, then this dependence may be desirable. In many experiments, however, user populations are not a focus. In these cases, it is preferable to use evaluation criteria which focus entirely on system characteristics.
- Precision depends on *solution applicability*—the likelihood that a similar case will have a similar solution—which depends on the contents of the case base. Although this is appropriate for judging a system as a whole, this dependence can cause difficulties in interpretation of results when it is desirable to separate the performance of similarity assessment from the coverage of the case base (e.g., when developing similarity criteria before the case base is fully populated).

In addition, precision and efficiency measurements do not directly address another important question for user satisfaction and acceptance: the quality of the *entire set* of cases and rankings presented *incrementally* at each step of the conversation. The obvious way to try to address this for precision is to apply precision measures to each case at each step in the conversation, but this still falls prey to the dependence on solution applicability. An analogous approach to incremental efficiency is a mere count of questions answered at each step, which would provide minimal information.

Rank quality was devised for CCBR system evaluation, addressing precision and efficiency's dependence on case selection and solution applicability, and providing information about the entire set of cases retrieved throughout the conversation. Rank quality compares two retrieval lists: The *candidate list* $L_{\hat{t}}$ is the list of cases retrieved given the incomplete target problem $\hat{t}$ available at any given point in a dialog. The *ideal list* L_t is the list of cases that would be retrieved if the complete target problem t were available[2]. Both lists are of length k, containing the k cases considered most similar to the target problem. Rank quality describes the "similarity" between the candidate and ideal lists with a value in $[0, 1]$, with 1 indicating maximum similarity. That is, rank quality measures how well the system is retrieving cases using only $\hat{t}$ instead of t.

Rank quality has been compared to precision, efficiency, and several other related measures [1]. It may also be compared to the "rank measure" in [4], in which candidate lists from different retrieval techniques are compared by ranking of the known best case; rank quality contrasts in considering the entire contents of the list.

Rank quality does not depend on solution applicability or case selection, and thus does not need to be assessed based on a simulated user. Furthermore, rank quality can naturally provide data about the *entire* candidate list *throughout* the dialog. We have presented empirical illustrations that a richer view of CCBR system performance can be gained with a suite of system evaluation metrics that includes rank quality [1,2].

However, previous work on rank quality also revealed that defining a rank quality measure involves surprisingly subtle issues, with the measure proposed there providing counter-intuitive results for certain domains. That work developed strategies for judging

---

[2] Rank quality as presented here is a measure for use in experimental settings, for which perfect information about the complete target problem is available in advance, and the experimenter reveals target problem attributes one-by-one. Alternatively, the so-called "ideal" list could actually be a hand-ordering of cases by an expert, or an ordering by some alternative system.

the suitability of that measure for a given domain, but left two open questions: 1) *how to define a rank quality measure immune to the observed pitfalls of previous formulations*, and 2) *how to systematically assess whether a given rank quality measure provides meaningful information*. This paper explores those questions.

This paper first summarizes previous work on rank quality and potential pitfalls for the previous rank quality measure when cases' similarity values appear tied. Second, it formalizes the desired properties of a rank quality measure. Third, it defines a new rank quality measure, and proves that it has the desired properties and is not susceptible to the previous pitfalls. Fourth, it presents an empirical demonstration illustrating that the defined rank quality measure's performance captures two important desiderata for rank quality: that rank quality values decrease as the noise in system distance measurements increases and as the probability of spurious ties increases.

2   Previous Rank Quality Formulations and Their Problems

An early form of the rank quality measure was presented in [5], and a stronger version in [1]. Informally, these measures compare the candidate and ideal lists. A weighted sum of distances between t and each case in the candidate list is computed. A sum is computed for the ideal list in the same way. The ideal list sum is the lowest possible weighted sum for t and the current case base. If the candidate list has a sum as small as the ideal list sum, then the rank quality is 1. The larger the candidate list's sum compared to the sum for the ideal list, the closer the rank quality is to 0.

In some domains, for some incomplete target problems $\hat{t}$, there may be many cases that are *estimated* to be equidistant from the actual target problem t. This is particularly common in domains with ordinal and nominal attributes. Such cases are *tied* in $L_{\hat{t}}$, and form a *tied sequence* of cases, which a system may order arbitrarily[3]. The historical approach for handling ties [6,7] involves averaging weights across the tied sequence so that order does not matter. However, it must be stressed that weight averaging is insufficient for the rank quality measure. Specifically, a tied sequence may extend beyond the end of $L_{\hat{t}}$, where cases cannot be trivially included in a weight-averaging scheme. We refer to this as *splitting the k-boundary*. In some k-boundary splitting situations, the rank quality measure of [1] degenerates to a zero value.

Assigning a zero rank quality value in such situations holds some intuitive appeal, because a candidate list with so many ties may be failing to properly distinguish the cases (e.g., if the system did not yet have enough information about the target problem to determine which cases were most relevant). Nevertheless, assigning zero rank quality here may also fail to distinguish candidate lists which can reasonably be distinguished. For example, for a system that presents 10 cases to the user, a zero would be given to candidate lists for calling the top 30 or the top 500 cases tied. However, everything else being equal, the list with a smaller set of tied top cases is likely superior. Thus, by using the zero score for candidate lists with many ties (generally, very poor candidate lists), some granularity is lost. Some domains are particularly susceptible to this problem of

---

[3] There may also be ties in L_t, but since rank quality computes a weighted sum of true (not estimated) distances, a reordering of cases with tied true distances does not affect the summation.

the zero score. This can be predicted based on relationships of their cases [1]. The previous rank quality formulation is not applicable to such domains.

In response, Bogaerts [2] examines several other possible rank quality formulations, using strategies such as a threshold to determine which cases to present to a user (rather than always presenting a fixed number), an overlap count, measures developed for assessing the ordering of Web search results, and approaches based on statistical measures of rank correlation. That analysis reveals that ultimately these approaches all fail at least in the same circumstances as the measure of [1], and sometimes in more serious ways.

2.1 The Target Behavior for Rank Quality

Amidst these challenges it is important to define more carefully what is needed in a rank quality measure. So, we define a highly intuitive, yet prohibitively expensive, rank quality formulation, which we will designate rq_{slow}. This is used only as a tool for analysis of rank quality. The definition of rq_{slow} requires the following notions:

- Given a candidate list $L_{\hat{t}}$ with any number of tied sequences, each with some arbitrary ordering of constituent cases, define a *consistent refinement* of $L_{\hat{t}}$ as any list identical to $L_{\hat{t}}$ except that one or more of the tied sequences has some alternative arbitrary ordering of their constituent cases. (The general notion of consistent refinements exists in other work in AI as well; for example, see [8].)
- Define the *untied rank quality*, $rq'(L_t, L_{\hat{t}})$, as a simple rank quality calculation that makes no consideration of ties. That is, arbitrary orderings within sequences of ties are treated as non-arbitrary:

$$rq'(L_t, L_{\hat{t}}) = 1 - \frac{\sum_i w_i \cdot dist(t, L_{\hat{t}}[i]) - \sum_i w_i \cdot dist(t, L_t[i])}{\sum_i w_i}$$

- w_i : Weight of a case of rank i in the corresponding list. These weights could come from expert input or could be learned from user feedback.
- $L[i]$: Case at rank i in the given list.
- $dist(t, c)$: Distance in $[0, 1]$ between t and c.

The intuition of rq' is as follows: if $L_{\hat{t}}$ is identical to L_t, then corresponding summations will be the same, resulting in an rq' value of 1. L_t leads to the lowest possible value for the corresponding summation, thus an $L_{\hat{t}}$ that is different from L_t must have a higher sum. The worse $L_{\hat{t}}$ is, the higher the corresponding summation will be, thus rq' approaches 0. An rq' of 0 is rare, and occurs only when L_t consists entirely of cases with distance 0 from t, while $L_{\hat{t}}$ consists entirely of cases with distance 1 from t.

Given this, we can define rq_{slow} as a rank quality formulation that handles ties in $L_{\hat{t}}$ by calculating the *average* untied rank quality over all consistent refinements. This is a very intuitive approach: *arbitrary outcomes are averaged for every possible result of the arbitrary process, thus the process has no net effect on the rq_{slow} result.*

Unfortunately, rq_{slow} is only appropriate as a *target for behavior* of the rank quality measure, rather than as a definitive formulation. This is due to its high time complexity when ties are present. In our analysis, let the distance calculation be the basic operation to be counted. For each computation of rq', each summation in the numerator takes $\Theta(k)$ time, for k the length of each list, so rq' takes $\Theta(k)$ time.

Given G tied sequences in a candidate list and assuming for simplicity that none split the k-boundary[4], with sequence g in $[1, G]$ of length s_g, there are $\prod_g s_g!$ consistent refinements. Each refinement requires computing rq', so rq_{slow} operates in $\Theta(k \prod_g s_g!)$ time. So this formulation could be acceptable for systems that retrieve small numbers of cases and/or are guaranteed to have few ties, but would be prohibitively expensive for some domains. Consequently, rq_{slow} is not a satisfactory formulation, and only serves as a target for desired behavior of a rank quality formulation.

3   New Rank Quality Definition

To resolve the above issues, rank quality is defined:

$$rq(L_t, L_{\hat{t}}) = 1 - \frac{\sum_i w_i \cdot \widehat{dist}(t, L_{\hat{t}}[i]) - \sum_i w_i \cdot dist(t, L_t[i])}{\sum_i w_i} \tag{1}$$

$$\widehat{dist}(t, L_{\hat{t}}[i]) = \begin{cases} dist(t, L_{\hat{t}}[i]) & L_{\hat{t}}[i] \text{ is not involved in a tie} \\ \mu_{m,n} & \text{otherwise} \end{cases}$$

$$\mu_{m,n} = \frac{\sum_{j=m}^{n} dist(t, \hat{L}_{\hat{t}}[j])}{(n - m + 1)}$$

- m and n : A tied sequence is said to start with the case at rank m and end with the case at rank n. (Note that there may be multiple tied sequences, each with its own m and n.)
- $\hat{L}_{\hat{t}}$: The expansion of $L_{\hat{t}}$ to length $max(n, k)$. That is, $\hat{L}_{\hat{t}}$ is the expanded list such that any tied sequence extending beyond rank k in $L_{\hat{t}}$ is fully included. If there is no such tied sequence extending beyond rank k, then $\hat{L}_{\hat{t}}$ is simply $L_{\hat{t}}$.

Rationale for the Measure: Replacing Weight-Averaging with Distance-Averaging The key insight underlying this formulation is to use a *distance-averaging* approach rather than the historical *weight-averaging* approach [6,7], in which the *weight* across the tied sequence is averaged. For any tied sequence, the average distance $\mu_{m,n}$ between t and each case in the sequence is used as the distance $\widehat{dist}(t, L_{\hat{t}}[i])$ for each case in the sequence. This is subtly yet crucially different from the weight averaging approach (see [2] for a detailed discussion).

The weight-averaging approach requires that either all or none of the cases in the sequence be included in the list, making sequences that split the k-boundary problematic. To see why either all or none must be included, first recall that only the *estimated* distances must necessarily be tied in a tied sequence, not the actual distances. That is, for each case index i and j in the tied sequence, $dist(\hat{t}, L_{\hat{t}}[i]) = dist(\hat{t}, L_{\hat{t}}[j])$, but it is not necessarily true that $dist(t, L_{\hat{t}}[i]) = dist(t, L_{\hat{t}}[j])$. Also recall that the rank quality calculation directly uses $dist(t, L_{\hat{t}}[i])$, not $dist(\hat{t}, L_{\hat{t}}[i])$. Thus, if the tied sequence extended beyond the k-boundary and only some of the tied cases (chosen arbitrarily) were

---

[4] If a tied sequence does split the k-boundary, then this will be of little consequence in the time complexity, but would complicate notation.

included in the rank quality calculation, then the result would depend on *which* were included, because not all $dist(t, L_{\hat{t}}[i])$ in the sequence are equal. This arbitrariness is unacceptable in a measure for evaluating rank quality, forcing a policy of including either all or none of the tied cases in order to assure a consistent result.

As proved in the following section, this problem is avoided in the new distance-averaging approach of Equation 1. Suppose as above that the tied sequence splits the k-boundary. With distance-averaging, the rank quality calculation is not affected by which cases in the tied sequence are included in $L_{\hat{t}}$, because the same $\widehat{dist}(t, L_{\hat{t}}[i])$ is used for each case in the sequence. A different arbitrary ordering would result in exactly the same rank quality, making the new rank quality formulation acceptable even for tied sequences splitting the k-boundary.

Time Complexity for the Measure: Consider the time complexity of computing rq, again with distance calculation the basic operation. The $dist(t, L_t[i])$ summation is computed in $\Theta(k)$, for k the length of the candidate list. For the $dist(t, L_{\hat{t}}[i])$ summation, note that for any case not in a tie, its distance is computed once. For any case that is in a tie, its distance is also computed once, in the $\mu_{m,n}$ computation. Thus, the $dist(t, L_{\hat{t}}[i])$ summation is also in $\Theta(k)$, and so the computation of rq is a $\Theta(k)$ operation — it is linear in the size of the candidate list, assuming a basic operation of distance calculation.

The remaining sections will give evidence for the appropriateness of this formulation.

4   Proof of the Effectiveness of the New Measure's Handling of Ties

We now prove the effectiveness of the tie-handling strategy of rq. Note that rq is significantly more efficient than rq_{slow}. Thus if we can show that in all possible scenarios, $rq = rq_{slow}$, then we may use the more efficient rq, while still achieving the desired target behavior. In the proof, three scenarios must be considered:

1. **Single Tied Sequence** in $L_{\hat{t}}$, not splitting the k-boundary
2. **Multiple Tied Sequences** in $L_{\hat{t}}$, none splitting the k-boundary
3. **Splitting the k-Boundary** with one sequence in $L_{\hat{t}}$, with possibly other tied sequences also present.

The following subsections discuss these related scenarios in turn. For more complete discussion, see [2]. For simplicity of notation, 1-based indexing will be used.

4.1   Single Tied Sequence

Suppose that there is a single tied sequence in $L_{\hat{t}}$, of length s, that does not split the k-boundary. Thus there are $s!$ consistent refinements of $L_{\hat{t}}$. Label these orderings $L_{\hat{t}}^j$ for each integer j in $[1, s!]$. In this scenario, we can define:

$$rq_{slow}(L_t, L_{\hat{t}}) = \frac{\sum_j rq'(L_t, L_{\hat{t}}^j)}{s!}$$

Claim: In the Single Tied Sequence scenario, $rq(L_t, L_{\hat{t}}) = rq_{slow}(L_t, L_{\hat{t}})$.

Proof: For convenience, define:

$$r(L_t, L_{\hat{t}}, [a, b]) \equiv \frac{\sum_{i=a}^{b} w_i \cdot dist(t, L_{\hat{t}}[i]) - \sum_{i=a}^{b} w_i \cdot dist(t, L_t[i])}{\sum_{i=1}^{k} w_i}$$

That is, $r(L_t, L_{\hat{t}}, [a, b])$ is the portion of rank quality calculated for interval $[a, b]$ where $1 \leq a, b \leq k$, assuming no tied sequences overlapping the interval.

Suppose that the sequence extends from index m to n (inclusive) in the candidate list. Then for i in $[1, m-1]$ and $[n+1, k]$, $\widehat{dist}(t, L_{\hat{t}}[i]) \equiv dist(t, L_{\hat{t}}[i])$ because there are no ties within those ranges. For i in $[m, n]$, $\widehat{dist}(t, L_{\hat{t}}[i]) \equiv \mu_{m,n}$. So rq^5 is:

$$rq(L_t, L_{\hat{t}}) = 1 - r(L_t, L_{\hat{t}}, [1, m-1]) \tag{2}$$
$$- \frac{\sum_{i=m}^{n} w_i \cdot \mu_{m,n} - \sum_{i=m}^{n} w_i \cdot dist(t, L_t[i])}{\sum_{i=1}^{k} w_i}$$
$$- r(L_t, L_{\hat{t}}, [n+1, k])$$

Similarly for rq_{slow}, within the i ranges $[1, m-1]$ and $[n+1, k]$, $L_{\hat{t}}^{j}[i] = L_{\hat{t}}[i]$ by definition of $L_{\hat{t}}^{j}$. After some minor algebraic manipulations we have:

$$\frac{1}{s!} \sum_{j} rq'(L_t, L_{\hat{t}}^{j}) = 1 - r(L_t, L_{\hat{t}}, [1, m-1]) \tag{3}$$
$$- \sum_{j=1}^{s!} \frac{\sum_{i=m}^{n} w_i \cdot dist(t, L_{\hat{t}}^{j}[i]) - \sum_{i=m}^{n} w_i \cdot dist(t, L_t[i])}{s! \sum_{i=1}^{k} w_i}$$
$$- r(L_t, L_{\hat{t}}, [n+1, k])$$

The right hand sides of equations (2) and (3) are identical except for the i in $[m, n]$ terms. Labeling these terms $A_{m,n}$ and $B_{m,n}$:

$$A_{m,n} \equiv \frac{\sum_{i=m}^{n} w_i \cdot \mu_{m,n} - \sum_{i=m}^{n} w_i \cdot dist(t, L_t[i])}{\sum_{i=1}^{k} w_i}$$

$$B_{m,n} \equiv \sum_{j=1}^{s!} \frac{\sum_{i=m}^{n} w_i \cdot dist(t, L_{\hat{t}}^{j}[i]) - \sum_{i=m}^{n} w_i \cdot dist(t, L_t[i])}{s! \sum_{i=1}^{k} w_i}$$

It remains only to prove that $A_{m,n}$ is equivalent to $B_{m,n}$. Algebraic simplification gives:

$$A_{m,n} = \frac{\sum_{i=m}^{n} w_i \cdot \mu_{m,n}}{\sum_{i=1}^{k} w_i} - \frac{\sum_{i=m}^{n} w_i \cdot dist(t, L_t[i])}{\sum_{i=1}^{k} w_i}$$

---

[5] Note that one or both of the intervals $[1, m-1]$ and $[n+1, k]$ may be degenerate (if $m = 1$ or $n = k$.) In these scenarios, the r-term is considered 0.

$$B_{m,n} = \frac{\sum_{j=1}^{s!} \sum_{i=m}^{n} w_i \cdot dist(t, L_{\hat{t}}^j[i])}{s! \sum_{i=1}^{k} w_i} - \frac{\sum_{i=m}^{n} w_i \cdot dist(t, L_t[i])}{\sum_{i=1}^{k} w_i}$$

So to prove that $A_{m,n}$ and $B_{m,n}$ are equivalent, after cancelling like terms it now remains only to prove that:

$$\sum_{i=m}^{n} w_i \cdot \mu_{m,n} = \frac{1}{s!} \sum_{j=1}^{s!} \sum_{i=m}^{n} w_i \cdot dist(t, L_{\hat{t}}^j[i]) \tag{4}$$

For convenience, name the right hand side of the above equation β. To show that equation (4) is true, we must consider the meaning of $L_{\hat{t}}^j$. Note that in the construction of a consistent refinement $L_{\hat{t}}^j$, after placing some case $L_{\hat{t}}[h]$ in position i there remain $s-1$ cases to place throughout the tied sequence. Thus there are $(s-1)!$ consistent refinements of $L_{\hat{t}}$ where case $L_{\hat{t}}[h]$ is in position i. So the term $w_i \cdot dist(t, L_{\hat{t}}[h])$ appears $(s-1)!$ times in the summations of β. Summing these up for each i, we get the sum of all terms involving $L_{\hat{t}}[h]$ at any position i in $[m, n]$:

$$\sum_{i=m}^{n} (s-1)! \cdot w_i \cdot dist(t, L_{\hat{t}}[h])$$

To get the sum of all terms in β, we must sum the above for all h in $[m, n]$:

$$\sum_{h=m}^{n} \sum_{i=m}^{n} (s-1)! \cdot w_i \cdot dist(t, L_{\hat{t}}[h])$$

and so:

$$\beta = \frac{1}{s!} \sum_{h=m}^{n} \sum_{i=m}^{n} (s-1)! \cdot w_i \cdot dist(t, L_{\hat{t}}[h])$$

$$= \sum_{i=m}^{n} w_i \frac{\sum_{h=m}^{n} dist(t, L_{\hat{t}}[h])}{s}$$

Recall that s is the tied sequence length, so $s = n - m + 1$:

$$\beta = \sum_{i=m}^{n} w_i \frac{\sum_{h=m}^{n} dist(t, L_{\hat{t}}[h])}{n - m + 1}$$

Finally, note that:

$$\mu_{m,n} = \frac{\sum_{h=m}^{n} dist(t, L_{\hat{t}}[h])}{n - m + 1}$$

when the tied sequence in $[m, n]$ does not split the k-boundary, and so:

$$\beta = \sum_{i=m}^{n} w_i \cdot \mu_{m,n}$$

That is, β, the right hand side of (4), is equivalent to the left hand side. So $A_{m,n} = B_{m,n}$. So $rq(L_t, L_{\hat{t}}) = rq_{slow}(L_t, L_{\hat{t}})$ in the Single Tied Sequence scenario. $\square$

4.2   Multiple Tied Sequences

Suppose there are multiple tied sequences in $L_{\hat{t}}$, none splitting the k-boundary. Enumerate them $[1, G]$, and let each sequence length be denoted by s_g for some integer g in $[1, G]$. Thus there are $\prod_g s_g!$ consistent refinements of $L_{\hat{t}}$. Label these orderings $L_{\hat{t}}^j$ for each integer j in $[1, \prod_g s_g!]$. So in this scenario, using the new range for j:

$$rq_{slow}(L_t, L_{\hat{t}}) = \frac{\sum_j rq'(L_t, L_{\hat{t}}^j)}{s!}$$

Claim: In the Multiple Tied Sequences scenario, $rq(L_t, L_{\hat{t}}) = rq_{slow}(L_t, L_{\hat{t}})$.
Proof: This proof is a trivial extension of the proof in the Single Tied Sequences scenario of Section 4.1. In that scenario, summations are split into the ranges $[1, m - 1]$, $[m, n]$, and $[n + 1, k]$. In the Multiple Tied Sequences scenario, denote m_g and n_g as the starting and ending indices (inclusive) of tie sequence g. Then the summations are split into the intervals $[1, m_1 - 1], [m_1, n_1], [n_1 + 1, m_2 - 1], [m_2, n_2], [n_2 + 1, m_3 - 1]$, ..., $[n_G, k]^6$. Each of these intervals leads to a summation of terms comprised either entirely of ties or entirely of non-ties. The summations of non-ties in rq and rq_{slow} break down and are equivalent in the same manner as in the Single Tied Sequences scenario. The summations of ties are also shown to be equivalent by the same process.   □

4.3   Splitting the k-Boundary

Note that tied sequences that do not split the k-boundary will be equivalent for rq and rq_{slow} by the argument in the Multiple Tied Sequences scenario above. Thus it is sufficient to consider only the single tied sequence that splits the k-boundary. Therefore, suppose that there is a tied sequence that splits the k-boundary in $L_{\hat{t}}$. Let the sequence be in the range $[m, n]$ inclusive, for sequence length $s = n - m + 1$, with $m \le k < n$.

Recall in the original presentation of rq above that the computation of $\mu_{m,n}$ uses the candidate list $\hat{L}_{\hat{t}}$, which is $L_{\hat{t}}$ expanded to include the entire sequence of ties. So $\hat{L}_{\hat{t}}$ is of length n, while the original candidate list $L_{\hat{t}}$ used in all other calculations is of length $k < n$. So in this scenario, only part of the sequence is within k: the cases in positions $[m, k]$. For convenience, define the length of the sequence within the k-boundary $\ell \equiv k - m + 1$. There are s cases to be distributed to those ℓ spots, so there are $\binom{s}{\ell} \cdot \ell!$ distinct consistent refinements of $L_{\hat{t}}$. (That is, of the s possible cases, choose any ℓ of them, and then order them in any of $\ell!$ permutations.) Label the distinct consistent refinements $L_{\hat{t}}^j$ for j in $[1, \binom{s}{\ell} \cdot \ell!]$. So in this scenario, we define:

$$rq_{slow}(L_t, L_{\hat{t}}) = \frac{\sum_j rq'(L_t, L_{\hat{t}}^j)}{\binom{s}{\ell} \cdot \ell!}$$

Claim: In the Splitting the k-Boundary scenario, $rq(L_t, L_{\hat{t}}) = rq_{slow}(L_t, L_{\hat{t}})$.

---

[6] Note that some of these intervals may be degenerate. For example, if $n_g = m_{g+1}$, then the interval $[n_g + 1, m_{g+1} - 1]$ is equivalent to $[n_g + 1, n_g]$, a degenerate interval. As in the Single Tied Sequences scenario, these degenerate intervals lead to corresponding summations of 0 and can therefore be ignored.

Proof: Similar to Section 4.1, we can split $rq(L_t, L_{\hat{t}})$ and $rq_{slow}(L_t, L_{\hat{t}})$:

$$rq(L_t, L_{\hat{t}}) = 1 - r(L_t, L_{\hat{t}}, [1, m-1]) \tag{5}$$

$$- \frac{\sum_{i=m}^{k} w_i \cdot \mu_{m,n} - \sum_{i=m}^{k} w_i \cdot dist(t, L_t[i])}{\sum_{i=1}^{k} w_i}$$

$$\frac{1}{\binom{s}{\ell} \cdot \ell!} \sum_j rq'(L_t, L_{\hat{t}}^j) = 1 - r(L_t, L_{\hat{t}}, [1, m-1]) \tag{6}$$

$$- \sum_{j=1}^{\binom{s}{\ell} \cdot \ell!} \frac{\sum_{i=m}^{k} w_i \cdot dist(t, L_{\hat{t}}^j[i]) - \sum_{i=m}^{k} w_i \cdot dist(t, L_t[i])}{\binom{s}{\ell} \cdot \ell! \sum_{i=1}^{k} w_i}$$

With simplifications as Section 4.1, it remains only to prove that:

$$\sum_{i=m}^{k} w_i \cdot \mu_{m,n} = \frac{1}{\binom{s}{\ell} \cdot \ell!} \sum_{j=1}^{\binom{s}{\ell} \cdot \ell!} \sum_{i=m}^{k} w_i \cdot dist(t, L_{\hat{t}}^j[i]) \tag{7}$$

Define β to be the right hand side of the above equation. To prove equation (7), we must consider the meaning of $L_{\hat{t}}^j$. In the construction of a consistent refinement $L_{\hat{t}}^j$, first place some case $\hat{L}_{\hat{t}}[h]$ in position i, where $m \leq i \leq k$. After this placement, there are $s - 1$ cases that can be placed in the remaining $\ell - 1$ positions in the portion of the tied sequence that is within the k boundary[7]. Thus there are $\binom{s-1}{\ell-1} \cdot (\ell-1)!$ distinct consistent refinements of $L_{\hat{t}}$ where case $\hat{L}_{\hat{t}}[h]$ is in position i. So the term $w_i \cdot dist(t, \hat{L}_{\hat{t}}[h])$ appears $\binom{s-1}{\ell-1} \cdot (\ell-1)!$ times in the summations of β. Summing these for each i, we get the sum of all terms involving $\hat{L}_{\hat{t}}[h]$ at any position in $[m, k]$:

$$\sum_{i=m}^{k} \binom{s-1}{\ell-1} \cdot (\ell-1)! \cdot w_i \cdot dist(t, \hat{L}_{\hat{t}}[h])$$

To get the sum of all terms in β, we must sum the above for all h in $[m, n]$ (that is, over all cases in the tied sequence at the end of $\hat{L}_{\hat{t}}$):

$$\sum_{h=m}^{n} \sum_{i=m}^{k} \binom{s-1}{\ell-1} \cdot (\ell-1)! \cdot w_i \cdot dist(t, \hat{L}_{\hat{t}}[h])$$

and so:

$$\beta = \frac{1}{\binom{s}{\ell} \cdot \ell!} \sum_{h=m}^{n} \sum_{i=m}^{k} \binom{s-1}{\ell-1} \cdot (\ell-1)! \cdot w_i \cdot dist(t, \hat{L}_{\hat{t}}[h])$$

$$= \sum_{i=m}^{k} w_i \frac{\sum_{h=m}^{n} dist(t, \hat{L}_{\hat{t}}[h])}{s}$$

---

[7] Recall that s is the length of the tied sequence, while ℓ is the length of the sequence that is within the k-boundary.

Recall that s is the tied sequence length, so $s = n - m + 1$:

$$\beta = \sum_{i=m}^{k} w_i \frac{\sum_{h=m}^{n} dist(t, \hat{L}_{\hat{t}}[h])}{n - m + 1}$$

Finally, note that:

$$\mu_{m,n} = \frac{\sum_{h=m}^{n} dist(t, \hat{L}_{\hat{t}}[h])}{n - m + 1}$$

and so:

$$\beta = \sum_{i=m}^{k} w_i \cdot \mu_{m,n}$$

That is, β, the right hand side of (7), is equivalent to the left hand side. So $A_{m,k} = B_{m,k}$. So $rq(L_t, L_{\hat{t}}) = rq_{slow}(L_t, L_{\hat{t}})$ in the Splitting the k-Boundary scenario. □

5   Experimental Demonstrations of Rank Quality

Given the mathematical equivalence of rq and rq_{slow} proven above, we now consider further empirical evidence that rq exhibits the following two central properties:

1. As noise in distance measurements increases, rank quality decreases.
2. As the probability of spurious ties increases, rank quality decreases.

The reader may find it obvious that this behavior *should* be observed. However, the experiments are needed to show whether, despite the non-trivial computations described above, the performance is reasonable. For example, similar experiments revealed counter-intuitive behavior associated with the k-boundary splitting problem of [1].

To assess how well the new rank quality measure conforms to these, we conducted experiments using the Indiana University Case-Based Reasoning Framework (IUCBRF) [9]. IUCBRF is a freely-available Java framework for the rapid and modular development of CBR systems.

5.1   Experimental Examination of Principle 1

Principle 1: *As noise in the distance measurements increases, rank quality decreases.*

Recall that rank quality is a measure of how well a candidate list matches an ideal list. If the candidate list is ever unequal to the ideal list for any target, then the estimated distance measure (based on $\hat{t}$ rather than t) is less effective in some way, leading to an incorrect ordering of cases. Typically this is due to missing case information that has not been obtained from the dialog yet. The extent to which an estimated distance is different from the actual distance should be reflected directly in the rank quality results.

An effective way to precisely control the difference between the estimated and actual distances is by adding noise to the estimated distance:

$$estDist(t, L_{\hat{t}}[i]) = dist(t, L_{\hat{t}}[i]) + N(0, \sigma)$$

```
for σ = 0.00 to 2.00 step 0.02 do
    for each target t in CB do
        Temporarily remove t from CB (leave-one-out)
        for each c in CB do
            estDist(t, c) ← dist(t, c) + N(0, σ)
        L_t ← k min c ∈ CB according to dist(t, c)
        L_t̂ ← k min c ∈ CB according to estDist(t, c)
        Compute rq(L_t, L_t̂)
        Add t back into CB
    Compute average rq(L_t, L_t̂) for current σ
```

Fig. 1. An experiment to examine the effect of distance noise on rank quality, ignoring ties. Retrievals are done with $k = 10$.

where $N(0, \sigma)$ denotes normally-distributed noise [8] with mean 0 and standard deviation σ. Thus if rank quality follows principle 1 above, then there should be a steady decrease in rank quality given increasing σ. Note that given the infinite number of distances that can result from this addition of noise, the probability of a tie is effectively 0.

The evaluation procedure is shown in Figure 1. For each σ, a leave-one-out process is followed in which rank quality is computed with the noisy estimated distance as defined above, for $k = 10$. Average rank quality is computed for each σ.

This experiment was run on four domains from [10]: Car, Hayes-Roth, Monks, and Zoo. The results of the Car domain are provided in Figure 2(a)[9]; other domains had nearly identical results. As expected, when there is no noise ($\sigma = 0$), the estimated distance is equivalent to the actual distance, and rank quality is 1.0. When there is just a small amount of noise (low σ), average rank quality remains fairly high. However, rank quality drops quickly as noise increases. Given that distance measures are in $[0, 1]$, a standard deviation of even 0.4 is quite high, capable of greatly distorting the ordering in a candidate list. After this point, the effect of increasing standard deviation on average rank quality is lessened. This is because after a time, ordering has become quite randomized in the candidate list already, and so further noise simply changes one very random ordering into another.

Thus, the results support Principle 1 for rq: As noise in the distance measurements increases, rank quality decreases.

5.2   Experimental Examination of Principle 2

Principle 2: *As the probability of spurious ties increases, rank quality decreases.*

---

[8] This addition of noise may push distances outside the [0,1] range. However, because we are using the distances for case ordering only, this differing magnitude is irrelevant to the results.

[9] Regarding the scale of the measure, note that rank quality is designed to be an absolute measure—measurements for one system are directly comparable to measurements for any other. Thus a rank quality of 0 indicates the worst retrieval conceivable, in which every retrieved case is maximally distant from the target. In practice this is very rare, if not impossible, for most case bases. So a rank quality of 0.5 or 0.6 is a "poor" retrieval on this scale.

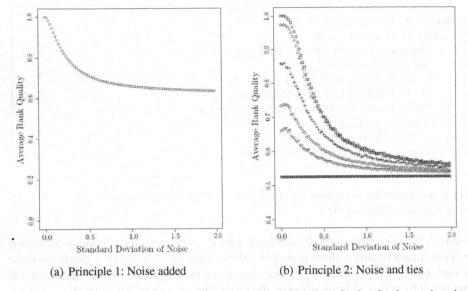

(a) Principle 1: Noise added   (b) Principle 2: Noise and ties

Fig. 2. (a) Principle 1: Average rank quality given standard deviation of noise, for the car domain. (b) Principle 2: Selected results of test for average rank quality given standard deviation of noise, for the Hayes-Roth domain, with $k = 10$ and various tie probabilities p. From top to bottom: $\square$: 0.00. $\triangle$: 0.66. $+$: 0.94. $\diamond$: 0.98. $\triangledown$: 0.99. $\boxtimes$: 1.00 (bottom horizontal line). Note that the vertical axis in (b) is cropped, from 0.4 to 1.0.

This experiment is designed to test the adherence of rq to the above principle. The probability of spurious ties can be controlled using the process of Figure 3.

It may appear by the experimental setup that the chosen p values are inappropriately skewed towards higher values. To see why the chosen values are appropriate, the effect of p on the average tied sequence length must be examined. For example, given a candidate list containing four cases in order, $[A, B, C, D]$, $p = 0.66$ means that it would be expected for, say, A, B, and C to be tied (thus two pairs tied) but not C and D (one pair not tied). That is, for this example, two ties for every one untied case, making an average sequence length of 3. In general, $p = 1 - 1/s$ where s is the average sequence length. So $p = 0.9$ leads to an average tied sequence of length 10. $p = .967$ leads to an average tied sequence length of 30. Thus, most of the substantial differences in sequence length come from high p values, and so these values are examined most closely.

This experiment was run on four domains from [10]: Car, Hayes-Roth, Monks, and Zoo. Results for each domain were very similar. Hayes-Roth results are shown in Figure 2(b). The trends discussed here are reflected in all results.

First consider the vertical slice at $\sigma = 0$. It is clear that as the probability of spurious ties increases, the average rank quality decreases. Spurious ties are an error in the formation of the candidate list. In fact, they are the only errors in a list with $\sigma = 0$. This corresponds to a list in perfect order, except for the sequences of ties. When more ties are present in this otherwise perfect candidate list, rank quality decreases, as expected.

Consider $p = 1$ (for any σ). This means that every case is thought to be tied to every other in the candidate list, so a random retrieval has been made. Rank quality accounts

```
Estimated Distance Noise, With Ties
    for each p in {0.00, 0.33, 0.66, 0.7, 0.8, 0.9, 0.92, 0.94, 0.96, 0.98, 0.99, 1.0} do
        for σ = 0.00 to 2.00 step 0.02 do
            for each target t in CB do
                Temporarily remove t from CB (leave-one-out)
                for each c in CB do
                    estDist(t, c) ← dist(t, c) + N(0, σ)
                Order L_t according to dist(t, c) for all c in CB
                Order L_t̂ according to estDist(t, c) for all c in CB
                makeTies(L_t̂, p)
                Compute rq(L_t, L_t̂)
                Add t back into CB
            Compute average rq(L_t, L_t̂) for current σ and p


    makeTies(L_t̂, p)
        r ← 1
        for each case c in L_t̂ do
            if U(0, 1) > p then
                r ← r + 1      // Don't make this case tied to the previous one
            setRank(c, r)      // Set rank of c to r, and set estDist(c) to first case of rank r
```

Fig. 3. An experiment to examine how distance noise affects rank quality, while controlling tie probability. makeTies($L_t̂, p$) is a procedure that makes cases tied with probability p. $U(0, 1)$ is a random number from a uniform distribution over $[0, 1]$. Retrievals are done with $k = 10$.

for this by assigning a value equal to the average rank quality of all possible random retrievals for a given target. (This was a key result proved in Section 4.) This average can then be averaged again over all targets, giving, in the case of Hayes-Roth, 0.525. This average is the same for all σ, because $p = 1$ means all cases are tied regardless of how much noise the estimated distances contain.

Now consider the progression of vertical slices as σ increases. This signifies the addition of more distance noise. As expected from the discussion in Section 5.1, rq decreases as σ increases. Interestingly, as σ increases, it can also be seen that the differences between lines for various p values decrease. This can be explained as follows. When σ is low, the addition of many ties is a serious deficiency in the candidate list. When σ is high, the candidate list is already quite poor, and so the addition of ties as well is of less consequence. That is, as the actual distances become increasingly noisy, the order is random enough that taking averages (in tie-handling) is no worse that using the untied estimated distances.

It appears that the lines for various p are asymptotically approaching the $p = 1.00$ line. That is, as $\sigma \to \infty$, there is no difference in average rank quality for various p values. This is because both σ and p decrease the quality of the candidate list as they increase. Ultimately, a candidate list cannot get any worse, at which point an increase of $\sigma \to \infty$ or $p \to 1.0$ has no effect.

Thus, it is clear that Principle 2 holds for rq: As the probability of spurious ties increases, rank quality decreases. Furthermore, as noise increases, the detrimental effect of ties is reduced, because the candidate list is already poor on account of the noise. That is, there is an important difference between finding averages and using the properly ordered distances, but there is not an important difference between finding averages and using improperly ordered differences.

6 Conclusion

Rank quality is an appealing measure for assessing conversational case-based reasoning systems, but previous formulations sometimes exhibited anomalous behaviors for tied cases [5,1]. This paper has presented a new definition of rank quality that addresses problems in those formulations. The measure provides an important complement to precision and efficiency as a measure of CCBR system evaluation. A formal proof of the match of its tie-handling to the behavior of an intuitive (but computationally infeasible) approach established that its behavior captures desired properties for consistency, and further experimental demonstrations provide support that its behavior meets expectations for adhering to two fundamental principles for a rank quality measure. Thus the new rank quality measure overcomes prior problems to provide a principled foundation for forming conclusions about CCBR systems.

References

1. Bogaerts, S., Leake, D.: What evaluation criteria are right for CCBR? Considering rank quality. In: Proceedings of the Eighth European Conference on Case-Based Reasoning (2006)
2. Bogaerts, S.: Rank Quality for Evaluating CCBR System Performance. PhD thesis, Indiana University, Bloomington, IN, USA (2007)
3. Aha, D., Breslow, L.: Refining conversational case libraries. In: Proceedings of the Second International Conference on Case-Based Reasoning, pp. 267–278. Springer, Berlin (1997)
4. Kontkanen, P., Myllymäki, P., Silander, T., Tirri, H.: On BAYESIAN case matching. In: Cunningham, P., Smyth, B., Keane, M. (eds.) Proceedings of the Fourth European Workshop on Case-Based Reasoning, pp. 13–24. Springer, Berlin (1998)
5. Bogaerts, S., Leake, D.: Facilitating CBR for incompletely-described cases: Distance metrics for partial problem descriptions. In: Funk, P., González, P. (eds.) ECCBR 2004. LNCS (LNAI), vol. 3155, pp. 62–76. Springer, Heidelberg (2004)
6. Kendall, M., Gibbons, J.D.: Rank Correlation Methods, 5th edn. Oxford University Press, New York (1990)
7. Mosteller, F., Rourke, R.E.K.: Sturdy Statistics: Nonparametrics and Order Statistics. Addison-Wesley Publishing Company, Reading (1973)
8. Ha, V., Haddawy, P.: Similarity of personal preferences: Theoretical foundations and empirical analysis. Artificial Intelligence 146(2), 149–173 (2003)
9. Bogaerts, S., Leake, D.: IUCBRF: A framework for rapid and modular CBR system development. Technical Report TR 617, Computer Science Department, Indiana University, Bloomington, IN (2005)
10. Blake, C., Merz, C.: UCI repository of machine learning databases (1998), http://www.ics.uci.edu/~mlearn/MLRepository.html

Provenance, Trust, and Sharing in Peer-to-Peer Case-Based Web Search*

Peter Briggs and Barry Smyth

Adaptive Information Cluster,
School of Computer Science & Informatics,
University College Dublin, Ireland
{Peter.Briggs,Barry.Smyth}@ucd.ie

Abstract. Despite the success of modern Web search engines, challenges remain when it comes to providing people with access to the right information at the right time. In this paper, we describe how a novel combination of case-based reasoning, Web search, and peer-to-peer networking can be used to develop a platform for personalized Web search. This novel approach benefits from better result quality and improved robustness against search spam, while offering an increased level of privacy to the individual user.

1 Introduction

Web search is one of the most important technologies in regular use, providing literally billions of users with access to online content every day; search activity reached more than 60 billion searches per month in 2007 [1]. However, Web search is far from perfect, and recent studies have highlighted the extent to which leading search engines struggle to provide users with relevant results. For example, Smyth et al. [2] describe how as many as 56% of Google Web searches fail to attract any result selections. Over the past few years, as "the business of search" has matured in to a major market sector, researchers have continued to look for new ways to enhance existing search engine technology. In this regard the idea of "social search" — that result-lists might usefully be influenced by the interests, preferences, or activities of other searchers — has gained some considerable attention as a way to improve search quality by personalizing result-lists.

Harnessing the search activities of users to improve result quality is a challenging task, but one that has benefited from a case-based perspective. The *collaborative Web search* (CWS) work of Balfe & Smyth [3] demonstrates how the search experiences (queries and result selections) of communities of like-minded users can be stored as search case bases and used as a source of result recommendations (*promotions* during future searches); in short, for a new target query, results that have been frequently selected by community members for similar queries in the past are promoted during the new search.

---

* This research was supported by Science Foundation Ireland Grant No. 03/IN.3/I361.

K.-D. Althoff et al. (Eds.): ECCBR 2008, LNAI 5239, pp. 89–103, 2008.

There are limitations to this standard approach to collaborative Web search. First, it relies on some explicit representation of a search community, with individual users expected to register and search within specific communities. The reality, of course, is that users simply want to search, and may not find it convenient to select a community context beforehand. Another limitation is that individual community members cannot be identified. In fact this is often cited as a privacy benefit, but in truth it has a downside when it comes to auditing the source of a promoted result. As the seminal work of Leake & Whitehead highlights, the origin, or *provenance*, of a case can be an important quality indicator [4]. This is especially true in CWS because it is possible for malicious users to influence result promotions [5]. By recording the source of a promotion (the searcher who originally selected the result), it is possible to present provenance information alongside the promoted result as a form of explanation. But, this is only possible if individual users can be distinguished within a community.

In this paper we present an alternative model of collaborative Web search; one that avoids the need for explicit communities, and which facilitates the identification of individual searchers to determine the provenance of promotions. We demonstrate how provenance information can be used to enhance the conventional CWS interface, and show how it can help to improve the quality of results in two important ways. Firstly, such information can be used as the basis for a computational model of user-trust, which we can apply to filter result promotions. Secondly, we argue that exposing the provenance of promotions through the search interface encourages the formation of social relationships between searchers, helping them to avoid making spurious result selections. Furthermore, we explain how the advantages of this trust-based approach can be achieved while preserving the privacy of individual searchers by implementing a distributed peer-to-peer search network. In this network, the search histories of individuals are maintained by their own local search-agent and only shared on the basis of trusted relationships between search peers. As an added benefit, we explain how this peer-to-peer architecture facilitates a more flexible approach to CWS by doing away with the need for explicit communities; essentially, an individual's search community evolves as they develop implicit relationships with other online searchers via the sharing and promotion of search experiences.

2   Background

This paper focuses on the personalization of search results, and, to this end, there is a growing body of literature covering the many ways in which individual and community preferences can be used to influence search. For example, the SOAP system [6] builds user profiles from bookmark collections and employs a collaborative filtering approach to result recommendation. Alternatively, Glance [7] describes a community search assistant which recommends similar (based on result overlap) queries from the previous searches of other community members.

In this paper we adopt an *experience-based* approach to personalization by harnessing the previous search sessions of searchers. This technique is naturally inspired by case-based reasoning, which of course emphasises the power of experience reuse in problem solving. Interestingly, work by [8] adopts a complementary perspective. In brief, searchers on the University of Oregon's library website are encouraged to supplement their queries with natural language questions that describe their information needs. New target queries are matched against any past questions that have led to result selections, and the matching questions are submitted alongside the user's actual query to identify additional results that may be of value to the user; see also the work of [2] for a similar approach.

If experience-reuse is an important feature of this work, then the idea of *experience sharing* is equally vital. It is interesting to reflect on recent Web developments that have emphasised the value of cooperation and sharing between users. The so-called Web 2.0 movement is based on a more flexible model of user cooperation and information sharing, and these ideas have helped to inspire and inform our own approach to Web search which, in this paper, is based very much on the free exchange of search experiences between searchers. Our experience-based approach relies on the idea that each user is associated with a case base that reflects their own past search experiences (queries submitted and results selected). As searches unfold, result recommendations are also harvested from the case bases of other, potentially numerous, users who are similar to the target user. This too echoes recent work by the CBR community on the use of multiple case bases during problem solving, where the benefits of such multiple sources of problem solving experiences have been convincingly demonstrated [9].

Other recent work in case-based reasoning has begun to explore how understanding the origins of cases is important when it comes to guiding their future reuse. In particular, the work of [4] argues for the storage and reuse of *provenance* information — information about where a case has come from or who provided the case, for example — in CBR systems as a way to improve problem solving performance and solution quality, especially where case learning is actively employed. This research has helped to clarify the importance of provenance-type information in our own work: given that search recommendations can come from the search experiences of other users, it is important to understand who these users are and how reliable their recommendations are likely to be. To this end, we use provenance information during search to advise the searcher about the source of a recommendation, but also as the basis for a computational model of trust that is used to filter out recommendations from unreliable searchers.

Finally, it is worth commenting briefly on research related to our use of a peer-to-peer search network. Peer-to-peer networks are not uncommon in Web search (see, for example, [10,11]), but in the main they have been used to distribute the computational load associated with search, with individual peer nodes storing and indexing a sub-set of the document collection. In our work, the core search functionality is provided by a traditional search engine, such as Google, and the peer-to-peer network is used as an experience overlay for the purpose of adapting traditional search results according to the past experiences of like-minded users.

3   Peer-to-Peer Collaborative Web Search

A peer-to-peer approach to collaborative Web search (P2P-CWS) envisages an overlay network of search agents, each capturing the search experiences of a user, U. This so-called *search network* facilitates the sharing of search experiences between agents. When a given user performs a search, their query (q_T) is used to access their local search experiences to identify relevant results that may be promoted. In addition, however, this query is also propagated along the search network links in order to probe the search expertise of trusted searchers with similar interests and identify further candidates for promotion (Figure 1). Any such promotions are then highlighted within, or added to, the result-list returned by the searcher's primary search engine, for example Google or Yahoo.

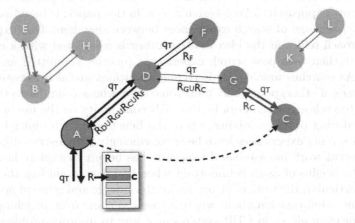

Fig. 1. The search network is made up of a set of individual user search agents each with a local store of search experiences. Queries propagate throughout the network, allowing the searcher to benefit from the recommendations of others.

The basic search agent architecture is shown in Figure 2, and in the following sections we will describe this novel approach to collaborative Web search in detail, focusing on how local search expertise is represented, shared, and reused throughout a search network. We will describe how local search results can be ranked and combined with the results from similar agents by using a computational model of trust that reflects the reliability of users within the search network. In turn, we will explain how this trust model is fine-tuned by the search interactions of pairs of users, and how the overall search network adapts to these evolving search relationships.

3.1   Experiences and Cases

Each search agent maintains a local case base of search experiences (C^U) such that each individual *search case* reflects the result selections of the user, U, for a particular query — accepting that these result selections may have been made

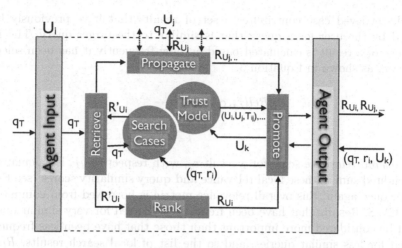

Fig. 2. The basic search agent architecture

over multiple search sessions. Thus each search case, c_i^U, is represented as a $n+1$-tuple made up of a query component and a result component; see Equation 1. The query component, q_i, is simply the set of terms that were used in the search query. The result component is made up of n result-pairs, with each comprised of a result-page id, r_j, and a hit-count, h_j, that reflects the number of times that U has selected r_j in response to q_i.

$$c_i^U = (q_i, (r_1, h_1), ..., (r_n, h_n)) \qquad (1)$$

It is important to note that, compared to the previous community-oriented versions of CWS [2], this peer-to-peer approach shifts the focus away from a community of searchers and on to the individual user. Instead of the case base corresponding to the community's search history, in this instance it corresponds to the search history of an individual. From a privacy viewpoint, however, it is worth highlighting that unlike the community-oriented version of CWS, where community case bases are stored centrally on a third-party server, this peer-to-peer approach facilitates a local, client-side store of search history information and thus provides the searcher with a further degree of security, privacy, and control over the use of their search data.

3.2 Retrieval and Ranking

The basic case retrieval implemented by each search agent is similar to that employed by community-based CWS [3]. In short, the target query, q_T, is compared to the search cases in the agent's local case base, and those cases that are deemed to be similar are retrieved (R'_{U_i}). Case similarity is based on a simple term-overlap metric (see Equation 2), although more sophisticated approaches can be applied and have been evaluated elsewhere [12].

$$Sim(q_T, c_i) = \frac{|q_T \cap q_i|}{|q_T \cup q_i|} \qquad (2)$$

Each retrieved case contributes a set of results that have previously been selected by the user for a query that is similar to the target query. The *local relevance* of a result is calculated based on how frequently it has been selected for a case, as shown in Equation 3.

$$Rel(r_j, c_i) = \frac{h_j}{\sum\limits_{k=1}^{n} h_k} \tag{3}$$

An *overall relevance* score for a result r_j, with respect to q_T, is calculated as the weighted sum of these local relevance and query similarity scores (see Equation 4); once again, this overall relevance metric is borrowed from community-based CWS. Results that have been frequently selected for very similar queries should be considered more important than those that have been less frequently selected for less similar queries, and so the list of local search results, R_{U_i}, is ranked according to these overall relevance scores.

$$WRel(r_j, q_T, c_1, ..., c_m) = \frac{\sum\limits_{i=1}^{m} Rel(r_j, c_i) \cdot Sim(q_T, c_i)}{\sum\limits_{i=1}^{m} Exists(r_j, c_i) \cdot Sim(q_T, c_i)} \tag{4}$$

3.3 Propagation and Collaboration

So far, we have described how a given agent retrieves and ranks a local set of search results based on its user's prior search experiences. Each agent is also connected to a number of peer nodes (search agents belonging to other users) in the search network. The agent propagates q_T to each of these peers in order to receive their local search recommendations, with each peer producing their recommendations using the same basic process. These agents will in turn propagate q_T on to *their* peers, and so on. As a practical matter, query propagation is limited to a fixed number of propagation steps according to a *time-to-live* counter that is decremented and passed on with each propagated query.

Ultimately, agents will be connected because there is some history of collaboration when it comes to prior search sessions. One agent may have suggested a search result which came to be selected by the receiving agent, for example. These positive examples of *search collaboration* serve to strengthen the trust between connected agents, which we shall discuss in the next section. Before we do, however, it is worth highlighting another way that the search network can adapt to search collaboration. As queries are propagated through the network, the *target agent* (the agent that is the original source of the target query) may receive recommendations from *distant* agents through a chain of network connections. If the target agent's user comes to select one of these distant recommendations, then it speaks to the potential for further positive search collaborations between these search agents in the future. This provides the basis for a simple approach to network adaptation: by connecting agents that collaborate. In Figure 1, we can see that the searcher corresponding to agent A selects a recommendation that has come from agent C, resulting in the creation of a direct link between A and C. For simplicity, in this work we create a connection at the first sign of such collaboration, but in reality there is significant scope for further research on this particular topic to look for a more robust mechanism for adaptation that is not mislead by what could be spurious collaborations. Similarly, if two connected agents fail to collaborate, then there is scope to sever their connections.

Of course, when a user joins the search network for the first time, a set of seed connections is needed to initialise their search network. There are a number of ways that such connections might be identified in practice. For example, the user might be asked to provide a list of friends, or connections might be selected automatically from a centralised list of reputable searchers. In our evaluation in Section 4 we simply choose a set of initial connections at random and let each user's local search network evolve from there.

3.4 Trust, Promotion and Provenance

Each agent is responsible for generating a set of result promotions based on the combination of its own *local recommendations* and the *remote recommendations* that have been returned by its neighbours as a result of query propagation. Remember that each of these recommendations is accompanied by a relevance score (as per Equation 4), and they must now be combined to produce a ranked promotion list. To do this, there is one further vital source of information that needs to be described: the *trust model*.

The previous section referred to the notion of collaboration between searchers via their search agents — in the sense that a result suggested by one user (or, more correctly, their agent) might be subsequently selected by another user — and how frequent collaboration could be used as the basis for a computational model of trust between users. Simply put then, we can model the trust between a pair of directly connected users, U_i and U_j, as the percentage of recommendations that U_j has made to U_i which have come to be selected by U_i (as shown in Equation 5). Obviously trust, as we have defined it, is an asymmetric relationship because U_j may be a better source of search recommendations to U_i than U_i is to U_j. This simple trust model is straightforward to implement, with each agent maintaining trust scores for its peers and updating them after each search session.

$$Trust(U_i, U_j) = \frac{SelectedRec(U_j, U_i)}{TotalRecs(U_j, U_i)} \qquad (5)$$

The key point is that we can use an agent's trust score as a way to weight its recommendations, so that the relevance score that accompanies a remote recommendation is modified by the trust score of its contributory agent as shown in Equation 6; where $WRel(r_k)$ is the weighted relevance score of result r_k which has been recommended by U_j to U_i.

$$TRel(U_i, U_j, WRel(r_k)) = Trust(U_i, U_j) \cdot WRel(r_k) \qquad (6)$$

But, via query propagation, users can also receive recommendations from agents that they are not directly connected to and that they have no trust score for. To accommodate this, the trust-weighted relevance score of the recommendation is updated at each step as it is propagated back to the agent that issued the query. In this way, the relevance score is scaled according to the trust scores that exist between connected agents. Thus, the *provenance* of a recommendation has a concrete influence on its final relevance score; see [4] for related work. If a remote recommendation propagates through a short chain of highly trusted peers, then its relevance score will be largely preserved. Alternatively, if a remote recommendation propagates through a long chain of less trustworthy peers, then its relevance score will be greatly discounted. Ultimately, the target agent will assemble a combined list of local and remote recommendations ranked according to their appropriate relevance scores. If a given recommendation has arrived from multiple sources, then its relevance scores can be combined additively.

The final step for the target agent is to promote the final set of recommendations within the result-list that is returned for the target query by the baseline search engine (e.g. Google, Yahoo etc.). In practice, this means highlighting those results in the result-list that also appear in the recommendation-list. Additionally, the *top-k* (with $k = 3$ usually) most relevant recommendations are promoted to the top of the result-list.

3.5   An Example Session

Figure 3 presents a simple example of this peer-to-peer approach to Web search in operation. In this case the query used, 'cbr', is ambiguous (at least to Google), and produces a result-list where none of the first page of results refer to case-based reasoning. In this example, the query has been propagated through a search network of peers, many of whom have an interest in various aspects of case-based reasoning and related AI research. Consequently, the top ranking recommendations that are returned provide a more relevant set of results for the searcher than the default Google list. In this case the top-3 most relevant results have been promoted, and each refers to an important CBR site.

It is worth highlighting how each result recommendation is annotated with icons that provide the searcher with hints as to the origins of the recommendation. For example, the icon that depicts a lone individual (see Figure 3) indicates that the result in question is a local recommendation that, by definition, has been previously selected by the current searcher for a similar query. In contrast, the icon that depicts a group of individuals indicates that the result is a remote recommendation from the searcher's peers. In the example shown, the top-ranking result is both a local and a remote recommendation. The screenshot also shows that "mousing-over" the group icon reveals further information about the origins of the recommendation, including the "names" of the contributing searchers and the queries that they have selected this result for in the past. In the example, we see that the searcher has chosen to view more information about the user 'mabes25', and is shown that this user has selected this particular result for two other queries: 'research cbr' and 'cbr publications'.

Fig. 3. A search result-list from Google enhanced by CWS recommendations

3.6   Discussion

Identifying the individuals responsible for a result promotion is an important departure from the traditional (community-based) model of CWS [2]. It is not without its challenges, but it does bring significant potential benefits when it comes to the facilitation of high quality search collaborations between users.

First and foremost, this new P2P collaborative Web search (P2P-CWS) approach is proposed as an effective strategy for coping with *recommendation spam*: previous versions of CWS were found to be somewhat susceptible to the actions of malicious users promoting irrelevant results [5]. The trust model used in this peer-to-peer approach provides for a very practical coping strategy in the face of such attacks, because promotions can only be made by a remote user if there is already a path of trust connections to the target searcher. Of course, this does not preclude more sophisticated forms of attack. For example, a particularly devious user might 'groom' the searcher by baiting them with good recommendations early on, in an attempt to gain their trust, before inserting irrelevant results into the recommendation stream. However, the searcher is likely to recognise and ignore such spurious promotions, which will quickly erode the false-trust that had been built up. Furthermore, the malicious user does not receive any direct feedback on the effectiveness of their efforts.

Ultimately, of course, trust is not simply a computational measure of collaboration between searchers. It is a social construct that develops as a result of social interactions. And the anonymous promotions of community-based CWS effectively limit the type of social relationships that can develop between searchers. It is clear from trial data that some searchers are better promotion sources than others, but this information is lost in community-based CWS. P2P-CWS is different. It provides information about the provenance of promotions by labeling recommendations with the names of the searchers who contributed to their recommendation. And this affords the searcher an opportunity to develop an implicit social connection with other searchers. If a searcher finds that they frequently benefit from the recommendations of a particular user then they will be naturally drawn to this user's recommendations in the future as they come to trust in their search experiences. Equally, if a searcher is seldom interested in the recommendations of another user then they will quickly learn to avoid recommendations from this user. All of this is independent of the computational model of trust that co-develops as such collaborations persist and mature.

Where community-based CWS neatly side-stepped the privacy issue by obscuring any personal search histories within community case bases, the new model's requirement of individual search histories clearly raises some significant privacy demons. The peer-to-peer architecture is a direct response to this. It provides for an increased level of privacy and security by eliminating the need for a *central* store of search histories. Instead, each user's searches are stored locally on their client and accessed by their personal search agent. This provides the individual user with a significant level of control over the sharing of their valuable search data. For example, it is feasible to allow the user to control their local search network and to influence which other search agents they are connected to. In this way, only other trusted users are permitted to contribute to, or benefit from, a given user's search experiences. When it comes to the propagation of queries, privacy is aided by the fact that when an agent receives a query request it knows only of the *forwarding agent*, and nothing of the agent that initiated the search. However, although agents handle such query requests automatically, it is possible for a motivated user to intercept them. Consequently, as is the case with search logs, personal information in the query could pose a privacy risk.

Finally, it has been noted that, with our current trust model, a peer who makes useful recommendations on one topic may have their trust score reduced unfairly if their recommendations for an entirely different topic are rarely selected. Future work may address this issue by adjusting the trust model so that scores are not reduced in such cases, or by maintaining topic-specific trust scores.

4   Evaluation

We have described an alternative approach to CWS which provides a searcher with personalized search recommendations that are drawn from the related search experiences of a set of trusted searchers. In this section we test this approach by evaluating the recommendations that are generated within an evolving search network. In addition to the traditional precision-recall study, we also examine the evolution of the search network as collaboration and cooperation between search agents unfold, with a view to better understanding how the trust model adapts during the course of an extended period of time.

4.1   Data

Ideally we would have liked to test P2P-CWS in a live-user setting, but this was not feasible. We considered a small-scale laboratory trial, but our previous experience tells us that such limited studies are rarely very revealing. At the same time, the alternative strategy of using simulated users is equally problematic even though it offers greater scope for large-scale evaluation. In this work we have chosen to adopt a middle-ground by using the search profiles of 50 real users as the basis for our search network, and then applying a leave-one-out methodology to evaluate various performance metrics such as precision and recall.

As a source of search data, we used the profiles of 50 users from the Del.icio.us[1] online social bookmarking service. In doing so, we follow the work of [13,14] by treating each bookmarked page as a result selection with the user's tags acting as query terms. Thus, each tag and its bookmarks acted as a proxy for a search case with its query and associated result selections. Obviously, the core assumption behind P2P-CWS is that there will be some opportunity for collaboration between the various searchers in the network, and this can only come about if there is overlap between their various search interests. Thus we focused on the first 50 users that Del.ico.us listed as having tagged the http://www.foaf-project.org URL (the home page of the *Friend of a Friend* project), on the grounds that there would be a reasonable opportunity for naturally overlapping search interests from this group without actually biasing the results by forcing overlap. For each user, we retrieved all their bookmarked URLs and their associated tags. This produced an average of 406 bookmarks (pages and queries) per user, with the typical profile containing an average of 242 unique tags (query terms).

The search network corresponding to these 50 users is initialised by randomly connecting each user to 10 other users, and all trust scores are set to the default of 0.5. An alternative would have been to connect each individual user to a set of other users based on some assessment of their similarity (for example, query or page overlap), but we chose this more challenging initialisation strategy in part because it provides a tougher test of network adaptation and trust evolution.

---

[1] http://www.del.icio.us

4.2 Methodology

To evaluate the performance of P2P-CWS, we adopt a leave-one-out method-ology in which each user in turn is designated as the target user to whom rec-ommendations will be made. We re-run each of the target user's search queries through the search network and examine whether the recommendations pro-duced contain any pages bookmarked by the target user for that current query. During each search we remove the corresponding search case from the target user's local search case base so that they cannot receive recommendations based on their own result selections. Obviously this is a fairly strict notion of result relevance. Many recommendations may actually be relevant to the query, but will not be judged as such unless the user had deemed to bookmark them in the past. Nevertheless, this approach at least provides a lower-bound on relevance and has the advantage that it can be fully automated.

The above methodology is repeated for a number of iterations or, *epochs*, to allow for the trust models to evolve as a result of sharing and collaboration between search agents. This also allows us to explore how search performance changes as the network adapts to search collaborations. After each search session, the trust model of the searcher is updated to reflect any selections — according to the above strict notion of relevance, we assume that the searcher will select any relevant recommendations that have been made.

4.3 The Evolution of Trust

Before we come to look at the precision-recall performance of P2P-CWS, it is interesting to examine how the search network and the trust models evolve during the experiment. In Figure 4(a), we present a graph of the number of network connections within the network. The experiment begins (epoch 0) with 500 connections (since each user is randomly connected to 10 other users), but as the experiment progresses we see new connections being formed as searchers collaborate successful. Interestingly, we see that the majority of new connections are forged during the first 4 epochs as the network structure quickly converges. As a matter for future work, it would be interesting to validate this convergence behaviour over different and larger-scale networks.

Just as the structure of the search network evolves over time, so too do the trust models employed by the individual search agents. The results in Figure 4(b) show a series of trust-score histograms that highlight the distribution of searcher-pairs with different trust scores; each histogram was generated at the end of a full epoch by counting the number of searcher-pairs with a trust score that fell within a given range of values. At the end of the first epoch, the majority of the trust relationships remain close to their default strength of 0.5; there are 579 trust relationships in our search network, and over 90% of these (529) have a score of between 0.5 and 0.75 at the end of epoch 1. However, the trust scores gradually settle as a result of search activity and, by the end of epoch 20, just under 30% of the relationships have a trust score in this range. Overall, we see a gradual flattening of the trust distribution curve, indicating that a broad range

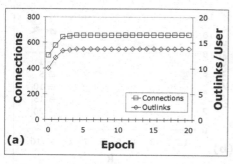
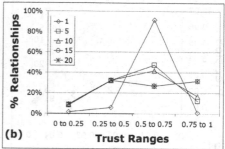

Fig. 4. (a) The number of peer-to-peer connections per epoch; (b) The changing distribution of trust scores per epoch

of trust scores are distributed throughout the network as searchers collaborate with varying degrees of success. Since, by design, the interests of this network of searchers are likely to overlap to some degree (they share a common interest in FOAF research), it is perhaps not surprising to see that, on the basis of the trust values presented, there is a considerable degree of productive collaboration within the network. For example, after 10 epochs we see that approximately 60% of trust scores fall in the 0.5-1 range, indicating a strong history of search collaboration between at least half of the search relationships encoded by the search network. Indeed, less that 10% of the relationships are weak, in the sense that they have trust scores below the 0.25 threshold.

4.4 Recommendation Quality

The traditional metrics of information retrieval success are precision and recall. The former measures the percentage of results (recommendations) that are relevant, while the latter measures the percentage of relevant results that are recommended. In Figure 5 (a), we present a precision-recall graph in which each plot represents the precision-recall characteristics for recommendation lists of various sizes ($k = 1, ..., 10$) during each epoch. For example, in Figure 5 (a) the points that represent epoch 1 are labeled with their respective values of k so that the point corresponding to $k = 1$ indicates that during the first epoch, when only the top recommendation was presented to the searcher, we found an average precision score of 0.03 and a recall score of 0.015.

There are a number of points to be made about these results. First, the precision and recall scores are unusually low, more because of the strict nature of our relevance judgement than any underlying shortcoming of the recommendations themselves. As is usually the case in this type of experiment, precision tends to decrease with increasing k, while recall tends to increase; as k increases it becomes less likely that additional recommendations will be relevant, but it is more likely that a greater number of relevant recommendations will be produced. Perhaps most importantly, we see a sustained improvement in precision-recall

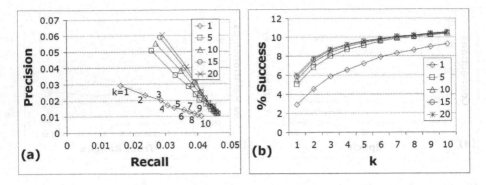

Fig. 5. (a) Precision versus recall for result-lists sizes from 1 to 10; (b) Percentage of sessions with recommendations containing a relevant result within the top k

during later epochs. This means that as the search network evolves, and as trust models adapt, better recommendations are being made. For example, by epoch 20 the precision and recall characteristics of the recommendations at the top of the list have effectively doubled.

In Figure 5 (b), we present an alternative performance graph which computes the average percentage of sessions that include a relevant result within the top k recommendations in sessions where recommendations are actually made. Once again, we see a steady increase in the percentage of *successful* recommendations as the trust network evolves. For example, during epoch 1, successful results are found in the top result-list position about 3% of the time, rising to just over 9% of the time if we consider the top 10 result-list positions. By epoch 20, this success rate has more than doubled for $k = 1$, with a success rate of over 6% at this position, and reaching nearly 11% for the top 10 results.

5   Conclusion

This work has been inspired by recent approaches to CWS [3] in which CBR techniques are used to harness the search experiences of communities of searchers. The research presented here is novel in that it provides for a more flexible CWS architecture; one that avoids the need for explicit search communities while delivering similar benefits in terms of search quality. Moreover, the peer-to-peer architecture provides a level of privacy and security that is sufficient to merit the use of individual user search profiles in place of community-based profiles, resulting in significant benefits when it comes to regulating the exchange of search experiences within the network. By profiling individual users, for example, it is possible to evaluate the reliability of searchers when it comes to recommending relevant results to others, and this can be used as an effective way to cope with search spam that may be introduced by malicious searchers within the network.

References

1. Search Engine Watch: Worldwide internet: Now serving 61 billion searches per month, http://searchenginewatch.com/showPage.html?page=3627304
2. Smyth, B., Balfe, E., Boydell, O., Bradley, K., Briggs, P., Coyle, M., Freyne, J.: A live-user evaluation of collaborative web search. In: Proceedings of the 19th International Joint Conference on Artificial Intelligence (IJCAI 2005), pp. 1419–1424 (2005)
3. Balfe, E., Smyth, B.: Case-Based Collaborative Web Search. In: Proceedings of the 7th European Conference on Cased Based Reasoning, pp. 489–503 (2004)
4. Leake, D.B., Whitehead, M.: Case provenance: The value of remembering case sources. In: Weber, R.O., Richter, M.M. (eds.) ICCBR 2007. LNCS (LNAI), vol. 4626, pp. 194–208. Springer, Heidelberg (2007)
5. O'Mahony, M.P., Smyth, B.: Collaborative Web Search: A Robustness Analysis. In: Artificial Intelligence Review, Special Issue on the 18th Artificial Intelligence and Cognitive Science Conference (AICS 2007) (to appear, 2007)
6. Voss, A., Kreifelts, T.: SOAP: Social Agents Providing People with Useful Information. In: Proceedings of the International ACM SIGGROUP Conference on Supporting Group Work, pp. 291–298. ACM Press, New York (1997)
7. Glance, N.S.: Community Search Assistant. In: Proceedings of the 6th International Conference on Intelligent User Interfaces (IUI 2001), pp. 91–96. ACM Press, New York (2001)
8. Jung, S., Harris, K., Webster, J., Herlocker, J.L.: Serf: integrating human recommendations with search. In: CIKM 2004: Proceedings of the thirteenth ACM international conference on Information and knowledge management, pp. 571–580. ACM, New York (2004)
9. Leake, D., Sooriamurthi, R.: When Two Cases Are Better Than One: Exploiting Multiple Casebases. In: Proceedings of the International Conference on Case-Based Reasoning. Springer, Heidelberg (2001)
10. Bender, M., Michel, S., Weikum, G., Zimmer, C.: Bookmark-driven query routing in peer-to-peer web search. In: Proceedings of the SIGIR Workshop on Peer-to-Peer Information Retrieval, 27th Annual International ACM SIGIR Conference (2004)
11. Suel, T., Mathur, C., wen Wu, J., Zhang, J., Delis, A., Kharrazi, M., Long, X., Shanmugasundaram, K.: Odissea: A peer-to-peer architecture for scalable web search and information retrieval. In: International Workshop on Web and Databases (WebDB), pp. 67–72 (2003)
12. Smyth, B., Balfe, E.: Anonymous personalization in collaborative web search. Inf. Retr. 9(2), 165–190 (2006)
13. Boydell, O., Smyth, B.: Enhancing case-based, collaborative web search. Case-Based Reasoning Research and Development 4626, 329–343 (2007)
14. Bao, S., Xue, G., Wu, X., Yu, Y., Fei, B., Su, Z.: Optimizing web search using social annotations. In: WWW 2007: Proceedings of the 16th international conference on World Wide Web, pp. 501–510. ACM, New York (2007)

Visualizing and Evaluating Complexity of Textual Case Bases

Sutanu Chakraborti[1], Ulises Cerviño Beresi[2], Nirmalie Wiratunga[2], Stewart Massie[2], Robert Lothian[2], and Deepak Khemani[3]

[1] Systems Research Lab
Tata Research Development and Design Centre
54B Hadapsar Industrial Estate, Pune, India
sutanu.chakraborti@tcs.com
[2] School of Computing,
The Robert Gordon University
Aberdeen AB25 1HG, Scotland, UK
{ucb,nw,sm,rml}@comp.rgu.ac.uk
[3] Department of Computer Science and Engineering
Indian Institute of Technology, Madras
Chennai – 36, India
khemani@iitm.ac.in

Abstract. This paper deals with two relatively less well studied problems in Textual CBR, namely visualizing and evaluating complexity of textual case bases. The first is useful in case base maintenance, the second in making informed choices regarding case base representation and tuning of parameters for the TCBR system, and also for explaining the behaviour of different retrieval/classification techniques over diverse case bases. We present an approach to visualize textual case bases by "stacking" similar cases and features close to each other in an image derived from the case-feature matrix. We propose a complexity measure called GAME that exploits regularities in stacked images to evaluate the alignment between problem and solution components of cases. GAME$_{class}$, a counterpart of GAME in classification domains, shows a strong correspondence with accuracies reported by standard classifiers over classification tasks of varying complexity.

1 Introduction

This paper presents a novel approach to visualizing textual case bases, and evaluating their complexity. Visualization is useful in the Textual CBR (TCBR) context for the following reasons:

1. easing knowledge acquisition from human experts
2. visually evaluating goodness of the underlying representation,
3. aiding case base maintenance, by revealing redundant features or noisy cases
4. presenting and explaining retrieved results to end users.

K.-D. Althoff et al. (Eds.): ECCBR 2008, LNAI 5239, pp. 104–119, 2008.

The first three are concerned with building and maintaining textual case bases, and are "off-line" activities in that they do not directly concern retrieval. In contrast, the fourth is an "on-line" activity, and is outside the scope of the current paper. Also, it may be noted that throughout this paper, we will focus on visualizing the case base in its entirety, and not individual cases.

Our second goal is to evaluate case base complexity. Complexity has different connotations in different contexts. In supervised classification tasks, a domain is complex if the classes are not easily separable, whereas in unsupervised tasks where we have a set of cases without any class labels, a complex domain is one which shows no neat clustering tendencies between the cases. Most TCBR domains are characterized by cases each having a problem and a solution component, both textual. Later in this paper, we will present an interpretation of complexity that estimates the competence of the system in solving a new problem by retrieving solutions to similar problems encountered in the past. It may be noted that complexity measures for supervised classification domains can be treated as a special case of this formulation, where the solution components map onto class labels. Complexity evaluation is important in facilitating the three off-line tasks mentioned above, particularly tasks 2 and 3. In case of task 2, a complexity measure would provide a quantitative basis for assessing the suitability of a representation, while visualizations aid qualitative judgements by humans. While visualization and complexity evaluation have often been treated in isolation, our current understanding is that they often share similar goals, and may exploit similar mechanisms to realize these goals as well.

Visualization is a well studied sub-field of text mining (TM) [5], and it is not surprising that most approaches investigated till date can be extrapolated to TCBR tasks. However, some differences are worth noting. Firstly, most visualization approaches in TM focus either on visualizing clusters of documents, or of words, but not both. In TCBR maintenance tasks, we often want to highlight the nature of interrelationships between words (alternately higher level TCBR features) and documents (cases) that give rise to the clustering patterns, and serve as an explanation for the underlying complexity. This helps in case base maintenance, as we can identify noisy cases or redundant features [7]. A second distinction, and one that has a strong bearing on complexity evaluation as mentioned above, is the TCBR emphasis on the split between problem and solution components of a textual case. We choose a representation that maximizes the "alignment" [4] between problem and solution components of texts. This issue has not been explored by researchers in TM visualization. Thirdly, TCBR representations are often more knowledge rich in comparison to those used in TM or Information Retrieval (IR). In contrast to shallow Bag Of Words (BOW) representations used in TM/IR, TCBR often uses "knowledge entities" ranging from domain specific terms, phrases or syntactic patterns from Information Extraction, as features [14]. However, this distinction is not critical here since our approaches are agnostic to the kind of features, though both visualization and complexity measures can take into account sophisticated domain-specific similarity measures associated with knowledge rich features.

Our first contribution in this paper is the idea of visualizing a textual case base as an image displaying a matrix of cases and features such that interesting associations and clusters within the case base are revealed. We present a simple algorithm that generates this image by exploiting regularities across cases and features. The resulting image has more than just a visual appeal; the compressibility of the image is used to arrive at a novel measure of complexity called GAME (for Global Alignment MEasure) that estimates alignment between problem and solution components of cases. We present experimental studies to show that GAME correlates well with classifier accuracies in classification problems of varying complexity.

2 The "Case Base as Image" Metaphor

Let us consider a set of textual cases, each case consisting of a set of features. For simplicity, we treat words in the text as features; the ideas presented can easily be extended to deal with more complex features. Also, we will restrict our attention to the problem side of cases, for the moment. To illustrate our ideas, we model the documents in the toy Deerwester collection [6] as cases. This is shown in Figure 1(a). An alternate representation is in the form of case-feature matrix shown in Figure 1(b); elements are 1 when a feature is present in a case, 0 otherwise. It is straightforward to map this matrix onto an equivalent image, shown in Figure 2(a), where the values 0 and 1 are mapped to distinct colours, a lighter shade denoting 1. We obtained this image, and for that matter all other images in this paper, using Matlab. Very simply put, this is the "case base as image" metaphor. However the image as it stands, is not very useful. Firstly, it conveys very little information about underlying patterns in terms of word or document clusters. Secondly, the image is highly sensitive to how the words and documents are arranged in the matrix; this is clearly undesirable. Thirdly, and we shall explore this in more detail in Section 3, the image tells us very little about the complexity of the underlying case base.

To address these limitations, we propose an algorithm that does a twofold transformation on the case-feature matrix to yield a matrix where similar cases (and similar features) are stacked close to each other. The output is a matrix, which when visualized as an image, captures the underlying regularities in the case base. Figure 3 shows a sketch of the algorithm. The broad idea is as follows. The first case row in the original matrix is retained as it is. Next, we compute the similarity of all other cases to the first case, and the case most similar to the first case is stacked next to it, by swapping positions with the existing second row. If more than one case is found to be equally similar, one of them is chosen randomly. In the next step, all cases excepting the two stacked ones are assessed with respect to their similarity to the second case. The case that maximizes a weighted combination of similarities to the first and second case (with higher weight assigned to the second case) is chosen as the third case, and stacked next to the second row. The process is repeated till all rows are stacked. In Step 2 of the algorithm, the same process is repeated, this time over the columns of the matrix generated by Step 1.

The weighted similarity evaluation is critical to the working of this algorithm and merits a closer look. The general rule for selecting the $(k+1)$ row (case) is to choose the one that maximizes

$$\sum_{i=1}^{k} w_i \, sim(c_i, c) \text{ such that for all } 1 \le i < k, \ w_{i+1} > w_i \tag{1}$$

where k is the number of already stacked rows, c_i is the ith stacked case, c is a case whose eligibility for $(k+1)$th position is being evaluated, $sim(c_i, c)$ is the cosine similarity

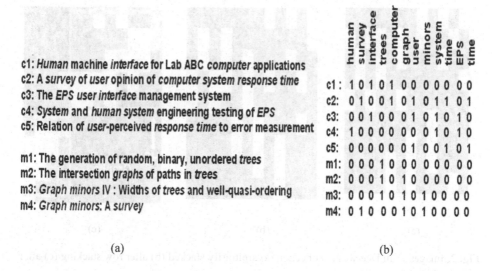

c1: *Human* machine *interface* for Lab ABC *computer* applications
c2: A *survey* of *user* opinion of *computer system response time*
c3: The *EPS user interface* management system
c4: *System* and *human system* engineering testing of *EPS*
c5: Relation of *user*-perceived *response time* to error measurement

m1: The generation of random, binary, unordered *trees*
m2: The intersection *graphs* of paths in *trees*
m3: *Graph minors* IV : Widths of *trees* and well-quasi-ordering
m4: *Graph minors*: A *survey*

	human	survey	interface	trees	computer	graph	user	minors	system	time	EPS	time
c1:	1	0	1	0	1	0	0	0	0	0	0	0
c2:	0	1	0	0	1	0	1	0	1	1	0	1
c3:	0	0	1	0	0	0	1	0	1	0	1	0
c4:	1	0	0	0	0	0	0	0	1	0	1	0
c5:	0	0	0	0	0	0	1	0	0	1	0	1
m1:	0	0	0	1	0	0	0	0	0	0	0	0
m2:	0	0	0	1	0	1	0	0	0	0	0	0
m3:	0	0	0	1	0	1	0	1	0	0	0	0
m4:	0	1	0	0	0	1	0	1	0	0	0	0

(a)   (b)

Fig. 1. Documents in the Deerwester Collection

between cases c_i and c, and w_i is the weight attached to the similarity of c with the ith stacked case. In our implementations, we used

$$w_i = 1/(k - i + 1) \tag{2}$$

The basic intuition behind this approach is that we want to ensure a gradual change in the way cases are grouped. This has implications for facilitating a meaningful display of clusters, and also for the complexity evaluation discussed in Section 3. If only $sim(c_k, c)$ were considered for the stacking process (which is equivalent to assigning 0 to all w_i, $i = 1$ to k-1) we may have abrupt changes resulting in an image that fails to reveal natural clusters. We note that for efficiency reasons, our implementation uses an approximation of (2), where we take into account only the previous 10 stacked cases and no more, since the weights associated with very distant cases are negligible and have no significant effect on the ordering. Choosing the starting case for ordering cases is an important issue, that we examine in the Section 4.

Figure 2(a) shows the image corresponding to an arbitrary arrangement of the documents in the Deerwester matrix. Figure 2(b) shows the image after the rows are stacked. Figure 2(c) is the final image after column stacking. It is interesting to see that the two broad topics within the collection, namely *Human Computer Interaction (HCI)* and *graphs* are clearly visible in Figure 2(c) as two "chunks" of contiguous light shades. Also, there is a gradual transition in shades from *HCI* to *graphs*. This is useful in identifying "bridge words" that can serve to connect two topics; an example is word 9 ("survey") in Figure 2(c) which is common to *HCI* and *graphs*. We can also visually identify cases that are in the topic boundaries and deal strongly with more than one topic. This has implications in case base maintenance tasks in terms of identification of noisy cases, and redundant cases and features [7]. We have designed a simple interface that allows users to "navigate" the image, and visualize the "topic chunks", and words that describe those chunks.

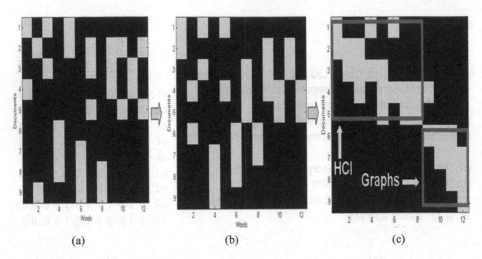

Fig. 2. Images from Deerwester collection (a) arbitrarily stacked (b) after row stacking (c) after column stacking

Step 1 (Stack Rows)
>   **Input :** Case-Feature Matrix M
>   **Output :** Case-Feature Matrix M_R which is M stacked by rows
>   **Method:**
>   Instantiate first row of M_S to first row M
>   for k = 1 to (noOfRows-1) /*the index of the last case (row) stacked*/
>>   for j = (k+1) to noOfRows /* check through all candidate cases*/
>>> $wsim_j$ = 0; /* $wsim_i$ weighted similarity of ith case */
>>>   for i = 1 to k /* already stacked rows*/
>>>> $wsim_j = wsim_j + wsim_j*(1/(k-i+1))*sim(c_i,c_j)$;
>>>   end
>>   end
>>   choose j that maximizes $wsim_j$ and interchange rows (k+1) and j
>   end

Step 2 (Stack Columns)
>   **Input :** Case-Feature Matrix M_R generated by step 1
>   **Output :** Case-Feature Matrix M_C which is M_R stacked by columns
>   **Method:** same as in Step 1 except that columns are interchanged (based on feature
>   similarity computed as cosine similarity between columns) instead of rows.

Fig. 3. The Stacking Algorithm

3   Complexity Evaluation Using Compression

In this section, we explore how the image metaphor can be exploited to obtain a measure
of the case base complexity. There are two reasons why complexity evaluation is useful.
Firstly, we can predict difficulty of domains (datasets) for a given choice of representation (feature selection/extraction and similarity measures). Secondly, we can compare

across different choices of representation over a fixed domain and choose the representation that minimizes complexity. We observe that complexity over a case base can be defined in two ways, namely Alignment Complexity (AC) and Collection Complexity (CC). The former, which is our main concern in this paper, measures the degree of "alignment" [4] between problem and solution components of textual cases. Measuring this helps us in answering the question "Do similar problems have similar solutions?" and thereby assessing the suitability of CBR (or alternatively the choice of representation) to that task. A special case of this problem is seen in classification domains, where the solution is replaced by class label. In measuring CC, the distinction between the problem and solution components of cases is ignored, and the complexity measure provides a measure of clustering tendencies exhibited by the case base. Thus a case base with cases uniformly distributed over the feature space has a high complexity; whereas, one with more well-defined clusters has a lower complexity [12]. Intuitively, since the stacked image captures regularities arising from topic chunks in the case base, we would expect that, all else being equal, stacked images from simpler domains will be more compressible, and thus have higher compression ratios, compared to ones from complex domains. This is because image compression algorithms typically exploit regularities to minimize redundancy in storage. Alternatively, a simple domain is one where case clustering serves as an explanation for feature clustering, and vice versa. We carry forth this intuition into our discussions of AC, since AC can be thought of as an extension of CC.

Alignment can be interpreted in two different ways. The first interpretation is a local one; an example is the case cohesion metric formulated by Lamontagne[4]. Here we look at a case, say C, in isolation, and determine two sets: set S_1, which comprises cases whose problem components are closest to the problem component of C (based on a threshold), and a set S_2, comprising cases whose solution components are closest to the solution of C. The overlap between S_1 and S_2 is used as a measure of alignment of C. This is a local metric, in that each case is evaluated on its own, and assigned a measure. The second interpretation is a global one based on how well the clusters derived from problem components of cases correspond to clusters derived from solution components. In this paper we adopt this second interpretation of alignment.

For measuring alignment, we construct two case-feature matrices: one based on problem components of cases, the other based on solution components. These two matrices are stacked as described in Section 2, to yield two images I_P and I_S respectively. I_P and I_S are now independently compressed to obtain compression ratios CR_P and CR_S respectively. For measuring alignment, it is interesting to compare the ordering of cases in I_P and I_S. One way of doing this is to create a fresh solution side image I_{SP} by stacking solution components of cases using the problem side ordering of cases as read out from I_P. We would intuitively expect I_{SP} to be less compressible than I_S, unless the case base is perfectly aligned. Compressing I_{SP} yields a new compression ratio CR_{SP}. Let CR_{SMIN} denote the minimum compression ratio that can be obtained by reordering the solution components independent of the problem components; CR_{SMIN} corresponds to the worst possible stacking of the solution side, where dissimilar cases are stacked next to each other, leading to an image having very few regularities and hence very poor compression ratio. The Global Alignment MEasure (GAME) is given by $(CR_S - CR_{SMIN})/(CR_S - CR_{SP})$. A higher value of GAME indicates a better alignment. An alternate measure can be obtained by considering I_{PS}, the problem side image with solution ordering imposed on it, instead of I_{SP}. However, our choice of I_{SP} over I_{PS} was governed by the observation that while we are keen on ensuring that similar problems have similar solutions, it is not of primal importance that similar solutions necessarily originate from similar problems. Using I_{SP} takes care of this asymmetry.

GAME can be extended to classification domains where the class label is treated as a solution. In this case, our interest is in determining whether near-neighbours in the problem side ordering (as obtained from I_P) belong to the same class. We obtain a string of class labels corresponding to the problems as they appear in the problem side ordering. This allows us to do away with the image compression and resort to a simpler string based compression instead. As an illustration, let us consider a two class problem of 10 cases in the email domain, where cases C_1 through C_5 belong to class S (for SPAM) and C_6 through C_{10} belong to L (for LEGITIMATE). Let us assume that the problem side ordering of the cases after stacking is $C_1C_2C_6C_4C_5C_7C_3C_9C_{10}C_8$. Replacing each case identifier with its class label, we obtain the class string SSLSSLSLLL. The most easily classifiable case base would have a string SSSSSLLLLL, and the most complex would have SLSLSLSLSL. A compression algorithm that exploits contiguous blocks (but not compound repeating patterns like SL) would thus be ideal; Run Length Encoding is one such scheme. Using this, the complexity is a direct function of the number of the flips (changes from one class label to another, L to S or S to L in the above example). We define GAME complexity measure for classification as

$$ \text{GAME}_{\text{class}} = \log\left(\frac{flips_{\max} - flips_{\min}}{flips - flips_{\min}}\right) = \log\left(\frac{(n-1) - (k-1)}{flips - (k-1)}\right) \tag{3} $$

where k is the number of classes, n is the number of cases ($n > k$), *flips* is the number of transitions from one class to another in the class string, $flips_{\min}$ is the value of *flips* for the simplest possible case base having n cases and k classes, and $flips_{\max}$ is the value of *flips* for the most complex case base. We note the most complex case-base presupposes a uniform class distribution; we then have $flips_{\max} = (n-1)$. A higher value of $\text{GAME}_{\text{class}}$ corresponds to a simpler domain; the most complex domain has $\text{GAME}_{\text{class}} = 0$. Thus we expect positive correlation of $\text{GAME}_{\text{class}}$ to accuracy results derived from classifiers. The logarithm has a dampening effect on the large values that could result when $n >> k$, *flips*. As a further detail, a small constant (say 0.01) should be added to the denominator to avoid division by zero when $flips = flips_{\min}$. Considering the inverse relation that exists between flips and compression ratio ($flips_{\min}$ corresponds to CR_S, and $flips_{\max}$ to CR_{SMIN}), and ignoring scaling due to logarithms, it is clear that $\text{GAME}_{\text{class}}$ can be viewed as an extension of GAME.

4   Experimental Results

Evaluating the general formulation of GAME involves a study of its correlation with an effectiveness measure (like precision/recall/F-measure) derived from subjective relevance judgments from experts over diverse case bases. Because of the difficulty in obtaining such TCBR datasets with relevance rankings, we evaluated the adapted version of GAME ($\text{GAME}_{\text{class}}$) over six different classification tasks.

For evaluating classification effectiveness in routing, we created datasets from the 20 Newsgroups [1] corpus. One thousand messages from each of the 20 newsgroups were chosen at random and partitioned by the newsgroup name [1]. We form the following four sub corpora: SCIENCE which has 4 science related groups, REC which has 4 recreation related groups, HARDWARE which has 2 problem discussion groups on PC and Mac, RELPOL which has 2 groups on religion and politics. We also used two datasets for evaluation on spam filtering: USREMAIL [11] which contains 1000 personal emails of which 50% are spam and LINGSPAM [8] which contains 2893 email messages, of which 83% are non-spam messages related to linguistics, the rest are spam. Equal sized stratified disjoint training and test sets were created, where each set contains 20 % of the dataset of documents randomly selected from the original corpus. For repeated trials, 15 such train test splits were formed. Documents were pre-processed by removing stop words and some special characters. We use an Information Gain based feature selection.

Figure 5 shows snapshots of stacked images obtained from the six datasets described above. The rows of each image correspond to cases, and the columns to features. The case rows are shaded to show the classes to which they belong. It is seen that USREMAIL has very neat separability between the classes with cases belonging to the same class packed closely to each other. LINGSPAM and RELPOL also display regularities with respect to ways cases belonging to the same class are packed. In contrast, HARDWARE is clearly a complex domain, with very little separability between classes, and very few pronounced topic chunks. This is perhaps explained by the presence of large number of features which are shared by classes PC and Mac. To increase effectiveness of classification in HARDWARE, one approach is to combine features to extract new features which are more discriminative of the two classes. We note that in the colour shading as in Figure 5 is only applicable to classification domain. In non-classification domains (where the solution is textual) one approach is to map the solution side similarities of cases having similar problem descriptions (and hence stacked next to each other) to different colour shades (lighter shades for relatively dissimilar solution components, say) and show the resulting "colour band" alongside the stacked image. This helps in identifying complex regions of the casebase, where similar problems do not have similar solutions.

Figure 4 shows the $GAME_{class}$ values obtained over the 15 trials in each of the six datasets. Of the two class problems, LINGSPAM and USREMAIL have high $GAME_{class}$ values indicating that they are simpler compared to HARDWARE which has a low $GAME_{class}$ value. Table 1 suggests that $GAME_{class}$ predictions are supported by accuracy figures recorded by seven classifiers. The first of these is the standard 3-nearest-neighbours classifier using a cosine similarity measure. The second and third are 3-NN classifiers based on Latent Semantic Indexing (LSI) [6] and its class-aware version sprinkled LSI (LSISPR in the table) [3] which are interesting in the TCBR context, since they lend themselves to instance based retrieval, and incremental learning. The fourth is a neural network classifier embedded in an architecture called the Extended Case Retrieval Network, presented in [15]. The Support Vector Machine (SVM) [2] has been shown to be very successful with textual data [5]; we have experimented with SVM with a linear kernel (which has been shown in [18] to work best for textual data) as our fifth classifier. The sixth is LogitBoost, which is a boosting approach grounded on weak learners in the form of decision stumps [5]. Finally, we also used a classifier based on Propositional Semantic Indexing (PSI) which

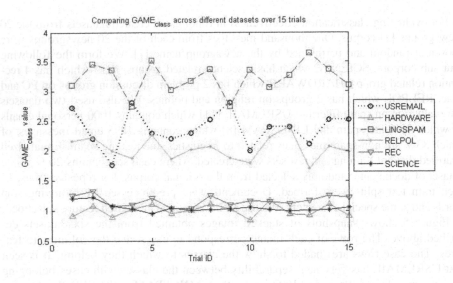

Fig. 4. GAME$_{class}$ values across different datasets

Table 1. GAME$_{class}$ and Accuracies obtained by different classifiers

	HARDWARE	RELPOL	USREMAIL	LINGSPAM	REC	SCIENCE
GAME measure	1.0028	2.0358	2.3728	3.2222	1.1629	1.0492
kNN-3	59.51	70.51	59.23	85.09	62.79	54.89
LSI + kNN-3	66.30	91.17	94.67	97.37	79.32	72.55
LSISPR + kNN-3	80.42	93.89	96.13	98.34	86.99	80.60
ECRN(Neural Network)	80.12	93.26	96.50	98.17	69.91	80.18
SVM	78.82	91.86	95.83	95.63	--	--
LogitBoost	77.99	79.67	92.67	95.80	87.15	73.77
PSI	80.1	91.2	94.83	95.8	76.2	59.9

Table 2. Correlation of GAME$_{class}$ with classifier accuracies over 4 binary classification problems

	kNN-3	LSI + kNN-3	LSISPR + kNN-3	ECRN (NN)	SVM	LogitBoost	PSI
ρ	0.7685	0.9176	0.9365	0.9360	0.9023	0.8820	0.9330

has been presented in the TCBR context [16]. Like LSI, PSI performs feature extraction; however the extracted features are more easily interpretable compared to LSI. The current formulation of GAME$_{class}$ allows for more meaningful comparisons between problems when they have the same number of classes. So we compared the binary and four-class problems separately. The correlation coefficient of the GAME$_{class}$ score against classification accuracies over the four binary problems are shown in Table 2. We note a strong positive linear correlation of GAME$_{class}$ to accuracies reported by all seven classifiers. It is also interesting to note a stronger correlation of GAME$_{class}$ to LSISPR as compared to LSI, hinting at the importance of class knowledge. It is pointless to do correlation over the four-class datasets since we have just two of them; however we observe that GAME$_{class}$ declares SCIENCE to be more complex than REC, and this is confirmed by all classifiers, excepting ECRN, where the neural network training failed to converge in the REC dataset. SVM being inherently a binary classifier was not tried on the 4-class datasets, though we plan to experiment with multi-class SVM in future. The GAME$_{class}$ results closely relate to the visualizations; for instance, comparing the stacked images in Figure 5 from RELPOL and USREMAIL reveal that RELPOL is sparser with less conspicuous chunks, thus partially explaining its lower GAME$_{class}$ value.

Figure 6 shows the result of stacking on a representation generated by LSI. LSI recovers from word choice variability, by inferring similarity between words that co-occur in similar contexts. This has the effect of reducing sparseness of the original representation. It is interesting to observe that the LSI image is a blurred version of the original; also the compressed LSI image is approximately 73% the size of the original compressed image. We note that both LSI and LSISPR results were at a dimensionality setting where they yielded best performances [3].

An important issue that merits closer attention is the choice of the starting case in the stacking process, and its influence on the visualization and complexity measure. Our experiments have shown that visualizations are not widely affected by the choice of starting cases, except for the shuffling in the order in which clusters are displayed. We carried out experiments to study the effect of choice of starting case on the GAME$_{class}$ complexity measure. 50 different starting cases were chosen for each dataset. Figure 7 shows histogram plots for variation in flips over these choices; each vertical bar in the graphs shows the number of choices (out of 50) that result in a certain range of flips values, which are plotted along the horizontal axis. The range indicators $flips_{max}$ and $flips_{min}$ are shown along with mean flips and standard deviations. It is observed that all graphs are either densely packed or have sharp peaking behaviour; in other words, they have low standard deviations in comparison to the range ($flips_{max}$ -- $flips_{min}$). This shows that the GAME$_{class}$ scores are statistically robust to choice of starting cases, when it comes to comparing complexity between casebases. From a purist standpoint, however, one would choose a starting case that that produces the maximum GAME$_{class}$ score. An obvious brute force approach, which is impractical for any case base of non-trivial size, is to exhaustively try each case as a starting case. More research needs to go into finding efficient ways of pruning the search space to make the process less computationally expensive. A graph theoretic perspective to this problem is briefly outlined in Section 6.

114   S. Chakraborti et al.

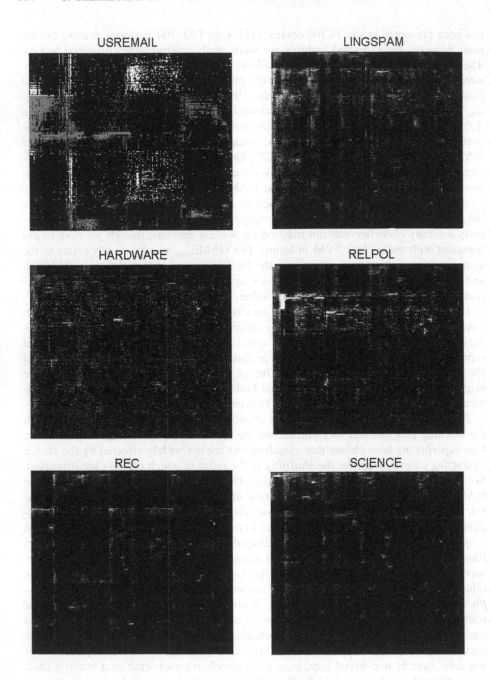

Fig. 5. Stacked Images

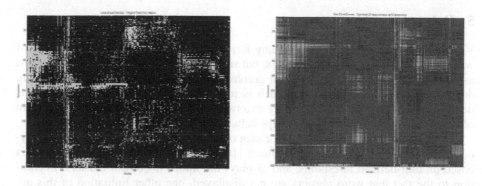

Fig. 6. Stacked images from USREMAIL before and after LSI

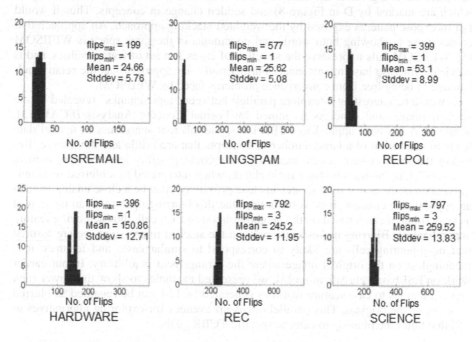

USREMAIL: flips_max = 199, flips_min = 1, Mean = 24.66, Stddev = 5.76

LINGSPAM: flips_max = 577, flips_min = 1, Mean = 25.62, Stddev = 5.08

RELPOL: flips_max = 399, flips_min = 1, Mean = 53.1, Stddev = 8.99

HARDWARE: flips_max = 396, flips_min = 1, Mean = 150.86, Stddev = 12.71

REC: flips_max = 792, flips_min = 3, Mean = 245.2, Stddev = 11.95

SCIENCE: flips_max = 797, flips_min = 3, Mean = 259.52, Stddev = 13.83

Fig. 7. The impact of choice of starting cases on the $GAME_{class}$ complexity measure

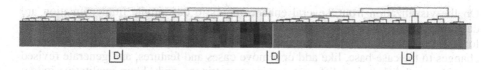

Fig. 8. A snapshot of hierarchical visualization (courtesy HCI Maryland website [10])

5 Related Work

Visualization techniques in Text Mining have typically attempted to display one of word associations or document clusters, but seldom both. Techniques to display word associations include word association graphs and circle graphs [5]. For visualizing document clusters, a common approach is multidimensional scaling which projects documents in a high dimensional space to a two dimensional one, under the constraint of preserving the similarity relationships between documents, as closely as possible.

An approach that comes close to our idea of stacking in terms of the generated layout is the Hierarchical Clustering Explorer [10] which dynamically generates clusters based on user-defined thresholds, and displays the mined document clusters. In addition to the fact that word clusters are not displayed, one other limitation of this approach is that there is no clear way of choosing the right ordering between several sub-trees under a given node. This may lead to discontinuities in the image (some of which are marked by D in Figure 8) and sudden change in concepts. Thus it would fail to expose patterns exposed by the weighted stacking approach. An approach that comes close to showing both words and documents in the same space is WEBSOM [5]. WEBSOM fails to preserve the structure of cases as a set of feature values, and is unwieldy for case base maintenance. Furthermore, our approach has the relative advantage of being free from convergence problems faced by WEBSOM.

It would be interesting to explore parallels between "topic chunks" revealed by the stacked image, and concepts as mined by Formal Concept Analysis (FCA) [13]. While FCA has been applied to TCBR tasks, the inherent sparseness of textual data leads to generation of a large number of concepts that are brittle and unintuitive. Relaxing the strict closure requirements of FCA could possibly lead to "approximate concepts". Our intuition is that a topic chunk, when interpreted as a blurred rectangular version of the actual light shades in close proximity, may be a close analog to such an approximate concept. It is worth noting that this blurring operation can be viewed as smoothing of cases based on the neighbourhood of each cell, thus achieving feature generalization. Blurring makes sense only on the stacked image since we are assured that neighbouring cells are likely to correspond to similar cases and features; it is meaningless on the original image where the arrangement is arbitrary. In our earlier work on LSI-based classification [3], we presented examples to show that lower rank approximations to case feature matrices generated by LSI can be regarded as blurred versions of the original. This parallel opens up avenues for exploring alternatives to LSI that tailor the blurring to cater to specific TCBR goals.

6 Future Work

On the visualization front, several enhancements to our simple implementation are desirable. Firstly, the visualization should facilitate interaction with the user, that allows him to view and annotate concepts that act as descriptors of topic chunks, make changes to the case-base, like add or remove cases and features, and generate revised stacking on the fly using different parameter settings, and obtain qualitative judgements for determining settings that work best. When case bases are large, the user should be able to zoom in on interesting regions of the image. Another interesting extension to our current interface would be a facility to show feature associations in each topic chunk in the style of association graphs [5] rather than displaying just a list of features. This may enhance its usability for the knowledge engineer.

As part of future work on global complexity measures, we would like to carry out an evaluation of the original GAME measure on unsupervised case bases over which relevance judgements are available, or can be inferred implicitly [17]. We are also investigating the problem of complexity evaluation from a graph theoretic perspective, where each case is a vertex, and each edge carries a weight equal to the similarity between the two cases it connects. Theoretically, the process of finding the best stacking arrangement maps onto finding an optimal tour that connects all cases in the graph, while minimizing a cost, which in our case is simply the sum of similarities (we could incorporate a weighting as in equations (1) and (2) above) across all edges involved in the tour. This is the classic Travelling Salesman Problem (TSP) [20] which is known to be NP-complete. We can obtain approximate solutions based on branch-and bound heuristics and distance measures that satisfy triangle inequality. An interesting alternative that leads to an exact solution is to find the minimum spanning tree (MST) instead. The greedy algorithm for the MST is the following: at each stage, build the cheapest (least cost) edge (in our case, an edge corresponding to highest similarity) that, when added to the already constructed graph, does not result in a cycle. It can be shown that this greedy algorithm results in a minimal cost spanning tree, and several efficient variants of the above algorithm have been proposed [20]. There are two ways in which the MST idea can be exploited. Firstly, it can help us in a more principled and efficient choice of the starting case. Secondly, the idea can be extended to devise a complexity measure based on forming MSTs independently of problem and solution components, and comparing these MSTs using one of several tree edit measures [19].

As a final point, we note that case bases are seldom static, so the importance of efficient update strategies that can handle additions, deletions or updates of cases (or features) cannot be over-emphasized. Though we have not experimented with dynamic collections, our current prescription is a lazy strategy that makes quick incremental but approximate updates whenever a change happens, and relegates the job of making accurate changes at a later "bulk update" stage. This saves the overhead of performing stacking each time a change is encountered. The basic idea is to trade off accuracy for efficiency, and is similar in sprit to the idea of folding-in [21] which is a popular method for updating LSI based representations.

7 Conclusions

We presented a simple approach to visualize textual case bases. The stacked image display can help knowledge engineers in getting a bird's eye view of the domain, thus facilitating knowledge acquisition. The visualization has three main advantages over other approaches. Firstly, it shows case and feature clusters in relation to each other, thus allowing case clusters to be explained in terms of feature clusters, and vice versa. Secondly, since stacking does not rely on any abstraction, it preserves the structure of cases and displays case and feature vectors as they are. This helps case base maintenance since noisy cases, redundant features or "bridge" features are revealed. Finally, stacking is fast and simple to implement, has no convergence problems, and is parameter-free for all practical purposes. We have also introduced a complexity measure founded on the idea of stacking. We showed that in classification tasks, an adapted version of this measure corresponds closely to accuracies reported by standard classifiers.

Acknowledgements

The authors are grateful to Dr. Derek Bridge for his interesting insights on various aspects of this work.

References

1. Mitchell, T.: Machine Learning. Mc Graw Hill International (1997)
2. Joachims, T.: Text Categorization with Support Vector Machines: Learning with Many Relevant Features. In: Proc. of ECML, pp. 137–142. ACM Press, New York (1998)
3. Chakraborti, S., Mukras, R., Lothian, R., Wiratunga, N., Watt, S., Harper, D.: Supervised Latent Semantic Indexing using Adaptive Sprinkling. In: Proc. IJCAI, pp. 1582–1587 (2007)
4. Lamontagne, L.: Textual CBR Authoring using Case Cohesion, in TCBR'06 - Reasoning with Text. In: Proc of the ECCBR 2006 Workshops, pp. 33–43 (2006)
5. Feldman, R., Sanger, J.: The Text Mining Handbook. Cambridge University Press, Cambridge (2007)
6. Deerwester, S.C., Dumais, S.T., Landauer, T.K., Furnas, G.W., Harshman, R.A.: ndexing by Latent Semantic Analysis. JASIST 41(6), 391–407 (1990)
7. Massie, S.: Complexity Modelling for Case Knowledge Maintenance in Case Based Reasoning, PhD Thesis, The Robert Gordon University (2006)
8. Sakkis, G., Androutsopoulos, I., Paliouras, G., Karkaletsis, V., Spyropoulos, C.D., Stamatopoulos, P.: A Memory-based Approach to Anti-Spam Filtering for Mailing Lists. Information Retrieval 6, 49–73 (2003)
9. Delany, S.J., Cunningham, P.: An Analysis of Case-base Editing in a Spam Filtering System. In: Funk, P., González Calero, P.A. (eds.) ECCBR 2004. LNCS (LNAI), vol. 3155, pp. 128–141. Springer, Heidelberg (2004)
10. HCE visualization, HCI Lab, University of Maryland, http://www.cs.umd.edu/hcil/hce/
11. Delany, S.J., Bridge, D.: Feature-Based and Feature-Free Textual CBR: A Comparison in Spam Filtering. In: Proc. of Irish Conference on AI and Cognitive Science, pp. 244–253 (2006)
12. Vinay, V., Cox, I.J., Milic-Fralyling, N., Wood, K.: Measuring the Complexity of a Collection of Documents. In: Lalmas, M., MacFarlane, A., Rüger, S.M., Tombros, A., Tsikrika, T., Yavlinsky, A. (eds.) ECIR 2006. LNCS, vol. 3936, pp. 107–118. Springer, Heidelberg (2006)
13. Díaz-Agudo, B., González-Calero, P.A.: Formal concept analysis as a support technique for CBR. Knowledge Based Syst. 14(3-4), 163–171 (2001)
14. Brüninghaus, S., Ashley, K.D.: The Role of Information Extraction for Textual CBR. In: Aha, D.W., Watson, I. (eds.) ICCBR 2001. LNCS (LNAI), vol. 2080, pp. 74–89. Springer, Heidelberg (2001)
15. Chakraborti, S., Watt, S., Wiratunga, N.: Introspective Knowledge Acquisition in Case Retrieval Networks for Textual CBR. In: Proc. of the 9th UK CBR Workshop, pp. 51–61 (2004)
16. Wiratunga, N., Lothian, R., Chakraborti, S., Koychev, I.: A Propositional Approach to Textual Case Indexing. In: Jorge, A.M., Torgo, L., Brazdil, P.B., Camacho, R., Gama, J. (eds.) PKDD 2005. LNCS (LNAI), vol. 3721, pp. 380–391. Springer, Heidelberg (2005)
17. White, R.W., Ruthven, I., Jose, J.M.: A Study of Factors Affecting the Utility of Implicit Relevance Feedback. In: Proc. of SIGIR 2005 (2005)

18. Joachims, T.: Text categorization with support vector machines: Learning with many relevant features. In: Nédellec, C., Rouveirol, C. (eds.) ECML 1998. LNCS, vol. 1398, pp. 137–142. Springer, Heidelberg (1998)
19. Bille, P.: A survey of tree edit distance and related problems. Theoretical Computer Science 337(1-3), 217–239 (2005)
20. Cormen, T.H., Leiserson, C.E., Rivest, R.L., Stein, C.: Introduction to Algorithms, 2nd edn. MIT Press and McGraw-Hill (2001)
21. Berry, M., Dumais, S., O'Brien, G.: Using linear algebra for intelligent information retrieval. SIAM Rev. 37, 573–595 (1995)

Learning Similarity Functions from Qualitative Feedback

Weiwei Cheng and Eyke Hüllermeier

FB Mathematik/Informatik, Philipps-Universität Marburg, Germany
{cheng,eyke}@mathematik.uni-marburg.de

Abstract. The performance of a case-based reasoning system often depends on the suitability of an underlying similarity (distance) measure, and specifying such a measure by hand can be very difficult. In this paper, we therefore develop a machine learning approach to similarity assessment. More precisely, we propose a method that learns how to combine given local similarity measures into a global one. As training information, the method merely assumes qualitative feedback in the form of similarity comparisons, revealing which of two candidate cases is more similar to a reference case. Experimental results, focusing on the ranking performance of this approach, are very promising and show that good models can be obtained with a reasonable amount of training information.

1 Introduction

The concept of similarity lies at the heart of case based reasoning (CBR), and the success of a CBR system often strongly depends on the specification of a suitable similarity measure. Unfortunately, domain knowledge provided by human experts is often not sufficient to define an optimal measure by hand. This problem remains despite the existence of "divide-and-conquer" techniques such as the "local–global principle", stating that the (global) similarity between two cases can be obtained as an aggregation of various local measures pertaining to different dimensions or features of a case [1].

In fact, even though it is true that *local similarity measures* can sometimes be defined in a relatively straightforward way, the proper *combination* of these local measures often remains a challenging problem. The reason is that, usually, the definition of a local measure only requires the comparison of properties or attribute values that are measured on the same scale and, therefore, are indeed comparable. However, to aggregate different local measures into a global one, one has to combine properties that may not be easily comparable, and whose importance may be highly subjective or context-dependent.

In this paper, we address the above problem by using machine learning methods to elicit global similarity measures on the basis of feedback in the form of examples. In this regard, the type of feedback expected as input by a learning method is of special importance. Roughly, two types of feedback can be distinguished, namely *absolute* and *relative*. Typically, the former corresponds to quantitative information about the degree of similarity between two cases,

K.-D. Althoff et al. (Eds.): ECCBR 2008, LNAI 5239, pp. 120–134, 2008.

whereas the latter only provides qualitative information about the (order) relation between similarities. Even though absolute feedback is convenient from a learning point of view, it is of course demanding and hence hard to acquire from human experts. In this paper, we therefore proceed from qualitative feedback which is much less difficult to obtain: Given a reference case and two cases to compare with, we only expect information about which of these two cases is more similar. Essentially, this is what Stahl in [2] refers to as *relative case utility feedback*.[1]

The paper is organized as follows: In Section 2, we detail the formal setting underlying our learning method. The method itself is then introduced in its basic form in Section 3 and evaluated empirically in Section 4. We discuss possible extensions of the basic model in Section 5 and related work in Section 6. The paper ends with concluding remarks in Section 7. Before proceeding, we mention that, formally, our approach will not be developed in terms of similarity functions but instead resort to the dual concept of a distance function.

2   Problem Setting

A case base is a subset $CB \subseteq \mathbb{C}$ with $|CB| < \infty$, where $\mathbb{C} \neq \emptyset$ denotes the set of all conceivable cases. We assume the existence of d *local distance measures*

$$\delta_i : \mathbb{C} \times \mathbb{C} \to \mathbb{R}_+ \quad (i = 1 \ldots d). \tag{1}$$

For each pair of cases $a, b \in \mathbb{C}$, $\delta_i(a, b) \in \mathbb{R}_+$ is a measure of the distance between these cases with respect to a certain aspect. For example, suppose cases to be represented as graphs, i.e., $\mathbb{C}$ is a set of graphs. A local distance $\delta_i(a, b)$ may then be defined by $|n(a) - n(b)|$, where $n(a)$ is the number of nodes in a, or by $\max(n(a), n(b)) - s$, where s is the size of the maximal common subgraph.

According to the *local–global principle*, the (global) distance between two cases can be obtained as an aggregation of the local distance measures (1):

$$\Delta(a, b) = \mathrm{AGG}\left(\delta_1(a, b), \delta_2(a, b) \ldots \delta_d(a, b)\right), \tag{2}$$

where AGG is a suitable aggregation operator. As a special case, consider a representation of cases in terms of d-dimensional feature vectors

$$a = (a_1, a_2 \ldots a_d) \in \mathbb{A}_1 \times \mathbb{A}_2 \times \ldots \times \mathbb{A}_d, \tag{3}$$

where $\mathbb{A}_i$ is the domain of the i-th attribute A_i. $\mathbb{C}$ is then given by the Cartesian product of these domains, $\mathbb{A}_1 \times \mathbb{A}_2 \times \ldots \times \mathbb{A}_d$, and the local distances are of the form

$$\delta_i : \mathbb{A}_i \times \mathbb{A}_i \to \mathbb{R}_+, \tag{4}$$

i.e., $\delta_i(a_i, b_i)$ assigns a distance to each pair of attributes $(a_i, b_i) \in \mathbb{A}_i \times \mathbb{A}_i$; obviously, (4) is a special case of (1). Even though a feature-based representation

---

[1] In a different context though quite similar way, relative feedback of that kind is also used in information retrieval [3].

is of course not always optimal (in terms of performance), it is often the most feasible approach and still predominant in practice [4]. In our experiments in Section 4, we shall use data sets with numerical attributes and local distances $\delta_i(a_i, b_i) = |a_i - b_i|$.

2.1   Linear Combination of Local Measures

For the time being, we shall focus on a special type of aggregation operator (2) which is simple and often used in practice, namely a linear combination:

$$\Delta(a, b) = \sum_{i=1}^{d} w_i \cdot \delta_i(a, b). \tag{5}$$

Note that it makes sense to require

$$w = (w_1 \ldots w_d) \geq 0 \tag{6}$$

in order to guarantee the monotonicity of the distance measure (2). That is, if a local distance increases, the global distance cannot decrease.

Despite its simplicity, the linear model (5) has a number of merits. For example, it is easily interpretable, as a weight w_i is in direct correspondence with the *importance* of a local measure. In principle, it thus also allows one to incorporate additional background knowledge in a convenient way, e.g., that attribute A_i is at least as important as attribute A_j ($w_i \geq w_j$). Finally, the linear model is attractive from a machine learning point of view, as it is amenable to efficient learning algorithms and, moreover, to non-linear extensions via "kernelization" [5]. We shall come back to this point in Section 5.

2.2   Learning Distance Measures and Learning to Rank

The problem we shall consider in the next section is to learn the weights w_i in (5) from user feedback. The kind of training information we assume to be given as input to a learner is *qualitative* feedback of the following form: case a is more similar to b than to c. Information of this type will be denoted by a triplet $(a, b, c) \in \mathbb{C}^3$. Note that qualitative feedback of the above kind is typically much easier to acquire than absolute feedback, that is, the degree of distance $\Delta(a, b)$ between two cases a and b.

A global distance function induces for any query a total order on the case base: Given a query $q = (q_1 \ldots q_d) \in \mathbb{C}$ and two cases $a, b \in \mathrm{CB}$,

$$a \succeq_{q, \Delta} b \stackrel{\mathrm{df}}{\Longleftrightarrow} \Delta(q, a) \leq \Delta(q, b).$$

Indeed, it is often only the *ordering* of cases that really matters, not the distance degrees themselves. For example, to retrieve the k nearest neighbors in NN retrieval, a correct ordering of the case base is sufficient. Seen from this point of view, it is actually not important to approximate the true distance (2) accurately in the sense of minimizing a norm $|\Delta - \Delta^{est}|$ (such as the $\mathcal{L}^2$ norm) on $\mathbb{C} \times \mathbb{C} \to \mathbb{R}_+$ mappings. Instead, it is more important to find an estimation Δ^{est} that induces (almost) the same rankings, i.e., an estimation for which

$$\succeq_{q,\Delta^{est}} \approx \succeq_{q,\Delta} . \tag{7}$$

In our experiments in Section 4, we shall therefore evaluate a distance function Δ^{est} by comparing the ranking induced by this function with the actually true ranking (in terms of standard distance measures for rankings).

3   The Learning Algorithm

Suppose to be given a set of training data $\mathbb{T}$, which consists of a finite number of exemplary similarity constraints (a, b, c), where $a, b, c \in$ CB. As mentioned previously, the basic learning problem is to find a distance function (5) which is as much as possible in agreement with these constraints and also satisfies the monotonicity property (6). Besides, this function should of course generalize as well as possible beyond these examples in the sense of (7).

3.1   Distance Learning as a Classification Problem

A key idea in our approach is to reduce the above learning problem to a *binary classification problem*. Due to the assumption of a linear distance model, this is indeed possible: The inequality $\Delta(a, b) < \Delta(a, c)$ required by a constraint (a, b, c) is equivalent to

$$\langle w, x \rangle = \sum_{i=1}^{d} w_i \cdot x_i > 0,$$

where $x_i \stackrel{\text{df}}{=} \delta_i(a, c) - \delta_i(a, b)$. From a classification point of view, $x = T(a, b, c)$ $= (x_1 \ldots x_d)$ is hence a positive example and $-x$ a negative one. That is, a similarity constraint (a, b, c) can be transformed into two examples $(x, +1)$ and $(-x, -1)$ for binary classification learning; see Fig. 1 for a schematic illustration. Moreover, the vector $w = (w_1 \ldots w_d)$ that defines the distance function (5) in a unique way also defines the model (hyperplane) of the associated classification problem.

3.2   Ensemble Learning

Binary classification is a well-studied problem in machine learning, and a large repertoire of corresponding learning algorithms is available. In principle, all these methods can be applied in our context. Here, we make use of an ensemble learning technique, mainly for two reasons. First, ensembles typically produce more accurate predictions than individual learners. Secondly, as will be detailed in Section 3.4, the ensemble technique is also useful in connection with the selection of informative queries to be given to the user.

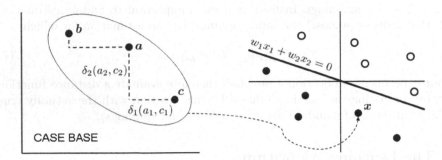

Fig. 1. Transformation of the distance learning problem to a classification problem: Each similarity constraint referring to a case triplet gives rise to a classification example

More specifically, we train an ensemble of m linear perceptrons, using the noise-tolerant learning algorithm proposed in [6], on permutations of the original training data; the j-th perceptron is represented by a weight vector $\boldsymbol{w}^{(j)} = (w_1^{(j)} \ldots w_d^{(j)})$. The output produced by this ensemble for an input $\boldsymbol{x} \in \mathbb{R}^d$ is given by the average of the individual outputs:

$$M(\boldsymbol{x}) = \frac{1}{m} \sum_{j=1}^{m} \sum_{i=1}^{d} w_i^{(j)} \cdot x_i = \sum_{i=1}^{d} w_i^* \cdot x_i. \tag{8}$$

The w_i^* can be taken as estimates of the w_i in the distance function (5).

In [7], it was shown that (8) approximates the center of mass of the version space and, hence, that this learning algorithm yields an approximation to a Bayes point machine. The latter seeks to find the midpoint of the region of intersection of all hyperplanes bisecting the version space into two halves of equal volume. This midpoint, the Bayes point, is known to be approximated by the center of mass of the version space.

3.3   Monotonicity

The monotonicity constraint (6) constitutes an interesting challenge from a machine learning point of view. In fact, this relatively simple property is not guaranteed by many standard machine learning algorithms. That is, a model that implements a distance function $\Delta(\cdot)$ may easily violate the monotonicity property, even if this condition is satisfied by all examples used as training data.

Fortunately, our learning algorithm allows us to incorporate the monotonicity constraint in a relatively simple way. The well-known perceptron algorithm is an error-driven on-line algorithm that adapts the weight vector $\boldsymbol{w}$ in an incremental way. To guarantee monotonicity, we simply modify this algorithm as follows: Each time an adaptation of $\boldsymbol{w}$ produces a negative component $w_i < 0$, this component is set to 0. Roughly speaking, the original adaptation is replaced by a "thresholded" adaptation.

In its basic form, the perceptron algorithm provably converges after a finite number of iterations, provided the data is linearly separable. We note that this property is preserved by our modification (proof omitted due to space restrictions). Obviously, monotonicity of the single perceptrons implies monotonicity of their average (8).

3.4 Active Learning

So far, we did not address the question of where the training data $\mathbb{T}$ actually comes from. The simplest assumption is that $\mathbb{T}$ is just a random sample, even though this assumption is of course not always justified in practice. In this section, we consider the interesting scenario in which additional training examples can be gathered by asking for feedback from the user of a CBR system. Thus, feedback is derived by selecting two cases b, c and a reference case a, and asking the user whether b or c is more similar to a.

Again, the simplest way to generate such a query is to choose it at random from CB. However, realizing that different queries can have different information content, the goal of this step should be the selection of a maximally informative query, i.e., an example that helps to improve the current distance function Δ^{est} as much as possible. This idea of generating maximally useful examples in a targeted way is the core of *active learning* strategies [8].

In the literature, numerous techniques for active learning have been proposed, most of them being heuristic approximations to theoretically justified (though computationally or practically infeasible) methods. Here, we resort to the *Query by Committee* approach [8]. Given an ensemble of models, the idea is to find a query for which the disagreement between the predictions of these models is maximal. Intuitively, a query of that kind corresponds to a "critical" and, therefore, potentially informative example. In our case, the models are given by the ensemble of perceptrons (cf. Section 3.2). Moreover, given a reference case a and two other cases b and c, two models Δ_1, Δ_2 disagree with each other if $\Delta_1(a, b) < \Delta_1(a, c)$ while $\Delta_2(a, b) > \Delta_2(a, c)$.

Various strategies are conceivable for finding a maximally critical query, i.e., a query for which there is a high disagreement among the ensemble. Our current implementation uses the following approach: Let $W = \{w^{(1)} \ldots w^{(m)}\}$ be the set of weight vectors of the perceptrons that constitute the current ensemble. In a first step, the two maximally conflicting models are identified, that is, two weight vectors $\{w^{(i)}, w^{(j)}\} \in W$ such that $\|w^{(i)} - w^{(j)}\|$ is maximal. Then, using these two weight vectors, two rankings π_i and π_j of the cases in CB are generated, respectively, taking a randomly selected reference case a as a query. Starting from the top of these rankings, the first conflict pair (b, c) is found, i.e., the first position k such that b and c are put on position k, respectively, by π_i and π_j, and $b \neq c$.[2] This conflict pair then gives rise to a query for the user. Depending on the answer, either (a, b, c) or (a, c, b) is added as an example to the training data $\mathbb{T}$ (and the learner is retrained on the expanded data set).

---

[2] In principle, an additional strategy is needed for the case where the two orderings are identical. However, even though this problem is theoretically possible, it never occurred in our experiments. Therefore, we omit further details here.

4   Experimental Results

This section presents the results of experimental studies that we conducted to investigate the efficacy of our approach. The aim of the experiments was twofold. A first goal was to show that the performance is convincing in absolute terms, which means that good predictions can be achieved with a reasonable amount of training information. Second, we wanted to provide evidence for the effectiveness of the special features of our learning algorithm, namely the incorporation of the monotonicity constraint, the use of an ensemble of models, and the active learning strategy.

4.1   Quality Measures

Let π^{est} denote the ranking of the case base induced by a learned distance function Δ^{est}. That is, when ordering all cases according to their estimated distance to the query, $\pi^{est}(a)$ is the position of case a. To evaluate Δ^{est}, we compare π^{est} with the ranking π induced by the true distance function Δ. To this end, we use three different quality measures: Kendall's tau, recall, and the position error.

Kendall's tau is a well-known and widely used rank correlation measure [9]. It calculates the number of pairwise rank inversions, i.e., the number of discordant pairs (a, b):

$$\# \left\{ (a, b) \mid \pi(a) < \pi(b), \pi^{est}(a) > \pi^{est}(b) \right\}.$$

More specifically, the Kendall tau coefficient normalizes this number to the interval $[-1, +1]$ such that $+1$ is obtained for identical rankings and -1 in the case of reversed rankings.

To complement the rank correlation, which takes the whole ranking into account, we employed a second measure that puts more emphasis on the top-ranks and is closely related to the recall measure commonly used in information retrieval. Let $\mathcal{K}$ be the set of top-k elements of the ranking π, that is, $\mathcal{K} = \{a \in \mathrm{CB} \mid \pi(a) \leq k\}$, where k is an integer that is usually small in comparison with the size of the case base (as a default value, we use $k = 10$); likewise, let $\mathcal{K}^{est}$ denote the top-k elements of π^{est}. We then define

$$\mathrm{recall}(\pi, \pi^{est}) \overset{\mathrm{df}}{=} \frac{\#(\mathcal{K} \cap \mathcal{K}^{est})}{k}. \tag{9}$$

This measure corresponds to the percentage of top-k cases of the ranking π that are also among the predicted top-k cases. It is motivated by the assumption that, typically, the top-k cases of a ranking are more important than the cases at lower ranks.

Focusing even more on the top and looking only at the case which is most similar to the query, we define the *position error* by the position of this case in the predicted ranking (minus 1): $\mathrm{pos}(\pi^{est}) \overset{\mathrm{df}}{=} \pi^{est}\left(\pi^{-1}(1)\right) - 1$, where π^{-1} is the inverse of π, i.e., $\pi^{-1}(1)$ is the topmost case in π.

4.2   Data

To analyze our algorithm under different conditions, we used data sets of varying size in terms of the number of features and the size of the case base: UNI (6/200), Iris (4/150), Wine (13/178), Yeast (24/2465), NBA (15,3924). The UNI data set is a ranking of the top-200 universities world-wide in 2006, provided by [10], where the universities are evaluated in terms of six numerical features (peer review score, recruiter review score, international faculty score, international students score, staff-to-student ratio, citation-to-staff ratio). Iris and Wine are widely used benchmark data sets that are publicly available from the UC Irvine machine learning repository [11]. Yeast is a genetic data set of phylogenetic profiles for the Yeast genome [12]. The genome consists of 2465 genes, and each gene is represented by an associated phylogenetic profile of length 24. The NBA data set records career statistics for regular seasons by NBA players. Each player is characterized by a set of 15 match statistics, e.g., scoring, rebound, turnover, steal, etc. This data set is part of the basketball player data set, which is published and maintained by *databasebasketball.com*.

4.3   Experiments

To answer the questions raised at the beginning of this section, we conducted three comparative studies:

– The first experiment investigates the advantage of using a modified perceptron learning algorithm that ensures monotonicity. We compare results for the standard perceptron algorithm (**standard**) with those for the modified one (**monotone**). For both variants, we use an ensemble of size $m = 10$ and non-active learning.
– The second experiment investigates the advantage of using an ensemble of models instead of a single model. Here, we compare the results obtained by training a single perceptron (**single**) with those of an ensemble of size $m = 10$ (**ensemble**). For both variants, we use monotone, non-active learning.
– Finally, we investigate the improvements due to our active learning strategy. To this end, we compare the active-learning strategy[3] (**active**) as described in Section 3 with the random strategy (**random**) that simply selects triplets $(a, b, c) \in$ CB at random.

In all experiments, we derived quality measures for different numbers of training data, ranging from 10 to 100. In a single experiment, we randomly generated a weight vector w (uniformly in $[0, 1]^d$) as the ground truth. A fixed number of training examples was then generated according to this vector, either by selecting triplets (a, b, c) at random or by using the active learning strategy. A model is then learned on this data. To evaluate its quality, a query is generated at random, and the ranking predicted for this query is compared to the true ranking; this is done repeatedly and results are averaged.

---

[3] Initialized with 10 randomly chosen triplets.

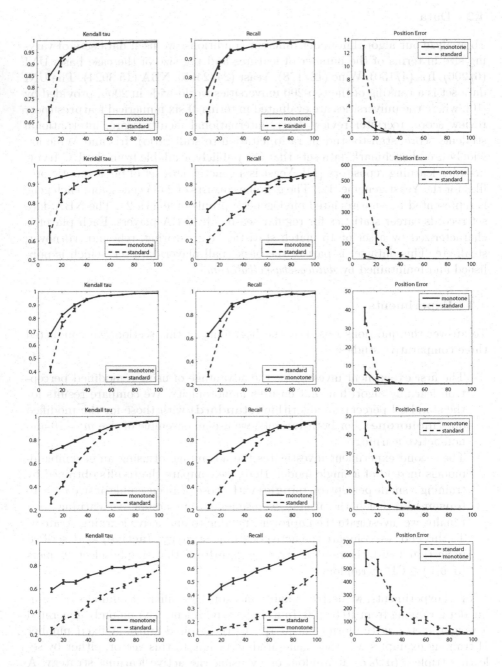

Fig. 2. Monotone vs. non-monotone learning: Experimental results in terms of rank correlation, recall, and position error as a function of the number of training examples (x-axis). Data sets from top to bottom: Iris, NBA, UNI, Wine, Yeast.

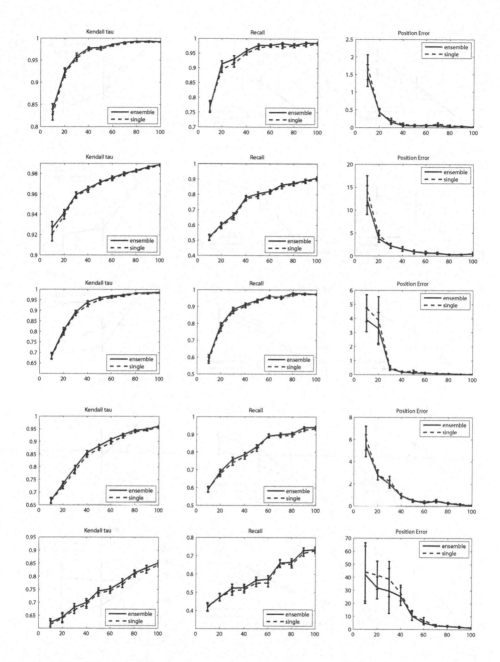

Fig. 3. Single vs. ensemble learning: Experimental results in terms of rank correlation, recall, and position error as a function of the number of training examples (x-axis). Data sets from top to bottom: Iris, NBA, UNI, Wine, Yeast.

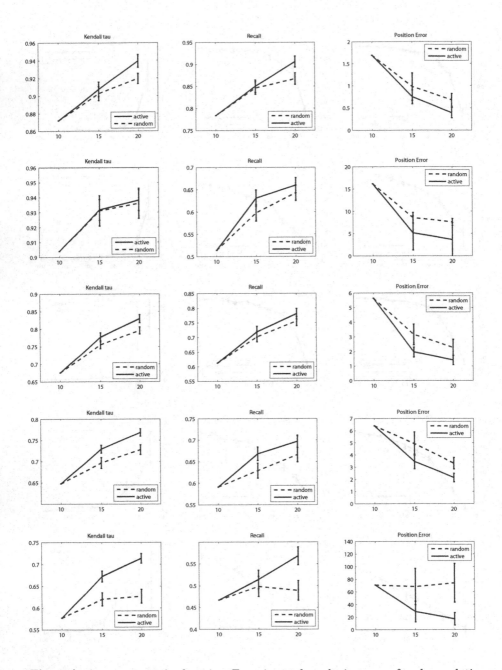

Fig. 4. Active vs. non-active learning: Experimental results in terms of rank correlation, recall, and position error as a function of the number of training examples (x-axis). Data sets from top to bottom: Iris, NBA, UNI, Wine, Yeast.

Figures 2, 3, and 4 show the results in terms of mean values and standard deviations obtained from 100 repetitions. As can clearly be seen from the learning curves in these figures, our approach to learning distance functions is indeed quite effective, and all its extensions do obviously pay off. This is especially true for the incorporation of the monotonicity constraint and the active learning strategy, where the learning curves show a visible improvement. The ensemble effect, on the other hand, yields only a slight improvement (the learning curves are often very close) which is, nevertheless, still statistically significant.

5   Extensions

The linearity assumption underlying model (5) is of course not always justified in practice. Instead, the aggregation (2) may be a nonlinear operator, and the classification examples $x = T(a, b, c)$ created by triplets of cases (cf. Fig. 1) will no longer be linearly separable. As our idea of transforming the distance learning problem into a classification problem, as outlined in Section 3.1, strongly exploits the linearity of (5), one may wonder whether this approach can be extended to the nonlinear case. Indeed, there are different options for such an extension, two of which will be sketched in this section.

5.1   Kernel-Based Learning

First, it is important to note that our transformation only exploits the linearity in the coefficients w_i, not the linearity in the local distances. Therefore, the approach can easily be extended to linear combinations of arbitrary functions of the local distances. An especially important example is a model which is, in a similar form, often used in fields like statistics and economics:

$$\Delta(a, b) = \sum_{i=1}^{d} w_i \cdot \delta_i(a, b) + \sum_{i=1}^{d} \sum_{j=i}^{d} w_{ij} \cdot \delta_i(a, b) \delta_j(a, b). \qquad (10)$$

The terms $\delta_i(a, b) \delta_j(a, b)$, which are called *interaction terms*, enable the modeling of interdependencies between different local distances.

It is noticeable that (10) is closely related to the transformation induced by a quadratic kernel $(x, x') \mapsto \langle x, x' \rangle^2$ in kernel-based learning. More generally, (10) is actually equivalent to (5) when looking at the local distances δ_i as *features*. Indeed, both models are special cases of the representation

$$\Delta(a, b) = v \cdot \phi(d(a, b)) = \sum_{\ell=1}^{k} v_\ell \cdot \phi_\ell(d(a, b)), \qquad (11)$$

where $d(a, b) = (\delta_1(a, b) \ldots \delta_d(a, b))$, and the ϕ_ℓ are properties of this vector of local distances. This provides the basis for "kernelizing" our approach. Without going into technical detail, we just mention that finding a model with maximal (soft) margin then comes down to solving a quadratic program defined as follows:

$$\min_{\boldsymbol{v},\xi_i} \frac{1}{2}\|\boldsymbol{v}\| + C \sum_{(\boldsymbol{a}_i,\boldsymbol{b}_i,\boldsymbol{c}_i)} \xi_i \quad \text{s.t.} \quad \begin{cases} \boldsymbol{v} \cdot (\phi(\boldsymbol{d}(\boldsymbol{a},\boldsymbol{c})) - \phi(\boldsymbol{d}(\boldsymbol{a},\boldsymbol{b}))) \geq 1 - \xi_i \\ \xi_i \geq 0 \end{cases},$$

where the $(\boldsymbol{a}_i, \boldsymbol{b}_i, \boldsymbol{c}_i)$ are the training examples and C is a regularization parameter. Eventually, this leads to learning a model that can be represented as

$$\Delta(\boldsymbol{a},\boldsymbol{b}) = \sum_i \alpha_i \left(K(\boldsymbol{d}(\boldsymbol{a},\boldsymbol{b}), \boldsymbol{d}(\boldsymbol{a}_i,\boldsymbol{c}_i)) - K(\boldsymbol{d}(\boldsymbol{a},\boldsymbol{b}), \boldsymbol{d}(\boldsymbol{a}_i,\boldsymbol{b}_i)) \right),$$

where $K(\cdot)$ is the kernel associated with the feature map $\phi(\cdot)$.

5.2 Nonlinear Classification and Sorting

Our original model as well as the extension (10) establish a one-to-one correspondence between the distance function $\Delta(\cdot)$ and the model for the induced classification problem. In fact, there is even a one-to-one correspondence between the parameters of $\Delta(\cdot)$ and the parameters of the corresponding (linear) classifier. A second extension is based on the observation that such a one-to-one correspondence, even if desirable, is in principle not needed.

Suppose we train a possibly nonlinear classifier $C(\cdot)$ that separates the classification examples induced by the similarity constraints given. From this model, it is perhaps not possible to recover the distance function $\Delta(\cdot)$ in explicit form. Still, given a query case $\boldsymbol{q}$ and any pair of cases $\boldsymbol{a}, \boldsymbol{b} \in$ CB, the classifier $C(\cdot)$ can answer the question whether $\boldsymbol{a}$ or $\boldsymbol{b}$ is more similar to $\boldsymbol{q}$: In the first case $C(\boldsymbol{x}) = +1$, while in the second case $C(\boldsymbol{x}) = -1$, where $\boldsymbol{x} = T(\boldsymbol{q}, \boldsymbol{a}, \boldsymbol{b})$. As this information is a sufficient prerequisite for applying a *sorting algorithm*, it is, in principle, again possible to order the case base for the query $\boldsymbol{q}$. Such an algorithm cannot be applied directly, however, as a non-perfect classifier may produce non-transitive preferences. Yet, there are "noise-tolerant" ranking algorithms that can handle non-transitive preferences and yield good approximations to a true ranking [13].

6 Related Work

The learning and adaptation of similarity or distance measures has received considerable attention is CBR and related fields. In particular, the work of Stahl [14,15,2,16] shares a number of commonalities with ours. In fact, the problem considered in [14] is basically the same, namely to learn the weights in a linear combination of local similarity functions. However, the setting of the learning problem is quite different, just like the learning method itself. Stahl [14] applies a conventional gradient descent algorithm to minimize an "average similarity error". To obtain this error, he assumes the availability of a "similarity teacher" who, given a query case, is able to provide feedback in the form of a ranking of a subset of cases of the case base. In [17], Stahl and Gabel also address the problem of learning *local* similarity measures. They propose evolutationary optimization techniques as an approach to adaptation.

Methods for feature weighing and selection have also been studied by many other authors, especially in the context of k-NN classification [18,19,20,21,22]. In an early work, Wettschereck and Aha have proposed a general framework for comparing feature weighting methods [23]. They distinguish such methods along five dimensions, namely feedback, weight space, representation, generality, and knowledge. More recent methods for feature weighing can also be found in machine learning research [24,25].

Finally, problems related to feature weighing, selection, and aggregation are of course also studied outside CBR and machine learning research, for example in fields like decision making and information fusion (e.g. [26]). A complete review of the literature, however, is beyond the scope of this paper.

7 Summary and Conclusions

To support the specification of similarity (distance) measures in CBR, we have proposed a machine learning algorithm that proceeds from predefined local distance functions and learns how to combine these functions into a global measure. The algorithm is quite user-friendly in the sense that it only assumes qualitative feedback in the form of similarity comparisons: Case *a* is more similar to *b* than to *c*. First experiments have yielded promising results, showing that the algorithm is effective and, moreover, that its special features (monotonicity, ensemble learning, active selection of examples) lead to increased performance.

Apart from technical aspects, we consider the general idea of the approach as especially interesting, as it allows one to reduce the problem of distance learning to a conventional classification problem. Thus, distance learning becomes amenable to a large repertoire of existing and well-understood algorithms. In this regard, we are currently elaborating on several extensions of our basic model, such as those outlined in Section 5.

References

1. Richter, M.M.: Foundations of similarity and utility. In: The 20th International FLAIRS Conference, Key West, Florida (2007)
2. Stahl, A.: Learning similarity measures: A formal view based on a generalized CBR model. In: Muñoz-Ávila, H., Ricci, F. (eds.) ICCBR 2005. LNCS (LNAI), vol. 3620, pp. 507–521. Springer, Heidelberg (2005)
3. Joachims, T.: Optimizing search engines using clickthrough data. In: KDD 2002, Proc. of the ACM Conference on Knowledge Discovery and Data Mining (2002)
4. Cunningham, P.: A taxonomy of similarity mechanisms for case-based reasoning. Technical Report UCD-CSI-2008-01, University College Dublin (2008)
5. Schölkopf, B., Smola, A.: Learning with Kernels: Support Vector Machines, Regularization, Optimization, and Beyond. MIT Press, Cambridge (2001)

6. Khardon, R., Wachman, G.: Noise tolerant variants of the perceptron algorithm. The Journal of Machine Learning Research 8, 227–248 (2007)
7. Herbrich, R., Graepel, T., Campbell, C.: Bayes point machines. Journal of Machine Learning Research 1, 245–279 (2001)
8. Seung, H., Opper, M., Sompolinsky, H.: Query by committee. In: Computational Learning Theory, pp. 287–294 (1992)
9. Kendall, M.: Rank correlation methods. Charles Griffin, London (1955)
10. O'Leary, J.: World university rankings editorial - global vision ensures healthy competition. The Times Higher Education Supplement (2006)
11. Asuncion, A., Newman, D.: UCI machine learning repository (2007)
12. Pavlidis, P., Weston, J., Cai, J., Grundy, W.: Gene functional classification from heterogeneous data. Journal of Comput. Biology 9, 401–411 (2002)
13. Cohen, W., Schapire, R., Singer, Y.: Learning to order things. Journal of Artificial Intelligence Research 10 (1999)
14. Stahl, A.: Learning feature weights from case order feedback. In: Aha, D.W., Watson, I. (eds.) ICCBR 2001. LNCS (LNAI), vol. 2080, pp. 502–516. Springer, Heidelberg (2001)
15. Stahl, A., Schmitt, S.: Optimizing retrieval in CBR by introducing solution similarity. In: Proc. Int. Conf. on Art. Intell., ICAI, Las Vegas, USA (2002)
16. Stahl, A., Gabel, T.: Optimizing similarity assessment in case-based reasoning. In: Proc. 21th National Conf. on Artificial Intelligence. AAAI, Menlo Park (2006)
17. Stahl, A., Gabel, T.: Using evolution programs to learn local similarity measures. In: Ashley, K.D., Bridge, D.G. (eds.) ICCBR 2003. LNCS, vol. 2689, pp. 537–551. Springer, Heidelberg (2003)
18. Bonzano, A., Cunningham, P., Smyth, B.: Using introspective learning to improve retrieval in CBR: A case study in air traffic control. In: Leake, D.B., Plaza, E. (eds.) ICCBR 1997. LNCS, vol. 1266, pp. 291–302. Springer, Heidelberg (1997)
19. Kononenko, I.: Estimating attributes: Analysis and extensions of RELIEF. In: European Conference on Machine Learning, pp. 171–182 (1994)
20. Ricci, F., Avesani, P.: Learning a local similarity metric for case-based reasoning. In: Aamodt, A., Veloso, M.M. (eds.) ICCBR 1995. LNCS, vol. 1010, pp. 301–312. Springer, Heidelberg (1995)
21. Wilke, W., Bergmann, R.: Considering decision cost during learning of feature weights. In: European Workshop on CBR, pp. 460–472 (1996)
22. Branting, K.: Acquiring customer preferences from return-set selections. In: Aha, D.W., Watson, I. (eds.) ICCBR 2001. LNCS (LNAI), vol. 2080, pp. 59–73. Springer, Heidelberg (2001)
23. Wettschereck, D., Aha, D.: Weighting features. In: Aamodt, A., Veloso, M.M. (eds.) ICCBR 1995. LNCS, vol. 1010, pp. 347–358. Springer, Heidelberg (1995)
24. Wu, Y., Ianakiev, K., Govindaraju, V.: Improvements in k-nearest neighbor classification. In: Singh, S., Murshed, N., Kropatsch, W.G. (eds.) ICAPR 2001. LNCS, vol. 2013, pp. 222–229. Springer, Heidelberg (2001)
25. Toussaint, G.: Geometric proximity graphs for improving nearest neighbor methods in instance-based learning and data mining. Int. J. Comput. Geometry Appl. 15(2), 101–150 (2005)
26. Torra, V., Narukawa, Y.: Modeling Decisions: Information Fusion and Aggregation Operators. Springer, Heidelberg (2007)

Conservative Adaptation in Metric Spaces

Julien Cojan and Jean Lieber

Orpailleur, LORIA, CNRS, INRIA, Nancy Universities,
BP 239, 54 506 Vandœuvre-lès-Nancy
{Julien.Cojan,Jean.Lieber}@loria.fr

Abstract. Conservative adaptation consists in a minimal change on a
source case to be consistent with the target case, given the domain knowledge. It has been formalised in a previous work thanks to the AGM theory
of belief revision applied to propositional logic. However, this formalism
is rarely used in case-based reasoning systems. In this paper, conservative adaptation is extended to a more general representation framework,
that includes also attribute-value formalisms. In this framework, a case
is a class of case instances, which are elements of a metric space. Conservative adaptation is formalised in this framework and is extended
to α-conservative adaptation, that relaxes the conservativeness. These
approaches to adaptation in a metric space transform adaptation problems to well-formulated optimization problems. A running example in
the cooking domain is used to illustrate the notions that are introduced.

Keywords: adaptation, belief revision, conservative adaptation, case
representation, metric spaces.

1 Introduction

Adaptation is an issue of CBR (case-based reasoning [1]) that still deserves a
big amount of research. Conservative adaptation is an approach to adaptation
that consists in a minimal change on a source case to be consistent with the
target case, given the domain knowledge. It has been formalised in a previous
work thanks to the AGM theory of belief revision applied to propositionnal logic
(PL).

However, PL is rarely used in CBR systems. In this paper, conservative adaptation is extended to the general representation framework of "metric space
formalisms", that includes PL and also attribute-value formalisms (which are
widely used in CBR [2]).

Section 2 is a reminder about adaptation in CBR and introduces the running
example in the cooking domain used throughout the paper. Section 3 presents
the metric space formalisms. Section 4 formalises conservative adaptation in
these formalisms. This approach to adaptation can be extended by relaxing the
conservativeness: this is the α-conservative adaptation, presented and studied in
section 5. Finally, section 6 concludes the paper and draws some future work.

K.-D. Althoff et al. (Eds.): ECCBR 2008, LNAI 5239, pp. 135–149, 2008.
© Springer-Verlag Berlin Heidelberg 2008

2   Adaptation in Case-Based Reasoning

2.1   Principles of CBR and of Adaptation in CBR

Case-Based Reasoning (CBR) is a reasoning paradigm using cases, where a case encodes a particular piece of experience. The aim of a CBR system is to complete a *target case* Target for which some information is missing. To do so, a case base is assumed to be available. A case base is a finite set of cases, called the *source cases*. The application of CBR on a target case Target consists in two main steps:

- *Retrieval* of a source case Source from the case base, similar to Target.
- *Adaptation*, that consists in completing Target into Target-completed from Source.

Target-completed might still have to be completed. If so, it is used as a new target case for a new CBR session. Therefore several source cases may be involved in the final completion of Target.

Much work has been done on retrieval, but adaptation still needs investigation work. In most CBR implementations, adaptation is either basic or domain specific. The purpose of this paper is to present a general method for adaptation based on the principle of minimal change.

2.2   An Adaptation Example

Cooking provides many case-based reasoning examples, a recipe book is indeed a kind of case base. For simplicity, the focus is put on ingredients rather than on preparation, a problem consists in requirements on ingredients and portions, a solution is a recipe satisfying these requirements, i.e. an ingredient list and a text of instructions.

Léon wants to cook a fruit pie for six persons but he only has pears at disposal (and thus, no apple). He finds an apple pie recipe for four servings but no pear pie recipe. This can be formulated as a CBR adaptation problem:

Target = a requested recipe for a 6 portion pie with pears and no other fruit.
Source = a 4 portion apple pie recipe with 2 apples, 40 grams of sugar, and 120 grams of pastry as ingredients.

It is quite natural for Léon to think of the following adaptation which can be split into two steps: a substitution of apples by pears and an increase by half of the amount of each ingredient. These two adaptation steps involve different pieces of knowledge. The first one involves similarity between apples and pears. The second one is the following principle: the amount of ingredients is proportional to the number of portions.

In addition to this adaptation knowledge, some more knowledge is needed. The amount of apples and pears is expressed in number of fruits, however the relevant quantity here is their mass, thus the average mass per apple and pear is needed, say 120 grams for an apple and 100 grams for a pear. Moreover, to preserve the pie sweet, the amount of added sugar should be adjusted so as to compensate the different sweet amount contained in apples and pears —say 13 grams per pear and 14 grams per apple.

Knowing all this, from the source recipe Léon should infer he needs the following ingredients for his fruit pie:

- 3 or 4 pears as these values make the variation of fruit mass per person $\left|\frac{120\times 2}{4} - \frac{100\times x}{6}\right|$ minimal (for x: a natural integer).
- 50 grams of sugar (resp., 63 grams) if 4 pears (resp., 3 pears) were used , as it makes the variation of sweet mass per person $\left|\frac{40+2\times 14}{4} - \frac{x+4\times 13}{6}\right|$ (resp., $\left|\frac{40+2\times 14}{4} - \frac{x+3\times 13}{6}\right|$) minimal (for x: a real number).
- 180 grams of pastry as it makes the variation of pastry mass per person $\left|\frac{120}{4} - \frac{x}{6}\right|$ minimal (for x: a real number).

3   Metric Space Formalism for Case and Domain Knowledge Representation

3.1   Background

Definition 1. *A similarity measure* on a set $\mathcal{U}$ is a mapping S from $\mathcal{U} \times \mathcal{U}$ to $[0, 1]$ *such that:*

$$\text{for all } x, y \in \mathcal{U} \qquad S(x, y) = 1 \quad \text{iff} \quad x = y$$

The notation S is extended on $y \in \mathcal{U}$ and $A, B \subseteq \mathcal{U}$:

$$S(A, y) = \sup_{x \in A} S(x, y) \qquad S(A, B) = \sup_{x \in A, y \in B} S(x, y) \tag{1}$$

with the following convention: $S(\emptyset, y) = S(A, \emptyset) = S(\emptyset, B) = 0.$

A similarity measure S can be defined from a mapping $d : \mathcal{U} \times \mathcal{U} \to \mathbb{R}_+$ satisfying the separation postulate of metrics —for all $x, y \in \mathcal{U}$ $d(x, y) = 0$ iff $x = y$— by the relation:[1]

$$\text{for all } x, y \in \mathcal{U} \qquad S(x, y) = e^{-d(x,y)} \tag{2}$$

3.2   Case Representation

Cases are assumed to be represented by concepts of a *concept language* $\mathcal{L}_C$ where a concept C is interpreted by a subset $\text{Ext}(C)$ of a set $\mathcal{U}$ (the "universe

---

[1] Any mapping $f : \mathbb{R}_+ \to [0, 1]$ continuous, strictly decreasing and such that $f(0) = 1$ and $\lim_{x \to +\infty} f(x) = 0$ can be used instead of $x \mapsto e^{-x}$. For instance, $f(x) = \frac{1}{1+x}$ is often chosen in CBR. This choice was made for simplifications (see further). And, as the values do not have any relevance but through comparisons by $\leq$, this choice has no other effect than simplicity.

of discourse"). $\mathcal{L}_C$ is supposed to be closed under negation, conjunction and the unary operators G^σ for $\sigma \in [0,1]$:

$$\text{if } C, D \in \mathcal{L}_C \quad \text{then} \quad \neg C, \; C \wedge D, \; G^\sigma(C) \in \mathcal{L}_C$$
$$C \vee D \quad \text{is defined by} \quad \neg(\neg C \wedge \neg D)$$

Moreover $\mathcal{L}_C$ is assumed to contain $\top$ and $\bot$. The semantics is given by the mapping Ext from $\mathcal{L}_C$ to $2^{\mathcal{U}}$ (the subsets of $\mathcal{U}$) satisfying:

$$\text{Ext}(\top) = \mathcal{U} \qquad\qquad \text{Ext}(C \wedge D) = \text{Ext}(C) \cap \text{Ext}(D)$$
$$\text{Ext}(\bot) = \emptyset \qquad\qquad \text{Ext}(C \vee D) = \text{Ext}(C) \cup \text{Ext}(D)$$
$$\text{Ext}(\neg C) = \mathcal{U} \setminus \text{Ext}(C) \qquad \text{Ext}(G^\sigma(C)) = \{x \in \mathcal{U} \mid S(\text{Ext}(C), x) \geq \sigma\}$$

Definition 2. *A model of $C \in \mathcal{L}_C$ is, by definition, an element of $\text{Ext}(C)$. The consequence $\vDash$ and equivalence $\equiv$ relations on $\mathcal{L}_C$ are defined by:*

$$C \vDash D \quad \text{if} \quad \text{Ext}(C) \subseteq \text{Ext}(D)$$
$$C \equiv D \quad \text{if} \quad \text{Ext}(C) = \text{Ext}(D)$$

A concept $C \in \mathcal{L}_C$ is satisfiable if $\text{Ext}(C) \neq \emptyset$, i.e. $C \nvDash \bot$. For $A \in 2^{\mathcal{L}_C}$ and $C \in \mathcal{L}_C$, $A \vDash C$ means that if $x \in \mathcal{U}$ is a model of each $D \in A$, then it is a model of C. If $C, C_1, C_2 \in \mathcal{L}_C$, $C_1 \equiv_C C_2$ if $C \wedge C_1 \equiv C \wedge C_2$: $\equiv_C$ is the equivalence modulo C.

In this paper, $\vDash$ (and thus, $\equiv$) are supposed to be computable: there is a program taking as inputs two concepts C and D and giving in finite time a boolean value that is equal to True iff $C \vDash D$.

The following notations are introduced for the sake of simplicity:

$$S(C, x) = S(\text{Ext}(C), x) \qquad S(C, D) = S(\text{Ext}(C), \text{Ext}(D)) \tag{3}$$
$$\mathcal{E} = \{\text{Ext}(C) \mid C \in \mathcal{L}_C\} \quad (\text{Thus, } \mathcal{E} \subseteq 2^{\mathcal{U}}) \tag{4}$$

3.3 Domain Knowledge Representation

Domain knowledge is about properties that can be inferred on cases. By contrast with adaptation knowledge that is about comparisons between cases, it is static, i.e. it applies to cases by their own. In the cooking example, the amount of fruit is inferred from the amount of apples and pears in the recipe. From the interpretation point of view, the domain knowledge comes to the restriction of the extension space, some interpretations are not *licit*. So, like cases, it can be represented by a concept DK provided that the language $\mathcal{L}_C$ is expressive enough, which is assumed. Thus, DK $\in \mathcal{L}_C$.

3.4 Attribute-Value Representation

Many CBR systems rely on attribute-values representation of cases. The formalism presented below is a general attribute-value representation formalism that specialises the (very) general framework presented above. In this formalism $\mathcal{U}$ is assumed to be a Cartesian product:

$$\mathcal{U} = V_1 \times V_2 \times \ldots \times V_n$$

where V_i are "simple values" spaces, i.e. either $\mathbb{R}$ (the real numbers), $\mathbb{R}_+$ (the positive or null real numbers), $\mathbb{Z}$ (the integers), $\mathbb{N}$ (the natural integers), $\mathbb{B} = \{\texttt{True}, \texttt{False}\}$, or another enumerated set given in extension ("enumerated type").

For $i \in \{1, \ldots, n\}$, the *attribute* a_i is the projection along the ith coordinate:

$$a_i(x_1, x_2, \ldots, x_i, \ldots, x_n) = x_i \tag{5}$$

The language $\mathcal{L}_C$ is made of expressions with boolean values on the formal parameters $a_1, a_2, \ldots, a_n$: $C = P(a_1, a_2, \ldots, a_n)$. The extension of such a concept C is:

$$\begin{aligned} \texttt{Ext}(C) &= \{x \in \mathcal{U} \mid P(a_1(x), a_2(x), \ldots, a_n(x)) = \texttt{True}\} \\ &= \{(x_1, x_2, \ldots, x_n) \in \mathcal{U} \mid P(x_1, x_2, \ldots, x_n) = \texttt{True}\} \end{aligned}$$

$\mathcal{L}_C$ is still considered as closed for negation and conjunction.

3.5 Propositional Logic as a Kind of Attribute-Value Representation

The set of formulas on propositional variables $p_1, \ldots, p_n$ ($n \in \mathbb{N}$) can be put under the attribute-value representation with $\mathcal{U} = \mathbb{B}^n$. Indeed, to a propositional logic formula f on $p_1, \ldots, p_n$, can be associated the mapping $P_f : \mathbb{B}^n \to \mathbb{B}$ such that, for an interpretation I of the variables $p_1, \ldots, p_n$, I is a model of f iff $P_f(I(p_1), I(p_2), \ldots, I(p_n)) = \texttt{True}$. Reciprocally, to a mapping $P : \mathbb{B}^n \to \mathbb{B}$ it can be associated a formula f unique modulo logical equivalence such that $P = P_f$.

For example, to $f = a \wedge \neg(b \vee \neg c)$ is associated $P_f : (x, y, z) \in \mathbb{B}^3 \mapsto P(x, y, z) = \texttt{and}(x, \texttt{not}(\texttt{or}(y, \texttt{not}(z))))$.

For $I \in \mathcal{U}$, $i \in \{1, \ldots, n\}$ and f a propositional formula on $p_1, \ldots, p_n$, let $a_i(I) = I(p_i)$ and $\texttt{Ext}(f) = \{x \in \mathcal{U} \mid P_f(a_1(x), a_2(x), \ldots, a_n(x)) = \texttt{True}\}$. The following equivalence identifies the obtained semantics with the propositional logic semantics: I is a model of f iff $I \in \texttt{Ext}(f)$. This justifies the use of section 3.1 formalism in section 4 to generalise conservative adaptation defined on propositional logic in [3].

3.6 Formalisation of the Cooking Example Adaptation Problem

The section 2.2 example can be formalised as follows. The following attributes are introduced:

- $a_1 = \texttt{servings}$ for the number of servings the recipe is meant to, $V_1 = \mathbb{N} \setminus \{0\}$.
- $a_2 = \texttt{sweet}$ for the total amount of sweet (in equivalent saccharose grams), $V_2 = \mathbb{R}_+$.

- $a_3 = $ sugar for the amount of saccharose, in grams, $V_3 = \mathbb{R}_+$.
- $a_4 = $ pastry-mass for the amount of pastry, in grams, $V_4 = \mathbb{R}_+$.
- $a_5 = $ fruit-mass for the amount of fruits, in grams, $V_5 = \mathbb{R}_+$.
- $a_6 = $ apples-nb for the number of apples, $V_6 = \mathbb{N}$.
- $a_7 = $ pears-nb for the number of pears, $V_7 = \mathbb{N}$.

The space is then $\mathcal{U} = (\mathbb{N} \setminus \{0\}) \times \mathbb{R}_+ \times \mathbb{R}_+ \times \mathbb{R}_+ \times \mathbb{R}_+ \times \mathbb{N} \times \mathbb{N}$. The attributes sugar, pastry-mass, apples-nb, and pears-nb correspond to the possible ingredients that can be used in the recipes. The values corresponding to the attributes sweet and fruit-mass are deduced from the values of the "ingredient" attributes and from the domain knowledge DK: the amount of fruits is the sum of apple and pear masses, similarly, the sweet is equal to the sugar plus the sweet contained in apples and pears:

$$DK = (\text{sweet} = \text{sugar} + 14 \times \text{apples-nb} + 13 \times \text{pears-nb})$$
$$\wedge \, (\text{fruit-mass} = 120 \times \text{apples-nb} + 100 \times \text{pears-nb})$$

The source case, an apple pie for four servings, is represented by the concept Source stating the number of servings and the amount of each ingredient:

$$\text{Source} = (\text{servings} = 4) \wedge (\text{pastry-mass} = 120) \wedge (\text{sugar} = 40)$$
$$\wedge \, (\text{apples-nb} = 2) \wedge (\text{pears-nb} = 0)$$

The target case, a pie for six servings, is represented by the concept Target stating the number of servings, the fact that no apple is available, and the fact that some fruit is required:

$$\text{Target} = (\text{servings} = 6) \wedge (\text{apples-nb} = 0) \wedge (\text{fruit-mass} > 0).$$

4 Conservative Adaptation in Metric Space Formalisms

4.1 Belief Revision

The belief revision theory aims at establishing how to incorporate new information into previous beliefs that can be inconsistent with this new information, i.e. to define an operator $\circ$ on beliefs such that if D is the new information to be added to prior beliefs C, then the resulting beliefs should be $C \circ D$. Requirements for a revision operator have been formalised in the AGM postulates [4]. In [5], Katsuno and Mendelzon give the following postulates which are equivalent to AGM postulates —they prove the equivalence in propositional logic but their demonstration is still valid in the formalism of section 3.1:

Basic postulates
$$\begin{cases} \text{(R1)} & C \circ D \models D \\ \text{(R2)} & \text{if } C \wedge D \text{ is satisfiable then } C \circ D \equiv C \wedge D \\ \text{(R3)} & \text{if } D \text{ is satisfiable then } C \circ D \text{ too} \\ \text{(R4)} & \text{if } C \equiv C' \text{ and } D \equiv D' \text{ then } C \circ D \equiv C' \circ D' \end{cases}$$

Minimality postulates
$$\begin{cases} \text{(R5)} & (C \circ D) \wedge F \models C \circ (D \wedge F) \\ \text{(R6)} & \text{if } (C \circ D) \wedge F \text{ is satisfiable} \\ & \text{then } C \circ (D \wedge F) \models (C \circ D) \wedge F \end{cases}$$

The postulate (R1) means that the new knowledge D must be kept, (R2) means that if C and D are compatible, then both should be kept. (R3) means that $C \circ D$ must be consistent whenever D is, (R4) states the irrelevance of syntax principle. (R5) and (R6) are less intuitive, according to [5], they express the minimality of change.

These postulates are not constructive and do not prove the existence nor the unicity of such a revision operator. However, provided a similarity measure S is given on $\mathcal{U}$, a candidate $\circ^S$ for being a revision operator is defined by $C \circ^S D$ where C and D are concepts and $\Sigma = S(C, D)$:

$$C \circ^S D = G^{\Sigma}(C) \wedge D \tag{6}$$

In terms of interpretations, this means that:

$$\text{Ext}(C \circ^S D) = \{x \in \text{Ext}(D) \,|\, S(C, x) \geq S(C, D)\} \tag{7}$$

The models of $C \circ^S D$ are the models of D which are the most similar to C.

Proposition 1.   *(i) $\circ^S$ satisfies postulates (R1), (R4), (R5), and (R6).*
(ii) The postulate $C \wedge D \vDash C \circ^S D$, weaker than (R2), is satisfied by $\circ^S$.
(iii) $\circ^S$ satisfies (R2) iff for all $A \in \mathcal{E}$ and $x \in \mathcal{U}$:

$$S(A, x) = 1 \;\; implies \;\; x \in A \tag{8}$$

(iv) $\circ^S$ satisfies (R3) iff for all $A, B \in \mathcal{E}$ with $B \neq \emptyset$:

$$if \, S(A, B) = \Sigma \;\; then \; there \; is \;\; x \in B \; such \; that \; S(A, x) = \Sigma \tag{9}$$

The proof of this proposition is given in appendix B.

4.2   Conservative Adaptation

Conservative adaptation consists in completing Target by a minimal change on Source.

In [3], conservative adaptation is defined for CBR systems where each case is assumed to be decomposable in a fixed manner in a problem part and a solution part, both expressed in propositional logic. Below, conservative adaptation is formalised in the more general framework of this paper. Given a target case Target, a source case Source, and domain knowledge DK, conservative adaptation returns Target-completed such that:

$$(\text{DK} \wedge \text{Source}) \circ (\text{DK} \wedge \text{Target}) \equiv_{\text{DK}} \text{Target-completed} \tag{10}$$

Therefore, conservative adaptation depends on the chosen revision operator $\circ$. Consider Katsuno and Mendelzon postulates meaning from the conservative adaptation point of view:

(R1) means that, modulo DK, Target-completed specialises Target, and thus, conservative adaptation realises a completion.

(R2) means that if Source is not incompatible with Target modulo DK, then it completes Target correctly and Target-completed $\equiv_{DK}$ Source $\wedge$ Target.

(R3) is a success guarantee, if Source is consistent modulo DK, then conservative adaptation returns Target-completed which is consistent with DK too.[2]

(R4) means that conservative adaptation satisfies the irrelevance of syntax principle.

(R5) and (R6) mean that the adaptation from Source should be minimal, it consists in a minimal change on Source to be consistent with Target.

Proposition 1 states that postulates (R2) and (R3) are only satisfied if some conditions on d are satisfied. The non satisfaction of (R2) is not really a problem, interpretations with a similarity of 1 to the original belief can arguably be included in the extension of the revision. The non satisfaction of postulate (R3) is more problematic, no solution can be found, not because Source is too different to Target —(R3) can even be contradicted with $S(\text{Source}, \text{Target}) = 1$— but because the similarity condition is too restrictive, the inferior boundary in the definition of S on subsets (1) may not be reached. This concern leads to the study of α-conservative adaptation in section 5.

4.3   Conservative Adaptation in the Cooking Example

In the cooking example formalisation (section 3.6) the source and target cases and the domain knowledge have been formalised. However, conservative adaptation also depends on a revision operator which is chosen here to be of the (6) kind where the similarity measure S is defined from a mapping d as in (2). d is taken under the form:

$$d(x, y) = \sum_{i=1}^{7} w_i d_i(x, y)$$

where $w_i > 0$ are weights and $d_i : \mathcal{U} \times \mathcal{U} \mapsto \mathbb{R}_+$ are defined as follows, for $x = (x_1, \ldots, x_7)$ and $y = (y_1, \ldots, y_7)$:

$$d_1(x, y) = |y_1 - x_1|, \quad \text{for } i \in \{2, \ldots, 7\}, \ d_i(x, y) = \left| \frac{y_i}{y_1} - \frac{x_i}{x_1} \right|$$

The choice of d_2 to d_7 expresses proportionality knowledge: the quantity of each product is to be considered relatively to the number of servings —2 apples for 4 servings and 3 apples for 6 servings correspond to the same amount of apples per serving.

The conservative adaptation built upon S gives a concept Target-completed from the source case Source and a target case Target satisfying:

$$(DK \wedge \text{Source}) \circ^S (DK \wedge \text{Target}) \equiv_{DK} \text{Target-completed}$$

---

[2] Note that the condition "Source is consistent with DK" should always be true: when adding a case Source to the case base, the consistency test $DK \wedge \text{Source} \not\models \bot$ should be done. Indeed, since we adhere to the irrelevance of syntax principle, a source case that is inconsistent with domain knowledge is useless.

According to (7), its extension is equal to:

Ext(Target-completed)

$$= \{x \in \text{Ext}(\text{DK} \wedge \text{Target}) \mid S(\text{DK} \wedge \text{Source}, x) \text{ is maximal}\}$$

$$= \{x \in \text{Ext}(\text{DK} \wedge \text{Target}) \mid d(\text{DK} \wedge \text{Source}, x) \text{ is minimal}\}$$

Therefore, at this point, conservative adaptation is reduced to an optimisation problem. The way this specific optimisation problem is solved is presented in appendix A. However, the choice of w_i values could not be completely justified, in particular two sets of weights are proposed for which conservative adaptation results are respectively Target-completed and Target-completed':

Target-completed$\equiv_{\text{DK}}$(servings $= 6$)$\wedge$(pastry-mass $= 180$) $\wedge$ (sugar $= 50$)

$\wedge$ (apples-nb $= 0$) $\wedge$ (pears-nb $= 4$)

Target-completed' $\equiv_{\text{DK}}$(servings $= 6$)$\wedge$(pastry-mass $= 180$) $\wedge$ (sugar $= 63$)

$\wedge$ (apples-nb $= 0$) $\wedge$ (pears-nb $= 3$)

In the following, the values set corresponding to Target-completed is chosen. However, the distance difference with DK $\wedge$ Source is small:

$$d(\text{DK} \wedge \text{Source}, \text{Target-completed}) = 20 + \frac{1}{6}(10 + 40 + 10 \times 3 + 10 \times 4) = 40$$

$$d(\text{DK} \wedge \text{Source}, \text{Target-completed'}) = 20 + \frac{1}{6}(3 + 60 + 10 \times 3 + 10 \times 3) = 40.5$$

It may be interesting to include both in the result. Indeed, the adaptation process presented in section 2.2 is exactly Target-completed $\vee$ Target-completed'. This can be done thanks to α-conservative adaptation.

5 α-Conservative Adaptation: A *Less* Conservative Adaptation

Keeping only the models of Target closest to those of Source can be too restrictive, in particular when (R3) is not satisfied, the conservative adaptation result is not satisfiable. Some flexibility in what is meant by "closest to Source" is needed. For instance as the similarity difference between four and five pears is small, both possibilities could be proposed to Léon letting him choose whether he would rather have more or less fruits on his pie. To do so, a flexibility is introduced in the revision operator conservative adaptation stands on, a stretchable margin is added in the extension delimitation. This has also the merit to reduce the sensitivity of the adaptation on some parameters of the similarity measure (such as the weights w_i).

5.1 α-Revision

Definition 3. *Given a similarity measure S, $\alpha \in [0, 1]$, and $C, D \in \mathcal{L}_C$, the α-revision of C by D is $C \circ_{\alpha}^{S} D$ defined as follows where $\Sigma = S(C, D)$:*

$$C \circ_{\alpha}^{S} D = G^{\Sigma \times \alpha}(C) \wedge D$$

which entails that

$$Ext(C \circ_\alpha^S D) = \{x \in Ext(D) \mid S(C,x) \geq \Sigma \times \alpha\}$$

Proposition 2. $\circ_1^S = \circ^S$, *and for all* $1 \geq \alpha \geq \beta \geq 0$:

$$C \circ^S D \equiv C \circ_1^S D \vDash C \circ_\alpha^S D \vDash C \circ_\beta^S D \vDash C \circ_0^S D \equiv D$$

Moreover, for $\alpha < 1$, $\circ_\alpha^S$ *satisfies postulates* $(R1), (R3), (R4),$ *and* $(R5)$.

A proof of this proposition is given in appendix B.

However, if $\circ^S$ does not satisfy (R2), then for any $\alpha \in [0,1], \circ_\alpha^S$ neither does. The fact that, for $\alpha < 1$, $\circ_\alpha^S$ may not satisfy postulate (R6) is not surprising as the minimality criteria is loosened in α-revision.

5.2 α-Conservative Adaptation

The α-conservative adaptation is defined from α-revision as conservative adaptation has been from revision. Given a target case `Target`, a source case `Source`, and domain knowledge `DK`, the α-conservative adaptation returns `Target-completed`$_\alpha$ such that:

$$(\mathtt{DK} \wedge \mathtt{Source}) \circ_\alpha^S (\mathtt{DK} \wedge \mathtt{Target}) \equiv_{\mathrm{DK}} \mathtt{Target\text{-}completed}_\alpha \qquad (11)$$

From proposition 2, it comes that, for all $1 \geq \alpha \geq \beta \geq 0$:

$$\mathtt{Target\text{-}completed} \equiv \mathtt{Target\text{-}completed}_1 \vDash \mathtt{Target\text{-}completed}_\alpha$$
$$\vDash \mathtt{Target\text{-}completed}_\beta \vDash \mathtt{Target\text{-}completed}_0 \equiv \mathtt{Target}.$$

5.3 α-Conservative Adaptation in the Cooking Example

In example 4.3, given `DK` and `apples-nb` $= 0$, three parameters fully determine a model of `Target`: `pears-nb`, `sugar`, `pastry-mass`. In `Target-completed`, these parameters are fixed to precise values (`pastry-mass` $= 180$, `sugar` $= 50$, and `pears-nb` $= 4$). For $\alpha < 1$, `Target-completed`$_\alpha$ is less restrictive than `Target-completed`, and leaves some freedom in the parameter values. The representation of `Target-completed`$_\alpha$ needs 3D. Figure 1 represents cuts of its extension by the plane corresponding to the pair (`sugar`, `pastry-mass`), for `pears-nb` $= 4$ and `pears-nb` $= 3$. A point (x,y) of the graph `pears-nb` $= k$ is in the zone corresponding to α iff (`servings` $= 6$) $\wedge$ (`pastry-mass` $= y$) $\wedge$ (`sugar` $= x$) $\wedge$ (`apples-nb` $= 0$) $\wedge$ (`pears-nb` $= k$) is a model of `Target-completed`$_\alpha$.

For instance, with $\alpha = e^{-0.5}$, the possible values for `pears-nb`, `sugar`, and `pastry-mass` are: `pears-nb` $= 3$, `sugar` $= 63$, and `pastry-mass` $= 180$; or `pears-nb` $= 4$ and any values for `sugar` and `pastry-mass` in the corresponding zone of the left graph. In particular `Target-completed'` $\vDash$ `Target-completed`$_\alpha$.

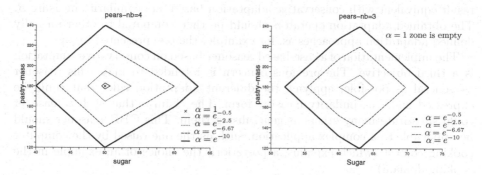

Fig. 1. Possible values for `sugar` and `pastry-mass` with `pears-nb` = 4 (left) and `pears-nb` = 3 (right). The graphs were made with Scilab [6].

6   Conclusion

The adaptation phase in CBR still lacks some formal definition. Conservative adaptation and its extensions can be considered as attempts of defining, at a semantic level, some approaches of adaptation based on revision operators. These latters may satisfy or not some of the AGM postulates, which has consequences on the properties of the adaptation function. A general question can be raised: *What are the adaptation approaches that can be covered by (more or less) conservative adaptation?* In [3], an answer is given in propositional logic. In the current paper, conservative adaptation is considered in the general framework of metric spaces.

Given a revision operator defined from a similarity measure S, conservative adaptation reduces the problem of adaptation to a problem of optimisation — determine the $x \in \mathcal{U}$ which maximise the function $y \mapsto S(\text{DK} \land \text{Source}, y)$ with the constraint $x \in \text{Ext}(\text{DK} \land \text{Target})$. The associated α-conservative adaptation is a relaxation of this optimisation problem —determine the $x \in \mathcal{U}$ such that $S(\text{DK} \land \text{Source}, x) \geq \alpha \times \sup_{y \in \text{ExtTarget}} S(\text{DK} \land \text{Source}, y)$— and is reduced to constraint programming problem. Powerful optimisation and constraint solvers as [7] could be used to solve large adaptation problems.

A prospect is to define fuzzy conservative adaptation that from a `Source` concept and `Target` concept would return a fuzzy concept `Target-completed` (an expression to be interpreted as a fuzzy subset `Ext(Target-completed)` of $\mathcal{U}$). The α-conservative adaptation is a first step towards it: from the parametered answer `Target-completed`$_\alpha$ can be built a fuzzy concept since a fuzzy set can be built from α-cuts [8]. However, in section 5, `Source` and `Target` are assumed to be classical concepts which prevents `Target-completed` to be further completed or retained as a new source case of the case base. The extension of fuzzy conservative adaptation to fuzzy concepts `Source` and `Target` is therefore a necessity for its coherence.

Another investigation direction is the construction of similarity measures so as to express adaptation rules, i.e. such that rule-based adaptation gives a result equivalent with conservative adaptation based on a similarity measure S. The obtained adaptation operators should be then compared to other formally defined adaptation approaches as, for example, the one presented in [9].

The implementation of a case-based reasoner based on conservative adaptation is a third objective. The previous concern is intended to make this reasoner as general as possible, applying the different adaptation rules that could be expressed under a similarity measure form. The claim is that such a reasoner could substitute many others as generalising them. This CBR reasoner should be applicable to a complex application, such as the one raised by the computer cooking contest (which explains, a posteriori, the choice of an example in the cooking domain).

References

1. Riesbeck, C.K., Schank, R.C.: Inside Case-Based Reasoning. Lawrence Erlbaum Associates, Inc., Hillsdale (1989)
2. Kolodner, J.: Case-Based Reasoning. Morgan Kaufmann, Inc., San Francisco (1993)
3. Lieber, J.: Application of the Revision Theory to Adaptation in Case-Based Reasoning: The Conservative Adaptation. In: Weber, R.O., Richter, M.M. (eds.) ICCBR 2007. LNCS (LNAI), vol. 4626. Springer, Heidelberg (2007)
4. Alchourrón, C.E., Gärdenfors, P., Makinson, D.: On the logic of theory change: partial meet functions for contraction and revision. Journal of Symbolic Logic 50, 510–530 (1985)
5. Katsuno, H., Mendelzon, A.: Propositional knowledge base revision and minimal change. Artificial Intelligence 52(3), 263–294 (1991)
6. Scilab software. Last consult (March 2008), http://www.scilab.org/
7. Puget, J.F.: A C++ implementation of CLP. In: Proceedings of the Second Singapore International Conference on Intelligent Systems, Singapore (1994)
8. Zadeh, L.A.: Fuzzy Sets. Information and Control 8, 338–353 (1965)
9. Hüllermeier, E.: Credible case-based inference using similarity profiles. IEEE Transactions on Knowledge and Data Engineering 19(6), 847–858 (2007)

A   Fruit Pie Adaptation Example Resolution

The minima of $x \mapsto d(\text{DK} \wedge \text{Source}, x)$ have to be found upon $\text{Ext}(\text{DK} \wedge \text{Target})$. However, some d_i are constant here, which simplifies the minima search, for all $x \in \text{Ext}(\text{DK} \wedge \text{Target})$, with the "$(x)$" dropped from the attributes:

$$d_1(\text{DK} \wedge \text{Source}, x) = |\text{servings} - 4| = 2$$

$$d_4(\text{DK} \wedge \text{Source}, x) = \left| \frac{\text{pastry-mass}}{6} - \frac{120}{4} \right| = 0$$

$$d_6(\text{DK} \wedge \text{Source}, x) = \left| \frac{\text{apples-nb}}{6} - \frac{2}{4} \right| = \frac{1}{2}$$

Indeed, `servings` $= 6$, `apples-nb` $= 0$, and `pastry-mass` has no constraint and can be taken equal to 180. What remains to be minimised is:

$$\frac{1}{6}\left(w_2 \left| \texttt{sugar} + 13 \times \texttt{pears-nb} - \frac{6}{4} \times 68 \right| + w_3 |\texttt{sugar} - 60| \right.$$

$$\left. + w_5 |100 \times \texttt{pears-nb} - 360| + w_7 \times \texttt{pears-nb} \right)$$

which is a sum of affine per parts functions with two parameters. Minima can be searched one parameter at a time. First, let us focus on `sugar`, `pears-nb` being taken as constant. The value of `sugar` should be a minimum of the function $x \mapsto w_2|x - (102 - 13 \times \texttt{pears-nb})| + w_3|x - 60|$, i.e.:

- If $w_2 > w_3$ then `sugar` $= 102 - 13 \times \texttt{pears-nb}$ and the sweet mass per person is preserved.
- If $w_2 < w_3$ then `sugar` $= 60$ the sugar mass per person is preserved.
- If $w_2 = w_3$, any value between 60 and $102 - 13 \times \texttt{pears-nb}$ can be given to `sugar`.

It is assumed that the preservation of `sweet` is to be preferred to the preservation of `sugar` —sugar is used in cooking to adjust the sweet taste. Therefore $w_2 > w_3$. What remains to be minimised is then:

$$w_3 |(42 - 13 \times \texttt{pears-nb})| + w_5 |100 \times \texttt{pears-nb} - 360| + w_7 \times \texttt{pears-nb}$$

As previously, some relative importance relation between term considerations reduce the set of alternatives to explore. `fruit-mass` preservation is more important than `pears-nb`'s, thus $100 \times w_5 > w_7$, 100 being the average pear mass: this coefficient is used in the inequality for normalisation. $x \mapsto w_5|100x - 360| + w_7 x$ decreases for $x \leq \frac{360}{100} = 3.6$, and increases for $x \geq 3.6$. $x \mapsto w_3|42 - 13x|$ also decreases for $x < \frac{42}{13} \approx 3.23$ and then increases. As both decrease before 3 and increase after 4, the minima is then reached for `pears-nb` $= 3$ or 4:

- For `pears-nb` $= 4$, the term value is $w_3 \times 10 + w_5 \times 40 + w_7 \times 4$.
- For `pears-nb` $= 3$, the term value is $w_3 \times 3 + w_5 \times 60 + w_7 \times 3$.

Which one is minimal depends on the sign of $20 \times w_5 - 7 \times w_3 - w_7$. The previous considerations cannot help to determine it, consider the following two sets of w_i:

- $w_1 = 10$, $w_2 = 5$, $w_3 = 1$, $w_4 = 1$, $w_5 = 1$, $w_6 = w_7 = 10$, the constraints $w_2 > w_3$ and $100 \times w_5 > w_7$ are satisfied and $20 \times w_5 - 7 \times w_3 - w_7 > 0$. The minima of $x \mapsto d(\text{DK} \wedge \text{Source}, x)$ with $x \in \text{Ext}(\text{Target})$ is then reduced to the single tuple $x = (6, 102, 50, 180, 400, 0, 4)$.
- $w_1 = 10$, $w_2 = 5$, $w_3 = 2$, $w_4 = 1$, $w_5 = 1$, $w_6 = w_7 = 10$, as before $w_2 > w_3$ and $100 \times w_5 > w_7$ but now $20 \times w_5 - 7 \times w_3 - w_7 < 0$. And $x \mapsto d(\text{DK} \wedge \text{Source}, x)$ with $x \in \text{Ext}(\text{Target})$ minima is reduced to a single tuple too: $y = (6, 102, 63, 180, 300, 0, 3)$.

Unlike for the constraint $w_2 > w_3$ any choice of values for the w_i will not guarantee that `sugar` preservation will be given priority over `pears-nb` preservation as in the first case or the opposite as in the second case, it depends on the case attributes values. In this paper, the first set of weights is chosen and conservative adaptation will return the concept `Target-completed`:

$$\texttt{Target-completed} \equiv_{\text{DK}} (\texttt{servings} = 6) \land (\texttt{pastry-mass} = 180) \land (\texttt{sugar} = 50)$$
$$\land\,(\texttt{apples-nb} = 0) \land (\texttt{pears-nb} = 4).$$

B Proofs

Proposition 1

(i) (R1) is satisfied by construction of $\circ^S$: $C \circ^S D = G^\Sigma(C) \land D \vDash D$.
   (R4): If $C \equiv C'$ and $D \equiv D'$, then $G^\Sigma(C) \equiv G^\Sigma(C')$ so
   $C \circ^S D = G^\Sigma(C) \land D \equiv G^\Sigma(C') \land D' = C' \circ^S D'$.
   For (R5) and (R6), two cases are to be considered:
   First case: $(C \circ^S D) \land F \vDash \bot$, (R5) and (R6) are automatically satisfied.
   Second case: $(C \circ^S D) \land F \nvDash \bot$, then $\text{Ext}((C \circ^S D) \land F) \neq \emptyset$. Let $x \in \text{Ext}((C \circ^S D) \land F)$. According to $\circ^S$ definition, since $x \in \text{Ext}(C \circ^S D)$:

$$S(C,x) = S(C,D) = \sup_{u \in \text{Ext}(D)} S(C,u) \geq \sup_{u \in \text{Ext}(D) \cap \text{Ext}(F)} S(C,u)$$
$$\geq S(C, D \land F)$$

However, according to (R1), $\text{Ext}(C \circ^S D) \subseteq \text{Ext}(D)$, so $x \in \text{Ext}(D \land F)$ and $S(C, D \land F) = \sup_{u \in \text{Ext}(D \land F)} S(C,u) \geq S(C,x)$, therefore $S(C,D) = S(C, D \land F)$. And finally:

$$(C \circ^S D) \land F = G^{S(C,D)}(C) \land D \land F = G^{S(C,D \land F)}(C) \land D \land F$$
$$= C \circ^S (D \land F) \quad \text{thus, (R5) and (R6) are satisfied.}$$

(ii) Satisfaction of $C \land D \vDash C \circ^S D$: the case $C \land D \vDash \bot$ is trivial. Consider now the case $C \land D \nvDash \bot$, let x be in $\text{Ext}(C \land D)$, $x \in \text{Ext}(C)$ thus $S(C,x) = 1$ and so $x \in \text{Ext}(G^1(C) \land D) = \text{Ext}(C \circ^S D)$. This shows that $\text{Ext}(C \land D) \subseteq \text{Ext}(C \circ^S D)$ and thus $C \land D \vDash C \circ^S D$.

(iii) **(8) implies (R2):** Assume $(S(A,x) \Rightarrow x \in A)$, then for $C \in \mathcal{L}_C$, $G^1(C) \equiv C$, indeed $\text{Ext}(G^1(C)) = \{x \in \mathcal{U} \mid S(\text{Ext}(C), x) = 1\} = C$. (R2) follows from this property: if $C \land D$ is satisfiable, then $\text{Ext}(C \land D) \neq \emptyset$ and $S(C,D) = 1$ ($\Sigma = 1$), thus

$$C \circ^S D = G^1(C) \land D \equiv C \land D$$

(R2) implies (8): Assume (R2) is satisfied, let A be in $\mathcal{E}$, x in $\mathcal{U}$, and C in $\mathcal{L}_C$ such that $\text{Ext}(C) = A$. Assume $S(A,x) = 1 > 0$, from the convention established in definition 1 it follows that $A \neq \emptyset$, so $A = \text{Ext}(C) = \text{Ext}(C) \cap \mathcal{U} = \text{Ext}(C) \cap \text{Ext}(\top) = \text{Ext}(C \land \top) \neq \emptyset$. (R2) implies that $C \circ^S \top \equiv C \land \top \equiv C$, thus $x \in \text{Ext}(C \circ^S \top) = \text{Ext}(C) = A$. and $x \in A$.

(iv) **(9) implies (R3):** Assume that (9) is satisfied, if D is satisfiable and $\Sigma = S(C, D)$, then (9) implies that there is an x in $\text{Ext}(D)$ such that $S(C, x) = \Sigma$. Thus $\text{Ext}(C \circ^S D) \neq \emptyset$ and $C \circ^S D$ is satisfiable.

  (R3) implies (9): Assume that (R3) is satisfied, let A and B be in $\mathcal{E}$ with $B \neq \emptyset$, $\Sigma = S(A, B)$, and C and D in $\mathcal{L}_C$ such that $\text{Ext}(C) = A$ and $\text{Ext}(D) = B$. D is satisfiable so, according to (R3), $C \circ^S D$ is satisfiable too. However $\text{Ext}(C \circ^S D) = \{x \in B \mid S(A, x) = \Delta\}$, it follows that there is an x in B such that $S(A, x) = \Sigma$.

Proposition 2

– $\circ_1^S = \circ^S$, indeed, for C and D in $\mathcal{L}_C$ with $\Sigma = S(C, D)$:

$$C \circ_1^S D = G^{\Sigma \times 1}(C) \wedge D = G^{\Sigma} \wedge D = C \circ^S D$$

– Similarly, for C and D in $\mathcal{L}_C$ $C \circ_0^S D \equiv D$, indeed $\text{Ext}(G^0(C)) = \{x \in \mathcal{U} \mid S(C, x) \geq 0\} = \mathcal{U}$, thus $G^0(C) \equiv \top$. Let $\Sigma = S(C, D)$,

$$C \circ_0^S D = G^{\Sigma \times 0} \wedge D = G^0(C) \wedge D \equiv \top \wedge D \equiv D$$

– For α and β such that $1 \geq \alpha \geq \beta \geq 0$, and C, D in $\mathcal{L}_C$ with $\Sigma = S(C, D)$:

$$\text{Ext}(G^{\Sigma \times \alpha}(C)) = \{x \in \mathcal{U} \mid S(C, x) \geq \Sigma \times \alpha\}$$
$$\subseteq \{x \in \mathcal{U} \mid S(C, x) \geq \Sigma \times \beta\} = \text{Ext}(G^{\Sigma \times \beta}(C))$$

Thus $G^{\Sigma \times \alpha}(C) \models G^{\Sigma \times \beta}(C)$ and

$$C \circ_\alpha^S D = G^{\Sigma \times \alpha}(C) \wedge D \models G^{\Sigma \times \beta}(C) \wedge D = C \circ_\beta^S D.$$

Opportunistic Acquisition of Adaptation Knowledge and Cases — The IAKA Approach

Amélie Cordier[1], Béatrice Fuchs[1], Léonardo Lana de Carvalho[3], Jean Lieber[2], and Alain Mille[1]

[1] LIRIS CNRS, UMR 5202, Université Lyon 1, INSA Lyon, Université Lyon 2, ECL
{Amelie.Cordier,Beatrice.Fuchs,Alain.Mille}@liris.cnrs.fr
[2] LORIA UMR 7503 CNRS, INRIA, Universités de Nancy
Jean.Lieber@loria.fr
[3] LEACM-Cris, Université Lyon 2, Institut de Sciences de l'Homme (ISH) LIESP,
Université Lyon 1, INSA Lyon
Leonardo.LanaDeCarvalho@univ-lyon2.fr

Abstract. A case-based reasoning system relies on different knowledge containers, including cases and adaptation knowledge. The knowledge acquisition that aims at enriching these containers for the purpose of improving the accuracy of the CBR inference may take place during design, maintenance, and also on-line, during the use of the system. This paper describes IAKA, an approach to on-line acquisition of cases and adaptation knowledge based on interactions with an oracle (a kind of "ideal expert"). IAKA exploits failures of the CBR inference: when such a failure occurs, the system interacts with the oracle to repair the knowledge base. IAKA-NF is a prototype for testing IAKA in the domain of numerical functions with an automatic oracle. Two experiments show how IAKA opportunistic knowledge acquisition improves the accuracy of the CBR system inferences. The paper also discusses the possible links between IAKA and other knowledge acquisition approaches.

1 Introduction

Case-based reasoning exploits knowledge, such as domain knowledge and adaptation knowledge, to perform inferences on cases. The more complete and accurate the knowledge is, the better the inferences are. Hence, building efficient knowledge bases is of particular importance. The building of the knowledge base for a CBR system is often done beforehand, during the design phase. However, in order to make systems capable of evolving, the knowledge base has to evolve as well, thus additional knowledge acquisition has to be possible during the system use. In systems offering such a possibility, the acquired knowledge is reused in further reasoning sessions to improve the solutions produced.

Several ways of performing knowledge acquisition have been explored in CBR related research. Knowledge engineers and domain experts can collaborate to model knowledge of the domain. This manual approach is efficient because it

K.-D. Althoff et al. (Eds.): ECCBR 2008, LNAI 5239, pp. 150–164, 2008.

allows the acquisition of relevant knowledge coming from the expert but it is rather constrained by the availability of the expert and of the knowledge engineer. Other approaches rely on the knowledge already available in the system (often in the cases) to infer new knowledge, like adaptation rules. These approaches are efficient in the sense that they automate the acquisition process but they produce a large amount of knowledge that has to be validated by an expert. Moreover, this validation phase is performed off-line, out of a specific context, thus it may be felt by an expert as an irksome task. Hybrid approaches, such as IAKA, combine the reasoning capabilities of the system with interactions with the expert to acquire missing knowledge in context.

Usually, knowledge acquisition approaches assume that the knowledge of the system is organized in separate knowledge containers and that the reasoning process is split into several distinct steps. These assumptions are helpful better to understand CBR, but they do not reflect the reality. Actually, knowledge containers are closely interconnected (not to say identical) and the steps of the CBR process contribute to the achievement of the same objective: problem solving. The adaptation-guided retrieval principle [11] is a good illustration of this point: adaptation knowledge is used to support retrieval, and retrieval and adaptation steps contribute to the problem solving. This paper advocates a unified view of CBR steps and knowledge containers. In IAKA, the CBR process is considered as a whole and the knowledge acquisition process focuses on *the knowledge of the system*: cases and adaptation knowledge are acquired at the same time.

This paper presents IAKA, an interactive and opportunistic approach for knowledge acquisition in CBR. IAKA is interactive in so far as it exploits interactions between the expert and the system during CBR sessions. Its opportunistic aspect is due to the fact that reasoning failures trigger the acquisition process: the system seizes this opportunity to identify missing knowledge and to acquire it. One of the main advantages of this approach is that it focuses on knowledge known to be needed, which constitutes a strong guidance for the knowledge acquisition process and alleviates the effort required by the expert. In IAKA, cases are adapted using adaptation knowledge. When a failure occurs, the applicability of the adaptation knowledge for this case has to be questioned. The expert plays two important roles: identifying the failure and correcting the faulty adaptation knowledge. As the adaptation knowledge is corrected in the context of the case being solved, it stays linked with the case. The case and its related adaptation knowledge are then added to the knowledge base.

The remainder of this paper is organized as follows. Section 2 compares several approaches of knowledge acquisition in CBR. Then, section 3 describes IAKA, a set of principles for interactive knowledge acquisition in CBR systems which perform approximate reasoning (i.e when the aim is to find an approximate solution for a problem). The modelling of the expert by an *oracle* is discussed. Formalizing the adaptation knowledge acquisition process is described and the classical assumption of CBR—similar problems have similar solutions— is questioned. Section 4 is dedicated to IAKA-NF, a prototypical CBR application implementing the principles of IAKA in the numerical functions domain and describes two experiments. Section 5 discusses the complementarity of the IAKA approach with other knowledge approaches introduced in section 2. Finally, section 6 concludes the paper and outlines some prospects for future work.

2 Knowledge Acquisition in CBR

It has long been argued that CBR was a solution to the knowledge acquisition bottleneck in knowledge-based systems because it is easier to collect cases than other pieces of knowledge. However, CBR only partly overcomes this problem because it also requires substantial effort to acquire the knowledge involved in the reasoning process. As with other knowledge-based systems, the implementation of knowledge-intensive CBR systems has to cope with the knowledge acquisition problem, and this issue has motivated significant research.

Adaptation-guided retrieval [11] aims at retrieving a prior case that is the easiest to adapt, given the available adaptation knowledge. Thus the adaptation step is central and adaptation knowledge plays a major role in CBR. For this reason, several studies focus on adaptation knowledge acquisition to improve the global quality of the system [9,2].

Knowledge acquisition takes place at different stages of the life cycle of a CBR system. Initial knowledge acquisition can be done with experts who manually model the domain knowledge, or with the assistance of automated learning methods. Such approaches are off-line in that they take place outside a CBR reasoning cycle. Among off-line methods, machine-learning techniques have been used for instance in [7]. In these methods, the case base is exploited to learn adaptation rules. Adaptation rules are generated by examining the differences between problems related to the differences between solutions. In the same vein, Craw et al. experiment further with this method by applying learning algorithms, such as C4.5, in the tablet formulation domain [3]. The CABAMAKA system uses a knowledge discovery process to acquire adaptation knowledge [4]. Data mining algorithms are applied to detect regularities which are candidates to become adaptation rules. Adaptation rules are then validated by a domain expert. Off-line methods have been successfully applied, nevertheless these methods do not make it possible to acquire knowledge that is not yet in the cases.

On-line methods take advantage of a reasoning cycle to learn from a problem-solving session. One of the first CBR systems, CHEF, a case-based planner in the cooking domain, experimented learning from failures [6]. CHEF learns by storing successfully adapted plans or repaired plans. When an adapted plan fails, CHEF builds a causal explanation of the failure in order to anticipate a future similar problem. Hammond qualifies his approach as an incremental repair process after a test or an execution: for a given problem, a first error-prone solution is produced and further tested and repaired incrementally using a causal model. CHEF differs in that it takes advantage of a failure to anticipate it in further reasoning cycles. DIAL is a disaster response planning system that retrieves and adapts prior similar past plans [10]. Adaptation is performed with help either of general adaptation rules, or of prior successful adaptation cases, or of the user.

Adaptation is a combination of transformations combined with memory search processes of knowledge required by the transformation. The adaptation effort is stored and reused for an adaptation-guided retrieval approach. FRAKAS [1] is a system for enriching domain knowledge when failures due to the incompleteness of the knowledge base occur. When such a failure occurs, a knowledge acquisition process involving the domain expert is triggered. Interactions with the expert allow the system to add new knowledge to its knowledge base and to collect an explanation of the failure. This knowledge is stored and reused to avoid the failure reoccurring in further reasoning. FRAKAS is an example of the opportunistic knowledge acquisition approach in which new knowledge is acquired from outside the system. Next section presents IAKA, a complementary approach to FRAKAS.

3   IAKA: InterActive Knowledge Acquisition

IAKA is an approach to interactive knowledge acquisition in CBR systems that produce approximate solutions. The main idea of the approach is to exploit reasoning failures and their repairs to acquire cases and adaptation knowledge. Indeed, the occurrence of a failure highlights the fact that knowledge is missing. When correcting a failure, the required knowledge is added to the knowledge base and is reused in the following reasoning sessions to improve the solutions. The acquisition process is made possible thanks to an *oracle* that is capable of correcting solutions and providing the necessary adaptation knowledge.

3.1   Definitions and Hypotheses

In this work, the notions of *problem* and *solution* are assumed to be well defined. If pb is a problem (resp., sol is a solution), then pb (resp., sol) is an expression in a knowledge representation formalism representing a problem (resp., a solution). $\mathcal{L}_{pb}$ denotes the problem space and $\mathcal{L}_{sol}$ denotes the solution space. Moreover, a binary relation on $\mathcal{L}_{pb} \times \mathcal{L}_{sol}$ is assumed to exist with the semantics "has for solution". This relation is generally not completely known by the system, but some of its instances are: they are the pairs $(srce, Sol(srce)) \in \mathcal{L}_{pb} \times \mathcal{L}_{sol}$, called *source cases*. The aim of the CBR process is to find a solution for the target problem denoted tgt. $\widetilde{Sol}(tgt)$ is a *candidate* solution of tgt, i.e. the solution produced by the CBR system.

In order to adapt the solution of a case, IAKA relies on *adaptation knowledge* mainly composed of *adaptation operators*.

Definition 1 (Adaptation operator —$AO_r = (r, \mathcal{A}_r)$)
An adaptation operator AO_r *is a pair* $(r, \mathcal{A}_r)$ *where* r *is a binary relation between problems* $(r \subseteq \mathcal{L}_{pb} \times \mathcal{L}_{pb})$. $\mathcal{A}_r$ *is an adaptation function:*
if $(srce, Sol(srce), tgt) \in \mathcal{L}_{pb} \times \mathcal{L}_{sol} \times \mathcal{L}_{pb}$ *and* $srce\, r\, tgt$
then $\mathcal{A}_r(srce, Sol(srce), tgt)$ *is a candidate solution of* $srce$.

Adaptation operators are organized in adaptation methods. An adaptation method is linked to a source case.

Definition 2 (Adaptation method —AM(srce))
The adaptation method AM(srce) associated with the case (srce, Sol(srce)) is a finite set of adaptation operators $AO_r = (r, A_r)$. An adaptation method may also contain strategic knowledge for managing the adaptation operators.

The notions of adaptation operators and adaptation methods can be likened respectively to adaptation specialists and adaptation strategies defined in [12]. The adaptation method is used to build a similarity path and an associated adaptation path.

Definition 3 (Similarity path —SP)
A similarity path from a problem srce to a problem tgt is a set of q triples (pb_{i-1}, r_i, pb_i) with :

- *pb_i : q + 1 problems;*
- *$pb_0 = srce$ and $pb_q = tgt$;*
- *$pb_{i-1} \; r_i \; pb_i$ (for $i \in \{1, \ldots, q\}$);*
- *r_i is such that (r_i, A_{r_i}) is an available adaptation operator.*

$\mathcal{P}(srce, tgt)$ denotes the set of similarity paths that can be built from srce to tgt.

The adaptation path is built after the similarity path.

Definition 4 (Adaptation path —AP)
The adaptation path AP associated to a similarity path SP is a set of q triples $(\widetilde{Sol}(pb_{i-1}), A_{r_i}, \widetilde{Sol}(pb_i))$ with :

- *$\widetilde{Sol}(pb_0) = Sol(srce)$ and $\widetilde{Sol}(pb_q) = \widetilde{Sol}(tgt)$;*
- *$\widetilde{Sol}(pb_i) = A_{r_i}(pb_{i-1}, \widetilde{Sol}(pb_{i-1}), pb_i)$.*

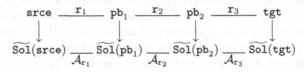

Fig. 1. A similarity path and the associated adaptation path

Figure 1 shows an example of a similarity path and its adaptation path. In order to choose between several similarity paths relating the same srce and tgt, the notion of length of a similarity path is introduced. This notion relies on the notion of estimated adaptation error.

Definition 5 (Adaptation error —e_r and its estimation —$\widetilde{e}_r$)
Each adaptation operator AO_r introduces a numerical error e_r, function of the problems srce and tgt related by r: $e_r(srce, tgt) \in \mathbb{R}_+$. This error is known by the oracle but the system only knows an estimated value $\widetilde{e}_r(srce, tgt)$ of it. Moreover, $\widetilde{e}_r$ is assumed to have the following property: $\widetilde{e}_r(srce, tgt) = 0$ if srce = tgt.

Definition 6 (Length of a similarity path —$\ell(\text{SP})$)

$$\ell(SP) = \sum_{i=1}^{q} \widetilde{e_r}(pb_{i-1}, pb_i)$$

Finally, the distance from a problem to another one is defined as the length of the shortest similarity path.[1]

Definition 7 (Distance between problems —$\text{dist}(\text{srce}, \text{tgt})$)
$dist(srce, tgt) = \min\{\ell(SP) \mid SP \in \mathcal{P}(srce, tgt)\}$

Given these definitions, the retrieval process consists in building a similarity path, and consequently an adaptation path, from srce to tgt that minimizes the length $\ell(\text{SP})$ and the adaptation process consists in following the adaptation path.

Illustration of the Definitions. This example is given in a fictive domain where problems consist of ordered pairs of shapes and solutions consist of single shapes. Shapes have two properties: number of edges and color. It must be remarked that there is no available rule allowing the computation of the solution knowing the problem. Figure 2 illustrates the concept of adaptation operator. The candidate solution for the target problem (on the right) is obtained by adaptation of the source case (on the left). The relation r between srce and tgt means: *to go from srce to tgt, a edge has to be added to the first shape of the pair.* Except this difference, all the relevant attributes of the shapes are identical. To r is associated the adaptation function $\mathcal{A}_r$ which meaning is: *If there is one more edge on the first shape of the target problem, then the source solution must be adapted by adding one edge to it.* Hence, $\widetilde{\text{Sol}}(\text{tgt})$ is obtained by application of $\mathcal{A}_r$ on $\text{Sol}(\text{srce})$.

3.2 Mechanisms of the IAKA Approach

The key idea of IAKA is to exploit failures to acquire cases and adaptation knowledge. In systems that produce approximate solutions, a failure occurs when the distance between the solution of the system and the "ideal solution" is too large. IAKA relies on the availability of an *oracle* which is able to say if a solution is satisfactory or not, to correct a non-satisfactory solution and to give adaptation operators for a case. Hence, the oracle is able to compute a distance between solutions and to compare it to a *tolerance threshold* denoted by ε ($\varepsilon > 0$): if the distance is larger than ε, the solution is not satisfactory.

In CBR, the occurrence of a failure means that a piece of knowledge that was used during adaptation has to be corrected or made precise. In the framework of IAKA, adaptation methods, adaptation operators and adaptation errors may be questioned.

---

[1] Technically, an inf should be used instead of a min: it is possible to find a series of similarity paths $(\text{SP}_n)_n$ such that $\ell(\text{SP}_n) > 0$ and $\lim_{n \to \infty} \ell(\text{SP}_n) = 0$. To avoid this theoretical problem, it is assumed that the number q of steps in a similarity path is bounded by a constant (e.g., $q \leq 10^{100}$).

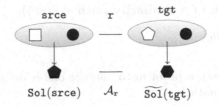

Fig. 2. An example of adaptation operator

A main advantage of the IAKA approach is that the different pieces of knowledge (in particular, the adaptation operators) are separated and tested independently thus enabling the faulty knowledge to be identified more easily. Indeed, when a solution is not satisfactory, the adaptation operators involved are tested by the oracle one after the other. If the oracle identifies a faulty adaptation operator, it corrects it. The new piece of knowledge is added to the knowledge base of the system and a new CBR cycle is performed in order to find a better solution for the current problem. Adaptation operators are corrected and a new CBR cycle is performed until a satisfactory solution is found.

Justification of the IAKA Approach. The CBR inference is based on the following principle (see, e.g., [5]):

Similar problems have similar solutions.   (CBR principle)

The similarity between problems is the knowledge of the retrieval step, often in the form of a similarity measure or a distance between problems. The similarity between solutions is linked with the adaptation: the higher the error caused by adaptation is, the less the solutions are similar.

This principle can be replaced by its contraposition:

Dissimilar solutions solve dissimilar problems.

Therefore, a failure of the CBR inference indicates:

(a) Either that srce and tgt are not (enough) similar;
(b) Or a failure in the CBR principle.

The failure (a) can also be split into two sub-situations:

(a1) There is no source case similar to the target problem;
(a2) There is at least a source case $(srce', Sol(srce')) \neq (srce, Sol(srce))$ that is similar to tgt but it has not been retrieved.

Each of the failures of type (a1), (a2), and (b) leads to a knowledge acquisition from the oracle.

When a failure of type (a1) occurs, the oracle may provide a new source case (with its associated adaptation method), that is similar to the target problem (for instance a case $(tgt, Sol(tgt))$ and an adaptation method $AM(tgt)$).

When a failure of type (a2) occurs, this questions the similarity between problems that constitute the retrieval knowledge: (srce, Sol(srce)) is closer to tgt than (srce', Sol(srce')) and it should be the contrary. With a similarity based on the estimated adaptation errors, the interactions with the oracle should lead to a modification of these estimated errors.

When a failure of type (b) occurs, the similar problems srce and tgt have no similar solution. In other words, in a neighborhood of srce, the solution varies in an irregular manner. This situation can be interpreted with the notion of (dis)continuity of numerical functions $f : \mathbb{R}^n \to \mathbb{R}$. Indeed, if $\mathcal{L}_{pb} = \mathbb{R}^n$, $\mathcal{L}_{sol} = \mathbb{R}$, and Sol(pb) solves pb if $f(pb) = $ Sol(pb), then the continuity of f is defined intuitively with the CBR principle: if x_1 is close to x_2 then $f(x_1)$ is close to $f(x_2)$. A type (b) failure means that there is a discontinuity close to srce. The interactions with the oracle may be useful to better locate the discontinuity points. It may occur that these discontinuity points involve a partition of the problem space in several points. For example, if $\mathcal{L}_{pb} = \mathbb{R}$ and 4 is a discontinuity point highlighted by the oracle, then $\mathcal{L}_{pb}$ is partitioned in $\{]-\infty, 4[, \{4\},]4, +\infty[\}$. This implies that two problems of two different parts of this partition should never be considered as similar. With the previous example, 3.99 is dissimilar to 4.01. Therefore, the knowledge of this discontinuity point can be used as pieces of retrieval knowledge.

This justification of the IAKA approach based on the CBR principle and the proximity of this principle to the notion of continuity suggest that it should be tested in domains where continuity is well-defined. The numerical functions constitute such domains. IAKA-NF, described in the following section, is a prototype implementing IAKA with numerical functions.

4 IAKA-NF: A Prototype Implementing the IAKA Approach

4.1 The IAKA-NF System

IAKA-NF is a prototypical CBR engine implementing the principles of IAKA in the application domain of the numerical functions ($f : \mathbb{R}^n \to \mathbb{R}$). The aim of this prototype is to solve problems by approximation, i.e., given n variables $(x_1, ..., x_n)$, the goal is to find an approximate value of $f(x_1, ..., x_n)$ by CBR.

In IAKA-NF, a problem is a n-tuple of real numbers and a solution is an approximation of the value of the function f for these values. f_{CB} denotes the approximation of the function f obtained from the CBR system using the case base CB (and the adaptation methods). To each case is associated an adaptation method containing n adaptation operators. In the numerical functions domain, an intuitive way to define adaptation operators is to use the notion of partial derivatives. Indeed, the influence of the variation of a problem variable on the solution can be expressed by the partial derivative of this variable.

The retrieval is performed according to the distance defined in definition 7. The adaptation consists in applying the different adaptation operators of the retrieved adaptation method. The solution is obtained by adding to the solution of srce the variations involved by the different variables of the problem (calculated using the partial derivatives).

The knowledge acquisition process is performed according to the principle introduced before: a candidate solution produced by the system is always tested by the oracle. If the solution is not satisfactory, the involved adaptation operators are tested and corrected if needed, until a satisfactory solution is found. Then, the newly solved case (tgt, Sol(tgt)) is added to the case base together with its adaptation method, given by the oracle.

The oracle is simulated by the function f and by a tolerance threshold $\varepsilon > 0$ (the maximal tolerated error). The oracle is capable of computing the distance between two solutions, to give the correct solution for a case and to give the adaptation methods.

The following example illustrates the mechanism of IAKA-NF with a function $f_a : \mathbb{R} \to \mathbb{R}$. The first part of the example describes the notations used and the knowledge available in the system:

Example: Oracle knowledge, source case and target problem are defined as follows:

$$f_a : \mathbb{R} \to \mathbb{R} \qquad f_a(x) = \begin{cases} 1 + \arctan(3x) & \text{if } x \geq 0 \\ -1 + \arctan(3x) & \text{if } x < 0 \end{cases}$$

$$\texttt{srce} = x^s \qquad \texttt{tgt} = x^t$$

$$\texttt{Sol}(\texttt{srce}) = y^s \qquad \widetilde{\texttt{Sol}}(tgt) = \tilde{y}^t$$

Moreover, there is only one adaptation operator $\texttt{AO}_r$ in the adaptation method $\texttt{AM}(\texttt{srce})$. It is defined by x^s r x^t holds for any x^s and x^t, and $\tilde{y}^t = \mathcal{A}_r(x^s, y^s, x^t)$ $= y^s + \frac{\partial y^s}{\partial x}(x^t - x^s)$.

4.2   Experiments

Several experiments have been conducted with IAKA-NF. Two of them are presented below.

Influence of the Tolerance Threshold of the Oracle. The aim of this experiment is to analyze the impact of ε (the tolerance threshold of the oracle) on the quality of the results produced by the system. The hypothesis is that the smaller ε is, the better the results are (for a constant number of solved problems).

In order to conduct this experiment, an initial knowledge base is built; it consists 20 cases randomly generated (and solved by the oracle $\mathcal{O}_{f_m}$) and their associated adaptation methods (also given by the oracle $\mathcal{O}_{f_m}$).

$$\mathcal{O}_{f_m} = (f_m, \varepsilon) \qquad f_m : \mathbb{R} \to \mathbb{R}$$
$$f_m(x) = x + 10 \sin(5x) + 7 \cos(4x)$$

Moreover, 70 target problems are randomly generated. The same initial knowledge base and set of problems are used for all the tests in this experiment.

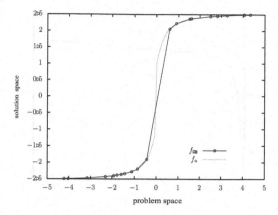

Fig. 3. Representation of the oracle knowledge f_a and of the system knowledge f_{CB} for an initial case base of 20 cases (circles represent cases)

Two systems are run in parallel: the control system and the IAKA system. The goal is to solve the 70 problems of the set of problems. In both systems, problems are solved according to the IAKA approach (test and repair of the knowledge of the system). The difference is that solved cases are not added to the case base in the control system whereas they are in the IAKA system.

The purpose of the experiment is to make ε vary, thus the experimental protocol described above is made 10 times with 10 different values for ε. For each experiment, we compare, for each case, the difference between the error made by the control system and by the IAKA system.

Two statistical tests are performed on the gathered data: the *Z-test* [8] and the *Wilcoxon test* [13] to measure the efficiency of the knowledge acquisition process. The value ρ, determined in each test, is the probability of obtaining the same results in a system performing knowledge acquisition as in a system without knowledge acquisition. For a IAKA system, the smaller ρ is, the lower the chances of obtaining such results with the control system are. Therefore, the smaller ρ is, the better the IAKA system is. The Z-test is a parametric test for two paired samples. As there is no guarantee that the initial distribution of cases and problems follows a normal law, the Wilcoxon test, a non-parametric test for two paired samples, is used to confirm the results of the first test. Figure 4 shows a graphical interpretation of the results of the Wilcoxon test (the results of the Z-test are similar).

On the charts, we observe that the smaller ε is, the smaller ρ is, i.e., the more effective the system is. A significant difference ($\rho < 0.01$ i.e. 1%) in terms of reduction of the size of the error is achieved when $\varepsilon = 10$ (which is a high value in this domain). The conclusion is that the higher the tolerance threshold of the oracle is, the bigger the probability for the system to make a mistake is, which confirms the hypothesis of this experiment. Similar tests have been performed with problems of two and three variables, giving similar results.

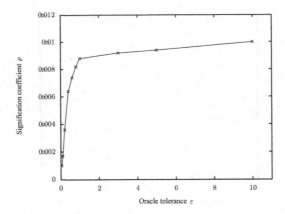

Fig. 4. Evolution of the value of ρ in function of ε for the Wilcoxon test

Impact of a Discontinuity on the CBR Process. The aim of this experiment is to analyze the behavior of a CBR system solving problems by approximation when there is a discontinuity in the domain. This experiment is motivated by the observation (b) discussed in section 3. The hypothesis is that more interactions with the oracle are needed when a problem is in the neighborhood of a discontinuity.

As for the previous experiment, an initial knowledge base of 20 cases randomly generated is built by the oracle $\mathcal{O}_{f_a}$, and 70 target problems are also randomly generated. The oracle is defined as $\mathcal{O}_{f_a} = (f_a, \varepsilon)$ with f_a as defined in section 4.1. The experiment consists in solving the 70 target problems with IAKA-NF. The results are processed to count the number of problem-solving episodes that have required a correction from the oracle. As an example, figure 5

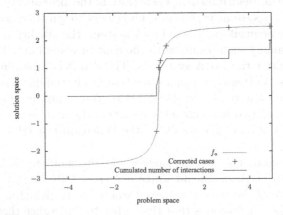

Fig. 5. Distribution of the corrected cases around a discontinuity (with $\varepsilon = 0.2$). The dotted line represents the function to approximate, the crosses are the solved cases that have required a correction from the oracle and the plain line represents the accumulation of the number of interactions with the oracle.

Table 1. Number of corrected cases and number of corrected cases around the discontinuity in function of the tolerance of the oracle

Value of ε	0.05	0.1	0.2	0.5	1.0	1.5	2.0	5.0	10
Number of corrected cases	20	13	6	5	3	3	2	0	0
Number of corrected cases around the discontinuity[a]	16	13	5	4	3	3	2	0	0

[a] The interval "around discontinuity points" is determined manually before the experiment.

shows a graphical interpretation of the result of an experiment conducted with a tolerance threshold $\varepsilon = 0.2$.

This experiment has been conducted several times with different values for ε (but still with the same initial knowledge base and the same series of problems). Table 1 gives the results of these experiments. Empirical results show that the number of cases learned around a discontinuity grows while the oracle tolerance threshold decreases. This tends to confirm the initial hypothesis of this experiment. The same experiment was also conducted with another function f_{ht} involving two problems variables.

$$\mathcal{O}_{f_{ht}} = (f_{ht}, \varepsilon) \qquad f_{ht} : \mathbb{R}^2 \to \mathbb{R}$$

$$f_{ht}(x, y) = \begin{cases} -3 - g(x, y) \text{ if } x^2 + y^2 \leq 4 \\ -g(x, y) \text{ if } x^2 + y^2 > 4 \end{cases}$$

$$g(x, y) = \sin \sqrt{x^2 + y^2} + \frac{x}{7}$$

For two-dimensional problems, the results and the conclusions are similar. Figure 6 illustrates the conclusion. In this example, the oracle is $\mathcal{O}_{f_{ht}}$, $\varepsilon = 1.0$ and 20.000 problems are solved. Only 149 cases had to be corrected by the oracle, 113 of which during the first 1000 solved problems.

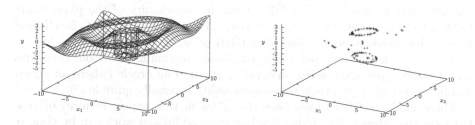

Fig. 6. Acquisition of cases around a discontinuity. The figure on the left represents the oracle knowledge. The figure on the right shows the cases learned by the system (after correction by the oracle): a high proportion of cases are acquired near discontinuity points. It must be remarked that there is a discontinuity around the top of the curve.

5   Discussion

IAKA is different from off-line approaches in that the knowledge, coming from the external world, is acquired incrementally. Off-line approaches generate a large amount of knowledge at once, leading to a significant work for the domain expert to interpret the results. In IAKA, the gradual acquisition alleviates the effort required by the oracle. IAKA may be used as a complement of a first acquisition phase: it offers an easy way to acquire additional knowledge.

Among on-line methods, CHEF learns from failures but differs from IAKA in that it exploits its own knowledge to explain failures and to avoid them in further reasoning. In DIAL, an adaptation case base is used to support an incomplete adaptation rule base but it does not evolve over time. By contrast, IAKA updates its existing adaptation methods whenever a failure occurs.

On-line learning in CBR is usually limited to the accumulation of cases and to their indexing. A failure due to system knowledge may reoccur several times if the involved knowledge is not corrected. In IAKA, the role of the oracle is to correct such knowledge. The effort required from the oracle might seem quite important but it is limited compared to the one required in off-line methods. Moreover, this effort cannot be avoided when focusing on knowledge that usually resists other knowledge acquisition approaches.

6   Conclusion

This paper has described IAKA, an approach for on-line acquisition of cases and adaptation knowledge based on interactions with an oracle (which can be considered as an "ideal expert"). IAKA has been designed using the idea of a unified view of the knowledge involved in the CBR process. The failures of the CBR inference are used to repair the knowledge base (adaptation knowledge within cases). The decomposition of the adaptation process into several steps makes the identification of the knowledge involved in the failure easier. IAKA-NF is a prototype for testing IAKA in the domain of numerical functions with an automatic oracle. The tests show that IAKA opportunistic knowledge acquisition improves the accuracy of the CBR system in the vicinity of the place where failures have occurred. They also show that this acquisition ceases to be efficient around discontinuity points, where the CBR principle is violated.

Although it has been tested, the IAKA approach remains to be compared with a real-world application, using an expert instead of an oracle (where an expert can be seen as "a noisy oracle whose availability is usually quite low").

Three kinds of failure have been described in this paper. Failures of type (b) were the subject of experiments. However, additional work can be done to improve the efficiency of the knowledge acquisition. For instance, when several failures occur in the same part of the space, the system could point it out to the expert. The interaction, that takes place off-line, may lead to the explicit modelling of additional knowledge in this part of the space (e.g. "there is a discontinuity in 4"). This knowledge could then be added to the system, thus avoiding the consideration that 3.99 and 4.01 are similar in further reasoning. Failures of types (a1) and (a2) may also lead to knowledge acquisition. With regard to type (a1) failures, experiments are currently conducted to measure the impact of the addition of intermediate cases (by the oracle) when there is no similar source case. The study of failures of type (a2) is possible future work.

The IAKA approach and its justification rely on the viewpoint of CBR as system producing approximate solutions. Another viewpoint is that of uncertain reasoning. A future work direction aims at generalizing the IAKA approach and its justification so that it considers both viewpoints.

As discussed in section 5, IAKA should inter-operate with other knowledge acquisition/extraction/learning approaches. Most of the time, these approaches are supposed to be applicable to different phases of CBR, with different goals and with different knowledge sources. However, IAKA adopts a unified view of the CBR process and its knowledge. Therefore, more work must be done to connect the various approaches in a more general framework. For instance, a future work is to elaborate a strategy that focuses on the type of faulty knowledge (adaptation knowledge, strategic knowledge, domain knowledge, etc.) to trigger an appropriate acquisition method. Although this is a long-term future work, the authors' opinion is that this is an important issue in the field.

References

1. Cordier, A., Fuchs, B., Lieber, J., Mille, A.: Failure Analysis for Domain Knowledge Acquisition in a Knowledge-Intensive CBR System. In: Weber, R.O., Richter, M.M. (eds.) ICCBR 2007. LNCS (LNAI), vol. 4626. Springer, Heidelberg (2007)
2. Cordier, A., Fuchs, B., Mille, A.: Engineering and Learning of Adaptation Knowledge in Case-Based Reasoning. In: Staab, S., Svátek, V. (eds.) EKAW 2006. LNCS (LNAI), vol. 4248, pp. 303–317. Springer, Heidelberg (2006)
3. Craw, S., Wiratunga, N., Rowe, R.: Learning adaptation knowledge to improve case-based reasoning. Artificial Intelligence 170(16-17), 1175–1192 (2006)
4. d'Aquin, M., Badra, F., Lafrogne, S., Lieber, J., Napoli, A., Szathmary, L.: Case Base Mining for Adaptation Knowledge Acquisition. In: Proceedings of the 20th International Joint Conference on Arti cial Intelligence (IJCAI 2007), pp. 750–755. Morgan Kaufmann, Inc., San Francisco (2007)
5. Dubois, D., Esteva, F., Garcia, P., Godo, L., de Màntaras, R.L., Prade, H.: Fuzzy Modelling of Case-Based Reasoning and Decision. In: Leake, D.B., Plaza, E. (eds.) ICCBR 1997. LNCS, vol. 1266, pp. 599–610. Springer, Heidelberg (1997)
6. Hammond, K.J.: Explaining and Repairing Plans That Fail. Artificial Intelligence 45(1-2), 173–228 (1990)
7. Hanney, K.: Learning Adaptation Rules from Cases. MSc Thesis, Trinity College Dublin, Ireland (1996)
8. Kendall, M.G., Stuart, A.: The advanced theory of statistics: Tome 1 distribution theory. Hafner, New York (1969)
9. Leake, D., Kinley, A., Wilson, D.: Learning to integrate multiple knowledge sources for case-based reasoning. In: Proceedings of the 15th International Joint Conference on Artificial Intelligence. Morgan Kaufmann, San Francisco (1997)

164   A. Cordier et al.

10. Leake, D.B., Kinley, A., Wilson, D.: Learning to Improve Case Adaptation by Introspective Reasoning and CBR. In: Aamodt, A., Veloso, M.M. (eds.) ICCBR 1995. LNCS, vol. 1010, pp. 229–240. Springer, Heidelberg (1995)
11. Smyth, B., Keane, M.T.: Retrieving Adaptable Cases: The Role of Adaptation Knowledge in Case Retrieval. In: Wess, S., Richter, M., Althoff, K.-D. (eds.) EWCBR 1993. LNCS, vol. 837, pp. 209–220. Springer, Heidelberg (1994)
12. Smyth, B., Keane, M.T.: Adaptation-Guided Retrieval: Questioning the SimilarityAssumption in Reasoning. Artificial Intelligence 102(2), 249–293 (1998)
13. Wilcoxon, F.: Individual comparisons by ranking methods. Biometrics 1, 80–83 (1945)

Noticeably New: Case Reuse in Originality-Driven Tasks*

Belén Díaz-Agudo[1], Enric Plaza[2],
Juan A. Recio-García[1], and Josep-Lluís Arcos[2]

[1] Department of Software Engineering and Artificial Intelligence,
Universidad Complutense de Madrid, Spain
belend@sip.ucm.es, jareciog@fdi.ucm.es
[2] IIIA, Artificial Intelligence Research Institute,
CSIC, Spanish Council for Scientific Research,
Campus UAB, Bellaterra, Catalonia, Spain
{enric,arcos}@iiia.csic.es

Abstract. "Similar problems have similar solutions" is a basic tenet of case-based inference. However this is not satisfied for CBR systems where the task is to achieve *original* solutions — i.e. solutions that, even for "old problems," are required to be noticeably different from previously known solutions. This paper analyzes the role of reuse in CBR systems in *originality driven tasks* (ODT), where a new solution has not only to be correct but noticeably different from the ones known in the case base. We perform an empirical study of transformational and generative reuse applied to an originality driven task, namely tale generation, and we analyze how search in the solution space and consistency maintenance are pivotal for ODT during the reuse process.

1 Introduction

A basic tenet of case-based inference is that similar problems have similar solutions. This is not only a useful way to explain Case Based Reasoning to laypeople but is the central core of so-called similarity-based inference in fuzzy logic. Based on this assumption developing a good CBR system basically has two requirements: (1) acquiring a good sample of cases, and (2) designing a predictive similarity measure (i.e. one that predicts a good solution when the cases are similar). Nevertheless, there are domains where the task is to achieve not only solutions but *new* solutions — i.e. solutions that, even for "old problems," are required to be noticeably different from previously known solutions. Domains like music composition and performance, story plotting and writing, or architecture design, require the solutions to be noticeably dissimilar from previously produced solutions, or at least from previous solutions from other authors. We will call these kind of tasks *originality-driven tasks*.

Moreover, several CBR approaches have dealt with originality-driven tasks for innovative design or for "creative" problem solving (as we discuss in Section 6).

---

* Supported by the MID-CBR project (TIN2006-15140-C03-02).

K.-D. Althoff et al. (Eds.): ECCBR 2008, LNAI 5239, pp. 165–179, 2008.

Focusing on the role of the Reuse process, this paper aims to analyze the issues relevant for CBR systems when dealing with originality-driven tasks in general. We will study how different Reuse techniques effect different search processes in order to elucidate the main issues relevant for the construction of a noteworthy new solution. Specifically, we will consider two existing reuse techniques (a transformational reuse technique and a generative reuse technique), and we will apply them to the domain of folk tale generation to analyze these issues and provide some guidelines for future originality-driven reuse techniques.

The structure of this paper is as follows. In Section 2, we present a search based framework to study Reuse processes and we define novelty (or originality) from the notions of solution space similarity and plagiarism. Section 3 characterizes the two reuse techniques and analyzes them with respect to originality driven tasks. Section 4 describes tale generation as an originality driven task. Section 5 presents the results of some experiments with different reuse approaches. Following a review of the related work in Section 6, Section 7 summarizes the main conclusions and the lines of future work.

2   Search, Reuse and Plagiarism

First, we find it useful to distinguish between analytic and synthetic tasks. In analytical tasks finding a solution is selecting one element from a known and enumerable collection of solutions; examples are classification, identification or single diagnosis. Synthetic tasks, on the other hand, do not not provide in advance with a collection of solutions; synthetic tasks define a collection of *solution elements*, and a solution is *constructed* by a certain combination of some solution elements. In general, a solution can be seen as a graph, where solution elements are nodes and edges are the relationships holding among the solution elements. In some synthetic tasks, like planning, a solution is a special kind of graph, like a sequence or a partial order among actions (the solution elements of the planning task). Clearly, originality-driven tasks are synthetic tasks, and novel solutions can be found by new combinations of the solution elements.

Let us now consider the main differences between the "similar problems have similar solutions" scenario (SPSS, see Figure 1) and the "originality-driven tasks" scenario (ODT, see Figure 2). In the SPSS scenario of Figure 1 a new problem x_0 is compared in the problem space using a similarity measure with other problems in the case base. Moreover, let us view the case base as a repository of the mappings from problem space to solution space given by the known cases $CB = \{(x_i, s_i)\}$. Assuming x_1 is the most similar problem to x_0, case based inference yields s_1 as the solution of case (x_1, s_1). Now, the "similar problems have similar solutions" hypothesis basically states that we expect to find s_0 (the solution for x_0) in the neighborhood of s_1 (depicted as a circle around s_1). The Reuse process, in abstract terms, is the one that moves from solution s_1 to solution s_0 in the solution space; depending on the reuse technique, this "trajectory" can be seen in different ways, but we will consider that in general (as argued in [1]) it is some form of search process. However, the bottom line

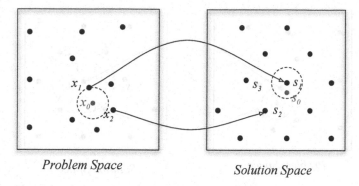

Problem Space   Solution Space

Fig. 1. Scenario 1: Similar problems have similar solutions in CBR

is that CBR systems have been designed with the underlying idea that a *short length trajectory* is desirable or even mandatory.

This assumption can not be satisfied, in general, for ODT using CBR. Figure 2 exemplifies this scenario where a solution to the new problem x_0 cannot be too close to the solutions of similar cases. Consider, for instance, that new problem x_0 is similar to case $C_1 = (x_1, s_1)$; an original solution to problem x_0 cannot be too close to s_1 — they have to be outside the grey circle in Figure 2 centered around s_1. Additionally, an original solution for x_0 must also not be too close to any other existing solutions. The Reuse process in ODT CBR systems has to build a trajectory such as that shown in Figure 2 from s_1 to s_0 — i.e. a trajectory that cannot be ensured to be short and that finds a consistent solution for x_0 in a relatively unpopulated region of the solution space. Therefore, we formulate the following hypothesis:

Hypothesis 1. *ODT CBR Reuse needs a similarity (or a distance) measure on the solution space S.*

Most CBR systems do not require a definition of a similarity measure on the space of solutions. There are exceptions, but we are not claiming any innovation here. We simply state that for the ODT scenario, it makes sense to consider as indispensable the definition of similarity measures on the space of solutions.

There is no problem, in principle, to find solutions in relatively unpopulated region of the solution space: domains where ODT are applicable have large solution spaces since the combination of their solution elements into complex structures is huge. However, there are technical requirements that should addressed by Reuse techniques when abandoning the "short length trajectory" assumption: (1) the Reuse technique needs to search the solution space in a systematic (or even exhaustive) way, and (2) the Reuse technique should ensure the validity and consistency of the solutions

Assumption (1) is necessary to be able to reach unpopulated regions of the solution space in large Reuse trajectories. Assumption (2) is needed because in the SPSS scenario often the validity and coherence of solutions are not ensured or

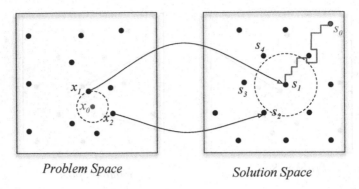

Problem Space   Solution Space

Fig. 2. Scenario 2: originality-driven tasks in CBR

explicitly tested: the "short length trajectory" assumption implies that, since few changes are made, if the solution of the retrieved case is valid and consistent then the Reuse process most likely will produce a valid and consistent solution. If not, the Revise process is designed to check and/or repair the solution (usually with a human in the loop). Validity and coherence of solutions play a different role in the Reuse process for originality-driven tasks. Since Reuse will perform a large search process it cannot simply present thousands of configurations to be Revised by a human. Moreover, since the solution space to explore is huge, a Reuse process that is able to prune most or all invalid or inconsistent partial solutions will be more efficient in the exploration of the solution space. Therefore, we formulate the following hypothesis for CBR systems in originality-driven tasks:

Hypothesis 2. *ODT CBR Reuse needs knowledge to assess the internal coherence of solutions and partial solutions meaning that (a) either the Reuse process is able to ensure that it will only deal with consistent solutions and partial solutions, or (b) partial solutions (intermediate points in the Reuse trajectory) may have some inconsistencies but they are temporary, detectable, and remediable.*

Later, in Section 3, we will see how generative reuse and transformational reuse employ respectively approaches (a) and (b) to address validity and consistency of solutions for "long length trajectory" reuse.

Indeed, ensuring validity and consistency of solutions requires additional domain knowledge, but it is an empirical question whether "more knowledge" is a large or modest amount. Anyway, domains where originality-driven tasks are usually applied to already have a rather rich ontology, and the *solution elements* and their possible relationships have to be represented in some formalism. Although we do not intend to address this issue in general, we address later in the paper the role of domain knowledge for the domain of folk tale generation, and how it differs in the specific generative and transformational reuse techniques we use.

Finally, we will address the notion of plagiarism in the context of originality-driven tasks. Plagiarism is an argument made against the quality of something being original on the grounds that it is (very) similar to some preexisting body of work. Although definitions of plagiarism in music, literature or architecture may vary in how to measure or assess similarity, or which similarity threshold may legally sustain a plagiarism lawsuit, the core idea of "plagiarism" seems quite stable and transversal. This core idea allows us to define originality or novelty for ODT case-based reasoning:

Definition 1 (Originality). *Given a case base* $CB = \{(x_i, s_i)\}$, *a distance measure* Δ *over the solutions space* $\mathcal{S}$, *and a plagiarism threshold* γ, *a solution* s_0 *is original iff* $\forall (x_i, s_i) \in CB : \Delta(s_0, s_i) > \gamma$.

This approach based on the plagiarism/originality dualism offers a pragmatic framework to deal with the issues of novelty and innovation. Instead of proposing some debatable definitions of what is or not "original" (or "novel" or "innovative"), we propose to consider a solution *original* as long as no argument of plagiarism attacks that solution; similarly, if there are plausible plagiarism arguments against some solution, then that solution may be considered of "debatable originality." Another reason for this approach is that we wanted to avoid having "degrees of innovation", i.e. we do not intend to distinguish between something being "very novel" (or "very creative") vs. being not very novel. We think this kind of phrasing mixes together an assessment of quality and an assessment of dissimilarity from an existing body of work. Discussion in this paper of *originality* refers to the definition above and does not imply any assessment about the quality of solutions; for instance, in the domain of folk tale generation presented later we deal with their originality but not with the "tale quality", although a certain consistency of solutions is guaranteed.

3   Reuse Techniques

The purpose of this paper is not to design new Reuse techniques for originality-driven tasks (ODT) in CBR, but rather to analyze existing CBR Reuse techniques inside a ODT framework in order to determine how well adapted they are for these tasks and which possible shortcomings should be addressed to improve CBR in originality-driven tasks. For this purpose we selected two broadly different Reuse techniques, one based on transforming an existing solution into a new solution (Figure 3a) and another based on generating or constructing a new solution (Figure 3b).

Transformational Reuse –or Transformational Adaptation (TA)– is the most widely used approach to case reuse; Figure 3a shows a schema of this approach (where DK means domain knowledge and CK means case knowledge). Although this schema is not intended to cover all existing techniques, it is useful to pinpoint their main features. Typically, a new case is solved by retrieving the most similar case in memory and copying the solution (although some techniques may use solutions from multiple cases); then a transformational process using domain knowledge (DK) and/or case-derived knowledge (CK) modifies that copy (which we consider a form of search) until a final solution adequate for the current problem is found. In the experiments described in Section 5, we used a local

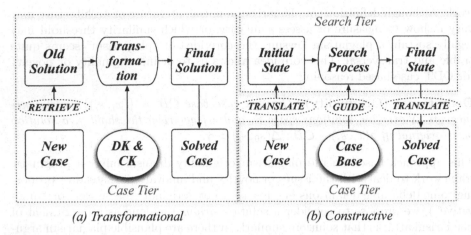

(a) Transformational   *(b) Constructive*

Fig. 3. Schemas of reuse processes based on (a) transforming an existing solution into a new solution, and (b) generating or constructing a new solution

search transformational reuse technique; basically, a node in the "working case" is substituted by finding another related node in a taxonomic hierarchy — e.g. a *sword* is a type of *weapon* in the folk tale generation domain, and may be substituted by another weapon like a *crossbow*. Moreover, Transformational Reuse is able to modify more than a single node: *deep substitution* allows to modify a whole subgraph in the solution — e.g. when substituting a character like the *evil wolf* by an *evil wizard* then the constituent aspects of the characters (role, sex, dwelling, physical appearance) are also substituted. Finally, consistency is maintained by the use of explicit *dependencies*; dependencies are used to detect nodes that need to be transformed after some nodes are substituted — e.g. the folk tales domain uses dependencies among actions to assure consistency, like *Release-from-captivity* depends-on *Kidnapping* (see Figure 4).

Generative or Constructive Reuse builds a new solution for the new case while using the case base as a resource for guiding the constructive process. Figure 3a shows the schema of *Constructive Adaptation* [1], a family of methods based on a heuristic search-based process —where the heuristic function guiding search is derived from a similarity measure between the query and the case base. Constructive Adaptation (CA) takes a problem case and translates it into an initial state in the *state space* (Figure 3b); i.e. transform a case representation into a state representation. Then a heuristic search process expands a search tree where each node represents a partial solution, until a final state (with a complete and valid solution) is found. Notice that final but non-valid states can be reached, but this simply means the search process will backtrack to expand other pending states.

This process is guided by a heuristic based on comparing the similarity from *states* (represented in the *state space*) to cases (represented in the *space of cases*); the nodes with higher similarity are expanded first during the search process. The result is that CA adds one node to a partial solution as it moves from one state

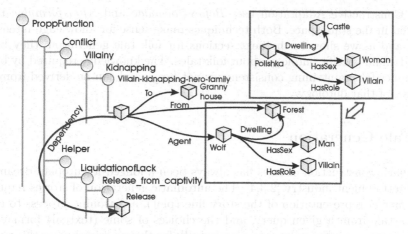

Fig. 4. Deep Substitution and Dependencies

to the next; that is to say, it builds a solution by piecemeal copies of nodes from similar cases. Notice that there is neither retrieval nor "single case adaptation" here since the component nodes are incrementally copied from multiple cases in the case base, depending only on the similarity measure that works on the whole case base. To ensure consistency, however, CA requires that each component is described with *Before-formulae* and *After-formulae* [1]. *Before-formulae* specify what properties are required to be true in order for the component to be validly added to a solution, while *After-formulae* state what properties are true by the incorporation of this component in the solution. A consistent solution is one that satisfies all the *Before-formulae* required by its components, and a valid solution is one that satisfies the current problem.

Thus, the main difference between these techniques is that TA works in the *space of cases* while CA works both in the *state space* and the *space of cases*. Additionally, we are able now to characterize both Reuse techniques in our framework of Reuse as a search process.

Concerning TA, we characterize it as follows: (1) *eager reuse* (copies an old solution as the first step, and later discards parts of it by substituting them); (2) based on *case space search*; and (3) *single-focus reuse* (since all transformations are effected upon a single case solution; this is true even when using substitutes from multiple cases, since parts of these cases are always substituted against the structure of a single "working case" being transformed).

Concerning CA, we characterize it as follows: (1) *lazy reuse* (adds one component at a time to the solution); (2) based on an interplay between *state space search* and similarity on *case space*; (3) *multi-focus reuse* (since components added to a solution come in principle from multiple cases); and (4) an *exhaustive search approach* that can provide solutions even when no similar cases (or no cases at all) are provided.

Finally, consistency is also approached in a different way in both reuse techniques. Transformational Reuse uses explicit dependencies in the space of cases, while Constructive Adaptation uses *Before-formulae* and *After-formulae* that are used in the state space. Both techniques make sense for knowledge-intensive CBR, and as we show in the next sections for folk tale generation, they both use a domain-specific ontology about folk tales. The knowledge required by both techniques for maintaining consistency is not large, and can be derived from an analysis of that ontology.

4 Tale Generation

Automatic construction of tales has always been a longed-for utopian dream in the entertainment industry [2,3,4]. The automatic generation of stories requires some *formal* representation of the story line (plot), a reasoning process to generate a tale from a given query, and the choices of some (textual) format for presenting the resulting plots. As a case study for the experiments, in this paper we present a CBR approach to the problem of obtaining a structured description of a tale plot from a given query. The problem of transforming the resulting plot into a textual rendition is out of the scope of this paper.

Previous work by the UCM group has shown that Ontologies and Description Logics are a very powerful combination as a resource for generating linguistically correct texts [5,6]. The UCM group has formalized an ontology including the primitives to represent a plot structure based on Vladimir Propp's theory [7]. Propp's original goal was to derive a morphological method of classifying tales about magic, based on the arrangements of 31 primitive actions or "functions", resulting in the description of folk tales according to their constituent parts, the relationships between those parts, and the relations of those parts with the whole. Propp's work has been used as a basis for a good number of attempts to model computationally the construction of stories [8,9].

The UCM group approach relies on Propp's main idea that folk tales are made up of components that change from one tale to another, and *actions* or *functions* that act as constants in the morphology of folk tales. What changes are the names and certain attributes of the characters, whereas their actions remain the same. For example, some Propp functions are: *Villainy, Departure, Acquisition of a Magical Agent, Guidance, Testing of the hero*, etc. The ontology (explained in [6]) includes various concepts that are relevant to tale generation and give semantic coherence and structure to the tales. Based on this formalization we previously proposed a CBR approach for storyline representation and adaptation [5]. That work described a process to retrieve one plot based on a user query specifying an initial setting for the story. Then a transformational reuse process modifies the retrieved plot according to the query.

The goal of this paper is studying the role of reuse in CBR systems in *Originality driven tasks*, like tale generation, where the underlying goal is creating a tale that is new and useful at the same time as maintaining narrative coherence. Although in the literature there are different definitions for concepts like *creativity, novelty* and *originality*, in this paper we characterize them using an *edit distance* measure[10].

Each case is a story plot that, according to Propp's structure, is formalized by its actions, and each action by its properties, like the participant characters and their roles (Donor, Hero, FalseHero, Prisoner, Villain), the place where the action takes place (City, Country, Dwelling), the involved objects, attributive elements or accessories (a ring, a horse). Each case is composed of a great number of interrelated individuals, i.e instances of concepts, from the ontology.

The basic components are the Propp's character functions that act as high level elements that coordinate the structure of discourse. There are some restrictions on the choice of functions that one can use in a given folk tale, given by implicit dependencies between functions: for instance, to be able to apply the *Interdiction Violated* function, the hero must have received an order (*Interdiction* function). There are many other examples, like the dependency between *Release-from-Captivity* and *Kidnapping*, or *Resurrection* and *Dead* functions.

Background domain knowledge required by the system is related with the respective information about characters, places and objects of our world. Domain knowledge is used to measure the semantical distance between similar cases or situations, and for maintaining an independent story plot structure from the simulated world. The domain knowledge of our application is the classic fairy tale world with magicians, witches, princesses, etc. The ontology is formalized in OWL and it includes about 230 concepts, 626 distinct individuals (246 appearing in the initial case base), and 94 properties. Each case representing a complete tale is typically composed of several interrelated actions. Each action refers to a Propp function, and gives answers to the *who* (character), *where* (place) and *what* (object) questions. We distinguish between *temporal* relations (before, after, during, starts-before, ends-before, etc.) and actions with *dependencies* (in which a change in one of them strongly affects the others). There are different types of dependencies like *place-dependency, character-dependency, object-dependency* and *propagation-dependency*. Dependencies are explicitly represented as relations that link the dependent elements in the ontology.

The initial case base in our system has 6 cases representing story plots for traditional fairy tales like "Fortune Teller", "Little Red Riding Hood", "Cinderella" and "Yakky Doodle". Each one of these cases is a complex structure where many individuals are interrelated. See Figure 5 (right) for a summary of the complexity and number of instances for each tale. The simpler one is "Cinderella" with 36 individuals including actions, characters, places and objects. The more complex is "Goldfish" with 77 individuals. Figure 5 (left) depicts the action structure of the "Little Red Riding Hood" story plot.

5   Experiments

The purpose of our experiments is to take a technique representative of transformational adaptation (TA) and another representative of constructive adaptation (CA) and study how they behave in our ODT framework. We have used jCOL-IBRI [11] to develop the Tales application and to perform the experiments. We will analyze the results for two specific implementations of TA and CA for case

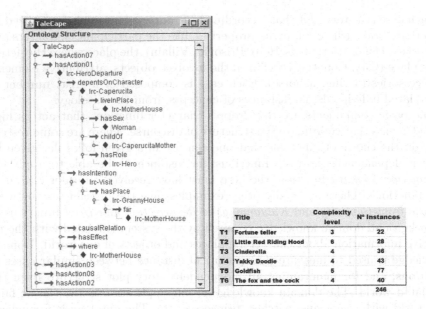

	Title	Complexity level	N° Instances
T1	Fortune teller	3	22
T2	Little Red Riding Hood	6	28
T3	Cinderella	4	36
T4	Yakky Doodle	4	43
T5	Goldfish	5	77
T6	The fox and the cock	4	40
			246

Fig. 5. Action structure of the Little Red Riding Hood story plot

reuse in the tale generation domain. First we describe the query structure and some other decisions taken during the implementation of both approaches, TA and CA. Then, for the same sets of queries we compare the distances between the generated solutions and the solutions in the case base, and the distribution of the generated solutions with respect to those preexisting in the case base.

Queries: The queries use the same vocabulary used to describe the cases in the case base, i.e., the domain ontology. As a query the user provides a set of actions, characters, places, and objects that (s)he would like to include in the tale. Actions in the query are neither ordered nor linked to specific characters, objects or places. For the experimentation we defined four collections of queries named Q1, Q3, Q5, Q7. Each collection was populated, respectively, with queries involving 1,3,5, and 7 instances of each first level concept (i.e. actions, characters, places, and objects); 20 queries were randomly generated for each collection.

Originality Measure: In order to assess the novelty of solutions we will measure an edit distance from a new solution to each solution in the case base. The distance between two tale structures will assess the dissimilarity between those solutions. We use the Zhang & Shasha's algorithm [12], where the cost of adding, deleting, or substituting a node in the tree depends on the distances of the elements in the domain ontology. Moreover, the distance between two tales is normalized by the size of the smaller one. We will analyze (1) the distances on the preexisting tales in the case base, and (2) the distances of the generated tales with respect to the case base for each query in both TA and CA.

We first analyze the distances among the tales preexisting in the case base. Since they are assumed to be original (in the sense that there is no plagiarism

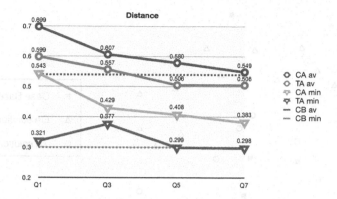

Fig. 6. Average and minimum distance of new solutions w.r.t the case base

among them), the distances among them will give us a qualitative measure of what is desirable for the generated tales to be considered original. The average edit distance over all pairs of the case base solutions is $CB_{av} = 0.54$. Moreover, the two solutions that are more similar have a distance $CB_{min} = 0.3$; thus we can consider this a lower threshold for originality since we assume that the tales in the case base are original. Therefore, if the distance of a generated solution to every solution in the case base is higher than $CB_{min} = 0.3$, we will consider it to be original. According to definition of originality in Section 2 the plagiarism threshold in the example domain would be $\gamma = 0, 3$.

Figure 6 shows the average distances of the solutions for query collections Q1, Q3, Q5, Q7 generated by TA and CA with respect to the case base. Both TA_{av} and CA_{av} have on average distances higher than the threshold distance $CB_{min} = 0.3$, so they can be considered, on average, to be original with respect to the cases they are built from. Moreover, their average distances TA_{av} and CA_{av} are around $CB_{av} = 0.54$, the average distance among the case base solutions. Therefore, the solutions generated by CBR are as original, on average, as the cases provided by the initial case base.

Another way to visualize this fact is shown in Figure 7, where solutions in the case base and solutions generated by TA and CA are mapped in a two-dimensional space. The original data is a matrix of pairwise distance values among all solutions, while the visualization is built using a force-directed graph-drawing algorithm where the repulsive force between two cases is proportional to their distance. In order to provide original solutions, a CBR system has to look for solutions that are situated in a sparse area of the solution space. We can see in Figure 7 that all solutions (initial and generated) are evenly distributed, without clumps or clusters.

Comparing TA and CA, in general CA tends to find solutions in the unpopulated region of the solution space while TA keeps closer to the previously existing cases. This effect was expected by hindsight: since TA works by transforming an existing solution, it seems reasonable to expect that it will change what needs to

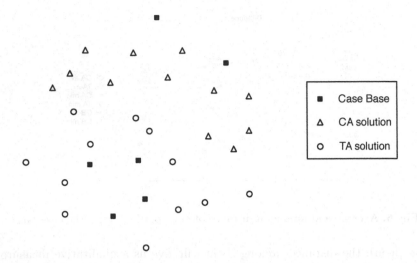

Fig. 7. Distribution of solutions regarding the original case base

be changed (following a parsimony principle) while CA builds the solution and opportunistically reuses parts of existing solutions in different cases.

This difference can also be seen in Fig. 6, where CA solutions are more distant on average from the case base than TA solutions. In relation to query complexity, both TA and CA techniques follow the same pattern of decreasing average distance to the case base as the query constraints increase from Q1 to Q7. Our explanation for this effect is that Q7 constrains much more the set of admissible solutions than Q1; e.g. Q7 specifies 7 actions, 7 characters, 7 places, and 7 objects (and they are generated randomly in our experiments). Nevertheless, Q7 solutions are around the average $CB_{av} = 0.54$ for the case base, which is good. These results indicate however that very specific queries may cause problems by being over-constraining and reducing admissible solutions to a rather small set; in this circumstance an originality driven task would basically require a lot of search and the usefulness of cases may be reduced. As future work, we suggest later that a conversational CBR approach could be useful in this scenario.

Finally, we have so far analyzed average distance, so we turn to the worst case scenario. Figure 6 also shows the minimal distances TA_{min} and CA_{min} from a solution to the case base for each query collection Q1, ..., Q7. Since both TA_{min} and CA_{min} are above or around $CB_{min} = 0.3$, we can safely say that even the generated solutions with lower distances can be safely considered original (with respect to the originality in the content of the case base). As before, CA provides solutions that are more distant from the case base than TA; the explanation is again the parsimony principle of TA, while CA reuses opportunistically parts of different cases in its constructive process.

Since both TA and CA produce solutions without knowing any threshold of "minimal distance" that need be surpassed, it may seem unexpected that all solutions end up being sufficiently original in our experiments. We think the reason is the ontology used in the task of folk tale generation and the handling of solution consistency in both TA and CA (albeit using different mechanisms). Essentially, reuse in TA and CA explore the solution space searching for solutions that satisfy the elements required in the query; this already put further the new solution from the case base. Moreover, the reuse process by either adding a new element (in CA) or transforming an element (in TA) triggers further constraints to be satisfied, which in turn require further additions/transformations. Thus, originality in folk tale generation is obtained by the consistency enforcement during the reuse process in the presence of a large solution space. Clearly, this need not be true for any originality-driven task using CBR; Section 7 we suggest future work where solution space distance is estimated as part of the reuse process for originality-driven tasks.

6   State of the Art

Related to our work are several CBR approaches for the task of innovative design. The FAMING system [13] is an example of the use of case adaptation for supporting innovative design of kinematic pairs; reuse in FAMING combines a structural model with constraint-based techniques for generating solutions different from the ones in the case base. The structural model is akin to our ontology in providing domain knowledge and constraint-based search provides a mechanism for preserving consistency in solutions. The FAMING system thus fits in our ODT framework of CBR systems, in that the originality of the solution is not pursued as such, but is a result of the domain knowledge and the consistency maintenance during reuse. However, the paper [13] is interested in showing that "different solutions" can be found by a CBR system in this way, but it is not intent on developing a framework for originality-driven CBR tasks. Another CBR approach is the IDEAL system [14], that produces innovative solutions by adapting solutions of design cases from one domain to another distant domain by using *structure-behavior-function* models. A survey of CBR approaches to design and innovation can be found in [15].

Regarding tale generation, there have been various attempts in the literature to create a computational model. Many existing systems are somehow related with the CBR paradigm, even if they do not explicitly mention it, because they are based on re-using a collection of plots with the structure of coherent tales [16,3,9,17,6]. Basically, these story creation systems retrieve a complete plot structure and reuse it by changing secondary elements of the story world, like places or characters. A related approach, that is also based on the Proppian morphology, is that of Fairclough and Cunningham [9]. They implement an interactive multiplayer story engine that operates over a way of describing stories based on Propp's work, and applies case-based planning and constraint satisfaction to control the characters following a coherent plot.

7 Conclusions and Future Work

The purpose of this paper was to analyze CBR in the context of a class of tasks we called *originality-driven tasks* (ODT). We characterized the *originality* of a CBR solution using the pragmatic notion of plagiarism: a solution is original if it cannot be accused of plagiarism with respect to previous solutions (i.e. to the solutions in the case base). Since plagiarism is defined as a measure of similarity between objects, originality of CBR solutions can easily be understood and measured by defining a distance measure (or equivalently a similarity measure) on the *space of solutions*. We then modeled the reuse process in ODTs as a search process that builds solutions that are not only new and valid with respect to the query but also distant enough in the space of solutions from preexisting solutions.

After establishing this conceptual framework, we examined how two different reuse techniques (one transformational and the other constructive) address the issues of originality-driven tasks in CBR; moreover, we designed and performed some experiments in the domain of folk tale generation where originality of solutions could be assessed and analyzed. We saw that the two reuse techniques indeed produced original solutions, even if transformational reuse seemed a priori more likely to produce solutions more similar to preexisting cases. Since existing reuse techniques do not internally use a distance measure in the space of solutions to enforce the originality of the new solution, we had to conclude that this "originality" was a kind of side effect. Solutions are original because of the interplay of two factors: the large solution space and the maintenance of solution consistency that forces the reuse process to search for solutions even more distant in order to build a consistent solutions.

The difference between transformational and constructive reuse was less than a priori expected. We assumed that transformational reuse would find solutions less distant than constructive reuse, as indeed can be observed in Fig. 6. The differences however are not large, and transformational reuse always found solutions that are original. One difference between transformational and constructive reuse is the way in which they maintain solution consistency while searching in the solution space, but this difference is minor compared with the fact that it is this consistency maintenance mechanism that forces changes in the solution and ends up building a solution far away from the initial case base.

Concerning future work we think that both TA and CA reuse for ODT should include a way to measure distances in the solution space to be able to ensure that solutions are original with respect to some appropriate domain threshold. Most CBR systems focus on exploiting similarity on the problem space, but few use similarity on the solution space; we think ODT is a class of problems where new CBR techniques that use similarity on the solution space can be developed. Moreover, the notion of plagiarism can be refined; we were using here a global measure among solutions, but plagiarism accusations can focus on specific parts of solutions (e.g. in music a few notes too similar to another song are grounds for plagiarism claims). This refined notion of plagiarism would require more introspective reuse techniques that estimate and maintain both consistency and originality over partial solutions during the reuse process.

Finally, the effect of over-constrained queries suggests that a conversational CBR approach would be best suited for folk tale generation, and maybe for ODTs in general. A conversational CBR approach could start with a smaller query, allowing the user to augment the query requirements incrementally while the CBR system would assess whether new requirements can be incorporated or compromise the originality of the solution.

References

1. Plaza, E., Arcos, J.L.: Constructive adaptation. In: Craw, S., Preece, A.D. (eds.) ECCBR 2002. LNCS (LNAI), vol. 2416, pp. 306–320. Springer, Heidelberg (2002)
2. Adams, S.: Storytelling and computer games: Past, present and future (2001)
3. Braun, N., Schneider, O., Habinger, G.: Literary analytical discussion of digital storytelling and its relation to automated narration. In: Workshop Understanding User Experience: Literary Analysis meets HCI, London, UK (2002)
4. Bringsjord, S., Ferrucci, D.: Artificial Intelligence and Literary Creativity: Inside the mind of Brutus, a StoryTelling Machine. Lawrence Erlbaum Associates, Hillsdale (1999)
5. Díaz-Agudo, B., Gervás, P., Peinado, F.: A CBR approach to story plot generation. In: Funk, P., González Calero, P.A. (eds.) ECCBR 2004. LNCS (LNAI), vol. 3155. Springer, Heidelberg (2004)
6. Peinado, F., Gervás, P., Díaz-Agudo, B.: A description logic ontology for fairy tale generation. In: Language Resources for Linguistic Creativity Workshop, 4th LREC Conference, Lisboa, Portugal (2004)
7. Propp, V.: Morphology of the Folktale. University of Texas Press (1968)
8. Malec, S.A.: Proppian structural analysis and XML modeling (2004), http://clover.slavic.pitt.edu/~sam/propp/theory/propp.html
9. Fairclough, C., Cunningham, P.: An interactive story engine. In: O'Neill, M., Sutcliffe, R.F.E., Ryan, C., Eaton, M., Griffith, N.J.L. (eds.) AICS 2002. LNCS (LNAI), vol. 2464, pp. 171–176. Springer, Heidelberg (2002)
10. Levenshtein, V.I.: Binary codes capable of correcting deletions, insertions and reversals. Soviet Physics Doklady 10, 707–710 (1966)
11. Díaz-Agudo, B., González-Calero, P.A., Recio-García, J., Sanchez-Ruiz, A.: Building CBR systems with jCOLIBRI. Journal of Science of Computer Programming 69(1-3), 68–75 (2007)
12. Zhang, K., Shasha, D.: Simple fast algorithms for the editing distance between trees and related problems. SIAM J. Comput. 18, 1245–1262 (1989)
13. Faltings, B., Sun, K.: FAMING: Supporting innovative mechanism shape design. The Knowledge Engineering Review 30(3), 271–276 (2005)
14. Bhatta, S., Goel, A.: Learning generic mechanisms for innovative strategies in adaptive design. Journal of Learning Sciences 6(4), 367–396 (1997)
15. Goel, A.K., Craw, S.: Design, innovation and case-based reasoning. The Knowledge Engineering Review 30(3), 271–276 (2005)
16. Turner, S.R.: Minstrel: a computer model of creativity and storytelling. PhD thesis, Los Angeles, CA, USA (1993)
17. Callaway, C.B., Lester, J.C.: Narrative prose generation. Artificial Intelligence 139, 213–252 (2002)

Experience-Based Design of Behaviors in Videogames

Gonzalo Flórez Puga, Belén Díaz-Agudo, and Pedro González-Calero

Department of Software Engineering and Artificial Intelligence,
Universidad Complutense de Madrid, Spain
gflorez@fdi.ucm.es, {belend,pedro}@sip.ucm.es

Abstract. Artificial intelligence in games is usually used for creating player's opponents. Manual edition of intelligent behaviors for Non-Player Characters (NPC) of games is a cumbersome task that needs experienced designers. Amongst other activities, they design new behaviors in terms of perception and actuation over the environment. Behaviors typically use recurring patterns, so that experience and reuse are crucial aspects for behavior design. In this paper we present a behavior editor (eCo) using Case Based Reasoning to retrieve and reuse stored behaviors represented as hierarchical state machines. In this paper we focus on the application of different types of similarity assessment to retrieve the best behavior to reuse. eCo is configurable for different domains. We present our experience within a soccer simulation environment (SoccerBots) to design the behaviors of the automatic soccer players.

1   Introduction

Artificial Intelligence for interactive computer games is an emerging application area where there are increasingly complex and realistic worlds and increasingly complex and intelligent computer-controlled characters. Interactive computer games provide a rich environment for incremental research on human-level AI behaviors. These artificial behaviors should provide more interesting and novel gameplay experiences for the player creating enemies, partners, and support characters that act just like human players [1].

The edition of intelligent behaviors in videogames (or simulation environments) is a cumbersome and difficult task where experience has shown to be a crucial asset. Amongst other activities, it implies identifying the entities which must behave intelligently, the kind of behaviors they must show (e.g. helping, aggressive, elusive), designing, implementing, integrating and testing these behaviors in the virtual environment.

Designing new behaviors could be greatly benefited from two features that are common in most of everyday videogames. First of all, modularity in behaviors. That means complex behaviors can be decomposed into simpler behaviors that are somehow combined. Second, simpler behaviors tend to recur within complex behaviors of the same game, or even in different games of the same genre. For instance, in a soccer game "defend" could be a complex behavior that is

K.-D. Althoff et al. (Eds.): ECCBR 2008, LNAI 5239, pp. 180–194, 2008.

composed of two simpler behaviors like "go to the ball" and "clear"; meanwhile "attack" could be composed of "go to the ball", "dribbling" and "shoot". Both features are useful to build new complex behaviors based on simple behaviors as the building blocks that are reused.

We are developing a graphical behavior editor that is able to store and reuse previously designed behaviors. Our editor (eCo) [2] is generic and applicable to different games, as long as it is configured by a game model file. The underlying technologies are Hierarchical Finite State Machines (HFSMs) [3] and Case Based Reasoning (CBR). In this paper we focus on the similarity assessment and retrieval processes and give some ideas about our future work on reuse.

HFSMs are appropriate and useful tools to graphically represent behaviors in games[4]. HFSMs facilitate the modular decomposition of complex behaviors into simpler ones, and the reuse of simple behaviors. The eCo behavior editor provides with a graphical interface which allows the user to manually create or modify behaviors just by "drawing" them. Using a CBR-based module, the user can make approximate searches against a case base of previously edited behaviors. Both technologies work tightly integrated. Initially, the case base is empty, so all the editing has to be done via the manual editing (graphic) tools. Once there are enough cases in the case base, new behaviors can be constructed by retrieving and reusing the stored ones.

First, in Section 2, we introduce some general ideas on behavior representation and present the approach followed by the eCo behavior editor. In Section 3 we show a small example of application of the editor to a simulation environment: SoccerBots. Section 4 describes the CBR module integrated in the editor focusing in the different ways of computing similarity. Finally, in Section 5 and 6, we present related work, future goals and conclusions.

2 Modeling Reusable Behaviors

In general terms, the execution of a computer video game can be viewed as the continuous execution of a loop of perceiving, deciding the behavior, acting and rendering tasks. The behavior for each NPC basically decides the set of actions or reactions performed by the controlled entity, usually in relation with its environment. In a computer game or simulation, each entity gathers information about its environment using a set of sensors, which could be compared to the senses of the living beings. Depending on this information, the entity performs certain actions, using a set of actuators. In general, the set of sensors and actuators is unique for all the entities of a game and is different for each game or simulation environment, although there will be similarities between games of the same genre. For example, sensors in a first-person-shooter (FPS) game will give access to the position, the steering, the health, the visibility of other entities or the remaining fuel of a vehicle. Regarding the actuators, the entity can shoot, look at or go to a place, talk to other entities, among others.

Several suitable techniques exist for the representation of behaviors. Due to its expressive power and simplicity, Finite State Machines (FSMs) is one of the most

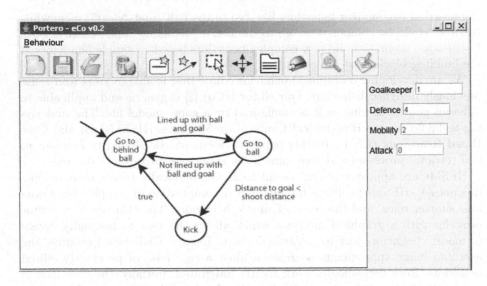

Fig. 1. Example of a HFSM

popular techniques. FSMs have been used successfully in several commercial games, like Quake [5], and in game editing tools, like Simbionic [6]. A FSM is a computation model composed of a finite set of states, actions and transitions between states. Simple states are described by the actions or activities which will take place in a state and the transitions point out changes in the state, and are described by conditions formulated over the sensors. One of the drawbacks of the FSMs is that they can be very complex when the number of states grows. To prevent this situation, we used Hierarchical Finite State Machines (HFSMs), which are an extension to the classic FSMs. In a HFSM , besides a set of actions, the states can contain a complete HFSM, reducing the overall complexity and favoring its legibility [3].

We have developed eCo, a game designer oriented tool that represents behaviors using HFSMs. The main module offers a graphical editor to manually "draw" the state machine representing a certain behavior. It includes tools for loading, saving and importing the behaviors from disk, drawing and erasing the nodes and edges, and specifying their content (actions or subordinate state machines, and conditions respectively). Once the behavior is complete, it is possible to use the code generation tool to generate the source code corresponding to the behavior. This tool uses the structure of the state machine together with the information in the *game model* to generate the source file. As the game model and the source file required are usually different for each game, the code generator will also be unique for each game.

The *game model* is a configuration file that describes some details of a game or a simulation environment. Each game model is an XML file, which includes the information about sensors and actuators, and a set of descriptors. The sensors and actuators are obtained from the game API. Descriptors are the attributes used by the CBR module to describe the behaviors and retrieve them from the case base. The descriptors are obtained through the observation of the characteristics of the different behaviors that exist in the domain of the game.

Every manually designed behavior is stored and indexed and, as behaviors tend to recur, there is a CBR module that allows retrieving and reusing behaviors previously stored. We use XML files to store the cases. Each case in the case base represents a behaviour using the following components. Next section describes an example using a Soccer simulation environment.

- Attributes: descriptors that characterize different properties of the behavior. The attributes are different for each game, although similar games (e.g. games of the same genre) will share similar attribute sets. The designer specifies as many attributes as necessary in the game model.
- Description: textual description of the behavior used to fine tune the description given by attributes.
- Enclosed behaviors: specifies which behaviors are hierarchically subordinated. This allows the user to retrieve behaviors which include a specific set of sub-behaviors or actuators.

3 SoccerBots Example

As we have already mentioned, the behavior editor described in Section 2, and the CBR system that we are describing in Section 4, are independent of any specific game. However, for the sake of an easier exposition we are explaining the basic ideas using a simple game. SoccerBots[1] is a simulation environment where two teams play in a soccer match. Simulation time, behavior of robots, colours, size of field, and many other features are configured from a text file. Basically, rules are similar to those from Robocup[2][7].

The first step when using eCo to generate behaviors for the SoccerBots environment is to define the game model with the information about sensors, actuators and CBR descriptors. In the SoccerBots API we can find sensors for example to check the X, Y position of the ball, its angle and distance. Some examples of actuators (i.e. actions that robots can take) are kicking the ball, change the speed of the robot, or change the direction the robot is facing.

Attributes (or descriptors) are obtained through the observation of the characteristics of the different possible behaviors. We used four numeric descriptors to characterize SoccerBots behaviors, namely *mobility* is the ability to move all over the playfield; *attack* is the ability of the robot to play as an attacker; *defence* is the ability of the robot to play as a defender; and *goalkeeper* is the ability of the robot to cover the goal. Next section describes how to deal with these and others ways of describing behaviors in the CBR system.

---

[1] http://www.cs.cmu.edu/ trb/TeamBots/index.html
[2] http://www.robocup.org/

4   CBR for Experience Based Behaviour Design

Case Based Reasoning is specially well suited to deal with the modularity and reuse properties of the behaviors; it assists the user in the reuse of behaviors by allowing her to query a case base. Each case of the case base represents a behavior. By means of these queries, the user can make an approximate retrieval of behaviors previously edited, which will have similar characteristics. The retrieved behaviors can be reused, modified and combined to get the required behaviors.

Initially, the case base is empty, so all the editing has to be done via the manual editing (graphic) tools. Once there are enough cases in the case base, new behaviors can be constructed by retrieving and adapting the stored ones. The number of cases necessary in the case base to obtain relevant results will vary from game to game, depending on the complexity of the descriptors and the heterogeneity of the behaviors that can be constructed for that particular game. In the example of the Soccerbots environment, we began with a small case base composed of five cases, and made it grow until we obtain reasonable results for the queries. This happened with a case base of 25 cases. There are two kinds of queries: functionality based queries and structure based queries. In the former, the user provides a set of attribute-value parameters to specify the desired functionality for the retrieved behavior. In the latter, a behavior is retrieved, whose composition of nodes and edges is similar to the one specified by the query.

4.1   Functionality Based Retrieval

The most common usage of the CBR system is when the user wants to obtain a behavior similar to a query in terms of its functionality. The functionality is expressed by means of a set of parameters, which can be any (or all) of the components of the cases described at the end of Section 2.

The parameters describing the query behavior are closely related to the game model. The more differences exist between two games, the more different the associated behaviors are and, hence, the parameters used to describe them. The eCo editor provides a query form, showed in figure 2 to enter the parameters and texts describing the functionality based queries, and a graphical tool to draw structural queries (see next section).

To obtain the global similarity value between the cases and the query, the similarity of the numeric and symbolic attributes is aggregated with the similarity due to the textual description of each behavior. The user can select the most appropriate operator to combine them in the query form. Some examples of operators could be the arithmetic and the geometric mean or the maximum. Functionality queries are provided by mean of a form where the user selects attributes, and gives a textual description of the required behaviour. (S)he also selects the similarity measure used to compare the query to the cases. Descriptor based similarity is based on standard similarity measures here, like the normalized difference value for numbers. Textual similarity metrics like the vector space model [8] are used to compare textual queries with a short textual description

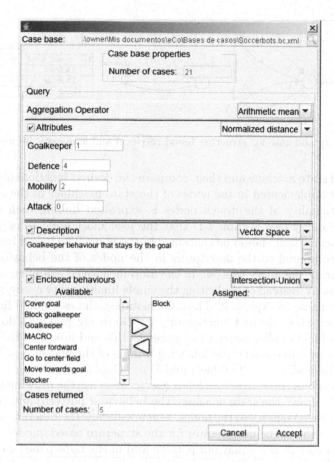

Fig. 2. Functionality based queries

included in the cases. For instance, in the previous example, the user is requesting a behavior that stays near the goal. This descriptor was not included in the game model, as it is not relevant for most of the behaviors.

4.2 Structure Based Retrieval

There are cases in which the behaviour designer knows the general structure of the state machine (i.e. the distribution of the nodes and edges and the generic functionality of them). In these cases, it would be easier and faster for the designer if he could "draw" the state machine and let the editor find a similar state machine in the case base. Finite state machines are directed graphs, so we can compare them using any of the existing techniques in the literature. Figure 3(left) shows an example of a structure based query.

Entering this data, the retrieved state machine would be similar to the query in terms of its shape, but the behaviour it implements could be any. Hence, we need to allow the behaviour designer to point out the desired functionality of

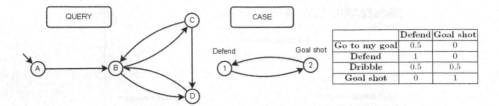

Fig. 3. Query and case for structure based retrieval and similarity between nodes

the retrieved state machine and then, compare the desired functionality with the functionality implemented in the nodes of the state machines in the case base.

The functionality of the drawn nodes is expressed linking each node to a functionality query (see Section 4.1) that the user must build to expresses the desired behaviour that should be contained in the node. The linked functionality queries are compared to the descriptors in the nodes of the behaviours in the case base during the query process. In the aforementioned example, and for the sake of simplicity, instead of expliciting the whole functionality query, we will use a descriptive name to express it. Thus, for instance, the user could link node A to a behaviour whose desired functionality is "Go to my goal". To do this (s)he must build a functionality query that expresses this and link it to the node. For the examples we will consider the following linking of the nodes: A = "Go to my goal"; B= "Defend"; C = "Dribble"; and D = "Goal shot".

Our approach to these *structure based queries* is to use the drawing facilities of the editor to "draw" the state machine (the behaviour pattern) and then assign functionality based queries to the nodes, which will show the functionality of each node. Figure 4 shows the query editor for the structure based queries. In the left pane the user can draw a behaviour pattern and in the right pane he can specify the desired functionality of the retrieved behaviour by entering a functionality query. Additionally, each node can be linked to another functionality query, as we have already mentioned, to tune up the search.

In the next section we review different techniques to calculate labelled graph similarity and how they can be applied to our specific problem.

Graph Similarity

The graph similarity problem is an issue that has been approached in several different ways in the literature. Each approach has its own advantages and disadvantages. In the following paragraphs we review some of them and explain how we adapted them to solve our current problem, the labelled graph similarity.

First approach

Bunke and Messmer's approach [9] is based in the calculation of the weighted graph edit distance, a generalization of the string edit distance [10]. They define a set of edit operations (namely, adding a node (A), deleting a node (D) and editing the label of a node (E), and adding an edge (A'), deleting an edge (D') and editing an edge(E')). Each operation has an associated cost (C_A, C_D, C_E,

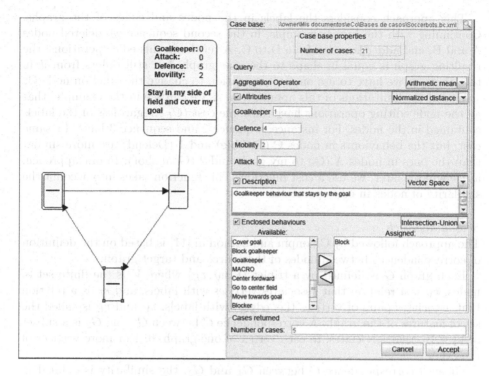

Fig. 4. Structure based query editor

etc.). Using different sets of cost values will lead us to different results. The edit distance ($dist$) is the minimum cost among all sequences of edit operations that transform the source graph into the target graph. The distance can be converted into a similarity measure by defining a function that uses the distance, like:

$$\text{sim}(G_1, G_2) = [1 + dist(G_1, G_2)]^{-1}$$

For instance, for the example in figure 3, valid sequences of edit operations are:

$$S_1 = \{D(A), D(C)\}$$
$$S_2 = \{D(A), D(B), E(C)[\text{Dribble} \rightarrow \text{Defend}], A'(D, C)\}$$
$$S_3 = \{E(A)[\text{Go to my goal} \rightarrow \text{Goal shot}], D(C), D(D), A'(B, A)\}$$

$C_1 = 2 \cdot C_D$	$C_2 = 2 \cdot C_D + C_E + C_{A'}$	$C_3 = 2 \cdot C_D + C_E + C_{A'}$

Intuitively, if C_E and $C_{A'}$ are greater than 0, the sequence S_1 has the lowest cost, and therefore, is the edit distance.

The sequence associated to the edit distance contains the operations needed to transform one graph into the other, and hence, it can be used to perform the adaptation of the retrieved behaviour later.

In the worst case, the complexity of the computation of the graph edit distance is exponential in the size of the underlying graphs, although it can be speeded up using heuristics and bound techniques.

This approach considers the labels in the nodes and edges of the graphs. Continuing with the former example, in the second sequence we deleted nodes A and B, and added an edge from D to C. After doing this edit operations, the resulting graph is equal in shape to the case graph, but still differs from it in the labels, so we have to use one edit operation to change the label on node C.

One of the limitations of this approach is, as we can see in the example, that all the node editing operations have the same cost (C_E) regardless of the labels contained in the nodes. For instance, sequence 2 and sequence 3 have the same cost, but the behaviours in nodes C (Dribble) and 1 (Defend) are more similar than the ones in nodes A (Go to my goal) and 2 (Goal shot). In our approach, as we will see later, we use a cost function. This function takes into account the similarity of nodes in edit operations.

Second approach

The approach followed by Champin and Solnon in [11] is based on the definition of correspondences between nodes of the source and target graph.

Each graph G is defined by a triplet $\langle V, r_V, r_E \rangle$ where V is the finite set of nodes, r_V is a relation that associates vertices with labels, and r_E is a relation that associates pairs of vertices (i.e. edges) with labels. r_V and r_E is called the set of features of the graph. A correspondence C between G_1 and G_2 is a subset of $V_1 \times V_2$, that associates, to each vertex of one graph, 0, 1 or more vertices of the other.

Given a correspondence C between G_1 and G_2, the similarity is defined in terms of the intersection of the sets of features (r_V and r_E) of both graphs with respect to C:

$$
\begin{aligned}
descr\,(G_1) \cap_C descr\,(G_2) = \\
\{(v,l) \in r_{V1}|\,(v,v') \in C \wedge (v',l) \in r_{V2}\} \cup \\
\{(v',l) \in r_{V2}|\,(v,v') \in C \wedge (v,l) \in r_{V1}\} \cup \\
\left\{(v_i,v_j,l) \in r_{E1}|\,(v_i,v_i') \in C \wedge (v_j,v_j') \in C \wedge (v_i',v_j',l) \in r_{E2}\right\} \cup \\
\left\{(v_i',v_j',l) \in r_{E2}|\,(v_i,v_i') \in C \wedge (v_j,v_j') \in C \wedge (v_i,v_j,l) \in r_{E1}\right\}
\end{aligned}
$$
$$(1)$$

$$
sim_C\,(G_1,G_2) = \frac{f\,(descr\,(G_1) \cap_C descr\,(G_2)) - g(splits(C))}{f\,(descr\,(G_1) \cup descr\,(G_2))}
$$

Where $splits$ is the set of vertices from $V_1 \cup V_2$ which are associated with 2 or more vertices by C. The total similarity value is the maximum similarity value of all the possible correspondences:

$$
sim\,(G_1,G_2) = \max_{C \subseteq V_1 \times V_2}\,\{sim_C\,(G_1,G_2)\}
$$

The complexity of this problem is, again, exponential in the number of vertices of the graphs being compared, but the use of heuristics and bounding functions can accelerate the search.

This approach is more sensible to the similarity of the labels in the edges. On the other hand, the possible values when comparing one label with another (whether it is a node or an edge label) can only express if they are identical or not. We need a way to compare, not only the shape of the behaviours but also their functionalities and, in the scenario we are dealing with, its uncommon to find two nodes or two edges which have exactly the same labels, so we will need some way to relax this comparison.

Third approach

The similarity measure proposed by Wang and Ishii in [12] is also based in the definition of correspondence relations between the nodes of the two graphs.

This method doesn't use the intersection, but an algebraic formula to obtain the final similarity measure. As in the previous approach, the similarity degree of two graphs G_1 and G_2 is the maximum similarity of G_1 and G_2 over all the possible correspondences:

$$\text{sim}(G_1, G_2) = \max_C \left\{ \text{sim}_C(G_1, G_2) \right\}$$

and the similarity of G_1 and G_2 over the correspondence C

$$\text{sim}_C(G_1, G_2) = \frac{F_n + F_e}{M_n + M_e}$$

$$F_n = \sum_{n \in V_1} \frac{W(n) + W(C(n))}{2} \cdot \text{sim}(n, C(n))$$

$$F_e = \sum_{e \in E_1} \frac{W(e) + W(C(e))}{2} \cdot \text{sim}(e, C(e))$$

$$M_n + M_e = \max \left(\sum_{n \in V_1} W(n), \sum_{n \in V_1} W(C(n)) \right) + \max \left(\sum_{e \in E_1} W(e), \sum_{e \in E_1} W(C(e)) \right)$$

where W is the weight of a node or an edge.

For this approach, the labels in the nodes and edges are single variables or constants, and their similarity is defined by the following functions:

- For nodes, if the value represented for the constant or variable in both nodes is the same, then the similarity is 1, and 0 in any other case.
- For edges, if the source and target nodes of the edges are related by C and the labels are equal, then the similarity is 1; if the labels are different, the similarity is 0.5 and is 0 in any other case.

In this case we can change this similarity function so we can obtain a more descriptive value. We use a functionality based similarity function (Section 4.1) to compare the descriptors of the nodes. As with the previous techniques, the complexity of this one is also exponential and its also possible to reduce the search space by the use of heuristics and bounding techniques.

Our Approach
Our approach to the similarity problem in finite state machines is based in both
the structure of the state machine and the labeling in the nodes. The labels
associated to the nodes are used to express the functionality of the behaviours
contained in them.

In our implementation we allow the user to select any of the three techniques
explained before to obtain the similarity measure in the structure based retrieval.

First approach
This approach is based in the calculation of the edit distance between two graphs.
The distance is obtained as the sum of the operations needed to transform one
graph into the other.

The cost assigned to each edit operation determines the final distance. In our
approach, we are considering the costs of edit operations, not as constants, but
as functions defined over the source and target nodes or edges. This way, we
can express the intuitive idea that changing one label for another is cheaper in
cost if the labels are more similar. For instance, the cost of the edit operation
$E(C)[\text{Dribble} \rightarrow \text{Defend}]$ is:

$$cost(E(C)[\text{Dribble} \rightarrow \text{Defend}]) = C_E \cdot (1 - \text{sim}(\text{Dribble}, \text{Defend}))$$

where Dribble and Defend are the labels of the nodes (actually, the labels are
the functional descriptors of the behaviours, but we used these descriptive names
to simplify the example) and the sim function is the similarity function used in
functionality based retrieval in Section 4.1.

We also impose the following restrictions on the possible values of the cost
functions, so the results of the distance function are reasonable:

1. $C_E \leq C_A + C_D$ and $C_{E'} \leq C_{A'} + C_{D'}$
   This means that editing the label of a node is cheaper than an addition and
   a deletion of the same node with different labels.
2. $C_A = C_D$ and $\text{sim}(X, Y) = \text{sim}(Y, X)$
   These two restrictions give symmetry to our distance measure.

For instance, to obtain the similarity between the query and the case in
Figure 3, if we use the costs $C_A, C_D, C_E, C_{A'}, C_{D'}, C_{E'} = 1$, and the sequences:

$$S_1 = \{D(A), D(C)\}$$
$$S_2 = \{D(A), D(B), E(C)[\text{Dribble} \rightarrow \text{Defend}], A'(D, C)\}$$
$$S_3 = \{E(A)[\text{Go to my goal} \rightarrow \text{Goal shot}], D(C), D(D), A'(B, A)\}$$

The distances are:

$$d_1 = 2 \cdot C_D = 2$$
$$d_2 = 2 \cdot C_D + C_E \cdot (1 - \text{sim}(\text{Dribble}, \text{Defend})) + C_{A'} = 2 + 0.5 + 1 = 3.5$$
$$d_3 = 2 \cdot C_D + C_E \cdot (1 - \text{sim}(\text{Go to my goal}, \text{Goal shot})) + C_{A'} = 2 + 1 + 1 = 4$$

As we can see, the result of d_2 is better than d_3 because the labels *Dribble*
and *Defend* are more similar than *Go to my goal* and *Goal shot*.

Second approach

This approach is based in the definition of a correspondence between the nodes of the query and the case graphs.

As has been seen in equation (1), in page 188, the intersection with respect to a correspondence C only takes into account the nodes and edges who share identical labels. In the case of finite state machines, it is convenient to consider a more relaxed similarity measure, so we can take into account the nodes that are not equal but similar. To address this problem we add a value β to each tuple in the intersection. This value represents the similarity between the labels of the nodes or edges:

$$descr\,(G_1) \cap_C descr\,(G_2) =$$
$$\{(v, v', \beta) \mid (v, v') \in C \wedge (v, l) \in r_{V1} \wedge (v', l') \in r_{V2} \wedge \beta = \text{sim}\,(l, l')\} \cup$$
$$\{((v_i, v_j), (v'_i, v'_j), \beta) \mid (v_i, v'_i) \in C \wedge (v_j, v'_j) \in C \wedge (v_i, v_j, l) \in r_{E1} \wedge$$
$$(v'_i, v'_j, l') \in r_{E2} \wedge \beta = \text{sim}\,(l, l')\}$$

$$\text{sim}_C\,(G_1, G_2) = \frac{f\,(descr\,(G_1) \cap_C descr\,(G_2)) - g(splits(C))}{F}$$

The similarity function we use is the functionality based retrieval similarity (Section 4.1).

The similarity value β is used by the function f to obtain the final similarity value, and the constant F is an upper bound of f that maintains the result in the interval $[0, 1]$. For instance, considering the example in figure 3, and the functions:

$$f(I) = \sum_{\text{for each node n in I}} (f_N(n)) + \sum_{\text{for each edge e in I}} (f_E(e))$$
$$f_N((v, v', \beta)) - \beta$$
$$f_E(((v_i, v_j), (v'_i, v'_j), \beta)) = \beta$$
$$g(S) = |S|$$
$$F = \max\{|r_{V1}|, |r_{V2}|\} + \max\{|r_{E1}|, |r_{E2}|\} = 4 + 6 = 10$$

we can have the following similarity values:

– for $C = \{(A, 1), (B, 1), (C, 2), (D, 2)\}$:

$$descr\,(G_1) \cap_C descr\,(G_2) = \{(A, 1, 0.5), (B, 1, 1), (C, 2, 0.5), (D, 2, 1),$$
$$((B, C), (1, 2), 1), ((B, D), (1, 2), 1),$$
$$((C, B), (2, 1), 1), ((D, B), (2, 1), 1)\}$$
$$splits(C) = \{(1, \{A, B\}), (2, \{C, D\})\}$$
$$\text{sim}_C(G_1, G_2) = \frac{(3 + 4) - 2}{10} = 0.5$$

- for $C = \{(A,1),(B,\emptyset),(C,1),(D,2)\}$:

$$descr(G_1) \cap_C descr(G_2) = \{(A,1,0.5),(C,1,0.5),(D,2,1),((C,D),(1,2),1)\}$$
$$splits(C) = \{(1,\{A,C\})\}$$
$$sim_C(G_1,G_2) = \frac{(2+1)-1}{10} = 0.2$$

To simplify this approach, we can consider only the nodes and edges whose β is greater than a certain threshold.

Third approach
The third approach is also based in defining the possible correspondences between the graphs being compared. In this case, the calculation includes the comparison of the similarity of labels. To adapt it to our scenario we use the functionality based retrieval similarity function, instead of the one proposed.

As a first approach we give all the nodes and edges the same weight (1). The resulting similarity measure is:

$$sim_C(G_1,G_2) = \frac{F_n + F_e}{M_n + M_e}$$
$$F_n + F_e = \sum_{n \in N_1} sim(n, C(n)) + \sum_{e \in E_1} sim(e, C(e))$$
$$M_n + M_e = |N_1| + |E_1|$$

For the example in figure 3 we can have the following results:

- for $C = \{(A,1),(B,1),(C,2),(D,2)\}$:

$$sim_C(G_1,G_2) = \frac{(0.5+1+0.5+1)+(1+1+1+1)}{4+6} = 0.8$$

- for $C = \{(A,1),(B,2),(C,1),(D,2)\}$:

$$sim_C(G_1,G_2) = \frac{(0.5+0+0.5+1)+(1+1+1+1)}{4+6} = 0.6$$

5   Related Work

There exist several tools oriented towards the edition of finite state machines. Most of them are general purpose state machine editors (like Qfsm or FSME), which allow a more or less elastic definition of the inputs and outputs (the sensors and actuators) and the generation of the source code corresponding to the state machine in one or more common languages like C++ or Python. Most of them don't allow the use of HFSMs, nor facilitates the use of CBR or some other tool to favour reusing the state machines.

Regarding game editors, most of them are only applicable to one game or, at the most, to the games implemented by one game engine (as is the case of the Valve Hammer Editor). Besides, the vast majority only allow map edition. The few that allow editing the entity behaviors are usually script based, like the Aurora Toolset for Neverwinter Nights.

Finally, there exist some tools like BrainFrame and, its later version, Simbionic, which are game oriented finite state machine editors. These editors allow the specification of the set of sensors and actuators for the game and the edition of HFSMs using that specification. The HFSMs generated by the editor are interpreted by a runtime engine that must be integrated with the game. Currently, there exist a C++ and a Java version of the runtime engine. There are two crucial differences between our approach and the approach used in Simbionic. First of all, the Simbionic editor doesn't offer any assistance for reusing the behaviors, like the CBR approximate search engine integrated into the eCo editor. And second, to integrate a behavior edited with the Simbionic editor with a game, it is mandatory to integrate the Simbionic runtime engine with the game. On the other hand, eCo offers capabilities to implement code generator to automatically generate the source for behaviors in any language.

6   Conclusions and Future Work

In this paper we have described an ongoing work using CBR to design intelligent behaviors in videogames. We have developed a graphical editor based on HFSM that includes a CBR module to retrieve and reuse stored behaviors.

One of the main advantages of our approach is that the editor and the CBR module are generic and reusable for different games. We have shown the applicability in a soccer simulator environment (SoccerBots) to control the behavior of the players. As part of the testing stage and to check the editor applicability we have proposed the integration of the eCo editor with other games with very different nature: SoccerBots is a sports simulator, Neverwinter Nights is a role playing computer game, JV^{2}M [13] is an action game and AIBO is a real life multipurpose robot) and with different integrating characteristics. For instance, while in JV^{2}M we define the set of sensors and actuators, it is fixed for the other environments; while Neverwinter Nights is highly event-oriented, the rest of the environments are basically reactive systems.

In this paper we have described the current state of the work but there are many open lines of work. We have finished the graphical editor, defined the structure of the cases and the game models, and we have been working on case representation, storage and similarity based retrieval. Current lines of work are automatic reuse of behaviors and learning.

Regarding structure based similarity, in this paper we have proposed three different approaches to compare finite state machines. Our next step is testing them to determine which is the most suitable approach and for what kind of cases.

The use of HFSM offers many possibilities to reuse and combine pieces of behaviors within other more complex behaviors. We are also working on the definition of an ontology about different games genres to be able to reuse behaviors, vocabulary and sets of sensors and actuators between different games of the same genre. This way we can promote the reuse of behaviors, even among different games, while making easier the use of the editor, since the user doesn't need to learn the characteristics of the game model for each game.

There exist numerous techniques, besides HFSMs, to represent behaviors, like decision trees, rule based systems, GOAP or Hierarchical Task Networks, for instance. One of the opened investigation lines is the study of the pros and cons of each one of them and the possibility of combining some of them to create the behaviors.

References

1. Bowling, M., Fürnkranz, J., Graepel, T., Musick, R.: Machine learning and games. Machine learning 63, 211–215 (2006)
2. Flórez Puga, G., Díaz-Agudo, B.: Semiautomatic edition of behaviours in videogames. In: Proceedings of AI 2007, 12th UK Workshop on Case-Based Reasoning (2007)
3. Girault, A., Lee, B., Lee, E.: Hierarchical finite state machines with multiple concurrency models. IEEE Transactions on Computer-Aided Design 18, 742–760 (1999); Research report UCB/ERL M97/57
4. Champandard, A.J.: AI Game Development - Synthetic Creatures with Learning and Reactive Behaviors. New Riders Games (2003)
5. Brownlee, J.: (Finite state machines (fsm)) (accessed March 14, 2008), http://ai-depot.com/FiniteStateMachines/FSM.html
6. Fu, D., Houlette, R.: Putting ai in entertainment: An ai authoring tool for simulation and games. IEEE Intelligent Systems 17, 81–84 (2002)
7. Kitano, H., Asada, M., Kuniyoshi, Y., Noda, I., Osawa, E.: RoboCup: The robot world cup initiative. In: Johnson, W.L., Hayes-Roth, B. (eds.) Proceedings of the First International Conference on Autonomous Agents (Agents 1997), pp. 340–347. ACM Press, New York (1997)
8. Manning, C.D., Raghavan, P., Schütze, H.: Introduction to Information Retrieval. Cambridge University Press, Cambridge (to appear, 2007)
9. Bunke, H., Messmer, B.T.: Similarity measures for structured representations. In: Wess, S., Richter, M., Althoff, K.-D. (eds.) EWCBR 1993. LNCS, vol. 837, pp. 106–118. Springer, Heidelberg (1994)
10. Wagner, R.A., Fischer, M.J.: The string-to-string correction problem. J. ACM 21, 168–173 (1974)
11. Champin, P.A., Solnon, C.: Measuring the similarity of labeled graphs. In: Ashley, K.D., Bridge, D.G. (eds.) ICCBR 2003. LNCS, vol. 2689, pp. 80–95. Springer, Heidelberg (2003)
12. Wang, Y., Ishii, N.: A method of similarity metrics for structured representations. Expert Systems with Applications 12, 89–100 (1997)
13. Gómez-Martín, P.P., Gómez-Martín, M.A., González-Calero, P.A.: Javy: Virtual Environment for Case-Based Teaching of Java Virtual Machine. In: Palade, V., Howlett, R.J., Jain, L. (eds.) KES 2003. LNCS, vol. 2773, pp. 906–913. Springer, Heidelberg (2003)

Considerations for Real-Time Spatially-Aware Case-Based Reasoning: A Case Study in Robotic Soccer Imitation

Michael W. Floyd, Alan Davoust, and Babak Esfandiari

Department of Systems and Computer Engineering
Carleton University
1125 Colonel By Drive
Ottawa, Ontario

Abstract. Case-base reasoning in a real-time context requires the system to output the solution to a given problem in a predictable and usually very fast time frame. As the number of cases that can be processed is limited by the real-time constraint, we explore ways of selecting the most important cases and ways of speeding up case comparisons by optimizing the representation of each case. We focus on spatially-aware systems such as mobile robotic applications and the particular challenges in representing the systems' spatial environment. We select and combine techniques for feature selection, clustering and prototyping that are applicable in this particular context and report results from a case study with a simulated RoboCup soccer-playing agent. Our results demonstrate that pre-processing such case bases can significantly improve the imitative ability of an agent.

1 Introduction

When using a case-based reasoning (CBR) system, the performance of the system is highly dependant on the quality of the case base that is used [1]. One aspect of case base quality is how well the cases in the case base represent the set of possible problems that the CBR system might encounter. If the case base contains too few cases (or cases that are highly similar to each other) then the case base might not adequately cover the problem space leading to a decrease in performance. One reason, which we will focus on in this paper, for a case base being a less than ideal size is if the CBR system must operate under a real-time constraint. Since the CBR system must search the case base in order to determine the solution to a problem, a larger case base will likely lead to a longer search time.

One specific area where CBR can be applied in a real-time setting is in the imitation of spatially-aware autonomous agents. These agents are able to identify objects that are visible to them in their environment and perform actions based on the configuration of those objects. Unless the agent has a complete world view, it is generally only able to see a subset of objects at any given time. In

K.-D. Althoff et al. (Eds.): ECCBR 2008, LNAI 5239, pp. 195–209, 2008.

addition to being able to only view a subset of the objects in the environment at a given time, the agent may also not know the total number of objects that exist in the environment.

When an agent is fully aware of each unique object in the environment and is able to differentiate between similar objects (for example, the agent can differentiate between two humans and does not just classify them both as *human*) then there would exist a *type* for each of the unique objects. However, if the agent is unable to differentiate between similar objects then multiple objects would belong to a single *type* and the objects of a similar type could be considered interchangeable.

The RoboCup Simulation League [2] is a realistic benchmark for examining the type of agents we described. RoboCup agents must deal with temporal events as well as with an environment consisting of a 2-D space (the soccer field) with objects and other agents within that space. The agent does not know its exact position on the field but must estimate it using the location of the objects that are visible to it. During each time period in a game, the server provides clients with world view and state information (subject to a noise model) using one of see, hear, or sense_body messages. Objects described in see messages may be players, the ball, goal nets, or the numerous lines and flags located on the field. Due to noise associated with *seeing* objects, a RoboCup agent often does not possess enough information to properly differentiate similar objects (for example, it may only be able to tell that it can see a player, though not which player it sees). The RoboCup Simulation league provides a suitable testbed to examine the methods described in this paper due to the real-time constraints and the difficulty in differentiating similar objects.

In the remainder of this paper we will examine several techniques (feature selection, clustering and prototyping) that can be used to increase the number of cases that can be examined within a real-time limit as well as methods of improving the diversity of cases contained in a fixed sized case base. It should be noted that assume that the case bases do not use any method of fast-indexing, although we feel that our techniques could be used as a complement to fast-indexing. Initially, in Section 2 we describe the case study we will perform to demonstrate the techniques presented in later sections of the paper. Section 3 will look at methods for representing a case and selecting the most useful features in a case to use will be covered in Section 4. The creation of prototype cases will be covered in Section 5. Related work will be examined in Section 6 followed by conclusions in Section 7.

2   Case Study: RoboCup Simulation League

Our case study involves a case-based reasoning system that is used to imitate the behaviour of a RoboCup [2] soccer player. Cases for this system are generated, in an automated manner, by observing the RoboCup player that will be imitated and logging the inputs to the player and the player's outputs [3,4]. Each case is comprised of the inputs to the player (what objects the player can see) as well as the outputs (actions the player performs) of the player in response to those inputs. The imitative CBR agent then uses those cases in an attempt to select appropriate actions based on what it can currently see (what objects are in its field of vision). The goal of such a system is to produce behaviour that is indistinguishable from the behaviour of the RoboCup player it is imitating.

In the RoboCup Simulation League, the environment contains objects that belong to a fixed number of *object types*. Although each individual object on the field in unique, the agent is often unable to distinguish between objects of the same type due to noise. For example, the agent would be able to see a teammate but might not be able to tell what specific teammate it is. For this reason, objects of the same type are treated as interchangeable. In the RoboCup Simulation League we define the following object types:

$$Type = \{Ball, Goalnet, Flag, Line, Teammate, Opponent, Unknownplayer\}$$

Each player may only perform an action once per discrete time interval, called a cycle. If the player does not perform an action each cycle then it will be at a disadvantage compared to other players who act more often. The entire process (Figure 1) of identifying what objects are currently visible to the agent, using CBR to select the appropriate actions to perform and performing those actions should then be completed within a cycle (of length 100ms). Also, given that the CBR process is not the only task the agent needs to complete within each cycle, we will set our time limit for performing CBR to half of the cycle (50ms).

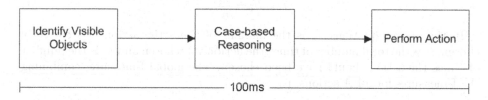

Fig. 1. The activities the agent must perform in one 100ms cycle

2.1   Metrics

The effectiveness of each approach will be measured using a combination of two criteria: how much time it takes to perform the case-based reasoning process and how well the agent performs imitation.

The time it takes to perform the CBR process will be measured as the time it takes from when the CBR system is given a problem (the objects an agent can currently see) to when it provides a solution (the action to perform). As was mentioned previously, we want this time to be as close to our imposed time limit of 50ms as possible. If the time is lower than 50ms we could add more cases to our case base, or if the time is greater than 50ms we would need to remove cases from the case base. Either adding or removing cases may have an impact of how well the imitative agent performs, so we also require a metric of agent performance.

If it takes an amount of time, T, to perform CBR using a case base of size N, then we can estimate the number of cases, N_{max}, that can be used within our real-time limit, T_{max}, as:

$$N_{max} \approx \frac{T_{max} * N}{T} \tag{1}$$

A simple measure of agent performance would be to measure the classification accuracy of the CBR system when performing a validation process. Each case in a testing set will be used as input to the CBR system and the output of the CBR system, the predicted action, will be compared to that case's known action. This provides a measure of the number of test cases that are classified correctly. However it can be misleading when the testing data contains a disproportional number of cases of a certain class. For example, in RoboCup soccer a player tends to *dash* considerably more often than it *kicks* or *turns*. A CBR system that simply selected the dominant class (dash) could gain a high classification accuracy while completely ignoring the other classes.

Instead, we use the *f-measure*. We define the f-measure, F, for a single action, i, as:

$$F_i = \frac{2 * precision_i * recall_i}{precision_i + recall_i} \tag{2}$$

with

$$precision_i = \frac{c_i}{t_i} \tag{3}$$

and

$$recall_i = \frac{c_i}{n_i} \tag{4}$$

In the above equations, c_i is the number of times the action was correctly chosen, t_i is the total number of times the action was chosen and n_i is the number of times the action should have been chosen. The global f-measure, combining the f-measures for all A actions, is:

$$F_{global} = \frac{1}{A} \sum_{i=1}^{A} F_i. \tag{5}$$

3   Case Representation and Comparison

As we focus on spatially-aware agents, an important issue is that of representing the agent's environment. Assuming a previous step in the considered system extracts symbolic information from a robot's sensor data, the "raw" information is a list of recognized objects with spatial coordinates, for example in polar coordinates with respect to the agent, as in the RoboCup context.

The standard inputs of most machine learning systems are *feature vectors*, and in most CBR publications (particularly in the RoboCup context) researchers have manually defined vectors from their input data, selecting features according to their expertise in the application domain. For soccer simulation, the feature vectors comprised such heterogeneous features as the distance from the ball to the net, the current score, counts of players in particular zones, etc. In previous work on this project [3,4,5] we have adopted an orthogonal approach, exploring techniques to manipulate the raw data received from the feature extraction step, minimizing application-specific bias and human intervention.

3.1   Raw Data Representation

The first representation that we consider here is a simple list representation of the visible objects with their exact coordinates. The main problem with this representation is that is does not form an ordered set of features of a fixed length. At a given time the agent only has a partial view of the world, and cannot necessarily differentiate objects of a given symbolic category. For example, a mobile robot navigating a city could label the objects surrounding it as cars, people, or buildings, but probably not identify each one according to some complete reference of all possible cars, people, or buildings.

Comparing two cases represented by such "bags of objects" involves comparing the sets of objects present in the scenes, matching as many objects from one set to objects of the other set, and secondly evaluating the actual physical distance in between matched objects. As permutations need to be considered, the cost of object-matching algorithms is very high, as reported by Lam et al. [4] and Karol et al.[6] in separate work. Objects of one scene which cannot be matched to an object of the other must also be accounted for, for example by a penalty added to the distance value.

3.2   Histogram Representation

In [5] we presented an alternative approach that creates a vector using all the spatial data without the bias of manual feature selection. Our approach takes inspiration from *grid occupancy maps* [7] used in mobile robotics, a technique where sections of the environment are assigned probabilistic indications that they contain obstacles. Such a representation aims to project all the available information (e.g. from a sonar) on a feature map that represents the entire known environment. Our representation is based on histograms of objects over a partition of the visible space, and transforms a list of objects into an image-like representation with customizable granularity.

As a feature vector, this representation supports practical similarity metrics and opens the door for the application of other machine learning techniques while avoiding the need of *a priori* manual feature selection. Distance and similarity metrics that we have experimented with include Euclidean distance and a similarity metric based on the Jaccard Coefficient, which has proved to give better results in our experiments (see [5]).

3.3   Fuzzy Histograms

Discretizing the visible space into intervals, although efficient in our practical experiments, has some drawbacks. Objects that are near the boundaries can be artificially separated into two different sections, whereas two relatively distant objects, at opposite ends of a section, would be lumped together. In fact, since we are removing the information of the exact coordinates of the objects, some cases which were only slightly different can now have the exact same representation. If these cases were associated to the same *solution* then it can be a way of removing redundant cases, but if the cases were associated to different solutions then the indistinguishability of the two cases becomes a problem.

In order to address these problems we can introduce fuzzy logic to the discretization. Fuzzy logic allows for the smooth spreading of the count of objects over neighbouring segments according to the actual position of the objects, and thus limits boundary effects. For fuzzy histograms, we can use the same distance or similarity metrics as for *crisp* (non-fuzzy) histograms.

3.4   Empirical Comparison

The case representation schemes we have described store the case features and calculate distance between cases in different manners. As such, we can expect the execution time of a CBR system to be different depending on which representation scheme we use. The goal of these experiments is to find out how large the case base can be for each representation (while still meeting our imposed 50ms time limit) and how well the CBR system performs when using a case base of that size.

The experiments will use the following parameters:

- The player we will attempt to imitate is Krislet [8]. Krislet uses simple decision-tree logic to express its behaviour, namely that the agent will always search for the ball, attempt to run towards it, and then attempt to kick it toward the goal. Although it may seem that simply inducing decision-trees from our data would be an obvious solution to imitate this agent, our preliminary studies found that this required more human intervention and performed less accurately than a case-based reasoning approach.
- All features will be given an equal weighting.
- The CBR system will use a 1-nearest neighbour algorithm.
- All case representations will work on identical datasets (although they will represent the data sets differently).
- The histogram approaches will discretize the data into a 5x8 grid.
- The histogram approaches use the Jaccard Coefficient similarity measure.

Case bases of varying sizes were used in order to determine the maximum number of cases that could be used within a 50ms timeframe. We can see that the histogram approaches can utilize far more cases, nearly 5 times more, that the raw data representation (Table 1). Also, the histogram approaches achieve higher f-measure scores in all categories except for *kicking*, with the crisp approach slightly outperforming the fuzzy approach.

Table 1. Comparison of case representation

	Max. cases	$f1_{global}$	$f1_{kick}$	$f1_{dash}$	$f1_{turn}$
Raw	3012	0.43	0.17	0.70	0.41
Crisp histogram	14922	0.51	0.12	0.84	0.57
Fuzzy histogram	14922	0.50	0.12	0.82	0.56

4   Feature Selection

The comparison between cases, usually a similarity or dissimilarity measure, occurs quite often in a single CBR cycle and can represent a majority of the computational time required by the CBR system. If the comparison between cases is a function of the features contained in the cases, such that the computation time of the comparison is proportional to the number of features, then removing unnecessary or redundant features can reduce the computational time required.

Wrapper algorithms [9] are a type of feature selection algorithm that search for an optimal feature weighting by evaluating the weightings when using them in a target algorithm (in our case, a CBR algorithm). This is in contrast to a *filter* algorithm [10] that selects features without using the target algorithm. Wrapper algorithms are often favoured because they directly use the algorithm that will use the feature weights, although they do have a higher computational cost.

The downside of existing wrapper algorithms, when taking into account the real-time concerns, is that they select the features that will optimize the performance of a given algorithm when using a fixed-sized training sample. One should note though that performing feature selection on a fixed-sized training sample will produce an optimum feature weighting for that training sample and will not take into account that every feature removed will result in more cases that can be evaluated. For example, the removal of a feature might not improve the performance of the target algorithm using a fixed-sized training set but the performance might be increased if that feature was removed so that more cases could be added to the training set (potentially improving the diversity of the training set).

Given the total time to solve a problem case using a CBR system, t_{tot}, when the CBR system uses a case base of size N, then the average execution time cost per case, t_{case}, is:

$$t_{case} = \frac{t_{tot}}{N} \tag{6}$$

And if the each case is composed of i types of features, then the average execution time cost per feature type, t_{feat}, is:

$$t_{feat} = \frac{t_{case}}{i} \tag{7}$$

It should be noted that this assumes that each type of feature has an equal execution cost. If this is not the situation, each feature type can have a different cost value. We can then apply the following algorithm to complement the use of any existing wrapper feature selection algorithm:

Algorithm 1. Dynamic Training Set Feature Selection

Inputs: WrapperAlgorithm, allCases, timeLimit, CBRAlgorithm
Outputs: optimum weights

```
DTSFS(WrapperAlgorithm, allCases, timeLimit, CBRAlgorithm)
    while(!WrapperAlgorithm.optimumWeightsFound()):
        weights = WrapperAlgorithm.nextWeightsToTest()
        caseCost = 0
        for(each non-zero weight in weights)
            caseCost += execution time cost of the feature being weighed
        end loop
        estimatedSize = timeLimit/caseCost
        trainingCaseBase = randomly select 'estimatedSize' cases from allCases
        CBRAlgorithm.setWeights(weights)
        CBRAlgorithm.setTrainingData(trainingCaseBase)
        performance = CBRAlgorithm.evaluatePerformance()
        WrapperAlgorithm.returnEvaluation(performance)
    end loop
    return WrapperAlgorithm.optimumWeights()
end
```

This algorithm dynamically changes the size of the training data used by a wrapper feature selection algorithm based on the estimated computational cost of the feature set that is currently being evaluated by the CBR system.

4.1   Experimental Results

This round of experiments looks to demonstrate the benefit of using the feature selection algorithm discussed in the previous section (Algorithm 1). For these experiments we will use a simple wrapper feature selection algorithm, a backward sequential selection (BSS) algorithm [11], as an input to Algorithm 1. We make a slight variation to this algorithm in that it does not directly evaluate weights using the CBR algorithm. Instead, it makes the current weights it wants to test available (as in the *nextWeightsToTest()* method in Algorithm 1) and waits to receive the performance of those weights (as in the *returnEvaluation(performance)* method in Algorithm 1). This wrapper algorithm requires two parameters. The first parameter is the minimum percentage a feature set must improve over the current best feature set in order to become the new best feature set. The second parameter is the number of feature sets we examine, without finding a new best feature set, before the algorithm terminates. For our experiments we will use a 0.01% minimum increase and up to 5 non-improving feature sets.

When the BSS wrapper algorithm is used to perform feature selection, with all three case representation schemes that were used in Section 3 (using the same parameters as those experiments), we find that all three schemes find the same set of features (ball and teammate) produce the largest performance improvement (Table 2). For all case representations we see noticeable increases in f-measure values by using this subset of object types instead of using all object types. Case base sizes were selected based on the experiments in Section 3 so that when using all of the features the CBR process would take approximately 50ms. We see that the feature selection algorithm found a set of features that did not contain all of the features. By removing the features that the feature selection algorithm did not select (and removing their computational cost) the CBR system will then be able to process more cases within the 50ms time limit. Does it then make sense to perform feature selection using a training case base of a fixed size if that fixed size is chosen in order to ensure the real-time constraint *when using all of the features*?

In fact, each feature set will allow for a different maximum case base size depending on the number of features that are included. If we use the same BSS wrapper algorithm as an input to Algorithm 1 we can see that it may be more beneficial to remove a feature, and as a byproduct allow for a larger case base size, then to keep the feature (Table 3). Using a fixed sized training case base, we found *ball* and *teammate* to be the features that should be included. However, using a dynamic sized training case base we find that only the *ball* should be included. The performance using a larger case base size, by removing the *teammate* feature, was larger than the performance of using a smaller case base size and including the *teammate* feature. It should be noted that the same can not be said about removing the *ball* feature and only keeping the *teammate* feature, as that actually caused a performance decrease.

5   Case Selection through Case-Base Clustering and Prototyping

The next method for improving case base diversity that we examine, in this section, is prototyping. Prototyping involves replacing a set of cases with a single case (a prototype case) that is representative of the entire set. In order for any type of prototyping to occur, the case base can first be divided into a number of smaller groups. Each of these clusters must contain similar cases so that the prototyping process can successfully produce a case that represents the entire cluster. Ideally, the cases within a specific cluster will be nearly identical to each other, so that the prototypical case would be highly similar to all cases in the grouping. However, if the cases in a grouping are highly dissimilar then the prototypical case will be a less precise representation of the cluster.

Many clustering algorithms work on the assumption that the distance metric, used to calculate the distance between two data points, follows the triangle inequality [12]. While we can make this assumption for the histogram distance calculation and data representation in Section 3.2, the same can not be said for

Table 2. Feature Selection Using Fixed Training Case Base

	Num. cases	Features	fl_{global}	fl_{kick}	fl_{dash}	fl_{turn}
Raw	3012	{ball,teammate}	0.52	0.30	0.79	0.47
Crisp histogram	14922	{ball,teammate}	0.57	0.25	0.87	0.60
Fuzzy histogram	14922	{ball,teammate}	0.55	0.26	0.82	0.58

Table 3. Feature Selection With Dynamic-sized Training Case Base

	Max. cases	Features	fl_{global}	fl_{kick}	fl_{dash}	fl_{turn}
Raw	21084	{ball}	0.60	0.42	0.84	0.55
Crisp histogram	104454	{ball}	0.61	0.30	0.90	0.64
Fuzzy histogram	104454	{ball}	0.60	0.30	0.88	0.62

the raw data representation and associated distance calculation (Section 3.1). This is due to the fact that each case can contain a different number of known values for features and features can be indistinguishable from each other. The way in which indistinguishable features are "matched" between cases [3] can lead to such a situation. For example, consider three cases A, B and C which contain features a, b and c respectively. We might find a situation where a and b are matched when comparing A and B, a and c are matched when comparing A and C but b and c are *not* matched when comparing B and C. This situation can lead to the triangle inequality not holding true. One type of clustering algorithm that could work on such data would be non-parametric clustering algorithms [13,14].

For the histogram representations we use a k-means clustering algorithm [15] to cluster the data. However, due to the distance calculation used by the raw data representation the k-means algorithm (along with a substantial number of other clustering algorithms) can not directly be applied due to the fact that each case contains a different number of known values for features. The data must first be transformed by converting it to a distance vector [13]. The distance vector for a case contains the distance between that case and each case in the case base. So if the case base contains N cases, then each case will be represented by a distance vector of size N. After this transformation is performed we can then apply the k-means algorithm to the distance vectors.

Assuming we can adequately cluster our case data, we will now examine two possible methods to create prototypical cases from the clustered data.

5.1 Using a Cluster Member

The simplest method for creating a prototypical case from a cluster of cases is to simply use a single case from the cluster, a cluster member, as the prototypical case and discard the remaining members of the cluster. This method is useful because it does not require creating a new case, but instead it reuses an existing case. By avoiding the creation of a new case the case base is guaranteed to be composed entirely of acquired cases.

For a cluster with n cases in it and containing the cases $\{C_i, \ldots, C_n\}$, we locate the prototypical case as:

$$C_{prot} = \arg \min_{C_i = C_1}^{C_n} \sum_{j=1}^{n} d(C_i, C_j) \tag{8}$$

This will find the case that is the minimum distance (where the distance between two cases is $d(C_i, C_j)$) from all other cases in the cluster. Likewise, we could modify the equation to find the maximum value when calculation a similarity between the cases.

5.2   Creating an Average Case

The second method of creating a prototypical case from a cluster of cases is to create an "average case". This entails determining an average position that spatial objects will be located when examining all cases in the cluster. Compared to the first method, this method constructs a novel case and does not reuse an existing case. The process of creating an average case when all cases have a fixed number of features is quite simple (the average case will contain the average value of each feature). The averaging process becomes more difficult in situations where cases can have different numbers of features. For example, with the raw data representation (Section 3.1) the issue of matching features between a pair of cases becomes substantially more difficult when matching between a set (cluster) of cases. To deal with the differing numbers of features we propose Algorithm 2.

This algorithm uses a case in the cluster that is central to the other cases (using Equation 8) and performs a pair-wise matching between that case and each of the other cases in the cluster. The resulting prototype will have the same number of features as the cental case and the feature values will be highly dependant on how the other cases matched to the central case. This means changing the case used as the cental case can result in different prototype cases being produced.

5.3   Experimental Results

In this section of experiments we demonstrate the results of applying the prototyping methods that we have described previously. For these experiments we will use the same parameters that we used in Section 3 and we will use the results from that section (the maximum-sized case base that can be searched in 50ms) as the benchmark.

Initially, each of the case bases (one for each case representation scheme) must be clustered. As was mention previously in this section, we will use the k-means clustering algorithm. The k-means algorithm requires a parameter, the *k-value*, to specify how many clusters the data will be partitioned into. For

---

Algorithm 2. Spatial Cluster-Average Prototype
Inputs: cluster of cases
Outputs: prototypical case

```
SCAP(cluster)
    remove the case, C, that is closest to all other cases
    for(each feature f in C):
        create an empty list and add the feature to that list
    end loop
    while(more cases exist in cluster):
        remove the next case in the cluster, N
        for(each feature in C):
            match the feature with a feature in N
            add the feature value from N to the list for this feature
        end loop
    end loop
    create a prototypical case, P, that contains no objects
    for(each feature in C):
        compute the average location of all features in the feature list
        add a feature with the average location to P
    end loop
    return P
end
```

---

each representation this value was found experimentally by finding the smallest k-value such that the resulting clusters were still homogeneous. A cluster is homogeneous if each case in the cluster has the same solution (the same action in the RoboCup domain).

With the resulting clusters we then applied the prototyping methods described in Section 5.1 and Section 5.2. Both prototyping methods resulted in the same decrease in number of cases and decreased execution time, since they used the same data partitioned into the same number of clusters. The difference between prototyping using a cluster member and prototyping using an average case (Table 4) can be seen in their influence on performance. While both methods result in a slight decrease in the f-measure, a tradeoff for the decrease in execution time, we see that the f-measure decreases less when prototyping using an average cluster.

Although we have focused exclusively on prototyping a case base that can already be searched within our real-time limit of 50ms, in order to compare with benchmarks set in previous experiments, the real benefit of such an approach is to compress a larger case base to fit within the time limit. Given that k-means allows the number of clusters produced to be specified, the case base can be partitioned into a number of clusters equal to the maximum allowable case base size. Each cluster can then be used to create a prototype case and the resulting case base will be exactly the maximum allowable size. The only limiting factor is that the more a case base is compressed the larger the potential performance decrease that will occur.

Table 4. Prototyping using cluster member and average case

	Initial cases	Final cases	Initial execution time	Final execution time	Initial $f1_{global}$	Member Final $f1_{global}$	Ave. Final $f1_{global}$
Raw	3012	2642	50ms	44ms	0.43	0.41	0.42
Crisp	14922	12335	50ms	41ms	0.51	0.47	0.49
Fuzzy	14922	11642	50ms	39ms	0.50	0.47	0.49

6 Related Work

In our previous work [4,3,5] we have exclusively looked at the application of CBR to the topic of agent imitation and the various algorithms and data representations used to facilitate that process. In that work we made no attempt at preprocessing the case base in order to improve search time and case base diversity.

Using CBR in the domain of RoboCup has been explored numerous times before, including the simulation [16,17,18], small-sized robot [19] and four-legged robot [20,6] leagues. These CBR systems are often given a complete worldview [17,18,19,6] or an artificially increased world-view (from opponents that communicate their location [20]) which may not be attainable in many real-world domains. The features contained in a case are selected by a human expert [16,17,18,19,20,6] and the cases are often authored [19,20] or filtered [16] by a human expert. The main difference between our approach and these works is that we use automatically generated cases, by observing another agent, that contain all objects the agent can see, thus reducing bias by avoiding feature selection by a human expert.

The topic of feature selection and feature weighting has been covered extensively in case based reasoning research. This work ranges from comparisons of various feature weighting methods [21] to applications of feature weighting [22]. While substantial work exists in the field of CBR, to our knowledge ours is the first to address the feature selection needs of a real-time agent. Similarly, prototyping and generalization have previously been examined and applied in CBR [23] but the way in which a spatial-aware agent represents a case complicates the prototyping processes and requires special consideration. Lastly, while it may appear that we ignored topics related to case base structure [24] and fast-indexing techniques, we feel that our techniques compliment such work and should be used in combination with, rather than as an alternative to them.

7 Conclusions

Throughout our case study we have experimented using three different methods of case representation. Our results have generally shown the histogram representations to significantly outperform the raw representation (using a t-test with p=0.01) and the crisp histogram outperformed the fuzzy version (p=0.05). There are two notable exceptions. Throughout we have found that the raw representation achieves higher f-measure values related to the action of kicking (p=0.01). This is likely because the artificial cell boundaries created by the histogram approach. Secondly, we find that the fuzzy histogram representation achieves better reduction in size while having no significant difference in f-measure score compared to the crisp histogram. This is because the fuzzy histogram approach produces fewer cases that have the same representation but different actions, since the fuzziness better encodes the exact position of features.

We have demonstrated throughout this paper that applying preprocessing techniques to a case base can increase the performance of a CBR system by allowing it to consider more cases within a real-time limit or increasing the diversity of the case base. We examined modifying the distance calculation used (as a byproduct of changing the case representation), selecting a feature set that optimize performance and clustering similar cases so that they may be used to generate a prototypical case. While we have shown these techniques to be successful in the domain of RoboCup soccer, and more specifically the imitation of soccer playing agents, they are applicable to any situation where a CBR system uses spatial data with real-time concerns.

Although the f-measure values attained may seem low (0.5 - 0.6 range), successful agent imitation can be observed when watching the imitative agent play a game of soccer. This study focused on data from a single agent (due to space limitations) but further analysis for agents of different complexity, data sets, source code and game videos can be found at http://rcscene.sf.net.

References

1. Smyth, B.: Case-base maintenance. In: Proceedings of the Eleventh International Conference on Industrial and Engineering Applications of Artificial Intelligence and Expert Systems (1998)
2. RoboCup: Robocup online (2008), http://www.robocup.org
3. Floyd, M.W., Esfandiari, B., Lam, K.: A case-based approach to imitating robocup players. In: Twenty-First International FLAIRS Conference, pp. 251–256 (2008)
4. Lam, K., Esfandiari, B., Tudino, D.: A scene-based imitation framework for robocup clients. In: Proceedings of the Workshop MOO at AAMAS 2006 (2006)
5. Davoust, A., Floyd, M.W., Esfandiari, B.: Use of fuzzy histograms to model the spatial distribution of objects in case-based reasoning. In: Bergler, S. (ed.) Canadian Conference on AI, pp. 72–83. Springer, Heidelberg (2008)
6. Karol, A., Nebel, B., Stanton, C., Williams, M.A.: Case based game play in the robocup four-legged league part i the theoretical model. In: RoboCup (2003)
7. Moravec, H., Elfes, A.E.: High resolution maps from wide angle sonar. In: Proceedings of the 1985 IEEE International Conference on Robotics and Automation, pp. 116–121 (1985)
8. Langner, K.: The Krislet Java Client (1999), http://www.ida.liu.se/frehe/RoboCup/Libs
9. Kohavi, R., John, G.H.: Wrappers for feature subset selection. Artificial Intelligence 97(1-2), 273–324 (1997)
10. John, G.H., Kohavi, R., Pfleger, K.: Irrelevant features and the subset selection problem. In: Proceedings of the Eleventh ICML, pp. 121–129 (1994)

11. Aha, D.W., Bankert, R.L.: A comparative evaluation of sequential feature selection algorithms. Learning from Data: AI and Statistics V, 199–206 (1996)
12. Xu, R., Wunsch, D.I.I.: Survey of clustering algorithms. IEEE Transactions on Neural Networks 16(3), 645–678 (2005)
13. Bicego, M., Murino, V., Figueiredo, M.A.T.: Similarity-based clustering of sequences using hidden markov models. In: Perner, P., Rosenfeld, A. (eds.) MLDM 2003. LNCS, vol. 2734, pp. 86–95. Springer, Heidelberg (2003)
14. Dubnov, S., El-Yaniv, R., Gdalyahu, Y., Schneidman, E., Tishby, N., Yona, G.: A new nonparametric pairwise clustering algorithm based on iterative estimation of distance profiles. Mach. Learn. 47(1), 35–61 (2002)
15. Hartigan, J.A.: Clustering Algorithms. John Wiley & Sons, Inc., New York (1975)
16. Berger, R., Lämmel, G.: Exploiting past experience – case-based decision support for soccer agents. In: Hertzberg, J., Beetz, M., Englert, R. (eds.) KI 2007. LNCS (LNAI), vol. 4667. Springer, Heidelberg (2007)
17. Steffens, T.: Adapting similarity measures to agent types in opponent modeling. In: Proceedings of the Workshop MOO at AAMAS 2004, pp. 125–128 (2004)
18. Ahmadi, M., Lamjiri, A.K., Nevisi, M.M., Habibi, J., Badie, K.: Using a two-layered case-based reasoning for prediction in soccer coach. In: Proceedings of the MLMTA 2003, Las Vegas, Nevada, pp. 181–185 (2003)
19. Marling, C., Tomko, M., Gillen, M., Alexander, D., Chelberg, D.: Case-based reasoning for planning and world modeling in the robocup small sized league. In: IJCAI Workshop on Issues in Designing Physical Agents for Dynamic Real-Time Environments (2003)
20. Ros, R., de Mántaras, R.L., Arcos, J.L., Veloso, M.: Team playing behavior in robot soccer: A case-based approach. In: Weber, R.O., Richter, M.M. (eds.) ICCBR 2007. LNCS (LNAI), vol. 4626, pp. 46–60. Springer, Heidelberg (2007)
21. Wettschereck, D., Aha, D.W.: Weighting features. In: First International CBR Research and Development Conference, pp. 347–358. Springer, Berlin (1995)
22. Jarmulak, J., Craw, S., Crowe, R.: Genetic algorithms to optimise CBR retrieval. In: 5th European Workshop on Advances in CBR, pp. 136–147 (2000)
23. Maximini, K., Maximini, R., Bergmann, R.: An investigation of generalized cases. In: Ashley, K.D., Bridge, D.G. (eds.) ICCBR 2003. LNCS, vol. 2689, pp. 261–275. Springer, Heidelberg (2003)
24. Lenz, M., Burkhard, H.-D.: Case retrieval nets: Basic ideas and extensions. Kunstliche Intelligenz, 227–239 (1996)

Retrieval Based on Self-explicative Memories

Albert Fornells[1], Eva Armengol[2], and Elisabet Golobardes[1]

[1] Grup de Recerca en Sistemes Intel·ligents
Enginyeria i Arquitectura La Salle, Universitat Ramon Llull
Quatre Camins 2, 08022 Barcelona (Spain)
{afornells,elisabet}@salle.url.edu
[2] IIIA - Artificial Intelligence Research Institute,
CSIC - Spanish Council for Scientific Research,
Campus UAB, 08193 Bellaterra, Catalonia (Spain)
eva@iiia.csic.es

Abstract. One of the key issues in Case-Based Reasoning (CBR) systems is the efficient retrieval of cases when the case base is huge and/or it contains uncertainty and partial knowledge. We tackle these issues by organizing the case memory using an unsupervised clustering technique to identify data patterns for promoting all CBR steps. Moreover, another useful property of these patterns is that they provide to the user additional information about why the cases have been selected and retrieved through symbolic descriptions. This work analyses the introduction of this knowledge in the retrieve phase. The new strategies improve the case retrieval configuration procedure.

Keywords: Case Retrieval, Case Memory Organization, Self-Explicative Memories, Soft Case-Based Reasoning, Self-Organizing Map.

1 Introduction

Case-Based Reasoning (CBR) [1] systems solve new problems through an analogical procedure based on experiences represented by a set of *cases* stored in a *case memory*. The way in which CBR works can be summarized in the following steps: (1) it retrieves the most similar cases from the case memory, (2) it adapts them to propose a new solution, (3) it checks if this solution is valid, and finally, (4) it stores the relevant knowledge used to solve the problem.

The building of the subset of cases similar to a given problem to perform an efficient *retrieval* of cases is an important key issue, which is closer related to the case memory organization. There are two possible organizations of the memory: flat and structured. The *flat* organization is the simplest way because cases are stored sequentially in a list. In such situation, the strategy for classifying a new problem p is to sequentially compare p with all the cases in that list using some similarity measure. The main shortcoming of this approach is that as more as cases contains the case base higher becomes the time of retrieval.

Concerning the structured memory organization, many authors have tackled this issue from many points of view, such as representing the attributes in

K.-D. Althoff et al. (Eds.): ECCBR 2008, LNAI 5239, pp. 210–224, 2008.
© Springer-Verlag Berlin Heidelberg 2008

tree structures [22] or graphs [16], grouping cases by their similarity [23], applying knowledge-intensive approaches [20] or data-intensive approaches [21]. Nevertheless, many of these methods pay more attention to how to structure the data than to the underlying features of the domain: uncertainty and partial knowledge. In this scenario, *Soft-Computing* techniques are more suitable than *Hard-Computing* techniques since they are able to manage this kind of knowledge [7,6]. In particular, *Self-Organizing Map* (SOM) [14] has become one of the most used Soft-Computing clustering techniques for visualizing and organizing data [18] thanks to its capability for discovering hidden patterns. SOM translates complex and nonlinear statistical relations contained in high-dimensional data into simple geometric relations on a low-dimensional space. This smart and powerful ability is the reason why some CBR's studies focus on indexing the case memory for improving the retrieve phase [5,8]. The idea is to identify groups of cases with certain characteristics in common and define a pattern for representing them. Then, the retrieval phase is done as follow: (1) select the set of clusters which contain the patterns most similar to the new input case, and (2) retrieve a set of cases from the selected clusters. Thus, the retrieve phase carries out a selective retrieval with fewer cases than with the original case memory.

We focus on an approach called SOMCBR (*Self-Organizing Map in a Case-Based Reasoning*) [13]. The main difference of SOMCBR in comparison with other combinations of SOM and CBR is that the Soft-Computing and the Knowledge-Discovery capabilities of SOM are introduced in all the CBR steps for enhancing the global performance rather than only in the retrieve phase: (1) The case retrieval is performed according to the data complexity and the user requirements [11]; (2) The relation between cases and clusters is used for improving the class prediction reliability [12]; and, (3) The knowledge is maintained from an incremental and semi-supervised point of view [10]. Another distinguishing aspect of SOMCBR is its capability for explaining the results [9] using symbolic descriptions extracted from each cluster by means of a generalization process based on the anti-unification concept [2]. The additional information provided allows user to understand why a set of cases is retrieved and what aspects share in common. This work analyses additional roles of explanations in the retrieval phase. In particular, their role in the case retrieval configuration.

The paper is organized as follows. Section 2 briefly reviews the self-explicative case memory organization. Section 3 outlines how explanations may improve the case retrieval strategies. Section 4 describes the experiments and discusses the results. Section 5 summarizes some related work about the characterization of clusters. Finally, section 6 ends with the conclusion and further research.

2   The Self-explicative Memory of SOMCBR

SOMCBR uses a *Self-Organizing Map* (SOM) [14] to identify patterns and organize the case memory through them with the aim of promoting all CBR phases.

SOM is a non supervised clustering technique that projects the original N-dimensional input space into a new space with fewer dimensions by highlighting

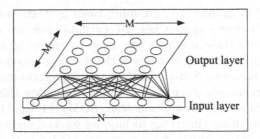

Fig. 1. SOM groups cases according to their similarity

the most important data features. Contrary to other neural networks approaches [4], the SOM's architecture is only composed of two layers. The input layer represents the new problem using as many neurons as input data features. On the other hand, the output layer describes the new low-dimensional space using as many neurons as the maximum number of expected clusters to identify. Each output neuron is connected to all input neurons. Although the output layer can represent any dimensionality lower than the original N-dimensional space, it usually represents a grid of two dimensions such as the example of Fig. 1. In this case, the output layer contains $M \times M$ clusters, where each one contains a group of similar cases represented by a pattern. A pattern can be described as a director vector (v_i) of N dimensions, where each one is the expected value of each attribute for belonging to this pattern. Even this pattern allows system to index the memory, it does not give an easy intuition of why some objects have been clustered together. For this reason, symbolic explanations from clusters were proposed in [9].

Symbolic explanations are built as a generalization of the objects of a cluster based on the anti-unification concept with some differences (see [9] for details). The descriptions are formed by the set of attributes that are common to all objects of the same class and, consequently, there are many explanations as many different classes are inside a cluster. Each one of these common attributes takes as value the union of values that it holds in the objects of the cluster. Let us illustrate with an example how explanations are built. Let m be the cluster formed by the four cases shown in the upper part of Fig. 2. The explanation D_m of these cases is shown in Fig. 2a. Attributes steroid, spleen-palpable, spiders, fatigue, malaise, liver-big, protime, and ascites are not in D_m because they are not common to all cases (i.e., steroid is not used in Obj-137). Attributes such as sex, antiviral and histology are not in D_m because all take all possible values, this means that the value of this attribute is irrelevant to describe m. Because m usually contains cases of several classes, a description $D_{m,j}$ can be built for each class j contained in m, taking into account only the subset of cases of the class j as Fig. 2b shows. Thus, a cluster m is described by a disjunction of descriptions $D_{m,j}$. Notice that each description $D_{m,j}$ also satisfies the global description D_m of a cluster.

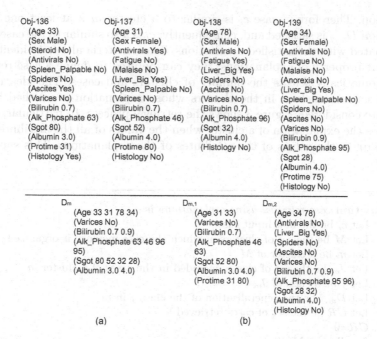

Obj-136	Obj-137	Obj-138	Obj-139
(Age 33)	(Age 31)	(Age 78)	(Age 34)
(Sex Male)	(Sex Female)	(Sex Male)	(Sex Female)
(Steroid No)	(Antivirals Yes)	(Antivirals No)	(Antivirals No)
(Antivirals No)	(Fatigue No)	(Fatigue Yes)	(Fatigue No)
(Spleen_Palpable No)	(Malaise No)	(Liver_Big Yes)	(Malaise No)
(Spiders No)	(Liver_Big Yes)	(Spiders No)	(Anorexia No)
(Ascites Yes)	(Spleen_Palpable No)	(Ascites No)	(Liver_Big Yes)
(Varices No)	(Varices No)	(Varices No)	(Spleen_Palpable No)
(Bilirubin 0.7)	(Bilirubin 0.7)	(Bilirubin 0.7)	(Spiders No)
(Alk_Phosphate 63)	(Alk_Phosphate 46)	(Alk_Phosphate 96)	(Ascites No)
(Sgot 80)	(Sgot 52)	(Sgot 32)	(Varices No)
(Albumin 3.0)	(Albumin 4.0)	(Albumin 4.0)	(Bilirubin 0.9)
(Protime 31)	(Protime 80)	(Histology No)	(Alk_Phosphate 95)
(Histology Yes)	(Histology No)		(Sgot 28)
			(Albumin 4.0)
			(Protime 75)
			(Histology No)

D_m	$D_{m,1}$	$D_{m,2}$
(Age 33 31 78 34)	(Age 31 33)	(Age 34 78)
(Varices No)	(Varices No)	(Antivirals No)
(Bilirubin 0.7 0.9)	(Bilirubin 0.7)	(Liver_Big Yes)
(Alk_Phosphate 63 46 96 95)	(Alk_Phosphate 46 63)	(Spiders No)
(Sgot 80 52 32 28)	(Sgot 52 80)	(Ascites No)
(Albumin 3.0 4.0)	(Albumin 3.0 4.0)	(Varices No)
	(Protime 31 80)	(Bilirubin 0.7 0.9)
		(Alk_Phosphate 95 96)
		(Sgot 28 32)
		(Albumin 4.0)
		(Histology No)

(a)   (b)

Fig. 2. Upper part shows the cases in M_i. Lower part shows the symbolic descriptions of Mi when (a) all objects belong to the same class. (b) Obj-136 and Obj-137 belong to the class C_1 and Obj-138 and Obj-139 belong to the class C_2.

We propose to use explanations for retrieval purposes in the same way as generalizations are used for instance in PROTOS [19]. The idea is that because the explanation contains attributes that are common to a subset of objects, a new problem sharing these attributes probably will be assessed as having higher similarity with these objects with respect to other objects of the base. Nevertheless, the point here is that a problem can share a different set of features with the explanations of several cluster. The next section analyses how this capability can be used to automatically select clusters and cases.

3   Introducing Explanations in the Retrieval Process

The case memory access in SOMCBR is based on a procedure of two steps where (1) a set of C clusters are selected according to the pattern of the new input case and, (2) a set of K cases from the selected clusters are retrieved. The optimal definition of the C and K values according to the data complexity and the user requirements are crucial issues for improving the performance [11].

Let c_i be the new input case, M be the set of clusters in which the case memory is organized and J_m be the set of solution classes included of cluster m. Let $D_{m,j}$ be the generalization of cases belonging to the cluster m for a class j. c_i satisfies a description $D_{m,j}$ if all the attribute' value are included in this description. Therefore, a case c_i is similar to a cluster m if at least one of the description $D_{m,j}$ is satisfied and, consequently, c_i is also similar to the cases from m associated with the satisfied descriptions. These criteria allows to identify an important property of explanations: they can be used to define a case retrieval that automatically selects the number of clusters and cases. The idea is that only the cases contained in the clusters whose explanation is satisfied by the case c_i are considered. Figure 3 shows the retrieval process. In particular, a case c_i satisfies the explanation of a cluster when the values of all the attributes of c_i are *similar* to the values of the attributes of the explanations. This similarity

```
1  Function case retrieval using explanations is
2  │  Let c_i be the new input case
3  │  Let M be the set of clusters in which the case memory is organized
4  │  Let m be a cluster of M
5  │  Let J_m be the set of classes included in the cases of a cluster m
6  │  Let j be a class of J_m
7  │  Let D_{m,j} be the generalization of the class j in m
8  │  Let CR be the set of cases retrieved
9  │  CR=∅
10 │  forall m ∈ M do
11 │  │  forall j ∈ J_m do
12 │  │  │  if c_i satisfies D_{m,j} then
13 │  │  │  │  CR=CR ∪ {cases from m associated to the D_{m,j}}
14 │  return CR

15 Function satisfies is
   │  input  : c_i, D_{m,j}
   │  output : True if c_i satisfies D_{m,j}. Otherwise, false
16 │  Let A be the set of the attributes contained in D_{m,j}
17 │  Let a be an attribute of A
18 │  Let V_a be the set of the possible values of a in D_{m,j}
19 │  Let v_a be one of the possible values of V_a
20 │  Let v_{a,i} be the value of the attribute a belonging to V_a for the case c_i
21 │  forall a ∈ D_{m,j} do
22 │  │  found=false
23 │  │  forall v_a ∈ V_a do
24 │  │  │  if a is numerical then
25 │  │  │  │  if (v_a − ϵ) ≤ v_{a,i} ≤ (v_a + ϵ) then  found=true; break;
26 │  │  │  else if a is symbolic then
27 │  │  │  │  if v_a=v_{a,i} then  found=true; break;
28 │  │  if found==false then  return false
29 │  return true
```

Fig. 3. Case retrieval strategy based on explanations

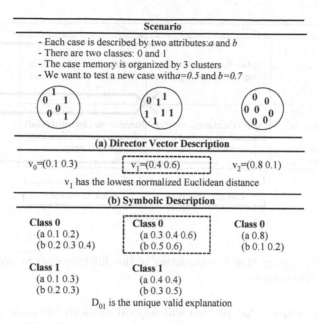

Scenario
- Each case is described by two attributes:*a* and *b* - There are two classes: 0 and 1 - The case memory is organized by 3 clusters - We want to test a new case with*a=0.5* and *b=0.7*

(a) Director Vector Description

v_0=(0.1 0.3) v_1=(0.4 0.6) v_2=(0.8 0.1)

v_1 has the lowest normalized Euclidean distance

(b) Symbolic Description

Class 0	Class 0	Class 0
(a 0.1 0.2)	(a 0.3 0.4 0.6)	(a 0.8)
(b 0.2 0.3 0.4)	(b 0.5 0.6)	(b 0.1 0.2)

Class 1	Class 1	
(a 0.1 0.3)	(a 0.4 0.4)	
(b 0.2 0.3)	(b 0.3 0.5)	

D_{01} is the unique valid explanation

Fig. 4. Both approaches select the same cluster m_1

is assessed as the equality of values when these values are symbolic (line 26 of the algorithm) and as belonging to an interval around the value hold by the explanation when the value is continuous (line 24 of the algorithm). The ϵ value depends on the attributes' range and the expected accuracy. For example, 0.2 could be considered as a confidence value if range is [0..1].

Nevertheless, this strategy is not as perfect as it seems at first sight. The similarity criteria using explanations is extremist (total or null) while the similarity based on distances in the interval [0..1] is more flexible. For example, if a problem is described by 100 attributes, the normalized distance between an input case and a director vector will not be significantly affected if three attributes are very different. However, using explanations the similarity is considered as different as when one of the attribute-value relations does not exist in the input case. Anyway, the major part of retrieved cases should be the same because both are based on the similarity between attributes. They key in the retrieval based on explanations is the specificity of explanations. If they are very specific, any cluster or case could be selected. In contrast, almost all clusters and cases could be selected if they are very general. Consequently, this issue is directly affects the performance. In our experiments we used epsilon to experiment with different specificity degree of the explanations. Figure 4 shows an example where both select the same cluster.

On the other hand, there is another issue to be careful when a high number of cases is retrieved: how system can order their similarity with respect to the new case if all are considered as 'equal' in terms of similarity. This can be a drawback during the reuse phase when the system uses a scheme voting on the

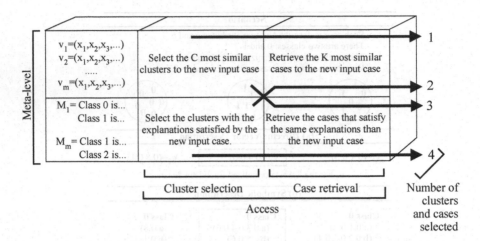

Fig. 5. The 3D Strategy Map is a taxonomy of the different ways in which the case retrieval can be performed

candidate classes since the solution will depend on both the class distribution and the number of cases in each class. Some criteria need to be defined to improve the reliability of the solution such as recomputing the similarity between the retrieved cases and the new input case. Therefore, we need to combine the benefits of both approaches: the capability of self-configuring C and K in explanations and, the accuracy of similarity distances.

Figure 5 describes a 3D Strategy Map. The concept of the *Strategy Map* was introduced in [11] and it is defined as a taxonomy of the different ways in which strategies can be performed according to the number of clusters selected and the number of cases retrieved from selected clusters (see x-axis and z-axis). In this case, the Strategy Map is composed by an additional axis which provides information related to the criteria used to represent the patterns: director vectors or explanations (see y-axis). As figure shows, four main strategies can be identified according to the way in which cluster and case selection is performed:

- Strategy 1: Clusters and cases are selected using a distance metric. The methodology presented in [11] helps to do it according to the user requirements.
- Strategy 2: Clusters are selected using explanations and cases of these clusters are selected using a distance metric. Although this capability simplifies the setting up process, there is a risk of not selecting clusters when the explanations are too specific. In contrast, general explanations can produce the selection of a high number of clusters and this fact ciuld negatively affect the system performance in terms of computational time.
- Strategy 3: Clusters are selected using a distance metric and cases of these clusters are selected using explanations. In this strategy is necessary to define the number of clusters to be used. Also, the problem is that it retrieves a set of cases which have the same similarity with respect the input case. Thus,

the class solution is obtained using a voting scheme that depends on the class distribution and the number of cases by cluster.

– Strategy 4: Clusters and cases are selected using explanations. The performance of this strategy depends on the accuracy of explanations.

In general lines, strategies 1 and 2 provide a good degree of similarity in structured domains where a reliable similarity distance is available. On the other hand, strategies 3 and 4 provide best results in unstructured and dynamic domains or when a reliable similarity function is not available because they manage best the data. Anyway, the performance of SOM in terms of defining 'good' clusters is directly related to the distance metric used for training the clusters. Thus, if is not possible to get a reliable similarity function will not be possible to build the clusters. The next section analyses the performance of the strategies proposed above on structured and static domains because they are preconditions to use SOM.

4   Experiments, Results and Discussion

The adequacy of the explanations is defined as the ability of them to select both the clusters and the cases more adequate for a given problem. For this reason, this section evaluates if this adequacy can be useful in the case retrieval process as has been proposed in section 3. Although explanations can deal with both symbolic and numerical values of attributes, in our experiments we selected datasets with only numerical attributes because we want to compare the results with those produced using the director vectors provided by SOM. The selected datasets from the *UCI Repository* are summarized in Table 1.

The strategies have been executed applying a 10-fold stratified cross-validation with the following common configuration: (1) The normalized Euclidean distance is used as distance metric. (2) No new cases are stored. (3) The map size is automatically computed as the map with the lowest error [13]. (4) 10 random seeds are used to minimize the random effects (the percentage of each fold is the mean of 10 random seeds). In addition, each strategy has some particularities. The adaptation phase proposes the solution through the majority class using K-NN with $K = 1$, 3 and 5 for the strategies 1 and 2. In the case of strategies 3 and 4, the solution is the majority class of all the selected cases. The strategies 1 and 3 uses three clusters since it is usually an optimal value [11].

4.1   Discussion

Tables 2, 3, 4, 5 and 6 show the averages of error percentage, standard deviation and mean percentage reduction of the number of cases selected for retrieval, for strategies 1, 2 and 4.

Tables 2 and 3 show results of SOMCBR using explanations for selecting clusters and the distance measure for selecting cases included in the clusters. In both situations we experimented with different values of K to compare the effects of producing a solution based in a higher number of cases. The difference

among both tables is the ϵ factor used to validate the explanations. As well as
the value of K is higher, the percentage of error decreases, however notice that
the increment of ϵ produces an increment of the error and a decrement of the
percentage of reduction of the number of cases retrieved. We do not interpret
this result as a malfunction of the explanation but as the explanations are too
specific and consequently some explanations are not satisfied because of the value
of only one or two attributes. Notice that the satisfaction of an explanation is
boolean, either *all* the attributes are satisfied or the explanation is not used. As
future work we plan to assess some satisfaction degree for the explanations.

Table 1. Description of the *datasets* used in experiments

Code	Dataset	Attributes	Instances	Classes
HE	hepatitis	19	155	2
GL	glass	9	214	6
TH	thyroids	5	215	3
HS	heart-statlog	13	270	2
IO	ionosphere	34	351	2
WD	wdbc	30	569	2
BA	bal	4	625	3
WB	wbcd	9	699	2
WI	wisconsin	9	699	2
VE	vehicle	18	846	4
TA	tao	2	1888	2
SE	segment	19	2310	7
WA	waveform	40	5000	3

Table 2. Error percentage (%Error), standard deviation (σ), and mean reduction percentage of cases retrieved (%R) using SOMCBR with strategy 2 and $\epsilon = 0.1$ with respect to use a flat memory

Code	1-NN %Error (σ) %R	3-NN %Error (σ) %R	5-NN %Error (σ) %R
BA	23.4 (3.2) 44.1	19 (2.9) 44.1	15.2 (2.6) 44.1
GL	40.5 (9.8) 69.8	37.1 (17.1) 45.8	39.2 (15.4) 45.8
HS	23.4 (6.4) 40.7	20.8 (5) 40.7	19.8 (5.7) 67.9
HE	20.5 (8) 69.1	16.2 (7.5) 69.1	15.4 (9.5) 69.1
IO	12.9 (6.4) 89.8	11.3 (6) 89.8	12.6 (5.8) 89.8
SE	3.2 (1.3) 55.1	4 (0.9) 55.1	5 (1.2) 55.1
TA	3.7 (1.6) 8.2	4.2 (2) 8.2	3.3 (1) 8.2
TH	3.3 (2.2) 17.6	7.1 (5.7) 17.6	7.1 (5.3) 17.6
VE	30.4 (4.9) 15	29.6 (4.5) 15	29.1 (6.2) 15
WA	26.8 (1.9) 14	22.7 (1.4) 21.7	20.8 (1.6) 14
WB	3.6 (3.6) 63.9	4 (3.6) 63.9	3.8 (2.4) 65.7
WD	5.1 (2.5) 59.8	3.7 (2.2) 59.8	3.4 (2) 34.2
WI	4.6 (2.7) 60.6	4.2 (1.7) 79.2	4.3 (2.8) 60.6
	14 52.4	11.6 61.7	9.8 52.4

Table 3. Error percentage (%Error), standard deviation (σ), and mean reduction percentage of cases retrieved (%R) using SOMCBR with strategy 2 and $\epsilon= 0.2$ with respect to use a flat memory

Code	1-NN %Error (σ) %R	3-NN %Error (σ) %R	5-NN %Error (σ) %R
BA	23.4 (3.2) 44.1	19 (2.9) 44.1	15.2 (2.6) 44.1
GL	39.3 (7.4) 45.3	38.9 (17.6) 42.2	39.9 (17.9) 42.2
HS	25 (8) 54.7	21.2 (5.5) 33.7	18.2 (5.1) 33.7
HE	21.5 (8.1) 61.9	16.3 (7.7) 61.9	15.6 (7.5) 61.9
IO	14.5 (4) 34.3	16.2 (3.9) 34.3	18.2 (4) 34.3
SE	2.9 (1.2) 32.7	4 (0.8) 32.7	4.9 (1.1) 32.7
TA	3.8 (1.6) 1.4	4.3 (2) 1.4	3.4 (0.9) 1.4
TH	3.3 (3.1) 17.1	6.1 (4.8) 17.1	6.1 (4.8) 17.1
VE	29.9 (4.1) 3.8	30 (4.9) 3.8	29.3 (4.8) 3.8
WA	27 (1.9) 0.4	22.6 (1.7) 1	21.1 (1.6) 1
WB	4.7 (2.8) 24.5	3.4 (1.5) 24.5	2.9 (2.1) 24.5
WD	5.3 (2.5) 12.7	3.5 (1.6) 25.4	3.4 (2) 26.6
WI	3.9 (1.6) 22.6	3.4 (1.1) 22.6	2.9 (1.9) 22.6
	13.6 33.4	11.2 33.4	9 33.4

Table 4. Error percentage (%Error), standard deviation (σ), and mean reduction percentage of cases retrieved (%R) using SOMCBR with strategy 1 with respect to use a flat memory

Code	1-NN %Error (σ) %R	3-NN %Error (σ) %R	5-NN %Error (σ) %R
BA	23.7 (3.9) 60	19.7 (2.8) 67.4	18.7 (4) 67.4
GL	33.6 (14.4) 47.9	31.3 (10.2) 21.4	33.2 (9.6) 21.4
HS	24.1 (8.8) 65.4	20.4 (5.8) 56	21.1 (3.7) 65.4
HE	19.4 (7.1) 67.6	13.6 (8.7) 56.1	16.8 (7.3) 56.1
IO	12.8 (4.5) 50.8	13.7 (4.9) 12.7	14.3 (4.8) 12.7
SE	4.7 (0.9) 56.5	5.7 (1.3) 56.5	6 (1.2) 56.5
TA	5.6 (1.7) 55.6	3.8 (1.8) 55.6	4.4 (2.1) 55.6
TH	2.8 (2.3) 3.1	7.9 (5.2) 52.8	5.1 (5) 3.1
VE	32 (4.6) 55.2	30.7 (6.7) 55.2	31.9 (5) 55.2
WA	27.2 (2.2) 76.5	23.8 (1.7) 54	21.8 (1.7) 55.4
WB	4.9 (1.5) 52.9	3.9 (2) 65.2	3.9 (1.9) 65.2
WD	4 (2.8) 44.3	3.3 (2) 44.3	4.2 (2.6) 53.9
WI	4 (1.2) 55.3	3.4 (1.7) 55.3	3.2 (1.2) 74.7
	13.9 57.7	11.6 61.4	11 71.1

The ability of the explanations for selecting clusters is shown by comparing the results from strategy 1 (see Tab. 4). Strategy 2 produces an error percentage equal or better than the produced by strategy 1 (although both results are not statistically different when applying a t-test at 95% of confidence level). Our interpretation is that strategy 2 tends to select a high number of clusters (commonly more than 3) and, consequently, this produces a wider picture of the

Table 5. Error percentage (%Error), standard deviation (σ), and mean reduction percentage of cases retrieved (%R) using SOMCBR with strategy 4 and $\epsilon = 0.1$ with respect to use a flat memory

Code	3×3			4×4			5×5		
	%Error	(σ)	%R	%Error	(σ)	%R	%Error	(σ)	%R
BA	39.8	(4.4)	44.1	42.2	(9.5)	60.1	38.9	(6)	87
GL	57.6	(11.4)	69.8	56.7	(10.4)	45.8	61.7	(12.1)	84.9
HS	33.1	(11.5)	40.7	37.7	(10.4)	67.9	37.6	(10.6)	79.4
HE	17.1	(6.4)	69.1	20.8	(9)	87.1	30.8	(17.2)	93.5
IO	29.8	(5.4)	69.8	35.3	(15.9)	66.3	14.5	(6.4)	89.8
SE	23.5	(3)	55.1	52.1	(8.5)	91.4	18.6	(3.8)	71
TA	36.4	(2)	1.9	33.7	(14.3)	59.3	22.5	(3.1)	8.2
TH	29.4	(4.3)	36.3	29.1	(4.2)	17.6	26.1	(5.7)	62.2
VE	60.9	(3.7)	15	57.8	(8.5)	43.9	58.4	(7.8)	57.2
WA	59.3	(1)	2.9	40.2	(1.3)	14	35.9	(3.1)	21.7
WB	18.1	(13.9)	63.9	22.2	(12.5)	65.7	10.9	(4.7)	83.9
WD	32.3	(6.3)	34.2	26	(10.7)	51.6	11.2	(7.5)	59.8
WI	13.2	(14.3)	60.6	11.6	(11.4)	76.5	4.7	(1.8)	79.2
	26.5		52.4	26.9		68.3	21.8		83.1

case base. This effect is hidden in the strategy 2 when $\epsilon = 0.1$ because a lot of cases are filtered due to the lack of flexibility of the explanations. However, this effect disappears when the explanation flexibility increases by taking $\epsilon = 0.2$. Our conclusion is that explanations are an automatic mechanism of cluster selection allowing the adjustment of cases exploration according to the specificity. From our point of view, this is an important issue because it simplifies the case retrieval configuration although further analysis should be done to evaluate the impact in performance related to the characteristics of the dataset.

Tables 5 and 6 show the results of strategy 4 with $\epsilon = 0.1$ and 0.2 respectively. To analyze the impact of the explanation flexibility, we performed experiments with different map sizes (3×3, 4×4 and 5×5). The higher the maps are the higher the number of clusters is and probably each cluster contains only few cases. In turn, clusters with low number of cases will produce specific explanations. This effect is shown in tables where the lowest error percentage and the maximum reduction of retrieval is achieved for the map of size 5×5. Nevertheless, by comparing these results with those produced by the other strategies we seen that probably the explanations have not been specific enough since the results for strategy 4 are worst than the produced by the other strategies. Notice also that in this strategy ϵ plays a different role. Now it is desirable that the explanations be restrictive enough since there is not a latter filtering process, whereas other strategies are more flexible in the selection of clusters because they have a filtering post-process (the distance measure).

On the other hand, the results of strategy 3 are not presented because they are very similar to the strategy 4 and, consequently, they do not provide any new comment.

Table 6. Error percentage (%Error), standard deviation (σ), and mean reduction percentage of cases retrieved (%R) using SOMCBR with strategy 4 and $\epsilon = 0.2$ with respect to use a flat memory

Code	3×3 %Error (σ) %R	4×4 %Error (σ) %R	5×5 %Error (σ) %R
BA	39.8 (4.4) 44.1	42.2 (9.5) 60.1	38.9 (6) 87
GL	61.1 (16.1) 45.3	59.6 (11.6) 42.2	65.7 (15) 57.8
HS	34.6 (10.6) 33.7	39.6 (6.5) 54.7	34.7 (9.1) 68.3
HE	18.5 (5.8) 61.9	19.7 (10.5) 83.5	24.1 (12.5) 87.8
IO	34.2 (5.7) 34.3	33.2 (14.4) 61	33.1 (5) 73.3
SE	46.8 (1.9) 32.7	60.3 (6.4) 88.2	44.7 (7.8) 42.9
TA	44.9 (2) 0.2	43.1 (7.6) 51.4	31 (7.3) 1.4
TH	29.8 (3.8) 17.1	29.4 (4.3) 11.4	26.5 (4.8) 32.6
VE	71 (3.5) 3.8	67.9 (5.5) 18.5	61.9 (2.9) 22.9
WA	66.1 (0.2) 0	65.6 (0.4) 0.4	64.9 (0.7) 1
WB	23.9 (12.2) 24.5	22.2 (15.1) 44.2	20.7 (13.1) 45.9
WD	35.2 (3.2) 12.7	31 (8.9) 26.6	32.4 (3.9) 25.4
WI	16.3 (12.9) 22.6	14.9 (12.8) 54.8	9.9 (9.5) 55.8
	28.1 33.4	28.6 57.5	24.4 71.4

Experiments have shown the role of explanations to support the simplification of the SOMCBR configuration. However, the use of explanation as mechanism for selecting cases have not produced as good results as expected because of their lack of flexibility. We conclude that is necessary to assess some similarity degree among explanations and problem to obtain more accurate results.

5   Related Work

An intelligent organization of the memory seems to be one of the key issues for an efficient case retrieval. Several approaches have been taken to produce useful organizations. Most of them are based on clustering cases in order to explore only a subset of cases. Bichindaritz [3] details several ways to organize the case-base memory. As the approach we presented in this paper, there are approaches based on constructing generalizations representing subsets of cases, and most of them use clustering techniques to determine the subset of cases to be represented by the same generalization.

For instance, PROTOS [19], one of the early CBR systems, defined categories of cases and also links that make explicit differences among clusters. Thus, when a new problem has to be classified, the retrieval of the most similar case is performed based on a combination of the similarity between the problem and both case features, categories and differences among particular cases. Zenko et al. [24] use the CN2 algorithm to induce rules that determine prototypes for each cluster. However this prototype is not symbolic but is a vector representing frequencies. As in our approaches, cluster prototypes are not discriminant therefore a problem could be include in several clusters. Because the CN2 algorithm can produce an ordered set of prototypes (rules), the problem is classified as belonging to the class represented by the first rule that is satisfied. In the modification proposed by Zenko et al., CN2 produces a non-ordered set of rules, therefore authors use class distributions of all rules to perform weighted voting.

The approach introduced by Lechevalier et al. [15] use the SOM algorithm for clustering the case base. Differently than in our approach, Lechevalier et al. combine SOM with a dynamic clustering algorithm called SCLUST that allows the use of symbolic data. Clusters are represented by symbolic descriptions and new problems are compared with these descriptions using the Hausdorff distance.

Malek and Amy [17] introduced a supervised approach focused on organizing the case-base of a CBR system. The case base is organized in two parts, prototypical and instance, and there is also a third part that contain cases than cannot be classified in any of these parts. For classifying a new problem the system tries to retrieve similar cases from those in the atypical part using some similarity measure with a threshold. When no atypical cases are retrieved then the problem is compared with the prototypes representing the classes. If the problem satisfies more than one prototype (i.e. it could be classified in more than one class), then it used k-NN to retrieve the most similar cases included in the clusters represented by the activated prototypes. Finally, when no prototype is satisfied by the problem the k-NN algorithm on the atypical cases is used.

A different approach was that taken by Bichindaritz [3] that proposed the use of techniques if information retrieval to organize the memory. The idea is to use a lexicon and an inverted index to organize the cases. Then, author proposes several strategies where both the lexicon and the indexes are combined to retrieve a subset of cases similar to the problem.

6   Conclusions and Future Work

SOMCBR is featured by organizing the case memory through SOM [14] to promote all the CBR phases [11,12,9,10]. Besides, SOMCBR is able to explain why a set of cases are grouped together and why they have been retrieved through descriptions built by a variant of the anti-unification operator [2]. This symbolic explanations describes the existent classes in the cluster through the generalization of its cases. This capability facilitate the revise task for two reasons: (1) explanations are more understandable than directors vectors, and; (2) explanations summarize best the common characteristics.

This work has analyzed if the smart properties of explanations can be introduced in the case access procedure with the aim of improving the case access. In particular, a 3D Strategy Map [11] has been defined as the combination of two criteria: (1) the distance computed between the new input case and the director vectors or between the new input case and the cases from the clusters, and (2) the satisfaction of the explanations extracted from the clusters. The results have been the definition of four different typologies of strategies: (1) cluster and case selection by the distance metric; (2) cluster selection by explanations and case selection by distance metric; (3) cluster selection by the distance metric and case selection by explanations, and; (4) cluster and case selection by explanations. The approaches 1 and 2 depend mainly on the distance metric while the approaches 3 and 4 depends on the specificity of descriptions. The analysis of strategies over several datasets has provided two important conclusions: (1) Approach 2 offers a similar performance than approach 1 and at the same time, it is easier to configure the strategy because user has not to select the number of clusters selected; (2) The approaches where the case selection depends on the explanations offer a very bad performance because the voting scheme is 'almost random' because it is related to the class distribution and the number of cases by cluster.

As further work we plan to refine the numerical management, work with unstructured and dynamic domains and introduce discriminant explanations.

Acknowledgments

We would like to thank the Spanish Government for the support in MID-CBR project under grant TIN2006-15140-C03 and the *Generalitat de Catalunya* for the support under grants 2005-SGR-00093 and 2005SGR-302. We would like to thank *Enginyeria i Arquitectura La Salle* of Ramon Llull University for the support to our research group as well.

References

1. Aamodt, A., Plaza, E.: Case-based reasoning: Foundations issues, methodological variations, and system approaches. AI Communications 7, 39–59 (1994)
2. Armengol, E., Plaza, E.: Bottom-up induction of feature terms. Machine Learning 41(1), 259–294 (2000)
3. Bichindaritz, I.: Memory organization as the missing link between case-based reasoning and information retrieval in biomedicine. Computational Intelligence 22(3-4), 148–160 (2006)
4. Bishop, C.M.: Neural Networks for Pattern Recognition. Oxford University Press, Oxford (1995)
5. Chang, P., Lai, C.: A hybrid system combining self-organizing maps with case-based reasoning in wholesaler's new-release book forecasting. Expert Syst. Appl. 29(1), 183–192 (2005)
6. Cheetham, W., Shiu, S., Weber, R.: Soft case-based reasoning. The Knowledge Engineering 0, 1–4 (2005)
7. Cordón, O., Herrera, E.: Special issue on soft computing applications to intelligent information retrieval on internet. Int. Jour. of Approximate Reasoning 34, 2–3 (2003)
8. Aiken, J., Corchado, E., Corchado, J.M.: Ibr retrieval method based on topology preserving mappings. Journal of Experimental & Theoretical Artificial Intelligence 16(3), 145–160 (2004)
9. Fornells, A., Armengol, E., Golobardes, E.: Explanation of a clustered case memory organization. In: Artificial Intelligence Research and Development, vol. 160, pp. 153–160. IOS Press, Amsterdam (2007)

10. Fornells, A., Golobardes, E.: Case-base maintenance in an associative memory organized by a self-organizing map. In: Corchado, E., Corchado, J.M., Abraham, A. (eds.) Innovations in Hybrid Intelligent Systems, vol. 44, pp. 312–319. Springer, Heidelberg (2007)

11. Fornells, A., Golobardes, E., Martorell, J.M., Garrell, J.M., Maciá, N., Bernadó, E.: A methodology for analyzing the case retrieval from a clustered case memory. In: Weber, R.O., Richter, M.M. (eds.) ICCBR 2007. LNCS (LNAI), vol. 4626, pp. 122–136. Springer, Heidelberg (2007)

12. Fornells, A., Golobardes, E., Martorell, J.M., Garrell, J.M., Vilasís, X.: Patterns out of cases using kohonen maps in breast cancer diagnosis. International Journal of Neural Systems 18(1), 33–43 (2008)

13. Fornells, A., Golobardes, E., Vernet, D., Corral, G.: Unsupervised case memory organization: Analysing computational time and soft computing capabilities. In: Roth-Berghofer, T.R., Göker, M.H., Güvenir, H.A. (eds.) ECCBR 2006. LNCS (LNAI), vol. 4106, pp. 241–255. Springer, Heidelberg (2006)

14. Kohonen, T.: Self-Organizing Maps, 3rd edn. Springer, Heidelberg (2000)

15. Lechevallier, Y., Verde, R., de Carvalho, F.: Symbolic clustering of large datasets. In: Data Science and Classification. Studies in Classification, Data Analysis, and Knowledge Organization, pp. 193–201. Springer, Heidelberg (2006)

16. Lenz, M., Burkhard, H.D., Brückner, S.: Applying case retrieval nets to diagnostic tasks in technical domains. In: Proc. of the 3rd European Workshop on Advances in Case-Based Reasoning, pp. 219–233. Springer, Heidelberg (1996)

17. Malek, M., Amy, B.: A pre-processing model for integrating cbr and prototype-based neural networks. In: Connectionism-symbolic Integration, Erlbaum, Mahwah (2007)

18. M. Oja, S. Kaski, and T. Kohonen. Bibliography of Self-Organizing Map (SOM) Papers: 1998-2001 (2003), http://www.cis.hut.fi/research/refs/

19. Porter, B.: Protos: An experiment in knowledge acquisition for heuristic classification tasks. In: Proceedings First International Meeting on Advances in Learning, Les Arcs, France, pp. 159–174 (1986)

20. Rissland, E.L., Skalak, D.B., Friedman, M.: Case retrieval through multiple indexing and heuristic search. In: Int. Joint Conf. on Art. Intelligence, pp. 902–908 (1993)

21. Vernet, D., Golobardes, E.: An unsupervised learning approach for case-based classifier systems. Expert Update. The Specialist Group on Artificial Intelligence 6(2), 37–42 (2003)

22. Wess, S., Althoff, K.D., Derwand, G.: Using k-d trees to improve the retrieval step in case-based reasoning. In: 1st European Workshop on Topics in Case-Based Reasoning, vol. 837, pp. 167–181. Springer, Heidelberg (1994)

23. Yang, Q., Wu, J.: Enhancing the effectiveness of interactive case-based reasoning with clustering and decision forests. Applied Intelligence 14(1) (2001)

24. Zenko, B., Dzeroski, S., Struyf, J.: Learning predictive clustering rules. In: Bonchi, F., Boulicaut, J.-F. (eds.) KDID 2005. LNCS, vol. 3933, pp. 234–250. Springer, Heidelberg (2006)

Increasing Precision of Credible Case-Based Inference

Thomas Gabel and Martin Riedmiller

Neuroinformatics Group
Department of Mathematics and Computer Science
Institute of Cognitive Science
University of Osnabrück, 49069 Osnabrück, Germany
{thomas.gabel,martin.riedmiller}@uni-osnabrueck.de

Abstract. Credible case-based inference (CCBI) is a new and theoretically sound inferencing mechanism for case-based systems. In this paper, we formally investigate the level of precision that CCBI-based retrieval results may yield. Building upon our theoretical findings, we derive a number of optimization criteria that can be utilized for learning such similarity measures that bring about more precise predictions when used in the scope of CCBI. Our empirical experiments support the claim that, given appropriate similarity measures, CCBI can be enforced to produce highly precise predictions while its corresponding level of confidence is only marginally impaired.

1 Introduction

Credible case-based inference (CCBI) has been recently proposed as a new retrieval paradigm for case-based problem solving [6]. It features a number of desirable theoretical properties and allows for deriving formal statements about its performance. Furthermore, it makes few assumptions regarding the application domain for which it can be used and concerning the case structure and similarity measures employed during the inference process.

The issue mentioned last – the use of fixed similarity measures – depicts one point of departure for the work described in the paper at hand. We are going to consider the similarity measure CCBI builds upon as a variable. The second point of departure stems from the fact that the level of precision obtained when doing inference with CCBI has been recently shown to be only of moderate quality. Combining these two issues, our goal is to increase the precision of CCBI's predictions by modifying and optimizing the similarity measures that CCBI builds upon.

In so doing, we will first formalize the notion of a precise retrieval result in the context of CCBI and prove a number of its theoretical properties (Section 3). Then, we suggest the learning of high-precision similarity measures using a recently proposed learning framework and utilizing a number of novel precision-oriented error functions that we develop (Section 4). Finally, we empirically evaluate our findings using several benchmark data sets (Section 5). Before starting off, we briefly summarize the core concepts of CCBI in Section 2.

K.-D. Althoff et al. (Eds.): ECCBR 2008, LNAI 5239, pp. 225–239, 2008.

2 Credible Case-Based Inference

In [6], Hüllermeier introduced credible case-based inference as a novel method for retrieving candidate solutions in case-based problem solving. CCBI is built upon a sound formalization of the CBR paradigm and allows for proving some of its theoretical properties. In this section, we briefly outline those specifics of CCBI and of its inference mechanism that are of relevance in the scope of this paper, and we also point to some possibilities for improving its performance.

2.1 Notation and Outline of CCBI

Throughout this paper, we denote by $\mathcal{X}$ a problem space and by $\mathcal{L}$ a solution space, where a case consists of a problem part $x \in \mathcal{X}$ and solution part $\lambda_x \in \mathcal{L}$. Further, a case base $\mathcal{M}$ is a collection of cases $\langle x_i, \lambda_{x_i} \rangle \in \mathcal{M}$, $1 \leq i \leq |\mathcal{M}|$.

Motivating CCBI, the well-known CBR hypothesis that "similar problems have similar solutions" has been equipped with the formal interpretation that

$$\forall x, y \in \mathcal{X} : sim_{\mathcal{L}}(\lambda_x, \lambda_y) \geq sim_{\mathcal{X}}(x, y). \tag{1}$$

Since, however, in practice this requirement will typically be frequently violated, [6] introduces the concept of a similarity profile ζ that is defined by

$$\zeta(\alpha) := \inf_{\substack{x, y \in \mathcal{X} \\ sim_{\mathcal{X}}(x,y)=\alpha}} sim_{\mathcal{L}}(\lambda_x, \lambda_y) \text{ for all } \alpha \in [0, 1].$$

As ζ is generally unknown, the notion of a *similarity hypothesis* $h : [0, 1] \rightarrow [0, 1]$ is introduced which is meant to approximate ζ. Of special interest are similarity hypotheses that are consistent with a given data set $\mathcal{M}$, i.e. for which it holds

$$\forall \langle x, \lambda_x \rangle, \langle y, \lambda_y \rangle \in \mathcal{M} : sim_{\mathcal{X}}(x, y) = \alpha \Rightarrow sim_{\mathcal{L}}(\lambda_x, \lambda_y) \geq h(\alpha).$$

One such data-consistent hypothesis that will play a major role throughout this paper takes the form of a step function over a partition A_k of the problem similarity interval $[0, 1]$ and is called *empirical similarity profile*. It is defined as a function $h_{\mathcal{M}} : [0, 1] \rightarrow [0, 1]$ with

$$h_{\mathcal{M}} : x \mapsto \sum_{k=1}^{m} \beta_k \cdot \mathbb{I}_{A_k}(x) \text{ and } \beta_k := \min_{\substack{\langle x, \lambda_x \rangle, \langle y, \lambda_y \rangle \in \mathcal{M} \\ sim_{\mathcal{X}}(x,y) \in A_k}} sim_{\mathcal{L}}(\lambda_x, \lambda_y) \tag{2}$$

where $A_k = [\alpha_{k-1}, \alpha_k)$ for $1 \leq k < m$, $A_m = [\alpha_{m-1}, \alpha_m]$ and $0 = \alpha_0 < \alpha_1 < \ldots < \alpha_m = 1$ ($\mathbb{I}_A(x) = 1$ if $x \in A$, $\mathbb{I}_A(x) = 0$ else, and $\min \emptyset = 1$ by definition). Thus, by definition the following relaxation of the constraint in Equation 1 holds

$$\forall \langle x, \lambda_x \rangle, \langle y, \lambda_y \rangle \in \mathcal{M} : sim_{\mathcal{L}}(\lambda_x, \lambda_y) \geq h_{\mathcal{M}}(sim_{\mathcal{X}}(x, y)).$$

In contrast to, for example, k-NN prediction, CCBI does not provide point predictions, but sets of candidate solutions. So, for predicting the label λ_q of a new query problem $q \in \mathcal{X}$, the notion of a *credible solution set* $C(q)$ is introduced and, when doing inference with a finite data set $\mathcal{M}$, it is suggested that the requested solution is an element of the following *estimated* credible solution set

$$C^{est}(q) = \bigcap_{c \in \mathcal{M}} \{\lambda | sim_{\mathcal{L}}(\lambda, \lambda_c) \geq h_{\mathcal{M}}(sim_{\mathcal{X}}(q, c))\}. \tag{3}$$

For this inference mechanism, an estimation can be derived concerning the probability that a correct prediction ($\lambda_q \in C^{est}(q)$) is made subject to $|\mathcal{M}|$ and m.

2.2   Weaknesses of CCBI

As indicated before, high confidence levels in CCBI typically come along with poor levels of precision, meaning that the solution set $C^{est}(q)$ returned for some query q, contains a large number of elements. While some extensions to pure CCBI have been suggested to combat that shortcoming (e.g. the use of probabilistic similarity profiles [6]), the underlying problem of low precision is not a flaw in CCBI's inferencing mechanism, but is actually caused by poor and unsuitable problem similarity measures employed. Consequently, our goal pursued in this paper is to improve the problem similarity measures in such a manner that the imprecision of returned credible solution sets is reduced, while we rely on the basic form of CCBI (cf. Equation 3) to actually perform the retrieval.

3   Imprecision in CCBI

Aiming at the reduction of imprecision in inferencing with CCBI by adjusting problem similarity, we start off by formally investigating what it means for a credible set C^{est} to be precise or imprecise.

3.1   Formalization

Precision is usually defined as the share of correct items retrieved to the overall number of items retrieved [1]. Therefore, intuitively, we might say that a credible solution set $C^{est}(q)$ as prediction for the solution of q is of maximal precision if it contains the correct solution λ_q and no further elements. However, in the scope of CCBI, we need to extend that view slightly.

Definition 1 (Precise Solution Set). *Let $\mathcal{M}$ be a case base and $\langle q, \lambda_q \rangle$ be a case with $q \in \mathcal{X}$ and $\lambda_q \in \mathcal{L}$ as corresponding solution. Then, we call*

$$C^{prec}(q) = \bigcap_{\langle c, \lambda_c \rangle \in \mathcal{M}} \{\lambda | sim_{\mathcal{L}}(\lambda, \lambda_c) \geq sim_{\mathcal{L}}(\lambda_q, \lambda_c)\}$$

the precise solution set for q.

The following lemma lets us conclude that $C^{prec}(q) \subseteq C^{est}(q)$ is the smallest, hence, maximally precise solution set that (a) will be returned when doing case-based inference with CCBI and that (b) is correct in the sense that $\lambda_q \in C^{est}(q)$. In other words, besides the correct solution λ_q, all other elements from $C^{prec}(q)$ are always included in $C^{est}(q)$, no matter which similarity profile h is used during retrieval.

Lemma 1. *For any similarity hypothesis h consistent with the case data $\mathcal{M}$ and any query q, the credible solution set $C^{est}(q)$ contains $C^{prec}(q)$ as a subset.*

Proof: Let $\lambda_d \in C^{prec}(q)$. So, for all $\langle c, \lambda_c \rangle \in \mathcal{M}$ it holds: $sim_{\mathcal{L}}(\lambda_d, \lambda_c) \geq sim_{\mathcal{L}}(\lambda_q, \lambda_c)$. As h is assumed to be consistent with the data in $\mathcal{M}$, it holds for all $\langle x, \lambda_x \rangle, \langle y, \lambda_y \rangle \in \mathcal{M}$ that $sim_{\mathcal{L}}(\lambda_x, \lambda_y) \geq h(sim_{\mathcal{X}}(x,y))$. Thus, for all $\langle c, \lambda_c \rangle \in \mathcal{M}$ it also holds $sim_{\mathcal{L}}(\lambda_d, \lambda_c) \geq h(sim_{\mathcal{X}}(q,c))$. Therefore, $\lambda_d \in \bigcap_{\langle c,\lambda_c\rangle \in \mathcal{M}} \{\lambda | sim_{\mathcal{L}}(\lambda, \lambda_c) \geq h(sim_{\mathcal{X}}(q,c))\} = C^{est}(q)$. (Note: $\lambda_q \in C^{prec}(q)$ by definition.) □

Note that for $|C^{prec}(q)| > 1$ to occur, we must require that there is at least one $\langle d, \lambda_d \rangle$ whose solution λ_d is at least as similar to all other solutions in $\mathcal{M}$ as λ_q. This situation is not as unrealistic as it might seem: It may occur even for symmetric and reflexive solution similarity measures, e.g. if they contain "plateaus" of maximal similarity (see Figure 1). In the remainder of this paper, however, we focus on regression tasks using the Euclidean distance as the basis for determining solution similarity, such that $sim_{\mathcal{L}}$ is a strongly monotonous function and therefore always $|C^{prec}| = 1$ (proof omitted).

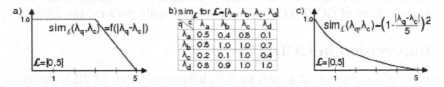

Fig. 1. Examples of solution similarity measures with $|C^{prec}| \geq 1$. In a), for $\lambda_q = 1$, for example, $C^{prec}(q) = \{\lambda_c | c \in \mathcal{M}, \lambda_c \in [1,3]\}$. In b), it holds $C^{prec}(a) = \{\lambda_a, \lambda_b, \lambda_d\}$, whereas in c), $sim_{\mathcal{X}}$ is decreasing strongly monotonically and hence $|C^{prec}(q)| = 1$.

3.2 Similarity Measures for High-Precision CCBI

We now focus on the relation between problem similarity measures, empirical similarity profiles that can be induced from them, and their impact on CCBI.

From Lemma 1, we observe that CCBI attains its maximal precision when it holds that $C^{prec}(q) = C^{est}(q)$ for all $q \in \mathcal{X}$. Assuming the case base $\mathcal{M}$ to be fixed and considering $sim_{\mathcal{X}}$ as a variable, improving the precision of CCBI means searching for a problem similarity measure such that $C^{est}(q)$ contains as few elements as possible for as many q as possible.

Definition 2 (Maximally Precise Problem Similarity Measure). *A function $sim_{\mathcal{X}}^{\star} : \mathcal{X}^2 \to [0,1]$ is called a maximally precise problem similarity measure for a given case base $\mathcal{M}$ and number of intervals m, if for the predictions produced by CCBI, based on the corresponding empirical similarity profile $h_{\mathcal{M}}^{sim_{\mathcal{X}}^{\star}}$, it holds that $Pr(C^{prec}(q) = C^{est}(q)) = 1$ for all $q \in \mathcal{X}$.*

Assuming the existence of an optimal problem similarity measure, it is straightforward to prove the following lemma.

Lemma 2. *Let $\mathcal{M}$ be a case base, $m > 0$ the number of intervals used for determining an empirical similarity profile $h_\mathcal{M}$, $sim_\mathcal{X}$ and $sim_\mathcal{L}$ be problem and solution similarity measures, respectively. If for all $\langle x, \lambda_x \rangle, \langle y, \lambda_y \rangle \in \mathcal{M}$ it holds that $sim_\mathcal{L}(\lambda_x, \lambda_y) = h_\mathcal{M}(sim_\mathcal{X}(x,y))$, then $sim_\mathcal{X}$ is a maximally precise problem similarity measure for $\mathcal{M}$, i.e. $h_\mathcal{M} = h_\mathcal{M}^{sim_\mathcal{X}^\star}$.*

Proof: We show $Pr(C^{prec}(q) = C^{est}(q)) = 1$ by proving by contradiction that, under the assumptions made, $C^{est}(q) \setminus C^{prec}(q) = \emptyset$ for all $q \in \mathcal{X}$. Assume there is a case $\langle u, \lambda_u \rangle \in \mathcal{M}$ such that $\lambda_u \in C^{est}(q) \setminus C^{prec}(q)$. The CCBI inference scheme tells that $\lambda_u \in C^{est}(q)$ implies that for all $\langle c, \lambda_c \rangle \in \mathcal{M}$ it holds $sim_\mathcal{L}(\lambda_u, \lambda_c) \geq h_\mathcal{M}(sim_\mathcal{X}(q,c))$. Knowing that $sim_\mathcal{L}(\lambda_x, \lambda_y) = h_\mathcal{M}(sim_\mathcal{X}(x,y))$ for all $\langle x, \lambda_x \rangle, \langle y, \lambda_y \rangle \in \mathcal{M}$ (precondition of Lemma 2), we conclude that $sim_\mathcal{L}(\lambda_u, \lambda_c) \geq sim_\mathcal{L}(\lambda_q, \lambda_c)$ $(\star)$ for all $\langle c, \lambda_c \rangle \in \mathcal{M}$. Further, as $\lambda_u \notin C^{prec}(q) = \bigcap_{\langle c, \lambda_c \rangle \in \mathcal{M}} \{\lambda | sim_\mathcal{L}(\lambda, \lambda_c) \geq sim_\mathcal{L}(\lambda_q, \lambda_c)\}$, there must exist a $\langle d, \lambda_d \rangle \in \mathcal{M}$ such that $sim_\mathcal{L}(\lambda_u, \lambda_d) \lneq sim_\mathcal{L}(\lambda_q, \lambda_d)$. This contradicts $(\star)$. $\square$

Accordingly, we can force predictions produced by CCBI to be of maximal precision for a given case base $\mathcal{M}$, if we manage to provide a problem similarity measure such that the corresponding empirical similarity profile $h_\mathcal{M}$ features no interval in which any two pairs of cases have different levels of solution similarity. For further investigations, we introduce the notion of the empirical similarity boundary that represents a kind of counterpart to an empirical similarity profile.

Definition 3 (Empirical Similarity Boundary). *Let A_k be a partition of $[0,1]$ as in Equation 2. We call*

$$\hat{h}_\mathcal{M} : x \mapsto \sum_{k=1}^{m} \gamma_k \cdot \mathbb{I}_{A_k}(x) \quad with \quad \gamma_k := \max_{\substack{\langle x, \lambda_x \rangle, \langle y, \lambda_y \rangle \in \mathcal{M}, \\ sim_\mathcal{X}(x,y) \in A_k}} sim_\mathcal{L}(\lambda_x, \lambda_y),$$

the empirical similarity boundary for $\mathcal{M}$ (here, $\mathbb{I}_A$ is the indicator function of set A and $\max \emptyset = 0$ by definition).

From Lemma 2, it follows that CCBI has maximal precision for $\mathcal{M}$, if the corresponding empirical similarity profile and boundary are identical for intervals containing data (and by definition, $\hat{h}_\mathcal{M}$ is zero while $h_\mathcal{M}$ is one for intervals that contain no data). Note, however, that the inverse statement is not generally true.

Corollary 1. *If, for a case base $\mathcal{M}$ and a similarity measure $sim_\mathcal{X}$, it holds $h_\mathcal{M}^{sim_\mathcal{X}}(x) \geq \hat{h}_\mathcal{M}^{sim_\mathcal{X}}(x)$, then $sim_\mathcal{X}$ is maximally precise, i.e. $sim_\mathcal{X} = sim_\mathcal{X}^\star$.*

3.3 Modifying Problem Similarity

Next, we investigate how to exploit the statements made so far for tuning similarity measures in order to increase CCBI's precision. Speaking about modifications applied to similarity measures, we stress that we consider the solution similarity measure $sim_\mathcal{L}$ to be fixed. By contrast, $sim_\mathcal{X}$ is a variable and may (at least in theory[1]) take any value from the space of functions definable over $\mathcal{X}^2 \to [0,1]$.

---

[1] In practice, we will usually confine ourselves to some "reasonable" or appropriately representable sub-space of functions.

3.3.1 Partitioning Problem Similarity

A naive approach that allows for frequently fulfilling the constraint from Corollary 1, i.e. $h_\mathcal{M}(x) = \hat{h}_\mathcal{M}(x)$ for many intervals, and so increases the probability for precise solution sets, can be realized by incrementing the number m of intervals used for determining the similarity profile and boundary (see Figure 2).

Lemma 3. *If for all $\langle x_1, \lambda_{x_1} \rangle, \langle y_1, \lambda_{y_1} \rangle, \langle x_2, \lambda_{x_2} \rangle, \langle y_2, \lambda_{y_2} \rangle \in \mathcal{M}$ with $sim_\mathcal{L}(\lambda_{x_1}, \lambda_{y_1}) \neq sim_\mathcal{L}(\lambda_{x_2}, \lambda_{y_2}))$ it holds $sim_\mathcal{X}(x_1, y_1) \neq sim_\mathcal{X}(x_2, y_2)$, then for any $m \geq |\mathcal{M}|$ there is a partition A_k (where $A_k = [\alpha_{k-1}, \alpha_k]$ for $1 \leq k \leq m$, $A_m = [\alpha_{m-1}, \alpha_m]$, $0 = \alpha_0 < \alpha_1 < \ldots < \alpha_m = 1$) so that $h_\mathcal{M}(x) \geq \hat{h}_\mathcal{M}(x) \; \forall x \in [0, 1]$.*

Proof: Let $\mathbb{S}_\mathcal{M} = \{sim_\mathcal{X}(x, y) | \langle x, \lambda_x \rangle, \langle y, \lambda_y \rangle \in \mathcal{M}\}$ be the set of all problem similarity levels occurring for cases within $\mathcal{M}$. Thus, $|\mathbb{S}_\mathcal{M}| \leq |\mathcal{M}|^2$, and $\forall s \in \mathbb{S}_\mathcal{M}$ the set $\{sim_\mathcal{L}(\lambda_x, \lambda_y) | \langle x, \lambda_x \rangle, \langle y, \lambda_y \rangle \in \mathcal{M}, sim_\mathcal{X}(x, y) = s\}$ contains exactly one element. We define $\mathbb{S}_\mathcal{M}^L = [s_1, \ldots, s_{|\mathcal{M}|}]$ as an ordered list that arranges all elements from $\mathbb{S}_\mathcal{M}$ in ascending order. Next, we set $\alpha_k = \mathbb{S}_\mathcal{M}^L[k]$ for $1 \leq k \leq m$, and for $k > |\mathbb{S}_\mathcal{M}|$ we set α_k distributed equidistantly over $[1 - \mathbb{S}_\mathcal{M}^L[|\mathbb{S}_\mathcal{M}|], 1]$. Obviously, A_k is a well defined partition. If $k > |\mathbb{S}_\mathcal{M}|$, then $1 = h_\mathcal{M}(x) > \hat{h}_\mathcal{M}(x) = 0$ for $x \in A_k$ by definition, because there are no $\langle x, \lambda_x \rangle, \langle y, \lambda_y \rangle \in \mathcal{M}$ with $sim_\mathcal{X}(x, y) \in A_k$. If, however, $k \leq |\mathbb{S}_\mathcal{M}|$ it holds that $|\{sim_\mathcal{L}(\lambda_x, \lambda_y) | \langle x, \lambda_x \rangle, \langle y, \lambda_y \rangle \in \mathcal{M}, sim_\mathcal{X}(x, y) \in A_k\}| = 1$. Consequently, $\min_{\langle x, \lambda_x \rangle, \langle y, \lambda_y \rangle \in \mathcal{M}, sim_\mathcal{X}(x,y) \in A_k} sim_\mathcal{L}(\lambda_x, \lambda_y) = \max_{\langle x, \lambda_x \rangle, \langle y, \lambda_y \rangle \in \mathcal{M}, sim_\mathcal{X}(x,y) \in A_k} sim_\mathcal{L}(\lambda_x, \lambda_y)$ and, hence, $h_\mathcal{M}(x) = \hat{h}_\mathcal{M}(x)$ for all $x \in A_k$. □

Lemma 3 suggests that increasing the value of m may support the precision of the solution sets returned by CCBI. Unfortunately, there are two important drawbacks to be considered. On the one hand, as shown in [6], increasing m also decreases the probability that the correct solution λ_q for some problem $q \in \mathcal{X}$ is not in the solution set, because $Pr(\lambda_q \notin C^{est}(q)) \leq 2m/(1 + |\mathcal{M}|)$.

On the other hand, even if $m \to \infty$, that lemma fails to guarantee maximal precision, if there exist pairs of cases in $\mathcal{M}$ whose problem parts have identical values of problem similarity, but whose solution parts differ in their solution similarities, i.e. $\exists \langle x_1, \lambda_{x_1} \rangle, \langle y_1, \lambda_{y_1} \rangle, \langle x_2, \lambda_{x_2} \rangle, \langle y_2, \lambda_{y_2} \rangle \in \mathcal{M} : sim_\mathcal{X}(x_1, y_1) = sim_\mathcal{X}(x_2, y_2)$ and $sim_\mathcal{L}(\lambda_{x_1}, \lambda_{y_1}) \neq sim_\mathcal{L}(\lambda_{x_2}, \lambda_{y_2})$. In particular, the latter problem can be avoided only by modifying the problem similarity measure $sim_\mathcal{X}$.

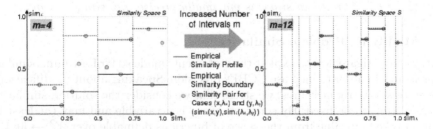

Fig. 2. By incrementing the number m of intervals, in principle maximal precision can be attained, although such an approach is not valuable in practice

3.3.2   Basic Problem Similarity Modifiers

Drawing from the preceding remarks, the need for adapting $sim_{\mathcal{X}}$ becomes obvious. As a very special case of Lemma 2, $sim_{\mathcal{X}}$ would trivially be a maximally precise problem similarity measure, if for all cases $\langle x, \lambda_x \rangle, \langle y, \lambda_y \rangle \in \mathcal{M}$ it held

$$sim_{\mathcal{X}}(x, y) = sim_{\mathcal{L}}(\lambda_x, \lambda_y). \tag{4}$$

This idea of employing the solution similarity measure as a kind of similarity teacher for learning a suitable problem similarity measure is not new. It has already been employed for practical tasks [5], has been formalized in [9], and empirically investigated in [3,4]. Although striving for a problem similarity measure that fulfills the constraint from Equation 4 in order to increase the precision of CCBI seems appealing at first glance, we must be aware that such a naive approach neglects all the knowledge about how the inferencing mechanism of CCBI (cf. Section 2.1) works and, hence, would waste useful background knowledge that can guide the search for a $sim_{\mathcal{X}}$ that yields high precision predictions.

By the same arguments, the strength of an empirical similarity profile ($h_{\mathcal{M}}^{sim_{\mathcal{X}}^1}$ is stronger than $h_{\mathcal{M}}^{sim_{\mathcal{X}}^2}$ iff. $h_{\mathcal{M}}^{sim_{\mathcal{X}}^1}(\cdot) \geq h_{\mathcal{M}}^{sim_{\mathcal{X}}^2}(\cdot)$, cf. [6]) as a function of the problem similarity measure and with m fixed is only of limited use, when searching for a $sim_{\mathcal{X}}$ that induces high-precision predictions. We will empirically support this claim in Section 5.

A final remark concerns the practical representation of similarity measures. When the problem domain $\mathcal{X}$ is finite, $sim_{\mathcal{X}}$ can be represented using a table and thus, $sim_{\mathcal{X}}(x, y)$ may be adjusted individually for any pair of problems from $\mathcal{X}^2$. Typically, however, $\mathcal{X}$ is a multi-dimensional, continuous space and problem similarity measures defined over $\mathcal{X}^2$ are represented in a parameterized way. For example, for $\mathcal{X} = \mathbb{R}^n$ one may set $sim_{\mathcal{X}}(x, y) = \frac{1}{1 + \|x - y\|_p}$, where $p \geq 1$ is a parameter determining the norm used (e.g. $p = 2$ for Euclidean distance). Here, when modifying p, $sim_{\mathcal{X}}$ is changed for vast parts of its domain. As a consequence of such a parameterized similarity measure representation, fulfilling the constraint from Equation 4 is in general infeasible (see Figure 3).

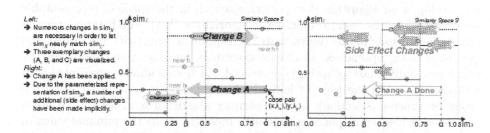

Fig. 3. Depending on the used representation for similarity measures, changing $sim_{\mathcal{X}}$ may entail changes in the problem similarity for numerous problems $x, y \in \mathcal{X}$. Here, for the case pair $\langle x, \lambda_x \rangle, \langle y, \lambda_y \rangle$ a change of $sim_{\mathcal{X}}(x, y)$ from α to β is desired. As indicated in the right part, conducting change A results in a number of side effect changes for other case pairs that may also cause the similarity profile h to change.

4   Precision-Oriented Tuning of Similarity Measures

Optimizing similarity measures in CBR is not a novel issue. A lot of work in this direction has been done, e.g. in the area of nearest-neighbor classification. Here, one tries to adjust feature weights by examining pre-classified training data [10,2,11]. Stahl [7] introduced a comprehensive methodology and a widely applicable framework for learning similarity measures which we utilize and further develop in the scope of this work. Optimizing similarity measures for the use within CCBI and with the goal of increasing the precision of predictions, however, is novel. In this section, we first briefly outline the learning framework mentioned. Subsequently, we develop and analyze required error measures that are geared towards improving the precision of case-based inferencing with CCBI.

4.1   A Framework for Learning Similarity Measures

The framework for learning similarity measures we utilize does not rely on absolute information of a case's utility for some query, but it allows for exploiting *relative* utility feedback [7]. A second important feature boosting its applicability is that it is not restricted to learning feature weights, but allows for optimizing a broad class of similarity measures [8].

For the representation of problem similarity, typical knowledge-intensive similarity measures consisting of feature weights w_i and feature-specific local similarity measures $sim_{\mathcal{X}_i}$ are assumed, where $\mathcal{X} = \mathcal{X}_1 \times \cdots \times \mathcal{X}_n$, and for the features of cases $x, y \in \mathcal{X}$ it holds that $x_i, y_i \in \mathcal{X}_i$:

$$sim_{\mathcal{X}}(x, y) = \sum_{i=1}^{n} w_i \cdot sim_{\mathcal{X}_i}(x_i, y_i). \tag{5}$$

Local similarity measures are commonly represented as similarity tables which assess all pairwise similarity values for symbolic features or as difference-based similarity functions which map feature differences to similarity values for numerical features (see [8] for an illustration).

For the task of optimizing feature weights as well as local similarity measures, we developed an algorithm that performs search in the space of representable similarity measures using evolutionary algorithms (EA). An EA maintains a population of individuals (individuals correspond to similarity measures) and evolves it using specialized stochastic operators (crossover and mutation) by which new individuals (offspring) are created. Each individual is associated with a fitness value and the least fit individuals are periodically excluded from the evolution process (selection). So, the learning algorithm searches for the *fittest individual*, whose corresponding similarity measure yields the minimal value of an error function on the training data. For more details on this learning approach and on the representation of similarity measures as individuals, we refer to [8].

Fitness Functions
A crucial component when using an evolution-based optimization technique is the fitness function used for assessing the usefulness of the respective individual.

Thus, for the task at hand, we must associate each similarity measure with a fitness value. While for learning similarity measures from relative case utility feedback, the retrieval *index error* [7] represents an appropriate fitness function, we found that more effort must be put into the fitness function's definition [3] when similarity measure optimization is to be performed for classification and regression tasks, where often only some kind of binary feedback (e.g. retrieved case has correct class or not) is available. Most of the corresponding fitness functions we investigated made use of a solution similarity measure and/or tried to induce relative utility feedback such that an index error was applicable. Being developed for usage in combination with k-nearest neighbor retrieval those error functions are unfortunately no longer usable if we work with CCBI and intend to improve the precision of the retrieved solution sets it returns. Hence, next we derive a number of candidate error functions that may be used as fitness functions when performing problem similarity measure optimization for CCBI.

4.2 Precision-Oriented Error Measures

Considering a fixed set of cases $\mathcal{M}$, a fixed number of intervals m, and a fixed solution similarity measure $sim_{\mathcal{L}}$, we can observe that

a) changing the problem similarity measure $sim_{\mathcal{X}}$ yields a shifting of data points in the similarity space $S = [0, 1] \times [0, 1]$ (see Figure 3) along the x-axis,
b) the precision of returned solution sets is heavily influenced by the data distribution in that space,
c) maximal precision can be attained, if the data is distributed in such a manner that the statement of Lemma 2 holds,
d) imprecision can arise, if there are cases $\langle x, \lambda_x \rangle, \langle y, \lambda_y \rangle$ such that $h_{\mathcal{M}}(sim_{\mathcal{X}}(x, y)) < sim_{\mathcal{L}}(\lambda_x, \lambda_y)$, in particular if this inequality holds for all $\langle y, \lambda_y \rangle \in \mathcal{M}$,

where we refer by $h_{\mathcal{M}}$ to the empirical similarity profile for the currently considered problem similarity measure $sim_{\mathcal{X}}$.

Departing from observation c), it is intuitive to employ the squared distance between the empirical similarity profile and boundary, summed over all intervals, as an error function (high fitness subsequently corresponds to a low error value).

Definition 4 (Boundary to Profile Error). *Given a case base $\mathcal{M}$, a partition A_k of $[0, 1]$ into m intervals, a problem and solution similarity measure $sim_{\mathcal{X}}$ and $sim_{\mathcal{L}}$, and the respective empirical similarity profile $h_{\mathcal{M}}$ and boundary $\hat{h}_{\mathcal{M}}$,*

$$E_{B2P}(sim_{\mathcal{X}}) = \sum_{i=1}^{m} \left(\hat{h}_{\mathcal{M}}(x_i) - h_{\mathcal{M}}(x_i) \right)^2$$

defines the boundary to profile error of $sim_{\mathcal{X}}$ for $\mathcal{M}$ (where $\forall x_i$, it holds $x_i \in A_i$).

Thus, $E_{B2P} = 0$ implies that $sim_{\mathcal{X}}$ is a maximally precise problem similarity measure. Despite this, E_{B2P} is apparently only of limited use, because the precision a problem similarity measure yields also strongly depends on the distribution of similarity pairs within each interval A_i (cf. observation b)). An example of two measures with $E_{B2P}(sim_\chi^1) = E_{B2P}(sim_\chi^2)$ where sim_χ^2 is the presumably more precise one, is shown in Figure 4. Thus, a straightforward extension of Definition 4 takes observation d) into account by summing the squared distances between individual data points in S and their respective profile values.

Definition 5 (Solution Similarity to Profile Error). *Using the same preconditions as before, the* solution similarity to profile error *is defined as*

$$E_{SS2P}(sim_\chi) = \sum_{\langle x,\lambda_x\rangle\in\mathcal{M}} \sum_{\langle y,\lambda_y\rangle\in\mathcal{M}} (sim_\mathcal{L}(\lambda_x,\lambda_y) - h_\mathcal{M}(sim_\chi(x,y)))^2 .$$

Again, although $E_{SS2P} = 0$ assures that $h = \hat{h}$ and although E_{SS2P} regards the distribution of similarity pairs within intervals more smartly than E_{B2P}, the distance between solution similarities and profile values is only a coarse indicator of whether imprecise solution sets C^{est} will occur.

Having taken a closer look at how $C^{est}(q)$ is defined, i.e. on Equation 3, and knowing that we obtain $C^{est} = C^{prec}$ if $h_\mathcal{M}(sim_\chi(x,y)) = sim_\mathcal{L}(\lambda_x,\lambda_y)$ everywhere, we can conclude that an "imprecise λ" is in one of the intersected sets $\{\lambda | sim_\mathcal{L}(\lambda,\lambda_c) \geq h_\mathcal{M}(sim_\chi(q,c))\}$, if there exists a $\langle u,\lambda_u\rangle \in \mathcal{M}$ with $sim_\mathcal{L}(\lambda_u,\lambda_c) \in (h_\mathcal{M}(sim_\chi(q,c)), sim_\mathcal{L}(\lambda_q,\lambda_c)]^2$. This gives rise to defining:

Definition 6 (Pairs in Imprecision Interval Error). *Let the same preconditions be given as before, and define* $I_{x,y} = (h_\mathcal{M}(sim_\chi(x,y)), sim_\mathcal{L}(\lambda_x,\lambda_y)]$ *as the imprecision interval for the case pair* $\langle x,\lambda_x\rangle, \langle y,\lambda_y\rangle$. *Then, we call*

$$E_{PII}(sim_\chi) = \sum_{\langle x,\lambda_x\rangle\in\mathcal{M}} \sum_{\langle y,\lambda_y\rangle\in\mathcal{M}} \sum_{\substack{\langle u,\lambda_u\rangle\in\mathcal{M} \\ u\neq x}} f(x,y,u)$$

where $f(x,y,u) = \begin{cases} 1 & \text{if } sim_\mathcal{L}(\lambda_u,\lambda_y) \in I_{x,y} \\ 0 & \text{else} \end{cases}$ *the* pairs in imprecision interval error.

Function f in Definition 6 indicates whether for two cases $\langle x,\lambda_x\rangle, \langle y,\lambda_y\rangle$ from the case base there is a $\langle u,\lambda_u\rangle \in \mathcal{M}$ $(u \neq x)$ such that $sim_\mathcal{L}(\lambda_u,\lambda_y) > h_\mathcal{M}(sim_\chi(x,y))$ and $sim_\mathcal{L}(\lambda_u,\lambda_y) \leq sim_\mathcal{L}(\lambda_x,\lambda_y)$. Consequently, one may say that the case pair $\langle x,\lambda_x\rangle$ and $\langle y,\lambda_y\rangle$ bears some potential for yielding imprecision (see Figure 4a for an illustration).

However, for $C^{est}(x) \setminus C^{prec}(x) \neq \emptyset$ to actually occur and for λ_u to be in that difference set, the two inequations mentioned in the previous paragraph must not just hold for y, but also for all $\langle z,\lambda_z\rangle \in \mathcal{M}$ $(z \neq y)$. In other words, if we can find a $\langle z,\lambda_z\rangle \in \mathcal{M}$ such that $sim_\mathcal{L}(\lambda_u,\lambda_z) < h_\mathcal{M}(sim_\chi(x,z))$, then the considered case pair $\langle x,\lambda_x\rangle$ and $\langle y,\lambda_y\rangle$ no longer bears potential for causing imprecision concerning λ_u. The following error function takes care of that fact.

---

[2] Note that λ_u is in the mentioned set *anyway*, if $sim_\mathcal{L}(\lambda_u,\lambda_c) > sim_\mathcal{L}(\lambda_q,\lambda_c)$, even if $h = \hat{h}$.

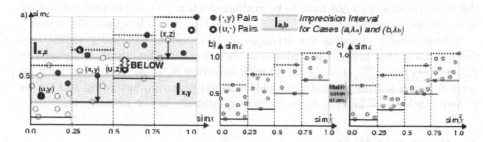

Fig. 4. In b+c), the similarity space for two problem measures sim_χ^1 and sim_χ^2 is shown (both yield the same value of E_{B2P}) which are presumed to be of different precision (see text). In a), an illustration for Definitions 6+7 is provided. Looking at case pair $\langle x, \lambda_x \rangle, \langle y, \lambda_y \rangle$, there are two data points $(\cdot, y)$ in the corresponding imprecision interval $I_{x,y}$. However, w.r.t. u, (x, y) bears no potential for yielding imprecision: Apparently, there exists a $\langle z, \lambda_z \rangle \in \mathcal{M}$ such that (u, z) is below $I_{x,z}$, which is why $\lambda_u \notin C^{est}(x)$.

Definition 7 (Pairs Causing Imprecision Error). *Let the same preconditions and definition of the imprecision interval for a case pair $\langle x, \lambda_x \rangle, \langle y, \lambda_y \rangle$ as well as the definition of f be given as before. Then, we call*

$$E_{PCI}(sim_\chi) = \sum_{\langle x, \lambda_x \rangle \in \mathcal{M}} \sum_{\langle y, \lambda_y \rangle \in \mathcal{M}} \sum_{\substack{\langle u, \lambda_u \rangle \in \mathcal{M} \\ u \neq x}} \left(f(x, y, u) \cdot \min_{\substack{\langle z, \lambda_z \rangle \in \mathcal{M} \\ z \neq y}} g(x, u, z) \right)$$

with $g(x, u, z) = \begin{cases} 0 \text{ if } sim_{\mathcal{L}}(\lambda_u, \lambda_z) < h_{\mathcal{M}}(sim_\chi(x, z)) \\ 1 \text{ else} \end{cases}$ *the pairs causing imprecision error.*

Assume, we are given a case base $\mathcal{M}$ with $M = |\mathcal{M}|$. Evaluating the fitness of a problem similarity measure sim_χ using one of the functions from Definitions 4 to 7, we have to acknowledge substantial differences in the computational effort required for computing E. First of all, the time complexity of (re-)calculating an entire empirical similarity profile[3] subject to a changed problem similarity measure is quadratic in the number of cases, as can be concluded from [6]. Thus, any fitness evaluation will *at least* have quadratic complexity in M.

Because evaluating E_{B2P} requires just one sweep over m intervals, the complexity does not rise, $E_{B2P} \in O(M^2)$. The same holds for E_{SS2P}, although here an additional sweep over all combinations of cases is required, thus $E_{SS2P} \in O(M^2)$. Counting the number of similarity points that fall into the imprecision interval $I_{x,y}$ for any pair of cases, necessitates another iteration over all cases, such that $E_{PII} \in O(M^3)$. Finally, for E_{PCI} the *min* operator (see Definition 7) must be evaluated. In the worst case, here the complexity of evaluating the inner sum can grow quadratically in the number of cases such that $E_{PCI} \in O(M^4)$, although a practical implementation may ease that by exploiting the fact that

---

[3] The effort for computing an empirical similarity boundary is the same as for the corresponding profile.

the *min* operator does not have to be evaluated when $f(\cdot) = 0$ or that evaluating *min* can be ceased as soon as a $\langle z, \lambda_z \rangle$ with $g(x, u, z) = 0$ has been discovered.

A final remark concerns the strength of an empirical similarity profile (see Section 3.3.2) that may, in accordance to the other error functions, be defined as $E_{STR}(sim_\mathcal{X}) = \sum_{i=1}^{m}(1 - h_\mathcal{M}(x_i))^2$ with arbitrary $x_i \in A_i$. Note that such an error function will in general not yield maximal precision according to Lemma 2. Nevertheless, we include E_{STR} in our experiments in the next section.

5   Empirical Evaluation

The focus of this evaluation is on a comparison of the performance of CCBI when doing inference utilizing a knowledge-poor default similarity measure sim_{def} (corresponding to the Euclidean distance) and the measures acquired during learning using the different error functions introduced above. All application domains we consider depict regression tasks, i.e. there is a single real-valued solution attribute for which we use a transformation of the Euclidean distance measure as solution similarity measure $sim_\mathcal{L}$. In accordance to [6], we measure the performance of CCBI in terms of confidence (share of retrievals with $\lambda_q \in C^{est}(q)$) and imprecision which is the length of the prediction interval (difference of the biggest and smallest element in C^{est}). Further, we provide the average point prediction errors for the respective regression task, where the point prediction of CCBI is determined as the center of the solution interval it predicts.

Note that the imprecision and point prediction of a retrieval result can only be calculated for $q \in \mathcal{X}$ for which $C^{est}(q) \neq \emptyset$. Therefore, we also provide an indication of the share of retrievals during which $C^{est} = \emptyset$ was returned. However, for larger case bases ($|\mathcal{M}| \geq 100$) it generally holds that $Pr(C^{est}(q) = \emptyset) < 0.01$, so that the influence of empty solution sets becomes negligible.

5.1   Proof of Concept

The atomic power plant domain is a small data set covering German nuclear power stations. Since German law dictates the discommisioning of all plants, the task here is to predict the remaining allowed running time of individual stations.

In this experiment, we pursued a leave-one-out validation strategy. Obviously, all error functions suggested are capable of yielding learning improvements regarding the level of precision CCBI achieves (see Figure 5). However, the computational complexity of an error measure seems to heavily correlate to its capabilities in reducing imprecision and the point prediction error. In particular, E_{PCI} reduces the length of the prediction interval represented by C^{est} after 60 evolutionary generations to 0.13 years[4], as opposed to an error of 1.78 years for sim_{def}. Interestingly, the confidence share ($Pr(\lambda_q \in C^{est}(q))$) is not impaired, i.e. stays above the confidence level of the default similarity measure.

---

[4] In 85% of all retrievals performed – in the remaining 15% it holds $C^{est}(q) = \emptyset$.

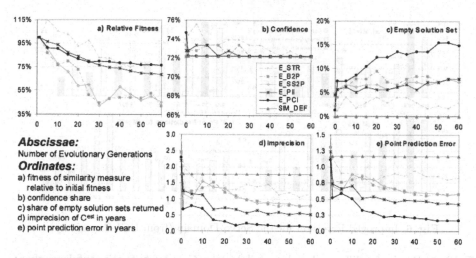

Fig. 5. Results for the Atomic Power Plant Domain (evaluations performed on a LOO basis where the experiments were repeated 10 times, $|\mathcal{M}| = 20$, and $m = 15$)

5.2   Benchmark Results

Next, we studied the behavior of our learning algorithms on several UCI data benchmark sets. In contrast to the experiments in Section 5.1 (LOO validation), we now split the case bases, learned on the first part of training cases, and conducted all evaluations of learning results on the remaining part of independent test cases.

The first question of our concern was on the influence of data-sparseness. Here, our findings are in line with [6], revealing that confidence strongly correlates to the size of $\mathcal{M}$. This dependency is even magnified when optimizing the problem similarity measures for increasing precision: Learning with small data sets, not only the imprecision, but also the level of confidence is clearly reduced. This effect is visualized in the top row of Figure 6 where for the *Servo* domain learning curves are shown for optimization processes with 25 and 50 training instances only. The bottom row shows how the situation improves when a more comprehensive training data set is used. Here, it can be concluded that in particular an optimization process using E_{SS2P}, E_{PII}, and E_{PCI} as error function yields excellent precision improvements while confidence stays at a satisfying level. Moreover, the point predictions that CCBI produces using that acquired optimized problem similarity measure clearly outperform the predictions of a k-NN regression ($k = 1, \ldots, 9$).

The results for further benchmark data sets are summarized in Table 1. Since we found that precision-improving similarity measures for CCBI can be reliably obtained for $|CB| \geq 100$, we have omitted the results for smaller training sets. As the orders of magnitude of the solution attributes vary across the domains we considered, we have provided percentual improvements/impairments of the confidence and imprecision levels relative to the corresponding values the default similarity measure yields. It is interesting to note that the changes of the point prediction error are similar to those of the imprecision, which is why the former are omitted in Table 1.

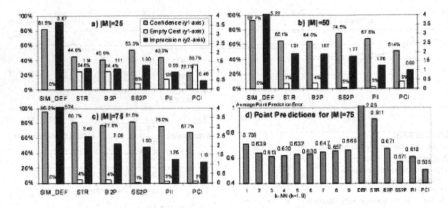

Fig. 6. Improved Precision for the Servo Domain (from UCI Repository)

Table 1. Results for different benchmark data sets. *Conf* refers to the confidence share and *Impr* to the level of imprecision, i.e. to the length of the predicted solution interval.

Domain Name	Train/ Test Data	E_{STR}		E_{B2P}		E_{SS2P}		E_{PII}		E_{PCI}	
		Conf	Impr	Conf	Impr	Conf	Impr	Conf	Impr	Conf	Impr
Abalone	200/1000	-2.0%	-3.2%	-3.1%	-5.8%	-7.7%	-41.2%	-11.3%	-40.0%	-6.1%	-32.9%
AutoMpg	200/198	-7.0%	+12.5%	-4.3%	+34.3%	-11.3%	-22.9%	-11.9%	-30.5%	-19.8%	-30.5%
Housing	200/306	-6.2%	-18.7%	-0.8%	+0.6%	-11.1%	-39.6%	-7.8%	-48.3%	-22.4%	-51.3%
Liver	200/145	-5.3%	-0.1%	-3.9%	+1.6%	-10.6%	-32.2%	-7.4%	-18.5%	-17.5%	-28.5%
Machines	100/109	-11.6%	+3.0%	-4.1%	+102%	-12.9%	-60.8%	-19.2%	-71.4%	-21.1%	-70.2%
Servo	75/91	-14.1%	-56.3%	-17.0%	-59.2%	-13.3%	-62.7%	-12.9%	-65.1%	-25.6%	-76.7%

While most of the results listed are based upon training data set of $|\mathcal{M}| = 200$ (except where noted) for learning on the basis of the pairs causing imprecision error E_{PCI}, we maximally employed 100 training instances, as the enormous computational complexity (cf. Section 4.2) prohibited the use of larger training sets. Consequently, due to effects of overfitting (comparable to, yet not as distinct as in the top row of Figure 6) the results given in the last two columns of the result table are likely to feature comparatively better imprecision and worse confidence levels than the other columns.

Summarizing, we can state that in most of the experiments conducted the gain achieved in reducing imprecision was significantly more distinct than the corresponding reduction of the confidence share. We thus can conclude that the proposed optimization of similarity measures using the error functions derived in Section 4 is highly beneficial for the performance of CCBI. Practically, our evaluation shows that the solution similarity to profile error E_{SS2P} as well as the pairs in imprecision interval error E_{PII} are most suitable for the realization of a precision-oriented similarity measure optimization. Averaged over our experiments they yield a confidence reduction of 11.3/11.8 percent[5] compared to

---

[5] We emphasize that this confidence reduction turns out to be much lower when the amount of training data is further increased (beyond $|\mathcal{M}| = 200$).

sim_{def} and a simultaneous reduction of imprecision of 43.2/45.6%. The performance of E_{PCI} is evidently superior, but, as mentioned, its computation becomes quickly intractable for increasing amounts of training case data.

6   Conclusion

The contribution of this paper is three-fold. First, we have theoretically examined the notion of precision in the context of credible case-based inference and proved several formal statements concerning the relation between similarity measures and the level of precision inferencing with CCBI may yield. Second, utilizing the theoretical properties of precision in CCBI, we have derived a number of potential error functions that can be employed for tweaking the problem similarity measures CCBI uses towards increased precision. Finally, we have evaluated the proposed optimization approach using several standard benchmark data sets and found that two of the error measures proposed create excellent improvements of the precision when generating candidate solutions with CCBI.

References

1. Baeza-Yates, R., Ribeiro-Neto, B.: Modern Information Retrieval. ACM Press, Addison-Wesley, New York (1999)
2. Bonzano, A., Cunningham, P., Smyth, B.: Using Introspective Learning to Improve Retrieval in CBR: A Case Study in Air Traffic Control. In: Proceedings of the 2nd International Conference on Case-Based Reasoning. Springer, Heidelberg (1997)
3. Gabel, T.: Learning Similarity Measures: Strategies to Enhance the Optimisation Process. Master thesis, Kaiserslautern University of Technology (2003)
4. Gabel, T., Stahl, A.: Exploiting Background Knowledge when Learning Similarity Measures. In: Proceedings of the 7th European Conference on Case-Based Reasoning, Madrid, Spain, pp. 169–183. Springer, Heidelberg (2004)
5. Gabel, T., Veloso, M.: Selecting Heterogeneous Team Players by Case-Based Reasoning: A Case Study in Robotic Soccer Simulation. Technical Report CMU-CS-01-165, Carnegie Mellon University (2001)
6. Hüllermeier, E.: Credible Case-Based Inference Using Similarity Profiles. IEEE Transactions on Knowledge and Data Engineering 19(6), 847–858 (2007)
7. Stahl, A.: Learning of Knowledge-Intensive Similarity Measures in Case-Based Reasoning, vol. 986, dissertation.de (2004)
8. Stahl, A., Gabel, T.: Using evolution programs to learn local similarity measures. In: Proceedings of the 5th International Conference on CBR, Trondheim, Norway, pp. 537–551. Springer, Heidelberg (2003)
9. Stahl, A., Schmitt, S.: Optimizing Retrieval in CBR by Introducing Solution Similarity. In: Proceedings of the International Conference on Artificial Intelligence (IC-AI 2002), Las Vegas, USA. CSREA Press (2002)
10. Wettschereck, D., Aha, D.: Weighting Features. In: Proceeding of the 1st International Conference on Case-Based Reasoning. Springer, Heidelberg (1995)
11. Zhang, Z., Yang, Q.: Dynamic Refinement of Feature Weights Using Quantitative Introspective Learning. In: Proceedings of the 16th International Joint Conference on Artificial Intelligence (1999)

Supporting Case-Based Retrieval by Similarity Skylines: Basic Concepts and Extensions*

Eyke Hüllermeier[1], Ilya Vladimirskiy[1], Belén Prados Suárez[2], and Eva Stauch[3]

[1] Philipps-Universität, FB Informatik, D-35032, Hans-Meerwein-Str.,
Marburg, Germany
{eyke,ilya}@mathematik.uni-marburg.de
[2] Department of Computer Science and Artificial Intelligence,
University of Granada, Spain
belenps@decsai.ugr.es
[3] Westfälische Wilhelms-Universität, Historisches Seminar, Robert-Koch-Str. 29,
D-48149, Münster, Germany
estauch@uni-muenster.de

Abstract. Conventional approaches to similarity search and case-based retrieval, such as nearest neighbor search, require the specification of a global similarity measure which is typically expressed as an aggregation of local measures pertaining to different aspects of a case. Since the proper aggregation of local measures is often quite difficult, we propose a novel concept called *similarity skyline*. Roughly speaking, the similarity skyline of a case base is defined by the subset of cases that are most similar to a given query in a Pareto sense. Thus, the idea is to proceed from a d-dimensional comparison between cases in terms of d (local) distance measures and to identify those cases that are maximally similar in the sense of the Pareto dominance relation [2]. To refine the retrieval result, we propose a method for computing maximally diverse subsets of a similarity skyline. Moreover, we propose a generalization of similarity skylines which is able to deal with uncertain data described in terms of interval or fuzzy attribute values. The method is applied to similarity search over uncertain archaeological data.

1 Introduction

Similarity search in high-dimensional data spaces is important for numerous application areas. In case-based reasoning (CBR), for example, it provides an essential means for implementing case retrieval, a critical step in case-based problem solving. In case-based retrieval, understood as the application of CBR paradigms to information retrieval tasks [3], similarity search becomes an even more central issue.

A commonly applied approach to case retrieval is nearest neighbor (NN) search. In fact, NN queries as proposed in [4] and their application to similarity

---

* Revised and significantly extended version of a paper presented at the ICCBR-07 workshop on "Uncertainty and Fuzziness in Case-Based Reasoning" [1].

K.-D. Althoff et al. (Eds.): ECCBR 2008, LNAI 5239, pp. 240–254, 2008.

search have been studied quite extensively in the past. Despite their usefulness for certain problems, NN methods exhibit several disadvantages. For example, they are usually sensitive toward outliers and cannot easily deal with uncertain data. Due to the "curse of dimensionality" [5], the performance of NN methods significantly degrades in the case of high-dimensional data.

Perhaps even more importantly, NN methods assume a *global* similarity or, alternatively, distance function to be specified across the full feature set. The specification of such a measure is often greatly simplified by the "local–global principle", according to which the global similarity between two cases can be obtained as an aggregation of various local measures pertaining to different features of a case [6]. However, even though it is true that local distances can often be defined in a relatively straightforward way, the *combination* of these distances can become quite difficult in practice, especially since different features may pertain to completely different aspects of a case. Moreover, the importance of a feature is often subjective and context-dependent. Thus it might be reasonable to free a user querying a system from the specification of an aggregation function, or at least to defer this step to a later stage.

In this paper, we propose a new concept, called *similarity skyline*, for supporting similarity search and case-based retrieval without the need to specify a global similarity measure. Roughly speaking, the similarity skyline of a case base is defined by the subset of cases that are most similar to a given query in a Pareto sense. More precisely, the idea is to proceed from a d-dimensional comparison between cases in terms of d (local) similarity or distance measures and to identify those cases that are maximally similar in the sense of the Pareto dominance relation.

The rest of the paper is organized as follows: Section 2 describes the application that motivates our approach, namely similarity search over uncertain archaeological data. The concept of a similarity skyline is introduced in Section 3. In Section 4, we propose a method for refining the retrieval result, namely by selecting a (small) diverse subset of a similarity skyline. Section 5 is devoted to a generalization of similarity skylines which is able to deal with uncertain data described in terms of interval or fuzzy attribute values. Finally, Section 6 presents some experimental results, and Section 7 concludes the paper.

2 Motivation and Background

Even though the methods introduced in this paper are completely general, they have been especially motivated by a particular application. As we shall report experimental results for this application later on, we devote this section to a brief introduction.

The DEADDY project aims at using knowledge discovery techniques to extract valuable information from archaeological databases. The domain under study is the analysis of graves in the Early Middle Ages. The data informs about graves, the persons buried therein, and the grave goods (objects which were put into the grave during the funeral ceremony according to religious rules

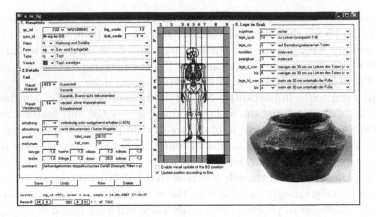

Fig. 1. Grave Good Form in the DEADDY Database

or traditions typical for the given historical moment). Fig. 1 shows a screen shot of the DEADDY user interface. One can see a data record with information about particular grave goods: type, material, position in the grave, etc.

To demonstrate our approach, we have chosen the graveyard Wenigumstadt, which dates from the Early Middle Ages and is situated in the south of Germany. The inhabitants of a small village were buried in this cemetery from the end of the Roman Empire to the Age of Charlemagne. The data set contains information about 126 graves and 1074 grave goods. Data were extracted from a relational database and put into a joint table containing attributes for graves, individuals and grave goods. In total there are 9 attributes, 3 of which describe a grave, 2 a person, and the remaining 4 the grave goods.

Imagine an archaeologist interested in discovering dependencies between wealth of the grave equipment and the age of the person buried therein. To make a first step in analyzing this question, a system should support similarity searches in a proper way. For example, an archaeologist may choose an *interesting* grave as a starting point and then try to find graves which are *similar* to this one. The techniques developed in this paper are especially motivated by the following experiences that we had with this field of application and corresponding users:

- While local similarity measures pertaining to different attributes or properties of a grave can often be defined without much difficulty, an archaeologist is usually not willing or not able to define a global distance measure properly reflecting his or her (vague) idea of similarity between complete graves.
- Both the data, such as age or spatial coordinates of a grave good, as well as the queries referring to the data are typically vague and imprecise, sometimes even context-dependent.

3   Similarity Search and the Similarity Skyline

We proceed from a description of cases in terms of d-dimensional feature vectors

$$\boldsymbol{x} = (x_1, x_2 \dots x_d) \in \mathbb{X} = \mathbb{X}_1 \times \mathbb{X}_2 \times \dots \times \mathbb{X}_d, \tag{1}$$

where $\mathbb{X}_i$ is the domain of the i-th feature X_i. A case base CB is a finite subset of the space $\mathbb{X}$ spanned by the domains of the d features. Even though a feature-based representation is of course not always suitable, it is often natural and still predominant in practice [7]. In this regard, we also note that a feature is not assumed to be a simple numerical or categorical attribute. Instead, a single feature can be a complex entity (and hence $\mathbb{X}_i$ a complex space), for example a structured object such as a tree or a graph. We only assume the existence of *local distance measures*

$$\delta_i : \mathbb{X}_i \times \mathbb{X}_i \to \mathbb{R}_+, \qquad (2)$$

i.e., each space $\mathbb{X}_i$ is endowed with a measure that assigns a degree of distance $\delta_i(x_i, y_i)$ to each pair of features $(x_i, y_i) \in \mathbb{X}_i \times \mathbb{X}_i$. According to the local–global principle, the distance between two cases can then be obtained as an aggregation of the local distance measures (2):

$$\Delta(\boldsymbol{x}, \boldsymbol{y}) = A\left(\delta_1(x_1, y_1), \delta_2(x_2, y_2) \ldots \delta_d(x_d, y_d)\right), \qquad (3)$$

where A is a suitable aggregation operator. As mentioned in the introduction, the specification of such an aggregation operator can become quite difficult in practice, especially for non-experts. Therefore, it might be reasonable to free a user querying a system from this requirement, or at least to defer this step to a later stage.

One may of course imagine intermediary scenarios in which *some* of the local similarity measures can be aggregated into measures at a higher level of a hierarchical scheme. In this scheme, the problem of similarity assessment is decomposed in a recursive way, i.e., a similarity criterion is decomposed into certain sub-criteria, which are then aggregated in a suitable way. In other words, each feature or, perhaps more accurately, *similarity feature* X_i in (1) might already be an aggregation

$$X_i = A_i(X_{i1}, X_{i2} \ldots X_{ik})$$

of a certain number of sub-features, which in turn can be aggregations of sub-sub-features, etc. Now, our assumption is that a further aggregation of the features $X_1 \ldots X_d$ is not possible, or at least not supported by the user. These (similarity) features, however, do not necessarily correspond to the attributes used to describe a single case. For example, suppose that two cars, each of which might be described by a large number of attributes, can be compared with respect to *comfort* and *investment* in terms of corresponding similarity measures. If a further combination of these two degrees into a single similarity score is difficult, then comfort and investment are the features in (1).

3.1   The Similarity Skyline

Note that a global similarity or distance function, if available, induces a *total* order on the set of all alternatives: Given a query $\boldsymbol{z} = (z_1 \ldots z_d) \in \mathbb{X}$ and two cases $\boldsymbol{x}, \boldsymbol{y} \in$ CB,

$$\boldsymbol{x} \succeq_z \boldsymbol{y} \stackrel{\text{df}}{\Longleftrightarrow} \Delta(\boldsymbol{z}, \boldsymbol{x}) \leq \Delta(\boldsymbol{z}, \boldsymbol{y}).$$

Instead of requiring a user to define a global distance measure and, thereby, to bring all alternatives into a total order, the idea of this paper is to compare alternatives in terms of a much weaker "closeness" or, say, "preference" relation, namely Pareto dominance: Given a query z and cases x, y,

$$x \succeq_z y \overset{\text{df}}{\Longleftrightarrow} \forall i \in \{1, 2 \ldots d\} : \delta_i(z_i, x_i) \leq \delta_i(z_i, y_i).$$

Thus, x is (weakly) preferred to y if the former is not less similar to z than the latter in every dimension. Moreover, we define strict preference as follows:

$$x \succ_z y \overset{\text{df}}{\Longleftrightarrow} x \succeq_z y \wedge \exists i \in \{1, 2 \ldots d\} : \delta_i(z_i, x_i) < \delta_i(z_i, y_i). \qquad (4)$$

When $x \succ_z y$, we also say that y is *dominated* or, more specifically, *similarity-dominated* by x. Note that the relation $\succeq_z$ is only a partial order, i.e., it is antisymmetric and transitive but not complete. That is, two cases $x, y \in$ CB may (and often will) be incomparable in terms of $\succeq_z$, i.e., it may happen that one can neither say that x is "more similar" than y nor vice versa.

However, when $x \succ_z y$ holds, x is arguably more interesting than y as a retrieval candidate. More precisely, the following observation obviously holds: $x \succ_z y$ implies $\Delta(z, x) < \Delta(z, y)$, regardless of the aggregation function A in (3), provided this function is strictly monotone in all arguments. As a result, y cannot be maximally similar to the query, as x is definitely more similar.

Consequently, the interesting candidates for case retrieval are those cases that are non-dominated. Such cases are called *Pareto-optimal*, and the set itself is called the Pareto set. This set corresponds to the set of cases that are potentially most similar to the query: If there exists an aggregation function A such that x is maximally similar to z among all cases in CB, then x must be an element of the Pareto set. For reasons that will become clear in the next subsection, we call the set of Pareto-optimal cases the *similarity skyline*:

$$\text{SSky}(\text{CB}, z) \overset{\text{df}}{=} \{ x \in \text{CB} \mid \forall y \in \text{CB} : y \not\succ_z x \} \qquad (5)$$

In passing, we note that only the ordinal structure of the local distance measures δ_i is important for this approach, which further simplifies their definition: For the $\mathbb{X} \to \mathbb{R}_+$ mapping $\delta_i(z_i, \cdot)$, it is only important how it orders x_i and y_i, i.e., whether $\delta_i(z_i, x_i) < \delta_i(z_i, y_i)$ or $\delta_i(z_i, x_i) > \delta_i(z_i, y_i)$, while the distance degrees themselves are irrelevant. In other words, the similarity skyline (5) is invariant toward monotone transformations of the δ_i.

3.2   Skyline Computation

The computation of a Pareto optimal subset of a given reference set has received a great deal of attention in the database community in recent years. Here, the Pareto optimal set is also called the *skyline*. A "skyline operator", along with a corresponding SQL notation, was first proposed in [8]. It proceeds from a representation of objects in terms of d *criteria*, i.e., "less-is-better" attributes C_i, $i = 1 \ldots d$, with linearly ordered domains $\mathbb{R}_+$; the corresponding data space is the Cartesian product of these domains, and an object is a vector in this space. In the simplest form, the skyline $\text{Sky}(P)$ of a d-dimensional data set P is defined by the subset of objects $(c_1 \dots c_d) \in P$ that are non-dominated, i.e., for which there is no $(c'_1 \dots c'_d) \in P$ such that $c'_i \leq c_i$ holds for all and $c'_i < c_i$ for at least one $i \in \{1 \dots d\}$.

To illustrate, consider a user choosing a car from a used-cars database, and suppose cars to be characterized by only two attributes, namely price and mileage. An example data set and its skyline are presented in Fig. 2. Point A (Acura) is dominated by point H (Honda), because the Honda is cheaper and has lower mileage. The six points (marked black) which are non-dominated by any other point form the skyline.

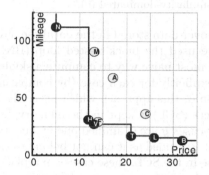

Car	Price, 1000$	Mileage, 1000km
Acura	17	68
BMW	32	13
Cadillac	24	37
Ford	14	29
Honda	12	33
Land Rover	26	16
Mercedes	13	91
Nissan	5	113
Toyota	21	18
Volkswagen	13	28

Fig. 2. Example of a two-dimensional skyline

Now, recall the problem of computing a *similarity skyline*, as introduced in the previous subsection: Given a case base CB and a query case z, the goal is to retrieve the set of cases $x \in$ CB that are non-dominated in the sense of (4). This problem can be reduced to the standard skyline problem in a relatively straightforward way. To this end, one simply defines the criteria to be minimized by the distances in the different dimensions. Thus, with $\delta_i : \mathbb{X}_i \times \mathbb{X}_i \to \mathbb{R}_+$ denoting the distance measure for the i-th feature, a case $x = (x_1 \dots x_d)$ is first mapped to a point

$$x' = T_z(x) \overset{\text{df}}{=} (\,\delta_1(x_1, z_1),\, \delta_2(x_2, z_2) \dots \delta_d(x_d, z_d)\,) \in \mathbb{R}_+^d. \qquad (6)$$

Geometrically speaking, this transformation is a kind of reflection that, using the reference point z as a center, maps all data points into the positive quadrant (see Fig. 3). The similarity skyline then corresponds to the standard skyline of the image of CB under the mapping T_z, i.e.,

$$\text{SSky}(\text{CB}, z) = \text{Sky}(T_z(\text{CB})).$$

Computing a skyline in an efficient way is a non-trivial problem, especially in high dimensions (cf. Section 6). In the database field, several main-memory algorithms (for the case where the whole data set fits in memory) as well as efficient

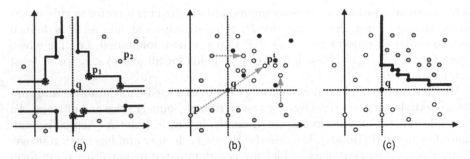

Fig. 3. Using the query point q as a center, the original data points (a) are mapped into the positive quadrant in a distance-preserving way (b). The skyline in the transformed space corresponds to the points that are not similarity-dominated (c).

methods for computation of skyline points over data stored in the database have been proposed. In our implementation, we used the block nested loop (BNL) algorithm for skyline computation [8]. The most naive way to compute a skyline is to check the non-dominance condition explicitly for each case (by comparing it to all other cases). BNL is a modification of this approach which proceeds as follows: The list of skyline candidate objects (SCL) is kept in the memory, initialized with the first case. Then, the other cases y are examined one by one: (a) If y is dominated by any case in the SCL, it is pruned as it can not belong to the skyline. (b) If y dominates one or more case in the SCL, these cases are replaced by y. (c) If y is neither dominated by, nor dominates any case in the SCL, it is simply added to the SCL. We refer to [9] for more details on BNL and a thorough review of alternative skyline computation algorithms. It is also worth mentioning that the concept of *dynamic skyline*, proposed in the same paper, provides a perfect algorithmic framework for implementing similarity skyline computation when the data is stored in an indexed database instead of main memory.

4   Refining Similarity Skylines

The similarity skyline (5) may become undesirably large, especially in high dimensions. A user may thus not always want to inspect the whole set of Pareto optimal cases. A possible solution to this problem is to select an interesting subset from $\mathbb{S} = \text{SSky}(\text{CB}, z)$, i.e., to filter $\mathbb{S}$ according to a suitable criterion. Here, we propose the criterion of *diversity*, which has recently attracted special attention in case-based retrieval [10,11]: To avoid redundancy, and to convey a picture of the whole set $\mathbb{S}$ with only a few cases, the idea is to select a subset of cases which is as diverse as possible.

An implementation of this criterion requires a formalization of the concept of diversity. What does it mean that a set $\mathbb{D} \subseteq \mathbb{S}$ is diverse? Intuitively, it means that the cases in $\mathbb{D}$ should be dissimilar amongst each other. It is important to note that, according to our assumptions, a formalization of this criterion must only refer to the local distance measures δ_i, $i = 1 \ldots d$, and not to a global measure.

We therefore define the diversity of a subset $\mathbb{D}$ of cases by the vector $\mathrm{div}(\mathbb{D}) = (v_1, v_2 \ldots v_d)$, where

$$v_i \stackrel{\mathrm{df}}{=} \min\{\, \delta_i(x_i, y_i) \mid \boldsymbol{x} = (x_1 \ldots x_d),\, \boldsymbol{y} = (y_1 \ldots y_d) \in \mathbb{D} \,\}$$

is the diversity in the i-th dimension. In principle, it is now again possible to apply the concept of Pareto optimality, i.e., to define a preference relation $\succeq$ on subsets of cases by $\mathbb{D} \succeq \mathbb{D}'$ iff $\mathrm{div}(\mathbb{D}) \geq \mathrm{div}(\mathbb{D}')$, and to look for Pareto optimal subsets of $\mathbb{S}$. However, this Pareto set will also include subsets that are very dissimilar in some dimensions but not at all dissimilar in others. From a diversity point of view, this is not desirable. To find subsets that are as "uniformly" diverse as possible, we therefore propose the following strategy: Suppose that a user wants to get a diverse subset of size K, which means that the set of candidates is given by the set of all subsets $\mathbb{D} \subseteq \mathbb{S}$ with $|\mathbb{D}| = K$. Moreover, for dimension i, consider the ranking of all candidate subsets $\mathbb{D}$ in descending order according to their diversity v_i in that dimension, and let $r_i(\mathbb{D})$ be the rank of $\mathbb{D}$. We then evaluate a candidate subset $\mathbb{D}$ by

$$\mathrm{val}(\mathbb{D}) \stackrel{\mathrm{df}}{=} \max\{\, r_i(\mathbb{D}) \mid i = 1 \ldots d \,\},$$

and the goal is to find a subset minimizing this criterion. Note that the latter is a minimax-solution, that is, a subset which minimizes its worst position in the d rankings; Fig. 4 gives an illustration. Interestingly, the above idea has recently been proposed independently under the name "ranking dominance" in the context of multi-criteria optimization [12].

Algorithmically, we solve the problem as follows. For every pair of cases $\boldsymbol{x}, \boldsymbol{y} \in \mathbb{S}$ and for each dimension i, one can precompute the rank $r_i(x_i, y_i)$ of their distance $\delta_i(x_i, y_i)$. For a fixed $v \in \mathbb{N}$, define a graph G_v as follows: the node set is $\mathbb{S}$, and for each $\boldsymbol{x}, \boldsymbol{y} \in \mathbb{S}$, an edge is inserted in G_v if $r_i(x_i, y_i) \leq v$. Obviously, a subset $\mathbb{D}$ with $\mathrm{val}(\mathbb{D}) \leq v$ corresponds to a K-clique in G_v. The optimization

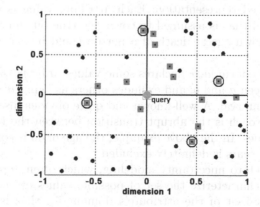

Fig. 4. A set of cases represented as points, the similarity skyline (boxes), and a diverse subset of size 4 (encircled boxes)

problem can thus be solved by finding the minimal $v \in \mathbb{N}$ such that G_v contains a K-clique.

Unfortunately, the K-clique problem is known to be NP-hard [13]. Nevertheless, there exist good heuristics. In our approach, we use a method similar to the one proposed in [14]. Moreover, to find the minimal value v, we employ the bisection method with lower bound 1 and upper bound v_{max}, where v_{max} is guessed at the beginning (and probably increased if $G_{v_{max}}$ does not contain a K-clique). Essentially, this means that the number of search steps is logarithmic in v_{max}.

We conclude this section by noting that a diverse subset $\mathbb{D}$ can be taken as a point of departure for "navigating" within a similarity skyline. For example, a user may identify one case $x \in \mathbb{D}$ as being most interesting. Then, one could "zoom" into that part of the skyline by retrieving another subset of cases from the skyline that are as similar to x as possible, using a criterion quite similar to the one used for diversity computation. Such extensions are being investigated in ongoing work.

5   Similarity Skyline for Uncertain Data

Motivated by our main application scenario, we have extended the concept of a similarity skyline to the case of uncertain data. In fact, the problem of uncertain and imprecisely known attribute values is quite obvious for archaeological data, though it is of course not restricted to this application field. Besides, note that the query itself is often imprecise. For example, consider a user looking for a case which is maximally similar to an "ideal" case, which is given as a query. This ideal case can be fictitious, and the user may prefer to specify it in terms of imprecise or fuzzy features like "a prize of about 1,200 dollars".

5.1   Uncertainty Modeling

Perhaps the most simple approach to handling imprecise attribute values is to use an interval-based representation: Each attribute value is characterized in terms of an interval that is assumed to cover the true but unknown value. For example, the unknown age at death of a person could be specified in terms of the interval $[25, 45]$.

An interval of the form $[a, b]$ declares some values to be *possible* or plausible, namely those between a and b, and excludes others as being *impossible*, namely those outside the interval. A well-known and quite obvious disadvantage of the interval-based approach is the abrupt transition between the range of possible and impossible values. In the above example, the age of 45 is considered as fully plausible, while 46 years is definitely excluded.

Another approach to uncertainty modeling, which often appears to be more appropriate, is to characterize the set of possible values of an attribute X_i in terms of a fuzzy subset of the attribute's domain $\mathbb{X}_i$, that is, by a mapping $F : \mathbb{X}_i \to [0, 1]$. Adopting a semantic interpretation of membership degrees in terms of *degrees of plausibility*, a fuzzy set F can be associated with a possibility

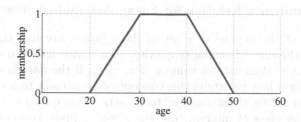

Fig. 5. Example of a fuzzy set modeling the linguistic concept "middle-aged"

distribution π_F: For every $x \in \mathbb{X}_i$, $\pi_F(x) = F(x)$ corresponds to the degree of plausibility that x equals the true but unknown attribute value x_i. A possibility distribution thus allows one to express that a certain value x is neither completely plausible nor completely impossible, but rather possible *to some degree*. For example, given the information that a person was middle-aged, all ages between 30 and 40 may appear fully plausible, which means that $\pi_F(x) = 1$ for $x \in [30, 40]$. Moreover, all ages below 20 or above 50 might be completely excluded, i.e., $\pi_F(x) = 0$ for $x \le 20$ and $x \ge 50$. All values in-between these regions are possible to some degree. The simplest way to model a gradual transition between possibility and impossibility is to use a linear interpolation, which leads to the commonly employed trapezoidal fuzzy sets (see Fig. 5). According to this model, $\pi_F(25) = 0.5$, i.e., an age of 25 is possible to the degree 0.5.

A possibility distribution π_F induces two important measures, namely a *possibility* and a *necessity* measure:

$$\Pi_F : 2^{\mathbb{X}_i} \to [0,1], \ A \mapsto \sup_{x \in A} \pi_F(x)$$

$$N_F : 2^{\mathbb{X}_i} \to [0,1], \ A \mapsto 1 - \sup_{x \notin A} \pi_F(x)$$

For each subset $A \subseteq \mathbb{X}_i$, $\Pi_F(A)$ is the degree of plausibility that $x_i \in A$. Moreover, $N(A)$ is the degree to which x_i is necessarily in A. The measures Π_F and N_F are dual in the sense that $\Pi_F(A) \equiv 1 - N_F(\mathbb{X} \setminus A)$. To verbalize, x_i is possibly in A as long as it is not necessarily in the complement $\mathbb{X} \setminus A$.

5.2 Transformation for Fuzzy Attribute Values

As outlined above, a first step of our approach consists of mapping a data point $x = (x_1 \ldots x_d) \in CB$ to the "distance space". According to (6), every attribute value x_i is replaced by its distance $x_i' = \delta_i(x_i, z_i)$ to the corresponding value of the query case $z = (z_1 \ldots z_d)$.

When both x_i and z_i are characterized in terms of fuzzy sets F_i and G_i, respectively, the distance x_i' becomes a fuzzy quantity F_i' as well. It can be derived by applying the well-known extension principle to the distance δ_i [15]:

$$F_i'(d) = \sup\{\min(F_i(x_i), G_i(z_i)) \mid \delta_i(x_i, z_i) = d\} \tag{7}$$

5.3   The Dominance Relation for Fuzzy Attribute Values

The definition of the skyline of a set of data points involves the concept of dominance. In the case of similarity queries, dominance refers to distance, i.e., a value x_i (weakly) dominates a value y_i if $x_i \leq y_i$. If the data is uncertain, an obvious question is how to extend this concept of dominance to attribute values characterized in terms of intervals or fuzzy sets. This question is non-trivial, since neither the class of intervals nor the class of fuzzy subsets of a totally ordered domain are endowed with a natural order.

Consider two objects (transformed cases) $\boldsymbol{x} = (x_1 \ldots x_d)$ and $\boldsymbol{y} = (y_1 \ldots y_d)$, and suppose that the true distance values x_i and y_i are characterized in terms of fuzzy sets F_i and G_i, respectively (derived according to (7)). The problem is now to extend the dominance relation so as to enable the comparison of two fuzzy vectors $\boldsymbol{F} = (F_1 \ldots F_d)$ and $\boldsymbol{G} = (G_1 \ldots G_d)$.

Let π_{F_i} and π_{G_i} denote, respectively, the possibility distributions associated with the fuzzy sets F_i and G_i. If these distributions can be assumed to be non-interactive, the degree of possibility and the degree of necessity of the event $x_i \leq y_i$ are given, respectively, by

$$p_i = \Pi(x_i \leq y_i) = \sup_{x \leq y} \min(\pi_{F_i}(x), \pi_{G_i}(y)),$$

$$n_i = N(x_i \leq y_i) = 1 - \sup_{x > y} \min(\pi_{F_i}(x), \pi_{G_i}(y)) \ .$$

Since the dominance relation requires dominance for *all* dimensions, these degrees have to be combined conjunctively. To this end, one can refer to a t-norm as a generalized logical conjunction [16]. Using the minimum operator for this purpose, one eventually obtains two degrees p and n, such that

$$p = \min(p_1 \ldots p_d) \geq \min(n_1 \ldots n_d) = n \ ,$$

which correspond, respectively, to the degree of possibility and the degree of necessity that the first object ($\boldsymbol{x}$) dominates the second one ($\boldsymbol{y}$). Thus, the (fuzzy) dominance relation between $\boldsymbol{x}$ and $\boldsymbol{y}$ is now expressed in terms of a possibility/necessity interval:

$$\text{FDOM}(\boldsymbol{x}, \boldsymbol{y}) = [n, p] \tag{8}$$

In principle, it would now be possible to use this "fuzzy" conception of dominance to define a kind of fuzzy skyline. More specifically, for each object $\boldsymbol{x}$ one could derive a degree of possibility and a degree of necessity for $\boldsymbol{x}$ to be an element of the skyline. A less complex alternative is to "defuzzify" the dominance relation first, and to compute a standard skyline afterward. Defuzzifying means replacing fuzzy dominance by a standard (non-fuzzy) dominance relation, depending on the two degrees p and n. Of course, this can be done in different ways, for example by thresholding:

$$\boldsymbol{x} \succ \boldsymbol{y} \overset{\text{df}}{\Longleftrightarrow} n \geq \alpha \text{ and } p \geq \beta \ , \tag{9}$$

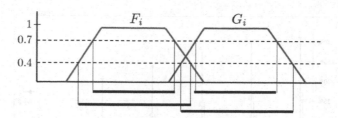

Fig. 6. Example in which the dominance relation (9) holds for $\alpha = 0.3$ (and $\beta = 1$) but not for $\alpha = 0.6$. In the latter case, the $(1 - \alpha)$-cuts of F_i and G_i intersect.

where $0 \leq \alpha \leq \beta \leq 1$. If α is small while $\beta = 1$, this means that $\boldsymbol{x} \succ \boldsymbol{y}$ iff dominance is considered fully plausible and also necessary to some extent. In fact, for $\beta = 1$, (9) has an especially intuitive meaning: A fuzzy interval F_i dominates a fuzzy interval G_i if the $(1 - \alpha)$-cut of F_i, which is the interval $[f_{1-\alpha}^l, f_{1-\alpha}^u] = \{x_i \mid F_i(x_i) \geq 1-\alpha\}$, dominates the $(1-\alpha)$-cut of G_i, $[g_{1-\alpha}^l, g_{1-\alpha}^u]$, in the sense that the former precedes the latter, i.e., $f_{1-\alpha}^u < g_{1-\alpha}^l$. The dominance relation hence tolerates a certain overlap of the fuzzy intervals, and the degree of this overlap depends on α; see Fig. 6 for an illustration.

As suggested by this example, the thresholds α and β can be used to make the dominance relation more or less restrictive and, thereby, to influence the size of the skyline: If α and β are increased, the dominance relation will hold for fewer objects, which in turn means that the skyline grows. In this regard, also note that α and β must satisfy certain restrictions in order to guarantee that $\boldsymbol{x} \succ \boldsymbol{y}$ and $\boldsymbol{x} \succ \boldsymbol{y}$ cannot hold simultaneously. Since $\text{FDOM}(\boldsymbol{y}, \boldsymbol{x}) = [1 - p, 1 - n]$, a reasonable restriction excluding this case is $\alpha + \beta > 1$.

6   Experiments

The get a first idea of the efficacy and scalability of our approach, we have conducted a number of experiments. In particular, we investigated how many cases are found to be *similar* to a query depending on the dimensionality of the case base and the strictness of the dominance relation (9), that we used for different values of α (while β was fixed to 1). Moreover, we addressed the issues of run time and scalability. Since the original data in the current version of our archaeological database is interval data, we turned intervals into fuzzy sets with triangular membership functions, using the mid-point of an interval as the core (center point) of the corresponding fuzzy set.

¿From the original 9-dimensional case base, 22 test sets of different dimension were constructed by projecting to corresponding subsets of the attributes. Each case of a case base CB was used as a query resulting in a total number of $n = |\text{CB}|$ queries. For the corresponding n answer sets (skylines), we derived the average and the standard deviation of the relative size of answer set (number divided by n); see Fig. 7. Likewise, the average run time and its standard deviation were measured; see Fig. 8. Finally, Fig. 9 shows run time results for

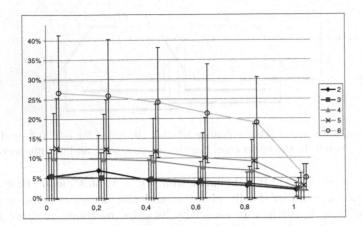

Fig. 7. Mean and standard deviation of the relative size of answer sets (y-axis) depending on the dimension (2–6) and the strictness level α (x-axis)

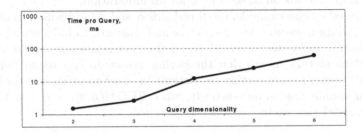

Fig. 8. Run time for skyline computation depending on the dimensionality of the case base

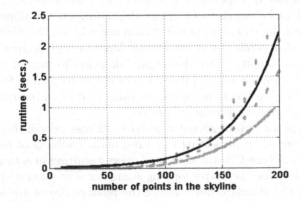

Fig. 9. Run time for the computation of diverse subsets of size 5 and dimensions 2–15 depending on the size of the original skyline

the computation of diverse subsets of size 5, depending on the size of the original skyline.

As it was to be expected, the cardinality of the answer set critically depends on the dimensionality of the case base and the strictness of the dominance relation. Run time increases correspondingly but remains satisfactory even for high-dimensional queries (171 ms on average for a 9-dimensional query). Similar remarks apply to the computation of diverse subsets.

In summary, our results confirm theoretical findings showing that the complexity of skyline computation, like most other retrieval techniques, critically depends on the dimension of a data set, in the worst case exponentially. Still, the results also show that problems of reasonable size (the number of features deemed relevant by a user in a similarity query is typically not very large) can be handled with an acceptable cost in terms of run time.

7   Conclusions

Motivated by an application in the field of archeology, we have proposed a new approach to similarity search. Our method is based on the concept of Pareto dominance and, taking an example case as a reference point, seeks to find objects that are maximally similar in a Pareto sense. It is especially user-friendly, as it does not expect the specification of a global similarity or distance function. Our first experiences are promising, and so far we received quite positive feedback from users.

Again motivated by our application, we have extended the computation of a similarity skyline to the case of uncertain (fuzzy) data. Apart from advantages with respect to modeling and knowledge representation, the fuzzy extension also allows for controlling the size of answer sets: Since one object can dominate another one "to some degree", the (non-fuzzy) dominance relation can be specified in a more or less stringent way. This effect is clear from our experimental results.

We believe that similarity search based on Pareto dominance is of general interest for CBR, and we see this paper as a first step to popularize this research direction. Needless to say, a lot of open problems remain to be solved. For example, as Pareto dominance is a rather weak preference relation, the number of cases "maximally similar" to the query can become quite large. Implementing additional filter strategies, such as diverse subset computation, is one way to tackle this problem. Another direction is to refine Pareto dominance, so that it discriminates more strongly between cases. This is a topic of ongoing work.

References

1. Vladimirskiy, I., Hüllermeier, E., Stauch, E.: Similarity search over uncertain archaeological data using a modified skyline operator. In: Wilson, D., Khemani, D. (eds.) Workshop Proceedings of ICCBR 2007, Belfast, Northern Ireland, pp. 31–40 (2007)
2. Aizerman, M., Aleskerov, F.: Theory of Choice. North-Holland, Amsterdam (1995)

3. Daniels, J., Rissland, E.: A case-based approach to intelligent information retrieval. In: Proc. 18th International ACM SIGIR Conference, Seattle, Washington, US, pp. 238–245 (1995)
4. Roussopoulos, N., Kelley, S., Vincent, F.: Nearest neighbor queries. In: Proc. SIGMOD 1995, New York, NY, USA, pp. 71–79 (1995)
5. Weber, R., Schek, H., Blott, S.: A quantitative analysis and performance study for similarity-search methods in high-dimensional spaces. In: Proc. VLDB 1998, San Francisco, CA, USA, pp. 194–205 (1998)
6. Richter, M.: Foundations of similarity and utility. In: Proc. FLAIRS-20, The 20th International FLAIRS Conference, Key West, Florida (2007)
7. Cunningham, P.: A taxonomy of similarity mechanisms for case-based reasoning. Technical Report UCD-CSI-2008-01, University College Dublin (2008)
8. Borzsony, S., Kossmann, D., Stocker, K.: The skyline operator. In: Proc. 17th International Conference on Data Engineering, San Jose, California, USA, pp. 421–430 (2001)
9. Papadias, D., Tao, Y., Fu, G., Seeger, B.: Progressive skyline computation in database systems. ACM Transactions on Database Systems 30(1), 41–82 (2005)
10. McSherry, D.: Diversity-conscious retrieval. In: Craw, S., Preece, A.D. (eds.) ECCBR 2002. LNCS (LNAI), vol. 2416, pp. 219–233. Springer, Heidelberg (2002)
11. McSherry, D.: Increasing recommendation diversity without loss of similarity. Expert Update 5, 17–26 (2002)
12. Kukkonen, S., Lampinen, J.: Ranking-dominance and many-objective optimization. In: IEEE Congress on Evolutionary Computation, Singapore, pp. 3983–3990 (2007)
13. Pardalos, P., Xue, J.: The maximum clique problem. Journal of Global Optimization 4(3), 301–328 (1994)
14. Tomita, E., Kameda, T.: An efficient branch-and-bound algorithm for finding a maximum clique with computational experiments. Journal of Global Optimization 37(1), 95–111 (2007)
15. Zadeh, L.: The concept of a linguistic variable and its applications in approximate reasoning. Information Science 8, 199–251 (1975)
16. Klement, E., Mesiar, R., Pap, E.: Triangular Norms. Kluwer Academic Publishers, Dordrecht (2002)

Using Case Provenance to Propagate Feedback to Cases and Adaptations*

David Leake and Scott A. Dial

Computer Science Department, Lindley Hall 215
Indiana University
Bloomington, IN 47405, U.S.A.
{leake,scodial}@cs.indiana.edu

Abstract. Case provenance concerns how cases came into being in a case-based reasoning system. Case provenance information has been proposed as a resource to exploit for tasks such as guiding case-based maintenance and estimating case confidence [1]. The paper presents a new bidirectional provenance-based method for propagating case confidence, examines when provenance-based maintenance is likely to be useful, and expands the application of provenance-based methods to a new task: assessing the quality of adaptation rules. The paper demonstrates the application of the resulting quality estimates to rule maintenance and prediction of solution quality.

1 Introduction

Case provenance concerns tracking how the cases in a case-based reasoning system came into being, whether from external sources or from internal reasoning processes [1]. Just as humans consider a case's sources when determining its trustworthiness [2], it may benefit a case-based reasoning system to consider the origins of externally-provided cases to estimate cases' applicability or reliability, and some systems have considered case sources in their reasoning [3,4]. More generally, internal provenance information provides a basis for CBR systems to refine their own processing through introspective reasoning (for an overview of introspective reasoning, see [5]). Leake and Whitehead [1] hypothesized that information about internal case provenance—how a CBR system derived a new case from other cases—can be exploited for many purposes in CBR system maintenance such as assessing case confidence, explaining system conclusions, and improving the ability of case-base maintenance to respond to delayed feedback (as might arise CBR tasks such as design or loan decisions) or case obsolescence (as might arise when predicting prices for a real estate domain). In principle, provenance-based methods could also help focus maintenance effort on knowledge containers beyond the case base, such as similarity information or adaptation knowledge.

Leake and Whitehead provided empirical illustrations of the value of provenance information to guide maintenance in the case of delayed feedback, and

---

* This material is based on work supported in part by the National Science Foundation under Grant No. OCI-0721674.

K.-D. Althoff et al. (Eds.): ECCBR 2008, LNAI 5239, pp. 255–268, 2008.
© Springer-Verlag Berlin Heidelberg 2008

demonstrated that provenance information about adaptation history could help to estimate case quality. The focus of these approaches is to use provenance to identify low-confidence cases and how those potentially problematic cases arose, in order to anticipate possible problems before the case is applied and, after feedback is available, to focus maintenance activities on cases or adaptation rules which may have contributed to the problems.

This paper builds on that work, focusing on how provenance considerations can enable more effective use of feedback at any time. It advances provenance-based maintenance in three ways. First, it proposes and tests a new bidirectional strategy for propagating case confidence, and provides a finer-grained examination of the use of provenance information to estimate case quality. Second, it examines how initial case-base quality affects the benefit of provenance-based feedback propagation. Third, it presents and evaluates a first study of the use of provenance information to guide maintenance of case adaptation rules, a novel area for CBR system maintenance. Experimental studies support the promise of these new directions for exploiting case provenance information.

2   Bidirectional Feedback Propagation

When a CBR system derives new cases from the cases in its case library, their provenance trace includes the cases from which they were derived and the adaptations used to derive them. Leake and Whitehead's work suggested that propagating feedback to related cases (as determined by adaptation history) provides a computationally practical and effective way of exploiting feedback concerning flawed conclusions. Their studies considered the effects of propagating feedback either to parents of a case—the cases from which the case was derived—or to the case's children—cases which had been derived from it prior to the feedback being received. Both methods were shown to improve performance, but downward propagation (to descendants) performed better in their tests [1].

To determine whether a bidirectional method could improve on both, we developed the algorithm shown in Figure 2. When the system receives feedback on a case, it propagates the feedback to the case's ancestors and repeats any adaptations to descendants (we will refer to this as *repairing* the case base). An example of a case base with adaptation provenance is shown in Fig. 1(a); Fig. 1(b) then gives an example of the propagation of feedback if the feedback was given for "Case 4." We note that adapting children to find solutions for the problems of their parent cases is not always possible. However, in practice the ability to adapt cases is often symmetric, and the algorithm assumes the ability to perform such adaptation.

Two factors complicate the propagation process:

1. Repeated ancestors: A single case may appear more than once in the ancestry trace.
2. Repeated descendants: A single case may appear underneath more than one parent (e.g., for k-NN with $k > 1$).

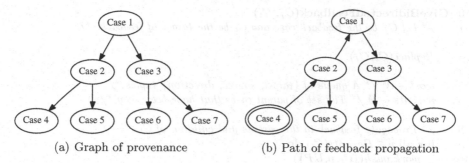

(a) Graph of provenance   (b) Path of feedback propagation

Fig. 1. Sample provenance and feedback propagation paths, beginning with "Case 4"

Consequently, bidirectional propagation must address the risk of cycles and multiple paths.

To address the problem of repeated ancestors, the algorithm only traverses the graph upwards to parents which have not yet been visited. Because the search is breadth-first, this ensures that the parent receives feedback along the shortest possible chain. By the heuristic of using chain length as a proxy for amount of knowledge degradation during propagation (which has been shown to give reasonable performance in some tests [1]), in the absence of finer-grained information we expect this to be the most reliable feedback.

To address the problem of repeated descendants, the algorithm simply recalculates the effect of each adaptation path in the provenance trace. When the same adaptation that was previously used still applies (e.g., for numerical averaging methods such as used by k-NN), this correctly reflects the change in each case's contribution to the solution. In general, if changes to the cases are small, we might assume that the same adaptations would apply, by the basic CBR assumption that similar problems (in this case, adaptation problems) should have similar solutions (in this case, adaptations). In domains for which updates to a case may invalidate the adaptation previously applied to it, how to handle propagation is an open question.

3 Estimating Confidence in Adaptation Rules

Because adaptation rules may be expected to provide somewhat approximate results, some loss of solution quality might be expected over long adaptation chains. Leake and Whitehead explored a very simple method for estimating case confidence based on the provenance trace: to predict a degradation of case quality proportional to the number of adaptations applied. Their experiments showed that in the absence of other feedback on case quality, this criterion can be a useful heuristic for choosing cases to maintain.

However, provenance information about adaptations may be used in another way, to guide maintenance of the adaptation rules themselves. If a solution is flawed, the flaw may result from flaws in the retrieval process (selecting the wrong case(s) as starting point), flaws in the case(s) from which the solution

```
 0: GiveBidirectedFeedback(C_f, C_t)
 1:     /* Let C_f be the feedback case and C_t be the target of feedback. */
 2:
 3:     Replace(C_t, C_f)
 4:
 5:     work ← ∅ /* A queue of {target, source, direction} tuples */
 6:     parents ← ∅ /* The set of parent cases that have been seen */
 7:
 8:     /* Propagate feedback to the parents and children of C_t. */
 9:     for all p ∈ Parents(C_t) do
10:         work.push({C_t, p, UP})
11:     end for
12:     for all c ∈ Children(C_t) do
13:         work.push({C_t, c, DOWN})
14:     end for
15:
16:     while work ≠ ∅ do
17:         {f, t, d} ← work.pop()
18:
19:         if d = UP ∧ t ∉ parents ∧ ¬IsReferenceCase(t) then
20:             Replace(t, Adapt(f, Problem(t)))
21:             parents ← parents ∪ {t}
22:
23:             /* Propagate feedback to the parents and children of t. */
24:             for all p ∈ Parents(C_t) do
25:                 work.push({C_t, p, UP})
26:             end for
27:             for all c ∈ Children(C_t) do
28:                 work.push({C_t, c, DOWN})
29:             end for
30:         else if d = DOWN then
31:             Replace(t, Adapt(Parents(t), Problem(t)))
32:
33:             /* Propagate feedback to the children of t. */
34:             for all c ∈ Children(C_t) do
35:                 work.push({C_t, c, DOWN})
36:             end for
37:         end if
38:     end while
```

Fig. 2. Algorithm for bidirectional feedback propagation in a case-base, guided by provenance information

was derived (e.g., due to obsolescence), flaws in the rules used to adapt those cases to the solution, or from a combination. If we assume that cases in the case base are approximately correct and retrieval is generally reliable, erroneous solutions can be attributed to problems in adaptation rules.

To explore the use of provenance to guide rule maintenance, we have developed a method to rank the performance of a system's adaptation rules, assuming that the cases to which they are applied are correct. Problem rules may then be flagged for expert assessment and maintenance if necessary. In what follows, we assume that a numerical error value can be assigned to any suboptimal solution.

Propagation approach: The rule ranking algorithm exploits a provenance trace, which for each case records all of the rules invoked for a given adaptation. When the system receives feedback about the performance of a solution in the case base, it recursively assigns blame to rules. The propagation process follows the same upward path as shown in Figure 1. However, feedback is not propagated downwards to children; feedback only has bearing on the adaptations that directly led to the creation of the case through the case's parents.

Blame assignment: The blame assignment process is inspired by back-propagation in neural networks [6]. The feedback on an erroneous case is treated as a training sample for a network, and each rule used in adaptation is treated as a weighted edge. The weight is modified in response to the error determined from feedback. The algorithm divides the local error evenly among all of the rules (a possible future refinement would be to estimate the relative influence of each rule). The algorithm then proceeds recursively through the ancestry (backwards) as in backpropagation.

Despite the natural relationship to backpropagation, the differing tasks result in a few differences:

1. Because the weights have no direct effect on the error of the system, local errors do not converge towards zero as propagation proceeds. Consequently, error weights tend to accumulate.
2. Unlike backpropagation, the algorithm does not visit all edges (rules) an equal number of times.
3. Because a new case may arise from adaptation rules in complicated ways, rather than from simple application of, e.g., backpropagation's sigmoid function, blame assignment could require sophisticated reasoning.

For our purposes, difference (1) is unimportant: We are concerned only in ranking rules by error levels, rather than in any specific error values. Difference (2) can be addressed by normalizing the weights by the number of times that they have been updated. The accumulation of error by a rule decreases confidence in that rule. The lower the confidence, the worse the average performance of the rule. This confidence information enables modifying or removing rules that are adversely affecting the performance of the system.

Difference (3), concerning the transfer of error, is more difficult to address. Because their is no canonical way to project backwards through the adaptation to assign blame to the inputs, we have chosen the simple approach of assigning a fixed proportion of the output's error to each rule. The fractional coefficient, or *decay rate*, reduces change to adaptation rule weights more distant from the feedback case. The decay reflects the assumption that less is known about sources of the error after it is passed backwards through an adaptation, and that it consequently should have less effect on more distant weights. The full algorithm is presented in Fig. 3.

```
0:  GiveRuleFeedback(C, E)
1:     /* Let case C be the target of feedback, E be the relative error of this case's
2:        solution, and let η be the decay rate. */
3:
4:     work ← ∅  /* A queue of {target, error} pairs */
5:     work.push({C, E})
6:     while work ≠ ∅ do
7:        {c, e} ← work.pop()
8:
9:        /* Adjust the weights of all of the rules invoked. */
10:       for all r ∈ Rules(c) do
```

11: $r_{weight} \leftarrow \left(1 - \frac{\eta \cdot e}{|Rules(c)|}\right) \cdot r_{weight}$

12: $r_{visited} \leftarrow r_{visited} + \frac{\eta}{|Rules(c)|}$

```
13:       end for
14:
15:       /* Add the parents to the work queue. */
16:       for all p ∈ Parents(c) do
17:          work.push(p, η · e)
18:       end for
19:    end while
```

Fig. 3. Algorithm for learning adaptation rule quality from feedback and provenance information. The result is a weighting reflecting each rule's contribution to system error.

4   Experimental Evaluation of Bidirectional Repair

To study the bidirectional feedback method, we performed experiments to address two questions:

1. How does the benefit of bidirectional repair compare to that of repair directed only to either ancestors or descendants?
2. When is provenance-based maintenance most useful?

For the second question, we focused on the effects of initial case-base quality (measured by solution accuracy) on the incremental benefit of provenance-guided feedback.

4.1   Experimental Design

Our system was developed using the Indiana University Case-Based Reasoning Framework (IUCBRF) [7]. We extended IUCBRF to automate the tracking of case provenance by maintaining a directed graph recording adaptation history for cases in the case base and to perform the record-keeping needed for the algorithms presented in this paper.

The first set of experiments tested the system using the Boston Housing dataset and the Abalone dataset from the UCI Machine Learning Repository

[8]. The Boston Housing dataset contains 506 cases with attributes capturing the quality of housing in the Boston area. This dataset includes an attribute denoting the median value of owner-occupied homes, and the system's task is to determine home values. The Abalone dataset contains 4177 cases with physical attributes for the Abalone, which are used to predict age.

For both datasets, the system used 3-NN retrieval with the similarity determined by weighted Euclidean distance, for which feature weights were determined by a multiple linear regression on the given cases. The three retrieved cases are adapted to the target problem by the scaling of a distance-weighted mean. The adapted solutions are retained as new cases in the case base. Feedback is given as the relative error of the solution.

In our trials, case bases were randomly populated with 100 cases, and the system then tested on 200 problems randomly selected from the remaining set. Each new solution was placed in the case base, with a case randomly selected and removed from the case base after each iteration to keep case base size constant. To evaluate the average accuracy during a trial, the system was tested by leave-one-out testing with all problems from the original dataset. The absolute error was measured, and the mean of these errors recorded as the mean absolute error (MAE) of the case base.

4.2   Comparing Bidirectional Feedback to Prior Methods

In order to be able to compare results from [1], we recreated the experiment from that paper. In this version of the system, we randomly choose a case to give feedback after each problem is posed. We repeated this experiment for 1000 trials to produce the average performance shown in Fig. 4 and Fig. 5.

The results show that in all cases, the bidirectional propagation has the lowest error compared to the previous best methods. With respect to the Boston Housing dataset, the improvement is not as great as that with the Abalone dataset. However, this is not entirely surprising because Leake and Whitehead noted that propagation to descendants proved more useful than the ancestors for that dataset, suggesting that the addition of propagation to ancestors might have less benefit.

4.3   How Case Base Quality Affects Benefits of Provenance-Based Propagation

An interesting question for any maintenance strategy is when it is likely to be most useful. This experiment assessed how the benefit of the bidirectional strategy depended on the original quality of the case base.

In this experiment, after selection of the original 100 cases and solution of 250 problems, the case bases were evaluated for quality of coverage. Twenty-five cases were then randomly selected from the case base to have their solutions replaced by correct feedback, simulating expert maintenance, with the case-base repaired by bidirectional propagation. The quality of coverage was then recalculated to determine to what degree the system was improved.

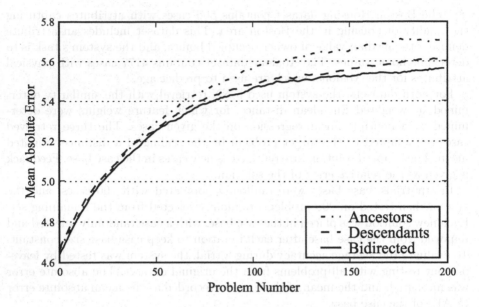

Fig. 4. Mean absolute error of the Boston Housing system for bidirectional propagation, propagation to ancestors, and propagation to descendants

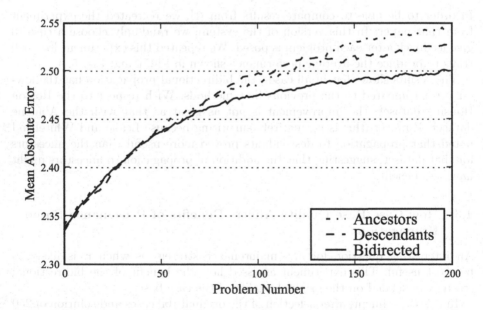

Fig. 5. Mean absolute error of the Boston Housing system for bidirectional propagation, propagation to ancestors, and propagation to descendants

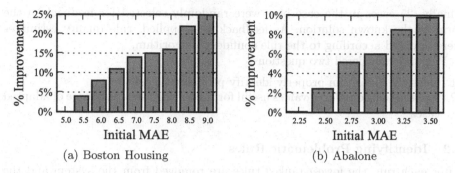

(a) Boston Housing

(b) Abalone

Fig. 6. Performance of the feedback propagation system for various ranges of initial MAE values

Figure 6 shows the results of this experiment as a histogram broken down by the initial error in the system. This shows a clear trend towards increased percent benefit with higher-error case bases.

5 Experimental Evaluation of Adaptation Rule Maintenance

In a second set of experiments, we investigated the ability of the provenance-based algorithm of Figure 3 to identify low-quality rules, in order to guide maintenance. We explored the question "Can the rule ranking algorithm identify rules whose removal will improve system accuracy?"

5.1 Experimental Design

Because this experiment required a domain for which a rich set of adaptation rules was available, for it we selected a domain conducive to the generation of adaptation rules. We extracted cases from the Homefinder.org website [9], which contains real estate listings for Bloomington, Indiana, U.S.A.. The extracted data contain a number of features useful for predicting the value of a home, as well as the listing price for each home, which was the target value for the system to predict. The collected data was filtered for erroneous values, and those cases were removed. The final dataset—a snapshot of listings on February 22, 2008— contains 333 cases.

To generate a large set of rules, we applied an algorithm based on the automatic adaptation rule acquisition work of Hanney [10], which also used a real estate domain. Our algorithm produced rules that consider only a single feature at a time, to simplify the implementation; more complex adaptations can be achieved by successively applying multiple rules. We generated 272 rules of this form.

As with our first experiment, for each run we populated the case base with 100 random cases with known solutions and tested the system with 200 problems.

Finally, 25 cases in the case base were randomly selected for feedback in the form of the known solution. As feedback was applied, rule quality estimates were updated according to the rule confidence algorithm.

We then considered two questions:

1. Does the algorithm properly identify problematic rules?
2. Are the rule confidence values useful for predicting case confidence of adapted cases?

5.2 Identifying Problematic Rules

After each run, the lowest-ranked rules are removed from the system and the trial is repeated with the same initial conditions. If the rule ranking identifies bad rules, we expect that the removal of those rules will improve the system's performance. As a baseline, the same tests were performed removing random rules.

The results of this experiment are shown in Fig. 7. Removing low-ranked rules yields a significant performance improvement for the system. Given the simple approach taken to generate rules, it is reasonable to expect a number of low-quality rules. We observe that benefits are achieved for removal of even large numbers of rules, though with diminishing returns as larger numbers of rules are removed. The fact that random removals often provide benefit is initially surprising. Given that our rule generation procedure produces rules with a wide range of quality, we hypothesize that this may result from occasional serendipitous removal of very low-quality rules, but this and the discrepancy between benefit of initial and later random deletions are subjects for further investigation.

Figure 8 shows the average marginal benefit of removing each rule. We hypothesize that two factors affect the diminishing returns shown by the graph. First, if the algorithm is performing as desired, the worst rules should tend to be removed first; additional removed rules tend to be of higher quality. Second, available feedback is limited, limiting the system's ability to assess rule quality for rules used infrequently. The improvement gained from removing rules based on insufficient feedback is similar to the effect of removing random rules.

5.3 Using Rule Confidence to Predict Case Confidence

Leake and Whitehead's [1] experimental test of provenance-based confidence prediction treated all adaptations identically. Here we exploit the availability of rule confidence information to explore a finer-grained approach, estimating solution confidence based on the system-generated adaptation rule confidence for the rules used to generate the solutions. After an adaptation, confidence in a solution is adjusted by the mean weight of the rules used to adapt it. We use the following confidence rule, where the parameter α controls how large of an effect the adaptation confidence has on the solution:

$$\text{SConfidence}(c) = \text{SConfidence}(\text{Parent}(c)) \cdot \left(\sum_{r \in Rules(c)} \frac{\text{RConfidence}(r)}{|\text{Rules}(c)|} \right)^{\alpha}$$

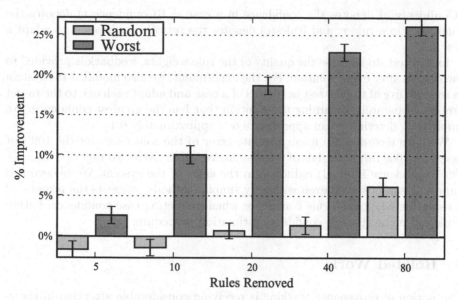

Fig. 7. Percent improvement in relative error after removing rules considered worst according to the rule confidence algorithm, compared to random rule deletion, based on the mean of 1000 runs. The error bars represent 95% confidence intervals.

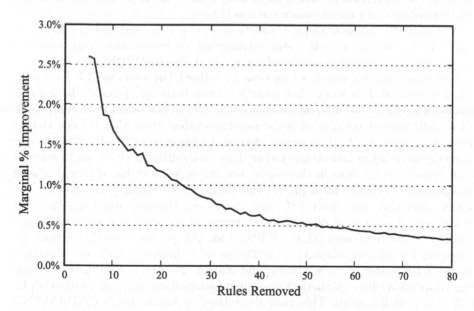

Fig. 8. A plot showing the amount of improvement per rule by removing a given number of worst rules. The plot shows 1000 trials of N rules being removed, where N extends from 5 to 80 rules.

SConfidence(c) denotes the confidence in a case c, RConfidence(r) denotes the confidence in a rule r, and Rules(c) denotes the set of rules invoked to adapt a case c.

In this test, to increase the quality of the rule weights, feedback is provided to the system after every solution. For the experiment, we also modified the system to retrieve five of the nearest neighbors of a case and adapt each one to the target problem separately, returning the solution that has the greatest confidence. We empirically determined an appropriate α – approximately 0.1.

We have recorded the mean absolute error of the solutions over the 100 test cases, for 1000 random trials of the system. We observed an average of a $4\% \pm 1\%$ (95% confidence interval) reduction in the error of the system. We believe this improvement, observed even with very simple methods, suggests the promise of considering adaptation rule confidence when predicting case confidence. Future work will refine the rule confidence estimation procedure.

6   Related Work

The notion of provenance tracking is receiving considerable attention in the e-Science community, for tracking the derivation of scientific data [11]—and even for case mining [12]—as well as in the semantic Web community (e.g., [13]). Tracing the derivation of beliefs has a long history in AI as well, extending to early work on truth maintenance systems [14].

Within CBR research, storage of meta-cases was proposed by Goel and Murdock [15] to capture a CBR system's reasoning for explanation, and reasoning traces are used for introspective failure repair in Fox's ROBBIE system [16].

Case-base maintenance has long been an active CBR area (see [17] for a sampling of some of this work), but there has been little attention to the maintenance of existing case adaptation knowledge. Often, the adaptation component of a CBR system consists of static expert-specified rules that do not change over the course of a CBR system's lifetime. Existing work has focused on augmenting adaptation knowledge, rather than on identifying problems in adaptation knowledge, as done in this paper. For example, work has explored mining adaptation knowledge from pre-existing cases, as by Hanney and Keane [18], Craw, Jarmulak and Rowe [19], and Patterson, Rooney, and Galushka [20]; other work has focused on capturing increasing adaptation knowledge by acquiring adaptation cases [21,22]. Wilke et al. [23] propose knowledge-light approaches for refining adaptation knowledge using knowledge already contained in the CBR system, and Patterson and Annad [24] propose methods for mining adaptation rules; McSherry's on-demand adaptation using adaptation triples [25] is in a similar spirit. This work also relates to Aquin et. al's CABAMAKA system, which combines case base mining with expert guidance [26]. Rial et al. [27] introduced a method for revising adaptation rules using belief revision [28].

7   Conclusion

Case provenance provides a promising source for reasoning to guide CBR system maintenance. This paper investigates the use of provenance to guide the propagation of feedback, describing a bidirectional propagation method. It also provides a first assessment of the case base characteristics for which such propagation is likely to be useful, providing support for the hypothesis that the highest percentage improvements arise for lower-quality case bases.

The paper also describes, to our knowledge, the first use of provenance information to guide maintenance of another knowledge container, the system's adaptation knowledge. It introduces an algorithm inspired by backpropagation to assign blame to adaptation rules, identifying low-quality rules for revision or removal. Evaluations suggest the promise of this approach and its potential application to assessing case confidence. In future research we expect to develop more refined methods for the evaluation of case and rule confidence and provenance-based identification of problematic rules.

References

1. Leake, D., Whitehead, M.: Case provenance: The value of remembering case sources. In: Weber, R.O., Richter, M.M. (eds.) ICCBR 2007. LNCS (LNAI), vol. 4626. Springer, Heidelberg (2007)
2. Evans, M.: Knowledge and Work in Context: A Case of Distributed Troubleshooting Across Ship and Shore. PhD thesis, Indiana University (2004)
3. Göker, M., Roth-Berghofer, T.: Development and utilization of a case-based helpdesk support system in a corporate environment. In: Althoff, K.D., Bergmann, R., Branting, L.K. (eds.) Proceedings of the Third International Conference on Case-Based Reasoning, pp. 132–146. Springer, Heidelberg (1999)
4. Leake, D., Sooriamurthi, R.: Case dispatching versus case-base merging: When MCBR matters. International Journal of Artificial Intelligence Tools 13(1), 237–254 (2004)
5. Cox, M.: Metacognition in computation: A selected research review. Artificial Intelligence 169(2), 104–141 (2005)
6. Werbos, P.: Beyond regression: New tools for prediction and analysis in the behavioral sciences. PhD thesis, Harvard University (1974)
7. Bogaerts, S., Leake, D.: IUCBRF: A framework for rapid and modular CBR system development. Technical Report TR 617, Computer Science Department, Indiana University, Bloomington, IN (2005)
8. Asuncion, A., Newman, D.: UCI machine learning repository. Technical report, University of California, Irvine, School of Information and Computer Sciences (2007)
9. Bloomington MLS, Inc.: homefinder.org (2007)
10. Hanney, K.: Learning adaptation rules from cases. Master's thesis, Trinity College, Dublin (1997)
11. Simmhan, Y., Plale, B., Gannon, D.: A survey of data provenance in e-Science. SIGMOD Record 34(3), 31–36 (2005)

12. Leake, D., Kendall-Morwick, J.: Towards case-based support for e-science workflow generation by mining provenance information. In: Proceedings of the Nineth European Conference on Case-Based Reasoning. Springer, Heidelberg (in press, 2008)
13. Murdock, J., McGuiness, D., da Silva, P.P., Welty, C., Ferrucci, D.: Explaining conclusions from diverse knowledge sources. In: Cruz, I., Decker, S., Allemang, D., Preist, C., Schwabe, D., Mika, P., Uschold, M., Aroyo, L.M. (eds.) ISWC 2006. LNCS, vol. 4273, pp. 861–872. Springer, Heidelberg (2006)
14. Doyle, J.: A truth maintenance system. Artificial Intelligence 12, 231–272 (1979)
15. Goel, A., Murdock, J.: Meta-cases: Explaining case-based reasoning. In: Proceedings of the Third European Workshop on Case-Based Reasoning, pp. 150–163. Springer, Berlin (1996)
16. Fox, S., Leake, D.: Modeling case-based planning for repairing reasoning failures. In: Proceedings of the 1995 AAAI Spring Symposium on Representing Mental States and Mechanisms, March 1995, pp. 31–38. AAAI Press, Menlo Park (1995)
17. Leake, D., Smyth, B., Wilson, D., Yang, Q. (eds.): Maintaining Case-Based Reasoning Systems. Blackwell. Special issue of Computational Intelligence 17(2) (2001)
18. Hanney, K., Keane, M.: The adaptation knowledge bottleneck: How to ease it by learning from cases. In: Proceedings of the Second International Conference on Case-Based Reasoning. Springer, Berlin (1997)
19. Craw, S., Jarmulak, J., Rowe, R.: Learning and applying case-based adaptation knowledge. In: Aha, D., Watson, I. (eds.) Proceedings of the Fourth International Conference on Case-Based Reasoning, pp. 131–145. Springer, Berlin (2001)
20. Patterson, D., Rooney, N., Galushka, M.: A regression based adaptation strategy for case-based reasoning. In: Proceedings of the Eighteenth Annual National Conference on Artificial Intelligence, pp. 87–92. AAAI Press, Menlo Park (2002)
21. Sycara, K.: Using case-based reasoning for plan adaptation and repair. In: Kolodner, J. (ed.) Proceedings of the DARPA Case-Based Reasoning Workshop, pp. 425–434. Morgan Kaufmann, San Mateo (1988)
22. Leake, D., Kinley, A., Wilson, D.: Acquiring case adaptation knowledge: A hybrid approach. In: Proceedings of the Thirteenth National Conference on Artificial Intelligence, pp. 684–689. AAAI Press, Menlo Park (1996)
23. Wilke, W., Vollrath, I., Althoff, K.D., Bergmann, R.: A framework for learning adaptation knowledge based on knowledge light approaches. In: Proceedings of the Fifth German Workshop on Case-Based Reasoning, pp. 235–242 (1997)
24. Patterson, D., Anand, S., Dubitzky, W., Hughes, J.: Towards automated case knowledge discovery in the M^2 case-based reasoning system. Knowledge and Information Systems: An International Journal, 61–82 (1999)
25. McSherry, D.: Demand-driven discovery of adaptation knowledge. In: Proceedings of the sixteenth International Joint Conference on Artificial Intelligence (IJCAI 2001), pp. 222–227. Morgan Kaufmann, San Mateo (1999)
26. d'Aquin, M., Badra, F., Lafrogne, S., Lieber, J., Napoli, A., Szathmary, L.: Case base mining for adaptation knowledge acquisition. In: Proceedings of the Twentieth International Joint Conference on Artificial Intelligence (IJCAI 2007), pp. 750–755. Morgan Kaufmann, San Mateo (2007)
27. Rial, R.P., Fidalgo, R.L., Rodriguez, A.G., Rodriguez, J.C.: Improving the revision stage of a CBR system with belief revision techniques. Computing and Information Systems 8, 40–45 (2001)
28. Alchourrón, C., Gärdenfors, P., Makinson, D.: On the logic of theory change: Partial meet contraction and revision functions. Journal of Symbolic Logic 50, 530–541 (1985)

Towards Case-Based Support for e-Science Workflow Generation by Mining Provenance⋆

David Leake and Joseph Kendall-Morwick

Computer Science Department, Indiana University, Lindley Hall 215
150 S. Woodlawn Avenue, Bloomington, IN 47405, U.S.A.
{leake,jmorwick}@cs.indiana.edu

Abstract. e-Science brings large-scale computation to bear on scientific problems, often by performing sequences of computational tasks organized into workflows and executed on distributed Web resources. Sophisticated AI tools have been developed to apply knowledge-rich methods to compose scientific workflows by generative planning, but the required knowledge can be difficult to acquire. Current work by the cyberinfrastructure community aims to routinely capture provenance during workflow execution, which would provide a new experience-based knowledge source for workflow generation: large-scale databases of workflow execution traces. This paper proposes exploiting these databases with a "knowledge light" approach to reuse, applying CBR methods to those traces to support scientists' workflow generation process. This paper introduces e-Science workflows as a CBR domain, sketches key technical issues, and illustrates directions towards addressing these issues through ongoing research on Phala, a system which supports workflow generation by aiding re-use of portions of prior workflows. The paper uses workflow data collected by the myGrid and myExperiment projects in experiments which suggest that Phala's methods have promise for assisting workflow composition in the context of scientific experimentation.

1 Introduction

e-Science takes a multidisciplinary approach to scientific investigation, allowing easy coupling of scientific research with computational studies, processes, numerical simulation, data transformations, and visualization to perform scientific research. e-Science is having profound scientific impact, enabling scientists to study phenomena such as weather systems or nuclear reactions through high-fidelity simulations with a low barrier to entry. The importance of the data produced by such studies has led to significant interest in recording the process by which results are generated—the *provenance* of the data products—for tasks

⋆ This material is based on work supported by the National Science Foundation under Grant No. OCI-0721674. Our thanks to Beth Plale, Yogesh Simmhan, and the rest of the Indiana University SDCI group at IU for their vital contributions to this work, and to Yogesh Simmhan and the anonymous reviewers for valuable comments on a draft of this paper.

K.-D. Althoff et al. (Eds.): ECCBR 2008, LNAI 5239, pp. 269–283, 2008.
© Springer-Verlag Berlin Heidelberg 2008

such as assessing data quality and validating results. Consequently, the capture and use of provenance has become an important e-Science research area [1].

Often, e-Science computational tasks are supported by a cyberinfrastructure that automates the management of data and computational tasks distributed over the Internet based on user specifications of *scientific workflows*. These workflows play a crucial role in enabling computational and data-driven science by providing the means for composing and running *in silico* experiments (e.g., [2]), and their importance has prompted interest in the use of artificial intelligence techniques to support workflow generation and use. Previous research has examined automated methods for workflow generation based on generative planning in situations where it is practical to perform the requisite knowledge acquisition [3,4], but this may be costly. In addition, studies of users suggest that they may be more interested in "quick ways of finding a relevant service" and "help for [the users] to build workflows themselves" than in "fancy knowledge-based descriptive techniques for services so that workflows would be composed automatically" [5]. This suggests interactive methods, such as retrieving related workflows and workflow fragments for users to analyze and incorporate [6].

Recent e-Science efforts aiming at large-scale capture and storage of data provenance information [7] present a new opportunity for applying provenance information, here as a source of cases to support e-Science. When traces of previous workflows are available, the traces may be mined for cases. We are investigating the use of this case information in intelligent interfaces to support scientists in defining workflows by suggesting additions to workflow designs under construction. This effectively acts as an aid to scientists for defining a new experiment based on prior experiments they have performed, or those performed by others. Our work builds on research into case-based methods for workflow reuse in other contexts [8,9,10] and other projects which we compare and contrast in Section 3. This application of CBR to provenance complements our work on case provenance to support CBR [11,12].

Applying CBR to support e-Science workflow generation will require special attention to four types of issues in addition to the standard issues for CBR:

1. **Case mining:** provenance provides a low-level view of a workflow's execution which, when mined into cases, must be made comparable to the user's abstract workflow specification.
2. **Scalability:** Scientific workflows are structured and may be large, but interactive support systems require fast response time, making efficient processing of large graph structures a significant concern.
3. **Interaction:** Effective user interfaces to support workflow generation will depend on addressing a host of intelligent user interfaces issues. These will include how best to integrate support into existing e-Science workflow composer interfaces, balancing automated and interactive authoring based on user expertise, and developing anytime methods [13] to enable providing "good enough" results when it would take too long to fully analyze all candidate cases for an optimal solution.

4. **Privacy and other social issues:** In a multi-user or multi-institution e-Science environment, addressing issues of privacy, attribution, and proprietary information is vital to acceptance (e.g., when scientific workflows are used in the service of drug design).

Our current focus is on addressing case mining and scalability issues.

Our research is grounded in a real-world project for large-scale provenance capture. Our testbed system, Phala, interoperates with the Karma provenance capture system [14].[1] Phala mines cases from execution traces to support human workflow generation with the XBaya Graphical Workflow Composer [15].

This paper begins by briefly introducing research in e-Science and provenance. The next section explains Phala's methods, and is followed by the results of experiments assessing Phala's performance and scalability and the usefulness of cross-user suggestions for sample workflow data, as a first test of the suitability of using cross-user cases to support e-Science workflow generation. We then compare Phala's approach to previous work and close the paper with conclusions and expectations for future work.

2 e-Science and Provenance

2.1 Mining Provenance for Cases

Grid computing and workflow technology are widely used by the scientific community for *in silico* experimental simulations, data analysis, and knowledge discovery [16]. Scientific workflows differ from those seen in other contexts, such as business processes, in that they are often deterministic and fully automated, with user intervention rarely required during execution.

Workflows supporting e-Science are used to coordinate control and data flow between individual Web services or processes through an annotated graph structure, as shown by the sample workflow in Figure 1. This example is a weather simulation experiment using the WRF forecasting model performed in the LEAD project [17], a large-scale project for mesoscale meteorology research and education which provides a test case for Phala. Input data is represented by the left-most node labeled "Assimilated ADAS Data/Config." Intermediate nodes represent web services which process data from the preceding nodes, and the edges between them represent data flowing from one service to another. Finally, the output of the workflow is represented by the right-most node labeled "WRF Output Data/Config".

The depicted workflow is small, but scientific workflows may contain a hundred steps or more, making them challenging for humans to compose. Also, the number of workflows that a scientist runs may be large. For example, ensemble simulation workflows run hundreds of highly similar workflows, differing slightly

---

[1] In Sanskrit, Karma means causality; the Karma project was named to reflect the capture of the causality of execution. In Sanskrit, Phala is the ripened fruit, so KarmaPhala is the fruit of provenance capture.

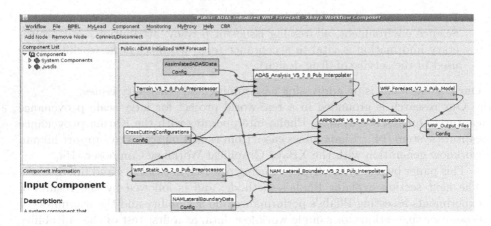

Fig. 1. The XBaya Graphical Workflow Composer

in structure or in parameters, to perform a parameter sweep study. In addition, the amount of data produced and consumed by services on the grid can be extremely large, and processing times long, making it important to generate the right workflow on the first attempt, to avoid wasting computational resources.

In the e-Science context, provenance is a type of metadata that describes the source and steps taken to derive a data product [7], which is collected by provenance management systems (such as Karma [14]).

Phala mines cases from process provenance gathered by the Karma provenance management system [14]. Karma collects provenance through software sensors embedded in the services represented as task nodes in workflows, operating independently of the workflow management system used. The information collected can be mined to produce workflow execution traces that identify producer/consumer relationships for data exchange by these services.

To generate cases, Phala mines the data flow between services within an instance of workflow execution. Workflows themselves would be equally useful as a source of data to mine (in fact, we mined a collection of workflows to generate data to evaluate our system), however we currently focus on building a tool for mining provenance because cyberinfrastructures using provenance management systems will have this data readily available on a long term basis and in a more homogeneous format. In addition, workflows can vary greatly in specification language used and support for various control and data flow patterns [18], but execution traces mined from provenance provide a simplified view of the execution of a workflow, while providing sufficient detail to support Phala's task of service recommendation.

2.2 The User Interface

Phala has been developed as a plug-in for the graphical workflow composer XBaya [15], an interface for authoring e-Science workflows composed of Web services (Figure 1 shows a portion of an XBaya screenshot). In XBaya, scientists interact with a graphical representation of workflows that abstracts away the details of workflow languages so that users who are not familiar with such languages can use the tool. Workflows are represented as directed graphs in which nodes represent services and control flow constructs within the workflow, and edges represent the transmission of data or control information between services.

Phala suggests "next steps," or extensions, from a partially authored workflow to an incrementally more developed workflow. The goal of providing these suggestions is twofold: first, to inform users about data and services that they might not have considered when authoring a workflow (e.g., by making new suggestions based on the workflows of others), and, second, making familiar components conveniently accessible for reuse (e.g., by making suggestions based on similarities to the user's own prior workflows).

At any point during the construction of a workflow, the current state of the workflow can be considered a query to the Phala plug-in. The plug-in sends that query to the Phala Web service, which searches prior cases for relevant information and, if successful, returns a collection of edges to new services. These queries are performed automatically every time the user makes a change to the workflow. If results are found, they are displayed as soon as they are received. No results are displayed if Phala determines that the quality of the suggestions is too low (based on a similarity threshold). An anytime algorithm is used to assure that suggestions will be generated in a reasonable time frame.

If Phala finds a sufficiently relevant suggestion, the system presents it as an additional highlighted node connected to the selected node. The user may then opt to have this extension automatically added to the workflow, sidestepping an otherwise possibly laborious process of manually determining which service to use, locating it in the registry, and loading/adding it to the available services in XBaya, before adding the service instance to the workflow.

3   Case-Based Support for e-Science Workflow Generation

Phala focuses on retrieval to support user extension of workflows under construction. When the user makes a change to the workflow, Phala forms a query from the new workflow and retrieves similar cases (execution traces). Phala replaces traditional adaptation with *extraction* and *re-capture*. Its extraction process determines which services used in the execution trace should be suggested as extensions to the query workflow. Once the workflow completes execution, the control decisions made during the execution are reflected in the recorded provenance, resulting in a more specific case on the execution path taken than the original workflow. That case is then captured for future use. This process is illustrated in Figure 2.

As a workflow is composed, Phala compares the state of the workflow being composed with cases in its case-base of execution traces to search for possible extensions. This similarity assessment problem differs from comparing workflows to other workflows because the set of control patterns in a workflow is more extensive. In the execution traces, only Sequence (the passing of control from one

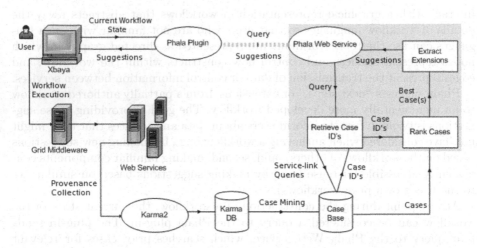

Fig. 2. Phala's re-use cycle

service to the next), AND-join (the merging of parallel processes) and AND-split (the splitting of one process into multiple parallel processes) control patterns exist. Also, segments of the workflow may appear any number of times in the processing trace depending on whether they were between an XOR split/join (exclusive choice of the next service to be executed) or part of a loop.[2]

Retrieval. Once non-deterministic control flow constructs are removed from a query to convert the form of the workflow to match that of the execution traces, similar execution traces are retrieved. The graph structure of the cases makes case matching potentially expensive for large e-Science case bases, but the services used in each node provide a promising set of content-based indices for more rapid retrieval. Consequently, Phala uses a two-step retrieval process: an inexpensive coarse-grained retrieval followed by a more expensive matching process to select the most promising candidates. Based on experiments discussed at the end of the following section, we believe that this simple approach is sufficiently efficient for medium to large case-bases of moderately sized cases.

For coarse-grained retrieval, Phala uses an indexing strategy similar to a filter used for comparing CAD models [19] and engineered to return results that will score highest according to its similarity assessment algorithm. Indices are the services (each node represents a unique service) combined with service links (an edge between two nodes solely identified by their services).

Phala retrieves from a database the entries for all workflows containing any one of the service links used in the query. In order to increase efficiency, only case identifiers are retrieved, rather than complete case structures. Because a stored case may have multiple matches with the services and service links in a query, cases are ranked by the number of times they are present in the results

---

[2] For a detailed discussion of workflow patterns see van der Aalst et. al [18] or the Workflow Patterns Web site: http://www.workflowpatterns.com

```
 1: INPUT: Q is a workflow
 2: IDS ← {} {IDS maps case id's to a relevance score}
 3: for all service links L in Q do {course-grained similarity assessment}
 4:     Retrieve all id's for workflows containing L
 5:     for all retrieved id's ID do
 6:         if IDS does not map ID to any value then
 7:             Map ID to 0 in IDS
 8:         else
 9:             Increment the value IDS maps to ID
10:         end if
11:     end for
12: end for
13: Insert id's from IDS into RANKED in decreasing order of their mapped values
14: Retrieve workflows for the top N id's in RANKED {N is a predefined limit}
15: Let C be a workflow with maximal mapping to Q {fine-grained similarity assess-
    ment}
16: Compute a map M between the nodes of Q and C {M identifies a sub-graph
    relationship}
17: for all pairs {NQ, NC} in M do
18:     for all edges {FROM, TO} in C such that FROM = NC do
19:         if M does not map any value to TO then
20:             Yield the edge {NQ, TO} as a suggestion
21:         end if
22:     end for
23: end for
```

Fig. 3. A sketch of Phala's re-use algorithm

of a query and only the top-ranked cases are fully retrieved and sent to the comparison phase. This process is represented by steps 3 - 14 in Figure 3.

Similarity Assessment. Once the top-ranked execution traces containing similar service links are retrieved, they are re-ranked by the size of the largest mapping produced between the query and the retrieved case (step 15 in Figure 3). The top ranked case (in the case of a tie, one is chosen at random) is then used to extract extension suggestions (steps 16 - 23 in Figure 3). This and other graph-based comparison methods for workflows are discussed by Goderis et. al. [6]. They found that graph matching algorithms can generate similarity rankings close to the average of those created by domain experts.

Phala's similarity assessment is based on a metric proposed by Minor et al.[20], with two significant differences. Apart from control structures, Minor et. al. consider each service within a workflow to be unique. Structural comparison can now be performed by summing the number of service links and services which are not common between the case and the query. The sum represents the edit distance between them, where an edit operation is the addition or deletion of a node or edge. Minor et. al. use this as a distance metric after normalizing by the number of all services and service links in the query and the case.

For Phala, comparing a query to a case for similarity does not involve determining how close to equality the two graphs are, but rather how close the query is to being a subgraph of the case. In fact, the case must be a supergraph of the portion of the query for which Phala is to produce suggestions. To determine similarity based on the minimum edit distance from the query to a subgraph of the case, it is sufficient for us to count how many services and service links are shared between the query and the case, in contrast to Minor et. al.'s method that counts non-common services and service links. In this scenario, a maximum similarity score (number of services and service links present in the query) represents a full subgraph relationship. Normalization is not required in Phala, because every comparison is only relevant to one query.

Phala's task also contrasts in that it must sometimes consider workflows with multiple instances of the same service, as is not uncommon in e-Science (we have encountered multiple instances in scientific workflows, e.g., within the my-Experiment [21] dataset). Phala supports workflows that re-use general-purpose computations at different points in processing by allowing for repeated use of services in the query and the case-base. Incorporating Minor et. al.'s methods of approximating similarity in the presence of repeated control structures could be useful for this purpose, but because the extraction task ultimately requires an accurate correspondence between the nodes of the query and the nodes of the case in order to generate suggestions, we are instead applying a greedy algorithm to search for an optimal mapping between the nodes of the query and the nodes of the case (cf. Champin and Solnon [22]). Such an optimization is necessary because, in the worst case (where only one service is used in both the case and the query), the problem of comparing workflows becomes the same as the subgraph isomorphism problem, which is NP-complete [22]. Once the mapping is complete, extensions are generated by identifying edges in the case from a node which is mapped, and to a node which is not mapped.

4   Evaluation

To assess Phala's performance and the potential to exploit available provenance data for case-based support, we performed experiments addressing four questions:

1. Given real data, how often will Phala produce relevant suggestions?
2. Given real data, how often will Phala be able to produce suggestions matching user choices?
3. How does performance vary when relying on a user's own prior workflows vs. workflows of others?
4. How scalable is Phala's retrieval method?

4.1   Ability to Produce Relevant Suggestions and Match User Choices

Data. For workflow data, we used the public database of workflows available from the myGrid/myExperiment projects[3] [21,23,24]. These projects facilitate

---

[3] These repositories can be found at "http://workflows.mygrid.org.uk/repository/" and "http://www.myexperiment.org," respectively.

workflow development through re-use of prior knowledge, by providing information enabling users to locate relevant services and re-purpose similar workflows [25]. Our data set contains 236 workflows from both the public myGrid repository and the myExperiment Web site. These workflows relate primarily to bio-informatics experiments and have 860 unique services and 2792 unique service links[4]. Some non-deterministic control data is present in a minority of these workflows, but it is discarded and only the data flow is considered for the purposes of our analysis.

Evaluation Method. The experiments for questions 1 and 2 were performed using leave-one-out testing with the myGrid/myExperiment data-set. Queries are formed for each workflow by deleting a single node and its connected edges. Each input edge leading into the deleted node is counted as an "opportunity" for a suggestion. These edges are then compared with the suggested extensions generated by Phala. If a suggested edge links *from* the same node as one of the deleted edges, an "attempt" is recorded. If the suggested edge also links *to* the same service as the deleted node, making the suggestion identical to the choice of the original workflow designer, a "success" is recorded. We will refer to the proportion of attempts to opportunities as the suggestion rate and the proportion of successes to attempts as the success rate.

As a baseline for comparison, we devised another knowledge light method of suggesting new edges that does not rely on the structure of individual cases, the "popular link" method. This method identifies the service to which the given node's service is most often linked, and links the node to an instance of that service. In the case that multiple services are tied for most-linked-to, one of them is selected at random. For comparison purposes, proportional success was recorded when the target service was within the set of possible suggestions, rather than making random choices. The popular link method relates to a similar method proposed by Xiang and Madey [3], which is discussed in Section 5.

Phala uses similarity as a predictive measure of the quality of the suggestions that the system makes. A user-determined similarity threshold controls a tradeoff between suggestion and success rates for a particular user. At threshold 0, all results are considered; at threshold 1, only results in which the query was a subgraph of the retrieved case are considered. Because the popular-link method is not case-based, it requires a different strategy for predicting suggestion quality. Here *suggestion quality* was considered to be the number of times the target service was linked proportionate to the number of times any service was linked.

To compare the different methods, for each method we tuned the method's quality threshold to generate a desired collection of suggestion rates, for which we could then compare the success rates. Using the popular-link method at a quality threshold of 0 (all suggestions are considered), a suggestion is made 79% of the time with a success rate of 47%. The results with the case-based method (also with a quality threshold of 0) are more conservative, making a suggestion

---

[4] We determined uniqueness differently for different types of nodes within the workflows. Where applicable, parameter values are ignored and service names, locations, and the exact texts of scripts are used to identify a service.

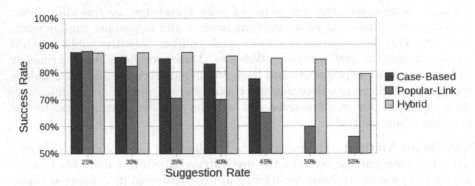

Fig. 4. Analysis of Suggestion Methods

45% of the time but with a much higher success rate of 77%. The success rates tended to rise and the suggestion rate strictly decreased as the threshold of consideration was raised. Figure 4 shows the results. Note that because the case-based method's maximum suggestion rate was 45%, no values are shown for that method at higher suggestion rates.

4.2 A Hybrid Method

The different strengths of the two methods suggested that a hybrid method might give the best results. We developed a hybrid method that generally uses the case-based suggestion but falls back on the popular-link method of suggestion when the popular-link quality is above a constant cut-off value and is expected to have higher quality than the case-based suggestion.[5] If a case-based suggestion is ever present in the set of suggestions generated by the popular-link method, it is used as the tie-breaking vote rather than choosing one at random. At a quality threshold of 0, this method produced a higher suggestion rate than the case-based method at 56.1%, allowing us to add additional comparisons to the popular-link method in Figure 4 at 50% and 55%.

A χ^2 test was used to determine the significance of differences in success rates between methods. Differences were considered significant when P was less than 0.05. No significant difference was found between the case-based method and the hybrid method for suggestion rates 25% through 40%, but the difference was significant at 45%. Because the case-based method attained a 47% suggestion rate at quality threshold 0 (the lowest possible setting), the success rate could not be measured at 50% or 55% for this method. There was no statistically significant difference in success rates between the popular-link and either of the case-based and hybrid methods at 25% and 30%. The differences were significant at all other suggestion rates.

It is important to note that relevance of services is difficult to determine (and is, in fact, an interesting research issue that we intend to explore), so we do not

---

[5] Though the quality measures for the case-based and popular-link methods cannot directly be compared, we developed a rough translation for this purpose.

consider our results to represent precision. Rather, the success rate we recorded represents a lower bound on precision, as services other than the service used in the deleted node may also be relevant.

4.3 Authorship Effects

Phala aims both to provide quick reminders of services the author has used in the past (potentially from the author's own workflows) and to provide suggestions for services the author might not have in mind (potentially from workflows of others). The following experiment explores how each source contributes to Phala's suggestions.

Evaluation Method. To test authorship effects, we used the authorship data included with the myGrid/myExperiment data set. Workflows on myExperiment are labeled with authors, contributors, and uploaders. Workflows in the myGrid repository are separated into different directories labeled with users' names. We re-ran our previous experiments in two new scenarios. In the first, the case-base for a given query was selected to be all of the other workflows credited to the same author as that of the query. In the second, the case-base included all workflows except those credited to the author of the query. The case-based method of generating suggestions was used in the analysis.

Results. Both the author's collection of workflows and the rest of the database turned out to be useful sources of data for suggestions. The results for each source separately were comparable to, though worse than, the original results when all workflows were included in the case-base. When only populating the case-base with workflows from the same authors, the suggestion rate was 36% and the success rate was 72%, compared to 37% and 70% when only populating the case-base with workflows that were not from the same author. This is compared to 45% and 77% when all workflows are included.

Though the results are encouraging, we believe that the authorship data we have may be incomplete, and that this may have increased scores for the scenario when the case-base is populated only with workflows that were not from the same author. We plan to repeat these experiments once more complete authorship data is available.

4.4 Scalability

Evaluation Method. To obtain a large set of test cases for this evaluation we generated artificial data. We generated execution traces with between 5 and 15 services drawn randomly from a predefined set of arbitrary service labels. Each node was randomly linked to one other node. We also developed a set of artificial workflow data that mirrored the myGrid/myExperiment data-set in terms of clustering statistics for our similarity metric and also in terms of statistics on frequency distribution of service links (cf. [26]).

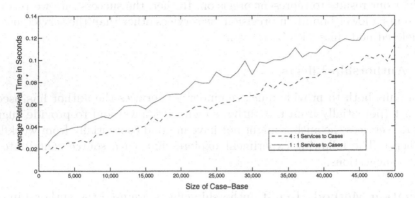

Fig. 5. Average Retrieval Time When Generating Case-Bases With Different Ratios of Services to Cases

This evaluation was performed with an average of 4 services per case in the generated cases, which is close to the ratio of the myGrid/myExperiment data-set. Because the myGrid/myExperiment data-set consists of only 236 workflows, and it is possible that the ratio with other case bases might differ, we also ran the evaluation with an average of 1 service per case, which we expected to reduce the efficiency of retrieval.

We loaded 1000 cases into the case-base and randomly selected 100 of them to be queries (this time leaving the queries in the case-base). We performed 500 iterations of this test, each time increasing the case-base size by 1000 cases. The results are shown in Figure 5. The evaluations were run on a 1.66 Ghz Intel Core Duo laptop with 1 GB of RAM and running Ubuntu 7.10 and mySQL.

Results. Retrieval times for both approaches started out near 0.02 seconds for case-bases of 1000 cases. When 50,000 cases were considered, retrieval times increased to 0.11 seconds when generating 4 services per trace. When generating 1 service per trace, retrieval times increased to 0.13 seconds. Both graphs are roughly linear. Although the number of services has a significant effect on retrieval time, we consider these times acceptable.

5   Related Work

A number of projects in the e-Science domain employ knowledge-rich generative methods. One such project called CAT (Composition Analysis Tool) and developed by Kim, Spraragen, and Gil, is a mixed-initiative system for developing workflows [4]. Their tool validates workflows and provides an interface that suggests edits to correct invalid workflows. Background knowledge and ontologies are combined with an AI planning framework to suggest node additions and replacements that move the workflow toward the goal of producing the desired outputs, at times allowing for abstract nodes to act as place holders for concrete, executable nodes. A main difference with Phala is that, instead of requiring a pre-constructed ontology, Phala depends on its case base; it needs no additional support other than the installation of a system for provenance collection.

Case-based methods have also been employed in a number of related projects. A project by Xiang and Madey uses a method similar to the 'popular-link' method of re-using past experience as part of a planning approach to assisting workflow composition [3], though without the quality metric used in our hybrid approach. In their work, users are presented with a ranked list of services which is constructed with semantic information and a table of service links mined from previous workflows. They also propose a planning approach that constructs a sequence of services linking to other services or abstract input / output requirements of a task. In general their work focuses on a more abstract process of composing a complete workflow from specifications, whereas the Phala project focuses on the specific task of suggesting minimal extensions to partially composed workflows. Their work also involves retrieving previously executed workflows similar to a workflow currently being authored. The user can then adapt features of the retrieved workflows into the workflow they are in the process of developing. Phala differs in its automatic extraction; Xiang and Madey's method provides more information to the user but requires more user assistance in adapting it.

Beyond the domain of e-Science, Minor et al. have developed a system for case-based agile workflow support [8,20]. In their system, cases represent a workflow revision as a pair of two workflows: one representing the workflow before the revision and the other representing the revised workflow. Along with contextual information and domain knowledge, these cases are retrieved in order to determine how a similar workflow can be altered. They also present a similarity metric which we have adapted to suit the characteristics of Phala's workflows. Weber et. al [9] also support workflow adaptation with CBR. Their tool, CBR-Flow, uses Conversational Case-Based Reasoning to adapt a workflow to new circumstances at execution time.

Madhusudan and Zhao have investigated case-based support for workflow modeling in the business process domain [10]. Their system, CODAW, utilizes workflow templates of varying degrees of generality, as well as concrete cases of previously defined workflows. Their work includes various indexing techniques and graph-based case retrieval. Their system also supports workflow composition through generative planning. Another related system, DWMSS, developed by Kim et. al. [27], stores cases in a hierarchical tree for facilitating user retrieval.

6   Conclusion and Future Work

Phala explores a case-based, knowledge-light approach to supporting production of e-Science workflows. We view the current results as encouraging for the ability of knowledge light case-based methods to draw on databases of workflows or provenance traces to assist the authors of scientific workflows.

Phala currently suggests single services. In our future work we expect to expand the types of suggestions Phala makes to include sequences of services or partial workflows, control information, and annotations, in addition to exploring the case-based suggestion of specific data products. We also intend to mine and directly exploit more of the semantic information existing in provenance and workflows, and to explore inclusion of user-driven generation of semantic information, such as tagging, which is used in the myExperiment project [21], or ontologies when available. In addition, we intend to develop Phala plug-ins for alternative workflow composition tools to allow larger-scale testing and to enable integration of Phala into mainstream e-Science experimentation.

References

1. Simmhan, Y., Plale, B., Gannon, D.: A survey of data provenance in e-Science. SIGMO Record 34(3), 31–36 (2005)
2. Gil, Y., Deelman, E., Blythe, J., Kesselman, C., Tangmunarunkit, H.: Artificial intelligence and grids: Workflow planning and beyond. IEEE Intelligent Systems 19(1), 26–33 (2004)
3. Xiang, X., Madey, G.R.: Improving the reuse of scientific workflows and their byproducts. In: ICWS, pp. 792–799. IEEE Computer Society, Los Alamitos (2007)
4. Kim, J., Spraragen, M., Gil, Y.: An intelligent assistant for interactive workflow composition. In: IUI 2004: Proceedings of the 9th international conference on Intelligent user interfaces, pp. 125–131. ACM, New York (2004)
5. Roure, D.D., Goble, C.: Six principles of software design to empower scientists. IEEE Software (January 2008)
6. Goderis, A., Li, P., Goble, C.: Workflow discovery: the problem, a case study from e-science and a graph-based solution. ICWS 0, 312–319 (2006)
7. Simmhan, Y.L., Plale, B., Gannon, D.: A survey of data provenance techniques. Technical Report 612, Computer Science Department, Indiana University (2005)
8. Minor, M., Tartakovski, A., Schmalen, D., Bergmann, R.: Agile workflow technology and case-based change reuse for long-term processes. International Journal of Intelligent Information Technologies (2007)
9. Weber, B., Wild, W., Breu, R.: CBRFlow: Enabling adaptive workflow management through conversational case-based reasoning. In: Funk, P., González Calero, P.A. (eds.) ECCBR 2004. LNCS (LNAI), vol. 3155, pp. 434–448. Springer, Heidelberg (2004)
10. Madhusudan, T., Zhao, J.L., Marshall, B.: A case-based reasoning framework for workflow model management. Data Knowl. Eng. 50(1), 87–115 (2004)
11. Leake, D., Whitehead, M.: Case provenance: The value of remembering case sources. In: Weber, R.O., Richter, M.M. (eds.) ICCBR 2007. LNCS (LNAI), vol. 4626. Springer, Heidelberg (2007)
12. Leake, D., Dial, S.: Using case provenance to propagate feedback to cases and adaptations. In: Proceedings of the Nineth European Conference on Case-Based Reasoning. Springer, Heidelberg (in press, 2008)
13. Dean, T., Boddy, M.: An analysis of time-dependent planning. In: Proceedings of the seventh national conference on artificial intelligence, pp. 49–54. Morgan Kaufmann, San Mateo (1988)
14. Simmhan, Y.L., Plale, B., Gannon, D.: Karma2: Provenance management for data driven workflows. International Journal of Web Services Research 5, 1 (2008)
15. Shirasuna, S.: A Dynamic Scientific Workflow System for the Web Services Architecture. PhD thesis, Indiana University (September 2007)

16. Oinn, T., Greenwood, M., Addis, M., Alpdemir, M.N., Ferris, J., Glover, K., Goble, C., Goderis, A., Hull, D., Marvin, D., Li, P., Lord, P., Pocock, M.R., Senger, M., Stevens, R., Wipat, A., Wroe, C.: Taverna: lessons in creating a workflow environment for the life sciences: Research articles. Concurr. Comput.: Pract. Exper. 18(10), 1067–1100 (2006)
17. Droegemeier, K.: Linked Environments for Atmospheric Discovery (LEAD): A Cyberinfrastructure for Mesoscale Meteorology Research and Education. AGU Fall Meeting Abstracts (December 2004)
18. van der Aalst W.M.P., ter Hofstede A.H.M., B., K., A.P., B.: Workflow patterns. Distributed and Parallel Databases 14(47), 5–51 (2003)
19. Anandan, S., Summers, J.D.: Similarity metrics applied to graph based design model authoring. Computer-Aided Design and Applications 3(1-4), 297–306 (2006)
20. Minor, M., Schmalen, D., Koldehoff, A., Bergmann, R.: Structural adaptation of workflows supported by a suspension mechanism and by case-based reasoning. In: Proceedings of the 16th IEEE Internazional Workshop on Enabling Technologies: Infrastructure for Collaborative Enterprises (WETICE 2007), pp. 370–375. IEEE Computer Society, Los Alamitos (2007)
21. Goble, C.A., Roure, D.C.D.: Experiment: social networking for workflow-using e-scientists. In: WORKS 2007: Proceedings of the 2nd workshop on Workflows in support of large-scale science, pp. 1–2. ACM, New York (2007)
22. Champin, P.A., Solnon, C.: Measuring the similarity of labeled graphs. In: Ashley, K.D., Bridge, D.G. (eds.) ICCBR 2003. LNCS, vol. 2689, pp. 80–95. Springer, Heidelberg (2003)
23. Stevens, R.D., Goble, A.R.,, C.A.: Grid: Personalised bioinformatics on the information grid. In: Proceedings 11th International Conference on Intelligent Systems in Molecular Biology, ISBN N/A (June 2003)
24. Oinn, T., Addis, M., Ferris, J., Marvin, D., Senger, M., Greenwood, M., Carver, T., Glover, K., Pocock, M.R., Wipat, A., Li, P.: Taverna: a tool for the composition and enactment of bioinformatics workflows. Bioinformatics 20(17), 3045–3054 (2004)
25. Wroe, C., Goble, C., Goderis, A., Lord, P., Miles, S., Papay, J., Alper, P., Moreau, L.: Recycling workflows and services through discovery and reuse: Research articles. Concurr. Comput. Pract. Exper. 19(2), 181–194 (2007)
26. Aha, D.W.: Generalizing from case studies: A case study. In: Proceedings of the Ninth International Conference on Machine Learning (1992)
27. Kim, J.H., Suh, W., Lee, H.: Document-based workflow modeling: a case-based reasoning approach. Expert Syst. Appl. 23(2), 77–93 (2002)

Knowledge Planning and Learned Personalization for Web-Based Case Adaptation

David Leake and Jay Powell

Computer Science Department, Indiana University
Bloomington, IN 47405, U.S.A.
{leake,jhpowell}@cs.indiana.edu

Abstract. How to endow case-based reasoning systems with effective case adaptation capabilities is a classic problem. A significant impediment to developing automated adaptation procedures is the difficulty of acquiring the required knowledge. Initial work on WebAdapt [1] proposed addressing this problem with "just-in-time" knowledge mining from Web sources. This paper addresses two key questions building on that work. First, to develop flexible, general and extensible procedures for gathering adaptation-relevant knowledge from the Web, it proposes a *knowledge planning* [2] approach in which a planner takes explicit knowledge goals as input and generates a plan for satisfying them from a set of general operators. Second, to focus selection of candidate adaptations from the potentially enormous space of possibilities, it proposes personalizing adaptations based on learned information about user preferences. Evaluations of the system are encouraging for the use of knowledge planning and learned preference information to improve adaptation performance.

1 Introduction

Case adaptation is a classic problem for case-based reasoning. From the early days of CBR research, endowing CBR systems with automated adaptation capabilities has been recognized as a substantial challenge [3,4], and fielded applications with automatic adaptation remain rare. A key impediment to automated adaptation is the difficulty of acquiring adaptation-relevant knowledge. In previous work, we proposed addressing this problem by "just-in-time" mining of Web sources [1]. This paper builds on that work by combining a new Web mining approach with personalization of adaptation based on learned user preferences.

Usually, the adaptation component of case-based reasoning systems rely on hand-built adaptation rules. However, in some domains the amount of adaptation knowledge needed or its dynamic nature can make it difficult to pre-code the needed knowledge (cf. [5]). For example, a general-purpose system for planning tourist itineraries might need to adapt plans involving thousands of destinations. In such domains, developers face two undesirable alternatives: fielding the system with incomplete adaptation knowledge—reducing knowledge acquisition cost but making adaptation failures more likely—or coding extensive knowledge, increasing development cost and including knowledge likely to go unused.

K.-D. Althoff et al. (Eds.): ECCBR 2008, LNAI 5239, pp. 284–298, 2008.

The difficulties of hand-building knowledge make it appealing to enable CBR systems to learn new adaptations (see Section 6 for a survey of this work). However, the enormous amount of knowledge now available on the Web presents opportunities for another approach, drawing on Web-based knowledge sources as needed. The WebAdapt system [1] was a first effort to support adaptation with as-needed mining of large-scale, publicly-available Web knowledge sources such as the formalized knowledge of OpenCyc [6], the informal natural language text of Wikipedia [7], and the geographical information of the Geonames GIS database [8]. The WebAdapt project aims to enable CBR systems to adapt a wide range of problems with minimal pre-coded knowledge. Evaluations of the initial version of the system were encouraging, with the system often able to propose good adaptations by relying only on its cases, knowledge sources external to the system, and a few simple hand-coded rules for mining those sources.

This paper addresses two questions to build on the WebAdapt approach and to increase its generality. First, it considers how to replace the hand-coded Web mining procedures of the initial WebAdapt system with a more flexible, general and extensible method for guiding the adaptation process and extracting Web-based adaptation knowledge. Its response is a *knowledge planning* [2] framework for Web mining, in which a planner takes explicit knowledge goals as input and generates a plan for satisfying them from a set of operators ranging from source-independent abstractions to concrete source-specific procedures. Second, it considers how to focus selection of specific adaptations, given the potentially enormous space of possibilities in large Web sources. Its response is to learn user preferences and apply those preferences to personalize the choice of adaptations. This personalization contrasts with standard perspectives on case adaptation, in which the same adaptations are proposed for all users.

The paper begins with an overview of the system's basic approach, architecture, and knowledge sources, followed by a description of its knowledge planning process to support adaptation. It then presents experiments assessing its knowledge planning and personalization processes, and closes with a comparison to related research. The experimental results suggest that the new approaches can play a valuable role in exploiting Web-based knowledge sources for adaptation.

2   WebAdapt's Approach

This section summarizes key aspects of WebAdapt's approach and user interaction (described in detail in [1]),[1] and introduces the system's new Web mining approach based on knowledge planning and learned preference information.

Viewing adaptation as transformation and memory search: Kass [9] proposed a view of adaptation in which adaptations are built from two components: (1) a small set of abstract structural transformations and (2) memory search strategies for finding the information needed to apply those transformations, by substituting appropriate components into the case structure. For example, in case-based

---

[1] The first two paragraphs of this section are adapted from [1].

explanation, search could find a new potential cause for an event, and transformation could re-structure the explanation to accommodate that cause [10]). However, rather than relying on a hand-coded search procedure for each possible adaptation, rather than searching internal memory, WebAdapt generates search procedures by a planning process, in a spirit similar to Leake, Kinley and Wilson's DIAL [11], and searches external Web resources.

The WebAdapt project focuses on substitution adaptations. It generates knowledge goals as sets of constraints to be satisfied (represented as item categories), based on examination of the item to be replaced and additional user preference information. It draws on information in Web-based sources both (1) to hypothesize constraints which a substitution adaptation must satisfy, and (2) to find replacement elements satisfying such constraints on the Web.

User Interactions: WebAdapt's task domain is sightseeing itinerary planning; its task is to adapt proposed itineraries to fit user preferences. Its initial case base contains eight travel itineraries taken from Frommer's Paris Travel Guide [12]. Users interact with WebAdapt by first selecting an itinerary and then designating any steps to modify. Such a system might be used to plan a customized itinerary in advance of a trip, or could be used on a portable wireless device to provide recommendations on-site (e.g., a traveler facing a long wait to ascend the Eiffel tower could request nearby alternatives to visit).

The system can automatically generate a substitution or support interactive user-guided adaptation by providing a ranked set of candidate alternatives. In interactive mode, the user can request an explanation of why any candidate was chosen, in terms of the constraints used, and can provide feedback on the appropriateness of the constraints as feedback for the system learning user preferences.

The Adaptation Process: WebAdapt's adaptation process and related learning are summarized in Figure 1. When the user requests a substitution for an itinerary item, WebAdapt formulates a knowledge goal for finding a substitution (Step 1). WebAdapt then selects a Web-based knowledge source to use to satisfy the request, based on a source performance profile and prior experience (Step 2). If possible, a prior plan, relevant to the formulated goals and already used successfully, is retrieved from memory. Otherwise a new plan is generated (Step 3). Next, the plan is executed to gather information from Web sources (Step 4) and candidate solutions are chosen, based on user preference information, for display (Step 5). The user can request explanations of how the displayed solutions were found (Step 6) before selecting a solution to use (Step 7). WebAdapt's knowledge and process are described in the following sections.

3   WebAdapt's Knowledge

The WebAdapt system relies on four main knowledge sources: (1) A model of user adaptation preferences, built up by user feedback during adaptations; (2) a domain model, built up by saving information retrieved by previous searches, (3) profiles of the Web sources it accesses, and (4) a case base of previous adaptations, used both to support decision-making about source selection and to guide new adaptations.

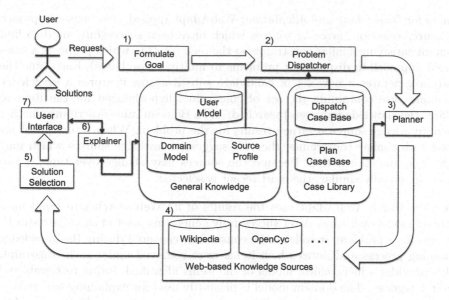

Fig. 1. WebAdapt's adaptation process and knowledge sources

User Model: As a user selects candidate adaptations, WebAdapt builds a simple model of user content preferences (i.e., of the constraints which, when used to guide knowledge source search, lead to acceptable substitutions). For example, if a user favors an adaptation falling under the constraint "Art museums in Paris," that constraint is stored as reflecting a possible area of user interest. WebAdapt also learns about categories in which a user is not interested, based on user feedback. This initial approach to user preferences provides a coarse-grained model of broad classes of preferences, which was suitable for proof of concept testing. However, we note that this simple approach does not yet address important aspects such as context-dependent preferences.

Source Profiles: Source profile statistics are available to influence source selection; users can interactively select weightings on these and how they should be balanced against content-based criteria (e.g., if the user is only interested in the top selection or wishes to compare alternatives). As WebAdapt queries Web sources, it maintains a *source performance* profile summarizing average access times and reliability (e.g., how often the source is available when queried), updated each time a source is accessed.

WebAdapt also maintains *source content* estimates for each knowledge source, reflecting coverage for past system queries and the diversity of results from that source. Source coverage is estimated from the percent of times the user found an acceptable item in the list of suggestions from the source in prior adaptations. Diversity is a measure of the average dissimilarity of items returned. Diversity is calculated based on Smyth and McClave's [13] approach, except that WebAdapt calculates diversity of knowledge returned for adaptations rather than of cases.

Cases for Dispatching and Adaptation: WebAdapt applied a case-based approach to source selection, favoring sources which have been successfully used to find content satisfying similar constraints in the past (cf. [14], which proposes a case-based approach to dispatching problems to multiple case bases). Each time the system generates a new set of candidate substitutions, it stores a knowledge planning case containing the set of constraints hypothesized for the item to adapt, the knowledge source(s) searched, and a Boolean value describing whether each knowledge source returned results for the problem. When future problems arise with similar constraints, the case suggests knowledge sources which may have relevant information. Because the sources may change over time, if two cases are equally similar, the most recent is selected.

Domain Model: WebAdapt uses the results of its Web searches to build up a domain model over time. After successfully generating a set of candidate substitutions for a problem, it collects the constraints captured during the knowledge planning process and notes which items were retrieved under each constraint. This provides a hierarchical model of the items identified during retrievals and their categories. The domain model is primarily used for explaining why particular items were proposed as candidate adaptations, as discussed in Section 4.2.

4   Knowledge Planning Process

4.1   Knowledge Planning Operators

WebAdapt's adaptation process relies primarily on fourteen abstract domain-independent search and transformation operators, which call upon basic source-specific operators to perform source-specific operations. The low-level operators currently include some simple text mining procedures (see [1] for an overview of WebAdapt's text mining process), and could be integrated with more sophisticated natural language processing. WebAdapt's knowledge planning is done by the regression planner UCPOP [15].

The preconditions of WebAdapt's operators specify knowledge required for their execution, while the postconditions specify the knowledge they generate, which is then available to later plan steps. Search operators affect only the system's knowledge state; transformation operators modify the structure of the case, based on inputs such as the case to be modified, item in the case to modify, and the type of modification to take place.

Each operator is defined in terms of a vocabulary of roles filled in during the planning process, either from the initial knowledge goal or based on intermediate results. The role-fillers include the knowledge source from which to retrieve, the constraints to be satisfied by the adaptation, and candidate items to be refined and ranked. Figure 2 illustrates the pre- and post-conditions for two operators used to hypothesize and expand constraints. Each operator contains:

1. A description of the problem solved after the execution of a step (described by the predicate *Problem_Solved*), to be matched with the knowledge goal to be satisfied during the regression planning process.

Hypothesize Constraints
  Preconditions :
    ?Q : Query
  Postconditions :
    Problem_Solved(Adapting(?I : InitialState, ?G : Goals), ?C : Constraints, ?T : StepSource)
    Constraints(?R : Role, ?K : KnowledgeEncoding, ?C : Constraints)
    Source_Of(?C : Constraints, ?S : KnowledgeSource, ?Q : Query)
    Is_A_Hypothesized_Constraint_Of(?C : Constraints, ?K : KnowledgeEncoding, ?S : KnowledgeSource)
Expand Constraints
  Preconditions:
    Constraints(?R : Role, ?K : KnowledgeEncoding, ?C : Constraints)
    Source_Of(?C : Constraints, ?S : KnowledgeSource, ?Q : Query)
  Postconditions :
    Problem_Solved(Adapting(?I : InitialState, ?G : Goals), ?HC : HypothesisCandidates, ?T : StepSource)
    Hypothesis(?R : Role, ?K : KnowledgeEncoding, ?HC : HypothesisCandidates, ?R : Refinement)
    Source_Of(?HC : HypothesisCandidates, ?S : KnowledgeSource, ?K : KnowledgeEncoding)
    Is_Constrained_By(?HC : HypothesisCandidates, ?C : Constraints, ?S : KnowledgeSource, ?R : Refinement)

Fig. 2. Example operators for hypothesizing and expanding constraints

2. Preconditions describing the knowledge necessary for execution (in the figure $Q : Query$)
3. A description of the knowledge acquired during execution (the postconditions *Constraints* and *Hypothesis*).
4. A description of the source to search for the acquired knowledge (*Source_Of*)
5. A description of what WebAdapt is expected to know after execution of a step (e.g., *Is_A_Hypothesized_Constraint_Of* and *Is_Constrained_By*), also matched with the knowledge goal to be satisfied

The slots in the operators fall into two categories: 1) slots that are filled during the problem dispatching stage, and 2) variables that are bound during plan execution. Examples of slots filled during problem dispatching are the knowledge source to use (e.g., $S : KnowledgeSource$ may be filled with *Wikipedia*), a frame representing a sub-unit of knowledge (e.g., *?page{?title}*), an encoding of a user query, and information describing how to refine knowledge from a source (e.g., the contextual information to search for in a Wikipedia entry).

The generic operator *Hypothesize Constraints* queries a knowledge source for an item (e.g., Eiffel Tower) and hypothesizes a set of seed constraints for the search process. The *?C : Constraints* variable is then bound to a list of sub-units of knowledge representing hypothesized constraints. When using source-specific Wikipedia operators, the hypothesized constraints are the categories under which an item falls and the category's URL, while OpenCyc constraints are the collections under which an item falls. The operator *Expand Constraints* takes a set of hypothesized constraints and recursively searches for a pool of related items, which can be presented to the user as hypothesized candidates.

4.2   Applying Knowledge Planning for Adaptation

Generating Knowledge Goals: WebAdapt generates top-level knowledge goals
in response to a user request to find substitutions for an itinerary item, or to
suggest constraints for search (Step 1 in figure 1). Lower-level knowledge goals
may be generated during the knowledge planning process. Knowledge goals are
represented in three parts: (1) a set of constraints to be satisfied by candidate
adaptations, (2) a set of constraints whose satisfaction would cause candidate
adaptations to be rejected (for example, used to avoid duplicating items already
in the itinerary), and (3) a ranking procedure for results (e.g., that results should
be ordered from most constrained to least constrained). A sample goal to acquire
candidate substitutions from an unspecified knowledge source and to rank them
according to a given model of the user's preferences is represented as:

Is_Constrained_By(?HC : HypothesisCandidates, ?C : Constraints, ?S : KnowledgeSource, ?R : Refinement)
Ordered_By_User_Preference(?R : Role, ?P : UserPreferences, ?HC : HypothesisCandidates)

Problem Dispatching: After a goal has been formulated, WebAdapt determines
which knowledge sources are best suited to achieve its goal (Step 2). WebAdapt
selects Web knowledge sources based on (1) prior cases for satisfying similar
knowledge goals, and (2) the source profiles reflecting estimated average source
coverage, speed, and reliability. These factors are balanced based on a user-
selected weighting. If WebAdapt has learned a set of preferred constraints for a
user, then WebAdapt ranks the retrieved cases by how closely the items found
by each case match the user's preferred constraints.

Selecting Operators: After knowledge source selection, the knowledge goal and
source are passed to a planning component (Step 3). That component first attempts to retrieve a prior plan satisfying the knowledge goals generated by the
system.[2] If no plan is found, one is generated from scratch using UCPOP. The
plan is then executed (step 4), and the resulting adaptation-relevant knowledge is
extracted from the sources, to instantiate empty role-fillers with the knowledge
from each source (e.g., constraints and candidate substitutions are extracted
from Wikipedia entries). In general, the role-fillers may include lists of alternative candidates. In the solution selection step (Step 5), candidate items are
refined using source specific techniques (e.g., searching for the word "Paris" in
a candidate's Wikipedia entry).

    Candidates are ranked based on the user preference model and constraints
captured during execution. For example, if a user prefers items satisfying the
constraint "Churches in Paris," candidates can be filtered by that constraint.
Once a set of candidates has been generated, the system's domain model is
updated with newly discovered candidates and constraints.

Preference Learning, Explanation and Feedback: Filtered candidate substitutions
are displayed to the user, who can request explanations of why a candidate was

---

[2] In the current implementation, planning cases are reused when possible but are not
adapted. A more flexible model is a subject for future research.

chosen for presentation (Step 6). WebAdapt explains the choice of candidates by describing the constraints they satisfy, based on its domain model and new constraints captured during knowledge plan execution, and how those constraints relate to the user's preferences. When the user chooses a substitution, the explanation module attempts to explain why a user chose a candidate to learn from the choice. The system refers to its user model of the constraints the user prefers and those in which the user is not interested to filter the constraints found and then adds the remaining new constraints to its user model, while incrementing the weight of constraints already present. The weights are used to help rank pools of substitutions matching several of a user's preferred constraints.

4.3 An Example of the Knowledge Planning Process, Suggestion and Explanation Processes

As an example, consider a user who requests an alternative to a planned visit to the Notre Dame cathedral. WebAdapt formulates a knowledge goal to hypothesize a set of candidate replacements ranked by user preferences. Suppose that WebAdapt's user model records that this user prefers *Art museums in Paris*, and *Churches in Paris*. WebAdapt chooses Wikipedia as the knowledge source to mine because its profile suggests that it has the best coverage and because past adaptations using Wikipedia described Notre Dame as a *Church in Paris*. After Web mining and ranking, the first item presented to the user is the Church of Saint-Merri, a small church located in Paris. When asked for an explanation, WebAdapt refers to its domain model and describes this church as a "Church in Paris," specifically a "Roman Catholic Church in Paris," and explains that the item was chosen because the user prefers "Churches in Paris."

5   Evaluation

Our evaluation addresses the following questions:

1. *Benefits of knowledge planning:* How do the results of WebAdapt's knowledge planning search compare to those of traditional keyword-based search?
2. *Benefits of preference learning:* When users have varying preferences for adaptations, will re-use of captured constraints from previous adaptations improve the suitability of mined adaptations?
3. *Benefits of source profile learning:* Can aggregate profile information improve the choice of knowledge sources to mine?

The experiments tested adaptation suggestions for a single itinerary taken from Frommer's Paris Travel Guide, *The Best of Paris in 3 Days*, a tour of 24 sites.

Experimental Design: To provide an easily quantifiable means for evaluating the ability of WebAdapt to reflect user preferences, we developed nine simple simulated users to interact with the system. Each user requested a set of candidate substitutions for each item in the sample itinerary, resulting in over 400 adaptations. Eight of the simulated users were associated with a set of 1–6 preferred

Table 1. List of preferred adaptation constraints for each simulated user

User	Preferred Categories	User	Preferred Categories
1	Museums in Paris	2	Roman Catholic Churches in Paris
3	Paris IVe arrondissement	4	Churches in Paris
			Roman Catholic Churches in Paris
5	Gothic architecture	6	Geography of Paris
	Paris IVe arrondissement		Visitor attractions in Paris
	Parks and open spaces in Paris		Art museums and galleries in Paris
	Tall structures in Paris region		Monuments and memorials in Paris
7	Art museums and galleries in Paris	8	Bridges over the River Seine in Paris
	Museums in Paris		Parks and open spaces in Paris
	Musee d'Orsay		River Seine
	Louvre		Boulevards in Paris
	Collections of the Louvre		Avenues in Paris
			Streets in Paris

constraints (typically corresponding to some theme, such as "Art Museums in Paris") that were unknown to WebAdapt. Table 1 lists the constraints used. The ninth user had no preferences, and served as a baseline.

Performance measures: Our experiments explore WebAdapt's ability to suggest the right items from a pool of candidate substitutions to present to the user, measured by precision of the pool of the top 5 or 10 candidates generated by the system.[3] As a coarse-grained impartial relevance criterion, we consider items relevant if they are mentioned in Frommer's Paris Travel Guide. Because it is possible that the system could suggest relevant items not mentioned in the guide, our criterion is a conservative measure of precision.

Choosing substitutions: From each pool of candidate substitutions generated by WebAdapt, the simulated user selected a substitution to use. The simulated user iterated through the pool of candidates in the order they were presented, requesting an explanation from WebAdapt for why each item was presented. WebAdapt then produced a list of constraints describing the candidate, captured during the search process. The first candidate encountered with at least one constraint matching a user's preferences was selected as the substitution, and the user's choice of that candidate was provided to the system as basic feedback, from which the system adjusted the user preference model. No feedback was given to the system if no suitable candidate was found.

Providing extended feedback on hypothesized preferences: During a second round of experiments, the simulated users were given the ability to critique WebAdapt's hypothesized set of adaptation preferences. After a set of substitutions was presented and a substitution selected, the simulated user provided feedback to the system on any constraints which WebAdapt used to explain the candidates'

---

[3] Although recall is typically shown with precision, here the goal is to select a small focused set of filtered results.

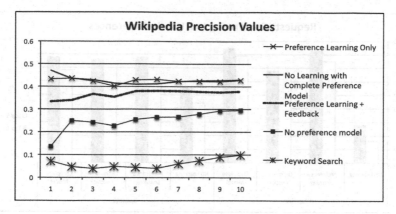

Fig. 3. Wikipedia precision trends

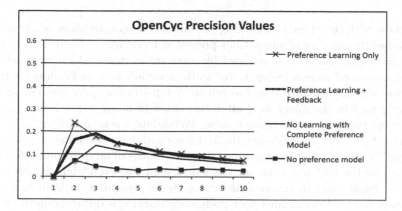

Fig. 4. OpenCyc precision trends

relevance but were not in the user's preferences. These were removed from We-bAdapt's user model.

Results for Questions 1 and 2: Benefits of knowledge planning and of preferences and preference learning: As a non-learning baseline to compare to the knowledge planning approach, keyword-based search was used to search Wikipedia for substitutions. Keywords consisted of a hypothesized constraint, combined with the item's location to establish the context, for a Google query.[4] Queries were executed for each hypothesized constraint, and the average precision was calculated for the first ten results returned from each query.

To assess the benefits of preference use and preference learning, two other non-learning baselines were also used—no preference model, or a complete model provided to the system—versus learning of preferences with or without feedback. Figures 3 and 4 show WebAdapt's average performance over all simulated users

---

[4] E.g., *site:en.wikipedia.org Visitor Attractions in Paris France.*

294   D. Leake and J. Powell

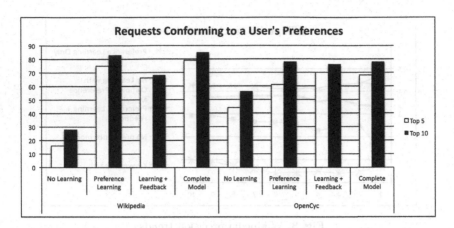

Fig. 5. Requests generating a match for a user in the top 5 and 10 candidates presented

and trials, with the three nonlearning baselines. The graphs show precision as a function of the number of suggestions presented to each simulated user. In some cases, precision figures were reduced by retrieval of items which were relevant but were counted as non-relevant, due to their omission from Frommer's guide.

Performance of keyword-based search on Wikipedia was quite low, because the keywords used in the query were often contained in many non-relevant articles, which were typically avoided when using WebAdapt's search strategy.

Without preference knowledge, the first few candidates presented are often not relevant. When the system is given a complete model of adaptation preferences, precision for the first few items increases noticeably, as WebAdapt is able to use the given constraints to ensure that the top items presented conform to a user's preference model. Performance with preference learning is quite competitive with performance with a complete user model. Adding feedback to basic preference learning did not improve performance, and was sometimes slightly detrimental.

Precision for OpenCyc remained low, as OpenCyc contains a large set of concisely defined knowledge which is difficult to filter. Our prior work [1] has shown that using multiple knowledge sources to filter OpenCyc's content produces greater accuracy, but these methods were not used here, in order to examine the effects of learning for a single source. Figure 5 illustrates the rates at which Wikipedia and OpenCyc suggested substitutions conforming to a user's preferences, as well as the percentage of substitutions picked by the simulated users in the top five and ten suggestions.

When hypothesizing a preference model for a user, WebAdapt tended to hypothesize constraints that were not in a user's true preference set, but were closely related to that user's preferences. For example, WebAdapt tended to over generalize its constraints and hypothesized that nearly every user preferred items that fell under the constraint "Visitor Attractions in Paris" when using Wikipedia, though only user 6 had this as a specific preference. Based on the incorrect hypothesis, WebAdapt would present a pool of items that were typically a mix of miscellaneous tourist attractions, as well as items that actually corresponded to a user's true preferences, resulting in the higher performance in Figure 5 when no feedback was given.

Discussion for questions 1 and 2: In the nonlearning conditions, WebAdapt's performance remains low. More specifically, the quality of the first few items is typically very low, which in practice might reduce a user's confidence in the system's ability to suggest substitutions. When WebAdapt is provided with a set of constraints, the quality of the top few items increases noticeably for Wikipedia, and slightly for OpenCyc, as shown in Figures 3 and 4. OpenCyc contains a large body of knowledge defined by a set of general constraints (e.g., Wikipedia defines a constraint for "Visitor attractions in Paris," while OpenCyc's closest equivalent is "Tourist Attraction"). When only taking knowledge from OpenCyc into account, it is difficult to remove items that are related to the travel domain but not to a specific city. Despite these limitations, WebAdapt was able to use discovered adaptation knowledge to improve the quality of the first ten items presented from OpenCyc.

WebAdapt was also able to successfully capture a set of constraints to improve adaptation quality, as shown in Figures 3 and 4. When no user feedback was given on the set of captured constraints, adaptation quality was comparable to when WebAdapt was provided with a complete set of constraints to use. Precision was slightly lower when WebAdapt received user feedback on the applicability of its captured constraint knowledge in the context of specific user preferences, due to filtering of items generated by constraints closely related to the user's, but not exactly matching them. We plan to explore more sensitive filtering processes to address this in the future.

Results for Question 3: Benefits of profile learning for dispatching: For an initial assessment of the usefulness of using source profiles when selecting Web sources, the average performance characteristics for Wikipedia and OpenCyc were stored during an initial set of 200 adaptations. These included information on average access time, failure rate, estimated result diversity, and estimated coverage. Wikipedia and OpenCyc had comparable measures for access time, estimated diversity, and reliability, but differed on estimated coverage: suitable adaptations were found for 86% of Wikipedia queries, vs. 33% of all OpenCyc queries. This information proved predictive not only of which source would yield usable suggestions more often, but of improved precision in the list of adaptations presented to the user. On a test set of another 200 adaptations, average precision with 5 suggestions was 45% with Wikipedia, 29% for random selection, and 14% for OpenCyc. Precision with 10 suggestions was 45% for Wikipedia, 30% for random selection, and 8% for OpenCyc. This suggests that source selection could make an important difference in performance, and we plan to investigate finer-grained strategies.

6   Related Work

Web search was used to gather information to support user adaptation in the Stamping Advisor [16], which suggested candidate search terms derived from the case being adapted, for the user to augment. In WebAdapt, the user makes a top-level request for an adaptation, and the system selects a knowledge source to query and generates a set of search constraints which are used for document retrieval. Relevance feedback occurs when a user selects a retrieved document to use as a substitution and the system builds an implicit model of preferred adaptation constraints to personalize future suggestions.

WebAdapt's on-demand Web mining of adaptation knowledge from semi-structured sources such as Wikipedia contrasts with CBR research on acquiring adaptation knowledge in advance from sources such as cases [17,18,19,20] and databases [21] whose content and structure are known. Finding useful knowledge on the Web requires a flexible knowledge acquisition framework capable of leveraging prior experience to adapt to the idiosyncratic content of external knowledge sources, which is reflected in the system's use of source profiles to determine which sources to use to solve problems.

Ponzetto [22] has shown that it is possible to use large web-based sources such as Wikipedia to derive taxonomic information that is comparable to professionally developed ontologies such as OpenCyc. WebAdapt uses the category network of Wikipedia to discover relationships between different Wikipedia entries, which is then captured as adaptation knowledge. In our experiments, this produces adaptations competitive with those the system generates from the formally represented knowledge of OpenCyc.

Aquin et al.'s CABAMAKA [23] also combines knowledge discovery with the CBR process, but unlike WebAdapt, assumes the existence of a domain ontology associated with the system's case-base to facilitate the explanation of mined adaptation rules. WebAdapt's approach is in the spirit of Leake, Kinley, and Wilson's DIAL [11]. However, DIAL relied on pre-specified role-filler constraints, rather than generating and learning those for particular users. Also, DIAL assumed that its pre-defined internal knowledge would be sufficient, rather than searching for knowledge outside the system.

Finally, Muñoz-Avila and Cox point to [24] case-based planning for information gathering as a new CBR direction raising interesting issues in its own right, especially for how to adapt information-gathering plans. WebAdapt's planning process currently combines generative planning with very simple case-based reuse, and we are exploring how to enrich this model.

7 Conclusion

This paper presents a framework for acquiring adaptation knowledge on demand from large-scale Web sources external to a CBR system. WebAdapt treats adaptation as involving transformation operations applied to knowledge mined on the fly by knowledge plans to satisfy explicit knowledge goals for the needed information. Preferred constraints for suggestions are learned from user choices in prior adaptations, personalizing the suggested adaptations.

Experimental results support the ability of the approach to generate good candidate adaptations and that learning preferences from prior adaptations can substantially improve adaptation quality. They also suggest that selective choice of Web sources may have an important effect on the quality of results, making that a promising area for future research. Additional future areas include better methods for exploiting feedback information, a richer user model and model of adaptation plan reuse, a reactive planning framework [25] to recover from information extraction failures, and richer NLP processes as low-level operators for adaptation plans.

References

1. Leake, D., Powell, J.: Mining large-scale knowledge sources for case adaptation knowledge. In: Weber, R., Richter, M. (eds.) Proceedings of the Seventh International Conference on Case-Based Reasoning, pp. 209–223. Springer, Berlin (2007)
2. Ram, A., Leake, D.: Learning, goals, and learning goals. In: Ram, A., Leake, D. (eds.) Goal-Driven Learning. MIT Press, Cambridge (1995)
3. Barletta, R.: Building real-world CBR applications: A tutorial. In: The Second European Workshop on Case-Based Reasoning (1994)
4. Kolodner, J.: Improving human decision making through case-based decision aiding. AI Magazine 12(2), 52–68 (Summer 1991)
5. Stahl, A., Bergmann, R.: Applying recursive CBR for the customization of structured products in an electronic shop. In: Proceedings of the Fifth European Workshop on Case-Based Reasoning, pp. 297–308. Springer, Heidelberg (2000)
6. Cycorp: OpenCyc (2007) (Accessed February 17, 2007), http://www.opencyc.org/
7. Wikimedia Foundation: Wikipedia (2007) (Accessed February 17, 2007), http://www.wikipedia.org
8. Geonames: Geonames (2007) (Accessed February 17, 2007), http://www.geonames.org
9. Kass, A.: Tweaker: Adapting old explanations to new situations. In: Schank, R., Riesbeck, C., Kass, A. (eds.) Inside Case-Based Explanation, pp. 263–295. Lawrence Erlbaum, Mahwah (1994)
10. Kass, A., Leake, D.: Case-based reasoning applied to constructing explanations. In: Kolodner, J. (ed.) Proceedings of the DARPA Case-Based Reasoning Workshop, pp. 190–208. Morgan Kaufmann, San Mateo (1988)
11. Leake, D., Kinley, A., Wilson, D.: Learning to improve case adaptation by introspective reasoning and CBR. In: Proceedings of the First International Conference on Case-Based Reasoning, pp. 229–240. Springer, Berlin (1995)
12. Frommer's: Frommer's Paris 2006. Frommer's (2006)
13. Smyth, B., McClave, P.: Similarity vs. diversity. In: Aha, D.W., Watson, I. (eds.) ICCBR 2001. LNCS (LNAI), vol. 2080, pp. 347–361. Springer, Heidelberg (2001)
14. Leake, D., Sooriamurthi, R.: Automatically selecting strategies for multi-case-base reasoning. In: Craw, S., Preece, A. (eds.) Advances in Case-Based Reasoning: Proceedings of the Fifth European Conference on Case-Based Reasoning, pp. 204–219. Springer, Berlin (2002)
15. Penberthy, J., Weld, D.: UCPOP: A sound, complete, partial order planner for ADL. In: Proceedings of the Third International Conference on Principles of Knowledge Representation and Reasoning, pp. 103–114. Morgan Kaufmann, San Francisco (1992)

16. Leake, D., Birnbaum, L., Hammond, K., Marlow, C., Yang, H.: Integrating information resources: A case study of engineering design support. In: Proceedings of the Third International Conference on Case-Based Reasoning, pp. 482–496. Springer, Berlin (1999)
17. Wilke, W., Vollrath, I., Althoff, K.D., Bergmann, R.: A framework for learning adaptation knowledge based on knowledge light approaches. In: Proceedings of the Fifth German Workshop on Case-Based Reasoning, pp. 235–242 (1997)
18. Patterson, D., Anand, S., Dubitzky, W., Hughes, J.: Towards automated case knowledge discovery in the M^2 case-based reasoning system. Knowledge and Information Systems: An International Journal, 61–82 (1999)
19. Hanney, K., Keane, M.: The adaptation knowledge bottleneck: How to ease it by learning from cases. In: Proceedings of the Second International Conference on Case-Based Reasoning. Springer, Berlin (1997)
20. Craw, S., Jarmulak, J., Rowe, R.: Learning and applying case-based adaptation knowledge. In: Aha, D., Watson, I. (eds.) Proceedings of the Fourth International Conference on Case-Based Reasoning, pp. 131–145. Springer, Berlin (2001)
21. Yang, Q., Cheng, S.: Case mining from large databases. In: Ashley, K.D., Bridge, D.G. (eds.) ICCBR 2003. LNCS, vol. 2689, pp. 691–702. Springer, Heidelberg (2003)
22. Ponzetto, S.P., Strube, M.: Deriving a large scale taxonomy from wikipedia. In: Proceedings of the Twenty-Second National Conference on Artificial Intelligence. AAAI Press / MIT Press (2007)
23. d'Aquin, M., Badra, F., Lafrogne, S., Lieber, J., Napoli, A., Szathmary, L.: Case base mining for adaptation knowledge acquisition. In: Proceedings of the Twentieth International Joint Conference on Artificial Intelligence (IJCAI 2007), pp. 750–755. Morgan Kaufmann, San Mateo (2007)
24. Muñoz-Avila, Cox, M.: Case-based plan adaptation: An analysis and review. IEEE Intelligent Systems (in press)
25. Firby, R.: Adaptive Execution in Complex Dynamic Worlds. PhD thesis, Yale University, Computer Science Department TR 672 (1989)

Cases, Predictions, and Accuracy Learning and Its Application to Effort Estimation

Jingzhou Li, Brenan Mackas, Michael M. Richter, and Guenther Ruhe

Department of Computer Science, University of Calgary, Canada
{jingli,bhmackas,mrichter,ruhe}@ucalgary.ca

Abstract. Estimation by analogy EBA (effort estimation by analogy) is one of the proven methods for effort prediction in software engineering; in AI this would be called Case-Based Reasoning. In this paper we consider effort predictions using the EBA () method AQUA and pay attention to two aspects: (i) The influence of the set of analogs on the quality of prediction. The set of analogs is determined by a learning process incorporating the number of nearest neighbors and the threshold of the similarity measure used, (ii) Analyzing and understanding the conditions under which the prediction can be expected to be the most or the least accurate.

We study two types of learning: One for finding the "best" set of analogs, and one for finding out factors for reliability. While both questions are relevant for different areas and disciplines, the focus of the paper is on estimation of effort in software engineering. For EBA method AQUA, the cases can be features or past projects characterized by attributes of various type. Classical estimation approaches just investigate the overall estimated quality of a system. However, in that case information is missing if and why estimation was performing the way it did. Bad estimates are often due to external influences. Therefore it is valuable for to find out under which conditions the estimates are more or less reliable.

Keywords: Software effort, estimation by analogy, accuracy, learning, AQUA.

1 Introduction

A central goal of the AQUA [1] effort estimation method is to estimate the needed effort for developing software products. Such estimates play an essential role in business planning, in particular in early development stages, e.g. in release planning. We are interested in estimates at an early stage in the development life cycle; this usually excludes the use of metrics because such numbers are not available.

A goal of any prediction is to achieve accuracy. A prediction system with a high average accuracy is called reliable. This kind of reliability is of interest to a company that may use the system. However, often results are distributed around the average and the company would like to know under which conditions they can trust an estimate and when one has to be suspicious. We assume we have an experienced estimator and we want to detect objective influence factors. For this, we assume that the reliability is influenced by the attributes and their values used in the cases. Besides that, we want to discover the situations where the success of the prediction is based on chance.

K.-D. Althoff et al. (Eds.): ECCBR 2008, LNAI 5239, pp. 299–311, 2008.

In principle, both tasks – prediction and reliability detection – are suitable for any domain; the specific approach will, however, depend on the application used. The domain of application of this paper is effort estimation and prediction and validation methods for software development projects. These problems were considered in algorithmic approaches (see [3], [4], [5], [6]) as well as analogy based methods (see [7], [8]). The term *analogy* in this area is often used in place of *case-based*. Both use expert knowledge, in either a compiled form or as past explicit experiences; in addition, *analogy* can also apply to an operation performed by humans utilizing the expert knowledge in their heads. A discussion can be found in [2]. Effort estimations have also be considered in CBR. A (critical) overview can be found in [9], see also [10]. In order to overcome several problems mentioned we describe a system AQUA that has approached the effort prediction problem in a comprehensive way, [1], [2]. The implementation was done in [1]. In [2] the target audience was quite different from the CBR audience and we found it useful to reformulate several techniques in CBR terms. In contrast to past approaches in software engineering, we combine the full power of statistical methods with those of case-based reasoning.

From the view point of CBR we emphasize two parameters that are used in most CBR systems but have not yet been investigated systematically. The first parameter N is the number of nearest neighbors considered and the second one is the size T of the threshold for similarity for cases in order to be considered. It should be noted that these parameters play a role only under certain circumstances. There need to be many cases that are well distributed; this is the case in our application. The parameters have also been considered in [11], but with a different focus.

The specification of a CBR system is done in terms of its utility (i.e., its usefulness), see [12]. The utility can be used as the specification for a similarity measure as pointed out in [12]. In order to meet the specification the similarity measure has to be chosen properly. In our situation the utility is the average reliability.

The CBR view results in AQUA in the presence of many elements that are not used in current software estimation approaches. The system AQUA contains a learning component which is based on evaluations of past experiences, i.e. past projects. We present an explorative study that was conducted not only for studying the quality of the estimates but also for improving the performance. The results were compared with results of other similar methods. In the present stage of AQUA there are currently three types of evaluations and two types of learning involved:

- **Evaluation 1:** A statistical evaluation for judging the overall quality of the approach in order to increase the confidence of the software company in the method. The main concern is the accuracy of these predictions.
- **Evaluation 2:** It was studied to see how each factor affecting the similarity measure influences the performance. This analysis deals mainly with the two parameters N (number of nearest neighbors), and T (threshold for the degree of similarity considered); in addition, the number of attributes, the number of qualitative attributes etc. was considered. This gave rise to the first kind of learning.
- **Evaluation3:** The analysis of (2) was then extended, based on the observation that good predictions do not only depend on the quality of the predictor. There are often circumstances that influence the accuracy that are outside of the control of the estimator. This is the motivation behind the second kind of learning.

Evaluation 1 is standard. There are several approaches to judge confidence in CBR systems, see for instance [13]. Evaluation 2 is not commonly used for CBR systems. Improvements of CBR systems are mainly obtained by weight learning, or, less often by learning local measures, see [14], [15]. Here the focus for learning is placed on the parameters N and T. For this reason it can be tolerated that all weights are set to 1.

The problem is now that a fixed and small number of cases, as assumed in existing analogy-based methods, may not produce the best accuracy of prediction. Therefore, a flexible mechanism based on learning of existing data is proposed for determining the appropriate values of N and T for offering the best accuracy of prediction. Some criteria for measuring the quality of predictions in terms of N and T are proposed. This is the goal of the first kind of learning.

Evaluation 3 provides an additional insight into the technique looking at total percent error only. This allows one to establish under what conditions (attribute values) the prediction result should be trusted as true. The evaluation allows one to establish when a high expected accuracy rate of the predictions is not simply caused by a number of lucky guesses. This kind of insight is the goal of the second kind of learning. The benefit of this type of learning is that it allows a company to keep a closer eye on a situation where the prediction method doubtful. Our principal method can be applied to other predictions like weather forecast or in economy.

We do not claim to have a universally applicable system. This is due to the fact that many aspects depend on the context, for instance, the type of projects a given company generally works on. The application affects the choice of which parameters are important and their weighting. However, our principal method can be applied once these parameters have been determined.

From the viewpoint of knowledge containers (see [16]) the vocabulary container contains the reliability knowledge; presently it cannot be seen how to shift it to other containers. The parameters N and T obviously carry some knowledge. Therefore it seems to be justified to regard them as knowledge containers; in fact, sub containers of the similarity container. This has not been investigated so far.

The paper is organized as follows: Section 2 discusses AQUA, section 3 presents the two leaning processes (3.1 and 3.2), and Section 4 gives a summary and outlook.

2 AQUA

2.1 Terminology and Basics

In the software community predictions of effort estimates are a common goal and many methods are employed. Some use experiences in ways that is called analogy reasoning. AQUA was originally targeted at the software community which is not very familiar with CBR. Therefore our approach varies somewhat from what is standard in CBR, and for that reason we introduce some concepts and partially reformulate the original AQUA concepts in CBR terms.

The cases are of the form (problem, solution) where the problem is usually given as an attribute value vector with attributes $A = \{a_1, a_2, ..., a_m\}$, and the solution is a number called *Effort*. The case base is $CB = \{r_1, r_2, ..., r_n\}$, and A is the set of attributes to describe the objects. The set $S = \{s_1, s_2, ..., s_t\}$ denotes the given objects to be estimated.

We discuss shortly how we use CBR techniques. The similarity measure is constructed in a standard way using the local-global principle, see [16]:

$$Gsim(s_g, r_i) = f(Lsim(a_1(s_g), a_1(r_i)), Lsim(a_2(s_g), a_2(r_i)), \ldots, Lsim(a_m(s_g), a_m(r_i)))$$

It should be remarked that our global measure is monotonic, i.e., $Gsim(s_g, r_i) > Gsim(s_g, r_j)$, $i \neq j$, if and only if $\exists a_k \in A$: $Lsim(a_k(s_g), a_k(r_i)) > Lsim(a_k(s_g), a_k(r_j))$) must be true to be useful for our considerations.

For simplicity we take f as a weighted sum. We will not discuss the local measures here. They are standard in CBR (but not so much in software estimation), depending mainly on the types of the attributes.

An essential problem is which attributes to choose. To ensure meaningful attributes, we assume that the set A of attributes is determined by applying the paradigm of goal-oriented measurement [17] or other possible methods. The attributes in our example data set were not quite ideal but we could not change them because they were given to us. Typical attributes used are contained in the set {Internal process, Data entry, Output form, Data query from database, Data query from file, Printing}.

We comment only on two types of attributes that represent uncertainties because they are not standard in software estimates. In particular, it is good to see how they are treated by the local measures.

One type is FUZ where the values of an attribute are fuzzy subsets of a crisp set C. For example, the attribute Funct% of a project describing its functionality is of FUZ type. There may be several types of functionality existing in one project, e.g. an internal process together with data entry and output form; each with a different percentage of total functionality, e.g. {0.70/Internal process, 0.1/Data entry, 0.1/Output form, 0.1/Data query from database, 0/Data query from file, 0/Printing}. The set of the degrees to which each functionality accounts for in the overall functionality of a project will be treated as a fuzzy subset of Funct%.

Given $a_j(s_g)$, $a_j(r_i) \in$ FUZ $a_j(s_g) = \{c_{g1}, c_{g2}, \ldots, c_{gn_c}\}$, $a_j(r_i) = \{c_{i1}, c_{i2}, \ldots, c_{in_c}\}$, they are treated as two vectors $\overline{a_j(s_g)}$ $(c_{g1}, c_{g2}, \ldots, c_{gn_c})$ and $\overline{a_j(r_i)}$ $(c_{i1}, c_{i2}, \ldots, c_{in_c})$, with the fuzzy set elements as their vector elements, where nc=|Cj|, Cj is the corresponding crisp set of aj. Seeing FUZ as a vector space, the local similarity is calculated using the Euclidean distance between the two vectors:

$$Lsim(a_j(s_g), a_j(r_i)) = \frac{1}{1 + \sqrt{\sum_{k=1}^{n_c} (c_{gk} - c_{ik})^2}}$$

The role of the parameters N and T is described by:

(P$_1$) number of cases considered is N, i.e. $|CB_{topN}(s_g)| = N$,

(P$_2$) the global similarity between s_g and all objects in CB_{topN} must be greater than the given threshold T: $Gsim(s_g, r_i^g) \geq T$ for all $r_i^g \in CB_{topN}$

(P$_3$) CB_{topN} includes only the closest N objects to s_g in R in terms of global similarity: $Gsim(s_g, r_i^g) \geq Gsim(s_g, r_x)$ for all $r_i^g \in CB_{topN}$ and all $r_x \in (CB \backslash CB_{topN})$ (the difference set).

The other type of attributes is RNG (range). These are numerical but instead of numbers intervals are taken. They are also useful in software engineering to represent imprecise information. For example, the time spent on developing a part of a requirement is estimated to be between 12 to 17 hours. Given a case r, $a_j(s_g)$, $a_j(r_i) \in$ RNG, let $a_j(s_g) = <l_{gj}, h_{gj}>$ and $a_j(r_i) = <l_{ij}, h_{ij}>$, then, the similarity between $a_j(s_g)$ and $a_j(r_i)$ is defined as:

$$Lsim(a_j(s_g), a_j(r_i)) = \begin{cases} 1 & l_{ij} \leq l_{gj} \text{ and } h_{gj} \leq h_{ij} \\ 0 & l_{ij} > h_{gj} \text{ or } l_{gj} > h_{ij} \\ \dfrac{min(h_{gj}, h_{ij}) - max(l_{gj}, l_{ij}) + 1}{max(h_{gj}, h_{ij}) - min(l_{gj}, l_{ij}) + 1} & \text{otherwise} \end{cases}$$

It can be seen that the similarity depends on the overlap between the two ranges.

In summary, an AQUA system is described by the following parameters:

<attributes, local measures *Lsim*, global measure *Gsim, N, T*>

The last two parameters are the subject of the first type of learning while the attributes are the basis for the second type of learning.

2.2 AQUA Predictions

The goal of the AQUA process itself is to generate predictions. Before performing the prediction itself we optimize the similarity system. The objects of the optimization are the values of the parameters N and T for a given project. This takes place in a learning procedure. For this, cross-validation based learning is performed to determine the accuracy distribution of predictions depending on varying parameters N and T. This is described below in the section 3.1 (first learning process).

The results of the optimization are then used to actually perform the effort prediction.

The predicted value for the effort of s_g is then taken as

$$\widetilde{Effort}(s_g) = \frac{\sum_{r_k \in R_{topN}(s_g)} (Effort(r_k) * Gsim(s_g, r_k))}{\sum_{r_k \in R_{topN}(s_g)} Gsim(s_g, r_k)}$$

where Effort is the real effort. This turns out to be an improvement of the analogy strategy used in former analogy-based methods, where a fixed and a small number of cases are considered regardless of the similarity threshold T.

2.3 Evaluation Data

AQUA has been tested on data set USP05 (University Students Projects 2005). It contains 197 different projects, each with 15 different attribute fields. The data set was split into two parts: USP05-FT and USP05-RQ for 76 features and 121 requirements respectively. The attributes of the data set are specified in Appendix 1.

The choice of the attributes is crucial for the results of further processing. They varied from abstract concepts such as the internal complexity of the project to more specific attributes like development tools. What matters is the information that is contained in the values of the attributes. The attributes are described in the Appendix. When AQUA was confronted with the data one could not influence the attributes used anymore; a posterior we found that not all attributes of interest had been used.

3 Learning

3.1 The First Learning Process

This process is concerned with the determination of the optimal parameter settings of N (number of nearest neighbors considered) and T (the threshold for the similarity). For a project P the optimal values of N and T are denoted by PN,T. These numbers have been investigated in software engineering in the past. For instance, N and T were tested separately in [12] as two strategies to determine the number of K-nearest neighbors. In existing analogy-based methods in software engineering, a small number of cases, typically from one to five, are used. This number is fixed for a given data set regardless of the similarity of the cases. In the following section we present the results of a more flexible approach in the form of an explorative study to gain further insight into the sensitivity between prediction accuracy and how similar the cases are, as well as how many cases are used.

For the explorative study the quasi-standard Leave-One-Out Cross Validation (LOOCV) method for validating effort estimation methods is used, (see [18)]). Given a data set CB with known efforts of all the objects, cross-validation is done on CB itself by estimating one object using others as cases each time, thus we have Gsim:CB×CB→[0, 1]. For our purposes, PN,T will be decided by varying values of both N and T. A statistical distribution of the accuracy in dependence of N and T is thus obtained after all the projects in the data set are estimated.

In addition to commonly used criteria as discussed in [5], the evaluations criteria contain the new criteria: support, strength, number of Top-N similar objects, and T.

In order to measure accuracy, different kinds of errors have been examined in the literature, they are more or less refined and we combine them. We go into some detail in order to be able to compare the results. The most important are (used here):

(1) Mean of magnitude of relative error (MMRE)

$$MMRE = \frac{1}{n} \sum_{r_k \in R} \frac{\left| Effort(r_k) - \widetilde{Effort}(r_k) \right|}{Effort(r_k)} \text{ for a fixed pair of values of } N \text{ and } T \text{ for all the}$$

objects in R in a single run of jack-knife, where $R = CB$ and $n=|CB|$; this is a relative error.

(2) Prediction at level α: $Pred(\alpha)$ measures the percentage of estimates that are within a given level of accuracy: $Pred(\alpha)=\tau/\lambda$, where λ is the total number of estimates, and τ the number of estimates with a MRE less than or equal to α. Greater $Pred(\alpha)$ with smaller α means

(3) Support and strength: Given an object $r_g \in R$ under estimation in the jack-knife process, if thresholds of N and T are set to N^* and T^* respectively, only when $|R_{topN}(r_g)| \geq 1$ can r_g have analogies and be able to be predicted. In other words, $R_{topN}(r_g)$ might be empty if T^* is too high or/and N^* is too big, hence r_g cannot be predicted without any eligible analogies. Therefore, the number of objects that can be estimated with given values of N and T is also an important measure for the prediction quality.

According to [5], the acceptable threshold values for $MMRE$ and $Pred(0.25)$ are suggested to be $MMRE \leq 25\%$, $Pred(1/4) \geq 75\%$, and Strength$\geq$ 0.3, respectively. We adopted these thresholds in order to be able to compare our results with those reported elsewhere. These criteria are combined using the criterion *MPS*:

$$MPS = \begin{cases} "Yes" & CMMRE \leq 0.25 \text{ and } CPred(25) \geq 0.75 \text{ and } CStrength \geq 0.3 \\ "No" & \text{Otherwise} \end{cases}$$

where *CMMRE*, *CPred(0.25)*, and *CStrength* are the maximum value of *MMRE*, minimum value of *Pred(1/4)* and minimum value of *Strength*, respectively. *Yes* means accepted and *No* means not accepted. Values of *N and T* for corresponding acceptable cases are called qualified *N* and *T*.

We split the sensitivity analysis of *MMRE* into two parts by varying *N* and *T* independently and simultaneously. The former is shown in [2] for data sets USP05-FT, USP05-RQ with two-dimensional scatter plots, the latter is shown in Fig.1. The only system so far that varied *N* and *T* simultaneously was GRACE (19).

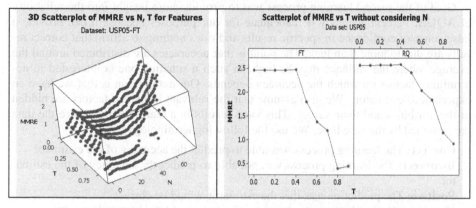

Fig. 1. MMRE for *N,T*   **Fig. 2.** MMRE for T only

The distinction between accurate and inaccurate was decided by whether or not the prediction percent error fell below a predetermined cutoff point *CO* which means that small prediction error counted as accurate. We chose to test the networks with cutoffs of 1%, 3%, 5%, 10%, and 15%. What can also be seen here is the expected fact that beyond a certain level increasing *T* does not add to the accuracy of the prediction, see the second learning.

The learning phase is a process of multiple runs of cross-validation which vary both *T* and *N*. The increment of *N* is set to 1 starting from 1, *T* to 0.01 or 0.02 starting from 0, depending on the size of the data set and the density of accuracy pursuing. In order to determine the best values of *T* and *N* we search for the smallest *MMRE*, greatest *Strength* and then greatest *Pred(0.25)*, with *MPS* measuring whether the best accuracy is acceptable or not. Let's assume that the data base of accuracy distribution is sorted by *MMRE* (ascending), *Strength* (descending), *Pred(0.25)* (descending), *T* (ascending), and *N* (ascending). We skip the details of this search process. At the end it is decided whether the expected prediction accuracy is acceptable or not depending on the value "*Yes*" or "*No*" of MPS_1 . An example for the exploration data is shown in table 1.

Table 1. Accuracy for USP05-FT

N	T	MMRE %	Pred(0.25) %	Strength %	Support (76)	MPS
1	0.86	17	86	75	57	Yes
1	0.8	20	82.26	82	62	Yes
1-24	0.94	4-18	76-92	33-70	25-53	Yes
20-26	0.92	13-18	75	42	32	Yes

3.2 The Second Learning Process

The experiments in this section should only be taken as an example for illustration. For a real statistical insight one would need more data. For this reason the shown results have not been investigated further.

Goal of the second learning process was to provide more insight into the reliability of AQUA. Percent accuracy is inadequate for our purposes because it can provide a false sense of confidence in specific results and does nothing to affirm that correct results are due to more than luck. The point is that accuracies are distributed around the average where the variance may be high. In such a situation one is interested in determining factors on which the accuracy depends. Our assumption is that we have an experienced estimator. We also assume that the relevant influence factors are hidden in the attributes and their values. This view results in a learning task where the data are provided by the case base. We use the following terminology:

Correct: The learning process was able to predict the accuracy of the estimator
Incorrect: The learning process was not able to predict the accuracy of the estimator
Positive: The prediction was that the estimator would be correct
Negative: The prediction was that the estimator would not be correct.

We use these terms to create a set of four possible outcomes, Correct Positive, Correct Negative, Incorrect Positive and Incorrect Negative predictions of estimator accuracy.

Step one: **Neural network application** (see [20]). The purpose was 1) show the results of AQUA are more than luck and 2) attempt to identify the cases, their attributes and values in which the results of AQUA should be deemed more or less reliable

For learning we used neural networks. All data processing was done with ruby scripts and the Java Neural Network Simulator (Java version of SNNS, ([21], [22])) was used for building and training the neural networks.

The input of the network is the attribute representation of the cases. We varied the number of hidden nodes. The net has two outputs, representing positive and negative predictions. This pair of outputs represents a statement about the accuracy of AQUA. During the training process these outputs were trained to binary XOR values according to the four possible outcomes. A percent error cut-off CO was chosen as in section 3.1. Each of the outputs may now be correct or incorrect, which leads to four possibilities. The training data were chosen randomly.

Concerning the attribute types mentioned above, a different strategy was used. Each percentage value in the fuzzy set of functionality percentages was assigned to a single input. Ranged values were split into two inputs, one for the minimum value and one for the maximum.

Once the networks were trained they were tested using a randomly chosen test subset of each dataset. Each result from the test set was placed into one of four categories: Correct Positive (CP), Incorrect Positive (IP), Correct Negative (CN), and Incorrect Negative (IN).

Step two: Analysis of results
The analysis of the results was done in two steps:

- Analysis at a per network level
- Analysis at a per attribute level.

On the network level the network outputs were classified for each project. The results are shown in Table 3. If a network is able to accurately classify the prediction of AQUA, it reinforces that AQUA is not simply making a lucky guess; in this case we have an additional conformation.

Secondly, the results were analyzed at an attribute per value level, which helps to identify not only the attributes that most adversely affect accuracy, but also the special cases for these attributes that have either very high or very low accuracy. For this purpose, for each attribute a, the case base was split into disjoint subsets according to the occurring values of the attribute and the same analysis step was performed. A part of the results are shown in Table 4.

Attributes of interest were identified by high percentage of correct classifications. Having a high percentage of Correct Positive classifications for a specific attribute/value pair should indicate that more confidence can be placed in the effort estimation of similar projects, whereas a high percentage of Correct Negative classifications points to problem scenarios where AQUA's prediction should be taken with a grain of salt. For a software company this means that the company should look mainly at the per attribute evaluation. If an attribute has certain critical values then one should not rely too much on the prediction.

The experimental results shown in Table 2 where done for 66 input nodes, 75 respectively. 150 hidden nodes, and two output nodes (with two variations a and b). The results show that AQUA was in general confirmed by the neural network for the positive answers but not so much for the negative ones. On a qualitative level one can say that more than luck was involved for the AQUA method.

In Table 3 we investigate as an example the attribute *internal complexity* that has in different projects different values 1, ...,5. The values 1 and 2 give more confidence than 3 or 5.

The USP05 was relatively useful for our purposes, in particular because there are several stand-out cases in which the networks were able to correctly guess the success of the effort estimation in not only the positive cases but also a number of the negative cases as well. This hints that this neural network verification method was able to learn some of the estimation behaviour of AQUA, and as such, that in the case of USP05 there may be more than luck involved. A table listing the test set classification statistics for the USP05 dataset is included in the appendix.

Table 2. Network based analysis

Cutoff Percent	Network	CP	IP	CN	IN
1	USP05_66_150_2a	11	1	2	4
1	USP05_66_150_2b	12	0	2	4
1	USP05_66_70_70_2a	12	0	1	5
1	USP05_66_70_70_2b	12	0	1	5
1	USP05_66_75_2a	12	0	0	6
1	USP05_66_75_2b	12	0	0	6
3	USP05_66_150_2a	14	0	0	4
3	USP05_66_150_2b	14	0	0	4
3	USP05_66_70_70_2a	12	2	0	4
3	USP05_66_70_70_2b	13	1	0	4
3	USP05_66_75_2a	14	0	0	4
3	USP05_66_75_2b	13	1	0	4
5	USP05_66_150_2a	14	0	1	3
5	USP05_66_150_2b	12	2	0	4
5	USP05_66_70_70_2a	13	1	0	4
5	USP05_66_70_70_2b	13	1	1	3
5	USP05_66_75_2a	12	2	0	4
5	USP05_66_75_2b	14	0	0	4
10	USP05_66_150_2a	13	1	1	3
10	USP05_66_150_2b	13	1	0	4
10	USP05_66_70_70_2a	13	1	1	3
10	USP05_66_70_70_2b	13	1	0	4
10	USP05_66_75_2a	14	0	0	4
10	USP05_66_75_2b	14	0	1	3
15	USP05_66_150_2a	13	1	1	3
15	USP05_66_150_2b	14	0	1	3
15	USP05_66_70_70_2a	14	0	1	3
15	USP05_66_70_70_2b	13	1	2	2
15	USP05_66_75_2a	12	2	2	2
15	USP05_66_75_2b	14	0	0	4

Table 3. Attribute based analysis

Attribute	Value	CP	IC	CN	IN
IntComplx	1	8	0	0	1
IntComplx	2	2	0	0	0
IntComplx	3	1	1	0	1
IntComplx	4	0	0	0	0
IntComplx	5	1	1	0	2

The belief that more than luck is involved for USP05 is further enhanced by analyzing the individual attribute value scores. Most of the attribute values with high occurrence count attributes are very heavily sided to either correct or incorrect. For space reasons were are not able to include a full listing of these per attribute per value scores, but numbers showing the results of one network for various values of internal complexity are shown in Table 2. From this table we can note that more confidence should be placed in AQUA's estimation of projects with internal complexity *1* or *2*, than *3* or *5*. The method can be further refined (in the same way as done here) by looking at effort overestimates and underestimates.

4 Summary and Outlook

In this paper we tackled a problem that is known to be notoriously difficult problem of effort estimation for software development. It is of high economic importance and therefore it has been approached in the past from many different angles. Here we used CBR methods, but added an aspect that is not common yet. We showed that considering the number of nearest neighbors and the similarity threshold can have a considerable influence on the prediction accuracy. Therefore these parameters were subject to optimization by a statistical learning process. A second type of learning was applied to get an insight into the factors that determine the reliability of the prediction in a single instance. This is again of importance to software companies. Both kinds of learning need further evaluations. For the second type of learning, alternative methods and configuration of neural networks need to be evaluated. The principal applicability of the approach has been demonstrated for the purpose of effort estimation of software projects, but is not limited to that.

There are several issues left for the future and we name only a few. The first is the question in how far the knowledge contained in N and T can also be expressed in terms of other subcontainers of the similarity measure, in particular the weights. Another problem is to try other learning methods instead of neural networks, for instance clustering or fuzzy clustering. This related to the question in how far the strict cut-off ca be replaced by a fuzzy representation.

Acknowledgements

The authors are grateful for the helpful comments of the referees and to Jim McElroy for corrections and proof reading.

References

1. Li, J.Z.: A Flexible Method for Software Effort Estimation by Analogy. PhD Thesis, University of Calgary, Department of Computer Science, Calgary (2007)
2. Li, J.Z., Ruhe, G., Al-Emran, A., Richter, M.M.: A flexible method for software effort estimation by analogy. Empirical Software Engineering 12(1), 65–106 (2007)

3. Angelis, L., Stamelos., I., Morisio, M.: Building a Software Cost Estimation Model Based on Categorical Data. In: METRICS 2001: Proceedings of the IEEE 7th International Symposium on Software Metrics, England, UK, pp. 4–15 (2001)
4. Ruhe, M., Jeffery, R., Wieczorek, I.: Cost Estimation for Web Application. In: ICSE 2003: Proceedings of 25th International Conference on Software Engineering, Oregon, USA, pp. 285–294 (2003)
5. Conte, S.D., Dunsmore, H., Shen, V.Y.: Software engineering metrics and models. Benjamin-Cummings Publishing Co. Inc. (1986)
6. Mendes, E., Watson, I., Chris, T., Nile, M., Steve, C.: A Comparative Study of Cost Estimation Models for Web Hypermedia Applications. Empirical Software Engineering 8(2), 163–196 (2003)
7. Shepperd, M., Schofield, C.: Estimating Software Project Effort Using Analogies. IEEE Transactions on Software Engineering 23(12), 736–743 (1997)
8. Walkerden, F., Jeffery, R.: An Empirical Study of Analogy-based Software Effort Estimation. Empirical Software Engineering 4(2), 135–158 (1999)
9. Delany, S.J., Cunningham, P., Wilke, W.: The Limits of CBR in Software Project Estimation. In: 6th German Workshop On Case-Based Reasoning, https://www.cs.tcd.ie/publications/tech-reports/reports.99/TCD-CS-1999-21.pdf
10. Kadoda, G., Michelle, C., Chen, L., Shepperd, M.: Experiences Using Case-Based Reasoning to Predict Software Project Effort. In: EASE 2000, Staffordshire, UK (2000)
11. Leake, D.B., Sooriamurthi, R.: Case dispatching versus case-base merging: when MCBR matters. International Journal on Artificial Intelligence Tools 13(1), 237–254 (2004)
12. Richter, M.M.: Foundations of Similarity and Utility. In: Proc. FLAIRS 2007, pp. 30–37. AAAI Press, Menlo Park (2007)
13. Cheetham, W.: Case Based Reasoning with Confidence. In: Blanzieri, E., Portinale, L. (eds.) EWCBR 2000. LNCS (LNAI), vol. 1898, pp. 15–25. Springer, Heidelberg (2000)
14. Wettschereck, D., Aha, D.W.: Weighting features. In: ICCBR 1995. Springer, Heidelberg (1995)
15. Stahl, A.: Learning of Knowledge-Intensive Similarity Measures in Case-Based Reasoning. Dissertation Kaiserslautern (2003)
16. Richter, M.M.: Similarity. In: Perner, P. (ed.) Case-Based Reasoning on Signals and Images, pp. 25–90. Springer, Heidelberg (2007)
17. Basili, V.R., Caldiera, G., Rombach, H.D.: The Goal Question Metric Approach. Encyclopedia of Software Engineering. John Wiley & Sons, Inc., Chichester (1994)
18. Efron, B., Gong, G.: A Leisurely Look at the Bootstrap, the Jackknife, and Cross-Validation. The American Statistician 37(1), 36–48 (1983)
19. Song, Q., Shepperd, M., Mair, C.: Using Grey Relational Analysis to Predict Software Effort with Small Data Sets. In: METRICS 2005: Proceedings of the 11th IEEE International Software Metrics Symposium, Como, Italy, pp. 35–45 (2005)
20. Mackas, B.: Prediction Accuracy Validation. In: Richter, M.M. (ed.) Teaching Machine Learning, Technical Report, University of Calgary (2007)
21. SNNS user manual, http://www.ra.informatik.uni-tuebingen.de/SNNS/UserManual/UserManual.html
22. Baldi, P., Hornik, K.: Neural networks and principal component analysis: learning from examples without local minima. Neural Network 2(1), 53–58 (1989)

Appendix A: Data Set UPS05

Attribute Name	Type	Values	Description
Funct%	Fuzzy	{Internal Process, Data entry/modification/deletion, Output, Data query from database/file, Printing, Report, Other}	Percentage of each type of functionality
Internal Complexity	Ordinal	1-Very low, 2-Low, 3-Medium, 4-High, 5-Very high	Complexity of internal calculations
Data File	Ordinal	Positive Integer	Number of data files/database tables accessed
DataEn	Ordinal	Positive Integer	Number of data entry items
DataOut	Ordinal	Positive Integer	Number of data output items
UFP	Ordinal	Positive Integer	Unadjusted function point count
Lang	Set	C++, Java, VB, Java Script, VB Script, SQL, Php, Perl, Asp, Html, XML, etc	Programming Languages used for implementation
Tools	Set	VJ++, VB, Delphi, VisualCafe, JUnit, PowerBuilder, BorlandC++, etc.	Development Tools and platforms used for implementation
ToolExpr	Range	Range of positive integers	Range of experience (in months) of the development team with the development tools and languages.
AppExpr	Ordinal	1-Very low, 2-Low, 3-Medium, 4-High, 5-Very high	Application experience level
TeamSize	Range	Range of positive integers	Range in size of development team over project. E.g. [2,5] indicates at any time the project had between 2 and 5 people actively working
DBMS	Set	Oracle, Access, SQLServer, MySQL, etc	Names of database systems used for project
Method	Set	OO, SA, SD, RAD, JAD, MVC, others	Programming methodologies used for implementation
SAType	Set	B/S, C/S, BC/S, Centered, other	Type of System/Application Architecture: B-Browser, C-Client, S-Server

Evaluation of Feature Subset Selection, Feature Weighting, and Prototype Selection for Biomedical Applications

Suzanne Little[1], Ovidio Salvetti[2], and Petra Perner[1]

[1] Institute of Computer Vision and Applied Computer Sciences, Germany
Suzanne.Little@ibai-institut.de, pperner@ibai-institut.de
[2] ISTI-CNR, Pisa, Italy
Ovidio.Salvetti@isti.cnr.it

Abstract. Many medical diagnosis applications are characterized by datasets that contain under-represented classes due to the fact that the disease appears more rarely than the normal case. In such a situation classifiers that generalize over the data such as decision trees and Naïve Bayesian are not the proper choice as classification methods. Case-based classifiers that can work on the samples seen so far are more appropriate for such a task. We propose to calculate the contingency table and class specific evaluation measures despite the overall accuracy for evaluation purposes of classifiers for these specific data characteristics. We evaluate the different options of our case-based classifier and compare the performance to decision trees and Naïve Bayesian. Finally, we give an outlook for further work.

Keywords: Feature Subset Selection, Feature Weighting, Prototype Selection, Evaluation of Methods, Methodology for Prototype-Based Classification, CBR in Health.

1 Introduction

Many medical diagnosis applications are characterized by datasets that contain under-represented classes due to the fact that the disease appears more rarely than the normal case. In such a situation classifiers that generalize over the data such as decision trees and Naïve Bayesian are not the proper choice as classification methods. Decision trees tend to over-generalize to the class with the most examples while Naïve Bayesian requires enough data for the estimation of the class-conditional probabilities. Case-based classifiers that can work on the samples seen so far are more appropriate for such a task.

A case-based classifier classifies a new sample by finding similar cases in the case base based on a proper similarity measure. A good coverage of the casebase, the right case description and the proper similarity are the essential functions that enable a case-based classifier to perform well.

In this work we studied the behavior of a case-based classifier based on different medical datasets with different characteristics from the UCI repository [1]. We chose

K.-D. Althoff et al. (Eds.): ECCBR 2008, LNAI 5239, pp. 312–324, 2008.

datasets where one or more classes were heavily under-represented compared to the other classes as well as datasets having more or less equally distributed samples for the classes for comparison purposes.

The case-based classifier has several options for improving its performance that can be chosen independently or in combination. Currently available options in our case-based classifier are: k-value for the closest cases; feature subset selection (FS); feature weight learning (FW) and prototype selection (PS). To conclusively determine which combination of options is best for the current problem is non-obvious and time-consuming and the hope of our study is to develop a methodology that assists a user to design and refine our case-based classifiers. We observe the influence of the different options of a case-based classifier and report the results in this paper. Our study is an on-going study; we also intend to investigate other options in casebase maintenance.

The aim of work here is to give the user a methodology for best applying our case-based classifier and how to evaluate the classifier particularly in situations where there is under-representation of specific classes. In Section 2 we describe our case-based classifier named ProtoClass while Section 3 describes the evaluation strategy. The datasets are described in Section 4. Results are reported in Section 5 and a discussion on the results is given in Section 6. Finally, we summarize our work and give an outlook of further work in Section 7.

2   Case-Based Classifiers

A case-based classifier classifies a sample according to the cases in a case base and selects the most similar case as output of the classifier. A proper similarity measure is necessary to perform this task but in most applications there is no a-priori knowledge available that suggests the right similarity measure. The method of choice to select the proper similarity measure is therefore to apply a subset of the numerous similarity measures known from statistics to the problem and to select the one that performs best according to a quality measure such as, for example, the classification accuracy. The other choice is to automatically build the similarity metric by learning the right attributes and attribute weights. The later one we chose as one option to improve the performance of our classifier.

When people collect samples to construct a dataset for a case-based classifier it is useful to select prototypical examples from this input. Therefore a function is needed to perform prototype selection and to reduce the number of examples used for classification. This results in better generalization and a more noise tolerant classifier. It is also possible for an expert to select prototypes manually. However, this can result in bias and possible duplicates of prototypes causing inefficiencies. Therefore a function to assess a collection of prototypes and identify redundancy is useful.

Finally, an important variable in a case-based classifier is the value used to determine the number of closest cases and the final class label.

Consequently, the design-options the classifier has to improve its performance are prototype selection, feature-subset selection, feature weight learning and the 'k' value of the closest cases (see Figure 1).

We choose a decremental redundancy-reduction algorithm proposed by Chang [2] that deletes prototypes as long as the classification accuracy does not decrease. The

feature-subset selection is based on the wrapper approach [3] and an empirical fea-
ture-weight learning method [4] is used. Cross validation is used to estimate the classification accuracy. A detailed description of our classifier ProtoClass is given in [6].
The prototype selection, the feature selection, and the feature weighting steps are
performed independently or in combination with each other in order to assess the
influence these functions have on the performance of the classifier. The steps are
performed during each run of the cross-validation process. The classifier schema
shown in Figure 1 is divided in the design phase (Learning Unit) and the normal classification phase (Classification Unit). The classification phase starts after we have
evaluated the classifier and determined the right features, feature weights, the value
for 'k' and the cases.

Our classifier has a flat case base instead of a hierarchical that makes it easier to
conduct the evaluations.

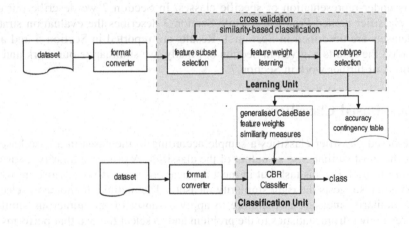

Fig. 1. Case-based Classifier

2.1   Classification Rule

This rule [5] classifies x in the category of its closest case. More precisely, we call
$x'_n \in \{x_1, x_2, \ldots, x_i, \ldots x_n\}$ a closest case to x if $\min d(x_i, x) = d(x'_n, x)$, where
$i = 1, 2, \ldots, n$.

The rule chooses to classify x into category C_n, where x'_n is the closest case to x
and x'_n belongs to class C_n.

In the case of the k-closest cases we require k-samples of the same class to fulfill
the decision rule. As a distance measure we use the Euclidean distance.

2.2   Prototype Selection by Chang's Algorithm

For the selection of the right number of prototypes we used Chang's algorithm [2].
The outline of the algorithm can be described as follows: Suppose the set T is given

as $T=\{t^1,...,t^i,...,t^m\}$ with t^i as the *i-th* initial prototype. The idea of the algorithm is as follows: We start with every point in T as a prototype. We then successively merge any two closest prototypes t^1 and t^2 of the same class by a new prototype t, if the merging will not downgrade the classification of the patterns in T. The new prototype t may simply be the average vector of t^1 and t^2. We continue the merging process until the number of incorrect classifications of the pattern in T starts to increase.

Roughly, the algorithm can be stated as follows: Given a training set T, the initial prototypes are just the points of T. At any stage the prototypes belong to one of two sets – set A or set B. Initially, A is empty and B is equal to T. We start with an arbitrary point in B and initially assign it to A. Find a point p in A and a point q in B, such that the distance between p and q is the shortest among all distances between points of A and B. Try to merge p and q. That is, if p and q are of the same class, compute a vector p^* in terms of p and q. If replacing p and q by p^* does not decrease the recognition rate for T, merging is successful. In this case, delete p and q from A and B, respectively, and put p^* into A, and the procedure is repeated once again. In the case that p and q cannot be merged, i.e. if either p or q are not of the same class or merging is unsuccessful, move q from B to A, and the procedure is repeated. When B becomes empty, recycle the whole procedure by letting B be the final A obtained from the previous cycle, and by resetting A to be the empty set. This process stops when no new merged prototypes are obtained. The final prototypes in A are then used in the classifier.

2.3 Feature-Subset Selection and Feature Weighting

The wrapper approach [3] is used for selecting a feature subset from the whole set of features and for feature weighting. This approach conducts a search for a good feature subset by using the k-NN classifier itself as an evaluation function. By doing so the specific behavior of the classification methods is taken into account. The leave-one-out cross-validation method is used for estimating the classification accuracy. Cross-validation is especially suitable for small data set. The best-first search strategy is used for the search over the state space of possible feature combination. The algorithm terminates if we have not found an improved accuracy over the last k search states.

The feature combination that gave the best classification accuracy is the remaining feature subset. We then try to further improve our classifier by applying a feature-weighting tuning-technique in order to get real weights for the binary weights.

The weights of each feature w_i are changed by a constant value, δ: $w_i := w_i \pm \delta$. If the new weight causes an improvement of the classification accuracy, then the weight will be updated accordingly; otherwise, the weight will remain as it is. After the last weight has been tested, the constant δ will be divided into half and the procedure repeats. The process terminates if the difference between the classification accuracy of two interactions is less than a predefined threshold.

3   Classifier Construction and Evaluation

Since we are dealing with small sample sets that may sometimes only have two samples in a class we choose leave one-out to estimate the error rate. We calculate the average accuracy and the contingency table (see Table 1) showing the distribution of the class-correct classified samples as well as the distribution of the samples classified in one of the other classes. From that table we can derive a set of more specific performance measures that had already demonstrated their advantages in the comparison of neural nets and decision trees [7] such as the classification quality (also called the sensitivity and specificity in the two-class problem).

Table 1. Contingency Table

		True Class Label (assigned by expert)				
		1	i	...	m	p_{ki}
Assigned Class Label (by Classifier)	1	c_{11}	...	...	c_{1m}	
	i	...	c_{ii}	...	...	
	...	...	...	...	...	
	m	c_{m1}	...	...	c_{mm}	
	p_{ti}					

In the fields of the table are recorded the true class distribution within the data set and the class distribution after the samples have been classified as well as the marginal distribution c_{ij}. The main diagonal is the number of correctly classified samples. From this table, we can calculate parameters that describe the quality of the classifier.

The correctness or accuracy p (Equation 1) is number of correctly classified samples according to the number of samples. This measure is the opposite to the error rate.

$$p = \frac{\sum\limits_{i=1}^{m} c_{ii}}{\sum\limits_{i=1}^{m} \sum\limits_{j=1}^{m} c_{ij}} \qquad (1)$$

The class specific quality p_{ki} (Equation 2) is the number of correctly classified samples for one class i to all samples of class i and the classification quality p_{ti} (Equation 3) is the number of correctly classified samples of class i to the number of correctly and falsely classified samples into class i:

$$p_{ki} = \frac{c_{ii}}{\sum\limits_{j=1}^{m} c_{ji}} \qquad (2)$$

$$p_{ti} = \frac{c_{ii}}{\sum\limits_{j=1}^{m} c_{ij}} \qquad (3)$$

These measures allow us to study the behavior of a classifier according to a particular class. The overall error rate of a classifier may look good but when examining the classification quality p_{ti} for a particular class we may find it not acceptable.

We also calculate the reduction rate, that is, the number of samples removed from the dataset versus the number of samples in the case base.

Since the classifier has several options: prototype-selection, feature subset selection and feature weighting that can be chosen combinatorially we performed the tests on each of these combinations in order to get an understanding for which data characteristics it is necessary to use what functions. Table 2 lists the various combinations and their order of application for the evaluations applied.

Table 2. Combinations of classifier options for testing

Test	Feature Subset Selection	Feature Weighting	Prototype Selection
1	1		
2		1	
3			1
4	1	2	3
5	2	3	1

4 Datasets and Methods for Comparison

A variety of datasets from the UCI repository [1] were chosen. The IRIS and EColi datasets are presented here as representative of the different characteristics of the datasets. Space constraints prevent the presentation of other evaluations in this paper.

The well-known, standard IRIS Plant dataset consists of sepal and petal measurements from specimens of IRIS plants and aims to classify them into one of three species. The dataset consists of 3 equally distributed classes of 50 samples each with 4 numerical features. One species (setosa) is linearly separable from the other two, which are not separable from each other. This is a simple and frequently applied dataset within the field of pattern recognition.

The EColi dataset aims to predict the cellular localization sites of proteins from a number of signal and laboratory measurements. The dataset consists of 336 instances with 7 numerical features and belonging to 8 classes. The distribution of the samples per class is highly unequal (143/77/2/2/35/20/5/52).

The Wisconsin Breast Cancer dataset consists of visual information from scans and provides a classification problem of predicting the class of the cancer as either benign or malignant. There are 699 instances in the dataset with a distribution of 458/241 and 9 numerical features.

Table 3. Dataset characteristics and class distribution

	No. Samples	No. Features	No. Classes	Class Distribution							
IRIS	150	4	3	setosa		versicolor			virginica		
				50		50			50		
E.Coli	336	7	8	cp	im	imL	imS	imU	om	omL	pp
				143	77	2	2	35	20	5	52
Wisconsin	699	9	2	benign				malignant			
				458				241			

For each dataset we compare the overall accuracy generated from:

1. Naïve Bayesian, implemented in Weka [11];
2. C4.5 decision tree induction, implemented in DECISION MASTER [12];
3. k-Nearest Neighbor (k-NN) classifier, implemented in Weka with the settings "weka.classifiers.lazy.IBk -K k -W 0 -A
   "weka.core.neighboursearch.LinearNNSearch -A
   weka.core.EuclideanDistance"";
4. case-based classifier, implemented in ProtoClass (described in section 2) without normalization of features.

Where appropriate, the k values were set as 1, 3 and 7 and leave-one-out cross-validation was used as the evaluation method. We refer to the different "implementations" of each of these approaches since the decisions made during implementation can cause slightly different results even with equivalent algorithms.

5 Results

The results for the *IRIS* dataset are reported in Table 4 to Table 6. In Table 4 you can see the results for Naïve Bayes, decision tree induction, k-NN classifier done with Weka implementation and the result for the combinatorial tests described in Table 2 with ProtoClass. As expected, decision tree induction performs well since the data set has an equal data distribution but not as well as Naïve Bayes.

In general we can say that the accuracy does not significantly improve when we do feature subset selection, feature weighting and prototype selection with ProtoClass. In case of k=1 and k=7 the feature subset remains the initial feature set. We marked this in Table 4 by an "X" indicating that no changes were made in the design phase and the accuracy is as in case of the initial classifier. This is not surprising since the data base contains only 4 features which are more or less well-distinguished. In case of k=3 we see a decrease in the accuracy although the stopping criteria for the methods for feature subset selection and feature weighting require the overall accuracy not to decrease. This accuracy is calculated within the loop of the cross validation cycle on the design data set and afterwards the single left out sample is classified against the new learnt classifier to calculate the final overall accuracy. Prototype selection where k=7 demonstrates the same behavior. This shows that the true accuracy must be calculated based on cross validation and not just on the design data set.

We expected that feature subset selection and feature weighting would change the similarity matrix and therefore we believed that prototype selection should be done afterwards. As can be seen from the table in case of k=3 we do not achieve any improvement in accuracy when running PS after the feature options. However, when conducting PS before FS and FW, we see that FS and FW do not have any further influence on the accuracy. When combining FS/FW/PS, the final accuracy was often the same as the accuracy of the first function applied. Therefore prototype selection prior to feature subset selection or feature weighting seems to provide a better result.

The contingency table in Table 5 gives us a better understanding what is going during the classification. Here we can see what samples get misclassified according to what class. In case of k=1 and k=3 the misclassification is more equitably distributed over the classes. If we prefer to accurately classify one class we might prefer k=7 since it can better classify class "virginica". It depends on the domain what requirements are expected from the system.

Table 6 shows us the remaining sample distribution according to the class after prototype selection. We can see that there are two or three samples merged for class "versicolor". The reduction of the number of samples is small (less than 1.4% reduction rate) but this behavior fits our expectations when considering the original data set. It is well known that the IRIS dataset is a sanitized dataset.

The *Ecoli* data set has the most unequally distributed classes among our selected datasets which matches the characteristics we are interested in.

Table 7 lists the overall accuracies for the different approaches using the EColi dataset. Naïve Bayesian shows the best overall accuracy and decision tree induction the worst one. The result for Naïve Bayesian is somewhat curious since we have to say that the Bayesian scenario does not hold for this data set. The true class conditional distribution can not be estimated for the classes with small sample number. Therefore, we consider this classifier as not applicable to such a data set. That it shows such a good accuracy might be due to the fact that the classifier can classify excellently the classes with large sample number (e.g., cp, im, pp) and the misclassification of sample from classes with a small number do not have a big impact on the overall accuracy. Although previous evaluations have used this data to demonstrate the performance of their classifier on the overall accuracy (for example in [11][12]) we suggest that this number does not necessarily reflect the true performance of the classifier. It is essential to examine the data characteristics and the class-specific classification quality when judging the performance of the classifier.

Table 4. Overall accuracy for IRIS dataset using leave-one-ou

k	Naïve Bayes	Decision Tree	kNN	ProtoClass	Feature Subset	Feature Weighting	Prototype Selection	FS+FW+PS	PS+FS+FW
1	95.33	96.33	95.33	96.00	X	X	96.00	96.00	96.33
3	na	na	95.33	96.00	96.33	96.33	96.00	96.33	96.00
7	na	na	96.33	96.67	X	96.00	96.00	96.33	96.00

Table 5. Contingency table for k=1,3,7 for the IRIS dataset and ProtoClass

IRIS	setosa			versicolor			virginica		
k	1	3	7	1	3	7	1	3	7
setosa	50	50	50	0	0	0	0	0	0
versicolor	0	0	0	47	47	46	3	3	4
virginica	0	0	0	3	3	1	47	47	49
Classification quality	100	100	100	94	94	97.87	94	94	92.45
Class specific quality	100	100	100	94	94	92	94	94	98

As in the former test, the k-NN classifier of Weka does not perform as well as the ProtoClass classifier. We can see for k=7 the best accuracy which is surprising but the contingency table (Table 8) confirms again that the classes with small sample number seem to have low impact to the overall accuracy.

Table 6. Class distribution and percentage reduction rate of IRIS dataset after prototype selection

	Iris-sertosa	Iris-versicolor	Iris-virginica	Reduction Rate in %
orig	50	50	50	0.00
k=1	50	49	50	0.67
k=3	50	49	50	0.67
k=7	50	48	50	1.33

Feature subset selection works on the EColi dataset. One or two features get dropped out but the same observations as of the IRIS data set are also true here. We can see an increase and a decrease of the accuracy. That means only on the accuracy estimated with cross-validation provides the best indication of the performance of feature subset selection. Feature weighting works only in case of k=1 (see table 9). There we can see an improvement of 1.79% in the accuracy.

The contingency table (Table 8) confirms our hypothesis that only the classes with many samples are well classified. In the case of classes with a very low number of samples (e.g., imL and imS) we get an error rate of 100% for the class. For these classes we have no coverage [8] of the class solutions space. The reduction rate on the samples after PS (Table 10) confirms again this observation. Some samples of the classes with high number of samples are merged but the classes with low sample numbers remain constant.

Results for the *Wisconsin Breast Cancer* dataset are summarized in Table 11 and 12. Due to the expensive computational complexity of the prototype implementation and the size of the dataset it was not possible to generate results for prototype selection. Therefore only results for feature subset selection and feature weighting have been completed. While the Wisconsin dataset is a two class problem, it still has the same disparity between the number of samples in each case. As expected in a reasonably well delineated two-class problem Naïve Bayes and Decision Trees both perform acceptably.

The k-value of 7 produces the best overall accuracy. The feature subset and feature weighting tasks both display slight improvements or maintenance of the performance for all values of k. The Wisconsin dataset has the largest number of features (9) of the datasets discussed here and it is to be expected that datasets with larger numbers of features will have improved performance when applying techniques to adjust the importance and impact of the features. However it is worth noting that the feature subset selection and feature weighting techniques used in this prototype assume that the features operate independently from each other. This may not be the case, especially in applying these techniques to classification using low-level analysis of media objects.

The contingency tables shown in table 12 provide a more in-depth view of the performance of the ProtoClass classifier than is possible using the overall accuracy value. In this instance the performance difference between classes is relatively stable and the k-value of 7 still appears to offer the best performance.

Overall the results from the three datasets summarised in this section demonstrate that measuring performance by using the overall accuracy of a classifier is inaccurate

Table 7. Overall accuracy for EColi dataset using leave-one-out

k	Naive Bayes	Decision Tree	Weka Nearest Neighbour	ProtoClass	Feature Subset (FS)	Feature Weighting (FW)	Prototype Selection (PS)	FS+FW+PS	PS+FS+FW
1	86.01	66.37	80.95	81.25	80.95	83.04	80.65	82.44	80.95
3	na	na	83.93	84.23	85.12	84.23	82.74	83.93	82.74
7	na	na	87.20	87.50	87.20	86.31	86.61	85.42	86.61

Table 8. Combined contingency table for k=1,3,7 for the EColi dataset and ProtoClass

k	cp 1	cp 3	cp 7	im 1	im 3	im 7	imL 1	imL 3	imL 7	imS 1	imS 3	imS 7	imU 1	imU 3	imU 7	om 1	om 3	om 7	omL 1	omL 3	omL 7	pp 1	pp 3	pp 7
cp	133	139	140	0	0	0	0	0	0	0	0	0	0	0	0	0	0	0	0	0	0	3	1	0
im	4	3	3	56	60	50	0	0	0	0	0	0	15	12	17	0	0	0	0	0	0	6	1	0
imL	0	0	0	1	1	1	0	0	0	0	0	0	1	1	1	0	0	0	0	0	0	0	0	0
imS	0	0	0	0	0	0	0	0	0	0	0	0	1	1	1	0	0	0	0	0	0	1	1	1
imU	1	1	1	15	16	12	0	0	0	0	0	0	17	22	19	16	17	17	0	0	0	0	3	0
om	0	0	0	0	0	0	0	0	0	0	0	0	0	0	0	17	17	17	1	1	1	2	0	2
omL	0	0	0	0	0	0	0	0	0	0	0	0	0	0	0	1	2	2	5	5	5	0	0	0
pp	5	4	4	1	1	1	0	0	0	0	0	0	0	0	0	0	0	0	5	5	5	44	45	47
P_d	93.66	93.92	93.92	72.73	76.92	78.95	0.00	0.00	0.00	0.00	0.00	0.00	52.78	56.67	64.71	85.00	85.00	85.00	71.43	71.43	71.43	88.89	80.00	84.62
P_a	93.01	97.20	97.90	72.73	76.92	78.95	0.00	0.00	0.00	0.00	0.00	0.00	48.57	62.86	54.29	100.00	85.00	85.00	83.33	100.00	100.00	84.62	86.54	90.38

Table 9. Learnt weights for EColi dataset

k	f1	f2	f3	f4	f5	f6	f7
1	0.5	1	1	1	0.75	1.5	1
3	1.5	0	1	1	1	1	1
7	0.75	0.5	1	1	1	1	1

Table 10. Class distribution and percentage reduction rate of EColi dataset after Prototype Selection

	cp	im	imL	imS	imU	om	omL	pp	Reduction rate in %
orig	143	77	2	2	35	20	5	52	0.00
k=1	140	73	2	2	34	20	5	49	3.27
k=3	142	72	2	2	31	20	5	52	2.97

and insufficient when there is an unequal distribution of samples over classes especially when one or more classes are significantly under-represented. In addition when the classifier uses the overall accuracy as the feedback measurement for feature subset selection, feature weighting and prototype selection is flawed as it encourages the classifier to ignore classes with a small number of members. Examining the contingency table and calculating the class specific quality measurements allows a more complete picture of classifier performance to be formed.

Table 11. Overall accuracy for Wisconsin dataset using leave-one-out

k	Naïve Bayes	Decision Tree	Weka Nearest Neighbour	ProtoClass	Feature Subset (FS)	Feature Weighting (FW)	Prototype Selection (PS)
1	96.14	95.28	95.56	94.42	95.14	94.71	na
3	na	Na	96.42	95.99	96.42	95.99	na
7	na	Na	96.85	96.85	96.85	97.14	na

Table 12. Combined contingency table for k=1,3,7 for the Wisconsin dataset using ProtoClass

	benign			malignant		
k	1	3	7	1	3	7
benign	444	445	447	14	13	11
malignant	25	15	11	216	226	230
class specific quality	94.67	96.74	97.6	93.91	94.56	95.44
classification quality	96.94	97.16	97.6	89.63	93.78	95.44

6 Discussion

We have studied the performance of some well-known classifiers such as Naïve Bayesian, decision induction and k-NN classifiers towards our case-based classifier. We liked to study it on datasets where some classes are heavily under-represented. This is a characteristic of many medical applications.

The choice of the value of k has a significant impact upon the classifier. If a k-value is selected that is larger than the number of cases in some classes in the data set then samples from those classes will not be correctly classified. This results in a classifier that is heavily generalized to over-represented classes and does not recognize the under-represented classes. For example, in the EColi dataset (described in section 4) there are two classes with only two cases. When the k-value is greater than 3, these cases will never be correctly classified since the over-represented classes will occupy the greater number of nearest cases. This observation is also true for Decision Trees and Naïve Bayesian classifiers. To judge the true performance of a classifier we need to have more detailed observations about the output of the classifier. This is given by the contingency table in Section 3 from which we derive more specific accuracy measures. We choose the class-specific classification quality described in Section 3.

The prototype selection algorithm used here has problems with the evaluation approach. Relying on the overall accuracy of the design dataset to assess whether two cases should be merged to form a new prototype tends to encourage over-generalization where under-represented classes are neglected in favor of changes to well-populated classes that have a greater impact on the accuracy of the classifier. Generalization based on the accuracy seems to be flawed and reduces the effectiveness of case-based classifiers in handling datasets with under-represented classes. We are currently investigating alternative methods to improve generalization in case-based classifiers that would also respect the concept of under-represented classes in spite of the well-represented classes.

What is important from the methodology point of view? FS is the least computationally expensive method because it is implemented using the best first search strategy. FW it is more expensive then FS but less expensive than PS. FS and FW go along into the same group of methods. That means FS changes the weights of a feature from "1" (feature present) to "0" (feature turned off). It can be seen as a feature weighting approach. When FS does not bring any improvement FW is less likely to provide worthwhile benefits. From the methodology point of view this observation indicates that it might be beneficial to not conduct feature weighting if feature subset selection shows no improvement. This rule-of-thumb would greatly reduce the required computational time.

PS is the most computationally expensive method. In case of the data sets from the machine learning repository this method did not have so much impact since the data sets have been heavily pre-cleaned over the years. For a real world data set, where redundant samples, duplicates and variations among the samples are common, this method has a more significant impact [6].

7 Future Work and Conclusions

The work described in this paper is a further development of our case-based classification work [6]. We have introduced new evaluation measures into the design of such a classifier and have more deeply studied the behavior of the options of the classifier according to the different accuracy measures.

The study in [6] relied on an expert selected image dataset that was considered by the expert as prototypical images for this application. It is a real-world data set. The study had in its central focus the conceptual proof of such an approach for image classification as well as to evaluate the usefulness of the expert selected prototypes. The study here was on more specific evaluation measures for such a classifier and focused on a methodology for handling the different options of such a classifier.

Rather than relying on the overall accuracy to properly assess the performance of the classifier, we create the contingency table and calculate more specific accuracy measures from it. Even for datasets with a small number of samples in a class, the k-NN classifier is not the best choice since this classifier also tends to prefer well-represented classes. Further work will evaluate the impact of feature weighting and changing the similarity measure. Generalization methods for datasets with well-represented classes despite the presence of under-represented classes will be further studied. This will result in a more detailed methodology for applying our case-based classifier.

References

[1] Asuncion, A., Newman, D.J.: UCI Machine Learning Repository. University of California, School of Information and Computer Science, Irvine, CA (2007), http://www.ics.uci.edu/~mlearn/MLRepository.html

[2] Chang, C.-L.: Finding Prototypes for Nearest Neighbor Classifiers. IEEE Trans. on Computers C-23(11), 1179–1184 (1974)

[3] Perner, P.: Data Mining on Multimedia Data. LNCS, vol. 2558. Springer, Heidelberg (2002)

[4] Wettschereck, D., Aha, D.W.: Weighting Features. In: Aamodt, A., Veloso, M.M. (eds.) ICCBR 1995. LNCS, vol. 1010, pp. 347–358. Springer, Heidelberg (1995)

[5] Aha, D.W., Kibler, D., Albert, M.K.: Instance-based Learning Algorithm. Machine Learning 6(1), 37–66 (1991)

[6] Perner, P.: Prototype-Based Classification. Applied Intelligence 28, 238–246 (2008)

[7] Perner, P., Zscherpel, U., Jacobsen, C.: A Comparision between Neural Networks and Decision Trees based on Data from Industrial Radiographic Testing. Pattern Recognition Letters 22, 47–54 (2001)

[8] Smyth, B., McKenna, E.: Modelling the Competence of Case-Bases. In: Advances in Case-Based Reasoning, 4th European Workshop, Dublin, Ireland, pp. 208–220 (1998)

[9] Witten, I.H., Frank, E.: Data Mining: Practical machine learning tools and techniques, 2nd edn. Morgan Kaufmann, San Francisco (2005)

[10] DECISION MASTER, http://www.ibai-solutions.de

[11] Horton, P.: Better Prediction of Protein Cellular Localization Sites with the it k Nearest Neighbors Classifier. In: Proceeding of the International Conference on Intelligent Systems in Molecular Biology, pp. 147–152 (1997)

[12] Ratanamahatana, C.A., Gunopulos, D.: Scaling up the Naive Bayesian Classifier: Using Decision Trees for Feature Selection. In: Proceedings of Workshop on Data Cleaning and Preprocessing (DCAP 2002), at IEEE International Conference on Data Mining (ICDM 2002), Maebashi, Japan (2002)

Case-Based Decision Support for Patients with Type 1 Diabetes on Insulin Pump Therapy

Cindy Marling[1], Jay Shubrook[2], and Frank Schwartz[2]

[1] School of Electrical Engineering and Computer Science
Russ College of Engineering and Technology
Ohio University, Athens, Ohio 45701, USA
marling@ohio.edu
[2] Appalachian Rural Health Institute, Diabetes and Endocrine Center
College of Osteopathic Medicine
Ohio University, Athens, Ohio 45701, USA
shubrook@ohio.edu, schwartf@ohio.edu

Abstract. This paper presents a case-based approach to decision support for diabetes management in patients with Type 1 diabetes on insulin pump therapy. To avoid serious disease complications, including heart attack, blindness and stroke, these patients must continuously monitor their blood glucose levels and keep them as close to normal as possible. Achieving and maintaining good blood glucose control is a difficult task for these patients and their health care providers. A prototypical case-based decision support system was built to assist with this task. A clinical research study, involving 20 patients, yielded 50 cases of actual problems in blood glucose control, with their associated therapeutic adjustments and clinical outcomes, for the prototype's case base. The prototype operates by: (1) detecting problems in blood glucose control in large quantities of patient blood glucose and life event data; (2) finding similar past problems in the case base; and (3) offering the associated therapeutic adjustments stored in the case base to the physician as decision support. Results from structured evaluation sessions and a patient feedback survey encourage continued research and work towards a practical tool for diabetes management.

1 Introduction

Not long ago, a waitress we will call Sally collapsed at the restaurant where she was working and was taken, unconscious, to the hospital emergency room. Sally, who has Type 1 diabetes, was in a coma due to severely depressed blood glucose levels, a problem known as hypoglycemia, or insulin reaction. The diabetic coma is a serious condition that can quickly lead to permanent brain damage or death. When efforts to restore Sally's blood glucose levels and revive her were successful, her physician turned his attention to preventing such occurrences in the future.

In Type 1 diabetes, the pancreas fails to produce insulin, an essential hormone required to convert food into energy. Therefore, patients with Type 1 diabetes

K.-D. Althoff et al. (Eds.): ECCBR 2008, LNAI 5239, pp. 325–339, 2008.

must depend on exogenous supplies of insulin to survive. Too little insulin results in elevated blood glucose levels, called hyperglycemia. Hyperglycemia can lead to numerous diabetic complications over time, including blindness, neuropathy and heart failure. Patients who take insulin to avoid hyperglycemia are subject to hypoglycemia, which occurs when they inadvertently take too much insulin. Hypoglycemia may cause weakness, confusion, dizziness, sweating, shaking, and, if not treated promptly, loss of consciousness or seizure. On the surface, the solution to Sally's problem may seem simple: she should take less insulin. Unfortunately, despite the best efforts to precisely balance insulin dosages with physical requirements, managing blood glucose levels is still a difficult and demanding task. It is a task faced by patients with Type 1 diabetes every day, who must keep their blood glucose levels as close to normal as possible, avoiding both hyper and hypoglycemia, to maintain their health and avoid serious disease complications [1].

In Sally's case, there was more to the story than just her physical manifestations. It turns out that Sally collapsed toward the end of her twelve-hour shift working as a waitress. Despite the facts that Sally had been wearing her insulin pump and had taken regular breaks for meals and snacks, the demands of her job created too much physical stress for her body to handle. In addition, from having had diabetes for many years, she no longer sensed the typical symptoms of hypoglycemia experienced by most people with diabetes. This condition, called hypoglycemia unawareness, made her especially vulnerable to hypoglycemia. For financial reasons, Sally needed to work as many hours as possible. Her employer urged her to work part-time, but Sally did not feel she could afford to do that. Her physician (the third author) proposed a compromise, in which she could still work a full forty hour week, but would not work more than eight hours in a single day. This solution worked for Sally, whose life has returned to normal.

Physical, social and lifestyle factors, with their myriad permutations and complex interactions, impact blood glucose levels in patients with Type 1 diabetes. To provide individualized decision support that can help each patient maintain good blood glucose control, we propose a case-based approach. The use of CBR to enhance rule-based and model-based reasoning for diabetes management was first introduced by the T-IDDM project [2]. Our work differs from this project in three important ways: (1) it uses CBR as the primary reasoning modality, rather than as an adjunct to other reasoning approaches; (2) it adds consideration of life event data, which may influence blood glucose fluctuations; and (3) it focuses on patients on insulin pump therapy, a more advanced and flexible treatment regime than that used by T-IDDM patients.

Traditionally, people with Type 1 diabetes recorded their daily blood glucose readings in paper log books. These logs were presented to the physician for review and analysis at office visits three or four times per year. Today, continuous glucose monitors can record blood glucose data every five minutes, and insulin pumps and glucose meters collect and store data daily. Patients can email this data to their physicians every day or every week. Commercially available software can acquire, transfer and plot data, but it does not, at present, provide data analysis. This leaves physicians with the complex and time-consuming task of interpreting voluminous blood glucose records and making appropriate therapeutic adjustments. Studies have shown that physicians may feel overwhelmed by data overload, which may lead to "clinical inertia," in which physicians do not even try to regularly adjust therapy for diabetes patients during their scheduled office visits [3,4].

Our goal is to ease the physician's task by automatically analyzing patient data and providing therapeutic recommendations comparable to those an endocrinologist or diabetologist would make. Initially, recommendations would be provided to physicians for review. We envision that, once proven safe and effective, decision support software could be embedded in patient medical devices, directly assisting patients with their daily diabetes management.

CBR seems especially appropiate for diabetes management for several reasons. First, the established guidelines for managing diabetes [5] are general in nature and must be customized to meet the needs of each patient. Cases can help to complement and individualize such general guidelines, as noted in [6]. Second, the factors that influence blood glucose control are both quantitative (e.g., blood glucose readings and insulin dosages) and qualitative (e.g., perceived stress and food preferences). CBR systems have long integrated the quantitative with the qualitative for applications ranging from generating expressive music [7] to menu planning [8] to recommender systems [9]. Finally, CBR has been successfully applied to other long-term medical conditions that can not be cured but must nevertheless be managed [10,11,12,13].

This paper presents a case-based approach to decision support for diabetes management in patients with Type 1 diabetes on insulin pump therapy. It describes the construction and evaluation of a research system prototype. It concludes with an overview of related research and plans for future work.

2   System Prototype Construction

2.1   Knowledge Acquisition and Representation

Existing diabetes information systems focus primarily on blood glucose levels and insulin dosages, and sometimes store limited data concerning the times of meals, carbohydrate consumption, and timing of exercise. As knowledge engineers shadowed physicians and conducted structured interviews, it became apparent that endocrinologists and diabetologists consider many more features when determining appropriate therapy for patients with Type 1 diabetes on insulin pump therapy. The most significant factors involved are shown in Figure 1.

Because these features are not routinely maintained, in either electronic or non-electronic form, it was not possible to build cases for the case base from existing patient records. Therefore, a preliminary clinical study involving 20 patients with Type 1 diabetes on insulin pump therapy was conducted to acquire cases for the system. A 44-table Oracle database with a Web-based user interface was designed and implemented to store the data provided by the patients participating in the study. Each patient submitted extensive daily logs documenting

Problem Description Features
High and Low Blood Glucose Target Levels
Actual Blood Glucose Levels throughout the Day
Insulin Sensitivity (patient specific reaction to insulin)
Carbohydrate Ratios (patient specific need for insulin with food)
Type of Insulin Used
Basal Rates of Insulin Infusion throughout the Day
Bolus Doses of Insulin with Food Consumption
Bolus Doses of Insulin Used to Correct for Hyperglycemia
Type of Bolus Wave for Each Bolus
Actions Taken to Self-Correct for Hypoglycemia
Meal Times
Amount of Carbohydrate Consumed at Each Meal
Specific Foods Consumed at Each Meal
Alcohol Consumption
Mechanical Problems with the Insulin Pump
Time of Change of Insulin Infusion Set
Location of Insulin Infusion Set on Patient's Body
Time, Type and Duration of Exercise
Work Schedule
Sleep Cycles
Menstrual Cycles
Stress (as subjectively determined by patient)
Illness (other than diabetes, such as cold or flu)

Fig. 1. Significant Features Used by Physicians to Determine Appropriate Therapeutic Adjustments for Patients with Type 1 Diabetes on Insulin Pump Therapy

their daily values for the features shown in Figure 1 over a six-week period. Once collected and reviewed by physicians, this data was used to structure cases. Each case represents one problem in blood glucose control for a specific patient, along with its associated physician-recommended solution and clinical outcome.

Patients participated in the preliminary study between February, 2006 and June, 2007. From one to four patients participated at a time. The number of patients who could supply data at once was limited by the available resources, including continuous glucose monitoring devices and physician time. Throughout the length of the study, knowledge engineers met with physicians weekly to review the patient data collected for that week. The immediate goal of each weekly meeting was for the physicians to examine the data, find problems in blood glucose control, and suggest therapeutic adjustments to help patients correct or prevent these problems. To facilitate this data review process, knowledge engineers provided the physicians with written data summary reports for each patient. They also built a data visualization tool to display all of the different types of data available for a patient over a 24-hour period.

Following each weekly meeting, physicians would contact patients to recommend therapeutic adjustments for the problems discovered in the data. In subsequent weeks, the data was monitored to evaluate the clinical outcome of each adjustment. A recommended adjustment might resolve a patient's problem, provide some degree of benefit but not completely resolve a problem, or fail to resolve a problem. Follow-up also ascertained if the patient had accepted and applied the recommended adjustment or not. Knowledge engineers then structured the problems, solutions (adjustments) and outcomes into cases for the case base. A total of 50 cases were built for the system prototype during the study.

2.2 Example Case: Problem of Nocturnal Hypoglycemia

The problem of nocturnal hypoglycemia was found in a 56-year-old female patient who had had Type 1 diabetes for 32 years. This patient had been on insulin pump therapy for eight years, and was generally well controlled, as evidenced by her HbA1c tests, which measure long-term blood glucose control. When her first week's data was displayed to her physician, as shown in Figure 2, it was evident that she had been hypoglycemic all night long without sensing it. This

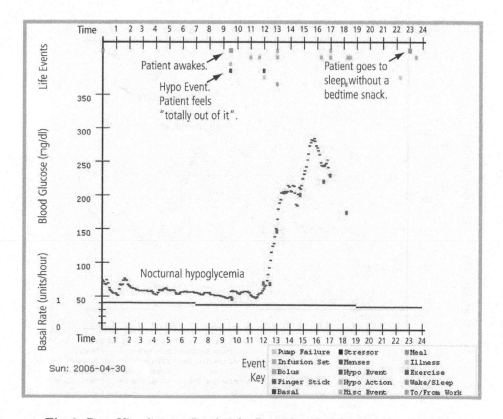

Fig. 2. Data Visualization Display for Patient with Nocturnal Hypoglycemia

is a serious problem, because untreated hypoglycemia can lead to diabetic coma and/or death.

In the data visualization display of Figure 2, blood glucose levels are indicated on the vertical axis, while time, beginning at midnight, is indicated by the horizontal axis. A curve, displayed in dark blue, shows the data captured by the continuous glucose monitoring device, while individual red dots show blood glucose values obtained through routine finger sticks. Life events recorded by the patient are denoted by markers at the top of the display. These are arranged by time of occurance, so that daily activities that impact blood glucose levels can be viewed together with the blood glucose values themselves. Clicking on a life event marker displays additional information as recorded by the patient.

In Figure 2, the patient's problem with nocturnal hypoglycemia is evidenced by the continuous glucose monitoring data curve between midnight and 9:30 AM. When she awakes at 9:30 AM, she takes a finger stick measurement, and reports that her blood glucose level is 46 mg/dl, which is dangerously low. She also reports that she feels "totally out of it" and is unable to take action to correct her hypoglycemia. The physician examined the rest of the data displayed to determine what might be causing this problem and what could be done to

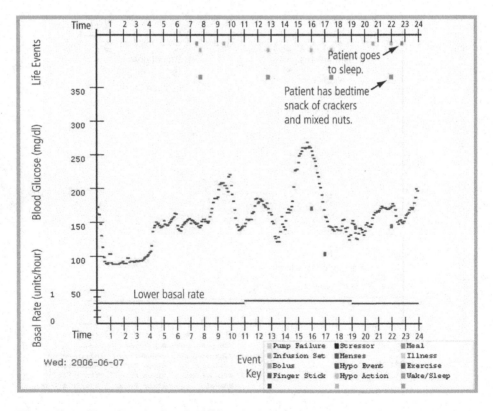

Fig. 3. Data Visualization Display of Successful Resolution of Nocturnal Hypoglycemia

eliminate it. By checking the meal markers at the top of the display, he could see that the patient was not eating snacks before bed. He recommended that she always eat a bedtime snack, and also that she lower her rate of basal insulin infusion by 0.1 units per hour between midnight and 7:00 AM. The basal rate is shown by the line at the very bottom of the display. The physician's recommended solution included adjustments to both diet and insulin intake. Having more food in a patient's system overnight helps to prevent blood glucose levels from falling. Because insulin depresses blood glucose levels even further, the basal rate of insulin infusion was decreased overnight.

In Figure 3, data for the same patient is displayed toward the end of her participation in the study. It is clear that she has taken the physician's advice, as her basal rate now appears lower and a meal marker indicates that she has eaten a bedtime snack. It is also clear from the blood glucose data displayed that the patient is no longer hypoglycemic overnight. This solution was therefore deemed to have a successful outcome.

This problem, solution and outcome comprise one of the 50 cases in the case base. Should another patient experience nocturnal hypoglycemia, this case may be recalled to suggest applicable therapeutic adjustments. A more detailed description of the abstract case representation is presented in [14]. Three cases are presented from a physician's perspective in [15]. Internally, a case is represented as an object of a hierarchical Java class containing over 140 data fields.

2.3   Reasoning with Cases

A prototypical case-based decision support system was built with the case base described above as its central knowledge repository. The system operates as shown in Figure 4. The patient enters daily blood gluose and life event data into the database via any available Web browser. Situation assessment software then searches the database to find problems in blood glucose control. Twelve different types of problems, defined during the preliminary study, can be detected. These problem types are listed in Figure 5. Next, the specific problems detected for the patient are displayed to the physician, who must select a problem of interest. The selected problem, with its associated values for all relevant features, becomes the input to the case retrieval module.

Cases are retrieved using a traditional two-step process in which: (a) a subset of potentially similar cases is identified; and (b) the most usefully similar cases are selected from that subset. The initial partition of the case base is based solely on problem type, as shown in Figure 5. For example, if a patient experiences hyperglycemia upon awakening, then other problems of this type or closely related types may be relevant. However, cases involving problems with hypoglycemia would not be useful or relevant, even if they share surface features like time of day or pattern of occurance.

To select the most usefully similar cases from the initial subset of potentially relevant cases, a standard nearest neighbor metric is used. Domain specific similarity functions compute the degree of correspondence between the input case and each potentially relevant case on 18 distinct problem features. An aggregate

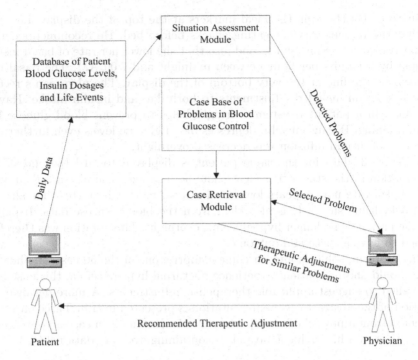

Fig. 4. Overview of Prototypical Decision Support System Operation

match score is then computed for each case by weighting the relative contribution of each feature toward the match. Next, the highest aggregate score is compared to a numeric threshold to determine if the best matching case is similar enough to the input case to contain a therapeutic adjustment of potential benefit. If so, the best matching case is displayed to the physician. Because similar problems often have similar solutions, the best matching case may aid the physician in determining an appropriate therapeutic adjustment for the current patient. It is up to the physician to determine whether or not, and in what form, to relay the retrieved solution to the patient.

The best matching case for the problem presented in Section 2.2 was recorded for an 18-year-old male patient. This patient reported waking up in a sweat at 2:00 AM with a blood glucose level of 49 mg/dl. In the first step of the retrieval process, this case is selected as potentially relevant, because both problems involve hypoglycemia. In the second step, the two cases are found to be similar in many respects, including time of day and relationships to meals, boluses, exercise and stress. They differ in the methods by which the problems were detected and also in the frequency with which the problems occurred. The physician's advice to the patient in the best matching case was, "The patient should have at least a small bedtime snack, perhaps a glass of milk." This solution overlaps with, although it is not identical to, the solution recommended for the patient in the input case.

---

1. Hyperglycemia upon wakening
2. Hypoglycemia upon wakening
3. Over-correction for hyperglycemia
4. Over-correction for hypoglycemia
5. Over-boluses for meals
6. Pre-waking hypoglycemia
7. Post-exercise hypoglycemia
8. Pre-meal hyperglycemia
9. Pre-meal hypoglycemia
10. Post-meal hyperglycemia
11. Post-meal hypoglycemia
12. Possible pump or infusion set malfunction

Fig. 5. Blood Glucose Control Problem Types Detected During Situation Assessment

3   Evaluation and Feedback

A patient exit survey and two structured feedback sessions for diabetes practitioners were administered to evaluate the feasibility of case-based decision support for patients with Type 1 diabetes on insulin pump therapy. The exit survey questioned patients about time requirements, ease of use, and benefits of participating in the study. Patients did not evaluate actual outputs from the prototype, as it was built after patients concluded their participation in the study. Diabetes practitioners evaluated the outputs from the situation assessment and case retrieval modules of the prototype.

Twelve patients completed the exit survey. Patients reported that the time required for data entry ranged from 15 minutes or less (5 patients) to between 30 and 60 minutes per day (7 patients). While 10 of 12 patients found the Web-based data entry system easy to use, 8 of 12 indicated a preference for having data entry capabilities available on their own insulin pumps or glucose meters. Ten of 12 patients indicated that their increased contact with health care professionals throughout the study was beneficial for their diabetes management. All patients confirmed that it would be beneficial to receive immediate feedback and therapeutic advice from an automated system. When asked, "How likely are you to adopt a therapy adjustment recommended by your doctor?" 10 patients marked *very likely* and 2 marked *fairly likely*. The exact same response was given to the question, "If a computerized therapy adjustment wizard were to recommend a therapy adjustment, how likely would you be to adopt it?" This patient acceptance of the concept of automated decision support suggests that further research could lead to a practical tool for patients, especially if the data entry burden were reduced.

To evaluate the situation assessment capabilities of the prototype, the situation assessment module was run retroactively on the completed patient database. A total of 352 problems in blood glucose control were detected for the patients who completed the study. Ten problem detections were randomly selected for re-

view by a panel of three physicians and one advance practice nurse specializing
in diabetes. Each problem detected was shown to the evaluators via the graphic
visualization display. Evaluators were then asked to indicate their agreement
with each of the following statements:

1. This is a correct identification of a problem
2. It would be useful to call this problem to the attention of the patient
3. It would be useful to call this problem to the attention of the physician

Evaluators agreed with the first statement 77.5% of the time, reported mixed
feelings 15% of the time, and disagreed 7.5% of the time. Evaluators agreed with
the second statement 87.5% of the time, had mixed feelings 10% of the time, and
disagreed 2.5% of the time. Evaluators agreed with the third 90% of the time,
reported mixed feelings 7.5% of the time, and disagreed 2.5% of the time.

Leave one out testing was performed to evaluate the case retrieval module of
the prototype. During testing, thresholding was turned off, so that the closest
match to an input case was always returned, whether or not there was a usefully
similar case in the base base. Ten of the 50 cases in the case base were randomly
selected as test cases for review by a panel of three physicians specializing in
diabetes. For each test case, physicians were given the problem descriptions and
recommended solutions of the case and its nearest neighbor. Then they were
asked to answer the following multiple choice questions:

1. The problem in the original case and the problem in the matching case are:
   (a) Very Similar
   (b) Somewhat Similar
   (c) Somewhat Dissimilar
   (d) Very Dissimilar
2. Applying the matching case's solution to the original problem would be:
   (a) Very Beneficial
   (b) Somewhat Beneficial
   (c) Neither Beneficial nor Detrimental
   (d) Somewhat Detrimental
   (e) Very Detrimental

Evaluators judged matching cases to be similar 80% of the time and dissimilar
20% of the time. They judged retrieved solutions to be beneficial 70% of the time,
neither beneficial nor detrimental 23% of the time, and detrimental 7% of the
time. Because not every case in the case base had a usefully similar nearest
neighbor, this performance is expected to improve as the case base grows in size.

4   Future Work

A second clinical research study has been designed and approved by Ohio University's Institutional Review Board (IRB). Twenty-eight patients with Type 1
diabetes on insulin pump therapy will participate for three months each. The

first goal of this study is to significantly grow the case base as a central knowledge repository, thereby increasing system competence.

The second goal is to develop patient specific case bases to remember recurrent problems with glucose control and the specific therapeutic solutions that are effective or ineffective for each patient. Each individualized case base will extend the general case base with cases documenting the individual patient's own problems, therapy adjustments and responses. This will enable the system to learn how an individual patient responds to changes in therapy so that the most effective therapy for a particular problem experienced by a specific patient can be recalled. The case retrieval metric will be extended to look first for similar problems experienced by the same patient and to search the central case base only when this does not yield an applicable solution.

The final goal of this clinical research study is to develop new similarity metrics to compare patients with Type 1 diabetes to each other. Then solutions known to work for similar problems in similar patients could be recommended. This is important, because even when problems are similar, lifestyle variations may preclude the successful transfer of therapeutic adjustments. For example, a retiree living alone might be willing to perform therapeutic actions that a teenager would not willingly perform in front of peers at school.

Longer term, we envision extending our work to patients with different types of diabetes, patients on different types of insulin or oral therapy, and patients with special needs, like elite athletes, pregnant women, and teenagers. We hope that eventually, following additional research, development, and safety testing, the software might be directly accessed by patients for continuous blood glucose monitoring and daily decision making support. We maintain contact with the manufacturers of diabetic equipment and supplies to ensure the future viability of our system for patients in the real world.

5   Related Research

The Telematic Management of Insulin-Dependent Diabetes Mellitus (T-IDDM) project was first to explore CBR for diabetes management [2,16,17]. The goals of T-IDDM were to: (a) support physicians in providing appropriate treatment for maintaining blood glucose control; (b) provide remote patients with tele-monitoring and tele-consultation services; (c) provide cost-effective monitoring of large numbers of patients; (d) support patient education; and (e) allow insulin therapy customization [2]. T-IDDM integrated CBR with rule-based reasoning and a probabilistic model of the effects of insulin on blood glucose over time. The role of CBR in T-IDDM was to specialize the behavior of rules, by tuning rule parameters, when rules could not provide optimal advice for patients. Cases were found to be especially helpful in providing advice for poorly controlled patients.

Our work shares T-IDDM's goal of supporting physicians in providing appropriate treatment for maintaining blood glucose control, but we have taken a different approach. This may be due, in part, to the differences between treating patients on conventional intensive insulin therapy and on insulin pump therapy.

The therapy regimen for a patient in the T-IDDM project consisted of from three to four insulin injections per day. Each patient had an insulin protocol in which he or she injected the same amount of insulin at the same time of day for each daily injection. The patient then attempted to regulate his or her daily food intake and activities in accordance with this insulin protocol, rather than adjusting the insulin intake to account for variations in daily routine. The data input to the probabilistic model for a patient was the insulin protocol plus three to four blood glucose measurements per day. A therapy adjustment consisted of changing the amount of insulin regularly taken for a daily injection. The model used by T-IDDM was a steady state model that did not account for daily variations in diet or lifestyle, but treated them as stochastic occurrences, or noise. This approach makes sense for conventional intensive insulin therapy, where available data and treatment options are limited. We expect CBR to provide even greater benefits to patients on insulin pump therapy, who can adjust a wider range of insulin and lifestyle parameters to manage their diabetes.

Telemedicine, which aims to enable remote access heath care, has been leveraged in T-IDDM and other research projects that aim to help patients manage their diabetes. Notable examples include VIE-DIAB [18], DIABTel [19], and the Intelligent Control Assistant for Diabetes (INCA) [20]. Telemedicine systems use mobile phones, email, and online applications to enhance data transfer and communication between patients and physicians. When human physicians are the primary sources of knowledge, AI decision support capabilities may be limited or non-existent. The problem with telemedicine approaches that incorporate limited, or no, intelligent decision support is that they can actually *increase* the workload on physicians. This effect was reported in [18], and also documented in a controlled trial of the fiscal and administrative aspects of telemedicine for patients with diabetes [21]. Certainly, the increased availability of patient data without automated data analysis capabilities created the physician overload that motivated our own work.

The dream of an artificial pancreas, which could someday supplant the diabetic patient's own deficient pancreatic function, has led to much work in developing formal models that depend on the relationship between blood glucose and insulin. These models may or may not include the effects of diet, but do not normally include other lifestyle factors, as these could not be automatically detected by an implanted device. The best known model, because of its ready availability for research and educational purposes via the Internet, is AIDA [22]. A number of researchers have tried integrating this model with other decision support techniques, including rule-based reasoning and neural networks [23]. Clearly, efforts to develop an accurate formal model complement efforts to develop intelligent decision support. However, a restricted focus on blood glucose/insulin models that can be embedded in an artificial pancreas presents at least two difficulties. First, the underlying physiological pharmacokinetic relationship is highly complex. Extensive modeling research dates back to the 1960s without the advent of a definitive model [24]. Second, should technical obstacles be surmounted, there will still be financial barriers to providing major surgery for the nearly five million patients who have Type 1 diabetes worldwide. Case-based decision support may provide a lower cost practical tool in the near-term, as well as account for observed individual variations not currently accounted for by formal models.

Finally, this research builds upon the work of CBR researchers in other medical domains. Workshops on CBR in the Health Sciences have been held for the past five years at the International and European Conferences on Case-Based Reasoning. Overviews of medical CBR have been published in [6,25,26,27]. Among the most closely related projects are MNAOMIA, in the domain of psychiatric eating disorders [10], CARE-PARTNER, for stem cell transplantation follow-up care [11], RHENE, in the domain of end-stage renal disease [12], and the Auguste Project, for the management of Alzheimer's Disease [13]. These research projects, like ours, aim to assist in managing long-term, or chronic, medical conditions. Special challenges in such domains include: (a) handling data that varies over time; (b) accounting for individual variation among patients; and (c) tailoring general guidelines to the needs of individual patients.

6   Summary and Conclusion

This paper has presented a case-based approach to decision support for diabetes management in patients with Type 1 diabetes on insulin pump therapy. A preliminary clinical research study, involving 20 patients with Type 1 diabetes on insulin pump therapy, was conducted. Through this study, 50 cases of problems in blood glucose control, with their associated therapeutic adjustments and clinical outcomes, were compiled in a case base. This case base became the central knowledge repository for a prototypical case-based decision support system. The prototype contains a Situation Assessment module that detects common problems in blood glucose control in large volumes of blood glucose and life event data. It contains a Case Retrieval module that finds the cases containing the most similar past problems in the case base. It displays the therapeutic adjustments from the best matching cases to the physician as decision support in therapy planning. The prototype was evaluated by means of a patient exit survey and two structured feedback sessions for diabetes practitioners. Preliminary results encourage continued research and work toward a practical tool for patients and their health care providers. The case-based approach presented herein has applicability to the management of all forms of diabetes and potential applicability to the management of other chronic medical conditions.

Acknowledgments

The authors gratefully acknowledge support from Medtronic MiniMed, Ohio University's Russ College Biomedical Engineering Fund, and the Ohio University Osteopathic College of Medicine Research and Scholarly Affairs Committee. We would also like to thank Eric Flowers, Thomas Jones, Tony Maimone, Wes Miller and Don Walker for their software development and knowledge engineering contributions.

References

1. The effect of intensive treatment of diabetes on the development and progression of long-term complications in insulin-dependent diabetes mellitus. New England Journal of Medicine 329, 977–986 (1993)
2. Bellazzi, R., Larizza, C., Montani, S., Riva, A., Stefanelli, M., d'Annunzio, G., Lorini, R., Gómez, E.J., Hernando, E., Brugués, E., Cermeno, J., Corcoy, R., de Leiva, A., Cobelli, C., Nucci, G., Prato, S.D., Maran, A., Kilkki, E., Tuominen, J.: A telemedicine support for diabetes management: The T-IDDM project. Computer Methods and Programs in Biomedicine 69, 147–161 (2002)
3. Grant, R.W., Buse, J.B., Meigs, J.B.: Quality of diabetes care in U.S. academic medical centers: Low rates of medical regimen change. Diabetes Care 28, 337–442 (2005)
4. Shah, B.R., Hux, J.E., Laupacis, A., Zinman, B., van Walraven, C.: Clinical inertia in response to inadequate glycemic control: Do specialists differ from primary care physicians? Diabetes Care 28, 600–606 (2005)
5. American Diabetes Association: American Diabetes Association Complete Guide to Diabetes. 4 edn. Bantam, New York (2006)
6. Bichindaritz, I., Marling, C.: Case-based reasoning in the health sciences: What's next? Artificial Intelligence in Medicine 36, 127–135 (2006)
7. López de Màntaras, R., Arcos, J.L.: AI and music from composition to expressive performance. AI Magazine 23, 43–58 (2002)
8. Marling, C.R., Petot, G.J., Sterling, L.S.: Integrating case-based and rule-based reasoning to meet multiple design constraints. Computational Intelligence 15(3), 308–332 (1999)
9. Bridge, D., Göker, M., McGinty, L., Smyth, B.: Case-based recommender systems. The Knowledge Engineering Review 20, 315–320 (2005)
10. Bichindaritz, I.: MNAOMIA: Improving case-based reasoning for an application in psychiatry. In: Artificial Intelligence in Medicine: Applications of Current Technologies, Stanford, CA. Working Notes of the AAAI 1996 Spring Symposium (1996)
11. Bichindaritz, I., Kansu, E., Sullivan, K.M.: Case-based reasoning in CAREPARTNER: Gathering evidence for evidence-based medical practice. In: Smyth, B., Cunningham, P. (eds.) EWCBR 1998. LNCS (LNAI), vol. 1488, pp. 334–345. Springer, Heidelberg (1998)
12. Montani, S., Portinale, L., Leonardi, G., Bellazzi, R.: Applying case-based retrieval to hemodialysis treatment. In: McGinty, L. (ed.) Workshop Proceedings of the Fifth International Conference on Case-Based Reasoning, Trondheim, Norway (2003)
13. Marling, C., Whitehouse, P.: Case-based reasoning in the care of Alzheimer's disease patients. In: Aha, D.W., Watson, I. (eds.) ICCBR 2001. LNCS (LNAI), vol. 2080, pp. 702–715. Springer, Heidelberg (2001)
14. Marling, C., Shubrook, J., Schwartz, F.: Towards case-based reasoning for diabetes management. In: Wilson, D.C., Khemani, D. (eds.) ICCBR 2007. LNCS (LNAI), vol. 4626, pp. 305–314. Springer, Heidelberg (2007)
15. Schwartz, F.L., Shubrook, J.H., Marling, C.R.: Use of case-based reasoning to enhance intensive management of patients on insulin pump therapy. Journal of Diabetes Science and Technology (in press, 2008)
16. Montani, S., Bellazzi, R.: Supporting decisions in medical applications: The knowledge management perspective. International Journal of Medical Informatics 68, 79–90 (2002)

17. Montani, S., Magni, P., Bellazzi, R., Larizza, C., Roudsari, A.V., Carson, E.R.: Integrating model-based decision support in a multi-modal reasoning system for managing type 1 diabetic patients. Artificial Intelligence in Medicine 29, 131–151 (2003)
18. Popow, C., Horn, W., Rami, B., Schober, E.: VIE-DIAB: A support program for telemedical glycaemic control. In: Dojat, M., Keravnou, E.T., Barahona, P. (eds.) AIME 2003. LNCS (LNAI), vol. 2780, pp. 350–354. Springer, Heidelberg (2003)
19. Gómez, E.J., Hernando, M.E., García, A., del Pozo, F., Cermeno, J., Corcoy, R., Brugués, E., de Leiva, A.: Telemedicine as a tool for intensive management of diabetes: the DIABTel experience. Computer Methods and Programs in Biomedicine 69, 163–177 (2002)
20. Hernando, M.E., Gómez, E.J., Gili, A., Gómez, M., García, G., del Pozo, F.: New trends in diabetes management: Mobile telemedicine closed-loop system. In: Duplaga, M., Zielinski, K., Ingram, D. (eds.) Transformation of Healthcare with Information Technologies. IOS Press, Amsterdam (2004)
21. Biermann, E., Dietrich, W., Rihl, J., Standl, E.: Are there time and cost savings by using telemanagement for patients on intensified insulin therapy? A randomised, controlled trial. Computer Methods and Programs in Biomedicine 69, 137–146 (2002)
22. Lehmann, E.D.: AIDA (2008) (accessed February, 2008), http://www.2aida.net/welcome/
23. Lehmann, E.D.: Research use of the AIDA www.2aida.org diabetes software simulation program: A review. Part 1. Decision support testing and neural network training. Diabetes Technology & Therapeutics 5, 425–438 (2003)
24. Boutayeb, A., Chetouani, A.: A critical review of mathematical models and data used in diabetology. Biomedical Engineering Online 5 (2006)
25. Schmidt, R., Montani, S., Bellazzi, R., Portinale, L., Gierl, L.: Case-based reasoning for medical knowledge-based systems. International Journal of Medical Informatics 64, 355–367 (2001)
26. Nilsson, M., Sollenborn, M.: Advancements and trends in medical case-based reasoning: An overview of systems and system development. In: Proceedings of the Seventeenth International Florida Artificial Intelligence Research Society Conference – Special Track on Case-Based Reasoning, pp. 178–183. AAAI Press, Menlo Park (2004)
27. Holt, A., Bichindaritz, I., Schmidt, R., Perner, P.: Medical applications in case-based reasoning. The Knowledge Engineering Review 20, 289–292 (2005)

Conversational Case-Based Reasoning
in Self-healing and Recovery

David McSherry[1], Sa'adah Hassan[2], and David Bustard[1]

[1] School of Computing and Information Engineering, University of Ulster
Coleraine BT52 1SA, Northern Ireland
{dmg.mcsherry,dw.bustard}@ulster.ac.uk
[2] Faculty of Computer Science and Information Technology, University Putra Malaysia
43400 UPM Serdang, Selangor, Malaysia
saadah@fsktm.upm.edu.my

Abstract. Self-healing and recovery informed by environment knowledge (SHRIEK) is an autonomic computing approach to improving the robustness of computing systems. Case-based reasoning (CBR) is used to guide fault diagnosis and enable learning from experience, and rule-based reasoning to enable fault remediation and recovery informed by environment knowledge. Focusing on the role of conversational CBR (CCBR) in the management of faults that rely on user interaction for their detection and diagnosis, we present a hypothesis-driven approach to question selection in CCBR that aims to increase the transparency of CCBR dialogues by enabling the system to explain the relevance of any question the user is asked. We also present empirical results which suggest that there is no loss of problem-solving efficiency in the approach. Finally, we investigate the effects of the environment awareness provided by autonomous information gathering in SHRIEK on the efficiency of CCBR dialogues.

Keywords: Autonomic computing, self-healing, environment awareness, fault management, case-based reasoning, explanation, transparency.

1 Introduction

Inspired by the autonomic computing concept of *self-healing* [1], SHRIEK is an approach to increasing the robustness of computing systems through self-healing and recovery informed by environment knowledge [2-3]. Soft Systems Methodology [4] is used in SHRIEK to build an explicit model of the system's environment (e.g., available resources) to inform self-healing and recovery from service failures. Case-based reasoning (CBR) is used to guide fault diagnosis and enable learning from experience, and rule-based reasoning to enable decision making informed by environment knowledge in fault remediation and recovery. Autonomous information gathering (AIG) also plays an important role in maintaining the environment awareness needed for effective problem solving in a dynamic environment.

While self-healing in autonomic computing has traditionally focused on fault diagnosis and remediation [1, 5-7], fault management in SHRIEK is based on the view that guiding user recovery from service failures is an equally important aspect of

K.-D. Althoff et al. (Eds.): ECCBR 2008, LNAI 5239, pp. 340–354, 2008.

robustness in a computing service. Environment knowledge needed to guide recovery from service failures includes staff responsibilities and availability as well as available resources and their locations. *Shriek*-Printer, for example, is an intelligent system for fault management in a local printer network based on the SHRIEK approach [2]. Recovery strategies suggested to the user by *Shriek*-Printer following the diagnosis of a printer fault might include:

- Waiting for assistance from a technician who has been notified about the problem and is known to be available
- Tackling the problem herself by taking remedial action suggested by the system (e.g., clearing a paper jam detected by AIG)
- Redirecting her print job to another available printer identified by the system

Another feature that distinguishes SHRIEK from existing approaches to self-healing in autonomic computing is the use of conversational CBR (CCBR) [8-12] in the management of faults that cannot be detected automatically by the system. For example, *Shriek*-Printer can detect simple problems such as an empty paper tray by AIG, but has no way of knowing if the quality of a printed document is acceptable to the user. To enable self-healing and recovery in the case of faults that rely on feedback from users for their detection and diagnosis, *Shriek*-Printer includes a CCBR system called *Shriek*-CBR which is available at workstation level to assist users with printing problems. As we show in Section 5, helping to minimize the number of questions the user is asked before a diagnosis is reached is an important benefit of the environment awareness provided by AIG.

One of the lessons learned from experience with our initial approach to CCBR in *Shriek*-CBR [2] is the need for greater transparency in CCBR dialogues. In contrast to CCBR approaches in which the user selects from a ranked list of questions [8], the user is asked one question at a time in *Shriek*-CBR, and can answer *unknown* to any question. While asking the user a few well-chosen questions often enables a diagnosis to be reached with a minimum of effort, one problem is that the relevance of questions selected by a CCBR system can be difficult to explain. Other important issues include how to recognize when a CCBR dialogue can be safely terminated without loss of solution quality, or when no solution is possible based on the available information. Although these issues have previously been discussed in relation to intelligent systems for interactive problem solving [10, 11, 13-16], there has been limited investigation of their implications for CCBR systems like *Shriek*-CBR in which the case structure is heterogeneous [8-9].

In this paper, we present a hypothesis-driven approach to question selection that aims to increase the transparency of CCBR dialogues by enabling the system to explain the relevance of any question it asks the user in terms of its current hypothesis. In Sections 2-4, we present the theory on which our approach to CCBR is based and demonstrate the approach in a new version of *Shriek*-CBR. We also present criteria for recognizing when a CCBR dialogue can be terminated without loss of solution quality and when no solution is possible given the available information. In Section 5, we investigate the trade-offs between efficiency and transparency in the approach and empirically demonstrate the effectiveness of AIG in helping to reduce the length of CCBR dialogues in *Shriek*-CBR. Our conclusions are presented in Section 6.

2 Conversational CBR in SHRIEK

In CCBR, a query describing a problem to be solved is incrementally elicited (or an initial query is extended) in an interactive dialogue, usually with the aim of minimizing the number of questions the user is asked before a solution is reached [8-9]. Factors that may influence a CCBR system's performance and acceptability to users include: (1) the strategy it uses to select the most useful questions, (2) its ability to explain the relevance of questions it asks the user and the conclusions it reaches, (3) its ability to solve problems for which the user is unable to provide a complete description, and (4) the criteria it uses to decide when to terminate a CCBR dialogue.

Following a brief overview of how these issues are addressed in our approach to CCBR, we describe how cases and queries are represented in *Shriek*-CBR, the similarity measure used in the system, and the role of AIG in fault diagnosis. The section finishes with a discussion of other basic concepts in our approach, such as *open*, *viable*, and *competitive* cases in a CCBR dialogue.

2.1 Question Selection and Explanation

Question selection (or ranking) in CCBR is often based on criteria (e.g., information gain, question frequency) in which the absence of a specific hypothesis makes it difficult to explain the relevance of questions the user is asked. In contrast, question selection in *Shriek*-CBR is *hypothesis driven* in that questions are selected with the goal of confirming a target case. As described in Section 4, a target case is selected by the system at the start of a CCBR dialogue and may later be revised in light of new information obtained as the description of the problem is extended. An important benefit is that the system can explain the relevance of any question it asks the user in terms of its current hypothesis. Also with the aim of increasing the transparency of the reasoning process, the user is shown the target case that the system is trying to confirm in each cycle of a CCBR dialogue, and is asked only questions in the target case. At the end of a CCBR dialogue, *Shriek*-CBR explains the solution it has reached, if any, by showing the user the most similar case and its matching and mismatching features.

2.2 Dialogue Termination and Incomplete Information

Recent research has highlighted the importance of CCBR systems being able to recognize when a problem-solving dialogue can be safely terminated without affecting solution quality [15]. The ability to solve problems for which the user is unable to provide a complete description is another important aspect of an intelligent system's performance. However, the possible benefit of allowing a problem-solving dialogue to continue when the user answers *unknown* to one or more questions must be balanced against the risk that no solution may be possible no matter what other questions the user might be asked [16].

In most CCBR approaches, a case is required to reach a minimum similarity threshold for its solution to be suggested by the system as a solution to the user's problem. However, simply presenting the solution of any case that reaches the similarity threshold as a solution to the user's problem ignores the risk that another case might exceed the similarity of the solution case if the dialogue is allowed to continue

[15]. This is a risk that cannot be lightly dismissed for CCBR similarity measures that use negative scoring for mismatching features as this means that even a single unanswered question can have a major impact on a case's similarity.

In Section 3, we present our approach to ensuring that a case's solution is suggested as a solution to the user's problem only when it is certain that the similarity of the solution case cannot be exceeded no matter how the user's query is extended. We also present a simple criterion for recognizing when no solution is possible based on the available information, thus ensuring that the user is never asked questions that cannot lead to a solution.

2.3 Case Structure and Query Representation

Below we briefly describe how cases and queries are represented in *Shriek*-CBR, and the similarity measure used in our approach. Table 1 shows an example case base that we use to illustrate the discussion. The example case base is a small subset of the case base used for fault diagnosis in *Shriek*-Printer, our intelligent system for fault management in a local printer network [2].

Case Structure. A case in *Shriek*-CBR consists of a case identifier, a problem description, a fault diagnosis, and, optionally, a remedial action (i.e., the action that was taken to correct the fault). The problem description is a set of question-answer (Q-A) pairs. As often in CCBR, the case structure is *heterogeneous* (i.e., a case includes only questions that are relevant for solution of the problem it represents) [9].

Query Representation. The current query Q in a CCBR dialogue is represented in *Shriek*-CBR as a set of Q-A pairs, including a Q-A pair for any question that the user answered *unknown*. In a CCBR dialogue based on the example case base in Table 1, the current query might be: $Q_1 = \{$able to print = N, power light on = unknown$\}$.

Table 1. Example case base for printer troubleshooting

Questions	Case 1	Case 2	Case 3	Case 4
Able to print?	N	N	N	Y
Toner level?			low	
Power light on?	N	N		
Printer switched on?	Y	N		
Printer plugged in?	N			
Print quality?				okay
Printing speed?				okay
Fault Diagnosis:	*Printer not plugged in*	*Printer switched off*	*Out of toner and refusing to print*	*Printer functioning normally*
Remedial Action:	*Connect printer to power outlet*	*Switch on the printer*	*Replace toner cartridge*	

Definition 1. For any case C, *questions*(C) is the set of questions in C.

Similarity Measure. Similarity assessment in *Shriek*-CBR is based on a measure commonly used in CCBR when the case structure is heterogeneous [8]. We define the similarity of any case C to a given query Q to be:

$$Sim(C, Q) = \frac{|matches(C,Q)| - |mismatches(C,Q)|}{|questions(C)|}. \tag{1}$$

In Equation 1, *matches*(C, Q) is the set of questions in C that are also in Q and have the same answer in C and Q, and *mismatches*(C, Q) is the set of questions in C that are also in Q, are not answered *unknown* in Q, and have different answers in C and Q. Thus a question that is answered *unknown* in a given query Q makes no contribution to the similarity of any case. The similarity measure's lack of symmetry is not an important issue in our approach as we use it only to assess the similarity of each case to a given query, and not the similarity between two cases. For the example query Q_1 = {able to print = N, power light on = unknown}, the similarities of Cases 1, 2, 3, and 4 in Table 1 are 0.25, 0.33, 0.50, and -0.33 respectively.

2.4 Autonomous Information Gathering

In general, the initial query in a CCBR dialogue may be empty, or the user may provide an initial query containing a partial description of the problem [8-9]. While the user is often the only source of information in a CCBR dialogue, some approaches support AIG from other sources [17-18]. When possible in *Shriek*-CBR, the initial query contains a partial description of the problem situation obtained by AIG from available sources in the computing environment. For example, when a user reports that she is having a problem with a printer, information that can normally be obtained directly from the printer includes toner level and paper status. The initial query in *Shriek*-CBR also includes the answers to any questions that can be inferred from the fact that this information can be obtained from the printer. For example, the printer must be switched on and connected to the power supply. There is also no need to ask the user if the power light is on.

Inferring the user's answer to one question from her answer to another question, a process known as dialogue inferencing (DI), is another approach to avoiding unnecessary questions in a CCBR dialogue [8-9]. However, even if a CCBR system can explain the additional reasoning steps needed for DI, a potential trade-off is that the overall reasoning process may be less transparent to the user. Moreover, we show in Section 5 that for the case base used for printer fault diagnosis in *Shriek*-Printer, rule-based DI appears to offer no improvement in the efficiency of CCBR dialogues based on the hypothesis-driven approach to question selection that we present in this paper. For these reasons, there is no DI in the current version of *Shriek*-CBR.

Also in Section 5, we demonstrate the effectiveness of AIG in helping to increase the efficiency of CCBR dialogues. In the interest of generality, however, we make no assumption in the rest of the paper about how the initial query in a CCBR dialogue is obtained.

2.5 Open, Viable, and Competitive Cases

Other basic concepts in our approach to CCBR include the *openness*, *viability*, and *competitiveness* of cases with respect to the current query in a CCBR dialogue.

Definition 2. For any query Q, *questions*(Q) is the set of questions that are answered in Q, including any questions that the user answered *unknown*.

Definition 3. For any case C and query Q, *unanswered*(C, Q) is the set of questions in C that are not yet answered in Q. That is, *unanswered*(C, Q) = *questions*(C) - *questions*(Q).

Definition 4. A case C is **open** with respect to a given query Q if *unanswered*(C, Q) $\neq$ $\varnothing$ (i.e., some of the questions in C are not answered in Q). Otherwise, C is **closed** with respect to Q.

In the example case base (Table 1), Case 3 is closed with respect to the query Q_2 = {able to print = N, toner level = unknown}, while Cases 1, 2, and 4 are open with respect to Q_2.

Definition 5. A query Q^* is an **extension** of another query Q if $Q \subseteq Q^*$.

Definition 6. For any case C and query Q, Q^C is the extension of Q such that *questions*(Q^C) = *questions*(Q) $\cup$ *questions*(C) and every question in *questions*(Q^C) - *questions*(Q) has the same answer in Q^C and C.

For the example case base in Table 1 and Q_1 = {able to print = N, power light on = unknown}, $Q_1^{\text{Case 2}}$ = {able to print = N, power light on = unknown, printer switched on = N}, while $Q_1^{\text{Case 3}}$ = {able to print = N, power light on = unknown, toner level = low}. It can also be seen that $Q^C = Q$ for any query Q and case C that is closed with respect to Q.

Definition 7. For any case C and query Q, *MaxSim*(C, Q) is the **maximum similarity** that can be reached by C over all possible extensions of Q.

In Theorem 1, we show how a case's maximum similarity can easily be determined with no need for exhaustive search over all possible extensions of a given query. Note that we make no assumption that the information provided by the user in a CCBR dialogue is consistent.

Theorem 1. For any case C and query Q,

$$MaxSim(C, Q) = Sim(C, Q^C) = Sim(C, Q) + \frac{|unanswered(C,Q)|}{|questions(C)|}.$$

Proof. The similarity of C to any extension of Q cannot exceed its similarity to Q^C. As the current query is extended from Q to Q^C, the similarity of C increases by $1/|questions(C)|$ for each $q \in unanswered(C, Q)$. $\square$

For any case C that is closed with respect to a given query Q, *MaxSim*(C, Q) = *Sim*(C, Q^C) = *Sim*(C, Q). For the example case base in Table 1 and Q_1 = {able to print = N, power light on = unknown}, *MaxSim*(Case 1, Q_1) = 0.75, *MaxSim*(Case 2, Q_1) = 0.67, *MaxSim*(Case 3, Q_1) = 1, and *MaxSim*(Case 4, Q_1) = 0.33.

Definition 8. A case C is **viable** with respect to a given query Q if $MaxSim(C, Q) \geq T$, where T is the minimum similarity threshold required for a case's solution to be re-used as a solution to the current problem.

A case that is *not* viable with respect to a given query Q can never reach the similarity threshold T no matter how Q is extended, and can thus be eliminated from considera-tion. In *Shriek*-CBR, the minimum similarity threshold required for a case's solution to be reused as a solution to the current problem is $T = 0.65$. For example, a case with four features (or Q-A pairs) in its description must have at least 3 matching features and no mismatching features. Other conditions for a case's solution to be suggested by *Shriek*-CBR as a solution to the user's problem are discussed in Section 3. For the example case base in Table 1 and Q_1 = {able to print = N, power light on = un-known}, only Cases 1, 2, and 3 are viable.

Definition 9. A case C_1 is **competitive** with respect to a given query Q if $MaxSim(C_1, Q) \geq MaxSim(C_2, Q)$ for all cases C_2.

At least one case must always be competitive, even if no case can reach a similarity of one. For the example case base in Table 1, Case 3 is the only competitive case with respect to Q_1 = {able to print = N, power light on = unknown}. However, a case that is not competitive with respect to the current query in a CCBR dialogue may later become competitive as the query is extended.

3   Knowing When to Stop Asking Questions

In Section 3.1, we present our approach to ensuring that a case's solution is suggested by *Shriek*-CBR as a solution to the user's problem only when it is certain that the similarity of the solution case cannot be exceeded no matter how the user's query is extended. Equally important when the user is unable to provide a complete descrip-tion of the problem is the ability to recognize when no solution is possible given the available information. In Section 3.2, we present our approach to ensuring that the user is never asked questions that cannot lead to a solution.

3.1   Recognizing When a Problem Has Been Solved

Our criterion for allowing a case's solution to be suggested as a solution to the user's problem in *Shriek*-CBR is that the case is *confirmed* by the current query in a CCBR dialogue. As soon as any case is confirmed, the dialogue is terminated and the solu-tion from the confirmed case is presented as a solution to the user's problem.

Definition 10. A case C_1 is **confirmed** by a given query Q if $Sim(C_1, Q) \geq 0.65$, C_1 is closed with respect to Q, and $Sim(C_1, Q) \geq MaxSim(C_2, Q)$ for all cases C_2.

Thus there are three conditions that a case C must satisfy for its solution to be sug-gested by *Shriek*-CBR as a solution to the user's problem. First, C must have reached the minimum similarity threshold ($T = 0.65$) for its solution to be reused as a solution to the current problem. Second, C must be closed with respect to the current query Q, thus ensuring that its similarity cannot *decrease* no matter how Q is extended. Third, there must be no other case that is more similar to Q or might exceed the similarity of

C if Q is extended. It is possible, though unlikely, for two or more cases to be confirmed at the same point in a CCBR dialogue. In this situation, the user can be shown the solutions from all the confirmed cases, or as currently in our approach, the solution from the confirmed case that appears first in case base.

A case C is clearly confirmed by any query Q such that $Sim(C, Q) = 1$, as C must be closed with respect to Q, and no case can exceed its similarity no matter how Q is extended. It is also possible for a case to be confirmed without reaching a similarity of one. For the example case base in Table 1, Case 1 is confirmed by the query $Q_3 = $ {able to print = unknown, power light on = N, printer switched on = Y, printer plugged in = N}. It can be seen from Table 1 that Sim(Case 1, Q_3) = 0.75, Case 1 is closed with respect to Q_3, and the maximum similarity that can be achieved by Case 4, the only other viable case, is 0.67.

Of course, the solution from a confirmed case cannot be guaranteed to solve the user's problem even if it has reached the maximum similarity of one. However, to enable learning from experience in *Shriek*-CBR, the user can *refer* any problem that remains unsolved by the system's recommendations to the person responsible for maintenance of the case base.

3.2 Recognizing When No Solution Is Possible

In Theorem 2, we present a simple criterion for recognizing when no solution is possible in a CCBR dialogue no matter how the current query is extended. An important benefit is that the user can be informed at the earliest possible stage when no solution is possible, and need never be asked questions that cannot lead to a solution.

Definition 11. A query Q is **inconclusive** if no case is (as yet) confirmed by Q.

Lemma 1. If at least one case is viable with respect to an inconclusive query Q, then all cases that are competitive with respect to Q are also open and viable.

Proof. If C_0 is a viable case, then for any competitive case C_1, $MaxSim(C_1, Q) \geq MaxSim(C_0, Q) \geq 0.65$, and so C_1 is also viable. As Q is inconclusive, it is also clear that C_1 cannot be closed with respect to Q, as this would imply that $Sim(C_1, Q) = MaxSim(C_1, Q) \geq 0.65$ and $Sim(C_1, Q) = MaxSim(C_1, Q) \geq MaxSim(C_2, Q)$ for all cases C_2, leading to the contradictory conclusion that C_1 is confirmed by Q.   □

Lemma 2. Any case C that is viable and competitive with respect to an inconclusive query Q is confirmed by Q^C.

Proof. If C_1 is any case that is viable and competitive with respect Q, then $Sim(C_1, Q^{C_1}) = MaxSim(C_1, Q) \geq 0.65$. It is also clear that C_1 is closed with respect to Q^{C_1}. It remains only to observe that, for all cases C_2, $Sim(C_1, Q^{C_1}) = MaxSim(C_1, Q) \geq MaxSim(C_2, Q) \geq MaxSim(C_2, Q^{C_1})$.   □

Theorem 2. A solution is possible by extending an inconclusive query Q if and only if at least one case is viable with respect to Q.

Proof. It is clear that no solution is possible by extending an inconclusive query if no case can reach the similarity threshold ($T = 0.65$) required for its solution to be applied to the current problem. Conversely, suppose that at least one case is viable with respect to an inconclusive query Q, and let C_1 be any case that is competitive with respect to Q. By Lemma 1, C_1 is also viable with respect to Q. It follows from Lemma 2 that C_1 is confirmed by Q^{C_1}. Thus if Q is incrementally extended in a CCBR dialogue by asking the user only questions in *unanswered*(C_1, Q), and all the user's answers are the same as in C_1, then C_1 must eventually be confirmed unless another case C_2 is confirmed (and the dialogue terminated) before Q^{C_1} is reached. In either case, we have established that a solution is possible by extending Q.   □

For example, none of the cases in Table 1 is viable with respect to the query Q_4 = {able to print = N, toner level = unknown, power light on = Y}. The user can thus be informed that no solution is possible after she has answered at most three of the seven questions in the case base. In *Shriek*-Printer, any fault that *Shriek*-CBR is currently unable to diagnose is automatically referred to the person responsible for maintenance of the case base and authoring of new cases for diagnosis of previously unseen faults. In this situation, possible recovery strategies suggested to the user by *Shriek*-Printer are likely to include redirecting her print job to another available printer.

4   Asking the Right Questions

In Section 4.1, we describe how an initial target case is selected in our hypothesis-driven approach to question selection in CCBR, and may later be revised as the query describing the problem is extended. In Section 4.2, we describe how the target case is used to guide the selection of the most useful question in each cycle of a CCBR dialogue. This is followed in Section 4.3 by a brief demonstration of *Shriek*-CBR based on the example case base in Table 1.

4.1   Selecting a Target Case

The target case used to guide question selection in *Shriek*-CBR is uniquely determined by the current query Q. To be selected as a target case, a case C must be competitive with respect to Q. If there is more than one competitive case, then the one with fewest *unanswered* questions in its problem description is selected as the target case. If there is still a tie between two or more competitive cases, then the one that appears first in the case base is selected as the target case. In a CCBR dialogue in which the user's problem is initially represented by an empty query Q, all cases are initially competitive as *MaxSim*(C, Q) = 1 for every case C. In this situation, the target case initially selected by *Shriek*-CBR is the first case with the smallest number of questions in the case base. Of course, the target case may later be revised in light of the user's answers to the system's questions.

Definition 12. The **target case** for an inconclusive query Q is the first competitive case C_1 in the case base such that |*unanswered*(C_1, Q)| ≤ |*unanswered*(C_2, Q)| for all competitive cases C_2.

Selecting the most similar case as the target case is one possible alternative to the proposed strategy. However, the most similar case may not be open, competitive, or even viable with respect to the current query. In Table 1, for example, the case that is most similar to $Q_5 = \{$able to print = N, toner level = unknown$\}$ is Case 3 (0.50). But Case 3 is not open, viable, or competitive with respect to Q_5. In contrast, only a competitive case can be selected as a target case in *Shriek*-CBR. As a CCBR dialogue is allowed to continue in *Shriek*-CBR only if there is at least one viable case, the target case must also be open and viable by Lemma 1. Another potential problem with target selection based on similarity is that a non-target case with the same answer to a question in the target case may obtain a greater increase in similarity than the target case if the user's answer is the same as in both cases. This may result in seemingly *inconstant* behavior (i.e., frequent changes from one target case to another).

4.2 Selecting the Most Useful Question

In *Shriek*-CBR, the user is asked only questions in the target case, which must include at least one unanswered question by Lemma 1. However, our approach to selecting the most useful question also takes account of question frequency, a criterion that has been shown to be effective in other CCBR approaches [8]. The most useful question at any stage of a CCBR dialogue in *Shriek*-CBR is the unanswered question in the target case that occurs most frequently in the viable cases. If two or more unanswered questions in the target case occur with maximum frequency in the viable cases, the one that occurs first in the target case is selected as the most useful question.

Definition 13. If C is the target case for an inconclusive query Q, then the **most useful question** is the first unanswered question in C that occurs with maximum frequency in all cases that are viable with respect to Q.

4.3 Example Dialogue in Shriek-CBR

The example dialogue in Fig. 1 that we use to demonstrate our approach to CCBR in *Shriek*-CBR is based on the example case base in Table 1 and a problem situation in which a user is attempting to use a printer that is not switched on. As printer status information cannot be obtained by AIG from a printer that is not switched on, the initial query is empty. Thus all cases in the example case base are initially open, viable, and competitive. As Case 3 has fewer questions (2) than any other case, it is initially selected as the target case. The question in Case 3 that occurs most frequently in the viable cases is 'Able to print?'. In light of the user's answer (N), the maximum similarity that Case 4 can reach falls to 0.33, so Case 4 is no longer viable. However, Cases 1, 2, and 3 remain open, viable, and competitive.

With $Q = \{$able to print = N$\}$ as the current query in the second cycle, Case 3 is again selected as the target case, and the user is asked about the toner level, the only question that remains unanswered in Case 3. However, the user does not know the toner level, with the result that Case 3 is no longer viable (i.e., its similarity can never reach 0.65). Though both less similar than Case 3 (0.50), Cases 1 and 2 (0.25 and 0.33) are still open, viable, and competitive. Case 2 is now selected as the target case because it has fewer unanswered questions (2) than Case 1 (3). As the two unanswered questions in Case 2 occur with equal frequency (2) in the viable cases, 'Power light on?' is selected as the most useful question because it appears first in the target case. The user's answer (N) increases the similarity of Case 2 to 0.67.

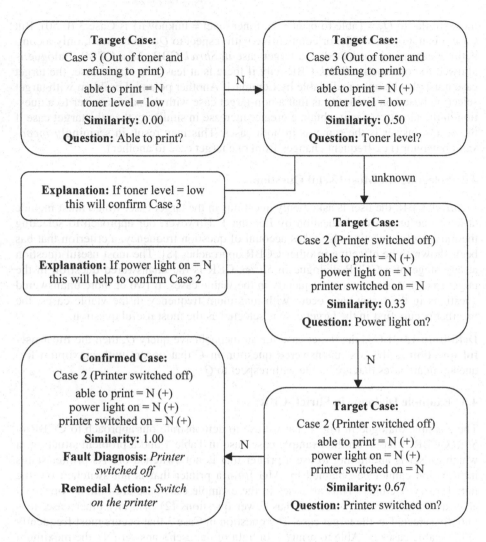

Fig. 1. An example CCBR dialogue in *Shriek*-CBR

Case 2 is again the target case in the fourth cycle as its only unanswered question is now 'Printer switched on?' while Case 1 still has two unanswered questions. When the user is asked if the printer is switched on, her answer (N) is enough to confirm Case 2 as it has now reached a similarity of one. Finally, the user is shown the solution (i.e., fault diagnosis and remedial action) from the confirmed case. A detail not shown in Fig. 1 is that *Shriek*-Printer also uses its environment knowledge to identify possible recovery strategies (e.g., waiting for assistance from an available technician) that the user may wish to consider.

The example dialogue also shows how *Shriek*-CBR can explain the relevance of any question it asks the user. Before answering any question, the user can ask why it is relevant. If so, *Shriek*-CBR explains that if the user's answer is the same as in the target case, this will confirm, or help to confirm, the target case. In each cycle of a CCBR dialogue, the user is also shown the target case that the system is trying to confirm, its matching (+) and mismatching (-) features, and its overall similarity to the current query. At the end of the dialogue, *Shriek*-CBR explains the solution it has reached by showing the user the confirmed case and its matching and mismatching features.

5 Empirical Study

The hypothesis that motivates the work presented is that the transparency of CCBR dialogues can be increased by a hypothesis-driven approach to question selection without loss of problem-solving efficiency. As shown in Section 4, our hypothesis-driven approach to question selection enables a CCBR system to explain the relevance of any question the user is asked. However, an important question is how the efficiency of CCBR dialogues based on this strategy compares with other approaches to question selection and ranking in CCBR. While approaches that assume a homogeneous case structure [11, 14-15] are not directly comparable to ours, an approach often used when the case structure is heterogeneous is to rank questions according to their frequency in the most similar cases [8]. The question-selection strategies compared in our evaluation are:

Random: Select any question at random
Frequency: Select the question that occurs most frequently in the most similar open cases
Target: Select the first unanswered question in the target case that occurs with maximum frequency in the viable cases.

Also of interest in our evaluation are the effects of AIG and DI on the efficiency of CCBR dialogues in *Shriek*-CBR. The case base used in our experiments is the one used for fault diagnosis in *Shriek*-Printer, our intelligent system for fault management in a local printer network [2]. It contains 20 cases, most of which have 3 or 4 Q-A pairs, and there are 12 questions in the case base. Because some printer faults (e.g., paper jams) cannot be arranged "to order" in a live environment, we use an off-line version of *Shriek*-Printer in which printer status information (e.g., toner level) normally obtained by AIG is provided in an initial query. The initial query also includes the answers to any questions that *Shriek*-Printer normally infers from its ability to communicate with the printer (if that is the case) as described in Section 2. When enabled in our experiments, DI is based on simple rules (e.g., if the power light is on, then the printer must be switched on).

We use a *leave-one-in* approach in which each case in the *Shriek*-Printer case base provides the description of a problem to be solved in a simulated CCBR dialogue. Any question that does not appear in the description of the left-in case is answered *unknown* in the CCBR dialogue. For any question that does appear in the left-in case, the answer given is the answer in the left-in case. The dialogue is allowed to continue until any case reaches a similarity of one. In our first experiment, this process is repeated for all cases and for each question-selection strategy with no AIG or DI. In our second experiment, the *Target* strategy is used with all combinations of AIG (on/off) and DI (on/off). In 90% of AIG-enabled dialogues, 7 of the 12 possible questions are already answered in the initial query. In the remaining 10%, the initial query is empty, for example because printer status information cannot be obtained by AIG from a printer that is not switched on.

In all CCBR dialogues, the left-in case was the *only* case to reach a similarity of one. Fig. 2 shows the minimum, average, and maximum lengths of CCBR dialogues (i.e., numbers of questions) observed in each question-selection strategy. Also shown is the *optimal* performance that could be achieved with any question-selection strategy, given that the number of questions asked before a case reaches a similarity of one cannot be less than the number of questions in the case. In the *Shriek*-Printer case base, the number of questions in a case ranges from 2 to 7 with an average of 3.3.

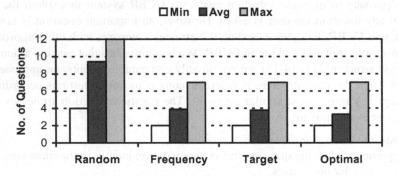

Fig. 2. Minimum, average, and maximum lengths of CCBR dialogues based on three question-selection strategies, and the optimal results achievable with any question-selection strategy

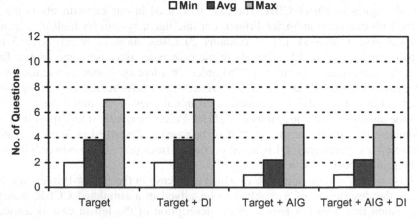

Fig. 3. Effects of AIG and DI on the efficiency of CCBR dialogues based on hypothesis-driven question selection in the *Shriek*-Printer case base

Average dialogue lengths in the *Target* and *Frequency* strategies (3.8 and 3.9) are much lower than in the *Random* strategy (9.4). In fact, average dialogue lengths in these two strategies are close to optimal (3.3). With the *Target* and *Frequency* strategies differing only slightly in average dialogue length, the results support our hypothesis that the transparency of CCBR dialogues can be increased by a hypothesis-driven approach to question selection without loss of efficiency.

Fig. 3 shows the effects of AIG and DI on the lengths of CCBR dialogues in the *Target* strategy. In the absence of DI, AIG reduced average dialogue length from 3.8 to 2.2, a reduction of 42%. Average dialogue length for the *Target* strategy with AIG (2.2) is 33% lower than the best possible average (3.3) that could be achieved with any question-selection strategy in the absence of AIG (Fig. 2). Whether or not AIG is enabled, however, rule-based DI appears to have no effect on the average length of simulated CCBR dialogues based on our hypothesis-driven approach to question selection in the *Shriek*-Printer case base.

6 Conclusions

In the SHRIEK approach to increasing the robustness of computing systems, CCBR is used to guide fault diagnosis and enable learning from experience in the management of faults that rely on user interaction for their detection and diagnosis [2-3]. In this paper, we presented a hypothesis-driven approach to question selection in CCBR that enables the system to explain the relevance of any question the user is asked. Also with the aim of increasing transparency, the user is shown the target case in each cycle of a CCBR dialogue and asked only questions in the target case.

Our empirical results suggest that there is no loss of efficiency in our approach relative to an approach often used in CCBR when the case structure is heterogeneous [8]. We also demonstrated a 42% reduction in the average length of CCBR dialogues as a result of the environment awareness provided by autonomous information gathering in *Shriek*-Printer. Finally, we presented CCBR techniques for ensuring that (1) the user is never asked questions that cannot lead to a solution, and (2) a solution is presented to the user only when no other case can exceed the similarity of the solution case no matter what additional questions the user might be asked.

Acknowledgements. Sa'adah Hassan's research is supported by the Ministry of Higher Education Malaysia. The authors would also like to thank Chris Stretch for his helpful comments on an earlier version of this paper.

References

1. Horn, P.: Autonomic Computing: IBM's Perspective on the State of Information Technology. In: Agenda 2001. IBM Watson Research Center, Scottsdale (2001)
2. Hassan, S., McSherry, D., Bustard, D.: Autonomic Self Healing and Recovery Informed by Environment Knowledge. Artificial Intelligence Review 26, 89–101 (2006)
3. Hassan, S., Bustard, D., McSherry, D.: Soft Systems Methodology in Autonomic Computing Analysis. In: UK Systems Society International Conference, pp. 106–115 (2006)
4. Checkland, P., Scholes, J.: Soft Systems Methodology in Action. Wiley, Chichester (1990)

5. Crapo, A.W., Aragones, A.V., Price, J.E., Varma, A.: Towards Autonomic Systems for Lifecycle Support of Complex Equipment. In: International Conference on Information Reuse and Integration, pp. 322–329. IEEE, Los Alamitos (2003)

6. Montani, S., Anglano, C.: Achieving Self-Healing in Service Delivery Software Systems by Means of Case-Based Reasoning. Applied Intelligence 28, 139–152 (2008)

7. Montani, S., Anglano, C.: Case-Based Reasoning for Autonomous Service Failure Diagnosis and Remediation in Software Systems. In: Roth-Berghofer, T.R., Göker, M.H., Güvenir, H.A. (eds.) ECCBR 2006. LNCS (LNAI), vol. 4106, pp. 489–503. Springer, Heidelberg (2006)

8. Aha, D.W., Breslow, L.A., Muñoz-Avila, H.: Conversational Case-Based Reasoning. Applied Intelligence 14, 9–32 (2001)

9. Aha, D.W., McSherry, D., Yang, Q.: Advances in Conversational Case-Based Reasoning. Knowledge Engineering Review 20, 247–254 (2005)

10. Gu, M., Aamodt, A.: Evaluating CBR Systems Using Different Data Sources: a Case Study. In: Roth-Berghofer, T.R., Göker, M.H., Güvenir, H.A. (eds.) ECCBR 2006. LNCS (LNAI), vol. 4106, pp. 121–135. Springer, Heidelberg (2006)

11. McSherry, D.: Interactive Case-Based Reasoning in Sequential Diagnosis. Applied Intelligence 14, 65–76 (2001)

12. Shimazu, H., Shibata, A., Nihei, K.: ExpertGuide: a Conversational Case-Based Reasoning Tool for Developing Mentors in Knowledge Spaces. Applied Intelligence 14, 33–48 (2001)

13. Cheetham, W.: A Mixed-Initiative Call Center Application for Appliance Diagnostics. In: AAAI 2005 Fall Symposium on Mixed-Initiative Problem-Solving Assistants. AAAI/MIT Press (2005)

14. McSherry, D.: Hypothetico-Deductive Case-Based Reasoning. In: ICCBR 2007 Workshop on Case-Based Reasoning in the Health Sciences, pp. 315–324 (2007)

15. McSherry, D.: Increasing Dialogue Efficiency in Case-Based Reasoning Without Loss of Solution Quality. In: 18th International Joint Conference on Artificial Intelligence, pp. 121–126 (2003)

16. McSherry, D.: Increasing the Coverage of Decision Trees through Mixed-Initiative Interaction. In: 18th Irish Conference on Artificial Intelligence and Cognitive Science, pp. 101–110 (2007)

17. Carrick, C., Yang, Q., Abi-Zeid, I., Lamontagne, L.: Activating CBR Systems through Autonomous Information Gathering. In: Althoff, K.-D., Bergmann, R., Branting, L.K. (eds.) ICCBR 1999. LNCS (LNAI), vol. 1650, pp. 74–88. Springer, Heidelberg (1999)

18. Giampapa, J., Sycara, K.: Conversational Case-Based Planning for Agent Team Coordination. In: Aha, D.W., Watson, I. (eds.) ICCBR 2001. LNCS (LNAI), vol. 2080, pp. 189–203. Springer, Heidelberg (2001)

Situation Assessment for Plan Retrieval in Real-Time Strategy Games

Kinshuk Mishra, Santiago Ontañón, and Ashwin Ram

Cognitive Computing Lab (CCL)
College of Computing
Georgia Institute of Technology
Atlanta, GA 30332/0280
{kinshuk,santi,ashwin}@cc.gatech.edu

Abstract. Case-Based Planning (CBP) is an effective technique for solving planning problems that has the potential to reduce the computational complexity of the generative planning approaches [8,3]. However, the success of plan execution using CBP depends highly on the selection of a correct plan; especially when the case-base of plans is extensive. In this paper we introduce the concept of a *situation* and explain a *situation assessment* algorithm which improves plan retrieval for CBP. We have applied situation assessment to our previous CBP system, Darmok [11], in the domain of real-time strategy games. During Darmok's execution using situation assessment, the high-level representation of the game state i.e. situation is predicted using a decision tree based Situation-Classification model. Situation predicted is further used for the selection of relevant knowledge intensive features, which are derived from the basic representation of the game state, to compute the similarity of cases with the current problem. The feature selection performed here is knowledge based and improves the performance of similarity measurements during plan retrieval. The instantiation of the situation assessment algorithm to Darmok gave us promising results for plan retrieval within the real-time constraints.

1 Introduction

Generative planning techniques are typically inapplicable for solving problems with extensive search spaces within real-time constraints. Case-based planning (CBP) [13] has the potential of reducing the computational complexity of traditional planning techniques. Specifically, CBP works by reusing previous stored plans for new situations instead of planning from scratch. Thus, CBP is a promising paradigm to deal with real-time domains. In this paper we will focus in Darmok, [11] a case-based planning system that is able to deal with the complexity of real-time strategy (RTS) games. Darmok was designed to play WARGUS, an open source implementation of the famous Warcraft II. However, the success of plan execution using CBP in such domains depends on the quality of plan selection within the real-time constraints. The performance of Darmok's plan

K.-D. Althoff et al. (Eds.): ECCBR 2008, LNAI 5239, pp. 355–369, 2008.

retrieval suffers when the case-base stores numerous plans representing several strategies played over maps of different sizes and terrain formations. In this paper we explain our work on situation assessment technique applied to Darmok for better plan retrieval in real-time.

A *Situation* is a high-level representation of the state of the world. For example, in the WARGUS domain the player might be in an *attacking* situation, or in a *base development* situation, among others. Depending on which situation the player is in, different aspects of the world state will be important to take decisions. Thus, in order to select which strategy to execute, it is important to know the current situation. Situations can be predicted based on raw features that can be directly computed from the game state, i.e. *shallow features*. However, shallow features by themselves are not strong enough for selection of a strategy in a game. Additional derived *deep features* for a situation are needed. For example, shallow features, like the ratio of a player's resources to that of the opponent, by themselves are less suggestive of usefulness of an appropriate strategy. However deeper features, like knowing the existence of path or a barrier between the player and its opponent, can help in choosing a rush or a tunneling strategy. Situation assessment is used to predict the situation of a game state based on the shallow features. This information is used to further select a set of deep features specific to the situation for choosing the best strategy. Formally, *Situation Assessment* is a process of gathering high-level information using low-level data to help in better decision making.

Our general situation assessment technique comprises of four steps: *shallow feature selection, model generation, model execution* and *case retrieval*. Firstly, a subset of shallow features is selected which are used for classification of a game state into a situation. Then three models: a) for classification of game state into situations based on shallow features, b) for mapping of situations to cases and c) for mapping of situations to deep features respectively are generated. Execution of these models helps Darmok to classify a game state into a situation and then retrieve the most optimal plan using situation specific deep features. Plan retrieval results in Darmok using situation assessment have been promising.

The rest of the paper is organized as follows. Section 2 presents a summary of the related work. Then, Section 3 briefly explains the architecture of the Darmok system. After that, Section 4 describes the process of situation assessment. Section 5 explains the situation assessment algorithm applied to Darmok System. Section 6 provides an illustration of the process. Finally, we summarize our experiment results in Section 7 and then end with a conclusions section.

2   Related Work

There are several relevant areas of work related to our approach, namely: situation assessment, feature selection, and the application of CBR to computer game AI. Concerning situation assessment, work has been done extensively in the area of information fusion [4] and defense related command and control projects [2], however little work has been done using CBR. Kolodner [10] defined situation assessment as the process of deriving additional features in a particular situation in order to compare it with previous experiences, but no CBR system to our knowledge implements such process. Kofod-Petersen and Aamodt [9] define a case-based situation assessment system for a mobile context-aware application. The system uses case-based reasoning to determine the situation in which the user might be in, and the possible goals associated with these situations. They define a situation as a context, and define a hierarchy of contexts in which the user might be in. The difference with our work is that we are interested in situation assessment as a way to select a subset of features that allows us to perform better case retrieval.

Plenty of work exists on feature selection in the machine learning literature. Hall and Holmes [7] present a nice overview and empirical evaluation of several feature selection techniques. Some well-known techniques include: information-gain based techniques [14], Principal Component Analysis, Correlation-based Feature selection [6], or Cross-validation methods (that simply run the learning algorithm repeatedly with different feature subsets and select the best one empirically). The main difference of our work with the existing feature selection techniques, is that the set of possible features from where we can select features is too large and the examples are few, and thus we need a more knowledge-based feature selection method (situation assessment) that does not involve trying feature-by-feature.

Concerning the application of case-based reasoning techniques to computer games, Aha et al. [1] developed a case-based plan selection technique that learns how to select an appropriate strategy for each particular situation in the game of WARGUS. In their work, they have a library of previously encoded strategies, and the system learns which one of them is better for each game phase. In addition, they perform an interesting analysis on the complexity of real-time strategy games (focusing on WARGUS in particular). Another application of case-based reasoning to real-time strategy games is that of Sharma et al. [12], where they present a hybrid case-based reinforcement learning approach able to learn which are the best actions to apply in each situation (from a set of high level actions). The main difference between their work and ours is that they learn a case selection policy, while our system constructs plans from the individual cases it has in the case-base. Moreover, our architecture automatically extracts the plans from observing a human rather than having them coded in advance.

3   Case-Based Planning and Execution in Wargus

In this section we will present an overview of WARGUS and of the Darmok system. WARGUS (Figure 1) is a real-time strategy game where each player's goal is to remain alive after destroying the rest of the players. Each player has a series of troops and buildings and gathers resources (gold, wood and oil) in order to produce more troops and buildings. Buildings are required to produce more advanced troops, and troops are required to attack the enemy. In addition, players can also build defensive buildings such as walls and towers. Therefore,

Fig. 1. A screenshot of the WARGUS game

WARGUS involves complex reasoning to determine where, when and which buildings and troops to build. For example, the map shown in Figure 1 is a 2-player version of the classical map "Nowhere to run nowhere to hide", with a wall of trees that separates the players. This maps leads to complex strategic reasoning, such as building long range units (such as catapults or ballistae) to attack the other player before the wall of trees has been destroyed, or tunneling early in the game through the wall of trees trying to catch the enemy by surprise.

The Darmok system [11] is a case-based planning system designed to play the game of WARGUS. Darmok learns plans (cases) by observing a human playing the game, and then reuses such plans combining and adapting them to play new games using case-based planning methods. Figure 2 presents the Darmok architecture that is split into two main processes: *Behavior Acquisition* and *Behavior Execution.* The *Behavior Acquisition* process is performed by the Revision and Case Learning modules in the following way. Each time a human plays a game, a trace is generated (containing the list of actions performed by the human). During revision, the human annotates that trace stating which goals he was pursuing with each action. This annotated trace is processed by the case learning module that extracts plans in form of cases from the trace. Each plan consists of two components:

- A Behavior: consisting of a goal and a plan. Basically, a behavior stores that, to achieve a particular goal, the human used a particular plan.
- An Episode: consisting of a reference to a behavior, a game state and an outcome. Episodes store how well a particular behavior performed in a particular game state. The outcome is a real number between 0 and 1, stating how much the behavior achieved its goal in the specified game state.

Thus, the case-base of Darmok is composed of behaviors, and each behavior is associated with a bunch of episodes. Behaviors are learnt from traces, and

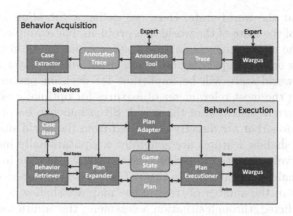

Fig. 2. Overview of our case-based planning approach

episodes can be learnt either from traces or from experience. The *Behavior Execution* process is performed by the rest of the modules in the architecture, and works as follows. Darmok starts off by giving the initial unexpanded goal "Win Wargus" to the Plan Expander. Each time the Plan Expander wants to expand a goal, it asks the Behavior Retriever for a behavior, which uses the case-base to select the best behavior for the goal at hand in the current game state. The Plan Adapter adapts the retrieved behaviors before they are inserted in the current plan, which is maintained by Darmok for execution. The Plan Executioner constantly tries to execute that plan that might be only partially expanded. Such a plan is maintained by the Plan Expander that looks for unexpanded goals in the plan and tries to expand them. Thus, the Plan Executioner tries to see if there is any part of the plan that has been expanded to the level of primitive actions that can be sent to the game, and executes such actions if possible. Some of the primitive actions in the game are like *move-unit*, *repair-building*, etc.

Finally, notice that WARGUS is a dynamic domain, thus the game state changes constantly. For that reason, the Plan Expander delays the adaptation of plans till the last moment (right before they have to start execution) to ensure they are adapted with the most up-to-date game state (Delayed Adaptation). In this paper we will focus on the behavior retrieval problem. See [11] for a detailed explanation of the Darmok system.

4   Situation Assessment for Case Retrieval

Traditionally, in Case-Based Reasoning the process of case retrieval is done by selecting the case from the case-base that has the closest similarity to the world state of the problem. This similarity is measured over the various features that are computed from the representation of the world state. The key to the most optimal case selection is choosing the set of most important features which improve the similarity measurement during the case selection process. The choice of features depends on their relevance in representing the high-level inferential knowledge about the world state. Here, we define a *Situation* as a high-level representation of the state of the world in a problem. For example, in the WAR-GUS domain the player might be in an *attacking* situation, or in a *base building* situation among others. Depending on which situation the player is in, different aspects of the world state will be important for decision making. Hence, the task of choosing the most relevant set of features for optimal case selection depends on the current situation of the world. Situations can be predicted based on the raw features that are directly computed from the world state i.e. *shallow features*. These shallow features are generally computationally inexpensive but lack the high-level inferential knowledge about the world. For instance, in the WARGUS domain, the features like ratio of player's gold resources versus that of the opponent or the number of trees in the map are shallow features. Once a situation is predicted, through situation assessment, the additional derived *deep features* specific to a situation are used for comparing the high-level knowledge represented by each case. For instance, in the WARGUS domain, the deep features like knowing the existence of path or a barrier between the player and its opponent, can help in choosing a rush or a tunneling strategy. The deep features are generally computationally expensive but provide information very relevant for case selection in specific situations. As we said before, situation assessment is a process of gathering high-level information using low-level data to help in better decision making. Thus, in the case of CBR, it is the process of gathering the important features and other pieces of information that will help us retrieve the most appropriate case.

Our general situation assessment algorithm is described in Figure 3. It comprises of four main steps:

- **Shallow Feature Selection:** During this first step, a situation annotated trace T is provided to a feature selection algorithm. An annotated trace consists of a sequence of world states annotated with the set of shallow features computed for each world state and the appropriate situation that world state corresponds to. This algorithm returns the set of shallow features F_s' which have high information gain. Specifically, in Darmok, we have used best-first greedy hill-climbing algorithm [5] for filtering the high information gain shallow features.
- **Model Generation:** In this step the following three models are generated:
  - The *Situation-Classification Model*, M_{cf}, is built by providing F_s' and T to a classification algorithm. This model is useful for classification of a world state to a situation using shallow features in F_s'. In Darmok, we have used a standard algorithm inducing a decision tree classifier model.
  - The *Situation-Case Model*, M_c, provides a mapping from the set of situations S to a subset of cases in the case-base C. It can be built using statistical or empirical analysis. This model captures the intuition that not all the cases will be useful in all the situations.
  - The *Situation-Deepfeature Model*, M_{df}, provides a mapping from S to deep features in the set F_d. This mapping is done using a feature selection algorithm or by using empirical knowledge.

Function SituationAssessment(C, T)
    1 Shallow Feature Selection
        $F'_s = $ SelectShallowFeatures(F_s, T)

    2 Model Generation
        $M_{cf} = $ GenerateClassificationModel(F'_s, T)
        $M_c = $ GenerateCaseModel(S, C)
        $M_{df} = $ GenerateDeepFeatureModel(S, F_d)

    3 Model Execution
        $s = $ GetCurrentSituation(M_{cf}, F'_s)
        $C' = $ GetRelevantCaseSubset(M_c, s)
        $F'_d = $ GetDeepFeatureSet(M_{df}, C')

    4 Case Retrieval
        Return RetrieveCase(C', F'_d, F_s)
End-Function

Fig. 3. General Situation Assessment Algorithm. Where C is the case-base, T is the situation annotated training set. F_s and F_d are the set of all shallow and deep features respectively. F'_s is the subset of high information gain features selected from F_s. M_{cf} is the Situation-Classification model. S is the universal set of all possible situations. M_c and M_{df} are the Situation-Case model and Situation-Deepfeature models respectively, built empirically in Darmok. s represents the current situation of the game state. C' is the most relevant subset of cases from the case-base obtained for s from the execution of M_c. F'_d is the subset of deep features obtained from execution of M_{df}. RetrieveCase returns the best case from C' using F'_d and F_s.

- **Model Execution:** In this third step, the models generated in the previous step are executed to get the current situation s, the subset of cases C' from the case-base C and the subset of deep features F'_d which are most relevant to s. s is obtained by running M_{cf} over F'_s. Once s is known, using M_c and M_{df}, C' and F'_d are obtained respectively.
- **Case Retrieval:** This is the last step where using F'_d and F_s the most similar case in retrieved from C' using normal retrieval techniques.

5   Situation Assessment Applied to Darmok

In this section we shall present the instantiation of the situation assessment algorithm in our system, Darmok, to improve the performance of its case-based plan retrieval. We apply the General Situation Assessment algorithm in Figure 3 to Darmok, but split in two stages:

- The Offline Stage: comprising of Feature Selection and Model Generation before the game-play.
- The Online Stage: comprising of Model Execution and Plan Retrieval during the game-play.

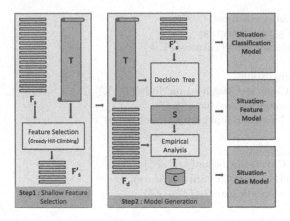

Fig. 4. Offline Stage of Situation Assessment. Where T is the trace, F_s is the set of shallow features, F_s' is the subset of shallow features after feature selection, F_d is the set of deep features, S is the set of situations and C is the case-base.

Table 1. Goal to Situation Mapping

Goals	Situations
ResearchGoal	Base Development, Defense, Dev-Defense
AbsoluteBuildUnitsGoal, RelativeBuildUnitsGoal	Base Development, Defense, Attack, Dev-Defense, Dev-Attack
ResourceInfrastructureGoal	Base Development
KillAllUnitsOfTypeGoal, KillUnitGoal, DefeatPlayerGoal	Attack
WinWargusGoal	Beginning

We perform situation assessment in two stages since the models required for predicting the situation during Darmok's game-play are built just once at the start. Therefore, the models can be easily generated offline using standard feature selection and classification algorithms.

5.1   Offline Stage

As shown in the Figure 4 the offline stage of the situation assessment algorithm in Darmok consists of the first two steps of the algorithm from Figure 3.

In the first step of shallow feature selection the set of shallow features F_s^w in WARGUS and the situation annotated trace T^w are provided to the best-first greedy hill-climbing-with-backtacking feature selection algorithm [5]. T^w is generated over various game states, with the values of all the shallow features, by forcing Darmok to play particular maps with the best strategies for those maps, which were demonstrated by an expert. In our experiments, trace generation and annotation was automated, based on the goals that Darmok was pursuing in those particular game states, because a goal being pursued is the high-level representation of the game state that helps in choosing a particular plan.

The feature selection algorithm we have used returns the set of shallow features $F_s^{w'}$, which have high information gain. Once $F_s^{w'}$ is generated it is provided along with T^w to a pruning enabled C4.5 decision tree algorithm [5] to learn a decision tree situation-classifier model M_{cf}^w. M_{cf}^w generated here is used in real-time during game-play for predicting the situation of the game state.

The Situation-Case model M_c^w is built using empirical knowledge of the WARGUS domain. The cases are mapped manually to situations based on the goal of the behavior in the plan represented in the case as shown in Table 1.

The Situation-Deepfeature model M_{df}^w is constructed manually by using an expert's empirical knowledge about usefulness of various deep features in certain situations. For example, using deep features like *attacking-speed-of-troops* and *attacking-radius-of-troop-formation* are more relevant in choosing a strategy while a player is in *attacking* situation as compared to when he is in *base development* situation.

5.2   Online Stage

This stage comprises of the last two steps of the algorithm of Figure 3 as shown in Figure 5. This stage in interleaved with the case-based planning and execution of Darmok. During Darmok's online game-play when the Plan Expander requests the Behavior Retriever for a new plan, Darmok, before the plan retrieval, first executes the model M_{cf}^w followed by the parallel execution of M_c^w and M_{df}^w respectively . Darmok computes the value of $F_s^{w'}$ from the current game state and evaluates the current situation through the decision tree based M_{cf}^w.

Once the current situation s is evaluated, mapping based M_c^w and M_{df}^w model suggest the case-base subset $C^{w'}$ and a deep feature subset $F_d^{w'}$ for the final plan retrieval.

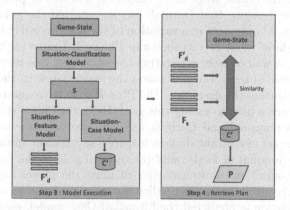

Fig. 5. Online Stage of Situation Assessment. Where s is the current situation, F_d' is the relevant subset of deep features, C' is the relevant subset of the case-base, F_s is the set of shallow features and P is the retrieved plan.

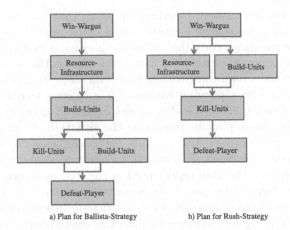

a) Plan for Ballista-Strategy   b) Plan for Rush-Strategy

Fig. 6. Plans for ballista and rush strategies for game-play in WARGUS. a) The ballista strategy comprises of initial resources development followed by building the units to strengthen the player base. Later the units are built and sent to kill the opponent units in parallel. b) The rush strategy comprises of quick resource development and building the units at the start in parallel followed by killing the opponent units.

In the last step of this stage the features in $F_d^{w'}$ and F_s^w are used to measure the similarity of the cases in $C^{w'}$ and return the plan having most similar goal and game state to the scenario during the game-play. The similarity is measured by placing more importance to the features in $F_d^{w'}$ as compared to F_s^w.

Let us illustrate this process with an example.

6   Example

Let us illustrate the online stage of the situation assessment process in Darmok with an example. Imagine that Darmok has just started the game-play against the built in game AI opponent in a variation of the well-known map "Nowhere to run nowhere to hide" (NWTR) as shown in Figure 1. Unlike the typical NWTR maps that have a wall of trees separating the opponent this map has a narrow opening in the wall of trees. Darmok starts the execution with the initial goal of "WinWargus". During the execution, the Plan Expander requests the Behavior Retriever to return a plan to satisfy this goal. Here, the online stage of situation assessment gets triggered and Darmok uses the decision tree based situation-classifier and the set of relevant shallow features, say, *lumber* (number of trees in the map), *food* (amount of food), *gold* (amount of gold of the player), *peasants* (number of peasants) and *units* (number of units the player has), which were chosen during the offline stage, to predict the current situation as *beginning*.

Once the situation is predicted the Situation-Case model, essentially a mapping of situations to plans based on the goals that the plans satisfy as shown in Table 1, is searched to find the subset of the plans which are relevant to the beginning situation. Since the beginning situation is mapped to plans satisfying the "WinWargus" goal, Darmok has successfully narrowed down its search space to the set of few relevant plans.

Darmok also refers to the Situation-Deepfeature model to get the set of most relevant features for the beginning situation: *ispath* (a boolean feature that is true when there is a path from the player base to the enemy base), *wallbarrierwidth* (the width of the biggest barrier between the player and the enemy) and *baseproximitydistance* (distance between the player's base and the enemy base).

Beginning situation is where player has to choose a game strategy which is most optimal for a particular map-terrain and opponent strength, to win the game. Assuming that there are just two plans as shown in Figure 6 for the beginning situation in the reduced case-base $C^{w'}$, each representing different game strategies, the task of the Darmok's Behavior Retriever is to choose the plan with the best strategy for the current game state.

The two plans in Figure 6 represent the *ballista* and *rush* strategies. Ballista strategy is good for maps where the player and the opponent are separated by a wall of trees while rush strategy is good when there is a path from player to the opponent in the map. The selection amongst these strategies depends highly on the measurement of the deep features like *ispath*, *wallbarrierwidth* and *baseproximitydistance* since the concept of existence of path between player and opponent bases, wall of trees and separation distance of base are not expressed through shallow features like gold, lumber, trees, etc. Also the other deep features like *attacking-speed-of-troops* and *attacking-radius-of-troop-formation* are more relevant for attack strategy selection rather than for game strategy selection and hence are not be considered for beginning situation. Using the three deep features and all the shallow features in a weighted manner Darmok's Behavior Retriever searches the two plans and retrieves the plan for the rush strategy since the game state's similarity is found to be higher for the episodes of plan representing rush strategy.

If no deep features were used, Darmok would have difficulty identifying which strategy to pick. Moreover, if no situation assessment is used, and all the deep features are always used for retrieval, the time consumed to compute all the deep features would be prohibitive (as we will show in the next section).

7 Experimental Evaluation

In our evaluation we found out that the performance of plan retrieval applying situation assessment algorithm (Figure 3) is better compared to plan retrieval without the application of situation assessment by conducting three set of experiments as follows:

- Exp_1: Darmok performed plan retrieval without the situation assessment algorithm. Darmok used only the *shallow* features for computing similarity during the retrieval stage and no situation prediction was performed.
- Exp_2: Darmok performed plan retrieval without the situation assessment algorithm. Darmok used only the *deep* features for computing similarity during the retrieval stage and no situation prediction was performed.

– Exp_3: Darmok performed plan retrieval using the situation assessment algorithm. It used selected shallow and deep features for similarity computation during the retrieval stage.

The experiments Exp_1, Exp_2 and Exp_3 were conducted over 11 variations of the "Nowhere to run nowhere to hide" (NWTR) map (with a wall of trees separating the opponents that introduces a highly strategic component in the game) and over "Garden of War" (GOW) map (large map having lot of open spaces, with tree and gold resources in the middle). Darmok was tested with 10 different strategies with slight variations, demonstrated over 6 out of the 11 different maps. The 10 strategies demonstrated were variations of the *ranged attack* (ballistas attack over the wall of trees), *rush* (footmen are built and quickly sent to attack the opponents when there is a path betweem them), *tunneling* (footmen and knights are built and tunnel through the wall of trees to attack the opponent) and *towering* (towers are built around the wall of trees to block the enemy).

We conducted the experiments with 10 traces in the case-base (that gives a total of 52 behaviors and 52 episodes in the case base) over 5 runs of the game and measured the performance of Darmok's plan retrieval in Exp_1 and Exp_3 over the following parameters: 1) number of wins, 2) number of draws, 3) number of losses, 4) player's score assigned by WARGUS, and 5) opponent's score assigned by WARGUS. We also report the average retrieval time for each plan by Darmok. For our experiments, and in order to properly validate retrieval, and retrieval only, episode learning and structural plan adaptation were disabled in Darmok.

Tables 2 and 3 show the results of Exp_1 and Exp_3 respectively. The first column shows the map in which a game was played, the next three columns show the number of wins, draws and losses respectively. The last two columns show the scores of player and the opponent which are assigned by WARGUS. The bottom row of each table shows a summarized view of Darmok's win ratio and average score ratio, where the win ratio is the number of wins divided by the total number of games played and the average score ratio is the average score of the player divided by the opponent's average score. As seen, there is a clear improvement in the results of the game-play in Exp_3; with win ratio of 0.683 which is thrice better than win ratio of 0.233 in Exp_1. Also, the average

Table 2. Exp_1 results

map	win	draw	loss	player score	opponent score
NWTR1	1	0	4	1068	1331
NWTR2	3	1	1	2410	562
NWTR3	2	0	3	2094	1613
NWTR4	1	0	4	1964	1791
NWTR5	1	0	4	1296	1700
NWTR6	1	1	3	1652	1128
NWTR7	1	0	4	1016	2161
NWTR8	2	0	3	1418	1560
NWTR9	0	0	5	832	2643
NWTR10	0	0	5	406	1997
NWTR11	0	0	5	82	1507
GoW	2	0	3	756	626
Win Ratio	0.233			Average Score Ratio	0.81

Table 3. Exp_3 results

map	win	draw	loss	player score	opponent score
NWTR1	2	3	0	7136	1386
NWTR2	5	0	0	3000	24
NWTR3	5	0	0	1800	0
NWTR4	4	0	1	1180	388
NWTR5	2	0	3	1794	1505
NWTR6	5	0	0	2450	50
NWTR7	5	0	0	3100	94
NWTR8	0	0	5	1750	2790
NWTR9	5	0	0	3356	60
NWTR10	5	0	0	1410	50
NWTR11	0	0	5	4466	3601
GoW	3	1	1	1355	585
Win Ratio	**0.683**			Average Score Ratio	**3.12**

score ratio in case of Exp_3 is four times better than Exp_1 (i.e. 3.12 as compared to 0.81), which indicates that Darmok wins convincingly and even its losses are well-fought. Situation assessment through its results, thus, can be seen to increase the performance of plan retrieval. An interesting observation is that on maps NWTR3, NWTR6, NWTR7, NWTR10 for which the expert demonstrated strategies, Darmok won on all 5 occassions in Exp_3. For the same maps in Exp_1, Darmok had marginal success and even complete failure in case of map NWTR10. In general Darmok performs better using situation assessment over all the maps except NWTR8 and NWTR11. For the map NWTR8, Darmok's performance in Exp_1 is marginally better compared to the performance in Exp_3. Darmok's performance suffers on map NWTR11 even after correctly retrieving the plan, demonstrated for map NWTR11 by the expert, from the case-base since in adversarial non-deterministic domain like WARGUS there are lots of factors which can influence winning a game. On the map NWTR11, Darmok's win ratio is same in Exp_1 and Exp_3, however, using situation assessment improved the average score ratio in Exp_3.

Using selective deep features like *ispath*, *wallbarrierwidth*, etc. based on the situations certainly improved the similarity metric for proper retrieval. Experiments were also conducted to measure the average plan retrieval time in seconds with all the deep features as shown in Table 4. Exp_2 was simply not feasible and experiments couldn't be run, retrieval time was some times over a minute, completely inappropriate for the dynamic nature of WARGUS. Using situation assessment we managed to reduce the time to a few seconds, which is acceptable for the speed at which WARGUS is played (notice that retrieval is only executed a few times during game-play, and thus spending a few seconds on selecting the appropriate plan paid off, as shown above). Interestingly, it was observed that using all the deep features makes the system use lots of irrelevant information during plan retrieval and reduces the efficiency. It is therefore necessary to filter

Table 4. Average retrieval time (in seconds) for Exp_1, Exp_2 and Exp_3

	Exp_1	Exp_2	Exp_3
retrieval time	0.016	46.428	4.990

the deep features and select only the relevant ones. Also, Situation assessment reduced the retrieval time by ten times through use of situation relevant deep features. The above observations indicate that deep features improve the retrieval performance only if chosen appropriately.

In the experiments conducted, Darmok's score in Exp_3 increased to 0.683 compared to 0.233 in Exp_1. The retrieval times with application of the situation assessment algorithm are also acceptable for Darmok's real-time performance and clearly show that quality of plan retrieval has improved.

8   Conclusions

In this paper we have presented situation assessment technique for plan retrieval in real-time strategy games. Our technique is a knowledge based approach for feature selection for improving the performance of case retrieval in case-based reasoning systems. Situation assessment essentially involves two major steps before case retrieval: the generation of models for case-base size reduction and feature selection and then their execution to get the reduced size case-base and set of high information features for case selection. The main characteristics of our approach are a) the capability to perform a knowledge based feature selection rather than a feature by feature, b) the ability to perform search in the case-base in a fast and focused manner by reducing the search space to the set of relevant cases using computationally inexpensive features, c) the capability to resize the dimensions of similarity metric based on the high-level representation of the game state i.e. situations. We have implemented the situation assessment algorithm inside the Darmok system that plays the game of WARGUS. The experiments conducted using situation assessment show a great improvement of performance in the system.

The main contributions of our technique are: 1) introduction of a domain independent situation assessment algorithm that can be applied for knowledge based feature selection to any domain; 2) the idea of case-base size reduction during the search operation through Situation-Case mapping; 3) the introduction of the concept of a situation as a high-level game state representation for effective plan selection for game strategies; 4) the idea of selective similarity-metric resizing based on the game state situation.

As future lines of work, we plan to explore strategies to fully automate the situation assessment procedure. Currently, the Situation-Case and the Situation-Deepfeature models are empirically determined by hand. Also, the subset of situations is defined by hand. Automated techniques to generate such models will greatly increase the applicability of the approach.

References

1. Aha, D., Molineaux, M., Ponsen, M.: Learning to win: Case-based plan selection in a real-time strategy game. In: Muñoz-Ávila, H., Ricci, F. (eds.) ICCBR 2005. LNCS (LNAI), vol. 3620, pp. 5–20. Springer, Heidelberg (2005)

2. Arritt, R.P., Turner, R.M.: Situation assessment for autonomous underwater vehicles using a priori contextual knowledge. In: 13th International Symposium on Unmanned Untethered Submersible Technology (UUST) (2003)
3. Bergmann, R., Muñoz-Avila, H., Veloso, M.M., Melis, E.: Cbr applied to planning. In: Case-Based Reasoning Technology, pp. 169–200 (1998)
4. Blasch, E., Kadar, I., Salerno, J., Kokar, M.M., Das, S., Powell, G.M., Corkill, D.D., Ruspini, E.H.: Issues and challenges of knowledge representation and reasoning methods in situation assessment (level 2 fusion). In: Proc. SPIE vol. 6235 (2006)
5. Frank, E., Hall, M.A., Holmes, G., Kirkby, R., Pfahringer, B.: Weka - a machine learning workbench for data mining. In: The Data Mining and Knowledge Discovery Handbook, pp. 1305–1314 (2005)
6. Hall, M.A.: Correlation-based feature selection for discrete and numeric class machine learning. In: ICML, pp. 359–366 (2000)
7. Hall, M.A., Holmes, G.: Benchmarking attribute selection techniques for discrete class data mining. IEEE Trans. Knowl. Data Eng. 15(6), 1437–1447 (2003)
8. Hammond, K.F.: Case based planning: A framework for planning from experience. Cognitive Science 14(3), 385–443 (1990)
9. Kofod-Pedersen, A., Aamodt, A.: Case-based situation assessment in a mobile context-aware system. In: Artificial Intelligence in Mobile System (AIMS 2003), pp. 41–49 (2003)
10. Kolodner, J.: Case-based reasoning. Morgan Kaufmann, San Francisco (1993)
11. Ontañón, S., Mishra, K., Sugandh, N., Ram, A.: Case-based planning and execution for real-time strategy games. In: Weber, R.O., Richter, M.M. (eds.) ICCBR 2007. LNCS (LNAI), vol. 4626, pp. 164–178. Springer, Heidelberg (2007)
12. Sharma, M., Homes, M., Santamaria, J., Irani, A., Isbell, C., Ram, A.: Transfer learning in real time strategy games using hybrid CBR/RL. In: IJCAI 2007. Morgan Kaufmann, San Francisco (2007)
13. Spalazzi, L.: A survey on case-based planning. Artificial Intelligence Review 16(1), 3–36 (2001)
14. Yang, Y., Pedersen, J.O.: A comparative study on feature selection in text categorization. In: ICML, pp. 412–420 (1997)

Optimization Algorithms to Find Most Similar Deductive Consequences (MSDC)

Babak Mougouie[1,2]

[1] University of Trier
Department of Business Information Systems II
Trier, Germany
[2] DFKI GmbH, Knowledge Management Department
Kaiserslautern, Germany
mougouie@dfki.de

Abstract. Finding most similar deductive consequences, MSDC, is a new approach which builds a unified framework to integrate similarity-based and deductive reasoning. In this paper we introduce a new formulation $\mathcal{OP}$-MSDC(q) of MSDC which is a mixed integer optimization problem. Although mixed integer optimization problems are exponentially solvable in general, our experimental results show that $\mathcal{OP}$-MSDC(q) is surprisingly solved faster than previous heuristic algorithms. Based on this observation we expand our approach and propose optimization algorithms to find the k most similar deductive consequences k-MSDC.

1 Introduction

Logic-oriented approaches for knowledge representation and reasoning have a long tradition in AI. Well known are also the limitations of pure logic-oriented approaches for real-world problems that involve uncertain or vague knowledge, that handle imprecise situations, or that search for approximate solutions to a problem instead of exact ones. During the past 30 years several approaches have been developed that combine logics with some kind of "softer" forms of reasoning. Famous examples are the fuzzy logic or rough set theory.

Also in case-based reasoning (CBR) [1,3], deductive reasoning is often combined with reasoning based on similarity. In CBR, problems are solved by first retrieving cases with similar problems from a case base and then adapting the solutions in these cases such that a solution of the new problem is constructed. The latter step often involves deductive reasoning that makes use of general adaptation knowledge represented in a logic-oriented manner. Hence, CBR combines specific knowledge represented as cases with general knowledge, e.g. for adaptation.

While reasoning with cases is usually done in a similarity-based manner, general knowledge is often represented in rules, constraints, or ontology definitions and is often applied in a deductive reasoning process. Therefore, the question of combining specific and general knowledge is strongly connected with the question of combining logic-oriented (deductive) and approximate reasoning[5].

K.-D. Althoff et al. (Eds.): ECCBR 2008, LNAI 5239, pp. 370–384, 2008.

In our previous paper [2], we presented MSDC as a new way of combining deductive and approximate reasoning in a unified manner. In this approach the specific knowledge about cases, similarity measure and additional general knowledge are combined and represented as a logical domain theory Σ (cases are encoded as facts and general knowledge as logical sentences and possibly additional facts). Given a query q and a similarity measure, k-MSDC is the problem of finding the k most similar cases to q that can be deduced from Σ.

In this paper we introduce a new formulation $\mathcal{OP}$-MSDC(q) of MSDC which is a mixed integer optimization problem. Mixed integer optimization problems are exponentially solvable in general [6]. However our experimental results show that $\mathcal{OP}$-MSDC(q) is surprisingly faster than our previous heuristic algorithms in [2]. Based on this observation we provide an algorithm $\mathcal{OP}$-k-MSDC to find k-MSDC. Furthermore we use the result of $\mathcal{OP}$-1-MSDC to initialize a *minimum acceptable similarity*, Min_Acc_Sim, to prune the search space of our previous heuristic algorithms.

The paper is organized as follows. In sec. 2, we define k-MSDC, construct a state-space to find deductive consequences of a domain theory and represent the heuristic algorithm dfs_MAS to find the most similar deductive consequences. In sec. 3, we define the alternating tree of a domain theory which is used to construct $\mathcal{OP}$-MSDC(q) in sec. 4. Optimization algorithms and experimental results will be provided in sections 5 and 6.

2 Finding Similar Deductive Consequences

Based on a domain theory Σ in which all knowledge of the domain including cases are represented, we look for the most similar case $q' = p(t'_1, ..., t'_n)$ that can be deduced from Σ to a query $q = p(t_1, ..., t_n)$ ($t_1, ..., t_n, t'_1, ..., t'_n$ can be constants or variables) given a similarity measure $sim_p : AF_p \times AF_p \mapsto [0, 1]$ where AF_p is the set of all atomic formulas starting with the n-ary predicate symbol p.

A *deduction* $\mathcal{D}$ of q' from Σ is defined as a finite sequence $\langle l_1, l_2, ..., l_d = q' \rangle$ of literals such that for each $l_j \in \mathcal{D}$ there exists a substitution σ_j such that either l_j is a fact in Σ or $v_j :\text{-} v_{j_1}, ..., v_{j_m}$ is a rule in Σ and $l_j = \sigma_j(v_j)$, $l_{j_1} = \sigma_j(v_{j_1}), ..., l_{j_m} = \sigma_j(v_{j_m})$ for $j_1, ..., j_m < j$ and $l_{j_1}, ..., l_{j_m} \in \mathcal{D}$.

We further formalize the similarity measure following the local-global principle: $sim_p(q, q') = \Omega(sim_1(t_1, t'_1), ..., sim_n(t_n, t'_n))$ such that Ω is an aggregate function that is monotonous in every argument and $0 \leq sim_i(t_i, t'_i) \leq 1$ for $i = 1, ..., n$ are local similarities. For the sake of simplicity, let $sim = sim_p$.

In this paper we restrict Σ to Horn logic such that recursive deduction is not allowed. MSDC is defined as follows:

Definition 1. (Most Similar Deductive Consequences, MSDC, k-MSDC)
The most similar deductive consequence is defined as follows:

$$MSDC(q) = \underset{q' \in closure_p(\Sigma)}{\arg\max} \; sim(q, q')$$

where $q = p(t_1, \ldots, t_n)$ and $closure_p(\Sigma) = \{p(t'_1, \ldots, t'_n) \mid \Sigma \vdash p(t'_1, \ldots, t'_n)\}$ is the deductive closure of Σ restricted to atomic formulas starting with the n-ary predicate symbol p.

This can be easily extended to k-MSDC which delivers the k-most similar deductive consequences: $k\text{-}MSDC(q) = \{q_1, \ldots, q_k\} \subseteq closure_p(\Sigma)$ such that $sim(q, q') \leq \min\{sim(q, q_i) \mid i = 1, \ldots, k\}$ $\forall q' \in closure_p(\Sigma) - \{q_1, \ldots, q_k\}$.

Example 1. Consider the following domain theory Σ_1 denoted in traditional notation for Prolog (the terms in the parenthesis are indices of the clauses)[1]:

```
(R1)  q(X,Y) :- c(X,Y).
(R2)  q(X,Y) :- c(X1,Y1), a(X,Y,X1,Y1).
(F1)  c(2,5).
(F2)  c(8,9).
(R3)  a(X,Y,X1,Y1) :- b(X), D is X-X1, D>0, D<3, Y is Y1+X-X1.
(F3)  b(1).
(F4)  b(2).
        .
        .
        .
(F12) b(10).
(F13) c(3,4,5).
```

One can verify that $closure_q(\Sigma_1) = \{q(2,5), q(8,9), q(3,6),\ q(4,7),\ q(9,10),$ $q(10,11)\}$ such that
$\mathcal{D}_1 = \langle c(2,5), q(2,5) \rangle$
$\mathcal{D}_2 = \langle c(8,9), q(8,9) \rangle$
$\mathcal{D}_3 = \langle b(3), 1 \text{ is } 3 - 2, 1 > 0, 1 < 3, 6 \text{ is } 5 + 3 - 2, a(3,6,2,5), c(2,5), q(3,6) \rangle$
$\mathcal{D}_4 = \langle b(4), 2 \text{ is } 4 - 2, 2 > 0, 2 < 3, 7 \text{ is } 5 + 4 - 2, a(4,7,2,5), c(2,5), q(4,7) \rangle$
$\mathcal{D}_5 = \langle b(9), 1 \text{ is } 9 - 8, 1 > 0, 1 < 3, 10 \text{ is } 9 + 9 - 8, a(9,10,8,9), c(8,9), q(9,10) \rangle$
$\mathcal{D}_6 = \langle b(10), 2 \text{ is } 10-8, 2>0, 2 < 3, 11 \text{ is } 9+10-8, a(10,11,8,9), c(8,9), q(10,11) \rangle$
are the deductions of the elements of $closure_q(\Sigma_1)$ respectively.

For the query $q(5,8)$ and the similarity measure $sim(q(t_1, t_2), q(T_1, T_2)) = (2sim_1(t_1, T_1) + 3sim_2(t_2, T_2))/5$ such that $sim_1(t_1, T_1) = 1 - (|t_1 - T_1|/10)$ and $sim_2(t_2, T_2) = 1 - (|t_2 - T_2|/7)$, it can be shown that $MSDC(q(5,8)) = q(4,7)$ and $sim((q(5,8), q(4,7)) \approx 0.874$. $\qquad\square$

2.1   State-Space Search and dfs_MAS

In [2], we transformed the problem of finding the elements of $closure_p(\Sigma)$ to a state-space search problem. The state-space $\mathcal{T}$ is such constructed that each state of $\mathcal{T}$ differs from its successor in one resolution step:

1. Set $(\langle q^* \rangle, q^*)$ with $q^* = p(T_1, \ldots, T_n)$ be the starting state of $\mathcal{T}$
   /* T_i are some new variables */
2. Let $\mathcal{S} = (\langle q_1, \ldots, q_d \rangle, \bar{q})$ be a state of $\mathcal{T}$;
   For all q_i $(i = 1, \ldots, d)$ do {

---

[1] In this paper, we provide a chain of examples to explain the procedure of constructing $\mathcal{OP}\text{-}MSDC(q)$ and let Σ_1 be known in all of them.

2.1. For each substitution σ such that $\sigma(q_i) \in \Sigma$
   (**trim** $(\langle \sigma(q_1), \ldots, \sigma(q_{i-1}), \sigma(q_{i+1}), \ldots, \sigma(q_d) \rangle), \sigma(\bar{q}))$
   is a direct successor state of $\mathcal{S}$;   /* Resolution with a fact*/
2.2. For each substitution σ such that $\sigma(q_i) = \sigma(r)$ for $r :\text{-} r_1, \ldots, r_m \in \Sigma$
   (**trim** $(\langle \sigma(q_1), \ldots, \sigma(q_{i-1}), \sigma(r_1), \ldots, \sigma(r_m), \sigma(q_{i+1}), \ldots, \sigma(q_d) \rangle), \sigma(\bar{q}))$
   is a direct successor state of $\mathcal{S}$;   /* Resolution with a rule*/ }.
trim$(list)$\{Delete each $q_i \in list$ from $list$ if it is a true built-in predicate\}.

$\mathcal{T}$ is constructed by iteratively applying step 2. of the above procedure. Final states of the form $(\langle \rangle, q')$ are elements of $closure_p(\Sigma)$ and it holds $\exists \sigma$ s.t. $\sigma(q^*) = q'$. Final states that are not of this form are search branches not leading to a logical consequence of Σ.

We assume Σ contains no recursion therefore $closure_p(\Sigma)$ has a finite number of elements. Even under this assumption, $\mathcal{T}$ might have a huge number of states. Since it is expensive to exhaustively explore the entire $\mathcal{T}$ (for instance by a depth first search (dfs)) to deliver the optimal $k\text{-}MSDC(q)$, we provided heuristic algorithms to prune the state-space in [2].

Below we recall the approximative algorithm dfs_MAS which surprisingly had the best performance, in terms of computation time and similarity error, among the developed heuristic algorithms.

dfs_MAS. This algorithm is a kind of dfs algorithm that cuts the state-space at the cost of not assuring to finding the optimal solution of k-MSDC. It ideally finds up to k solutions with a similarity higher than a minimum acceptable similarity Min_Acc_Sim. We run **dfs_MAS**$(q, \mathcal{S}, k\text{-}MSDC, k, Min\_Acc\_Sim)$ such that $\mathcal{S}$ is initiated to $(\langle q^* \rangle, q^*)$ with $q^* = p(T_1, \ldots, T_n)$ and $k\text{-}MSDC$ is an empty list:

dfs_MAS(query q, state $\mathcal{S}$, list $k\text{-}MSDC$, int k, int Min_Acc_Sim)\{
   If **length**$(k\text{-}MSDC) = k$ **stop**;
   If $\mathcal{S} = (\langle \rangle, q')$ and $sim(q, q') \geq Min\_Acc\_Sim$ then **append**$(q', k\text{-}MSDC)$
   else for all direct successors $\mathcal{S}'$ of $\mathcal{S}$ run **dfs_MAS**$(q, \mathcal{S}', k\text{-}MSDC, k)$;\}

dfs_MAS achieved a good performance in [2] because we set Min_Acc_Sim very close to the real similarity $sim(q, MSDC(q))$ found by a complete dfs in advance. dfs_MAS turns out to be very weak if Min_Acc_Sim is initialized using a faster but inaccurate algorithm such as *hill climbing*(hc). To have a fast and good approximation of Min_Acc_Sim, we developed $\mathcal{OP}$-MSDC(q) which is constructed from the alternating tree of a domain theory Σ for a query.

3   Alternating Tree of Σ

A useful picture of deductions from a domain theory Σ is a tree of deductions rather than just some sequences. We call this tree the *alternating tree* $G_{q^*}(\Sigma) = (\mathcal{N}, \mathcal{E})$ of Σ for a query $q^* = p(T_1, \ldots, T_n)$ such that $T_1, \ldots, T_n$ are some variables. $G_{q^*}(\Sigma)$ is a labeled directed tree consisting of:

- a set $\mathcal{N} = \langle l_1, l_2, ..., l_\beta, s \rangle$ of nodes such that s is a dummy node and for each node l_i, $i = 1, ..., \beta$, there exists a substitution σ_i such that $l_i = \sigma_i(l_i')$ and l_i' is a literal of a fact or rule of Σ,
- a set $\mathcal{E}$ of edges such that $e = [l_i, l_j]^R \in \mathcal{E}$ is a directed edge from l_i to l_j labeled with a label R.

Additionally $G_{q^*}(\Sigma)$ has the following properties:

1) $G_{q^*}(\Sigma)$ is a tree with finite number of nodes and edges. A domain theory Σ which allows no recursion has $G_{q^*}(\Sigma)$ with finite number of nodes and edges.

2) There exist disjoint sets of edges $[l, l_1']^{R_1}, ..., [l, l_f']^{R_f} \in \mathcal{E}$ that are *extensionally clustered* such that $l_i' = p'(T_1^i, ..., T_m^i)$ for $i = 1, ..., f$ in which $T_1^i, ..., T_m^i$ are constants or variables and p' is an m-ary predicate symbol.

In sec. 3.1, we construct *subtrees* of $G_{q^*}(\Sigma)$ using the above clusters (each subtree contains at most one edge $[l, l_\gamma']^{R\gamma}$ from each cluster). Additionally we show a subtree is either *valid* or *invalid* and for each valid subtree $\langle l_1, l_2, ..., l_d \rangle$ there exists a unique substitution $\bar{\sigma}$ such that $\langle \bar{\sigma}(l_1), ..., \bar{\sigma}(l_d) = \bar{\sigma}(q^*) \rangle$ is a deduction of $\bar{\sigma}(q^*)$ from Σ.

We construct $G_{q^*}(\Sigma)$ by indexing the rules and facts of Σ, initially setting $\mathcal{N}$ to $\langle s \rangle$ and $\mathcal{E}$ to empty set and calling **Generate_alternating_tree** $(s, q^*, -)$.

Generate_alternating_tree(literal l, literal l', label R){

If l' is a built-in predicate then {**insert**$(l', \mathcal{N})$; **insert**$([l, l']^R, \mathcal{E})$}

else{ Find all literals $\sigma_1(l'), ..., \sigma_f(l')$ such that σ_i is a substitution and either $\sigma_i(l')$ is a fact in Σ or $\sigma_i(l') = \sigma_i(r^i)$ for $r^i \text{ :- } r_1^i, ..., r_m^i \in \Sigma$;

For $(i = 1, ..., f)$ {

insert$(\sigma_i(l'), \mathcal{N})$;

Let RF_i be the index of the fact $\sigma_i(l')$ or the rule $r^i \text{ :- } r_1^i, ..., r_m^i$;

If $l = s$ then $e_i = [l, \sigma_i(l')]^{RF_i}$ else $e_i = [l, \sigma_i(l')]^{R,RF_i}$;

insert$(e_i, \mathcal{E})$;

If RF_i is the index of the rule $r^i \text{ :- } r_1^i, ..., r_m^i$ then

For $(j = 1, ..., m)${**Generate_alternating_tree** $(\sigma_i(r^i), \sigma_i(r_j^i), RF_i)$};}

Cluster the edges $e_1, ..., e_f$;}}.

Example 2. $G_{q^*}(\Sigma_1)$ is shown in Fig. 1. in which the clustered edges are connected with a dashed-line together.   □

Definition 2. (Binding): *Let* $[l, \sigma(l')]^R \in G_{q^*}(\Sigma)$. *In the course of the algorithm* **Generate_alternating_tree**, *let* l' *be a literal of the form* $p'(T_1, ..., T_m)$ *and* $\sigma(l') = p'(T_1, ..., T_{i-1}, t_i, T_{i+1}, T_m)$ *be a generated node such that* t_i *is a constant. We say* $\sigma(l')$ *binds* T_i *to* t_i.

3.1   Subtrees of $G_{q^*}(\Sigma)$

In this section we construct the subtrees of $G_{q^*}(\Sigma)$. Before we explain this, let's suppose that $G_{q^*}(\Sigma)$ of a domain theory Σ has no extensionally clustered edges. It means for each literal l' in Σ there exists at most one fact $\sigma(l')$ or rule with head literal r (where $\sigma(l') = \sigma(r)$) in Σ such that σ is a substitution. Consequently, it can be shown that $closure_p(\Sigma)$ has at most one element.

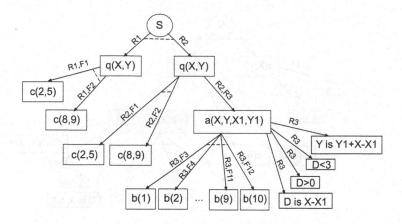

Fig. 1. The alternating tree $G_{q^*}(\Sigma_1)$

A domain theory Σ does not have the above property in general. However since finding deductions from Σ can be reduced to finding subsets $\bar{\Sigma}_i$ of Σ with this property, we construct subtrees of $G_{q^*}(\Sigma)$ which are nothing else but graphical representations of $\bar{\Sigma}_i$. Formally speaking, $\bar{\Sigma}_i$ is a domain theory consisting of a subset of facts and rules of Σ such that for $l = q^*$ the statement 1. holds.

1. There exists exactly one fact $\sigma(l)$ or rule with head literal r (where $\sigma(l) = \sigma(r)$) in $\bar{\Sigma}_i$ such that σ is a substitution. If r is a head literal of a rule R then the statement 2. holds.
2. Let r :- $r_1, ..., r_m$ be a rule in $\bar{\Sigma}_i$ labeled with R. The statement 1. holds for all $l = r_1, ..., r_m$ which are not built-in predicates.

Consequently, we can derive that $closure_p(\bar{\Sigma}_i)$ contains at most one element.

Now if we construct all such possible domain theories $\bar{\Sigma}_i$, we can find the elements of the deductive closure of Σ from some of the constructed domain theories (there might exist a domain theory $\bar{\Sigma}_j$ such that $closure_p(\bar{\Sigma}_j) = \emptyset$).

Definition 3. *(Subtree):* *A subtree of $G_{q^*}(\Sigma)$ is a subset of the nodes and edges of $G_{q^*}(\Sigma)$ constructed as follows: delete s and for each set of extensionally clustered edges $[l, l_1]^{R_1}, ..., [l, l_f]^{R_f} \in \mathcal{N}$, keep one node l_δ for $1 \leq \delta \leq f$ and prune[2] l' for all $l' \in \{l_1, ..., l_f\}\backslash l_\delta$ from $G_{q^*}(\Sigma)$.*
All such permutations give the set of the subtrees of $G_{q^*}(\Sigma)$.

Example 3. The subtrees of $G_{q^*}(\Sigma_1)$ are:
$\mathcal{V}_1 = \langle c(2,5), q(X,Y)\rangle$
$\mathcal{V}_2 = \langle c(8,9), q(X,Y)\rangle$
$\mathcal{V}_3 = \langle b(1), BI, a(X,Y,X1,Y1), c(2,5), q(X,Y)\rangle$
$\vdots$

---

[2] We prune $l' \in G_{q^*}(\Sigma)$ by deleting l', all its successors l'' and the edges connecting l' to l''.

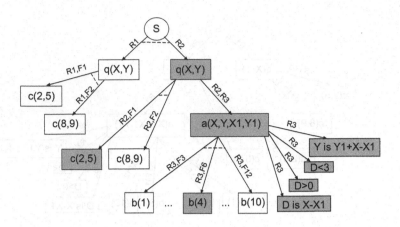

Fig. 2. The subtree $\mathcal{V}_6$ of $G_{q^*}(\Sigma_1)$

$\mathcal{V}_{21} = \langle b(9), BI, a(X,Y,X1,Y1), c(8,9), q(X,Y)\rangle$
$\mathcal{V}_{22} = \langle b(10), BI, a(X,Y,X1,Y1), c(8,9), q(X,Y)\rangle$
such that $BI = D$ is $X - X1, D > 0, D < 3, Y$ is $Y1 + X - X1^3$.

Fig. 2. shows $G_{q^*}(\Sigma_1)$ in which the subtree $\mathcal{V}_6$ is colored gray.

$\mathcal{V}_6$ is the graphical representation of the following domain theory $\bar{\Sigma}_1$:

    (R2)   q(X,Y) :- c(X1,Y1), a(X,Y,X1,Y1).
    (F1)   c(2,5).
    (R3)   a(X,Y,X1,Y1) :- b(X), D is X-X1, D>0, D<3, Y is Y1+X-X1.
    (F6)   b(4).   □

It can be proven that each subtree of $G_{q^*}(\Sigma)$ gives a subset of the facts and rules of Σ which constructs a domain theory $\bar{\Sigma}$ such that for every query $\bar{q}$, if $\bar{\Sigma} \vdash \bar{\sigma}(\bar{q})$ then the substitution $\bar{\sigma}$ is unique. Furthermore

Lemma 1. *Let* $\mathcal{V} = \langle l_1, l_2, ..., l_d\rangle$ *be a subtree of* $G_{q^*}(\Sigma)$. *Then there exists a unique substitution* $\bar{\sigma}$ *such that either* $\bar{\mathcal{V}} = \langle \bar{\sigma}(l_1), ..., \bar{\sigma}(l_d)\rangle$ *is a deduction of* q^* *from* Σ *or at least one literal* $\bar{\sigma}(l_j)$ *for* $j = 1, ..., d$ *fails.* □

Example 4. Consider Σ_1 and its subtrees $\mathcal{V}_i$ in *Example 3*. There exist unique substitutions $\bar{\sigma}_i$ such that $\bar{\mathcal{V}}_i = \bar{\sigma}_i(\mathcal{V}_i)$ and:

$\bar{\mathcal{V}}_1 = \langle c(2,5), q(2,5)\rangle$
$\bar{\mathcal{V}}_2 = \langle c(8,9), q(8,9)\rangle$
$\bar{\mathcal{V}}_3 = \langle b(1), -1$ is $1-2, -1 > 0, -1 < 3, 4$ is $5+1-2, a(1,4,2,5), c(2,5), q(1,4)\rangle$
$\vdots$

---

[3] We have represented a subtree $\mathcal{V}$ in form of a list of nodes $\langle l_1, l_2, ..., l_d\rangle$. This is unambiguous since for each two nodes $l, l' \in \mathcal{V}$, if $[l, l']^R \in G_{q^*}(\Sigma)$ then $[l, l']^R \in \mathcal{V}$. This means we can obtain the edges of a subtree by having its nodes and $G_{q^*}(\Sigma)$.

$\bar{\mathcal{V}}_{21} = \langle b(9), 1 \text{ is } 9-8, 1 > 0, 1 < 3, 10 \text{ is } 9+9-8, a(9,10,8,9), c(8,9), q(9,10) \rangle$
$\bar{\mathcal{V}}_{22} = \langle b(10), 2 \text{ is } 10-8, 2>0, 2<3, 11 \text{ is } 9+10-8, a(10,11,8,9), c(8,9), q(10,11) \rangle$.

For example $\bar{\mathcal{V}}_1 = \bar{\sigma}_1(\mathcal{V}_1)$ such that $\bar{\sigma}_1 = \{2/X, 5/Y\}$ and $\bar{\mathcal{V}}_{22} = \bar{\sigma}_{22}(\mathcal{V}_{22})$ such that $\bar{\sigma}_{22} = \{10/X, 11/Y, 8/X1, 9/Y1, D/2\}$.

$\bar{\mathcal{V}}_1, \bar{\mathcal{V}}_2, \bar{\mathcal{V}}_5, \bar{\mathcal{V}}_6, \bar{\mathcal{V}}_{21}, \bar{\mathcal{V}}_{22}$ are equal to $\mathcal{D}_1, ..., \mathcal{D}_6$ represented in *Example 1*. respectively. $\mathcal{V}_1, \mathcal{V}_2, \mathcal{V}_5, \mathcal{V}_6, \mathcal{V}_{21}$ and $\mathcal{V}_{22}$ are valid subtrees and the rest are invalid subtrees of $G_{q^*}(\Sigma_1)$. One can verify that for each invalid subtree $\mathcal{V}_i$, $\bar{\mathcal{V}}_i$ contains one built-in predicate which fails. For example $\bar{\mathcal{V}}_3$ contains $-1 > 0$. □

Definition 4. (Valid and Invalid Subtree of $G_{q^*}(\Sigma)$): $\mathcal{V}$ is a valid *subtree* of $G_{q^*}(\Sigma)$ iff $\bar{\mathcal{V}}$ is a deduction of $\bar{\sigma}(q^*)$ from Σ. $\mathcal{V}$ is invalid *otherwise.*

4   Optimization Problems

One way to obtain the subtrees of $G_{q^*}(\Sigma)$ is to solve the *optimization problem*:

$$\mathcal{OP}\text{-}\mathcal{T} = \max\ x(s)$$
$$\text{s.t. } h(x(s), x(l_1), ..., x(l_\beta)) = 0$$
$$x(l_i) \in \{0, 1\} \qquad \forall i = 1, ..., \beta$$

such that $x(s), x(l_1), ..., x(l_\beta)$ are some 0-1 variables assigned to the nodes s, $l_1, ..., l_\beta$ of $G_{q^*}(\Sigma)$ respectively. Besides $h(x(s), x(l_1), ..., x(l_\beta)) = 0$ is a set of *assignment constraints* that assigns each solution $\overrightarrow{X} = (x(l_1), ..., x(l_\beta))$ of $\mathcal{OP}\text{-}\mathcal{T}$ to a subtree $\mathcal{V} = \langle ..., l_i, ... \rangle$ of $G_{q^*}(\Sigma)$ such that $l_i \in \mathcal{V}$ iff $x(l_i) = 1$ and $l_i \notin \mathcal{V}$ otherwise. $h(x(s), x(l_1), ..., x(l_\beta)) = 0$ is generated as follows:

Generate_Assignment_Constraints{
    Set $x(s) = 1$;
    For each set of extensionally clustered edges $[l, l_1]^{R_1}, ..., [l, l_f]^{R_f} \in G_{q^*}(\Sigma)$
        {generate the assignment constraint: $x(l_{1_{R_1}}) + ... + x(l_{f_{R_f}}) = x(l)$;}
    For all other edges $[l, l']^{R'}$ in $G_{q^*}(\Sigma)$ (such that $[r, l]^R$ in $G_{q^*}(\Sigma)$)
        {generate the assignment constraint: $x(l_R) = x(l'_{R'})$;}}.

Example 5. Assign each node $l' \in G_{q^*}(\Sigma_1)$ to the 0-1 variables:

- $x(p_{R,RF})$ if $l' = p(T_1, ..., T_m)$ and $[l, l']^{R,RF} \in G_{q^*}(\Sigma_1)$,
- $x(p_R)$ if $l' = p(T_1, ..., T_n)$ and $[s, l']^R \in G_{q^*}(\Sigma_1)$,
- $x(bi(X_1, ..., X_r))$ if $l' = bi(X_1, ..., X_r)$ is a built-in predicate.

The set of the generated assignment constraints is:
$$x(q_{R1}) + x(q_{R2}) = x(s) = 1;$$
$$x(c_{R1,F1}) + x(c_{R1,F2}) = x(q_{R1});$$
$$x(c_{R2,F1}) + x(c_{R2,F2}) = x(q_{R2});$$

$$x(a_{R2,R3}) = x(q_{R2});$$
$$x(b_{R3,F3}) + ... + x(b_{R3,F12}) = x(a_{R2,R3});$$
$$x(D \text{ is } X - X1) = x(a_{R2,R3});$$
$$x(D > 0) = x(a_{R2,R3});$$
$$x(D < 3) = x(a_{R2,R3});$$
$$x(Y \text{ is } Y1 + X - X1) = x(a_{R2,R3});$$

One can verify that the generated $\mathcal{OP}\text{-}\mathcal{T}$ has 22 solutions. For example:

$\vec{X}_1 = (x(q_{R1}) = 1, x(c_{R1,F1}) = 1, 0, ..., 0),$

$\vec{X}_2 = (x(q_{R2}) = 1, x(c_{R2,F2}) = 1, x(a_{R2,R3}) = 1, x(b_{R3,F12}) = 1, x(D \text{ is } X - X1)$
$\qquad = 1, x(D > 0) = 1, x(D < 3) = 1, x(Y \text{ is } Y1 + X - X1) = 1, 0, ..., 0),$

$\vec{X}_3 = (x(q_{R2}) = 1, x(c_{R2,F1}) = 1, x(a_{R2,R3}) = 1, x(b_{R3,F3}) = 1, x(D \text{ is } X - X1)$
$\qquad = 1, x(D > 0) = 1, x(D < 3) = 1, x(Y \text{ is } Y1 + X - X1) = 1, 0, ..., 0)$

are some of the solutions of $\mathcal{OP}\text{-}\mathcal{T}$. □

Note 1. The notation used to show the solutions $\vec{X}_1$, $\vec{X}_2$ and $\vec{X}_3$ in *Example 5.* is a standard optimization notation. In this notation, the variables of a solution are sorted so that the ones equal to 1 are on the left hand side of the ones equal to 0. For example $\vec{X}_1 = (x(q_{R1}) = 1, x(c_{R1,F1}) = 1, 0, ..., 0)$ means the variables $x(q_{R1})$ and $x(c_{R1,F1})$ are equal 1 and the rest are equal to 0. □

Lemma 2. *Let a solution $\vec{X} \in \mathcal{OP}\text{-}\mathcal{T}$ be assigned to a set of nodes $\mathcal{V}$. Then $\mathcal{V}$ can be sorted so that it is a subtree of $G_{q^*}(\Sigma)$.*

Example 6. It can be verified that the solutions $\vec{X}_1$, $\vec{X}_2$, $\vec{X}_3$ in *Example 5.* are assigned to the subtrees $\mathcal{V}_1, \mathcal{V}_{22}, \mathcal{V}_3$ in *Example 3.* respectively. □

Pruning Constraints. In order to retrieve only solutions assigned to valid subtrees of $G_{q^*}(\Sigma)$, we add some *pruning constraints* $h'(x(l_1), ..., x(l_\beta)) \leq 0$ to $\mathcal{OP}\text{-}\mathcal{T}$ which give the new 0-1 optimization problem $\mathcal{OP}\text{-}\mathcal{VT}$.

For each built-in predicate $bi(T_1, ..., T_r)$ of a subtree $\mathcal{V}$ of $G_{q^*}(\Sigma)$ let the nodes $l_1, ..., l_m \in \bar{\mathcal{V}}$ bind $T_1, ..., T_r$ to $t_1, ..., t_r$. If $bi(t_1, ..., t_r)$ fails then

$$x(l_1) + ... + x(l_m) \leq m - 1 \qquad (1)$$

is a pruning constraint assuming that Σ is a well-defined domain theory.

Definition 5. (Well-Defined Domain Theory): *Let a domain theory Σ and a query q^* be given. For each variable X of a literal of Σ, let $l'_1, ..., l'_f$ be all non built-in predicates that bind X. Σ is well-defined iff $[l, l'_1]^{R_1}, ..., [l, l'_f]^{R_f}$ are extensionally clustered in $G_{q^*}(\Sigma)$.*

Note 2. We can directly derive from the above definition that for a well-defined domain theory Σ, whenever $\mathcal{V}$ is an invalid subtree of $G_{q^*}(\Sigma)$, then only built-in predicates of $\bar{\mathcal{V}}$ fail.

We will provide examples of well-defined domain theories in [4] and show that this property is not a restriction on a domain theory. □

Example 7. Consider $G_{q^*}(\Sigma_1)$ and its invalid subtrees presented in *Example 4*. We construct the following pruning constraints:

$$x(c_{R2,F1}) + x(b_{R3,F3}) \leq 1 \quad \text{prunes the solution assigned to } \mathcal{V}_3$$
$$x(c_{R2,F1}) + x(b_{R3,F4}) \leq 1 \qquad " \qquad\qquad\qquad \mathcal{V}_4$$
$$x(c_{R2,F1}) + x(b_{R3,F7}) \leq 1 \qquad " \qquad\qquad\qquad \mathcal{V}_7$$
$$x(c_{R2,F1}) + x(b_{R3,F8}) \leq 1 \qquad " \qquad\qquad\qquad \mathcal{V}_8$$
$$\vdots$$
$$x(c_{R2,F2}) + x(b_{R3,F9}) \leq 1 \qquad " \qquad\qquad\qquad \mathcal{V}_{19}$$
$$x(c_{R2,F2}) + x(b_{R3,F10}) \leq 1 \qquad " \qquad\qquad\qquad \mathcal{V}_{20}$$

$\square$

Up to now, given a domain theory Σ and a query q^*, we have constructed $\mathcal{OP}$-$\mathcal{VT}$ which gives the solutions assigned to valid subtrees of $G_{q^*}(\Sigma)$. Now we can add some similarity functions to $\mathcal{OP}$-$\mathcal{VT}$ to construct $\mathcal{OP}$-MSDC(q).

4.1 $\mathcal{OP}$-MSDC(q)

Let a domain theory Σ, an instantiated query $q = p(t_1,...,t_n)$ and $q^* = p(T_1,...,T_n)$ be given such that $t_1,...,t_n$ are either real numbers or variables and $T_1,...,T_n$ are variables. Additionally let the following be given:

- the similarity measure $sim(q,q^*) = \sum_{j=1}^{n} w_j sim_j(t_j, T_j) / \sum_{j=1}^{n} w_j$,
- the local similarities: $0 \leq sim_j(t_j, T_j) = 1 - |t_j - T_j|/n_j \leq 1$ and $sim_j(t_j, T_j) = 1$ if t_j is a variable,
- $w_j \geq 0$ and $n_j \geq \max|t_j - T_j|$ for all possible values of t_j and T_j.

We transform the above similarity measure to some similarity functions and add them to $\mathcal{OP}$-$\mathcal{VT}$ to construct $\mathcal{OP}$-MSDC(q). $\mathcal{OP}$-MSDC(q) is also an optimization problem in which 0-1 variables are assigned to the nodes of $G_{q^*}(\Sigma)$ and each solution $\overrightarrow{X} \in \mathcal{OP}$-MSDC($q$) is assigned to a valid subtree of $G_{q^*}(\Sigma)$. With the new similarity functions, the *optimal solution* of $\mathcal{OP}$-MSDC(q) is assigned to a valid subtree $\mathcal{D}^* = \langle l_1,...,l_d \rangle$ such that $\bar{D}^* = \langle \bar{\sigma}(l_1),...,\bar{\sigma}(l_d) \rangle$ and $MSDC(q) = \bar{\sigma}(l_d)$. $\mathcal{OP}$-MSDC(q) is formalized as follows:

$$\mathcal{OP}\text{-MSDC}(q) = \max SIM$$
$$\text{s.t. } h(\overrightarrow{X}) \leq 0$$
$$SIM \leq \sum_{j=1}^{n} w_j SIM_j / \sum_{j=1}^{n} w_j$$
$$SIM_j \leq 1 - (t_j - T_j)/n_j \qquad \forall j = 1,...,n$$
$$SIM_j \leq 1 - (T_j - t_j)/n_j \qquad "$$
$$T_j = \sum_{i=1}^{\beta_j} \tau_i^j x(l_i^j) \qquad "$$
$$SIM, SIM_j, T_j \in \mathbb{R} \qquad "$$
$$x(l_i^j) \in \{0,1\} \qquad \forall l_i^j \in G_{q^*}(\Sigma)$$

such that

- $h(\overrightarrow{X}) \leq 0$ is the set of assignment and pruning constraints generated in previous section,
- each 0-1 variable $x(l_i^j)$ is assigned to a node $l_i^j \in G_{q^*}(\Sigma)$,

- $q = p(t_1, ..., t_n)$ such that $t_1, ..., t_n$ are the same real numbers or variables in both MSDC and $\mathcal{OP}$-MSDC(q),
- $q^* = p(T_1, ..., T_n)$ such that $T_1, ..., T_n$ are the same real variables in both MSDC and $\mathcal{OP}$-MSDC(q). Besides $l_1^j, ..., l_{\beta_j}^j$ are all nodes that bind T_j to real numbers $\tau_1^j, ..., \tau_{\beta_j}^j$ respectively for $j = 1, ..., n$,
- SIM, SIM_j are some real variables for $j = 1, ..., n$.

By solving $\mathcal{OP}$-MSDC(q)

- the variables $x(l_i^j)$ will be set to 0 or 1. If $x(l_i^j) = 1$ then $l_i^j \in \mathcal{D}^*$ and $x(l_i^j) = 0$ otherwise.
- T_j is set to τ_j such that $\tau_j \in \{\tau_1^j, ..., \tau_{\beta_j}^j\}$ for $j = 1, ..., n$. We call $q' = p(\tau_1, ..., \tau_n)$ the *optimal deductive consequence* of $\mathcal{OP}$-MSDC(q).
- SIM_j is equal to $sim_j(t_j, \tau_j)$ for $j = 1, ..., n$.
- $SIM^*(\mathcal{OP}$-MSDC(q)) = $sim(q, MSDC(q))$ is the *optimal objective value* of $\mathcal{OP}$-MSDC(q).

In the following section, we construct the constraints $T_j = \sum_{i=1}^{\beta_j} \tau_i^j x(l_i^j)$ for $j = 1, ..., n$ which we call T_j_Constraints.

4.2 T_j_Constraints

In a well-defined domain theory, a variable T_j of the query $q^* = p(T_1, ..., T_n)$ is either bound by some nodes of $G_{q^*}(\Sigma)$ with a substitution or determined by arithmetic built-in predicates. Therefore for each of the above cases, we provide a different algorithm to generate T_j_Constraints.

1) T_j **Bound with Substitution:** Let T_j be bound by some nodes of $G_{q^*}(\Sigma)$ with a substitution. T_j_Constraints are then generated by calling the algorithm **Generate_T_j_Constraint**(q^*, T_j) for $j = 1, ..., n$:

Generate_T_j_Constraint(literal $p(T_1, ..., T_n)$, variable T_j){
    Find all nodes $l_i^j \in G_{q^*}(\Sigma)$ that bind T_j to a real number τ_i^j for $i = 1, ..., \beta_j$
    and add $T_j = \sum_{i=1}^{\beta_j} \tau_i^j x(l_i^j)$ to $\mathcal{OP}$-MSDC(q).
}.

2) T_j **Determined by Arithmetic Built-in Predicates:** Sometimes the values of T_j in a domain theory are determined by arithmetic built-in predicates. For example the arithmetic built-in predicate Y is Y1 + X - X1 gives the value of the variable Y in Σ_1. Therefore we need to generate an arithmetic function $Y = Y_1 + X - X_1$ to calculate the values of the real variable Y in $\mathcal{OP}$-MSDC(q). Furthermore T_j_Constraints for Y_1, X, X_1 should be generated. This is done by the following version of the algorithm **Generate_T_j_Constraint**:

Generate_T_j_Constraint(literal $p(T_1, ..., T_n)$, variable T_j){
    - Find all nodes $l_i^j \in G_{q^*}(\Sigma)$ that bind T_j to a real number τ_i^j for $i = 1, ..., \beta_j$.

- Find all nodes $\sigma(l_k'^j) \in G_{q*}(\Sigma)$ for $k = 1, ..., \gamma_j$ such that $l_k'^j :\text{-} ..., f_k(T_j,$
  $T_{k_1}^j, ..., T_{k_r}^j)$ is a rule in Σ and $f_k(T_j, T_{k_1}^j, ..., T_{k_r}^j)$ is an arithmetic built-in
  predicate with variables $T_{k_1}^j, ..., T_{k_r}^j$ which calculates the values of T_j.
- Add the constraint $T_j = \sum_{i=1}^{\beta_j} \tau_i^j x(l_i^j) + \sum_{k=1}^{\gamma_j} \bar{T}_k^j x(l_k'^j)$ to $\mathcal{OP}$-MSDC(q)
  such that $\bar{T}_1^j, ..., \bar{T}_{\gamma_j}^j$ are some new real variables.
- For $(k = 1, ..., \gamma_j)$ construct an arithmetic function $f_k(\bar{T}_k^j, T_{k_1}^j, ..., T_{k_r}^j)$ and
  add it to $\mathcal{OP}$-MSDC(q) (we assume that there exists a procedure performing
  such a construction for built-in predicates of the domain theory).
- For $(i = k_1, ..., k_r)$ **Generate_T_j_Constraint**$(f_k(\bar{T}_k^j, T_{k_1}^j, ..., T_{k_r}^j), \bar{T}_i^j).\}$.

Example 8. Given $G_{q*}(\Sigma_1)$ and the similarity measure of *Example 1.*, the similarity function and T_j constraints:

$SIM \leq (2SIM_1 + 3SIM_2)/5;$
$SIM_1 \leq 1 - (5 - T_1)/10;$
$SIM_1 \leq 1 - (T_1 - 5)/10;$
$SIM_2 \leq 1 - (8 - T_2)/7;$
$SIM_2 \leq 1 - (T_2 - 8)/7;$
$T_1 = 2x(c_{R1,F1}) + 8x(c_{R1,F2}) + 1x(c_{R3,F3}) + 2x(c_{R3,F4}) +$
$\qquad 3x(b_{R3,F5}) + 4x(b_{R3,F6}) + 5x(b_{R3,F7}) + 6x(b_{R3,F8}) +$
$\qquad 7x(b_{R3,F9}) + 8x(b_{R3,F10}) + 9x(b_{R3,F11}) + 10x(b_{F12,R3});$
$T_2 = 5x(c_{R1,F1}) + 9x(c_{R1,F2}) + \bar{T}^2 x(a_{R2,R3});$
$\bar{T}^2 = Y_1 + X - X_1;$
$Y_1 = 5x(c_{R1,F1}) + 9x(c_{R1,F2});$
$X = 1x(c_{R3,F3}) + 2x(c_{R3,F4}) + 3x(b_{R3,F5}) + 4x(b_{R3,F6}) + 5x(b_{R3,F7}) +$
$\qquad 6x(b_{R3,F8}) + 7x(b_{R3,F9}) + 8x(b_{R3,F10}) + 9x(b_{R3,F11}) + 10x(b_{F12,R3});$
$X_1 = 2x(c_{R1,F1}) + 8x(c_{R1,F2});$
$SIM, SIM_1, SIM_2, T_1, T_2, \bar{T}^2, Y_1, X, X_1 \in \mathbb{R}; x(i) \in \{0,1\}$

as well as the assignment and pruning constraints in examples 5. and 7. constitute the set of constraints of $\mathcal{OP}$-MSDC$(q(5,8))$. It can be verified that

$(x(q_{R2}) = 1, x(c_{R2,F1}) = 1, x(a_{R2,R3}) = 1, x(b_{R3,F6}) = 1, x(D$ is $X - X1) = 1,$
$x(D > 0) = 1, x(D < 3) = 1, x(Y$ is $Y1 + X - X1) = 1, 0, ..., 0),$

is the optimal solution of $\mathcal{OP}$-MSDC$(q(5,8))$ assigned to the valid subtree:

$\mathcal{V}_6 = \langle b(4), D$ is $X - X1, D > 0, D < 3, Y$ is $Y1 + X - X1, a(X,Y,X1,Y1),$
$\qquad c(2,5), q(X,Y) \rangle.$

Besides $T_1 = 4$, $T_2 = 7$, thus $q(4,7)$ is the optimal deductive consequence of
$\mathcal{OP}$-MSDC$(q(5,8))$ with the optimal objective value ≈ 0.874. Again $\bar{\mathcal{V}}_6 = \mathcal{D}_4$:

$\mathcal{D}_4 = \langle b(4), 2$ is $4 - 2, D > 0, 2 < 3, 7$ is $5 + 4 - 2, a(4,7,2,5), c(2,5), q(4,7) \rangle. \square$

4.3 $\mathcal{OP}$-MSDC(q) for Symbolic Domain Theories

In previous sections, we constructed $\mathcal{OP}$-MSDC(q) for a domain theory whose
variables were bound to numbers. However, real domain theories also have variables bound to symbols. A known challenge raised by Richter [5] is:

"*How to extend approximation techniques to symbolic domains and integrate them smoothly with logical reasoning methods?*"

To solve this problem, we transform the symbols of a domain theory into integers by replacing each symbol with a unique integer. For example, let a domain theory Σ_{car} contain the facts fuel_type('super') and fuel_type('benzin'). We can replace these facts with fuel_type(1) and fuel_type(2). Clearly the similarity measures with symbols should also be transformed into numerical similarity functions. For example the local similarity $sim_i(t, T)$

$$sim_i('super', 'super') = 1; \qquad sim_i('benzin', 'benzin') = 1;$$
$$sim_i('super', 'benzin') = 0.5; \qquad sim_i('benzin', 'super') = 1;$$

is transformed into the similarity functions

$$SIM_i + x_1 \leq (\textstyle\sum_{j=1}^{\beta_1} 1 \cdot x(l_j^1)) + 1; \qquad SIM_i + x_2 \leq (\textstyle\sum_{j=1}^{\beta_2} 1 \cdot x(l_j^2)) + 1;$$
$$SIM_i + x_1 \leq (\textstyle\sum_{j=1}^{\beta_2} 0.5 \cdot x(l_j^2)) + 1; \qquad SIM_i + x_2 \leq (\textstyle\sum_{j=1}^{\beta_1} 1 \cdot x(l_j^1)) + 1;$$

such that $x(l_1^1), ..., x(l_{\beta_1}^1)$ binds T to 1 ($\equiv$ 'super'), $x(l_1^2), ..., x(l_{\beta_2}^2)$ binds T to 2 ($\equiv$ 'benzin'), $x_1 = 1$ iff $t = 1$ ($\equiv$ 'super') and $x_2 = 1$ iff $t = 2$ ($\equiv$ 'benzin').

It is important to mention that SIM_i is an approximation of sim_i.

5   Optimization Algorithms

We use the free package *lp_solve*[4] to solve optimization problems[5]. Assuming that lp_solve($\mathcal{OP}$) is a program that provides an optimal solution, an optimal objective value and an optimal deductive consequence of an optimization problem $\mathcal{OP}$, we develop $\mathcal{OP}$-k-MSDC to find k similar deductive consequences.

$\mathcal{OP}$-k-**MSDC.** The idea of this algorithm is straightforward. Given a query $q = p(t_1, ..., t_n)$, we first solve lp_solve($\mathcal{OP}$-MSDC(q)) and retrieve the optimal solution of $\mathcal{OP}$-MSDC(q). Then we add a pruning constraint to $\mathcal{OP}$-MSDC(q) to prune the retrieved optimal solution and solve the new optimization problem. Keeping a list k-$MSDC$ of the retrieved optimal solutions, we continue the same procedure until no further solution is found or k-$MSDC$ contains k solutions. The algorithm $\mathcal{OP}$-k-**MSDC**($\mathcal{OP}$-MSDC(q), $\langle\rangle$, k, 1) is formalized as follows.

$\mathcal{OP}$-k-**MSDC**(problem $\mathcal{OP}$, list k-$MSDC$, int k, int *counter*){
  If *counter* $\leq k$ then {
    Run lp_solve($\mathcal{OP}$),
    If a solution $\vec{X}$ assigned to $\bar{\mathcal{V}} = \langle l_1, ..., l_\beta \rangle$ is retrieved then{
      insert($\bar{q}, k$-$MSDC$) s.t. $\bar{q}$ is the optimal deductive consequence of $\mathcal{OP}$;
      $\mathcal{OP} = \mathcal{OP} \cup x(l_1) + ... + x(l_\beta) \leq \beta - 1$;
      $\mathcal{OP}$-k-**MSDC**($\mathcal{OP}$, k-$MSDC$, k, *counter* + 1);}
    else return k-$MSDC$;}
  else return k-$MSDC$;}.

---

[4] lp_solve: http://tech.groups.yahoo.com/group/lp_solve/
[5] There exist also commercial packages such as ILOG-CPLEX which is frequently used in research institutions: http://www.ilog.com/products/cplex/

dfs_MAS_$\mathcal{OP}$ and dfs_MAS_hc. These algorithms are the same as dfs_MAS in which Min_Acc_Sim is set to $sim(q, q') - \epsilon$ such that q' is found by $\mathcal{OP}$-1-MSDC or hill climbing and ϵ is a small deviation e.g. 2%, 4% .... An upper bound for ϵ can only be retrieved using statistics. A possible strategy is to apply several experiments and make ϵ bigger and bigger until k solutions are found.

6 Experimental Results

To evaluate the performance of the algorithms with respect to computation time and similarity error caused by approximating the similarity measure or pruning heuristics, they are implemented in SWI-Prolog[6]. As test domains we employ:

1. the domain theory Σ_{pc} which formalizes a case-based configuration scenario that deals with the configuration of PCs. The deductive closure of the related domain theory contains 287280 elements,
2. the domain theory Σ_{car} which formalizes a car buying scenario to find the most appropriate car for a user. The deductive closure of the related domain theory Σ_{car} contains 304721 elements.

All experiments were executed on the same Intel Pentium 4 computer (1.8 GHz, 480 MB Ram). Each algorithm was executed with the parameter $k = 10$ for the same 400 randomly generated queries, each of which describes a demand for a PC or a car.

The results of the algorithms are shown in Table 1. with the following setting: for each query we measured the average computation time for the search (AET) as well as the average number of solutions found (AFS). One of the test algorithms is the complete dfs which computes k-MSDC exactly and serves as a base line for the similarity of the k-best solutions. This allows to determine the errors of other algorithms caused by approximating the similarity measure or the heuristic pruning. We determined the similarity error, i.e. the difference in similarity of the retrieved ith-best solution found with some algorithm and the similarity of the ith-best solution found by dfs. The following measures were introduced: MinEr1 is the minimal similarity error for the best solution over all 400 queries. Correspondingly, MaxEr1 is the maximum error and AveEr1 is the average error for the best solution. Further MinEk, MaxEk, and AveEk denote the minimum, maximum, and average similarity error averaged over all k solutions retrieved for each query.

Discussion of Results. Table 1. shows the results of the algorithms which are more or less the same for both domain theories Σ_{pc} and Σ_{car}. We have used a better **insert** procedure to organize the list k-$MSDC$ and therefore the results for dfs in this paper are better than those in [2]. However dfs still explores the whole state-space and is the slowest algorithm. In contrast, dfs_MAS_hc and dfs_MAS_$\mathcal{OP}$ are both fast but the latter provides a lot better solutions than

---

[6] SWI-Prolog: http://www.swi-prolog.org/.

Table 1. Comparison of the algorithms for Σ_{pc} and Σ_{car}

Algorithm	Theory	ϵ	AET	AFS	MinEr1	MaxEr1	AveEr1	MinEk	MaxEk	AveEk
dfs	Σ_{pc}	-	24.55	10	0	0	0	0	0	0
dfs_MAS_hc	Σ_{pc}	5%	0.16	9.75	0	0.40	0.141	0	0.43	0.152
dfs_MAS_$\mathcal{OP}$	Σ_{pc}	2%	4.02	9.84	0	0.05	0.008	0	0.06	0.010
dfs_MAS_$\mathcal{OP}$	Σ_{pc}	4%	2.84	10	0	0.07	0.027	0	0.08	0.030
$\mathcal{OP}$-k-MSDC	Σ_{pc}	-	0.73	10	0	0.05	0.002	0	0.07	0.003
dfs	Σ_{car}	-	33.39	10	0	0	0	0	0	0
dfs_MAS_hc	Σ_{car}	5%	3.48	9.49	0	0.31	0.049	0	0.32	0.051
dfs_MAS_$\mathcal{OP}$	Σ_{car}	2%	5.91	10	0	0.02	0.007	0	0.02	0.008
$\mathcal{OP}$-k-MSDC	Σ_{car}	-	0.84	10	0	0.005	0.0002	0	0.06	0.001

the former. Clearly, $\mathcal{OP}$-k-MSDC is the best choice since it is not only fast but also provides results with least errors.

In our current research we are improving the formulation of $\mathcal{OP}$-MSDC(q) by applying pre-compilation. Detailed results will be presented in future papers.

Acknowledgment. The author would like to thank Ralph Bergmann for his help, guidance and comments on this paper.

References

1. Aamodt, A., Plaza, E.: Case-based reasoning: foundational issues, methodological variations, and system approaches. AI Communications 7(1), 39–59 (1994)
2. Bergmann, R., Mougouie, B.: Finding Similar Deductive Consequences – A New Search-Based Framework for Unified Reasoning from Cases and General Knowledge. In: Roth-Berghofer, T.R., Göker, M.H., Güvenir, H.A. (eds.) ECCBR 2006. LNCS (LNAI), vol. 4106. Springer, Heidelberg (2006)
3. KER; The Knowledge Engineering Review: Special Issue on Case-Based Reasoning, vol. 20(3). Cambridge university press, Cambridge (2005)
4. Mougouie, B.: Integration of Similarity-Based and Deductive Reasoning for Knowledge Management. Ph.D. thesis (to appear, 2008)
5. Richter, M.M.: Logic and Approximation in Knowledge Based Systems. In: Lenski, W. (ed.) Logic versus Approximation. LNCS, vol. 3075, pp. 33–42. Springer, Heidelberg (2004)
6. Wolsey, L.: Integer Programming. John Wiley, Newyork (1998)

Understanding Dubious Future Problems

Oğuz Mülâyim and Josep Lluís Arcos

IIIA, Artificial Intelligence Research Institute
CSIC, Spanish Council for Scientific Research
Campus UAB, 08193 Bellaterra, Spain
{oguz,arcos}@iiia.csic.es

Abstract. Being able to predict the performance of a Case-Based Reasoning system against a set of future problems would provide invaluable information for design and maintenance of the system. Thus, we could carry out the needed design changes and maintenance tasks to improve future performance in a proactive fashion. This paper proposes a novel method for identifying regions in a case base where the system gives low confidence solutions to possible future problems. Experimentation is provided for RoboSoccer domain and we argue how encountered regions of dubiosity help us to analyse the case base and the reasoning mechanisms of the given Case-Based Reasoning system.

1 Introduction

When we use Case-Based Reasoning (CBR) [1] for solving problems, we count on the main assumption underlying this methodology[2], viz. *similar problems have similar solutions*. Wouldn't it be nice if we could anticipate to what extent the CBR assumption holds for future problems? A positive feedback in this direction would increase the reliability of the system. Contrariwise, we would be aware of the need for carrying out the required design and maintenance tasks throughout our system to improve its future performance in a proactive fashion [3].

Indeed, this preanalysis would give us important clues about the future. For instance, we could discover deserted regions in our case base (CB) where we do not have available cases to reason with, or we could encounter overcrowded zones in which we would have difficulty to classify our problem among cases of diverse classes.

Furthermore, this analysis would not only yield predictions about the case base but it could also give us valuable insight about the reasoner itself helping us to verify the functioning of CBR mechanisms like retrieval and reuse in advance.

The question, of course, is how this preanalysis could be performed. Case-Base Maintenance (CBM) techniques proved useful for improving the performance of CBR systems. Most of the existing CBM techniques focus on removing redundant or erroneous cases while preserving the system's competence [4,5,6]. More recent research introduces a complexity measure for highlighting areas of uncertainty within the problem space [7]. The common assumption of these techniques is that analysis of the cases provided in the case base is a good approach for estimating

K.-D. Althoff et al. (Eds.): ECCBR 2008, LNAI 5239, pp. 385–399, 2008.

the performance of the system for future cases. This assumption is known as the representativeness assumption. Nevertheless, new problems are expected to be slightly different from the existing cases.

Thus, the possibility of systematically assessing the performance of a system in a set of problems different from the existing cases becomes an interesting issue. One way for such an assessment is confronting the CBR system with possible future problems to detect deficiences beforehand. Though the idea sounds intuitive, the task of finding possible future problems that lead to system deficiencies is far from being trivial for most of the domains where the problem space is too vast or even infinite depending on the features that characterise a domain.

A common approach to attacking such a vast space is to use heuristics that guide the search. We believe that confidence measures can be used as effective heuristics to find system deficiences as they state how sure the system is about the solution it proposes for a given problem (where a solution with a low confidence indicates an inaccurate solution). The importance of the availability of such a measure is emphasised in recent research introducing possible confidence indicators and calculations for a CBR system [8,9,10].

In preliminary work [11] we have proposed a method inspired on evolutionary techniques to detect problematic future problems in terms of confidence. We call these future problems with low confidence solutions *Dubious Future Problems* (DFPs). In this paper we extend the previous work for detecting and characterising dubious regions in the problem space.

To effectively scan the problem space for finding dubious regions, we propose a method based on four steps: First, we explore the problem space to find dubious future problems. Then, we carry out an exploitation phase to better identify these problems by focusing the search on additional future problems in their neighborhoods. Next, to help the understanding of the regions where dubious future problems are located, we associate each DFP with a neighborhood pattern (e.g. hole, border). Finally, to focus on regions in the case base that suffer from the same deficiency rather than dealing with individual problems, we group DFPs according to these patterns.

In Section 2 we summarize our evolutionary approach for scanning the problem space to find dubious future problems. The definitions of dubiosity patterns and the grouping algorithm are described in Section 3. In Section 4 we give an example of how to explore dubious future problems and how to group them by patterns that they exhibit in a Robosoccer system. We interpret the results showing how they helped us to analyse our CBR system. We finally conclude discussing the outcomes of the methodology introduced in this paper and giving directions for future work in Section 5.

2   Exploring Dubious Future Problems

Given a domain ontology associated with a CBR system, we are interested in identifying possible future problems that: 1) are similar enough to the current cases and, 2) that the confidence on their solutions provided by the CBR system is low. Thus, the exploration of the problem space to find DFPs requires only three knowledge components in a CBR system: a domain ontology (specifying at least the features and their data types used for defining cases); a similarity metric; and a confidence measure that attaches a confidence value to each solution proposed by the CBR system.

In the search for dubious problems, the search space is the space of all problems that can be generated according to the domain ontology. As indicated above, this space can be too vast or even infinite depending on the features that characterise the domain. To find DFPs we use Genetic Algorithms (GA) as they have demonstrated their capabilities for exploring such vast search spaces. They have the advantage of scanning the search space in a parallel manner using a fitness function as heuristics and their implementations can be domain independent.

With a diverse initial population of possible future problems and an appropriate fitness function, DFPs will evolve as the GA runs, where the less confident the CBR system is about a problem's solution the more it will prefer to regard that problem as a DFP. However, as commonly seen in practice, GAs might have a tendency to converge towards local optima [12]. In our case, this would result as getting stuck to a low confidence zone and generating problems only within that locality instead of scanning a wider region in the problem space. In many GAs, mutation is the trusted genetic operator to avoid this problem as it introduces diversity to the population, nevertheless it is usually not a guarantee.

Our approach to effectively search the problem space and to avoid local minima has been to divide the search into two steps, namely *Exploration* and *Exploitation* of dubious future problems. In the Exploration step, the aim is to find DFPs which are similar enough to existing cases and which are as dissimilar as they could be to each other. The similarity to existing cases argument is to avoid dealing with irrelevant(although possibly not unlikely) problems which have no neighbour cases in the CB. The confidence for a solution to a generated problem which has no similar neighbours would probably be very low, but since this would already be an expected result, it would not be of much interest to bring these problems to the expert's inspection. Additionally, the dissimilarity between DFPs is for the sake of obtaining diversity in the results of Exploration to achieve a richer set of future problems and their neighbours after the Exploitation step.

Successively, in the Exploitation step our objective is to find future neighbours of the DFPs encountered in the Exploration step for providing a more precise analysis of the low confidence local regions.

Both, Exploration and Exploitation steps, incorporate two proximity limits in terms of similarity to an existing case or a future problem. These limits define the preferred region in the problem space during the search for DFPs and their neighbours. We will explain both limits in detail for each step in the next subsections. We also added a *Diversity Preservation* feature to our GAs for both steps to keep the population's diversity at a desired level.

The following sub-sections describe the details of the Exploration and Exploitation steps.

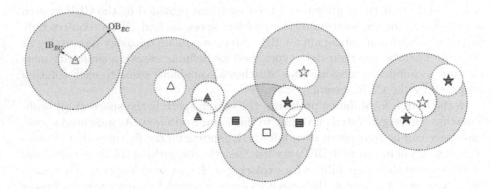

Fig. 1. Graphical representation of the Exploration step. Hollow shapes are existing cases (where different shapes refer to different classes); filled shapes are the encountered Dubious Future Problems; IB_{EC} and OB_{EC} are, respectively, inner and outer bounds.

2.1   Exploration

The goal of the Exploration step is to identify an initial set of dubious problems similar enough to the cases defined in a case base. A problem is considered dubious when its confidence is lower than a given threshold. Since the minimum value for considering a solution as confident may vary in each CBR application, the decision about the confidence threshold is domain dependent.

For the Exploration step, the proximity limits mentioned above define the preferred region of the search for dubious problems. The outer limit OB_{EC} defines the border for the less similar problems, while the inner limit IB_{EC} defines the border for the most similar ones to an existing case in the CB. We also use the inner limit to draw a border around the found DFPs since we are looking for DFPs that are as diverse as possible in this step. A graphical representation of the Exploration step is provided in Figure 1.

The decision of the proximity limits depends on the answer of how similar a problem can be to a case to be regarded as a relevant problem for the domain and application. The similarity among existing cases may give an idea of the range of possible values for these limits. For example; if these two limits are chosen so that their sum is closer to the similarity value between two nearest cases of different classes, then preffered proximities will overlap thus giving us the possibility to discover borders for the classes in the CB.

Throughout the execution of the GA for Exploration, we maintain a list of encountered future problems with low confidence solutions $\mathcal{LCFP}$. During the evaluation of a population, each time we come across a chromosome representing a dubious problem we add it to the $\mathcal{LCFP}$ list.

The concepts used in the GA for the Exploration step are explained below:

Chromosomes: Each chromosome in our population represents a future problem where each gene is a feature of the problem. The value of a gene is thus one of the possible values for the associated feature.

Initial Population: The initial population is formed by chromosomes generated by the *Random-Problem-Generator* function (RPG). RPG is a function able to generate a new problem by assigning random values for each problem feature. Values for problem features can be easily generated using the definitions of features in the domain ontology (feature definitions explicitly state the data type and the set of possible values for a feature). It should also be considered that in the existence of domain constraints, the Random-Problem-Generator function generates valid problems that conform to those constraints. Otherwise, generated future problems might be non-valid or irrelevant in the domain. The size of the population directly depends on the vastness of the problem space of the CB that is being worked on.

Fitness Function: The fitness of a chromosome is determined by two parameters: the confidence value of the solution to the problem represented by the chromosome and the similarity of the problem to the nearest problem in the CB. The fitness function has to be adapted in each different domain or CBR system. However, the following guidelines should be used in Exploration regardless of the domain or the application:

- The lower the confidence value is for a chromosome, the better candidate is that chromosome.
- A chromosome in the preferred proximity of an existing case is a better candidate than a chromosome which is not in this proximity.
- The confidence factor of the fitness is more significant than the similarity factor. This is not surprising since we are searching for dubious problems.

Our proposal for the fitness function definition is the following:

$$Fitness(c) = Confidence(c)^2 \times SimilarityFactor(c)$$

where c is the chromosome to be evaluated; $Confidence$ returns the confidence value supplied by the CBR application after solving c; and $SimilarityFactor$ takes into account the similarity to both cases and DFPs. $SimilarityFactor$ is calculated as follows:

$$SimilarityFactor(c) = partSimEC(c) + partSimDFP(c)$$

where $partSimEC$ refers to the similarity of c to existing cases and $partSimDFP$ refers to the similarity of c to DFPs in $\mathcal{LCFP}$. $partSimEC$ is defined as:

$$partSimEC(c) = \begin{cases} 1 - (OB_{EC} + IB_{EC} - Sim(c, CB)) & \text{if } Sim(c, CB) \geq IB_{EC} \\ 1 - Sim(c, CB) & \text{otherwise} \end{cases}$$

where $Sim(c, CB)$ is the similarity value of c to the most similar case in the CB (i.e. the highest similarity); IB_{EC} and OB_{EC} are, respectively, the inner and outer bounds of similarity to the existing cases. $partSimDFP(c)$ is defined as:

$$partSimDFP(c) = \sum_{p \in FP} (similarity(c, p) - IB_{EC})$$

where $FP \subset \mathcal{LCFP}$ is the set of future problems to which c is more similar than the allowed value IB_{EC} and $similarity(c,p)$ is the similarity value of c to the problem p.

Following the previously defined guidelines, $SimilarityFactor$ penalizes the chromosomes that are too close to either cases or future problems discovered in previous iterations (i.e. inside the radius defined by the inner threshold).

It should also be noted that for a desired chromosome (i.e. representing a dubious future problem which is in the preferred proximity of an existing case) our proposed function produces a fitness value which is lower than a non-desired one.

Selection: We defined a fitness-proportionate selection method. Fitness-proportionate selection is a commonly used and well studied selection mechanism where each chromosome has a chance proportional to its fitness value to be selected as a survivor and/or parent for the next generations. However, since we are interested in chromosomes with lower fitness values as explained above, to comply with our fitness function, selection of a chromosome was inversely proportional to its fitness value.

Crossover: We use single-point crossover as it is simple enough and widely used. Depending on the observed convergence of the GA, this method could easily be replaced by Two-Point or n-Point crossover methods.

Mutation: Generally, one random gene value is altered for a number of offspring chromosomes in the population. If a local minima problem is observed, more genes and/or more chromosomes can be mutated.

Diversity Preservation: We decided to use a diversity threshold that can be tuned for each application. Specifically, at each generation when the number of twins exceeds the diversity threshold, they are removed probabilistically using as probability their fitness value (i.e. twins with higher fitness have a higher probability to be deleted).

In our approach, the validity of a problem is another important issue. Due to the application of genetic operators in the evolution cycle, they are likely to reproduce offspring chromosomes which are non-valid. We may deal with these chromosomes basically in two ways: we may replace them with new valid chromosomes or we may let some of them survive hoping them to produce nice offspring in the following generations. In the former option, the replacement can be done in the Diversity Preservation. In the latter option, either a validity check can be incorporated into the fitness function reducing the fitness of non-valid chromosomes or simply non-valid chromosomes can be excluded from the $\mathcal{LCFP}$ after the termination of the Exploration step. In the current implementation we adopted this last solution.

Termination: The termination criterion for the GA can be reaching a number of generations or a number of dubious future problems. We let the population evolve for a certain number of generations.

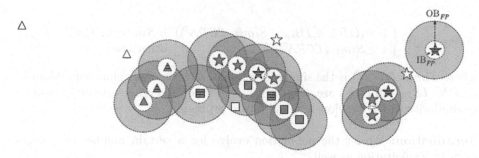

Fig. 2. Graphical representation of the Exploitation step. Hollow shapes are existing cases; filled shapes are the encountered and exploited Dubious Future Problems. IB_{FP} and OB_{FP} are, respectively, inner and outer bounds.

Result: As the result of the GA we obtain the list of future problems with low confidence solutions $\mathcal{LCFP}$.

2.2   Exploitation

The goal of the Exploitation step is to explore the neighbourhood of the low-confidence problems discovered in the Exploration step. Similarly to the Exploration step, during the execution of the GA for the Exploitation step we maintain a list of Low Confidence Problem Neighbours $\mathcal{LCPN}$. We initialise this list with the members of the $\mathcal{LCFP}$. In other words, the members of this list are the dubious future problems that we want to exploit.

For the Exploitation phase, the proximity limits define the preferred region of the search for neighbour problems. The outer limit OB_{FP} defines the border for the less similar problems, while the inner limit IB_{FP} defines the border for the most similar ones to any member of the $\mathcal{LCPN}$. A graphical representation of the Exploitation step is provided in Figure 2. Notice that, comparing with the Exploration step, the proximity limits for Exploitation step are narrower since in this step we are looking for neighbours of the DFPs.

All DFPs satisfying the proximity limits are added to the $\mathcal{LCPN}$ list. The confidence threshold for dubiosity is the same value used in the Exploration.

The concepts used in the GA for the Exploitation step are the following:

Chromosomes, Selection, Crossover, Mutation, Diversity Preservation: These concepts have the same definitions as the corresponding ones previously given in the Exploration step.

Initial Population: We partially feed the initial population with the $\mathcal{LCFP}$ set hoping to reproduce similar problems. We use the Random-Problem-Generator to reach to the desired initial population size when needed.

Fitness Function: The fitness of a chromosome c in the Exploitation step depends only on its neighbourhood to any member of $\mathcal{LCPN}$. The fitness function is defined as follows:

$$Fitness(c) = \begin{cases} 1 - (OB_{FP} + IB_{FP} - Sim(c, \mathcal{LCPN})) & \text{if } Sim(c, \mathcal{LCPN}) \geq IB_{FP} \\ 1 - Sim(c, \mathcal{LCPN}) & \text{otherwise} \end{cases}$$

where $Sim(c, \mathcal{LCPN})$ is the similarity value of c to the most similar problem in $\mathcal{LCPN}$; IB_{FP} and OB_{FP} are, respectively, the inner and outer proximity bounds of similarity to the previously found future problems.

Termination: We let the population evolve for a certain number of generations in Exploitation as well.

Result: At the end, the Exploitation step provides the list $\mathcal{LCPN}$ which contains dubious future problems found both in the Exploration and Exploitation steps.

3   Regions of Dubiosity

Exploration and Exploitation of DFPs give us a foresight of a possible bad performance of the CBR system. To inspect the underlying reasons of such a malfunction, the encountered DFPs may be presented directly for the domain expert's attention. Experts in turn may use this future map of the case base to initiate maintenance tasks if needed. However, depending on their number, analysing DFPs manually may become a difficult task as domain experts would have to check each DFP together with its neighbours to reveal the system deficiencies.

To be able to assist the domain experts in the endeavour of analysing DFPs, we have defined six dubiosity patterns. Each DFP is tagged with a dubiosity pattern which indicates the possible reason of being classified as dubious. Furthermore, when we have a numerous list of DFPs, we propose a grouping algorithm for helping the expert to focus on regions in the case base that suffer from the same deficiency.

3.1   Dubiosity Patterns

DFPs are good pointers to possible future system weaknesses as their solutions have low confidence values. But to identify the cause of the low confidence result, and thus, the needed policies for eliminating these weaknesses, DFPs themselves alone are not much of a help. This is because confidence measures, in general, do not provide detailed explanations of the judgement they make while attaching a confidence value to a solution. Thus, for analysing why DFPs were considered as dubious the expert should inspect the indicators of confidence used by the confidence measure of the CBR system.

On the other hand, since usually the similarity measure plays an important role in confidence calculus[9,10], looking at the neighbour cases of a DFP would give strong clues for analizing DFPs. For this aim, we have defined six dubiosity

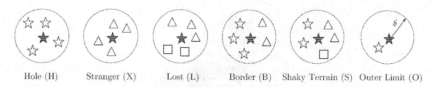

Hole (H)   Stranger (X)   Lost (L)   Border (B)   Shaky Terrain (S) Outer Limit (O)

Fig. 3. Graphical representation of DFP Patterns. Hollow shapes are cases and the filled one is a Dubious Future Problem. Each shape represents a different solution class. δ is the similarity threshold delimiting the neighbourhood of a DFP.

patterns according to the solution classes of a DFP and of its neighbour cases. Given a similarity threshold δ defining the neighbourhood, we say that a DFP exhibits a pattern of type (see Figure 3 for a graphical representation):

- **Hole (H).** When all of its neighbour cases are of the same class as the DFP;
- **Stranger (X).** When all of its neighbour cases are of the same class which is different from the DFP's;
- **Lost (L).** When there are at least two different groups of neighbour cases, according to their solution classes, where none of the groups is of the same class as the DFP;
- **Border (B).** When its neighbour cases can be grouped into two groups with different solution classes and one group shares the same class as the DFP;
- **Shaky Terrain (S).** When its neighbour cases can be grouped into at least three groups of different solution classes and one group shares the same class as the DFP. This pattern indicates regions where adding or removing a case might redraw borders for multiple classes.
- **Outer Limit (O).** When it has only one neighbour case sharing the class. This pattern may indicate outer limits for a particular class or it may point out isolated cases in the case base.

After the Exploitation step, for each DFP in $\mathcal{LCPN}$ we check the solution classes of its neighbour cases together with its own and we associate a pattern to each DFP according to the above pattern definitions. The similarity threshold δ value should be coherent to the OB_{EC} value in the Exploration step since we were looking for similarity between DFPs and existing cases. We propose to choose a value slightly bigger than the OB_{EC} value for the δ.

3.2   Grouping Dubious Future Problems

Preliminary experiments for exploring DFPs have shown that depending on the features that characterise a domain and on the CBR inference mechanism we may end up with a lengthy list of explored DFPs. In one sense, a high number of DFPs is attractive since the more DFPs we encounter the more possible future deficiencies we are discovering. However, using this lengthy list to carry out maintenance tasks may turn out to be a tedious task in both manual and automated maintenance of a CBR system. Although the associated dubiosity

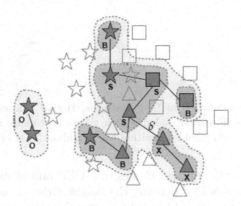

Fig. 4. Regions of Dubiosity. Hollow shapes are cases and filled shapes are DFPs. Subscripts point out the patterns associated to each DFP.

patterns help us to analyse DFPs, each DFP still requires special attention to identify the needed maintenance tasks.

To overcome this overhead when we have too many DFPs to deal with, we propose to group the DFPs according to their patterns and the similarity of the DFPs among each other. Grouping DFPs in this way makes it easier to identify regions in the problem space that suffer from the same deficiency. Thus, any maintenance task that eliminates a common deficiency in such a region will probably make the CBR system more confident of its solutions for similar future problems that will fall into that region. We call these regions *Regions of Dubiosity*.

Given the list $\mathcal{LCPN}$ and a similarity threshold δ', the grouping algorithm performs the following two steps:

1. **Identification** of the Regions of Dubiosity by transitively grouping all DFPs that are neighbours at similarity δ'. This step forms different isolated regions. Each region is a graph where the nodes are the DFPs and edges connect two nodes when their similarity is, at least, δ'.
2. **Characterization** of the Regions of Dubiosity by grouping all the DFPs that share the same pattern and are directly connected. Thus, each subregion is a subgraph highlighting a pattern.

δ' should be coherent(if not equal) with the OB_{FP} value in the Exploitation step since we are looking for similarity between DFPs for grouping them.

At the end, the regions of dubiosity that we obtain from the above algorithm help us to identify the problematic zones in the CBR system. Moreover, each subregion of shared patterns serves to detect zones that suffer from the same deficiency, thus preventing us from having to deal with individual DFPs.

A graphical representation of an example for identifying Regions of Dubiosity is given in Figure 4. In the figure two different regions have been detected. The first one on the left only has two DFPs identified as outer limits. The big region on the right has three border sub-regions, one stranger sub-region, and one central shaky terrain sub-region. Connecting lines between two DFPs show that they are neighbours according to a given similarity threshold δ'. Note that region surfaces are only painted with the purpose of highlighting the dubiosity regions in the problem space.

4   Experimentation

We have performed the analysis of DFPs on a CBR system developed for the Four-Legged League (RoboCup) soccer competition [13]. In RoboCup two teams of four Sony AIBO robots compete operating autonomously, i.e. without any external control. The goal of the CBR system is to determine the actions (called *gameplays*) the robots should execute given a state of the game.

The state of the game is mainly represented by the position of the ball and the positions of the players (both teammates and opponents). The positions are constrained by the field dimensions (6 m long and 4 m wide). Moreover, since robots occupy a physical space in the field, a state of the game is considered valid whenever the distances among the robots are higher than their dimensions (30 cm long and 10cm wide).

The 68 cases stored in the system can be grouped into three main behaviors: cooperative behaviors (where at least two teammates participate); individualistic behaviors (only one player is involved); and back away behaviors (where the position of the opponents forces a player to move the ball back).

The confidence measure provided by the application took into account not only the similarity of the problem to the cases but also the actual distance of the current position of the players to the ball. Therefore, although all similar cases share the same solution, when the players are away from the ball the confidence of the solution is low.

The first goal of our experiments was to foresee whether there exist states of the game where the CBR system has difficulties in determining the best behavior, i.e. the confidence on the proposed solution is low. The secondary goal was to detect if there were any bad performing mechanisms of the CBR system.

The experimentation settings were the following: 40% of the population was selected as survivors to the next generation; 60% of the chromosomes were selected as parents to reproduce offspring; mutation was applied to a randomly chosen 5% of the offspring modifying a gene's value for each chosen chromosome; the diversity threshold for the twin chromosomes was 5% (we kept this amount of twins in the new generation and replaced the rest of them with new ones created by the RPG).

Taking into account the similarities among existing cases, we chose the test range [0.93, 0.99] for the proximity limit values and we kept the proximity for Exploitation narrower than Exploration (see subsections 2.1 and 2.2). The similarity threshold (δ in Figure 3) for associating patterns to DFPs was always a value slightly bigger than the OB_{EC} value in the Exploration step. Analogously, the similarity threshold for grouping DFPs (δ' in Figure 4) to form Regions of Dubiosity, was the same as the OB_{FP} value in the Exploitation step (see

Table 1. Average (Avg) and standard deviation (σ) of DFPs discovered in the Exploration ($\mathcal{LCFP}$) and Exploitation ($\mathcal{LCPN}$) steps in 63 experiments. RD shows the number of the Regions of Dubiosity created from DFPs. H, X, L, B, S, O are, respectively, the percentage of the number of the experiments in which *Hole*, *Stranger*, *Lost*, *Border*, *Shaky Terrain*, and *Outer Limit* patterns appeared.

	$\mathcal{LCFP}$	$\mathcal{LCPN}$	RD
Avg	59.26	183.21	55.95
σ	34.12	105.78	30.89

H	X	L	B	S	O
95%	100%	50%	85%	15%	85%

subsections 3.1 and 3.2). Finally, the test range for confidence threshold was chosen as [0.3, 0.7].

We ran different experiments for analysing the sensitivity in identifying DFP regions by changing parameters such as the size of the initial population, the number of generations, the confidence threshold, and the proximity limits. Moreover, because of the random nature of GAs, for each setting we executed the Exploration and Exploitation steps several times to get an average value for the number of identified DFPs and regions of dubiosity.

Throughout experimentation we have seen that we may encounter a higher number of DFPs when, the initial population is larger in size or GAs evolve during enough generations or the preferred proximity is wider.

The results show (see Table 1 left) that the number of the DFPs encountered in the Exploration step is closely related to the number of the Regions of Dubiosity. The difference between these two numbers is due to linking of DFPs found in Exploration with other DFPs found in the Exploitation step. This happens when we reach a DFP previously found in the Exploration step while we are exploiting another DFP problem found in the same step. Therefore, when no linking is achieved between such DFPs, the number of the Regions of Dubiosity is equal to the number of the DFPs found in the Exploration step.

Another interesting result is the analysis of the DFP patterns discovered in the experiments (Table 1 on the right summarizes the percentage of experiments where each pattern is detected). This analysis allows a better understanding of the regions of the problem space where the CBR system is not performing confidently:

– Holes in the soccer domain occured when although all the closer cases shared the same individualistic solution, the players were far from the ball. This was due to the provided confidence measure explained above. To obtain more confident solutions the neighbourhood of holes can be populated with new cases.

– Stranger DFPs were problems that proposed cooperative behavior but whose neighbours were individualistic cases. We saw that this was because of the design of the system for favouring cooperative behavior. If there is a close cooperative case to the problem, the application proposes cooperative solution even if there are more similar cases with different solutions. Stranger DFPs helped us to discover regions where the influence of the cooperative cases was excessive. To improve the confidence, we proposed to reduce that influence for similar regions.

– Lost DFPs were problems that proposed cooperative behavior in a region where their neighbours were individualistic and back away cases. This was again due to the excessive influence of a cooperative case nearby. The proposed maintenance task was the same as in the previous pattern.

– Border DFPs identified the regions where neither individualistic nor cooperative behaviors reach a significantly better confidence. The confidence in these regions could be improved by incorporating new cases into the case base to be able to mark the borders better between these two classes.

– Shaky terrain DFPs does not seem to be significant in the Robosoccer domain due to the distribution of the cases in the CB. There are only three solution classes and back away behaviors are mainly close to individualistic behaviors. Hence, in only 15% of the experiments we encountered this pattern when the proximity limits were chosen to be too wide and the proximity of the cases of all three classes were overlapping in some regions.

– Finally, the encountered Outer Limit DFPs were either in the proximity of isolated cases in deserted regions of the CB or they were on the outskirts of the proximity of cases which were themselves at the border of a class.

In Figure 5 a visualisation of an example a dubious region in the Soccer domain is provided. Hollow and filled squares represent respectively cases and DFPs with cooperative solutions. Analogously, hollow and filled stars represent respectively cases and DFPs with indivudualistic solutions. The visualisation of cases and DFPs was built using a force-directed graph-drawing algorithm where the repulsive force between two cases is proportional to their distance. The dotted line indicates the border of the dubiosity region. We have drawn dubiosity groups at two similarity levels by using two different values for δ' (dark and light colors in figure). Neighborhood lines have been omitted for facilitating the understanding of the figures.

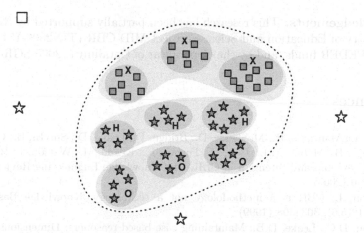

Fig. 5. Visualizing a dubious region in the Soccer problem. DFPs with individualistic solutions are represented as stars. Squares represent DFPs with cooperative solutions. H, X and O, respectively, indicate Hole, Stranger and Outer Limit patterns attached to the cases in the darker coloured regions of dubiosity.

5   Conclusions and Future Work

In this paper we have presented a novel method for identifying future low confidence regions given an existing case base. The method was based on four steps. First, we explored the problem space to find dubious future problems. Then, we exploited these problems to better locate them in the case base within their future neighbourhood. Both steps used an evolutionary approach to scan the problem space. Next, to help the understanding of the regions where dubious future problems are located, we associated each problem with one of the six dubiosity patterns defined in the paper. These patterns were based on the neighbourhood of future problems to the existing cases. Finally, we have proposed an algorithm for grouping dubious future problems according to these patterns to identify regions of dubiosity. We argued that these regions enabled us to focus on the regions in the case base that suffer from the same deficiency rather than dealing with individual problems, thus facilitating maintenance tasks.

We described the experiments performed in a Robosoccer application and have shown how DFPs associated with dubiosity patterns helped us to detect dubious regions in the case base and to analyse bad performing mechanisms of the CBR system.

We believe that the proposed method is useful for improving the performance of CBR systems in a proactive fashion. The proposed method uses only the domain ontology for generating future problems and evaluates them by using the confidence and similarity measures provided by the CBR system.

As future work we plan to relate the dubiosity patterns to possible maintenance tasks and to design a graphical tool for navigating through the problem space. We plan to join the method described in this paper with a visualisation method for case base competence based on solution qualities presented in [14].

Acknowledgements. This research has been partially supported by the Spanish Ministry of Education and Science project MID-CBR (TIN2006-15140-C03-01), EU-FEDER funds, and by the Generalitat of Catalunya (2005-SGR-00093).

References

1. Lopez de Mantaras, R., McSherry, D., Bridge, D., Leake, D., Smyth, B., Craw, S., Faltings, B., Maher, M.L., Cox, M., Forbus, K., Keane, M., Watson, I.: Retrieval, reuse, revision, and retention in CBR. The Knowledge Engineering Review 20(3), 215–240 (2005)
2. Watson, I.: CBR is a methodology not a technology. Knowledge Based Systems 12(5,6), 303–308 (1999)
3. Wilson, D.C., Leake, D.B.: Maintaining case-based reasoners: Dimensions and directions. Computational Intelligence 17(2), 196–213 (2001)
4. Smyth, B., Keane, M.T.: Remembering to forget: A competence-preserving case deletion policy for case-based reasoning systems. In: Proceedings of IJCAI 1995, pp. 377–382 (1995)

5. Smyth, B., McKenna, E.: Building compact competent case-bases. In: Althoff, K.-D., Bergmann, R., Branting, L.K. (eds.) ICCBR 1999. LNCS (LNAI), vol. 1650, pp. 329–342. Springer, Heidelberg (1999)
6. Smyth, B., McKenna, E.: Competence models and the maintenance problem. Computational Intelligence 17(2), 235–249 (2001)
7. Massie, S., Craw, S., Wiratunga, N.: When similar problems don't have similar solutions. In: Weber, R.O., Richter, M.M. (eds.) ICCBR 2007. LNCS (LNAI), vol. 4626, pp. 92–106. Springer, Heidelberg (2007)
8. Cheetham, W.: Case-based reasoning with confidence. In: Blanzieri, E., Portinale, L. (eds.) EWCBR 2000. LNCS (LNAI), vol. 1898, pp. 15–25. Springer, Heidelberg (2000)
9. Cheetham, W., Price, J.: Measures of solution accuracy in case-based reasoning systems. In: Funk, P., González Calero, P.A. (eds.) ECCBR 2004. LNCS (LNAI), vol. 3155, pp. 106–118. Springer, Heidelberg (2004)
10. Delany, S.J., Cunningham, P., Doyle, D., Zamolotskikh, A.: Generating estimates of classification confidence for a case-based spam filter. In: Muñoz-Ávila, H., Ricci, F. (eds.) ICCBR 2005. LNCS (LNAI), vol. 3620, pp. 177–190. Springer, Heidelberg (2005)
11. Mulayim, O., Arcos, J.L.: Exploring dubious future problems. In: Petridis, M. (ed.) Twelfth UK Workshop on Case-Based Reasoning, pp. 52–63. CMS Press (2007)
12. Michalewicz, Z.: Genetic Algorithms+Data Structures=Evolution Programs, 3rd edn. Springer, New York (1996)
13. Ros, R., Lopez de Mantaras, R., Arcos, J.L., Veloso, M.: Team playing behavior in robot soccer: A case-based approach. In: Weber, R.O., Richter, M.M. (eds.) ICCBR 2007. LNCS (LNAI), vol. 4626, pp. 46–60. Springer, Heidelberg (2007)
14. Grachten, M., Garcia-Otero, A., Arcos, J.L.: Navigating through case base competence. In: Muñoz-Ávila, H., Ricci, F. (eds.) ICCBR 2005. LNCS (LNAI), vol. 3620, pp. 282–295. Springer, Heidelberg (2005)

Conversational Case-Based Recommendations Exploiting a Structured Case Model

Quang Nhat Nguyen and Francesco Ricci

Free University of Bozen-Bolzano
{qnhatnguyen,fricci}@unibz.it

Abstract. There are case-based recommender systems that generate personalized recommendations for users exploiting the knowledge contained in past recommendation cases. These systems assume that the quality of a new recommendation depends on the quality of the recorded recommendation cases. In this paper, we present a case model exploited in a mobile critique-based recommender system that generates recommendations using the knowledge contained in previous recommendation cases. The proposed case model is capable of modeling evolving (conversational) recommendation sessions, capturing the recommendation context, supporting critique-based user-system conversations, and integrating both ephemeral and stable user preferences. In this paper, we evaluate the proposed case model through replaying real recommendation cases recorded in a previous live-user evaluation. We measure the impact of the various components of the case model on the system's recommendation performance. The experimental results show that the case components that model the user's contextual information, default preferences, and initial preferences, are the most important for mobile context-dependent recommendation.

1 Introduction

Product suggestions provided by recommender systems (RSs) are useful when users are overwhelmed by a large number of options to consider or when they do not have enough knowledge about a specific domain to make autonomous decisions [2].

Case-based recommender systems [3, 7] are knowledge-based RSs [5] that exploit case-based reasoning [1] to generate personalized recommendations. A case-based RS maintains a set of cases (i.e., a case base) of previously solved recommendation problems and their solutions. In many case-based RSs (e.g., [4, 8, 9, 16]), the authors assume that the case base is the product catalogue, i.e., the solutions of the recommendation problem, and the "problem" is the user's query that is essentially a partial description of her desired product. In this approach, the case does not store the user needs/preferences or the context that originates the recommendation problem, and the solution of the case is the case itself, i.e., the product recommended. Hence, this product-based case modeling approach does not capture the link between the problem, i.e., the user's preferences and the recommendation context, and the solution, i.e., the user's selected product, as in traditional CBR systems. Moreover, here no learning takes place, since no new knowledge is stored after a problem is solved, and no adaptation of a previously solved case is done.

K.-D. Althoff et al. (Eds.): ECCBR 2008, LNAI 5239, pp. 400–414, 2008.

Besides the product-based case modeling approach, there have been a few attempts to exploit more extensively the CBR methodology in RSs. In the approach presented in [14], a case models a user's interaction with the system in the recommendation session, and consists of four components: the collaborative features, which are the user's general characteristics, wishes, constraints, and goals; the queries executed during the recommendation session, representing the user's additional preferences and constraints on products; the selected products; and the ratings (evaluations) given to the selected products. To build the recommendation list, the system first retrieves the products that satisfy the user's current query, and then ranks the retrieved products according to their similarity to the products selected in past similar recommendation cases. In another approach, discussed in [17], a case is composed of a user's query (the problem part) and the selected product (the solution part). Given a user's query, the system's construction of the recommendation list consists of two steps. First, the system builds the retrieval set that is a union of 1) the set of the products in the product catalogue most similar to the user's query and 2) the set of the products selected in the past cases most similar to the current case. Then, the system applies a weighted majority voting rule to the retrieval set, because different items in the retrieval set may refer to the same product, to build the recommendation list. Both these approaches show how cases can be generated and reused in the recommendation task.

In addition, we observe that many RSs, e.g., collaborative filtering [2], follow the single-shot recommendation strategy, where given a user's request for recommendations the system computes and shows to the user the recommendation list, and the session ends. Conversely, in conversational RSs a recommendation session does not terminate immediately after the first recommendation list is shown to the user, but it evolves in a dialogue where the system tries to elicit step-by-step the user's preferences to produce better recommendations [3]. In conversational RSs a recommendation case should record not only the user's query and her selected products but also the important information derived from the human-computer dialogue. So, for instance, in critique-based conversational RSs [4, 8, 6, 10, 16] the information contained in the user's critiques should also be stored in the recommendation case.

Moreover, most of the existing case-based RSs have been designed for Web users, not for mobile users who move from place to place and access the system using mobile devices such as PDAs or mobile phones. In mobile RSs the contextual information, such as the user's position and the time of her request, is important, and should be included in the case model and exploited in the recommendation process.

In a previous paper [15], we presented our critique-based recommendation approach and its implementation in MobyRek, a mobile case-based RS that helps mobile users find their desired travel products (restaurants). In that paper, we also presented a live-user evaluation of MobyRek, and the experimental results showed that our recommendation methodology is effective in supporting mobile users in making product selection decisions. We also showed in [12] that the composite query representation employed in our recommendation methodology results in a better recommendation quality over a simpler query representation using either a logical or similarity query, and in [13] that the exploitation of both long-term and session-specific user preferences does improve recommendation performance compared to the exploitation of a single preferences component.

In this paper, we present the case model employed in our mobile recommendation methodology, which extends the case modeling approaches presented in [14] and [17]. In our approach, a mobile recommendation session is modeled as a case that is built when a user requests a product suggestion, and it is incrementally updated throughout the conversational recommendation session. The CBR problem solving strategy is used to exploit (reuse) the knowledge contained in the past recommendation cases to build the user-query representation, and to adapt the current case to the user's critiques. In this paper, we also present off-line experiments aimed at evaluating the impact, on the system's recommendation performance, of the different case components. In particular, we compare the full case model with the other partial case models. These off-line experiments exploit the log data of real recommendation cases recorded in the previous live-user evaluation of MobyRek [15]. The experimental results show that the full case model does improve the system's recommendation performance over the partial ones, and that the case components that model the user's contextual information, default preferences, and initial preferences, are the most important for mobile context-aware recommendation. In summary, the paper makes the following contributions.

• A new and more comprehensive case model for the mobile conversational recommendation problem.
• A case-based approach for building and revising the user-query representation.
• A number of off-line experiments that show the impact of the different case components on the system's recommendation performance.

The rest of the paper is organized as follows. In Section 2, we present the product and the user-query representations, and discuss the recommendation process. Section 3 presents the proposed case model and discusses our case-based approach to building and revising the user query representation. In Section 4, we present the experimental evaluation of the proposed case model. Finally, Section 5 gives the conclusions and discusses future work.

2 The Recommendation Approach

In the proposed approach, a product is represented as a feature vector $x = (x_1, x_2, ..., x_n)$, where a feature value x_i may be numeric, nominal, or a set of nominal values. For instance, the restaurant $x = $ ("Dolomiti", 1713, {pizza}, 10, {air-conditioned, smoking-room}, {Saturday, Sunday}, {credit-card}) has name $x_1 = $ "Dolomiti", distance $x_2 = 1,713$ meters (from the user's position), type $x_3 = $ {pizza}, average cost $x_4 = 10$ Euros, characteristics $x_5 = $ {air-conditioned, smoking-room}, opening days $x_6 = $ {Saturday, Sunday}, and payment method $x_7 = $ {credit-card}.

In a recommendation session, the user-query representation encodes the user's preferences and is used by the system to compute the recommendation list. The user-query representation is managed in the case. (The case-based construction and adaptation of the query representation are discussed later in Section 3.) The user query q consists of three components, $q = (q_l, p, w)$.

• The logical query (q_l) models the conditions that the recommended products must satisfy. The logical query is a conjunction of constraints, $q_l = (c_1 \wedge c_2 \wedge ... \wedge c_m)$.

- The favorite pattern (p), represented in the same vector space of the product representation, $p = (p_1, p_2, ..., p_n)$, models the conditions that the recommended products should match as closely as possible. These wish conditions allow the system to make trade-offs.
- The feature importance weights vector (w) models how much important each feature is for the user with respect to the others, $w = (w_1, w_2, ..., w_n)$, where $w_i \in [0,1]$ is the importance weight of feature f_i. The system exploits the feature importance weights when it makes trade-offs or when it needs to find query relaxation solutions [15].

For example, the query $q = (q_l = (x_2 \leq 2000) \wedge (x_6 \supseteq \{\text{Saturday, Sunday}\}); p = (?, ?, \{\text{pizza}\}, ?, ?, ?, ?); w = (0, 0.4, 0.2, 0, 0, 0.4, 0))$ models a user who looks for restaurants within 2 km from her position that are open on Saturday and Sunday and prefers pizza restaurants. For the user the distance and the opening days are the most important, followed by the restaurant type, and she is indifferent to the other features.

In our approach, a case models a recommendation session starting when a user asks for a product recommendation (see Fig. 1a) and ends either when the user selects a product or when she quits the session with no product selection. A recommendation session evolves in cycles. In each recommendation cycle, the system shows the user a ranked list of recommended products (see Fig. 1b) that she can browse and criticize (see Fig. 1c), and the cycle ends when a new recommendation list is requested and shown. We note that users are supported to make critiques on all the product features, not just on distance and cost.

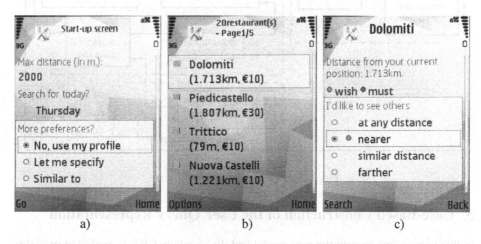

a)   b)   c)

Fig. 1. MobyRek user interface. a) Search initialization options. b) The recommendation list. c) Critique on a numeric feature.

In a recommendation cycle, the current query representation, $q = (q_l, p, w)$, is used by the system to compute the recommendation list, i.e., the system first retrieves the products that satisfy q_l and then ranks the retrieved products according to their similarity to (p, w). Only the k best products in this ranked list, i.e., those which satisfy q_l and are most similar to (p, w), are shown to the user as the recommendation result for the current cycle.

In the retrieval phase, if no products in the catalog satisfy q_l, then the system automatically finds a minimum number of constraints that if discarded from q_l make it satisfiable. In this automatic relaxation process, the constraints involving less important features are considered before those involving more important ones. The discarded constraints are converted to wish conditions and put in p. Similarly, in case no products satisfy a critique stated as must, the critique is converted to a wish condition and put in p. (More details on the recommendation list computation are presented in [15]).

Given a user's request asking for some product suggestions (see Fig. 1a), the system integrates the user's initial input and her long-term preferences to build a case that models the current recommendation session. Next, the system retrieves past recommendation cases similar to the current one, and uses the knowledge contained in these retrieved cases to update the current case. Then, the current case is iteratively adapted through a system-user dialogue that interleaves the system's recommendations with the user's critiques to the proposed products. When the session finishes, the current recommendation case is retained in the system's case base and the knowledge about the newly solved problem is stored. The case retention allows the system to exploit past recommendation cases in making recommendations for users in the future [1]. The model of the recommendation process is shown in Fig. 2.

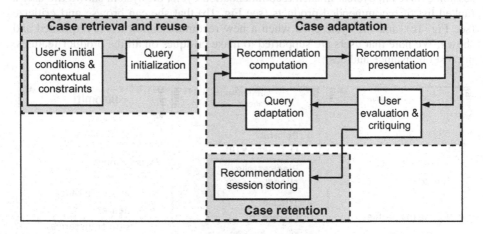

Fig. 2. A mobile recommendation case

3 Case-Based Construction of the User Query Representation

In this section, we present the case model and discuss how CBR is exploited in building and revising the user-query representation.

3.1 The Case Model

In the definition of the case model we considered the following requirements.

- Capture the problem definition, i.e., the knowledge necessary to compute personalized recommendations, and the solution (recommendations) of a mobile recommendation session.

- Support the critique-based conversational recommendation approach.
- Include the contextual information useful to solve a recommendation problem.
- Model both the user's ephemeral preferences (i.e., the user's query) and the user's stable ones.

Given a user's request for a product suggestion, the system exploits the user's initial input together with her stable preferences to initialize the case. In our approach, a recommendation case is modeled as:

$$C = (SAH, CTX, UDP, UIS, IQR, CTZ, SEL);$$

where:

- *SAH* stores the user's product selections (e.g., a selected hotel) made earlier (using a different web system, NutKing) and related to the current recommendation session. The idea is that if, for instance, users u1 and u2 selected the same hotel h before going to destination and user u2 selected also restaurant r; then the system would consider restaurant r to be a good product for user u1.
- *CTX* stores the contextual information of the current recommendation case. We note that in our tests (reported in Section 4) *CTX* stores only the user's position and the time of her recommendation request. The user's position is automatically detected by the system, or is approximated by the co-ordinates of a close landmark specified by her.
- *UDP* stores the preferences on product features that are explicitly set by the user as her default preference settings, i.e., $UDP = (u_1, u_2, ..., u_n)$, where u_i is a default favorite value set by the user. For example, the user may set a default preference of non-smoking room.
- *UIS* stores the conditions that are explicitly specified by the user at the beginning of the session, i.e., $UIS = (v_1, v_2, ..., v_n)$, where $v_i = (c_i, s_i)$, and c_i is an initial condition, and $s_i \in \{wish, must\}$.
- *IQR* stores the system's initial user-query representation.
- *CTZ* stores the sequence of the critiques that the user makes in the session.
- *SEL* stores the user's product selection at the end of the (mobile) session.

Given a user's request for a product suggestion, together with all the other information contained in the case, the system builds the initial representation of the user query (discussed in the next section): $IQR = q^0 = (q_l^0, p^0, w^0)$, where q_l^0 is the system's initial representation of the user's must conditions, p^0 is the system's initial representation of the user's wish conditions, and w^0 is the system's initial representation of the user's feature importance weights.

After the system outputs a recommendation list the user can browse it and criticize any recommended product (see Fig. 1c). A sequence of critiques is modeled as:

$$CTZ = null \mid (Ctz\_Rec)^*;$$

$$Ctz\_Rec = (prdPos, recSize, prdID, fID, ctzOpt, ctzVal);$$

where *Ctz_Rec* is a critique record, *prdPos* is the criticized product's position in the recommendation list in the current cycle, *recSize* is the number of the products in the recommendation list in the current cycle, *prdID* is the identity of the criticized product, *fID* is the identity of the criticized feature, *ctzOpt* is the critique operator applied, and *ctzVal* is the value of the criticized feature. An example of a critiques sequence is as follows.

(1, 20, Prd$_4$, f$_2$, Opt$_{(<)}$, 2000) →
(2, 12, Prd$_7$, f$_5$, Opt$_{(-\supset)}$, {parking, smoking-room}) →
(1, 12, Prd$_3$, f$_4$, Opt$_{(-=)}$, 15)

In this example, the user first makes a critique of "must be nearer than 2 km", then she "wishes to have the parking and smoking-room characteristics", and finally she "wishes a price around 15 Euros".

A recommendation session ends either when the user selects a product or when she quits the session with no product selected. The former case is referred as a successful recommendation case whereas the latter a failed one. Hence, the final result (i.e., the solution part) of a mobile recommendation case is modeled as:

$$SEL = \text{null} \mid (prdPos, recSize, prdID, postRating);$$

where *prdPos* is the position of the selected product in the recommendation list in the final cycle, *recSize* is the number of the products in the recommendation list in the final cycle, *prdID* is the identity of the selected product, and *postRating* is the user's rating of the selected product (i.e., before visiting it) to indicate how close it is to her needs and preferences.

3.2 Exploiting Past Cases in Building the User Query Representation

The user-query representation initialization starts when the user requests the system for product recommendation and ends before the first recommendation list is produced and shown to her. In the initialization process, both the past information (e.g., past recommendation cases) and the current information (e.g., the user's explicit initial conditions) are exploited. At the end of the initialization process, the system builds the *IQR* case component, $IQR = q^0 = (q_l^0, p^0, w^0)$.

The discussions on how the system builds the initial logical query (q_l^0) and the initial feature weights vector (w^0) components are presented in [15, 11]. Basically, q_l^0 is built exploiting the user's space-time constraints and her initial conditions stated as must, and w^0 is built exploiting the history of the user's critiques expressed in her past recommendation sessions (i.e., recorded in the *CTZ* case component).

In this section, we focus the discussion on how the system initializes the favorite pattern component (*p*) exploiting the knowledge contained in past recommendation cases, together with the user's default preferences (stored in her mobile device's memory) and her initial conditions stated as wish. The initial favorite pattern component (p^0) is built in the three following steps.

- First, find the past recommendation case which 1) contains a product selection (i.e., the value of the *SEL* case component is not null) and 2) is the most similar to the current case.
- Then, take out the product selected in that most similar case (i.e., stored in the *SEL* case component).
- Finally, merge the three preferences sources (i.e., the product selected in the most similar case, the user's default preferences, and the user's initial conditions stated as wish) to build the initial favorite pattern component (p^0). (This merging step is discussed later.)

As discussed in the previous section, the case model consists of seven components. However, at the time when the user-query initialization takes place only the first four components of the current case are known.

$$C^* = (SAH^*, CTX^*, UDP^*, UIS^*, ?, ?, ?)$$

The most similar case is found by computing the dissimilarities of the past cases to the current one C^*. In particular, the dissimilarity of a past case C to the current one C^* is given by the following distance function.

$$d(C, C^*) = [1 / (w_{SAH} + w_{CTX} + w_{UDP} + w_{UIS})] .$$
$$[w_{SAH} . d^{SAH}(C, C^*) + w_{CTX} . d^{CTX}(C, C^*) + \qquad (1)$$
$$w_{UDP} . d^{UDP}(C, C^*) + w_{UIS} . d^{UIS}(C, C^*)];$$

where the weights w_{SAH}, w_{CTX}, w_{UDP}, and w_{UIS} model the relative importance of the case components SAH, CTX, UDP, and UIS, respectively. We note that the weights of these case components are fixed (predefined) in the tests discussed in Section 4.

The dissimilarity of a past case C to the current one C^* with respect to case component COM (i.e., either SAH or CTX or UDP or UIS) is given by:

$$d^{COM}(C, C^*) = \frac{\sum_{i=1}^{k} w_i^{COM} . d(COM_i(C), COM_i(C^*))}{\sum_{i=1}^{k} w_i^{COM}} \qquad (2)$$

where k is the number of the features of case component COM, $d(COM_i(C)$, $COM_i(C^*))$ is the local dissimilarity function for the i-th feature of case component COM, and w_i^{COM} is the weight of the i-th feature of case component COM.

For the three case components SAH, CTX, and UDP, the local dissimilarity functions, $d(x_i, y_i)$, are defined for different feature types as follows.

- $d(x_i, y_i) = 1$, if x_i or y_i is undefined.
- For a numeric feature f_i, $d(x_i, y_i) = |x_i - y_i| / (max_i - min_i)$, where max_i and min_i are the maximum and minimum values of feature f_i.
- For a nominal feature f_i, $d(x_i, y_i)$ is equal to zero if $(x_i = y_i)$, and is equal to one if otherwise.
- For a nominal-set feature f_i, $d(x_i, y_i) = 1 - (|x_i \cap y_i| / |x_i \cup y_i|)$.

As discussed in Section 3.1, the UIS case component models the preferences that the user explicitly specifies at start-up. When specifying initial preferences, the user also indicates the strength of each initial preference; i.e., if an initial preference is a must or a wish. Therefore, the case similarity computation relative to the UIS case component must involve these strengths. In particular, the local dissimilarity functions, $d_{UIS}(x_i, y_i)$, used for the UIS case component are defined as follows.

- $d_{UIS}(x_i, y_i) = 1$, if x_i or y_i is undefined.
- For a numeric feature f_i, $d_{UIS}(x_i, y_i)$ is equal to $d(x_i, y_i)$ if both x_i and y_i are must conditions or both are wish ones, and is equal to $[d(x_i, y_i)]^\alpha$ ($\alpha \in (0,1)$) if otherwise.

- For a nominal feature f_i, $d_{UIS}(x_i, y_i)$ is equal to zero if $(x_i = y_i)$ and both x_i and y_i are must conditions or both are wish ones, and is equal to β $(\beta \in (0,1))$ if $(x_i = y_i)$ and x_i and y_i have different strength, and is equal to one if $(x_i \neq y_i)$.

- For a nominal-set feature f_i, $d_{UIS}(x_i, y_i) = (1/n_i)\sum_{j=1}^{n_i} d_{UIS}(x_{ij}, y_{ij})$, where n_i is the size (i.e., the number of the elements) of feature f_i.

The similarity of a past case C to the current one C^* is then computed as:

$$sim(C, C^*) = 1 - d(C, C^*) \tag{3}$$

Having found the case C^{sim} most similar to the current one C^*, the system merges the following preferences sources to build the initial favorite pattern (p^0).

- The user's initial conditions stated as wish stored in the UIS component of the current case C^*. (We note that the UIS component stores both the initial conditions stated as must and those stated as wish.)
- The user's default preferences (i.e., those kept in her mobile device's memory) stored in the UDP component of the current case C^*.
- The product selected in the most similar case C^{sim}, i.e., the solution part (SEL) of the most similar case C^{sim}.

The preference merging is done at the feature level, i.e., for each feature the preference expressed in the highest priority knowledge source overwrites that in the other sources. The order of the priority among the three knowledge sources is: the user's initial conditions, followed by the user's default preferences, and finally the product selected in the most similar case. For example, if the user specifies a wish condition on cost, then it is used to set the initial preference on cost (p_4^0); otherwise, the system sets p_4^0 by the preference on cost indicated in the user's default preferences. If no preference on cost indicated in the user's default preferences, the system sets p_4^0 by the cost of the product selected in the most similar case.

3.3 Adaptation of the User Query Representation through the User Critiquing

At the end of the initialization process, the system produces the initial user-query representation $q^0 = (q_l^0, p^0, w^0)$, i.e., the content of the IQR case component. However, this initial user-query representation may be far from the user's true preferences. To refine this initial representation, the user is involved in a dialogue where the system suggests some products and the user makes some critiques. The elicited preferences help the system to revise its current guess; i.e., adapt its current user-query representation. So, cycle by cycle, a more precise knowledge of the user's needs and preferences is obtained and the critiques are used to adapt the case.

When making a critique to a recommended product, the user indicates the strength of the preference (e.g., in Fig. 1c the user's critique is stated as a wish). A critique expressed as a must is incorporated in the logical query component (q_l), which makes the system focuses on a certain region of the product space, and the weight w_i of the criticized feature f_i is updated. A critique expressed as a wish is incorporated in the favorite pattern component (p), which makes the system re-rank the recommendation list, and the weight w_i of the criticized feature f_i is updated. After the user makes a critique the system updates the CTZ case component incorporating (appending) the new critique.

We note that our critique-based approach is different from the existing ones in several aspects. First, in our approach users are supported to make critiques on feature-level, but not on item-level (like the preference-based approach in [8]). Second, in our approach, given a user's critique, only the user's preference expressed on the criticized feature, but not the values of the other features in the criticized item (as in [4, 8, 6, 10]), is used to adapt the query representation. The rationale is that, due to the peculiar characteristics of the mobile usage environment (e.g., small screens), it is not practical to assume, or require, that the user looks at all the recommended items, or all the features of an item, before making a critique. Third, in our approach, when making a critique, the user is supported to indicate the preference strength (i.e., wish or must) of the critique.

4 Experimental Evaluation

The proposed recommendation approach has been implemented in MobyRek – a mobile case-based RS that supports mobile users in the selection of their desired travel products (restaurants). The MobyRek system was validated with real users, employing a catalog of 84 restaurants [15]. The log data of this live-user evaluation consists of fifteen successful recommendation cases.

In a previous work [13], we introduced the two system variants, *sysMR* and *sysSS*, using the same composite query representation, but in building the initial user-query representation *sysMR* exploited the past recommendation cases while *sysSS* did not. We ran off-line experiments that, exploiting the log data of the real recommendation cases, compared the average position of the user selected product in the first recommendation list in the two variants. The experimental results showed that *sysMR* produced a better quality of the first recommendation list over *sysSS*, i.e., the average position of the selected product in *sysMR* was 23.19% higher than that in *sysSS* [13]. This initial comparative result proves the benefit of exploiting past recommendation cases for generating the first recommendation list. Here, we shall extend this result evaluating the impact of the different case components on the system's recommendation performance. In this evaluation, we compare five system variants exploiting different case components.

- **"Full case model"**: the full case model is exploited.
- **"without *COM*"**: not exploiting case component *COM*, where *COM* ∈ {*SAH*, *CTX*, *UDP*, *UIS*}.

Here we are also exploiting the log data of the recommendation cases recorded in the previous live-user evaluation of MobyRek. First we compare the performance of the five system variants with respect to the quality of the first recommendation list. Then, we compare the performance of these variants with respect to the quality of the whole (simulated) recommendation session.

4.1 Quality of the First Recommendation List

In this first test, each variant incrementally **replayed the first recommendation cycle** of each tester's case. Here, "replayed" means that the initial user-query representation in the original case was recomputed, considering or not certain case components.

The test procedure, followed by all the five system variants, consists of three main steps (see [13] for another application of this evaluation methodology). First, for each tester's original case the system builds the initial user-query representation $q^0 = (q_l^0, p^0, w^0)$, as discussed in Section 3.2. Second, the system uses the initial query representation to compute the first recommendation list. We note that in this first test the system produces the full recommendation list, not top-k as discussed in Section 2. Third, the system checks in the first recommendation list the position of the product selected by the tester in her original case. For each system variant the average position of the selected product is computed over all the simulated cases. We assume that the best variant is the one achieving the highest average position of the selected product.

The performance of the five variants is shown in Fig. 3 with the "all cases" label. The results in Fig. 3 show that the variant exploiting the full case model outperformed the other variants exploiting a partial case model. In particular, the average position of the selected product in the first recommendation list was 15, 15.87, 19.73, 17.73, and 27 for "*Full case model*", "*without SAH*", "*without CTX*", "*without UDP*", and "*without UIS*", respectively (the lower the better, as 1 means the first position in the list). In Fig. 3, by comparing the "*Full case model*" variant with the others we can understand how much a case component influences the quality of the first recommendation list. As shown in Fig. 3, the *SAH* case component has a small impact, since the exclusion of this case component caused just a 5.8% increase of the average position of the selected product. However, each of the *CTX*, *UDP*, and *UIS* case components has a major impact, since its exclusion caused a larger increase of the average position of the selected product, i.e., 31.53%, 18.2%, and 80% for *CTX*, *UDP*, and *UIS*, respectively.

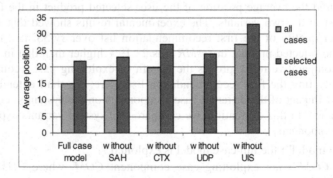

Fig. 3. The average position of the selected product in the first recommendation list

Since in the live-user evaluation of MobyRek we used the full case model, one might conjecture that a product has been selected just because it appeared in the first screen of the first recommendation list, and therefore the comparison could be biased in favor of the "*Full case model*" variant. Hence, in order to obtain a possibly more fair comparison, we also considered just the selected products that did not appear in the first screen (i.e., top 3, in the mobile phone interface) of the first recommendation list [13]. The performance, on this subset of simulated cases, of the five system variants is shown in Fig. 3 with the "selected cases" label. Even for these selected cases, the "*Full case model*" variant, which exploited the full case model, still achieved the best quality of the first recommendation list. In particular, the average position of the selected product in the first recommendation list was 21.7, 23, 27, 24.1, and 33 for *"Full case model"*, *"without SAH"*, *"without CTX"*, *"without UDP"*, and *"without UIS"*, respectively. Hence, the conclusions made above are still true under this probably less biased evaluation.

4.2 Quality of the Full Recommendation Session

In the second test, each system variant incrementally **replayed the whole sessions**. Here, "replayed" means that in a simulated recommendation case the system first re-computed the initial query representation, considering or not certain case components, and then re-applied, one by one in the original order, the user's critiques. To replay a real recommendation case, we had to define different ways of re-applying (i.e., simulating) user critiques. That is because the case models employed by the four variants *"without SAH"*, *"without CTX"*, *"without UDP"*, and *"without UIS"* were different from that employed by MobyRek. Therefore, at each simulated cycle the recommendation list produced by a variant (hereafter called "the output list") can be different from that produced in the real session, and moreover the real criticized product can be absent from the output list. Hence, for each variant, we tried different critique-simulation methods, and measured its performance using the best (or average) result obtained over all these methods. In this way, we are trying to be unbiased, i.e., not in favor of any variant.

In a recommendation session, the cause and motivation for a critique made in a cycle may be inferred based on the product criticized at that cycle or the one selected at the end of the session. Hence, for each system variant, we tried the four critique-simulation methods listed below. (See [12] for more details and another application of these simulation methods).

- *Just repeat the critique.* This method assumes that a user's critique is influenced by her preferences, rather by the products shown. In this method, the critique is re-applied even if the criticized product does not appear in the output list.
- *Critique according to the selected product.* This method assumes that a user's critique is motivated by her selected product. Hence, for a simulated critique the value of the criticized feature in the selected product is used to adapt the user-query representation.
- *Critique according to the product similar to the criticized one.* In case the criticized product is not found in the output list, this method assumes that the user makes a similar critique to a product (in the output list) similar to the criticized one. In particular, if the criticized product is found in the top N of the output list, then the critique is repeated; otherwise, the product most similar to the criticized one is identified, and the value of the criticized feature in that product is used to adapt the user-query representation.
- *Critique according to the product similar to the selected one.* In case the criticized product is not found in the output list, this method assumes that the user makes a similar critique to a product (in the output list) similar to the selected one.

The simulation test procedure, followed by all the five system variants, consists of four main steps [12]. At Step 1, for each tester's original case the system builds the initial user-query representation (as discussed in Section 3.2), considering or not certain case components, and retrieves the list of the original critiques that are recorded in the *CTZ* case component. At Step 2, the system uses the current query representation to compute the output list (as discussed in Section 2). At Step 3, the system checks if one of the termination conditions is met; if not, the system proceeds to Step 4. The simulation of a tester's original case ends either when the selected product appears in the view window of the output list (a successfully simulated case) or when all the original critiques have been re-applied but the selected product is still not found (an unsuccessfully simulated case). In this test procedure, the view window models the number of products that the simulated user is supposed to look at. At Step 4, the system takes the next critique from the original critiques list, and simulates it using one of the four critique-simulation methods. The simulated critique is then used by the system to adapt the query representation (see Section 3.3), and the simulation process proceeds to the next cycle (at Step 2). Finally, for each system variant the number of successfully simulated cases and the average session length are measured.

Fig. 4 shows the results obtained for a view-window size of 5 items. For each system variant, Fig. 4 shows the best result among the four critique-simulation methods and the average result over these methods.

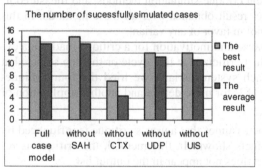 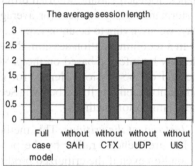

Fig. 4. The number of successfully simulated cases and the average session length, for the view-window size of 5

We first look at the number of successfully simulated cases (success rate). When comparing on the best result, both the *"Full case model"* and *"without SAH"* variants achieved the same highest success rate. This confirms the result of the previous test where the average position of the selected product in the first recommendation list in the *"without SAH"* variant was just a bit lower (5.8%) than that in *"Full case model"*. Also, the *"without SAH"* variant, applying the user critiques, achieved the same success rate as *"Full case model"*. Conversely, the success rates of the three variants *"without CTX"*, *"without UDP"*, and *"without UIS"* were 53.33%, 20%, and 20%, respectively, lower than that of *"Full case model"*. Hence, these three variants achieved a lower quality of the first recommendation list (see Fig. 3) and a lower success rate. Looking at the average result we observe that *"Full case model"* and *"without SAH"* achieved the same success rate, but the success rates of *"without CTX"*, *"without UDP"*, and *"without UIS"* were lower than that of *"Full case model"*. These comparative results show that the three case components CTX, UDP, and UIS are important for the mobile recommendation problem, since their exclusion from the case model causes a decrease of the system's recommendation performance.

We now look at the average session length (i.e., the average number of recommendation cycles). We note that in the simulated recommendation cases, the length of the dialogue was rather short, i.e., just 2-3 recommendation cycles. This average session length is much shorter than those of Web critique-based RSs [16, 8, 6, 10], and it is due to the mobile usage context, i.e., mobile users tend to spend less time and effort than Web users do in searching for some information or products. As shown in Fig. 4, the three variants *"without SAH"*, *"without UDP"*, and *"without UIS"* took the average session lengths approximately to that taken by *"Full case model"*. However, the *"without CTX"* variant consumed a longer (55.56%) average session length than *"Full case model"*. In fact, the exclusion of the *CTX* component from the case model caused not only a poor success rate but also a longer session length.

5 Conclusions and Future Work

In this paper, we have described a case-based approach for modeling mobile context-aware recommendation problems and solutions. The proposed case model is capable of modeling evolving recommendation sessions, capturing the recommendation context, supporting critique-based user-system conversations, and integrating both ephemeral and stable user preferences. We have discussed the exploitation of the proposed case model to build and revise the user query representation. We have illustrated an experimental evaluation aimed at testing the impact of different case components on the system's recommendation performance. The experimental results showed that the exploitation of the full case model results in a better recommendation, hence proving the correctness of our design choices, and that the case components that model the user's contextual information, default preferences, and initial preferences, play the most important role in the mobile recommendation problem.

In the proposed approach, when searching the case base for similar cases, the system uses a fixed set of pre-defined importance weights for the case components (see Equation 1). However, a case component may be very important in a recommendation situation, but less important in another one. Hence, in the future we want to define an appropriate approach for learning and adapting the importance weights of the case components for a given user in a particular recommendation situation. Also, in our approach the *CTX* case component contains only the user's position and the time of the request. In fact, the recommendation contextual information may include not only spatial-temporal information but also other situational information such as if the user goes to the restaurant alone or with a friend, on a date or for a casual dinner, etc. We plan to deal with this extension of the contexts exploitation in a future project.

References

1. Aamodt, A., Plaza, E.: Case-based Reasoning: Foundational Issues, Methodological Variations, and System Approaches. AI Communications 7(1), 39–59 (1994)
2. Adomavicius, G., Tuzhilin, A.: Toward the next Generation of Recommender Systems: A Survey of the State-of-the-Art and Possible Extensions. IEEE Trans. Knowledge and Data Engineering 17(6), 734–749 (2005)

3. Bridge, D., Göker, M., McGinty, L., Smyth, B.: Case-based Recommender Systems. Knowledge Engineering Review 20(3), 315–320 (2005)
4. Burke, R.: Interactive Critiquing for Catalog Navigation in E-Commerce. Artificial Intelligence Review 18(3-4), 245–267 (2002)
5. Burke, R.: Hybrid Web Recommender Systems. In: Brusilovsky, P., Kobsa, A., Nejdl, W. (eds.) The Adaptive Web: Methods and Strategies of Web Personalization, pp. 377–408. Springer, Heidelberg (2007)
6. Chen, L., Pu, P.: Preference-based Organization Interface: Aiding User Critiques in Recommender Systems. In: 11th International Conference on User Modeling, pp. 77–86. Springer, Heidelberg (2007)
7. Lorenzi, F., Ricci, F.: Case-based Recommender Systems: A Unifying View. In: Mobasher, B., Anand, S. (eds.) Intelligent Techniques for Web Personalization, pp. 89–113. Springer, Heidelberg (2005)
8. McGinty, L., Smyth, B.: Adaptive Selection: An Analysis of Critiquing and Preference-based Feedback in Conversational Recommender Systems. International Journal of Electronic Commerce 11(2), 35–57 (2006)
9. McSherry, D.: Completeness Criteria for Retrieval in Recommender Systems. In: 8th European Conference on Case-Based Reasoning, pp. 9–29. Springer, Heidelberg (2006)
10. McSherry, D., Aha, D.W.: Mixed-Initiative Relaxation of Constraints in Critiquing Dialogues. In: 7th International Conference on Case-Based Reasoning, pp. 107–121. Springer, Heidelberg (2007)
11. Nguyen, Q.N., Ricci, F.: User Preferences Initialization and Integration in Critique-Based Mobile Recommender Systems. In: 5th International Workshop on Artificial Intelligence in Mobile Systems, pp. 71–78. Universitat des Saarlandes Press (2004)
12. Nguyen, Q.N., Ricci, F.: Replaying Live-User Interactions in the Off-Line Evaluation of Critique-based Mobile Recommendations. In: Recommender Systems 2007, pp. 81–88. ACM Press, New York (2007)
13. Nguyen, Q.N., Ricci, F.: Long-Term and Session-Specific User Preferences in a Mobile Recommender System. In: 2008 International Conference on Intelligent User Interfaces, pp. 381–384. ACM Press, New York (2008)
14. Ricci, F., Venturini, A., Cavada, D., Mirzadeh, N., Blaas, D., Nones, M.: Product Recommendation with Interactive Query Management and Twofold Similarity. In: 5th International Conference on Case-Based Reasoning, pp. 479–493. Springer, Heidelberg (2003)
15. Ricci, F., Nguyen, Q.N.: Acquiring and Revising Preferences in a Critique-based Mobile Recommender System. IEEE Intelligent Systems 22(3), 22–29 (2007)
16. Shimazu, H.: Expertclerk: A Conversational Case-based Reasoning Tool for Developing Salesclerk Agents in E-Commerce Webshops. Artificial Intelligence Review 18(3-4), 223–244 (2002)
17. Stahl, A.: Combining Case-Based and Similarity-Based Product Recommendation. In: 8th European Conference on Case-Based Reasoning, pp. 355–369. Springer, Heidelberg (2006)

k-NN Aggregation with a Stacked Email Representation

Amandine Orecchioni, Nirmalie Wiratunga, Stewart Massie, and Susan Craw

School of Computing,
The Robert Gordon University,
Aberdeen AB25 1HG, Scotland, UK
{ao,nw,sm,smc}@comp.rgu.ac.uk

Abstract. The variety in email related tasks, as well as the increase in daily
email load, has created a need for automated email management tools. In this paper, we provide an empirical evaluation of representational schemes and retrieval
strategies for email. In particular, we study the impact of both textual and non-
textual email content for case representation applied to Email task management.
Our first contribution is STACK, an email representation based on stacking. Multiple casebases are created, each using a different case representation related with
attributes corresponding to semi-structured email content. A k-NN classifier is
applied to each casebase and the output is used to form a new case representation. Our second contribution is a new evaluation method allowing the creation
of random chronological stratified train-test trials that respect both temporal and
class distribution aspects, crucial for the email domain. The Enron corpus was
used to create a dataset for the email deletion prediction task. Evaluation results
show significant improvements with STACK over single casebase retrieval and
multiple casebases retrieval combined using majority vote.

1 Introduction

Over time, email has evolved from a simple medium of communication to one involving complex management tasks. Nowadays, it is not enough to simply read and reply
to emails. One must also prioritise reading order, filter spam and phish emails, avoid
viruses, organise and maintain information repositories and manage social networks
and diaries. This increase in email related tasks coupled with the increase in email handling load has created the need for automated email management tools.

Research in email management recognises five key areas [19,9]: information management, task management, time management, contact management and security pro-
tection. Machine learning research applied to email has focused on individual prediction
tasks within each area such as delete [8], reply [23,18], attach [12], forward [22], filter [20,15,10] and classify [2,4]. However, since each area typically involves several
chronologically organised email tasks, these tasks can be seen as email workflows. Table 1 presents four workflows by decomposing each management activity into a set
of chronologically organised tasks. The *Contact Workflow* combines contact management and email classification tasks, while the *Task Workflow* combines automated email
response, reply prediction and email classification tasks. The advantage of the email
workflow view is that it provides a template that can be used to guide prediction. For
instance, consider an incoming email, it would be useful to predict what action the user

K.-D. Althoff et al. (Eds.): ECCBR 2008, LNAI 5239, pp. 415–429, 2008.

Table 1. Email Workflow Examples

Task Workflow Helpdesk Query	Information Workflow Paper Recommendation	Time Workflow Meeting Announcement	Contact Workflow New Contact Detail
1. Read Email	1. Read Email	1. Read Email	1. Read Email
2. Reply	2. Open Attachment	2. Open calendar	2. Open Address Book
3. Keep as "open queries"	3. Print Attachment	3. Add reminder	3. Add contact
4. Receive follow-up question	4. Save Attachment	4. Keep email in inbox	4. Save contact
5. Reply	5. Delete Email	5. Delete email after meeting	5. Delete email
6. File in "closed queries"			

might take. Is the email going to be forwarded, if so to whom? Is the user likely to reply, if so can the reply be semi-authored? Should the email be deleted, if so when?

An email prediction task requires a learner to handle both local interactions between emails and potentially evolving email concepts. CBR's ability to handle these challenges were demonstrated on an email filtering task [10]. An email is commonly represented as a bag-of-words of its textual content. However, there is also separate evidence to suggest the utility of non-textual email attributes for email classification [11,17]. In this paper, we present a systematic evaluation of email attribute extraction from both textual and non-textual content. Our work differs from existing feature selection and extraction research in that we establish the importance of email sub-sections in case representation instead of that of features. Since every workflow in Table 1 terminates in the delete or filing tasks, we choose to focus our study on deletion prediction using the Enron corpus.

The rest of this paper is organised as follows. Section 2 discusses related work. Multiple email representations are defined in Section 3 and how they can be used in multiple casebases in Section 4. Section 5 defines a new evaluation methodology allowing the creation of random chronological stratified train-test trials that respect both temporal and class distribution aspects. The evaluation and results are presented in Section 6. Finally, our conclusions and future work are highlighted in Section 7.

2   Related Work

This section presents three different aspects of related work. We will start by discussing email representation and possible email attributes. We will then report the benefits of ensemble of classifiers documented in the literature. Finally, we will highlight the drawbacks of current evaluation methods for the email domain.

Research in email categorization is commonly focused by classification into topical folders [2] or into speech-acts [4], email prioritisation [16] and Spam filtering [10]. A standard information retrieval approach for document representation is to use a bag-of-words representation. However, research focused on the acquisition of indexing vocabulary for email identifies three types of features:

- *structured*: features extracted from the header such as *date, from, to*;
- *textual*: keywords from the free text sections such as *subject* and *body*; and

– *handcrafted*: features created from preprocessing the emails such as *email length* and *number of special characters* [11].

It was shown that handcrafted features typically do not improve prediction accuracy and so are not considered further in this paper.

Email features can be incorporated in a single feature vector. However, previous work has highlighted the benefits of using an ensemble of classifiers, based on different feature subsets, over a single feature vector [7]. Performance improvements with ensembles are due to the aggregation of *base-learners* which are essentially *local* specialists. This gets round the problem of feature weight optimisation otherwise needed with a single feature vector [5]. Feature subsets can be generated randomly [1] or using feature selection [6]. One possible ensemble aggregation method is stacking, which is typically used to combine different types of *base-learners* into a *meta-learner* [25]. The idea is to use the prediction of each *base-learner* as input for the *meta-learner*. This requires each case in the *meta-learner* casebase to be represented with values corresponding to predictions of the *base-learners*. Stacking has been successfully applied to spam filtering by combining a memory-based classifier and a Naive Bayes classifier [21].

The temporal aspect of email is an important issue to consider when generating train-test splits for evaluation. Indeed, test set emails must be more recent than train set emails. In a real life situation, it would be impossible to make a decision about an incoming email based on emails not yet received. This aspect is not taken into account by standard evaluation methodologies such as cross-validation, leave one out or hold out. A possible approach is to order emails chronologically and use the earlier half for training and the later half for testing [17]. However, a single split of the dataset is problematic to evaluate statistical significance as it only permits one trial. Another approach is to create multiple splits from a chronologically ordered dataset. The classifier is trained on the first N messages and tested on the following N, then trained on the first $2N$ messages and tested on the following N, then trained on the first $3N$ messages and tested on the following N and so on [2]. This approach is similar to the previous in that it ensures a chronological ordering of the data. But, it also allows statistical significance testing as it creates N-1 trials instead of a single trial. However, class distribution should also be respected, and these approaches are only suitable when emails from each class are evenly distributed over time.

3   Case Representation for Emails

The decomposition of a semi-structured document into constituents, such as *from*, *to*, *subject* and *body* in emails, allows case retrieval to focus on each of them separately. This is particularly useful when they have their own indexing vocabulary as they are further decomposable into feature vectors.

The top-half of Table 2 presents nine attributes identified in relation to email sections. *Date* and *From Address* are nominal attributes while the others are textual attributes represented as binary feature vector. For instance, all the email addresses from the *To* field of the emails in the casebase form the indexing vocabulary of *To Address*. This attribute is represented for each email as a feature vector of the indexing vocabulary, where the

Table 2. Case representations for email

	Descriptor	Email Representation
Single-Attribute	Date	$Date = date$
	From Address	$from_@ = (Address_{from_1}, ...Address_{from_i})$
	From Name	$from_N = (Name_{from_1}, ...Name_{from_j})$
	To Address	$to_@ = (Address_{to_1}, ...Address_{to_k})$
	To Name	$to_N = (Name_{to_1}, ...Name_{to_l})$
	CC Address	$Cc_@ = (Address_{cc_1}, ...Address_{cc_m})$
	CC Name	$cc_N = (Name_{cc_1}, ...Name_{cc_n})$
	Subject	$subject = (keyword_{subj_1}, ...keyword_{subj_n})$
	Body	$body = (keyword_{body_1}, ...keyword_{body_n})$
Multi-Attribute	From	$from = (from_@, from_N)$
	To	$to = (to_@, to_N)$
	CC	$cc = (Cc_@, cc_N)$
	Recipients	$recipients = (to_@, to_N, cc_@, cc_N)$
	Text	$text = (subject, body)$
	All	$all = (Date, from_@, from_N, to_@, to_N, Cc_@, cc_N, subject, body)$

value for each feature is 1 if the email's *To* field contains the feature or 0 otherwise. *From Name, To Name, CC Address, CC Name, Subject* and *Body* are represented similarly. Accordingly, an email can be represented with a single-attribute representation or a multi-attribute representation using alternative combinations of attributes (see bottom-part of Table 2). For instance, *From* combines feature attributes *From Address* and *From Name* and *Text* represents all textual content by including attributes *Subject* and *Body*.

The advantage of a representation that preserves document structure is that similarity computations can be confined to corresponding email sections. Figure 1 illustrates the aggregation of local similarities S_i into a global similarity $S(E_1, E_2)$ between emails E_1 and E_2. Local similarities are computed for each corresponding attribute and aggregated using average.

An obvious approach to represent email is to include all attributes in a single feature vector representation which we call *All*. The similarity between two emails with such a representation is computed as above. However, since seven out of the nine attributes are

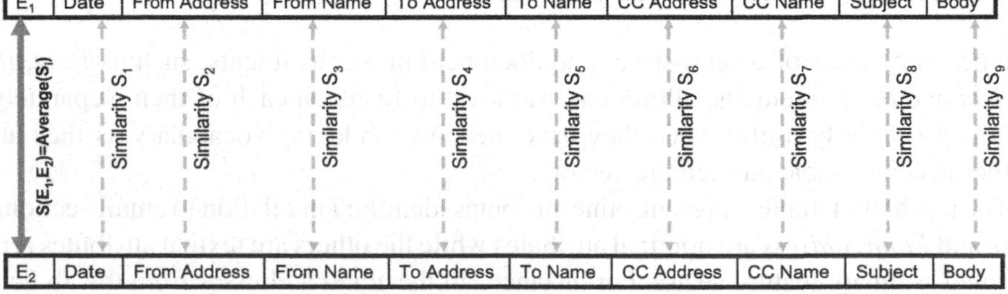

Fig. 1. Similarity computation with semi-structured document representations

binary feature vectors, we considered multiple casebases where every casebase contains the same set of emails but uses a different case representation. Each casebase uses one of the single-attribute representations listed in the top-half of Table 2. The prediction task involves aggregating retrieval results from multiple casebases. Essentially, our interest is to study how best to combine similarities from separate email sections.

4   Retrieval with Multiple Casebases

Previous work has shown that retrieval over multiple casebases can be achieved with ensembles of *k*-NN classifiers [7]. Each *k*-NN classifier constitutes a CBR system which we refer to as a *base-learner*. The final prediction is obtained by combining the predictions of each *base-learner*. Figure 2 illustrates majority voting, a common aggregation strategy. Each *base-learner* uses the same casebase, but with a different case representation, and the final prediction of the new email is the majority vote of the *base-learners* predictions.

However, voting only makes sense if the classifiers perform comparably well. If, for instance, six of the nine classifiers make incorrect predictions, the majority vote will be incorrect. Majority vote is therefore unsuitable when the relevances of *base-learners* vary. This is because it is unclear which classifier to trust and a dynamic weighting would have to be applied to capture the importance of each classifier in difference circumstances. For instance, when a case is represented using *Date*, the classifier is typically unable to make a prediction. However, when a prediction is made, it is highly likely to be correct. Therefore, when this classifier is able to make a prediction, its weight should be high, but otherwise low. In this work, since each classifier learns from the same set of emails represented differently, if each classifier performed comparably well, one classifier would suffice. The goal in using multiple classifiers is to exploit the complementarity of email attributes. Stacking combines multiple models differently by introducing the concept of *meta-learner*. It tries to learn which classifiers are reliable

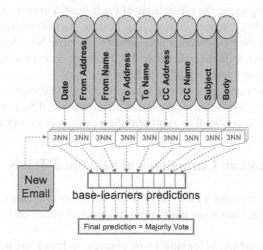

Fig. 2. Aggregation with majority voting

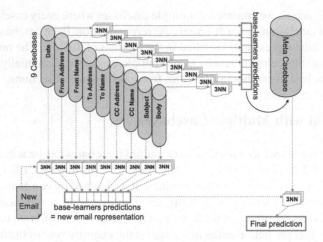

Fig. 3. STACK representation

using another learning algorithm to discover how best to combine the predictions of the *base-learners*. It is suited to situations where *base-learners* are reliable in different circumstances [24].

Stacking is generally used to combine different types of *base-learners*. Here, we use stacking to combine the same type of *base-learners*, k-NN classifiers, but where each classifier uses a different case representation. Each *base-learner* provides a prediction, like in majority voting, but the *meta-learner* combines these predictions into a new case. Therefore, cases in the casebase used by the *meta-learner*, or meta-casebase, have as many attributes as there are *base-learners*.

In this work, a new case is classified by nine *base-learners*, one for each single-attribute representation. The predictions are used to create a new case representation for the *meta-learner* called STACK. The top-part of Figure 3 illustrates how the meta-casebase is created by using the predictions of each *base-learners* to create a new case representation, or STACK representation. The bottom-part illustrates the classification of a new case. First, the new email is classified by the nine *base-learners* to obtain its STACK representation. It is then classified by the *meta-learner* which uses the meta-casebase where cases are represented with STACK.

The hypothesis supporting the STACK representation is that the *base-learners* predictions of similar emails follow the same pattern. For instance, if two emails are classified similarly by the *base-learners*, their representation in the meta-casebase will be similar.

5   Creating Random Chronological Stratified Trials

We introduce a new evaluation method, n-RCST, in order to create random chronological stratified trials that maintain the temporal aspect of email and respect the overall class distribution.

Given a set of n emails belonging to m classes, n-RCST creates chronologically ordered email subsets E_i corresponding to each class. Each subset E_i is further split into k even splits E_{ij}. Typically $k=2$, where one split is used for training and the other for testing. When using stacking, $k=3$: the new representation for the *meta-learner* is obtained for E_{i1} and E_{i2} using E_{i2} and E_{i3} respectively for training. Next, *k-1* suitable dates d_j are identified in order to create k chronological splits E'_{ij} for each class c_i, such that all emails in class c_i received between d_{j-1} and d_j form E'_{ij}. This enforces the temporal aspect on our trials because emails in any j^{th} split are more recent than emails in any $j+1^{th}$ split. Multiple stratified trials can then be generated by randomly selecting a number of emails according to c_i's distribution from E'_{ij} for testing and E'_{ij+1} for training. This algorithm is detailed in Figure 4 to illustrate its generality.

Figure 5 illustrates n-RCST applied to a DELETE/KEEP classification task. First DELETE emails are separated from KEEP emails and put into chronologically ordered subsets. Assuming 2 splits are required, one for testing and one for training, each subset is further decomposed into 2 even splits (e.g. D_1 and K_1). The date at which the oldest email of each split has been received is identified (e.g. d_{D1} and d_{K1}). Finally, a date d is chosen between d_{D1} and d_{K1}. Splits can be recreated so that $delete'_1$ and $keep'_1$ are all emails, from each class respectively, received after d, whilst $delete'_2$ and $keep'_2$ are those received before d. Trials are now created by randomly selecting emails from $delete'_1$ and $keep'_1$ for testing and $delete'_2$ and $keep'_2$ for training. We are now ensured that emails in the test set are more recent than those in the training set.

Let assume we have a dataset of 1500 emails, including 900 emails labeled as DELETE and 600 emails labeled as KEEP. Imagine we want to create N trials, respecting the overall class distribution and the chronological order of the dataset, where each trial

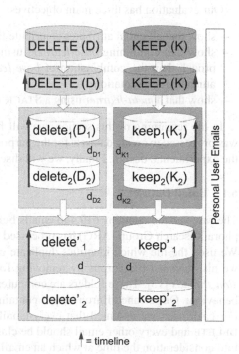

$E = \{e_1, ..., e_n\}$, set of emails
$C = \{c_1, ..., c_m\}$, set of classes
$D = \{d_1, ..., d_k\}$, set of dates
k the number of splits required
$d(e_i)$ date at which email e_i was received
$c(e_i)$ class of email e_i

Create a subset E_i per class
  $\forall c_i \in C, \exists E_i \subset E$ where, $\forall e \in E_i, c(e) = c_i$
Order subset chronologically
  $\forall E_i$, order so that $\forall e_j \in E_i, d(e_j) < d(e_{j+1})$
Create k even splits E_{ij} for each subset E_i
  $\forall E_i, E_i = E_{i1} \cup ... \cup E_{ik}$
  and $|E_{i1}| \approx ... \approx |E_{ik}|$
Get the date of the oldest email in each split E_{ij}
  $\forall E_{ij}, d_{ij} = d(e^*)$,
  where $e^* \in E_{ij}$ and $\forall e \in E_{ij}, d(e^*) < d(e)$
Create a set D_j with the dates of the oldest email in the jth split of all E_{ij} subsets
  $D_j = \bigcup_i \{d_{ij}\}$
Select a date d_j between the most recent and the oldest date in D_j
  $\forall D_j, min(D_j) < d_j < max(D_j)$

Create k chronological splits E'_{ij} per class c_i,
  $\forall e \in E, E'_{ij} = E_{ij} \cap \{e\}$,
  where $d_{j-1} > d(e) > d_j$, and $c(e) = c_i$
  so that $\forall e_j \in E_j = \bigcup_i E_{ji}, d(e_j) > d(e_{j+1})$

Fig. 4. n-RCST algorithm

Fig. 5. n-RCST for delete prediction

represents 10% of the dataset and contains 1/3 for testing and 2/3 for training. A trial must therefore contain 90 emails labeled as DELETE and 60 emails labeled as KEEP. Out of the 90 DELETE, 30 are used for testing and 60 for training. Similarly, out of the 60 KEEP, 20 are used for testing and 40 for training. After n-RCST is applied to the dataset (as in Figure 5), a training set is formed by randomly selecting 60 emails from $delete'_2$ and 40 from $keep'_2$ and the test set formed with 30 emails from $delete'_1$ and 20 from $keep'_1$. Multiple trials can now be generated similarly, ensuring each is stratified by selecting the correct number of emails from each class, and are chronological, as the emails from the test set have been received after the emails from the training set.

6   Evaluation and Results

In this paper, we compare different email representations for the prediction of email deletion. An ideal dataset should contain the time at which an email has been deleted. Indeed, an email can be deleted for different reasons. If an email is irrelevant, it is likely to be deleted as soon as it is received. An email regarding a meeting or an event is likely to be kept until a certain date then deleted when it becomes obsolete. Therefore, prediction of email deletion should also include the time at which the email should be deleted. A dataset containing deletion time is not currently available and is hard to obtain for ethical reasons. Therefore, in this paper, we experiment on a binary classification task where an email is classified either as DELETE or KEEP.

Our evaluation has three main objectives:

- show that all email attributes contribute to the performance of a classifier
- show that combining *base-learners* using a STACK representation is a better approach than the combination of *base-learners* using majority voting or a multi-attribute representation
- show that a *meta-learner* using a STACK representation is more stable across users.

In the remaining of this section, we will first present the Enron Corpus and how it was processed to create datasets for the purpose of our experiments. We will then define the experimental design. Finally, we will discuss the results for each objective.

6.1   Email Dataset

The raw version contains 619,446 emails belonging to 158 users [3]. The Czech Amphora Research Group (ARG) has processed the Enron corpus into 16 XML files [14]. We used the file which identifies duplicate emails to remove all duplicate emails and we also cleaned the corpus by removing folders such as *all_documents* and *discussion_threads* [13]. These folders are computer generated folders and do not reflect user behaviour. Our cleaned Enron corpus contains 288,195 emails belonging to 150 users. For each user, we assumed that every email in *deleted_items* should be classified as DELETE and every other email should be classified as KEEP. We therefore do not take into consideration the time at which an email has been deleted.

6.2   Experimental Design

n-RCST could not be applied to some Enron users because the time period covered by emails labeled as DELETE and the time period covered by email labeled as KEEP do not overlap or do not have an overlapping period large enough to create train-test trials. We extracted 14 Enron users for which n-RCST was suitable and generated 25 trials for each. The class distribution and the number of emails for these users is detailed in Table 3.

Table 3. Class distribution and Number of Email for selected Enron Users

User	% of Deleted Emails	User	Number of Emails
Dean-C	0.205	Lucci-P	753
Watson-K	0.214	Bass-E	754
Heard-M	0.270	Giron-D	767
Quigley-D	0.376	Shively-H	769
White-S	0.426	Heard-M	833
Schoolcraft-D	0.447	Quigley-D	988
Giron-D	0.495	Mims-Thurston-P	1028
Zipper-A	0.511	Zipper-A	1056
Bass-E	0.533	Thomas-P	1099
Parks-J	0.612	Schoolcraft-D	1321
Thomas-P	0.621	Dean-C	1540
Mims-Thurston-P	0.661	Parks-G	1661
Lucci-P	0.754	Watson-K	1974
Shively-H	0.765	White-S	2296

Three splits were generated for each user using n-RCST. In order to evaluate the email representations listed in Table 2, one test set and one train set are required. A trial is created by randomly selecting emails from the most recent split for testing and from the second most recent split for training. In order to evaluate the stack representation, one test set and one train set of emails represented with STACK are required. Emails from the most recent split are classified by the *base-learners* using the second most recent split for training. Similarly, emails from the second most recent split are classified by the *base-learners* using the third split for training. This provides us with a stack representation for emails in the first and second splits, allowing us to use the first split for testing and the second for training. The creation of trials is illustrated in Figure 6 and Figure 7. We maintain consistency in that, for all representations, test sets and training sets are identical.

Once the trials are generated, a casebase is created for each case representation for each trial. All *base-learners* and the *meta-learner* are k-Nearest-Neighbour classifiers with $k = 3$. Further research on the optimal number of neighbours to consider for each *base-learner* would be beneficial but is not considered further in this paper. For binary feature vectors attributes, the similarity is computed using the Euclidean distance. For nominal attributes, the similarity is 1 if the values are identical, 0 otherwise. During retrieval, any ties between multiple candidates are resolved randomly. Alternative representations are compared using classification accuracy. Since our data is not normally

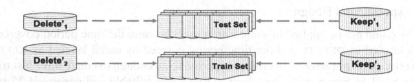

Fig. 6. Trial creation for single feature vector representation

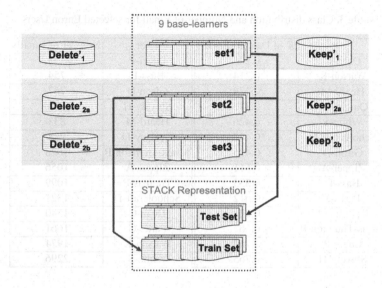

Fig. 7. Trial creation for STACK representation

distributed, significance results are based on a 95% confidence level when applying the Kruskal Wallis test to three or more datasets and 99% confidence when applying the Wilcoxen signed-rank test to two data sets.

6.3 Is Using *All* Attributes Best?

We compared the classification accuracy using the 12 email representations listed in Table 2. Our results show that using only the textual attributes (*Subject*, *Body* and *Text*) or using all the attributes (*All*) result in significantly better results compared to using any of the other attributes. Additionally, using *All* attributes gives significantly better results across users than *Subject*, *Body* and *Text*. This suggests that representing emails only using the textual attributes is not enough and that useful information for retrieval can be extracted from non-textual attributes. However, it is important to note that the accuracy achieved with the best single-attribute representation (*All*) is outperformed by simply predicting the majority class for 8 users out of 14. This is clearly illustrated in Figure 8, where the accuracy achieved with the four best representations is compared to the accuracy achieved by systematically predicting the majority class. We can note that *All* tends to perform well when classes are evenly distributed but struggles on highly skewed data.

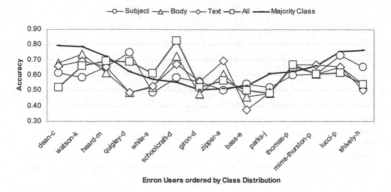

Fig. 8. Accuracy achieved with different email representations

6.4 What Is the Best Way to Combine *Base-Learners*?

The *All* representation, where all email attributes are included in a feature vector, is the simplest way to combine email attributes. Since a classifier using such a representation does not perform well on highly skewed data, we evaluated an alternative approach. A casebase is created for each single-attribute representation. The performance of k-NN using *All* representation is compared to an ensemble of 9 k-NN classifiers combined using majority vote (MAJORITY), each using a different casebase.

Unlike *All*, MAJORITY implicitly captures the importance of each attribute by giving a weight to each classifier based on the similarity between the retrieved neighbours and the new case. This is because the prediction of each *base-learner* is a numeric value between 0 and 1 based on the similarity of the new case to the 3 nearest neighbours. For instance, for a given *base-learner*, let the similarities between the new case and the 3 nearest neighbours 0.2, 0.6 and 0.8 and their class KEEP, DELETE and DELETE respectively. The prediction for this base learner is $(0.2*0+0.6*1+0.8*1)/(0.2+0.6+0.8) = 0.875$. If the prediction is smaller than 0.5, the email is classified as KEEP, otherwise it is classified as DELETE. The closer the prediction is to 0 or 1, the more the *base-learner* is confident that the class for the new case should be KEEP or DELETE respectively. The majority vote is calculated by averaging the predictions of all the *base-learners*. We therefore expect MAJORITY to perform better than *All*. However, significance test show that both approaches perform comparably. This is clearly illustrated with a scatter-plot in Figure 9. This suggests that the global similarity, or similarity across all attributes, is equivalent to the combination of local similarities, or similarities of individual attributes.

We then compared STACK to both previous approaches. Results show that k-NN using STACK representation performs significantly better than MAJORITY or k-NN using *All* representation. The scatter-plot in Figure 10 provides a closer look at STACK and MAJORITY results. The performance achieved using the STACK representation can be explained by its ability to generate predictions based on similarity values computed over the predictions of multiple *base-learners*. When combining email attributes using MAJORITY, a good performance is expected only if *base-learners* tend to agree on a prediction. However, STACK further exploits the fact that if the ensemble of *base-learners*

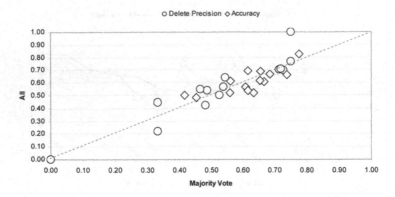

Fig. 9. Accuracy and Delete precision for 15 Enron users using MAJORITY and *All*

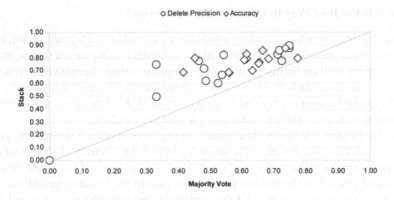

Fig. 10. Accuracy and Delete precision for 15 Enron users using MAJORITY and STACK

agree and disagree in a similar way then the emails are also similar. For instance, if *k*-NN using *Date* predicts DELETE and *k*-NN using *From* predicts KEEP, MAJORITY would struggle to make a judgment whilst STACK will decide based on other emails classified similarly.

It is interesting to note that STACK is also more robust to highly skewed data. Figure 11 shows how STACK significantly outperforms a classifier consistently predicting the majority class.

6.5 Is a *Meta-Learner* More Consistent Across Users Than a *Base-Learners*?

Email management is challenging because every individual deals with emails in a different way. A classifier can perform very well for one user and very poorly for another. In this work, the availability of emails from 14 different users permits us to compare the consistency of the 3 approaches. The accuracy, for each user, achieved with the 4 best email representations from Table 2 are illustrated in Figure 8. It is clear that all approaches achieve inconsistent results across users. The accuracy with *Subject* varies from 0.49 to 0.75; *Body* from 0.46 to 0.74; *Text* from 0.37 to 0.70 and *All* from 0.48 to

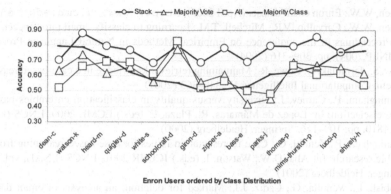

Fig. 11. Accuracy using different aggregation methods

0.83. Even if *All* significantly performs better, it is clearly inconsistent. It may perform extremely well for some users such as *Schoolcraft* but extremely poorly for others such as *Bass*. Such an approach is therefore unsuitable in a real life system.

The classification accuracy using MAJORITY, *All* and STACK appear in Figure 11. MAJORITY seems to be comparable to STACK in terms of consistency, but STACK still significantly outperforms MAJORITY in terms of overall accuracy.

7   Conclusions and Future Work

An email representation including both structured and non-structured content results in significantly better retrieval when compared to a bag-of-word representation of just the textual content. Semi-structured content can be dealt with at the representation stage by incorporating it into a single feature vector or alternatively at the retrieval stage by use of multiple casebases, each using a different representation. Multiple casebases, when combined with a stacked representation, perform significantly better than when combined using majority voting. STACK, MAJORITY and other alternative representation strategies are evaluated using n-RCST; a novel evaluation technique to create stratified train-test trials respecting the temporal aspect of emails. This methodology is applicable to any classification task dealing with temporal data. Future work will investigate the impact of feature selection techniques to optimise case representation in each casebase and the allocation of weights to the prediction of each classifier. It is also important to evaluate the generality of the STACK representation for other email management tasks (e.g Reply, Forward, File). Finally, it would be interesting to compare this approach with other machine learning methods such as Support Vector Machines and Naive Bayes.

References

1. Bay, S.D.: Combining nearest neighbor classifiers through multiple feature subsets. In: Proceedings of the International Conference on Machine Learning (ICML 1998), pp. 37–45 (1998)
2. Bekkerman, R., McCallum, A., Huang, G.: Automatic categorization of email into folders: Benchmark experiments on Enron and Sri Corpora. Technical report, UMass CIIR (2004)

3. Cohen, W.W.: Enron email dataset (April 2005), http://www.cs.cmu.edu/~enron/
4. Cohen, W.W., Carvalho, V.R., Mitchell, T.M.: Learning to classify email into "speech acts". In: Proceedings of the conference on Empirical Methods in Natural Language Processing (EMNLP 2004), pp. 309–316 (2004)
5. Craw, S., Jarmulak, J., Rowe, R.: Maintaining retrieval knowledge in a case-based reasoning system. Computational Intelligence 17, 346–363 (2001)
6. Cunningham, P., Carney, J.: Diversity versus quality in classification ensembles based on feature selection. In: López de Mántaras, R., Plaza, E. (eds.) ECML 2000. LNCS (LNAI), vol. 1810, pp. 109–116. Springer, Heidelberg (2000)
7. Cunningham, P., Zenobi, G.: Case representation issues for case-based reasoning from ensemble research. In: Aha, D.W., Watson, I. (eds.) ICCBR 2001. LNCS (LNAI), vol. 2080. Springer, Heidelberg (2001)
8. Dabbish, L., Venolia, G., Cadiz, J.J.: Marked for deletion: an analysis of email data. In: Proceedings of the Conference on Human Factors in Computing Systems (CHI 2003), pp. 924–925 (2003)
9. Dabbish, L.A., Kraut, R.E., Fussel, S., Kiesler, S.: Understanding email use: Predicting action on a message. In: Proceedings of the Conference on Human Factors in Computing Systems (SIGCHI 2005), pp. 691–700 (2005)
10. Delany, S.J., Cunningham, P., Coyle, L.: An assessment of case-based reasoning for spam filtering, vol. 24, pp. 359–378. Springer, Heidelberg (2005)
11. Diao, Y., Lu, H., Wu, D.: A comparative study of classification based personal e-mail filtering. In: Terano, T., Chen, A.L.P. (eds.) PAKDD 2000. LNCS, vol. 1805. Springer, Heidelberg (2000)
12. Dredze, M., Blitzer, J., Pereira, F.: Sorry, I forgot the attachment: email attachment prediction. In: Proceddings of the Conference on Email and Anti-Spam (CEAS 2006) (2006)
13. Dvorský, J., Gajdos, P., Ochodkova, E., Martinovic, J., Snásel, V.: Social network problem in enron corpus. In: Proceedings of the East-European Conference on Advances in Databases and Information Systems (ADBIS 2005) (2005)
14. Amphora Research Group, http://arg.vsb.cz/arg/Enron_Corpus/default.aspx
15. Gupta, A., Sekar, R.: An approach for detecting self-propagating email using anomaly detection. In: Proceedings of the International Symposium on Recent Advances in Intrusion Detection (2003)
16. Kiritchenko, S., Matwin, S.: Email classification with co-training. In: Proceedings of the Conference of the Centre for Advanced Studies on Collaborative research (CASCON 2001) (2001)
17. Klimt, B., Yang, Y.: The Enron Corpus: A new dataset for email classification research. In: Boulicaut, J.-F., Esposito, F., Giannotti, F., Pedreschi, D. (eds.) ECML 2004. LNCS (LNAI), vol. 3201. Springer, Heidelberg (2004)
18. Lamontagne, L., Lapalme, G.: Textual reuse for email response. In: Funk, P., González Calero, P.A. (eds.) ECCBR 2004. LNCS (LNAI), vol. 3155, pp. 242–256. Springer, Heidelberg (2004)
19. Mackay, W.E.: Diversity in the use of electronic mail: a preliminary inquiry. ACM Transactions on Information Systems 6(4), 380–397 (1988)
20. Palla, S., Dantu, R.: Detecting phishing in emails. In: Spam Conference 2006 (2006)
21. Sakkis, G., Androutsopoulos, I., Paliouras, G., Karkaletsis, V., Spyropoulos, C.D., Stamatopoulos, P.: Stacking classifiers for anti-spam filtering of e-mail. In: Proceedings of the Conference on Empirical Methods in Natural Language Processing, pp. 44–50 (2001)

22. Smith, M.A., Ubois, J., Gross, B.M.: Forward thinking. In: Proceedings of the Conference on Email and Anti-Spam (CEAS 2005) (2005)
23. Tyler, J.R., Tang, J.C.: 'When can I expect an email response?': a study of rhythms in email usage. In: Proceedings of the European Conference on Computer-Supported Cooperative Work (2003)
24. Witten, I.H., Frank, E.: Data Mining: Practical Machine Learning Tools and Techniques, 2nd edn. Morgan Kaufmann, San Francisco (2005)
25. Wolpert, D.H.: Stacked generalization. Neural Networks 5(2), 241–259 (1992)

Case-Based Reasoning and the Statistical Challenges

Petra Perner

Institute of Computer Vision and applied Computer Sciences, IBaI, Germany
pperner@ibai-institut.de, www.ibai-institut.de

Abstract. Case-based reasoning (CBR) solves problems using the already stored knowledge, and captures new knowledge, making it immediately available for solving the next problem. Therefore, CBR can be seen as a method for problem solving, and also as a method to capture new experience and make it immediately available for problem solving. The CBR paradigm has been originally introduced by the cognitive science community. The CBR community aims to develop computer models that follow this cognitive process. Up to now many successful computer systems have been established on the CBR paradigm for a wide range of real-world problems. We will review in this paper the CBR process and the main topics within the CBR work. Hereby we try bridging between the concepts developed within the CBR community and the statistics community. The CBR topics we describe are: similarity, memory organization, CBR learning, and case-base maintenance. Then we will review based on applications the open problems that need to be solved. The applications we are focusing on are meta-learning for parameter selection, image interpretation, incremental prototype-based classification and novelty detection and handling. Finally, we summarize our concept on CBR.

Keywords: Case-Based Reasoning, Incremental Learning, Similarity, Memory Organization, Signal Processing, Image Processing, CBR Meta-learning.

1 Introduction

CBR [1] solves problems using the already stored knowledge, and captures new knowledge, making it immediately available for solving the next problem. Therefore, CBR can be seen as a method for problem solving, and also as a method to capture new experience and make it immediately available for problem solving. It can be seen as an incremental learning and knowledge-discovery approach, since it can capture from new experience general knowledge, such as case classes, prototypes and higher-level concepts.

The CBR paradigm has originally been introduced by the cognitive science community. The CBR community aims at developing computer models that follow this cognitive process. For many application areas computer models have successfully been developed based on CBR, such as signal/image processing and interpretation tasks, help-desk applications, medical applications and E-commerce-product selling systems.

In this paper we will explain the CBR process scheme in Section 2. We will show what kinds of methods are necessary to provide all the necessary functions for such a

K.-D. Althoff et al. (Eds.): ECCBR 2008, LNAI 5239, pp. 430–443, 2008.

computer model. Then we will focus on similarity in Section 3. Memory organization in a CBR system will be described in Section 4. Both similarity and memory organization are concerned in learning in a CBR system. Therefore, in each section an introduction will be given as to what kind of learning can be performed. In Section 5 we will describe open topics in CBR research for specific applications. We will focus on meta-learning for parameter selection, image interpretation, incremental prototype-based classification and novelty detection and handling. In Section 5.1 we will describe meta-learning for parameter selection for data processing systems. CBR based image interpretation will be described in Section 5.2 and incremental prototype-based classification in Section 5.3. New concepts on novelty detection and handling will be presented in Section 5.4. While reviewing the CBR work, we will try bridging between the concepts developed within the CBR community and the concepts developed in the statistics community. In the conclusion, we will summarize our concept on CBR in Section 6. The paper presented here is a short version of a more extended version [55] presented to the European Network of Business and Industry Statistics Community.

2 Case-Based Reasoning

CBR is used when generalized knowledge is lacking. The method works on a set of cases formerly processed and stored in a case base. A new case is interpreted by searching for similar cases in the case base. Among this set of similar cases the closest case with its associated result is selected and presented to the output.

In contrast to a symbolic learning system, which represents a learned concept explicitly, e.g. by formulas, rules or decision trees, a CBR learning system describes a concept C implicitly by a pair (CB, sim) where CB is the case base and sim the similarity, and changes the pair (CB, sim) as long as no further change is necessary because it is a correct classifier for the target concept C.

Formal, we like to understand a case as the following:

Definition 1. A case F is a triple (P,E,L) with a problem description P, an explanation of the solution E and a problem solution L.

The problem description summarizes the information about a case in the form of attributes or features. Other case representations such as graphs, images or sequences may also be possible. The case description is given a-priori or needs to be elicited during a knowledge acquisition process. Only the most predictive attributes will guarantee us to find exactly the most similar cases.

Equation 1 and definition 1 give a hint as to how a case-based learning system can improve its classification ability. The learning performance of a CBR system is of incremental manner and it can also be considered as on-line learning. In general, there are several possibilities to improve the performance of a case-based system. The system can change the vocabulary V (attributes, features), store new cases in the case base CB, change the measure of similarity sim, or change V, CB and sim in combinatorial manner.

That brings us to the notion of knowledge containers introduced by Richter [2]. According to Richter, the four knowledge containers are the underlying vocabulary (or features), the similarity measure, the solution transformation, and the cases. The first three represent compiled knowledge, since this knowledge is more stable. The cases are interpreted knowledge. As a consequence, newly added cases can be used directly. This enables a CBR system to deal with dynamic knowledge. In addition, knowledge can be shifted from one container to another container. For instance, in the beginning a simple vocabulary, a rough similarity measure, and no knowledge on solution transformation are used. However, a large number of cases are collected. Over time, the vocabulary can be refined and the similarity measure defined in higher accordance with the underlying domain. In addition, it may be possible to reduce the number of cases, because the improved knowledge within the other containers now enables the CBR system to better differentiate between the available cases.

The abstraction of cases into a more general case (concepts, prototypes and case classes) or the learning of the higher-order relation between different cases may reduce the size of the case base and speed up the retrieval phase of the system [3]. It can make the system more robust against noise. More abstract cases which are set in relation to each other will give the domain expert a better understanding about his domain. Therefore, beside the incremental improvement of the system performance through learning, CBR can also be seen as a knowledge-acquisition method that can help to get a better understanding about the domain [4][5] or learn a domain theory.

The main problems with the development of a CBR system are the following: What makes up a case?, What is an appropriate similarity measure for the problem?, How to organize a large number of cases for efficient retrieval?, How to acquire and refine a new case for entry in the case base?, How to generalize specific cases to a case that is applicable to a wide range of situations?

3 Similarity

Although similarity is a concept humans prefer to use when reasoning over problems, they usually do not have a good understanding of how similarity is formally expressed. Similarity seems to be a very incoherent concept.

From the cognitive point of view, similarity can be viewed from different perspectives [8]. A red bicycle and a blue bicycle might be similar in terms of the concept "bicycle", but both bicycles are dissimilar when looking at the colour. It is important to know what kind of similarity is to be considered when reasoning over two objects. Overall similarity, identity, similarity, and partial similarity need to be modelled by the right flexible control strategy in an intelligent reasoning system. It is especially important in image data bases where the image content can be viewed from different perspectives. Image data bases need to have this flexibility and computerized conversational strategies to figure out from what perspective the problem is looked at and what kind of similarity has to be applied to achieve the desired goal. From the mathematical point of view, the Minkowski metric is the most used similarity measure for technical problems:

$$d_{ii'}^{(p)} = \left[\frac{1}{J} \sum_{j=1}^{J} \left|x_{ij} - x_{i'j}\right|^p\right]^{1/p} \tag{1}$$

the choice of the parameter p depends on the importance we give to the differences in the summation. Metrical properties such as symmetry, identity and unequality hold for the Minkowski metric.

If we use the Minkowski metric for calculating the similarity between two 1-dimensional curves, such as the 1-dimensional path signal of a real robot axis, and the reconstructed 1-dimensional signal of the same robot axis [9], calculated from the compressed data points stored in a storage device, it might not be preferable to chose $p = 2$ (Euclidean metric), since the measure averages over all data points, but gives more emphasis to big differences. If choosing $p = 1$ (City-Block metric), big and small differences have the same influence (impact) on the similarity measure. In case of the Max-Norm ($p = \infty$) none of the data point differences should exceed a predefined difference. In practice it would mean that the robot axis is performing a smooth movement over the path with a known deviation from the real path and will never come in the worse situation to perform a ramp-like function. In the robot example the domain itself gives us an understanding about the appropriate similarity metric.

Unfortunately, for most of the applications we do not have any a-priori knowledge about the appropriate similarity measure. The method of choice for the selection of the similarity measure is to try different types of similarity and observe their behaviour based on quality criteria while applying them to a particular problem. The error rate is the quality criterion that allows selecting the right similarity measure for classification problems. Otherwise it is possible to measure how well similar objects are grouped together, based on the chosen similarity measure, and at the same time, how well different groups can be distinguished from each other. It changes the problem into a categorization problem for which proper category measures are known from clustering [24] and machine learning [30].

In general, distance measures can be classified based on the data-type dimension. There are measures for numerical data, symbolical data, structural data and mixed-data types. Most of the overviews given for similarity measures in various works are based on this view [10][12][16]. A more general view to similarity is given in Richter [11].

Other classifications on similarity measures focus on the application. There are measures for time-series [54], similarity measures for shapes [53], graphs [29], music classification [13], and others.

Translation, size, scale and rotation invariance are another important aspect of similarity as concerns technical systems.

Most real-world applications nowadays are more complex than the robot example given above. They are usually comprised of many attributes that are different in nature. Numerical attributes given by different sensors or technical measurements and categorical attributes that describe meta-knowledge of the application usually make up a case. These n different attribute groups can form partial similarities $Sim_1, Sim_2,..., Sim_n$ that can be calculated based on different similarity measures and may have a meaning for itself. The final similarity might be comprised of all the partial similarities. The simplest way to calculate the overall similarity is to sum up over all partial similarities: $Sim = w_1 Sim_1 + w_2 Sim_2 ... + w_n Sim_n$ and model the influence of the particular similarity by different weights w_i. Other schemas for combining similarities are possible as well. The usefulness of such a strategy has been shown for meta-learning of segmentation parameters [14] and for medical diagnosis [15].

The introduction of weights into the similarity measure in equation 1 puts a different importance on particular attributes and views similarity not only as global similarity, but also as local similarity. Learning the attribute weights allows building particular similarity metrics for the specific applications. A variety of methods based on linear or stochastic optimization methods [18] , heuristics search [17], genetic programming [25], and case-ordering [20] or query ordering in NN-classification, have been proposed for attribute-weight learning.

Learning distance function in response to users' feedback is known as relevance feedback [21][22] and it is very popular in data base and image retrieval. The optimization criterion is the accuracy or performance of the system rather than the individual problem-case pairs. This approach is biased by the learning approach as well as by the case description.

New directions in CBR research build a bridge between the case and the solution [23]. Cases can be ordered based on their solutions by their preference relations [26] or similarity relation [27] given by the users or a-priori known from application. The derived values can be used to learn the similarity metric and the relevant features. That means that cases having similar solutions should have similar case descriptions. The set of features as well as the feature weights are optimized until they meet this assumption. Learning distance function by linear transformation of features has been introduced by Bobrowski et. al [19].

4   Organization of Case Base

The case base plays a central role in a CBR system. All observed relevant cases are stored in the case base. Ideally, CBR systems start reasoning from an empty memory, and their reasoning capabilities stem from their progressive learning from the cases they process [28].

Consequently, the memory organization and structure are in the focus of a CBR system. Since a CBR system should improve its performance over time, imposes on the memory of a CBR system to change constantly.

In contrast to research in data base retrieval and nearest-neighbour classification, CBR focuses on conceptual memory structures. While k-d trees [31] are space-partitioning data structures for organizing points in a k-dimensional space, conceptual memory structures [30][29] are represented by a directed graph in which the root node represents the set of all input instances and the terminal nodes represent individual instances. Internal nodes stand for sets of instances attached to that node and represent a super-concept. The super-concept can be represented by a generalized representation of the associated set of instances, such as the prototype, the mediod or a user-selected instance. Therefore a concept C, called a class, in the concept hierarchy is represented by an abstract concept description (e.g. the feature names and its values) and a list of pointers to each child concept $M(C)=\{C_1, C_2, ..., C_i, ..., C_n\}$, where C_i is the child concept, called subclass of concept C.

The explicit representation of the concept in each node of the hierarchy is preferred by humans, since it allows understanding the underlying application domain.

While for the construction of a k-d tree only a splitting and deleting operation is needed, conceptual learning methods use more sophisticated operations for the construction of the hierarchy [33]. The most common operations are splitting, merging, adding and deleting. What kind of operation is carried out during the concept hierarchy construction depends on a concept-evaluation function. There are statistical functions known, as well as similarity-based functions.

Because of the variety of construction operators, conceptual hierarchies are not sensitive to the order of the samples. They allow the incremental adding of new examples to the hierarchy by reorganizing the already existing hierarchy. This flexibility is not known for k-d trees, although recent work has led to adaptive k-d trees that allow incorporating new examples.

The concept of generalization and abstraction should make the case base more robust against noise and applicable to a wider range of problems. The concept description, the construction operators as well as the concept evaluation function are in the focus of the research in conceptual memory structure.

The conceptual incremental learning methods for case base organization puts the case base into the dynamic memory view of Schank [32] who required a coherent theory of adaptable memory structures and that we need to understand how new information changes the memory.

Memory structures in CBR research are not only pure conceptual structures, hybrid structures incorporating k-d tree methods are studied also. An overview of recent research in memory organization in CBR is given in [28].

Other work goes into the direction of bridging between implicit and explicit representations of cases [34]. The implicit representations can be based on statistical models and the explicit representation is the case base that keeps the single case as it is. As far as evidence is given, the data are summarized into statistical models based on statistical learning methods such as Minimum Description Length (MDL) or Minimum Message Length (MML) learning. As long as not enough data for a class or a concept have been seen by the system, the data are kept in the case base. The case base controls the learning of the statistical models by hierarchically organizing the samples into groups. It allows dynamically learning and changing the statistical models based on the experience (data) seen so far and prevents the model from overfitting and bad influences by singularities.

This concept follows the idea that humans have built up very effective models for standard repetitive tasks and that these models can easily be used without a complex reasoning process. For rare events the CBR unit takes over the reasoning task and collects experience into its memory.

5 Applications

CBR has been successfully applied to a wide range of problems. Among them are signal interpretation tasks [35], medical applications [36], and emerging applications such as geographic information systems, applications in biotechnology and topics in climate research (CBR commentaries) [37]. We are focussing here on hot real-world topics such as meta-learning for parameter selection, image&signal interpretation, prototype-based classification and novelty detection & handling. We first give an overview on CBR-based image interpretation system.

5.1 Meta-learning for Parameter Selection of Data/Signal Processing Algorithms

Meta learning is a subfield of Machine learning where automatic learning algorithms are applied on meta-data about machine-learning experiments. The main goal is to use such meta-data to understand how automatic learning can become flexible as regards solving different kinds of learning problems, hence to improve the performance of existing learning algorithms. Another important meta-learning task, but not so widely studied yet, is parameter selection for data or signal processing algorithms. Soares et. al [39] have used this approach for selecting the kernel width of a support-vector machine, while Perner and Frucci et. al [14][40] have studied this approach for image segmentation.

The meta-learning problem for parameter selection can be formalized as follows: For a given signal that is characterized by specific signal properties A and domain properties B find the parameters of the processing algorithm that ensure the best quality of the resulting output signal:

$$f : A \cup B \rightarrow P_i \tag{2}$$

with P_i the i-th class of parameters for the given domain.

What kind of meta-data describe classification tasks, has been widely studied within meta-learning in machine learning. Meta-data for images comprised of image-related meta-data (gray-level statistics) and non-image related meta-data (sensor, object data) are given in Perner and Frucci et. al [14][40]. In general the processing of meta-data from signals and images should not require too much processing and they should allow characterizing the properties of the signals that influence the signal processing algorithm.

The mapping function f can be realized by any classification algorithm, but the incremental behaviour of CBR fits best to many data/signal processing problems where the signals are not available ad-hoc but appear incrementally. The right similarity metric that allows mapping data to parameter groups and in the last consequence to good output results should be more extensively studied. Performance measures that allow to judge the achieved output and to automatically criticize the system performances are another important problem.

Abstraction of cases to learn domain theory are also related to these tasks and would allow to better understand the behaviour of many signal processing algorithms that cannot be described anymore by standard system theory [41].

5.2 Case-Based Image Interpretation

Image interpretation is the process of mapping the numerical representation of an image into a logical representation such as is suitable for scene description. This is a complex process; the image passes through several general processing steps until the final result is obtained. These steps include image preprocessing, image segmentation, image analysis, and image interpretation. Image pre-processing and image segmentation algorithm usually need a lot of parameters to perform well on the specific image. The automatically extracted objects of interest in an image are first described by primitive image features. Depending on the particular objects and focus of interest, these features can be lines, edges, ribbons, etc. Typically, these low-level features have to be mapped to high-level/symbolic features. A symbolic feature such as *fuzzy margin* will be a function of several low-level features.

The image interpretation component identifies an object by finding the object to which it belongs (among the models of the object class). This is done by matching the symbolic description of the object to the model/concept of the object stored in the knowledge base. Most image-interpretation systems run on the basis of a bottom-up control structure. This control structure allows no feedback to preceding processing components if the result of the outcome of the current component is unsatisfactory. A mixture of bottom-up and top-down control would allow the outcome of a component to be refined by returning to the previous component.

CBR is not only applicable as a whole to image interpretation, it is applicable to all the different levels of an image-interpretation system [42][12] and many of the ideas mentioned in the chapters before apply here. CBR-based meta-learning algorithms for parameter selection are preferable for the image pre-processing and segmentation unit [14][40]. The mapping of the low-level features to the high-level features is a classification task for which a CBR-based algorithm can be applied. The memory organization [29] of the interpretation unit goes along with problems discussed for the case base organization in Section 5. Different organization structures for image interpretation systems are discussed in [12]. The organization structure should allow the incremental updating of the memory and learning from single cases more abstract cases. Ideally the system should start working with only a few samples and during usage of the system new cases should be learnt and the memory should be updated based on these samples. This view at the usage of a system brings in another topic that is called life-time cycle of a CBR system. Work on this topic takes into account that a system is used for a long time, while experience changes over time. The case structure might change by adding new relevant attributes or deleting attributes that have shown not to be important or have been replaced by other ones. Set of cases might not appear anymore, since these kinds of solutions are not relevant anymore. A methodology and software architecture for handling the life-time cycle problem is needed so that this process can easily be carried out without rebuilding the whole system. It seems to be more a software engineering task, but has also something to do with evaluation measures that can come from statistics.

5.3 Incremental Prototype-Based Classification

The usage of prototypical cases is very popular in many applications, among them are medical applications [43], Belazzi et al. [45] and by Nilsson and Funk [44], knowledge management systems [46] and image classification tasks [48]. The simple nearest-neighbour- approach [47] as well as hierarchical indexing and retrieval methods [43] have been applied to the problem. It has been shown that an initial reasoning system could be built up based on these cases. The systems are useful in practice and can acquire new cases for further reasoning during utilization of the system.

There are several problems concerned with prototypical CBR: If a large enough set of cases is available, the prototypical case can automatically be calculated as the generalization from a set of similar cases. In medical applications as well as in applications where image catalogues are the development basis for the system, the prototypical cases have been selected or described by humans. That means when building the system, we are starting from the most abstract level (the prototype) and have to collect more specific information about the classes and objects during the usage of the system.

Since a human has selected the prototypical case, his decision on the importance of the case might be biased and picking only one case might be difficult for a human. As for image catalogue-based applications, he can have stored more than one image as a prototypical image. Therefore we need to check the redundancy of the many prototypes for one class before taking them all into the case base.

According to this consideration, the minimal functions a prototype-based classification system should realize are: classifications based on a proper similarity-measure, prototype selection by a redundancy-reduction algorithm, feature weighting to determine the importance of the features for the prototypes and to learn the similarity metric, and feature-subset selection to select the relevant features from the whole set of features for the respective domain.

Statistical methods focus on adaptive k-NN that adapts the distance metric by feature weighting or kernel methods or the number k of neighbours off-line to the data. Incremental strategies are used for the nearest- neighbour search, but not for updating the weights, distance metric and prototype selection.

A prototype-based classification system for medical image interpretation is described in [48]. It realizes all the functions described above by combining statistical methods with artificial intelligence methods to make the system feasible for real-world applications. A system for handwriting recognition is described in [49] that can incrementally add data and adapt the solutions to different users' writing style. A k-NN realization that can handle data streams by adding data through reorganizing a multi-resolution array data structure and concept drift by realizing a case forgetting strategy is described in [50].

The full incremental behaviour of a system would require an incremental processing schema for all aspects of a prototype-based classifier such as for updating the weights and learning the distance metric, the prototype selection and case generalization.

5.4 Novelty Detection by Case-Based Reasoning

Novelty detection [51], recognizing that an input differs in some respect from previous inputs, can be a useful ability for learning systems.

Novelty detection is particularly useful where an important class is underrepresented in the data, so that a classifier cannot be trained to reliably recognize that class. This characteristic is common to numerous problems such as information management, medical diagnosis, fault monitoring and detection, and visual perception.

We propose novelty detection to be regarded as a CBR problem under which we can run the different theoretical methods for detecting the novel events and handling the novel events [34]. The detection of novel events is a common subject in the literature. The handling of the novel events for further reasoning is not treated so much in the literature, although this is a hot topic in open-world applications.

The first model we propose is comprised of statistical models and similarity-based models. For now, we assume an attribute-value based representation. Nonetheless, the general framework we propose for novelty detection can be based on any representation. The heart of our novelty detector is a set of statistical models that have been learnt in an off-line phase from a set of observations. Each model represents a caseclass. The probability density function implicitly represents the data and prevents us from storing all the cases of a known case-class. It also allows modelling the uncertainty in the data. This unit acts as a novel-event detector by using the Bayesian decision-criterion with the mixture model. Since this set of observations might be limited, we consider our model as being far from optimal and update it based on new observed examples. This is done based on the Minimum Description Length (MDL) principle or the Minimum Message Length (MML) learning principle [52].

In case our model bank cannot classify an actual event into one of the case-classes, this event is recognized as a novel event. The novel event is given to the similarity-based reasoning unit. This unit incorporates this sample into their case base according to a case-selective registration-procedure that allows learning case-classes as well as the similarity between the cases and case-classes. We propose to use a fuzzy similarity measure to model the uncertainty in the data. By doing that the unit organizes the novel events in such a fashion that is suitable for learning a new statistical model.

The case-base-maintenance unit interacts with the statistical learning unit and gives an advice as to when a new model has to be learnt. The advice is based on the observation that a case-class is represented by a large enough number of samples that are most dissimilar to other classes in the case-base.

The statistical learning unit takes this case class and proves based on the MML-criterion, whether it is suitable to learn the new model or not. In the case that the statistical component recommends to not learn the new model, the case-class is still hosted by the case base maintenance unit and further up-dated based on new observed events that might change the inner-class structure as long as there is new evidence to learn a statistical model.

The use of a combination of statistical reasoning and similarity-based reasoning allows implicit and explicit storage of the samples. It allows handling well-represented events as well as rare events.

6 Conclusion

In this paper we have presented our thoughts and work on CBR under the aspect "CBR and Statistical Challenges". CBR solves problems using already stored knowledge, and captures new knowledge, making it immediately available for solving the next problem. To realize this cognitive model in a computer-based system we need methods known from statistics, pattern recognition, artificial intelligence, machine learning, data base research and other fields. Only the combination of all these methods will give us a system that can efficiently solve practical problems. Consequently, CBR research has shown much success for different application areas, such as medical and technical diagnosis, image interpretation, geographic information systems, text retrieval, e-commerce, user-support systems and so on. CBR systems work efficiently in real-world applications, since the CBR method faces on all aspects of a well-performing and user-friendly system.

We have pointed out that the central aspect of a well-performing system in the real-world is its ability to incrementally collect new experience and reorganize its knowledge based on these new insights. In our opinion the new challenging research aspects should have its focus on incremental methods for prototype-based classification, meta-learning for parameter selection, complex signals understanding tasks and novelty detection. The incremental methods should allow changing the system function based on the newly obtained data.

Recently, we are observing that this incremental aspect is in the special focus of the quality assurance agency for technical and medical application, although this is in opposition to the current quality performance guidelines.

While reviewing the CBR work, we have tried bridging between the concepts developed within the CBR community and the concepts developed in the statistics community. At the first glance, CBR and statistics seem to have big similarities. But when looking closer at it one can see that the paradigms are different. CBR tries to solve real-world problems and likes to deliver systems that have all the functions necessary for an adaptable intelligent system with incremental learning behavior. Such a system should be able to work on a small set of cases and collect experience over time. While doing that it should improve its performance. The solution need not be correct in the statistical sense, rather it should help an expert to solve his tasks and learn more about it over time.

Nonetheless, statistics disposes of a rich variety of methods that can be useful for building intelligent systems. In the case that we can combine and extend these methods under the aspects necessary for intelligent systems, we will further succeed in establishing artificial intelligence systems in the real world.

Our interest is to build intelligent flexible and robust data-interpreting systems that are inspired by the human CBR process and by doing so to model the human reasoning process when interpreting real-world situations.

Acknowledgement

The work presented here is a short version of an invited talk presented at the ENBIS 7 conference of the European Network of Business and Industry Statistics Community.

We like to thank the steering committee of ENBIS for encouraging us to present our ideas on that topic and for their cooperation in establishing the link between CBR and Statistics.

References

[1] Althoff, K.D.: Case-Based Reasoning. In: Chang, S.K. (ed.) Handbook on Software Engineering and Knowledge Engineering (2001)

[2] Richter, M.M.: Introduction to Case-Based Reasoning. In: Lenz, M., Bartsch-Spörl, B., Burkhardt, H.-D., Wess, S. (eds.) Case-based Reasoning Technology: from Foundations to Applications. LNCS (LNAI), vol. 1400, pp. 1–16. Springer, Heidelberg (1998)

[3] Smith, E.E., Douglas, L.M.: Categories and Concepts. Havard University Press (1981)

[4] Branting, L.K.: Integrating generalizations with exemplar-based reasoning. In: Proc. Of the 11th Annual Conf. of Cognitive Science Society, vol. 89, pp. 129–146. MI Lawrence Erlbaum, Ann Arbor (1989)

[5] Bergmann, R., Wilke, W.: On the role of abstraction in case-based reasoning. In: Smith, I., Faltings, B. (eds.) Advances in Case-Based Reasoning. LNCS (LNAI), vol. 1168, pp. 28–43. Springer, Heidelberg (1996)

[6] Iglezakis, I., Reinartz, T., Roth-Berghofer, T.: Maintenance Memories: Beyond Concepts and Techniques for Case Base Maintenance. In: Funk, P., González Calero, P.A. (eds.) ECCBR 2004. LNCS (LNAI), vol. 3155, pp. 227–241. Springer, Heidelberg (2004)

[7] Minor, M., Hanft, A.: The Life Cycle of Test Cases in a CBR System. In: Blanzieri, E., Portinale, L. (eds.) EWCBR 2000. LNCS (LNAI), vol. 1898, pp. 455–466. Springer, Heidelberg (2000)

[8] Smith, L.B.: From global similarities to kinds of similarities: the construction of dimensions in development. In: Smith, L.B. (ed.) Similarity and analogical reasoning, pp. 146–178. Cambridge University Press, New York (1989)

[9] Fiss, P.: Data Reduction Methods for Industrial Robots with Direct Teach-In Programming, Diss Λ, Technical University Mittweida (1985)

[10] Pekalska, E., Duin, R.: The Dissimilarity Representation for Pattern Recognition. World Scientific, Singapore (2005)

[11] Richter, M.: Similarity. In: Perner, P. (ed.) Case-Based Reasoning on Images and Signals, Studies in Computational Intelligence, pp. 1–21. Springer, Heidelberg (2008)

[12] Perner, P.: Why Case-Based Reasoning is Attractive for Image Interpretation. In: Aha, D.W., Watson, I. (eds.) ICCBR 2001. LNCS (LNAI), vol. 2080, pp. 27–44. Springer, Heidelberg (2001)

[13] Cl. Weihs, U., Ligges, F., Mörchen, D.: Classification in music research. Journal Advances in Data Analysis and Classification 3(1), 255–291 (2007)

[14] Perner, P.: An Architecture for a CBR Image Segmentation System. Journal on Engineering Application in Artificial Intelligence, Engineering Applications of Artificial Intelligence 12(6), 749–759 (1999)

[15] Song, X., Petrovic, S., Sundar, S.: A Case-Based Reasoning Approach to Dose Planning in Radiotherapy. In: Wilson, D.C., Khemani, D. (eds.) The Seventh Intern. Conference on Case-Based Reasoning, Belfast, Northern Irland, Workshop Proceeding, pp. 348–357 (2007)

[16] Wilson, D.R., Martinez, T.R.: Improved Heterogeneous Distance Functions. Journal of Artificial Intelligence Research 6, 1–34 (1997)

[17] Wettschereck, D., Aha, D.W., Mohri, T.: A review and empirical evaluation of feature weighting methods for a class of lazy learning algorithms. Artificial Intelligence Review 11, 273–314 (1997)

[18] Zhang, L., Coenen, F., Leng, P.: Formalising optimal Feature Weight Settings in Case-Based Diagnosis as Linear Programming Problems. Knowledge-Based Systems 15, 298–391 (2002)

[19] Bobrowski, L., Topczewska, M.: Improving the K-NN Classification with the Euclidean Distance Through Linear Data Transformations. In: Perner, P. (ed.) ICDM 2004. LNCS (LNAI), vol. 3275, pp. 23–32. Springer, Heidelberg (2004)

[20] Stahl, A.: Learning Feature Weights from Case Order Feedback. In: Aha, D.W., Watson, I. (eds.) ICCBR 2001. LNCS (LNAI), vol. 2080. Springer, Heidelberg (2001)

[21] Bhanu, B., Dong, A.: Concepts Learning with Fuzzy Clustering and Relevance Feedback. In: Perner, P. (ed.) MLDM 2001. LNCS (LNAI), vol. 2123, pp. 102–116. Springer, Heidelberg (2001)

[22] Bagherjeiran, A., Eick, C.F.: Distance Function Learning for Supervised Similarity Assesment. In: Perner, P. (ed.) Case-Based Reasoning on Images and Signals, Studies in Computational Intelligence, pp. 91–126. Springer, Heidelberg (2008)

[23] Bergmann, R., Richter, M., Schmitt, S., Stahl, A., Vollrath, I.: Utility-Oriented Matching: A New Research Direction for Case-Based Reasoning. In: Schnurr, H.-P., et al. (eds.) Professionelles Wissensmanagement, pp. 20–30. Shaker Verlag (2001)

[24] Jain, A.K., Dubes, R.C.: Algorithms for Clustering Data, 320 pages. Prentice Hall, Inc., Upper Saddle River (1988)

[25] Craw, S.: Introspective Learning to Build Case-Based Reasoning (CBR) Knowledge Containers. In: Perner, P., Rosenfeld, A. (eds.) MLDM 2003. LNCS, vol. 2734, pp. 1–6. Springer, Heidelberg (2003)

[26] Xiong, N., Funk, P.: Building similarity metrics reflecting utility in case-based reasoning. Journal of Intelligent & Fuzzy Systems, 407–416

[27] Perner, P., Perner, H., Müller, B.: Similarity Guided Learning of the Case Description and Improvement of the System Performance in an Image Classification System. In: Craw, S., Preece, A.D. (eds.) ECCBR 2002. LNCS (LNAI), vol. 2416, pp. 604–612. Springer, Heidelberg (2002)

[28] Bichindaritz, I.: Memory Structures and Organization in Case-Based Reasoning. In: Perner, P. (ed.) Case-Based Reasoning on Images and Signals, Studies in Computational Intelligence, pp. 175–194. Springer, Heidelberg (2008)

[29] Perner, P.: Case-base maintenance by conceptual clustering of graphs. Engineering Applications of Artificial Intelligence 19(4), 295–381 (2006)

[30] Fisher, D.H.: Knowledge Acquisition via Incremental Conceptual Clustering. Machine Learning 2(2), 139–172 (1987)

[31] Bentley, J.: Multidimensional binary search trees used for associative searching. Communication of the ACM 18(9), 509–517 (1975)

[32] Schank, R.C.: Dynamic Memory. A theory of reminding and learning in computers and people. Cambridge University Press, Cambridge (1982)

[33] Jaenichen, S., Perner, P.: Conceptual Clustering and Case Generalization of two dimensional Forms. Computational Intelligence 22(3/4), 177–193 (2006)

[34] Perner, P.: Concepts for Novelty Detection and Handling based on a Case-Based Reasoning Scheme. In: Perner, P. (ed.) ICDM 2007. LNCS (LNAI), vol. 4597, pp. 21–34. Springer, Heidelberg (2007)

[35] Perner, P., Holt, A., Richter, M.: Image Processing in Case-Based Reasoning. The Knowledge Engineering Review 20(3), 311–314

[36] Holt, A., Bichindaritz, I., Schmidt, R., Perner, P.: Medical applications in case-based reasoning. The Knowledge Engineering Review 20(3), 289–292
[37] De Mantaras, R.L., Cunningham, P., Perner, P.: Emergent case-based reasoning applications. The Knowledge Engineering Review 20(3), 325–328
[38] CBR Commentaries, The Knowledge Engineering Review 20(3)
[39] Soares, C., Brazdil, P.B.: A Meta-Learning Method to Select the KernelWidth in Support Vector Regression. Machine Learning 54, 195–209 (2004)
[40] Frucci, M., Perner, P., di Baja, G.S.: Case-based Reasoning for Image Segmentation by Watershed Transformation. In: Perner, P. (ed.) Case-Based Reasoning on Signals and Images. Springer, Heidelberg (2007)
[41] Wunsch, G.: Systemtheorie der Informationstechnik. Akademische Verlagsgesellschaft, Leipzig (1971)
[42] Perner, P.: Using CBR Learning for the Low-Level and High-Level Unit of a Image Interpretation System. In: Singh, S. (ed.) Advances in Pattern Recognition, pp. 45–54. Springer, Heidelberg (1998)
[43] Schmidt, R., Gierl, L.: Temporal Abstractions and Case-Based Reasoning for Medical Course Data: Two Prognostic Applications. In: Perner, P. (ed.) MLDM 2001. LNCS (LNAI), vol. 2123, pp. 23–34. Springer, Heidelberg (2001)
[44] Nilsson, M., Funk, P.: A Case-Based Classification of Respiratory Sinus Arrhythmia. In: Funk, P., González Calero, P.A. (eds.) ECCBR 2004. LNCS (LNAI), vol. 3155, pp. 673–685. Springer, Heidelberg (2004)
[45] Belazzi, R., Montani, S., Portinale, L.: Retrieval in a Prototype-Based Case-Library: A Case Study in Diabetes Therapy Revision. In: Smyth, B., Cunningham, P. (eds.) EWCBR 1998. LNCS (LNAI), vol. 1488, pp. 64–75. Springer, Heidelberg (1998)
[46] Bichindaritz, I., Kansu, E., Sullivan, K.M.: Case-Based Reasoning in CARE-PARTNER: Gathering Evidence for Evidence-Based Medical Practice. In: Smyth, B., Cunningham, P. (eds.) EWCBR 1998. LNCS (LNAI), vol. 1488, pp. 334–345. Springer, Heidelberg (1998)
[47] Aha, D.W., Kibler, D., Albert, M.K.: Instance-based learning algorithm. Machine Learning 6(1), 37–66 (1991)
[48] Perner, P.: Prototype-Based Classification. Applied Intelligence (online available) (to appear)
[49] Vuori, V., Laaksonen, J., Oja, E., Kangas, J.: Experiments with adaptation strategies for a prototype-based recognition system for isolated handwritten characters. International Journal on Document Analysis and Recognition 3(3), 150–159 (2001)
[50] Law, Y.-N., Zaniolo, C.: An Adaptive Nearest Neighbor Classification Algorithm for Data Streams. In: Jorge, A.M., Torgo, L., Brazdil, P.B., Camacho, R., Gama, J. (eds.) PKDD 2005. LNCS (LNAI), vol. 3721, pp. 108–120. Springer, Heidelberg (2005)
[51] Markou, M., Singh, S.: Novelty Detection: A Review-Part 1: Statistical Approaches. Signal Processing 83(12), 2481–2497 (2003)
[52] Wallace, C.S.: Statistical and Inductive Inference by Minimum Message Length. Series: Information Science and Statistics. Springer, Heidelberg (2005)
[53] Shapiro, L.G., Atmosukarto, I., Cho, H., Lin, H.J., Ruiz-Correa, S.: Similarity-Based Retrieval for Biomedical Applications. In: Perner, P. (ed.) Case-Based Reasoning on Signals and Images. Springer, Heidelberg (2007)
[54] Sankoff, D., Kruskal, J.B.: Time warps, string edits, and macromolecules: the theory and practice of sequence comparison. Addison-Wesley, Reading (1983)
[55] Perner, P.: Case-Based Reasoning and the Statistical Challenges, Quality and Reliability Engineering International (to appear)

Evaluation Measures for TCBR Systems

M.A. Raghunandan[1], Nirmalie Wiratunga[2], Sutanu Chakraborti[3],
Stewart Massie[2], and Deepak Khemani[1]

[1] Department of Computer Science and Engineering,
Indian Institute of Technology Madras, India
`maraghu@cse.iitm.ac.in, khemani@iitm.ac.in`
[2] School of Computing,
The Robert Gordon University, Scotland, UK
`{nw,sm}@comp.rgu.ac.uk`
[3] Tata Research Development and Design Centre,
Pune, India
`sutanu.chakraborti@tcs.com`

Abstract. Textual-case based reasoning (TCBR) systems where the problem and solution are in free text form are hard to evaluate. In the absence of class information, domain experts are needed to evaluate solution quality, and provide relevance information. This approach is costly and time consuming. We propose three measures that can be used to compare alternate TCBR system configurations, in the absence of class information. The main idea is to quantify alignment as the degree to which similar problems have similar solutions. Two local measures capture this information by analysing similarity between problem and solution neighbourhoods at different levels of granularity, whilst a global measure achieves the same by analyzing similarity between problem and solution clusters. We determine the suitability of the proposed measures by studying their correlation with classifier accuracy on a health and safety incident reporting task. Strong correlation is observed with all three approaches with local measures being slightly superior over the global one.

1 Introduction

Textual case-based reasoning (TCBR) systems often contain problems and solutions in the form of natural language sentences [1]. Unlike classification domains where a solution (class label) is associated with a group of cases, problem descriptions map onto unique solutions. Other forms of CBR systems such as in configuration and design domains are also less likely to contain groups of cases with identical solutions. However with problem decomposition, these tasks are often resolved using classification approaches [2]. Evaluation methods for text classification tasks are well studied, and measures such as accuracy, or information retrieval measures such as precision and recall are commonly employed [3,4]. These measures evaluate the correspondence between the actual and proposed class labels. With TCBR systems comparison of actual and proposed textual solution content is hard due to variability in vocabulary usage and uniqueness of solutions. Intuitive measures of relevance to the problem, instead of solution comparisons based on exact matches, are required.

K.-D. Althoff et al. (Eds.): ECCBR 2008, LNAI 5239, pp. 444–458, 2008.

The applications of evaluation measures in TCBR are four-fold. Firstly, they help predict the effectiveness of the system in solving unseen problems. A challenge here is to arrive at competent estimates without relying on human relevance judgements, which are hard to obtain. Secondly, during the design phase of a CBR system, decisions have to be taken regarding the contents of the knowledge containers [5] in relation to case representation, indexing and similarity measures, adaptation, and case authoring. Evaluation measures are useful in guiding these design choices. Thirdly, evaluation measures are useful in facilitating maintenance of the case base. Examples of maintenance tasks are the deletion of noisy or redundant cases or features, addition of representative cases and refinement of case representation or similarity measures. Visualization tools, which we briefly explore in this paper, are specifically relevant in this context. Finally, evaluation measures can be used to measure and compare the complexity of different TCBR problem domains, for a given choice of representation.

Empirical evaluation measures in TCBR remain an open area of research. Although a few measures have been proposed, to date no systematic comparison across these measures has been reported. Recent work reported in the literature exploit the basic tenet of CBR that "similar problems have similar solutions". The general approach involves devising measures that quantify the extent to which this assumption holds good given different system configurations. Local alignment measures capture the similarity of problems and solutions in the neighbourhood of individual cases. In contrast global alignment compares case clusters generated separately from the problem and solution spaces, derived from the entire case base.

In this paper we provide a meta-evaluation of TCBR alignment measures by analyzing correlation of evaluation measures with standard evaluation measures such as accuracy. Such a study presupposes that textual cases are also labelled with class information. In our experiments, we use a real-word dataset from the medical health and safety incident reporting domain. Each case consists of both a textual problem and solution but importantly also has an incident-related class label associated with it. We have created several case bases from this domain with different levels of difficulty. This provides CBR systems exhibiting a range of accuracy values thereby facilitating the correlation study with local and global textual alignment measures.

Section 2 discusses related work in evaluation and visualization. Section 3 presents the main idea of this paper, namely the relationship between classification accuracy and problem-solution space alignment. Next, Section 4 describes the local alignment measures, followed by the global alignment measure in Section 5. An evaluation of alignment measures on a real-world health and safety reporting task is presented in Section 6, with conclusions in Section 7.

2   Related Work

Estimating data complexity is a fundamental task in machine learning. In supervised classification tasks, which have been the focus of most work reported so far, data complexity helps in explaining behaviour of different classifiers over diverse datasets. It is also useful in parameter tuning, an example being selecting feature combinations that minimize complexity of the classification problem. Several approaches for measuring complexity have been proposed: statistical ones based on overlap between probability distributions of classes [6], information theoretic approaches based on estimating information needed to encode all feature values in a given class with class labels [7], graph theoretical approaches based on constructing Minimum Spanning Trees connecting data points to their nearest neighbours, and observing the number of adjacent points sharing opposite class labels [8], and approaches based on splitting the feature space into hypercubes (hyperspheres) and measuring class purity of these hypercubes [9]. Many of these approaches can be extended to complexity evaluation of supervised text classification problems, with allowance for the fact that textual data is characterized by high dimensionality, and often leads to sparse representations.

Unfortunately, most real world TCBR tasks cannot be neatly mapped onto run-of-the-mill classification tasks. Hence, from a practical TCBR perspective, two other relatively less well studied problems turn out to be interesting. The first: can we estimate the complexity of a text collection, without resorting to any additional information (like class labels)? The second: Can we estimate the complexity of given text collections, each of which has a problem and solution component?

In case of the first problem, complexity would measure the clustering tendency within the collection. The work by Vinay et al [10] falls into this category; they use the Cox-Lewis measure to test whether the data points are well-clustered, or spread randomly in the feature space. In the context of the second problem, complexity reflects the degree to which we can expect the system to be competent in answering a new problem, by retrieving solutions to similar problems in the repository. This involves study of alignment between problem and solution components of texts, and our current work belongs to this category.

Local measures of case base alignment have been independently studied by Lamontagne [11] and Massie et al [12] in the context of very different TCBR applications. Global measures explored by Chakraborti et al [13] have not been evaluated beyond a supervised setting. Our work attempts to fill in the void and propose a global alignment measure, which can be compared against the two local alignment measures in a level playing field. Absence of readily available human judgments makes evaluation a formidable problem in TCBR, which researchers often tend to sweep under the rug; or alternatively, make grossly simplifying assumptions (like availability of class knowledge) which are defeated in the real-world. In addition to proposing and comparing new alignment approaches, our current work adopts a novel evaluation strategy, which is central to our comparative empirical analysis. The study consolidates past and novel work, so that TCBR researchers can choose the appropriate measure based on their domain nuances, and also propose further enhancements.

3   Problem and Solution Alignment

In CBR the *"similar problems have similar solutions"* assumption is often taken for granted, whereas, in fact it is a measure not only of the suitability of CBR for the domain but also of the competence of the system design. Essentially quantifying the alignment between problem and solution space allows us to measure the degree to which the similarity assumption is respected by a CBR system.

The complexity of a domain in CBR is a measure of the difficulty of the problem being faced. Complexity is dependent on the extent to which a natural structure exists within the domain over which we have no control. However, complexity also depends on the contents of the knowledge containers in terms of the availability of cases and of the case representation and similarity knowledge chosen, over which we have at least some control. In designing a CBR system choices are made about the contents of the knowledge containers with the aim of making some aspects of the underlying natural structure apparent. This process results in clusters of cases being formed within the problem space that identify groups of recurring concepts, as shown in the problem space of Figure 1. In Information Retrieval data complexity has been estimated by measuring the extent to which documents in a dataset form into clusters as opposed to a random distribution [10].

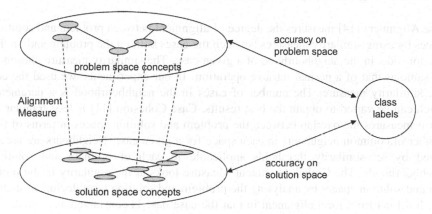

Fig. 1. Similarity assumption and alignment

However, CBR is a problem-solving methodology and cases consist of problem-solution pairs. This adds another layer to complexity. There is no guarantee that a strong structure in the problem space will lead to a competent CBR system. For example, consider an accident reporting system in which the problem representation captures and organises problems in relation to "type of industry". The system may be poor at identifying solutions to similar accidents that occur equally across all industry sectors. Here the problem and solution spaces are not aligned to the same concepts.

The solution space also has a natural structure and forms clusters that are determined by the chosen design configuration (as depicted in Figure 1). In unsupervised tasks the structure or concepts in the solution space emerge from the nature of the domain and the knowledge chosen to represent the solution. A competent CBR system requires a strong relationship between the concepts identified in the problem and solution spaces. It is this problem-solution alignment that we aim to measure in this paper.

We use a relatively large Health and Safety dataset in this paper where each case is composed of three parts: problem and solution description together with the class label. This allows us to compare concepts identified in the problem and solution spaces with those identified by the domain expert as class labels. By comparing the correlation between alignment measurements and accuracy we are able to provide a more comprehensive evaluation of local and global techniques for measuring alignment in unsupervised problems.

In the next sections we compare and contrast three measures of case base alignment: Case Cohesion; Case Alignment and Global Alignment. The first two are local alignment measures, which first calculate the alignment of a case in its neighbourhood, and then aggregate the alignment values of all cases to obtain a value for the entire case base. The third is a global measure, which calculates the alignment value for the case base as a whole.

4   Local Alignment Measures for TCBR

Case Alignment [14] measures the degree of alignment between problem and solution spaces by using similarity measures between the cases both on the problem and on the solution side, in the neighbourhood of a given case. The similarity measure chosen is the same as that of a normal retrieve operation. In our experiments, we used the cosine similarity measure. The number of cases in the neighbourhood is a parameter which can be varied to obtain the best results. Case Cohesion [11] is less granular in that it measures the overlap between the problem and solution spaces in terms of the number of common neighbours in each space for a given case. Neighbours are ascertained by set similarity thresholds applicable to each of problem and solution neighbourhoods. The Global Alignment Measure looks at the regularity in the problem and solution spaces by analysing the problem and solution term-document matrices. It differs from local alignment in that the case base is considered as a whole, to calculate the alignment.

4.1   Case Alignment

Case alignment measures how well the neighbourhood of cases are aligned on the problem and solution side. A leave-one-out test is used to calculate alignment of each target case, t, with reference to its k nearest neighbours, $\{c_1,...,c_k\}$, on the problem side.

$$Align(t,c_i) = 1 - (D_{soln}(t,c_i) - D_{smin})/(D_{smax} - D_{smin})$$

The function $D_{soln}(t,c_i)$ is a measure of distance between the target case t and the case c_i on the solution side, and $D_{prob}(t,c_i)$ is that on the problem side. The initial neighbours, $\{c_1,...,c_k\}$, are identified using $D_{prob}(t,c_i)$. Here D_{smin} is the minimum distance from t to any case on the solution side, and D_{smax} is the maximum. $Align(t,c_2)$, $Align(t,c_3)$,....,$Align(t,c_k)$ are calculated in the same way.

The case alignment for the case t in its neighbourhood is a weighted average of the individual alignments with each of the cases:

$$CaseAlign(t) = (\sum_{i=1 \text{ to } k} (1-D_{prob}(t,c_i))*Align(t,c_i)) / (\sum_{i=1 \text{ to } k} (1-D_{prob}(t,c_i)))$$

An alignment value closer to 1 would indicate that the problem and solution spaces are well aligned around the case, whereas a value closer to 0 would indicate poor alignment.

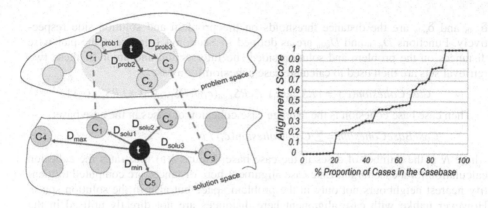

Fig. 2. a) Case alignment calculation b) Case base alignment profile

Figure 2(a) illustrates the alignment computation for a target case t, with 3 nearest neighbours from the problem side, $\{c_1, c_2, c_3\}$. Notice how the relative distances of problem space neighbours differ in the solution space. It is this difference that is being captured by the alignment measure and normalised by the nearest and farthest neighbour distances in the solution space. A plot of the alignment values for all the cases sorted in increasing order gives the local alignment profile of the case base. An example alignment profile for a set of 50 cases from a health and safety case base is shown in Figure 2(b). The area under this curve provides an average local alignment score for a given case base:

$$CaseBaseAlign = \sum CaseAlign(c_i) / N$$

where N is the number of cases in the case base.

Like with complexity profiles used in classification tasks [12], alignment profiles provide useful insight into individual cases as well as groups of cases that exhibit similar alignment characteristic. We expect that such profiles can be exploited for maintenance purposes in the future, for instance, the focus of case authoring could be informed by areas of poor alignment.

4.2 Case Cohesion

Case cohesion is a measure of overlap between retrieval sets in the problem and solution side. This is measured by looking at the neighbourhood of a target case in both the problem and the solution side. We retrieve cases which are close to the case in the problem as well as solution side, within some threshold, to form the sets RS_{prob} and RS_{soln}. The degree to which RS_{prob} and RS_{soln} are similar is an indication of the cohesion of the case. Cases which have RS_{prob} and RS_{soln} identical will have a strong cohesion, and those which have RS_{prob} and RS_{soln} completely different will have weak cohesion. This concept is defined below.

The nearest neighbour set of a case, t, on the problem and solution sides are given by:

$$RS_{prob}(t) = \{ c_i \in CB: D_{prob}(t, c_i) < \delta_{prob} \}$$
$$RS_{soln}(t) = \{ c_i \in CB: D_{soln}(t, c_i) < \delta_{soln} \}$$

δ_{prob} and δ_{soln} are the distance thresholds on the problem and solution side respectively. Functions D_{prob} and D_{soln} are as defined in Section 4.1 and compute pair-wise distances on the problem and solution side. The intersection and union of these two retrieval sets are then used to calculate case cohesion for a case:

$$CaseCohesion(c_i) = |\ RS_{prob}(c_i) \cap RS_{soln}(c_i)|/|\ RS_{prob}(c_i) \cup RS_{soln}(c_i)\ |$$

Then case base cohesion is the average case cohesion of cases in the case base:

$$CaseBaseCohesion = \sum CaseCohesion(c_i) / N$$

where N is the number of cases in the case base. Figure 3(a) illustrates the cohesion calculation for a case target. Like case alignment here distances are computed to identify nearest neighbours not only in the problem space but also in the solution space. However unlike with case alignment here distances are not directly utilised in the cohesion computation. Instead it is the retrieval sets that are compared. As a result case cohesion scores are less granular compared to alignment scores. This can be clearly observed when comparing the cohesion profile for a case base in Figure 3b with its alignment profile in Figure 2b.

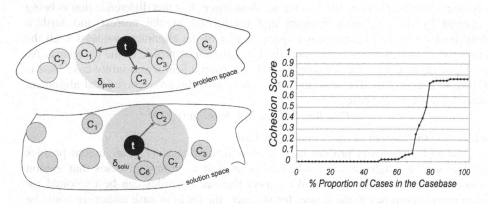

Fig. 3. a) Case cohesion calculation b) Case base cohesion profile

5 Global Alignment Measure

A global alignment measure derives alignment scores by comparing problem and solution space clusters. Although local case base profiles provide a map of well aligned and poorly aligned areas of the case base they do so without showing interesting patterns, regularities and associations in the case base in relation to the features. For this purpose, work in [13] has adopted a "case base image" metaphor as the basis for a Global Alignment Measure: whereby a textual case base is viewed as an image generated from its case-feature matrix such that visually interesting associations are revealed. Unique to this approach is that clusters can be used to observe both cases as well as features. Importantly for alignment this approach can be used to form and compare clusters in both the problem and solution space.

5.1 Image Metaphor

Consider the trivial case-feature matrix in Figure 4 taken from [15]. Here examples of nine textual cases and their corresponding binary feature vector representation appear in a matrix where shaded cells indicate presence of a keyword in the corresponding case. Very simply put, such a matrix, with shaded cells, is the "case base as image" metaphor. A 2-way stacking process is applied to transform such a matrix into its clustered image where useful concepts in the form of underlying term associations or case similarity patterns can be observed.

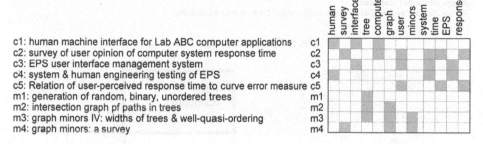

c1: human machine interface for Lab ABC computer applications c1
c2: survey of user opinion of computer system response time c2
c3: EPS user interface management system c3
c4: system & human engineering testing of EPS c4
c5: Relation of user-perceived response time to curve error measure c5
m1: generation of random, binary, unordered trees m1
m2: intersection graph pf paths in trees m2
m3: graph minors IV: widths of trees & well-quasi-ordering m3
m4: graph minors: a survey m4

Fig. 4. Binary vector representation of 9 cases taken from the Deerwester Collection [15]

5.2 Case-Feature Stacking Algorithm

The aim of the 2-way stacking algorithm is to transform a given matrix such that similar cases as well as similar features are grouped close together. Given a random initial ordering of cases and features, an image of the case base is obtained by row stacking followed by column stacking (see Figure 5). Given the first row, stacking identifies the most similar row from the remaining rows and makes that the second row. Next the row that is most similar to the first two rows is chosen to be the third row. But in calculating this similarity, more weight is given to the second row than the first. This process continues till all rows are stacked. A similar iterative approach is applied to column stacking, but this time, columns are selected instead of rows. Essentially column stacking employs feature similarity while row stacking is based on case similarity.

The weighted similarity employed here ensures that more recently stacked vectors play a greater role in deciding the next vector to be stacked. This ensures continuity in the image whereby a gradual transition in the image is achieved by a decaying weighting function. Unlike a step function which only considers the most recent stacking and disregards previously stacked vectors a decaying function avoids abrupt changes across the image. Figure 6 shows the resultant images for the matrix in Figure 4 after row and column stacking is applied.

5.3 Stacked Global Alignment Measure

Alignment can be measured by comparing the stacked matrices resulting from problem and solution side stacking. The matrix Mp obtained by stacking the problem side

452   M.A. Raghunandan et al.

```
Stack_Rows(M)
MR: empty matrix with just the first row from M

for i = 2 to noOfRows   // next case to be stacked
  for j = i to noOfRows  // check all candidate cases
    wsim_j = 0;          // wsim_i weighted sim of ith case
    for k = 1 to i-1     // already stacked rows
      wsim_j = wsim_j + (1/(i-k))*sim(c_k,c_j) ;
    end
  end
  choose j that maximizes wsim_j and swap rows i and j
end
Return MR // columns stacked matrix
```

```
Stack_Columns(M)
MC: empty matrix with first column from M

for i = 2 to noOfCols   // next feature
  for j = i to noOfCols  // check all other features
    wsim_j = 0;          // wsimi weighted sim of ith feature
    for k = 1 to i-1     // already stacked columns
      wsim = wsim + (1/(i-k))*sim(f_k,f_j) ;
    end
  end
  choose j that maximizes wsim_j and swap columns i and j
end
Return MC // columns stacked matrix
```

```
Image_metaphor (casebase)
Return (Stack_Columns(Stack_Rows(casebase)) // 2-way stacked casebase
```

Fig. 5. The stacking algorithm

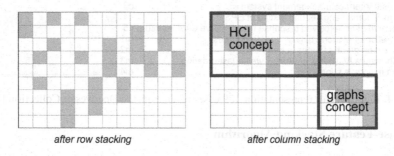

after row stacking   after column stacking

Fig. 6. Images from Deerwester Collection after row stacking and column stacking

shows the best possible ordering of the problem space and Ms similarly from the solution side. In order to establish alignment between Mp and Ms a third matrix is generated Msp by stacking the solution space using the case ordering obtained by problem side stacking. Figure 7 demonstrates how case stacking from the problem side is enforced on the solution side to obtain matrix Msp (the matrix in the middle). Here the 5 cases are ordered similar to that with Mp while the 4 features are ordered according to Ms. The more similar the case ordering of Msp to that of Ms the greater the alignment between problem and solution space. We quantify this alignment by measuring the average similarity between neighbouring cases in matrix Ms and Msp.

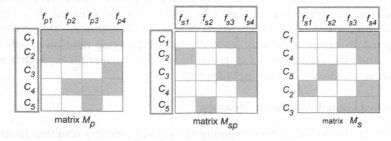

matrix M_p matrix M_{sp} matrix M_s

Fig. 7. Three matrices used in the global alignment measure

The average similarity of a case to its neighbours in the matrix (except the first) is given by:

$$Sim(c_i) = \sum_{j=1 \, to \, k} \quad sim(c_i, c_{i-j}) * (1/j)$$

This is a weighted sum of similarity values to the k previously allocated cases in the matrix with the weight decreasing exponentially. $sim(c_i, c_j)$ is the cosine similarity function in our experiments. The average similarity value for the matrix is:

$$Sim(M) = (\sum_{i=2 \, to \, N} Sim(c_i) \,) / (N-1)$$

We calculate the average similarity values for the matrices Ms and Msp, to get $Sim(Ms)$ and $Sim(Msp)$. The global alignment value is now calculated as:

$$GlobalAlign = Sim(Msp) / Sim(Ms)$$

Ms is the optimally stacked matrix, and Msp is the matrix obtained by arranging the cases according to the problem side ordering. Hence, $Sim(Ms) \geq Sim(Msp)$. For well aligned datasets, the best problem side ordering should be close to the best solution side ordering and the $GlobalAlign$ ratio will be close to 1. On the other hand, for poorly aligned datasets, there will be considerable difference between the problem and solution side orderings and the $GlobalAlign$ ratio should be much less than 1.

6 Evaluation and Experimental Results

We wish to evaluate the effectiveness of the local and global alignment measures. To do this we evaluate how well each measure correlates with classifier accuracy, over 10 case bases. A strong correlation indicates that the measure is performing well and provides a good indication of case base alignment.

In our experiments we use cosine similarity to measure pair-wise similarity between cases in the alignment algorithms and, in conjunction with k-Nearest-Neighbour (k-NN) with weighted voting, to calculate classifier accuracy. A leave-one-out experimental design is used and for each algorithm a paired series of results for alignment and accuracy are calculated and compared to give the correlation coefficient.

6.1 Dataset Preparation

The evaluation uses the UK National Health Service (Grampian) Health and Safety dataset, which contains incident reports in the medical domain. The cases consist of the description of the situation or incident, and the resolution of the situation, or what action was taken when the incident occurred. The cases also have a class label called "Care Stage," which can be used as a solution class for this dataset.

The NSHG dataset contains a total of 4011 cases distributed across 17 classes. We generated 10 different datasets, each containing about 100 cases and varying number of classes, from 2 to 10. The cases are preprocessed using the OpenNLP library, available as a part of the jCOLIBRI [16] framework. First, cases are organized into paragraphs, sentences, and tokens, using the OpenNLP Splitter. Stop words are removed; words are stemmed and then tagged with part-of-speech. The remaining features are pruned to remove terms which occur in less than 2% of the cases. After these operations, the vocabulary size of each dataset is not more than 200.

6.2 Evaluation Methodology

Alignment measures are compared to each other by their correlation to problem side accuracies. How confident are we that problem side accuracy based on class labels can be used so? To answer this, we analysed classifier accuracies on problem and solution sides. Essentially a leave-one-out test on each case base was used to calculate classifier accuracy for problem and solution sides separately. We use weighted 3-NN with the problem-side representation using class labels as pseudo-solutions, to calculate the problem-side accuracy (a similar approach was followed for solution side accuracies).

The 10 datasets and their problem and solution-side accuracies appear in Figure 8. The acronym of each dataset includes the number of classes and approximate size of the case base. For example, the acronym CB3-100 indicates a case base with 3 classes and a total of 100 cases.

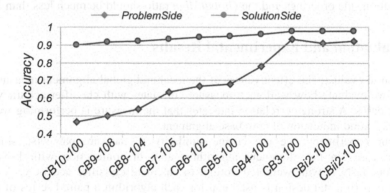

Fig. 8. Problem and Solution side accuracy values

The problem-side accuracies vary from a low 47% (10-class) to a high 93% (2-class) and highlights different complexities of our case bases. The solution side accuracy is a measure of confidence associated with the class labels of each dataset. These remain mostly constant and high (i.e. from 90% to 98%) indicating that the solution side concepts have a strong relationship with the class labels. Hence we are justified in our use of class labels to calculate classifier accuracy on the problem side. We now have an objective measure of the datasets, which can be used to judge our alignment measures. Essentially this allows us to correlate alignment values obtained for all the datasets, with their problem side classifier accuracy values.

6.3 Results with Local and Global Alignment

The case alignment measure for each dataset was calculated with different values of the parameter k, as explained in Section 4.1. Fig 9 shows a graph of Case Alignment

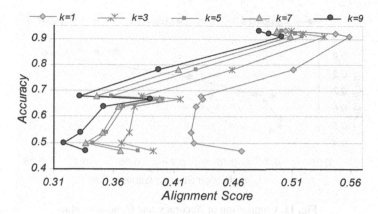

Fig. 9. Comparison of Accuracy and Case Alignment values

values plotted against accuracy for all the datasets. Generally the values of Case Alignment follow the values of accuracy closely for all values of k, i.e., the case bases with low accuracy also have low alignment, and vice-versa. We found positive correlation with all values of k with maximum correlation, i.e., 0.935, with $k=9$.

Unlike case alignment, with case cohesion (Section 4.2) we need to specify two parameters: the problem and solution neighborhood thresholds, δ_{prob} and δ_{soln}. Figure 10 plots the correlation with accuracy for case cohesion with different values of δ_{prob} and δ_{soln}. Each correlation point on the graph is obtained by comparing cohesion values for all 10 datasets with the accuracy values for a given δ_{prob} and δ_{soln}. Here the x-axis consists of 4 δ_{prob} threshold values and each graph line corresponds to results with 1 of 4 δ_{soln} threshold values. Generally cohesion is sensitive to the threshold values and best correlation (0.983) is achieved with $\delta_{soln}=0.8$ and no correlation (i.e. close to zero) with $\delta_{soln}= 0.4$. Figure 11 provides a closer look at the 10 cohesion values obtained for each dataset with $\delta_{soln}=0.8$, for different values of δ_{prob}. Best correlation of 0.983 is achieved with $\delta_{prob}=0.4$ and $\delta_{soln}=0.8$.

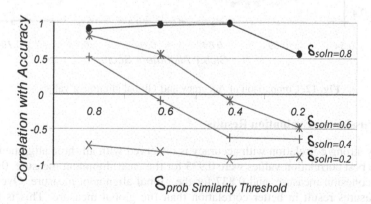

Fig. 10. Cohesion-Accuracy correlation with different δ_{prob} and δ_{soln} threshold values

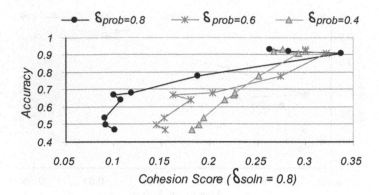

Fig. 11. Comparison of Accuracy and Cohesion values

The global alignment measure for each dataset was calculated as explained in Section 5. Figure 12 plots these values against the accuracy values for different k. Here the k parameter refers to the number of previously stacked cases that contribute to the weighted similarity computation. As with the local measures, global alignment also has good correlation with accuracy. However like cohesion it is also sensitive to the k parameter in that correlation increases with k at first, from 0.63 (with $k=3$) to 0.84 (with $k=30$), and decreasing thereafter.

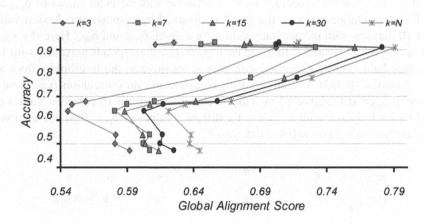

Fig. 12. Comparison of Accuracy and Global alignment values

6.4 Discussion on Evaluation Results

Generally strong correlation with accuracy is observed with all three alignment measures. The best correlation values were 0.935 for the case alignment measure, 0.983 for the case cohesion measure, and 0.837 for the global alignment measure. Overall, the local measures result in better correlation than the global measure. This is because local measures are better able to capture k-NN's retrieval performance. However positive correlation with the global measure is encouraging, because unlike local measures its visualisation aspect (i.e. the case base image metaphor) creates interesting opportunities for TCBR interaction and maintenance.

All three approaches require parameter tuning. Case cohesion is very sensitive to the threshold values (δ_{prob} and δ_{soln}) and so these must be chosen carefully. The global alignment measure is slightly less sensitive, whilst the case alignment measure shows very little variation with k and therefore is most consistent of the three.

7 Conclusions

Evaluation is a challenge in TCBR systems. However to our knowledge there have been no comparative studies of evaluation measures. Here we consolidate existing and novel TCBR evaluation measures in a correlation study with accuracy. Results show strong correlation thus allowing us to conclude that such measures can be suitably applied to evaluate TCBR systems, in the absence of class knowledge. Local measures showed stronger correlation with accuracy compared to the global alignment measure. It is our observation that the local case alignment measure is most consistent because it is least sensitive to parameter tuning.

In future work evaluation measures could be utilized to optimize TCBR systems. In particular we would be interested in applying alignment measures as a fitness function for feature weighting or selection algorithms. The measures could also be applied for maintenance, in particular to identify neighbourhoods with poorly aligned problem and solution concepts. Local profiles and stacked images of case bases provide useful insight with potential for interactive knowledge acquisition tools.

Acknowledgements

RGU and IIT exchanges are funded by UKIERI. The dataset for this work was provided by NHS Grampian, UK.

References

1. Weber, R., Ashley, K., Bruninghaus, S.: Textual CBR. Knowledge Engineering Review (2006)
2. Wiratunga, N., Craw, S., Rowe, R.: Learning to adapt for case based design. In: Proc. of the 6th European Conf. on CBR, pp. 421–435 (2002)
3. Bruninghaus, S., Ashley, K.: Evaluation of Textual CBR Approaches. In: AAAI 1998 workshop on TCBR, pp. 30–34 (1998)
4. Joachims, T.: Text Categorization with Support Vector Machines: Learning with Many Relevant Features. In: Proc. of European Conf. on ML, pp. 137–142 (1998)
5. Richter, M.: Introduction. In: Case-Based Reasoning Technology: From Foundations to Applications, pp. 1–15 (1998)
6. Glick, N.: Separation and probability of correct classification among two or more distributions. Annals of the Institute of Statistical Mathematics 25, 373–383 (1973)
7. Wallace, S., Boulton, D.M.: An information theoretic measure for classification. Computer Journal 11(2), 185–194 (1968)

8. Marchette, D.J.: Random Graphs for Statistical Pattern Recognition. Wiley Series in Probability and Statistics (2004)
9. Singh, S.: Prism, Cells and Hypercuboids. Pattern Analysis & Applications 5 (2002)
10. Vinay, V., Cox, J., Milic-Fralyling, N., Wood, K.: Measuring the Complexity of a Collection of Documents. In: Proc of 28th European Conf on Information Retrieval, pp. 107–118 (2006)
11. Lamontagne, L.: Textual CBR Authoring using Case Cohesion. In: 3rd TCBR 2006 - Reasoning with Text, Proceedings of the ECCBR 2006 Workshops, pp. 33–43 (2006)
12. Massie, S., Craw, S., Wiratunga, N.: Complexity profiling for informed case-base editing. In: Proc. of the 8th European Conf. on Case-Based Reasoning, pp. 325–339 (2006)
13. Chakraborti, S., Beresi, U., Wiratunga, N., Massie, S., Lothian, R., Watt, S.: A Simple Approach towards Visualizing and Evaluating Complexity of Textual Case Bases. In: Proc. of the ICCBR 2007 Workshops (2007)
14. Massie, S., Wiratunga, N., Craw, S., Donati, A., Vicari, E.: From Anomaly Reports to Cases. In: Proc. of the 7th International Conf. on Case-Based Reasoning, pp. 359–373 (2007)
15. Deerwester, S., Dumais, S., Landauer, T., Furnas, G., Harshman, R.: Indexing by Latent Semantic Analysis. JASIST 41(6), 391–407 (1990)
16. JCOLIBRI Framework, Group for Artificial Intelligence Applications, Complutense University of Madrid,
    http://gaia.fdi.ucm.es/projects/jcolibri/jcolibri2/index.html

CBR for CBR:
A Case-Based Template Recommender System for Building Case-Based Systems

Juan A. Recio-García[1], Derek Bridge[2],
Belén Díaz-Agudo[1], and Pedro A. González-Calero[1]

[1] Department of Software Engineering and Artificial Intelligence,
Universidad Complutense de Madrid, Spain
jareciog@fdi.ucm.es, {belend,pedro}@sip.ucm.es
[2] Department of of Computer Science, University College Cork, Ireland
d.bridge@cs.ucc.ie

Abstract. Our goal is to support system developers in rapid prototyping of Case-Based Reasoning (CBR) systems through component reuse. In this paper, we propose the idea of *templates* that can be readily adapted when building a CBR system. We define a case base of templates for case-based recommender systems. We devise a novel case-based template recommender, based on recommender systems research, but using a new idea that we call *Retrieval-by-Trying*. Our experiments with the system show that similarity based on semantic features is more effective than similarity based on behavioural features, which is in turn more effective than similarity based on structural features.

1 Introduction

It is an aspiration of the software industry that software development proceeds, at least in part, by a process of reuse of components. The anticipated benefits are improvements in programmer productivity and in software quality.

Compositional software reuse consists of processes such as: identifying reusable components; describing the components; retrieving reusable components; adapting retrieved components to specific needs; and integrating components into the software being developed [1]. These are difficult processes, made more difficult by the high volume of reusable components with which a software developer must ideally be acquainted.

Over the last twenty years, researchers have been looking at ways of providing software support to programmers engaged in software reuse. A lot of this research has drawn ideas from Case-Based Reasoning (CBR). The CBR cycle [2], retrieve-reuse-revise-retain, has obvious parallels with the processes involved in software reuse [3]. For example, an ambitious CBR system for software reuse is proposed in [4]. Its design combines text retrieval on component documentation with similarity-based retrieval on a case base of software components represented in LOOM. In [5], information about a repository of Java class definitions is extracted using Java's reflection facilities, and this information is used (along with

K.-D. Althoff et al. (Eds.): ECCBR 2008, LNAI 5239, pp. 459–473, 2008.

human annotations) to index the repository for similarity-based retrieval. In [6] retrieval is from a case base of Java 'examplets' (that is, snippets that demonstrate Java usage), using a mixture of text retrieval and spreading activation over a graph-based representation of the examplet token stream.

The most sustained research effort is that of Gomes [7]. In his ReBuilder system, cases represent designs and design patterns expressed as class diagrams in the Unified Modeling Language (UML). The work is unusual in providing some support for automated adaptation of the user's retrieved cases.

There has been surprisingly little work in which CBR applications have themselves been the target of case-based reuse: CBR for CBR! Perhaps the only example is the work reported in [8,9], where CBR is used at the corporate level to support organization learning in software development projects, including CBR projects.

On the other hand, there are now several *frameworks* for building CBR systems, including myCBR[1], IUCBRF[2], and, the most developed, jCOLIBRI[3].

jCOLIBRI, for example, is a Java framework for building CBR systems. Building a CBR system with jCOLIBRI is a process of configuration: the system developer selects *tasks* that the CBR system must fulfil and, for every primitive task, assigns one of a set of competing *methods* to achieve the task, where a method is an actual Java implementation. Non-primitive tasks decompose into subtasks, which themselves may be primitive (achieved by methods) or non-primitive (requiring further decomposition). Ideally, every task and method that a system designer needs will already be defined; more realistically, s/he may need to implement some new methods and, more rarely, to define some new tasks.

In jCOLIBRI 1, the emphasis was on supporting the novice system developer. A developer could build a CBR system using a visual builder, i.e. s/he used a graphical tool to select tasks and methods in point-and-click fashion. While easy to use, this offered low flexibility. For example, it was not easy to implement new methods; and to keep the visual builder simple, non-primitive tasks could be decomposed only into *sequences* of subtasks.

jCOLIBRI 2 is a more 'open' system: a white-box framework that make it easier for programmers to add new methods to its repository. Non-primitive task decomposition now supports conditionals and iteration, as well as sequence. This raises the question of how best to support system developers who wish to use jCOLIBRI 2 to build CBR systems. For novices building simple systems, a visual builder might again be appropriate, although as yet a visual builder for jCOLIBRI 2 has not been written. But for more complex systems, students, inexperienced designers and even experienced designers may benefit from greater support. In this paper, we explain how we have extended jCOLIBRI to have a case base of past CBR systems and system *templates*, and how we explain how we can give case-based support to these users of the jCOLIBRI framework: truly, CBR for CBR.

---

[1] http://mycbr-project.net/
[2] http://www.cs.indiana.edu/ sbogaert/CBR/index.html
[3] http://gaia.fdi.ucm.es/grupo/projects/jcolibri/

The contributions of this paper are as follows. We define the idea of templates, as abstractions over past systems (Section 2). We show how a case base of systems can be defined, where each can be described in terms of the templates from which it was constructed and features drawn from an ontology of CBR systems, and we describe Retrieval-by-Trying, which we have implemented in a case-based recommender system for case-based recommender systems (Section 3). We define alternative similarity measures that can be used in Retrieval-by-Trying (Sections 4). We give an example of our system in operation (Section 5). And we use ablation experiments to evaluate the different similarity measures (Section 6).

2   Template-Based Design

2.1   Templates

A *template* is a predefined composition of tasks. Each template is an abstraction over one or more successful systems (in our case, CBR systems). A template may contain primitive tasks, for which there will exist one or more methods that implement that task. A template may also contain non-primitive tasks, for which there may be one or more decompositions, each defined by a further, lower-level template. As already mentioned, in jCOLIBRI 2 tasks can be composed in sequence, conditionals and iteration. Templates are defined by experts who have experience of building relevant systems and are capable of abstracting over the systems they have built.

A system developer can rapidly build a new prototype CBR system by retrieving and adapting relevant templates, a process we will refer to as *template-based design*. The designer will select among retrieved templates, among decompositions of non-primitive tasks, and among methods that implement primitive tasks. There may be occasions too when the designer must modify templates, e.g. inserting or deleting tasks or altering control flow; and there may be times when s/he must implement new methods. The degree to which these more radical adaptations are needed will depend on the extent to which the template library covers the design space. It also depends on the extent to which CBR is suitable for CBR, i.e. the extent to which problems recur, and similar problems have similar solutions.

There is a knowledge acquisition bottleneck here: experienced CBR designers must define the templates. Furthermore, templates are not concrete instances. They are abstractions over successful designs. Nevertheless, we believe that this is feasible for CBR systems. They have a strong, recurring process model, whose essence the expert can capture in a relatively small number of templates.

As proof-of-concept, we have built a library of templates for case-based recommender systems. The second author of this paper acted as expert, while the other authors acted as knowledge engineers. Within a few hours, we obtained a library of templates with, we believe, good coverage, which we have refined, but not substantially altered, over the last twelve months. We will describe some of these templates in the next section. More of them are described in [10].

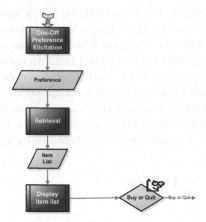

Fig. 1. Single Shot Systems

2.2 Templates for Case-Based Recommender Systems

We have defined twelve templates for case-based recommender systems, based in part on the conceptual framework described in the review paper by Bridge et al. [11]. We take the systems' interaction behaviour as the fundamental distinction from which we construct templates:

- *Single-Shot Systems* make a suggestion and finish. Figure 1 shows the template for this kind of system, where *One-Off Preference Elicitation* (for soliciting the user's 'query') and *Retrieval* (for finding items to recommend) are complex tasks that are solved by decomposition methods having other associated templates.
- After retrieving items, *Conversational Systems* (Figure 2) may invite or allow the user to refine his/her current preferences, typically based on the recommended items. *Iterated Preference Elicitation* might be done in navigation-by-proposing fashion [12] by allowing the user to select and critique a recommended item thereby producing a modified query, which requires that one or more retrieved items be displayed (Figure 2 left). Alternatively, it might be done in navigation-by-asking fashion [12] by asking the user a further question or questions thereby refining the query, in which case the retrieved items might be displayed every time (Figure 2 left) or might be displayed only when some criterion is satisfied (e.g. when the size of the set is 'small enough') (Figure 2 right). Note that both templates share the *One-Off Preference Elicitation* and *Retrieval* tasks with single-shot systems.

In the diagrams, non-primitive tasks are shown as red/dark grey rectangles. These tasks are associated with one or more further, lower-level templates. For the purposes of this paper, we will describe the decompositions of the *Retrieval* task, because it is common to all case-based recommender systems and because it will be familiar to everyone in a CBR audience. For information about the decompositions of the other non-primitive tasks in Figures 1 and 2, see [10].

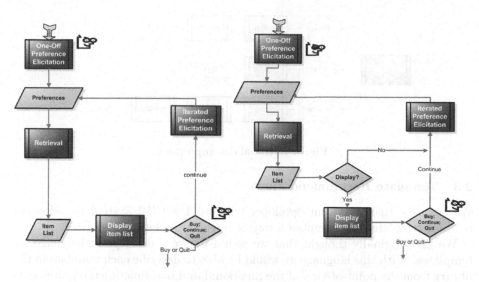

Fig. 2. Conversational Systems A and B

Retrieval is a complex task, with many alternative decompositions. Although Figure 3 shows only three decompositions, each of these three contains non-primitive tasks which themselves have more than one decomposition Commonly, for example, *Retrieval* comprises a scoring process followed by a selection process (Figure 3 top). For example, in similarity-based retrieval (k-NN), items are scored by their similarity to the user's preferences and then the k highest-scoring items are selected for display. Most forms of diversity-enhanced similarity-based retrieval follow this pattern too: items are scored by similarity, and then a diverse set is selected from the highest-scoring items [13,14,15].

But there are other types of recommender system in which *Retrieval* decomposes into more than two steps (Figure 3 bottom). For example, in some forms of navigation-by-proposing, first a set of items that satisfy the user's critique is obtained by filter-based retrieval, then these are scored for similarity to the user's selected item, and finally a subset is chosen for display to the user.

For completeness we mention also that some systems use filter-based retrieval (Figure 3 middle), where the user's preferences are treated as hard constraints. Although this is not commonly used in CBR in general, it can be found in some recommender systems. Despite its problems [16] it is still used in many commercial web-based systems. Also, systems that use navigation-by-asking often use filter-based retrieval: questions are selected using, e.g. information gain, and cases are retrieved in filter-based fashion [17].

A final observation about Figure 3 is that it shows optional tasks for updating a 'tabu list'. The tabu list can be used to prevent certain items from being recommended. A common use, for example, is to prevent the system from recommending an item that it has recommended previously.

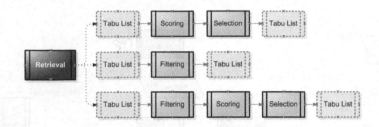

Fig. 3. Retrieval decomposition

2.3 Template Recommendation

We envisage that a system developer will build a CBR system by adapting relevant templates. This implies a way of retrieving relevant templates.

We had originally thought that we would devise a description language for templates. With this language we would be able to describe each template in the library from the point-of-view of the functional and non-functional requirements that it might satisfy. The same description language could then be used by the CBR system developer to construct a query description of the functional and non-functional requirements of the system s/he is building. A retrieval engine would then find the best-matching templates from the template library.

We soon realized that this raised two formidable problems. There is the difficulty for system developers of expressing their requirements as a query. But more fundamentally, we realized that templates often do not lend themselves to a useful level of description. It is easier to say useful things about *systems*, rather than *templates*.

This insight led us to define the case-based template recommender system that we describe in the next section.

3 Case-Based Template Recommendation

3.1 Cases

In line with the insight of the previous section, each case in our case-based template recommender represents a successful CBR system (in our case, each is a case-based recommender system). But the templates that characterize the system are stored in the case as well. One can think of the system itself and its templates as the 'solution' part of the case.

The description part of the case is a set of feature-value pairs. The feature set includes the tasks of the system, the methods of the system, and semantic features from an ontology defined by the domain expert. We postpone a detailed explanation of the features to Section 4.

In some situations, the systems in the case base may be original systems, collected over the years. In other situations, this may not be possible. It was not the way in which we built our case base of case-based recommender systems, for example. The original systems, such as Entree [18] and ExpertClerk [12], are not available. How then did we build a case base of systems? Very simply, we re-implemented versions of these systems and included these, along with their templates, in the case base. It is testimony to jCOLIBRI's repository of templates, tasks and methods that it did not take long to re-implement simplified versions of each of the main case-based recommender systems from the research and development literature. The case base we use in the rest of this paper contains fourteen such systems, although others could easily be implemented.

3.2   Retrieval-by-Trying

In Section 2.3, we noted two problems with a simple approach to template recommendation. We have overcome one of these problems (that the most useful descriptions apply to systems rather than to templates) by basing our case base on systems (see above). The other problem was that system developers would find it difficult to express their requirements as a query.

This problem is not unique to case-based template recommendation. In other recommender systems domains, it is not uncommon for users to find it difficult to articulate their preferences. But recommender systems research offers a solution.

In some of the most influential recommender systems, users make their preferences known through one or other of the many forms of navigation-by-proposing [18,19,12,20]. In navigation-by-proposing, the user is shown a small set of products from which s/he selects the one that comes closest to meeting his/her requirements. The next set of product s/he is shown will be ones that are similar to the chosen product, taking into account any other feedback the user supplies.

This is the idea we adopt in our case-based template recommender. We show the user (the system developer) two systems. In the style of McGinty & Smyth's *comparison-based recommendation*, s/he may choose one, and the system will try to retrieve more systems that are like the chosen one. This overcomes the problem that system developers may not be able to articulate their requirements.

But it raises another problem. On any iteration, how will the system developer know which system to choose? If all we do is show the names of the systems or abstruse descriptions of the systems, s/he is unlikely to be able to make a decision. But, what the user is choosing between here are implemented systems. Therefore, we allow the user to *run* these system. We call this *Retrieval-by-Trying*: the user can actually *try* the recommended items (in this case, the recommended recommender systems) to inform his/her choice.

Retrieval-by-Trying is a natural approach for systems that are relatively simple and interactive, like case-based recommender systems. The approach may not extend to other kinds of CBR system that are more complicated (e.g. case-based planners) or non-interactive (e.g. case-based process controllers).

In the next three subsections, we explain the following: how our implementation of Retrieval-by-Trying selects the initial pair of systems that it shows to the user; how it selects the pair of systems that it shows to the user on subsequent iterations; and how the user's feedback on every iteration is handled.

3.3 Entry Points

Initially, our system selects two systems to show to the user. One is as close to the 'median' of the case base as possible; the other is as different to the median as possible. A similar idea is used in ExpertClerk system [12], except that it selects three cases, one near the median and two dissimilar ones. Whether it is better to show three systems rather than two is something we can evaluate in future work. We decided to use two in our initial prototype because it simplifies the comparisons the user must make.

The first system that we retrieve is the most similar case to the median of the case base. The median of the case base is an artificial case where the value for every numerical attribute is obtained as the median of the values of that attribute in the case base, and the value for non-numerical attributes is set to the most frequent value for that attribute in the case base.

The second system initially retrieved is chosen to be as different to the median of the case base as possible. We compute for every case in the case base the number of 'sufficiently dissimilar' attributes between that case and the median case, and select the one with the largest number of dissimilar attributes. Two values of a numerical attribute are sufficiently dissimilar when their distance is larger than a predefined threshold. Two values of a non-numerical attribute are sufficiently dissimilar simply when they are different.

Although the process of selecting the initial two cases may be computationally expensive, it does not need to be repeated until new cases are added to the case base.

3.4 Diversity-Enhanced Retrieval for Comparison-Based Recommendation

The user is shown a pair of systems, which s/he may try. In the style of preference-based feedback, s/he may then select one, and we will retrieve a new pair of systems that are similar to the one s/he chooses.

We need to ensure that the two systems that we retrieve are similar to the user's choice but are different from each other. If they are too similar to each other, the chances that at least one of the systems will satisfy the user are reduced. In recommender systems terminology, we want to enhance the *diversity* of the retrieved set [13]. There are several ways to achieve this. We use the well known Bounded Greedy Selection algorithm which enhances diversity while remaining reasonably efficient [13].

3.5 Preference-Based Feedback

The case that the user chooses gives us information about his/her preferences. But the rejected case also gives important feedback. Therefore we have implemented several of the preference feedback elicitation techniques described in [19].

The *More Like This* (MLT) strategy just uses the selected case as the new query for the following iteration. A more sophisticated version named *Partial*

More Like This (pMLT) only copies attributes from the selected case to the query if the rejected case does not contain the same value for that attribute. Another option is the *Less Like This* (LLT) strategy that takes into account the values of the rejected case that are different from the values of the selected one. In the subsequent iteration, cases with these 'rejected values' will be filtered before retrieving the cases. Finally, the *More and Less Like This* strategy combines both MLT and LLT behaviors. Given that it is difficult for users to express their requirements as a query (as we have explained above), it is an advantage that none of these approaches requires the user him/herself to deal explicitly with features and their values.

Our tool to retrieve templates can be configured to work with any of these strategies. We compare them empirically in Section 6.

4   Similarity in Case-Based Template Recommendation

The description part of each case is a set of feature-value pairs. The feature set includes the tasks of the system, the methods of the system, and semantic features from an ontology defined by the domain expert. Thus we can compute similarity based on *what* the systems do (by comparing system task structure); we can compute their similarity based on *how* they do what they do (by comparing their methods); and we can compute their similarity using semantic features defined by an expert to describe structural and behavioural characteristics of the systems. Or, of course, we can use combinations of these. We will describe each of them in more detail in the next three subsections.

4.1   Task Structure Similarity

We take a simple approach to task similarity for the moment, which relies to an extent on the fact that our 'top-level' templates (Figures 1 and 2) contain very similar non-primitive tasks. A more complex approach might be needed for case bases whose templates share less top-level structure. Let G be the set of non-primitive tasks $\{C_1, C_2, C_3, \ldots, C_n\}$, (such as *Retrieval*) and Q the set of possible decompositions of tasks in G into primitive tasks $Q = \{Q_1, Q_2, Q_3, \ldots, Q_n\}$. Each sequence Q_i is composed of a set of primitive tasks $S = \{S_1, S_2, S_3, \ldots, S_n\}$ (e.g. see *Retrieval* decompositions in Figure 3).

We define one attribute for each non-primitive task in G. The allowed values of these attributes are the specific sequences of primitive tasks Q used in this case. Comparing two cases by their structure means comparing the attributes of their templates using the equals function that returns 1 if they have the same value and 0 otherwise.

4.2   Methods Similarity

Computing system similarity based on *how* the systems do what they do means comparing their methods. To be able to do that we include in the case representation structure different attributes, one for each primitive task. The allowed

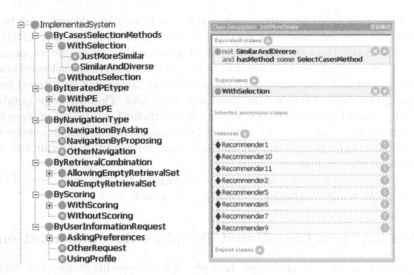

Fig. 4. Semantic features classification

values for each one of these attributes are the set of methods that implement the primitive task. If a primitive task occurs more than once, then it is represented by different attributes.

To be able to compare methods we have created a concept in CBROnto for each method, and we have organized them into subconcepts of the *Method* concept. These method concepts are hierarchically organized according to their behaviour. Then we apply the ontological similarity measures implemented in jCOLIBRI2 to compare the methods. This family of ontological measures use the structure of the ontology to compute the similarity between instances. The CBROnto ontology and the similarity measures are described in [21].

4.3   Semantic Feature Similarity

As well as comparing systems by their tasks and methods, we let the expert define semantic features to describe structural and behavioural characteristics of the systems. In the recommenders domain, for example, we can classify systems depending on their preference elicitation approach: navigation-by-asking (asking questions to the user) or navigation-by-proposing (showing items to the user). We can also classify them according to their retrieval process: filtering, scoring or both. These features (navigation type and retrieval) define two different ways of classifying recommenders, and by extension the templates associated with those systems. There are other axes to classify systems, like the type of interaction with the user and the type of user information that it collects. The left-hand side of Figure 4 illustrates some of these semantic features.

Each case (system) in the case base is represented by an individual and is assigned properties describing the tasks and methods that define its behaviour. Using the classification capabilities of a Description Logic reasoner, each

		Median Case	Recommender 5	Recommender 8
Generic Template		Conversational A	ConversationalA	ConversationalB
Task Structure	One-Off P.E.	Form_Filling	Form_Filling	Ask_Question
	Retrieval	Filtering_Scoring_Selection	Filtering_Scoring_Selection	Filtering
	Iterated P.E.	Create_Complex_Query	Create_Complex_Query	ExpertClerk_Iterated_P.E.
	Display	Display	Display	ExpertClerk_Display
Methods	FormFilling	FormFillingWithInitialValues	FormFillingWithoutInitialValues	
	SelectQuestion	InformationGain		InformationGain
	AskQuestion	ObtainQueryWithAttributeQuestion		ObtainQueryWithAttributeQuestion
	ReadProfile	ObtainQueryFromProfile		
	Scoring	ExpertClerkMedianScoring		
	SelectCases	SelectTopK		
	DisplayCases	DisplayCasesTableWithCritiques		
	Filtering	FilterBasedRetrievalMethod	FilterBasedRetrievalMethod	FilterBasedRetrievalMethod
	Scoring	NNScoringMethod	NNScoringMethod	NNScoringMethod
	Selection	SelectTopK	SelectTopK	BoundedGreedySelection
	RemoveTabu	null		
	Display	DisplayCasesTableWithCritiques	DisplayCasesTableWithCritiques	DisplayCasesTableWithCritiques
	UpdateTabu			
	FormFilling	FormFillingWithInitialValues		
	SelectQuestion	InformationGain		InformationGain
	AskQuestion	ObtainQueryWithAttributeQuestion		ObtainQueryWithAttributeQuestion
	CreateComplexQuery	MoreLikeThis	MoreLikeThis	MoreLikeThis
Global Features	CasesSelectionMethods		JustMoreSimilar	SimilarAndDiverse
	IteratedPEtype		ModifyingQueryWithUserSelection	ModifyingQueryWithUserSelection
	NavigationType		NbP	NbP and NbA
	RetrievalCombination		NotEmptyRetrievalSet	NotEmptyRetrievalSet
	Scoring		BasicScoring	BasicScoring
	UserInformationRequest		AskingUserForAllPreferences	AskingUserForSomePreferences

Fig. 5. Case values during retrieval

individual (system) is classified into the concepts that this individual fulfils, based on the properties of the individual. The concepts into which each individual is classified define different relevant features of the recommender. For example, in the right-hand side of Figure 4 we show the definition of the feature "JustMoreSimilar". It is a defined concept described as follows:

$$JustMoreSimilar \equiv \textbf{not } SimilarAndDiverse \textbf{ and}$$
$$hasmethod \textbf{ some } SelectCasesMethod$$

This definition applies to systems whose retrieval methods do not use any mechanism to enhance diversity but which do contain some method for selecting cases. The right-hand side of Figure 4 shows the systems in our case base that have been automatically classified as instances of this defined concept: eight of the fourteen recommenders are classified according to this feature.

The ontology allows us to compare two systems by classifying them into the hierarchy and comparing the concepts under which they are classsified. We use one of the ontological similarity metrics included in jCOLIBRI: the cosine function [21]. Similarity in the different semantic features can be computed separately as each feature represents a subtree in the hierarchy. Then the similarity results for each feature are aggregated.

5   Example

Let's illustrate the first step of our Retrieval-by-Trying template recommender. When the system is launched, it finds the most similar case to the median of the case base and the case that has most different attributes with respect to this median case. Figure 5 shows the content of the two retrieved cases and the median

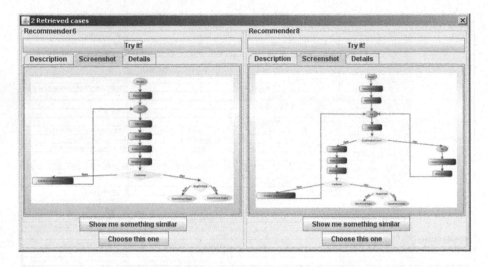

Fig. 6. Templates recommender screenshot

case computed by our method. The table contains the value of the attributes for each component of the case description: tasks, methods and semantic features. The first group of attributes describes the task decomposition of the templates associated with each case. Our templates have five non-primitive tasks: *One-Off Preference Elicitation, Retrieval, Display* and *Iterated Preference Elicitation*. Each one of these tasks can be decomposed into several sequences of primitive tasks as shown in Figure 3. This way, the values of this set of attributes reflect the decomposition into primitive tasks. The method attributes describe which methods were assigned to solve each task of the template to obtain the recommender. Finally, the semantic features refer to the roots of each classification hierarchy of our ontology (shown in Figure 4). The values of these features are the leaves of the hierarchy where each recommender is classified by the Description Logic reasoner.

The median case is a Conversational A recommender where each attribute has the most repeated value among all cases. This median case has no semantic features because it does not correspond to a real system in the case base. Recommender 6 is the closest case to the median and it is also a Conversational A system. Finally, Recommender 8 is the most different case to the median and to Recommender 6. The first feature that makes it different is that it is a Conversational B recommender. Also, our application has retrieved this recommender because it is an implementation of the ExpertClerk system [12] and thus has several features that make it different from other recommenders. For example, it acts both as a navigation-by-asking and a navigation-by-proposing system.

The result displayed to the user is shown in Figure 6. The user can read descriptions of the two recommender systems and choose to execute one or both. Once the user has selected the closest recommender to his/her preferences, s/he can ask the system for something similar. The system uses the Bounded Greedy algorithm to select the next pair of recommenders.

6   Evaluation

Our experimental evaluation is an ablation study. It is a leave-one-in study, where a chosen case from the case base is taken to be the user's target system. We simulate user preferences by deleting some of the case's attributes and take the resulting partial description to be a representation of the user's preferences.

Six representative recommenders were selected to act as target systems/ queries (two Single-Shot systems, two Conversational A systems, and two Conversational B systems). We used random deletion, and hence we repeated each cycle twenty times to allow for deletion of different sets of attributes.

Our experiments measured the number of steps required to retrieve the same recommender using our tool. Obviously, the number of steps (or depth) when using 100% of the attributes is always 0 but depth will increase when using only 75%, 50% and 25% of the attributes.

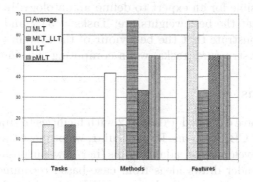

Fig. 7. Similarity approaches comparison

During the first stage of our experiment we used only one of the three similarity approaches: either tasks, methods or semantic features. We also tried each preference feedback elicitation strategy: MLT, LLT, pMLT, MLT_LLT (see Section 3.5). Figure 7 shows, for every similarity approach and every preference feedback elicitation strategy, the percentage of queries where that particular combination results in the minimum number of retrieval steps. Averaging those results we find that task-based similarity provides the best results in 10% of the queries, method-based in 40% and feature-based in 50%. As might be expected, the semantic feature similarity is most often the best because it is a knowledge-intensive measure.

Next we tested our hypothesis that the best similarity measure would be a weighted combination of the three similarity approaches using as weights the percentages discovered in the previous experiment. This hypothesis was actually confirmed in the experiments as shown in Figure 8 (left) where the proposed weight combination is shown to outperform other weight combinations (70%-15%-15%, 15%-70%-15%, and 15%-15%-70%), and Figure 8 (right) where it outperforms pure task, method and semantic feature approaches.

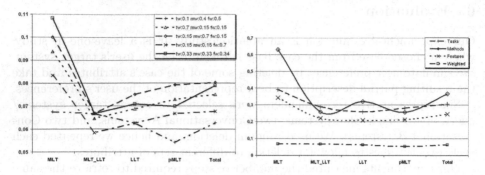

Fig. 8. Optimum weighted combination of similarity approaches

We can also propose a set of weights to use in the case where semantic features are not available. It is important to consider this scenario because it may not always be possible for an expert to define an ontology. In this case, our experiments show that the best weights are: Tasks = 34% and Methods = 66%. These values demonstrate that the behaviour of the system (methods) is more important than its structure (tasks) when computing the similarity.

7   Conclusions

In this paper, we have extended jCOLIBRI 2 with facilities to support reuse during the construction of CBR systems. In particular, we propose the use of templates, which a system developer can adapt to his/her new purposes. Our case-based template recommender draws ideas from case-based recommender systems research, and uses a new approach that we call Retrieval-by-Trying. We have illustrated the ideas by building a case-based recommender system for case-based recommender systems. We have defined and empirically evaluated different approaches to the measurement of similarity. We found, as might be expected, that knowledge-intensive semantic features are more important than behavioural features, which are in turn more important than structural features.

We will soon report on an empirical evaluation in which students template-based and other approaches to build recommender systems. In the future, we want to apply these ideas to CBR systems other than recommender systems. For example, we are looking at textual CBR systems. And we want to gain more practical experience of using the approach for rapid prototyping in educational, research and industrial environments.

References

1. Smolárová, M., Návrat, P.: Software reuse: Principles, patterns, prospects. Journal of Computing and Information Technology 5(1), 33–49 (1997)
2. Aamodt, A., Plaza, E.: Case-based reasoning: Foundational issues, methodological variants, and system approaches. Artificial Intelligence Communications 7(1), 39–59 (1994)

3. Tautz, C., Althoff, K.-D.: Using case-based reasoning for reusing software knowledge. In: Leake, D.B., Plaza, E. (eds.) ICCBR 1997. LNCS, vol. 1266, pp. 156–165. Springer, Heidelberg (1997)
4. Fernández-Chamizo, C., González-Calero, P.A., Gómez, M., Hernández, L.: Supporting object reuse through case-based reasoning. In: Smith, I., Faltings, B. (eds.) EWCBR 1996. LNCS, vol. 1168, pp. 135–149. Springer, Heidelberg (1996)
5. Tessem, B., Whitehurst, A., Powell, C.L.: Retrieval of java classes for case-based reuse. In: Smyth, B., Cunningham, P. (eds.) EWCBR 1998. LNCS (LNAI), vol. 1488, pp. 148–159. Springer, Heidelberg (1998)
6. Grabert, M., Bridge, D.: Case-based reuse of software examplets. Journal of Universal Computer Science 9(7), 627–640 (2003)
7. Gomes, P.: A Case-Based Approach to Software Design. PhD thesis, Departamento de Engenharia Informática, Faculdade de Ciêcias e Tecnologia, Univerisdade de Coimbra (2003)
8. Althoff, K.D., Birk, A., von Wangenheim, C.G., Tautz, C.: CBR for experimental software engineering. In: Lenz, M., Bartsch-Spörl, B., Burkhard, H.-D., Wess, S. (eds.) Case-Based Reasoning Technology. LNCS (LNAI), vol. 1400, pp. 235–254. Springer, Heidelberg (1998)
9. Jedlitschka, A., Althoff, K.D., Decker, B., Hartkopf, S., Nick, M.: Corporate information network: The Fraunhofer IESE Experience Factory. In: Weber, R., von Wangenheim, C. (eds.) ICCBR 2001, pp. 9–12 (2001)
10. Recio-García, J.A., Bridge, D., Díaz-Agudo, B., González-Calero, P.A.: Semantic templates for designing recommender systems. In: Procs. of the 12th UK Workshop on Case-Based Reasoning, University of Greenwich, pp. 64–75 (2007)
11. Bridge, D., Göker, M.H., McGinty, L., Smyth, B.: Case-based recommender systems. Knowledge Engineering Review 20(3), 315–320 (2006)
12. Shimazu, H.: ExpertClerk: A conversational case-based reasoning tool for developing salesclerk agents in e-commerce webshops. Artificial Intelligence Review 18(3–4), 223–244 (2002)
13. Smyth, B., McClave, P.: Similarity vs. diversity. In: Aha, D.W., Watson, I. (eds.) ICCBR 2001. LNCS (LNAI), vol. 2080, pp. 347–361. Springer, Heidelberg (2001)
14. McSherry, D.: Diversity-conscious retrieval. In: Craw, S., Preece, A.D. (eds.) ECCBR 2002. LNCS (LNAI), vol. 2416, pp. 219–233. Springer, Heidelberg (2002)
15. McSherry, D.: Similarity and compromise. In: Ashley, K.D., Bridge, D.G. (eds.) ICCBR 2003. LNCS, vol. 2689, pp. 291–305. Springer, Heidelberg (2003)
16. Wilke, W., Lenz, M., Wess, S.: Intelligent sales support with CBR. In: Lenz, M., Bartsch-Spörl, B., Burkhard, H.D., Wess, S. (eds.) Case-Based Reasoning Technology: From Foundations to Applications, pp. 91–113. Springer, Heidelberg (1998)
17. Doyle, M., Cunningham, P.: A dynamic approach to reducing dialog in on-line decision guides. In: Blanzieri, E., Portinale, L. (eds.) EWCBR 2000. LNCS (LNAI), vol. 1898, pp. 49–60. Springer, Heidelberg (2000)
18. Burke, R.D., Hammond, K.J., Young, B.C.: The FindMe approach to assisted browsing. IEEE Expert 12(5), 32–40 (1997)
19. McGinty, L., Smyth, B.: Comparison-based recommendation. In: Craw, S., Preece, A.D. (eds.) ECCBR 2002. LNCS (LNAI), vol. 2416, pp. 575–589. Springer, Heidelberg (2002)
20. Smyth, B., McGinty, L.: The power of suggestion. In: Gottlob, G., Walsh, T. (eds.) Procs. of the IJCAI 2003, pp. 127–132. Morgan Kaufmann, San Francisco (2003)
21. Recio-García, J.A., Díaz-Agudo, B., González-Calero, P.A., Sánchez, A.: Ontology based CBR with jCOLIBRI. In: Procs. of the 26th SGAI Int. Conference AI-2006. Springer, Heidelberg (2006)

Forgetting Reinforced Cases

Houcine Romdhane and Luc Lamontagne

Departement of Computer Science and Software Engineering
Laval University, Québec, Canada, G1K 7P4
{houcine.romdhane,luc.lamontagne}@ift.ulaval.ca

Abstract. To meet time constraints, a CBR system must control the time spent searching in the case base for a solution. In this paper, we presents the results of a case study comparing the proficiency of some criteria for forgetting cases, hence bounding the number of cases to be explored during retrieval. The criteria being considered are case usage, case value and case density. As we make use of a sequential game for our experiments, case values are obtained through training using reinforcement learning. Our results indicate that case usage is the most favorable criteria for selecting the cases to be forgotten prior to retrieval. We also have some indications that a mixture of case usage and case value can provide some improvements. However compaction of a case base using case density reveals less performing for our application.

Keywords: Case base management, Reinforcement learning, Anytime CBR.

1 Introduction

Games are an interesting laboratory for CBR as they involve interactivity, complex situations and evolving scenarios. As games often depict complex environments for which an exact model is difficult to build, they present some opportunities for the insertion of approximate approaches relying on example-based reasoning. Our work pertains to the application of CBR to games involving uncertainty and real-time response where time available to make a decision might vary with the context. Temporal constraints in games might be resulting from a change of level, a situation presenting increased complexity or a variation of tempo in the occurrence of events.

Computational time in a CBR cycle depends on the time dedicated to retrieval and adaptation. In a nearest neighbor setting, retrieval time depends on the number of cases being considered for making recommendations. Hence to meet time constraints a CBR system would either have to forget cases prior to case retrieval or to filter cases while performing retrieval. For this work, we adopt a forgetting approach to limit retrieval time. Characterization of adaptation time is more complex as this phase is less standardized. As most applications do not require adaptation or make use of simple case modification heuristics, we assume that most of the overall CBR computational time depends on the number of cases being considered during retrieval.

Forgetting cases involves removing those less valuable to the task being accomplished in order to maintain run-time performance and competence to an acceptable level. Means are required to assess the value of individual cases. As most games are

K.-D. Althoff et al. (Eds.): ECCBR 2008, LNAI 5239, pp. 474–486, 2008.

sequential in nature, reinforcement learning [15] is an interesting framework for determining the contribution or payoff expected from each case for solving some problems. Recent progress has been made in this direction [1, 2, 3, 9, 11] and we adopt this approach to assign values to individual cases.

In this paper, our goal is to determine if values obtained through reinforcement learning could provide a good indication on which cases a CBR system should forget to reduce the size of a case base. We conduct this work as a case study using Tetris, a game with simple rules presenting relevant time constraints. In section 2, we briefly survey the related CBR techniques used to manage a case base. Section 3 describes our research motivations and section 4 presents the reinforcement learning scheme we used for training a case base. In sections 5 and 6, we compare reinforcement value to other criteria such as case usage and case density to assess its importance as guidance for case forgetting. We also present in section 7 some experiments conducted with variants of a case deletion strategy proposed in [13] to determine if the compaction of case base is relevant to our problem.

2   Related Work

Managing the size of case bases has been addressed mostly by the community of CBR researchers working on case base maintenance strategies. Markovitch and Scott [6] showed that additional knowledge can degrade the performance of learning system and that removing some of this knowledge can help to correct the situation. Minton [7] proposed a deletion technique for explanation based learning systems. Racine and Yang [8] proposed to reduce the size of a textual case base by exploiting redundancy and incoherence relationships between cases.

Smyth and McKenna [13] proposed a technique for constructing compact case bases. Their approach relies on the notions of coverage and reachability [12], two criteria for estimating the competence of a case base when case adaptation is possible. This work highlights the importance of finding a trade-off between the competence and the efficiency of a CBR system. This is in opposition to machine learning deletion approaches mostly concentrating on computational time reduction.

It is important to mention that an alternative to removing cases prior to retrieval would be to filter cases during retrieval, and hence avoiding an exhaustive search of the case base. Schaaf [10] proposed *Fish and Shrink*, an approach where the similarity between two cases depends on how they are related to other cases already visited during retrieval. Also *Footprint-Based Retrieval* [14] is a retrieval procedure where a search is guided by a limited number of cases (the footprint set) covering all of the other cases in the case base. Following the selection of a reference case from the footprint set, the search is extended to covered cases, i.e. those that can be solved following adaptation of the reference case.

The main specificity of our work is that we make use of reinforcement learning to guide the forgetting of cases. Reinforcement learning (RL) in CBR has recently been studied by some authors. Gabel and Riedmiller make use of CBR to approximate RL versions of temporal difference learning [2] and Q-Learning [5]. Sharma et al. [11] proposed an approach for conducting RL/CBR in games. In our previous work [9], we experimented with Q-Learning for evaluating existing case bases. Finally Aha & Molineaux [1] proposed a model for the reinforcement of continuous actions in CBR systems.

3 Motivations

As mentioned previously, we are interested in the application of CBR to games where
time to make a decision varies for different situations. To conduct our study, we make
use of Tetris [9]. Tetris consists of placing a dropping piece onto a set of columns to
complete rows and avoid accumulation of pieces (Figure 1). Seven different shapes of
pieces exist in the game. Placing each of them involves various combinations of rotation and sliding. This game presents interesting time constraints as a decision must be
made before the piece touches the upper row of cubes. Time constraints in Tetris are
caused by the following:

- As a piece is dropping, time is limited to make a decision.
- As the upper row of cubes rises up, space is reduced to rotate and translate
  the dropping piece.
- As the level of the game increases, the dropping speed increases.

This has an impact on the number of cases that can be processed to select a move.
For instance, in most implementations of the game, a dropping figure takes less then a
second for going down one step at level 0. And for each additional level, the time
allocated for each step is reduced by tens of milliseconds. For our current implementation, this means that less than 25 000 cases could be explored for each step at level 0
during the retrieval phase. And each subsequent time reduction would corresponds to
approximately 1000 cases that could not be used by the CBR component to meet its
constraints.

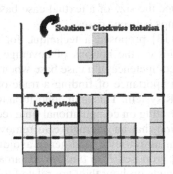

Fig. 1. Playing Tetris with CBR local patterns (from [9])

We assume for the moment that adaptation efforts are limited. In our current setting, adapting a solution consists of rotating and translating the dropping figure. This
can be easily accomplished by comparing cases and determining where some target
patterns are located on the surface of the board (for additional details, see details in
[9]). As this computation is negligible compared to retrieval time, temporal constraints would not influence how adaptation is performed.

We are interested to determine which cases should not be considered by the CBR
system when time is limited. To do so, we need some selection criteria to momentar-
ily forget some of the cases. Such criteria would be associated to a performance profile indicating how the removing cases impact on the competence of a CBR system.

As mentioned in section 2, criteria such as usage, recency and density could be considered. However, Tetris is a sequential game where a decision on how to place a figure impact on the next moves that can be done. This suggests that it is possible through reinforcement learning to assign a value to each case that would indicate the payoff expected from its usage. As reported in the next section, we made use of a Q-Learning scheme to determine such case values.

Given some profiles on how forgetting cases impact on CBR performance, we would need a framework to manage how to exploit these while reasoning online. Work on anytime reasoning could constitute an interesting framework to explore this issue. Case based reasoning could be formulated as an interruptible algorithm that can provide answers without running through a full completion of the reasoning cycle. As soon as one case has been consulted, the CBR system could be interrupted and return a solution whose quality might be partially satisficing. Quality measures are then required to guide a CBR component to keep searching for the amount of time being given. So our current goal is to learn how to characterize these performance profiles for CBR systems.

In the next sections, we will explore how reinforcement of learning is used to evaluate the payoff of a group of cases. Then we conduct a case study for evaluating the influence of various criteria on the performance of a CBR component for the game of Tetris.

4   Evaluation of Cases through Reinforcement Learning

Reinforcement learning [15] is a practical approach to learn consistent evaluations from observed rewards for complex Markov decision processes (MDPs). RL can be used to estimate the value of a state through temporal difference techniques or to evaluate state-action pairs through Q-Learning. For our application, we adopt a Q-Learning approach to evaluate a case base and the general training procedure is described in Figure 2.

Training relies on conducting multiple problem solving episodes with the CBR component. The case-based reasoning cycle (function CHOOSE-CBR-MOVE) used for this work contains the usual phases of CBR, i.e. retrieval and reuse. For our Tetris application, retrieval is performed by matching pattern cases with a subset of the columns on the board [9]. A pattern is represented as the heights of a sequence of N columns where a specific piece type can be dropped. This process returns the k best matching patterns. Case selection (function SELECT-BEST-CASE) is based on the value assigned to a case and returns, during exploitation, the most valued neighboring case. Case evaluation is performed using a Q-Learning procedure and is explained in the next paragraphs. Finally case adaptation (function ADAPT-SOLUTION) in Tetris is done by modifying the orientation of a dropping piece. This can easily be determined by placing the piece where a pattern was matched and by applying the move (i.e. the rotation) recommended by the selected case.

The training procedure (EVAL-CB-WITH-QLEARNING) for evaluating cases provided by a case base goes as follows. We start with some initial evaluations *Value* corresponding to the rewards assigned by Tetris to each of the cases of the case base. Then we let the CBR component play games during which cases are selected and

```
procedure EVAL-CB-WITH-QLEARNING (CB)
    inputs:  CB, the case base used by the CBR cycle.
    local variables:
        State, the current state of the game (i.e. the height of the columns, initially empty).
        Problem, a problem to solve (i.e. a new piece P presented with orientation O)
        Case, one specific case (a pattern of columns + a piece + its orientation + a move)
        Previous_Case, the case recommended in the previous cycle.
        Solution, a move (i.e. the rotation and translation of the piece P).
        R, the reward obtained by applying Solution to State

    repeat
        Problem ← GENERATE-NEW-PROBLEM();  // Select randomly a piece to be placed
        Case, Solution ← CHOOSE-CBR-MOVE(Problem, State, CB);
        Previous_Case.Value ← UPDATE-CASE-VALUE (Previous-Case, Case, R)
        R, State ← reward and new state resulting from the application of Solution to State
        Case.usage ← Case.usage + 1
        Previous-Case ← Case
    until some stopping criterion is satisfied

function CHOOSE-CBR-MOVE(New-problem, State, CB)  returns a case and a solution
    local variables:
            k, the number of nearest neighbors being considered
            Case, one specific case (a pattern of columns + a piece + its orientation + a move)
            Candidates, some similar cases
            New-solution, a move (i.e. the rotation and translation applied to the piece P).
    // Retrieval
    Candidates ← FIND-KNN(k, New-Problem, State, CB)
    // Reuse
    Case ← SELECT-BEST-CASE(Candidates, New-Problem, State)
    New-solution ← ADAPT-SOLUTION(Case, New-Problem, State) // rotate and translate the piece
    return Case, New-solution
```

Fig. 2. CBR problem-solving cycle for the reuse of reinforced cases with its interpretation for the game of Tetris

modified. For a case C_t selected at time t, a revision of its value is performed by UP-DATE-CASE-VALUE using the following function:

$$Value(C_t) = (1-\alpha)Value(C_t) + \alpha \left(R(C_t, state_t) + \gamma \max_{C_{t+1}} Value(C_{t+1}) \right) \quad (1)$$

where R is the reward obtained by applying the move adapted from C_t to the new target surface at time t. The discount factor γ assigns some importance to future moves and α determines the trade-off between the current value of a case and its potential future payoff.

In the update equation (1), C_{t+1} corresponds to the case selected by the CBR system at the iteration $t+1$. This captures the idea that an efficient CBR system should seek the maximum payoff expected from future moves. Hence the value of future moves should be backed up in the value of C_t. As the CBR cycle always chooses the most valued case present in the case base (function SELECT-BEST-CASE), we assume that the next selected case C_{t+1} is a good approximation of the maximum solution to be applied to $state_{t+1}$. From an implementation point of view, the value of C_t is updated during the CBR cycle at time $t+1$.

In order to prevent falling into local optima regions, the training process is allowed to explore the search space by selecting non maximal cases from the set of nearest neighbors. This is captured by a softmax rule [16] where the probability of selecting one of the nearest neighbors is given by

$$P(case) = \frac{e^{Value(case)/\tau}}{\sum_{case_i \in knn} e^{Value(case_i)/\tau}} \quad (2)$$

where τ is an exploration factor (or temperature). This factor is reduced progressively with time to bring the training algorithm to adopt a greedy exploitation behavior (i.e. select the most valued case). And exploration is not allowed during the exploitation of the case base once training is completed.

5 Forgetting Cases Using Reinforcement Values

The first issue we addressed was to determine if reinforcement learning helps to provide good indications on how to reduce the size of a case base. We conducted an experiment with an initial case base of 55 000 cases trained with Q-Learning and softmax exploration as described in the previous section. All the results were obtained using the Tieltris testbed and we made use of the rewards assigned by this implementation of Tetris to update the value of the cases.

The two following parameters for each case were determined following the training session:

- Case value (V) : the reinforcement value resulting from successive updates of a case during training;
- Case usage (U): the number of times a case was selected during the training experiment.

For evaluating the impact of these two criteria on the performance of the CBR component, we built performance profiles as follows:

- We impose a threshold value on one of the criteria and we remove all cases presenting lower characteristics;
- We play a number of games to evaluate the performance obtained by using the remaining cases. In our experiments, 100 games were played for each trial. And for each game, the pieces to be dropped were selected randomly.
- We increase the cutoff threshold and repeat this evaluation until the case base gets empty.

Performance profiles for both criteria are presented in Figure 3. Performance is characterized by the number of lines removed during a Tetris game. We obtained similar results for indicators such as game scores and the number of moves played during a game. Hence these are not presented in this experimentation section as they would lead to similar conclusions.

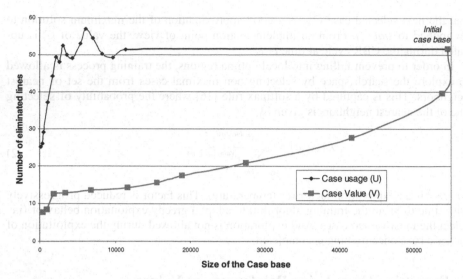

Fig. 3. Performance profiles for case usage and case reinforcement value. These are perform-ance profiles obtained by progressively removing cases from an initial case base of 55 000 cases.

Our experimental results indicate that progressively removing cases based on their reinforcement value prematurely yields an important degradation of performance (see curve *V*). By deleting about one thousand of the least valued cases (i.e. 2% of the initial case base), the CBR component removes on average 25% fewer lines during a game. We conjecture that some of these cases are applied to difficult moves offering little payoff. These states might often be visited during the course of a game and, by removing them from the case base, the CBR system is left with no guidance on how to manage these situations. Then by progressively removing additional cases, we notice a performance degradation which is almost linear. Finally, the system becomes totally inefficient when less than a thousand cases are used by the system.

Case usage presents a much different performance profile. The number of lines be-ing removed remains constant even after removing 40 000 of the less frequently used cases (i.e. 2/3 of the initial case base). However with a CBR system operating with between 2000 and 12 000 cases, the performance starts to oscillate. In this transition phase, we notice some peak performance even surpassing results obtained from larger case bases. However no guarantee for improvements can be made due to the instabil-ity of the performance profile in this region. Finally, as we keep removing the last few cases (< 1000), the performance drops rapidly to lower values as the number of cases becomes insufficient.

Hence, from this experiment, we can conclude that case usage (*U*) provides a better decision criterion for progressive forgetting of cases for our application. Results also indicate that reinforcement value (*V*) is not by itself an informative criterion for re-ducing the size of the case base. It is also interesting to note that the size of the CBR memory can significantly be reduced without impacting severely on its performance.

6 Combining Multiple Criteria

Based on the results of the previous experiment, we tried to combine both criteria to see if additional improvements could be obtained using a mixture of them. We considered 2 variants:

- Additive form: a linear combination of the two criteria.

$$f\left(Case\right)=\alpha\ Case.U+\beta\ Case.V$$

- Product form: a product of the two criteria where V is normalized to remove negative reinforcement values.

$$f\left(Case\right)=\alpha\ Case.U\times(Case.V+\beta)$$

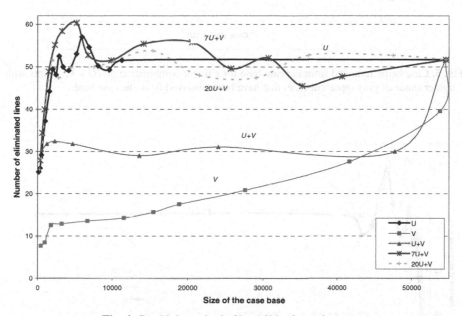

Fig. 4. Combining criteria U and V for forgetting cases

Figure 4 displays some experimental profiles we obtained for these forms. For most of the coefficients α and β, making a linear combination of V and U represents a compromise between these two criteria. Hence the resulting combination generates a performance profile that stands between those of the individual criteria. For instance, the curve $U+V$ is a slight improvement over V but does not nearly surpass the performance profile of U. And as the component U becomes more important in the mixture, the performance profile of the combination resembles the profile of the case usage criteria. We tried different linear combinations and we found that, for our Tetris application, the best results were obtained when $\alpha/\beta\approx7$. While some significant improvements can be expected from this combination, we can not however conclude that such a linear combination guarantees better results for any number of cases. However it seems to be an advantageous option for case bases comprising less then 20 000 cases.

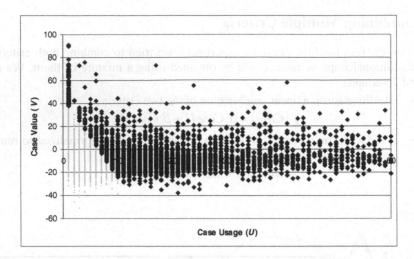

Fig. 5. Case being removed from the case base for a linear combination of $7U + V$. Points with a lighter shade of gray represent cases that have been removed from the case base.

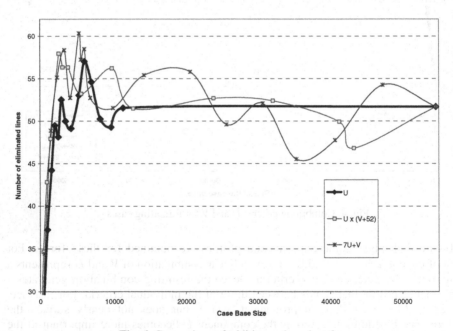

Fig. 6. Comparison of additive and product forms

Figure 5 illustrates the composition of the case base when reduced to 5200 cases (i.e. less than $1/10^{th}$ of its initial size) by applying a linear combination of $7U + V$ (i.e. a ratio of $\alpha/\beta = 7$). If we refer to Figure 4, this corresponds to the optimum peak value obtained by this performance profile. The dark points correspond to those cases left in the case base while the gray points correspond to those being removed. We notice that while more than 90% of the cases have been removed, those are highly concentrated in the bottom left part of the figure. This region depicts cases with both lower usage and reinforcement values. This suggests that this is a region where it is beneficial to concentrate its forgetting efforts.

Finally a comparison of the additive and product forms of combination, as illustrated in Figure 6, clearly indicates that the product form does not provide any additional advantage over the best results obtained using an additive form.

7   Compacting the Case Base

Smyth and McKenna proposed in [13] a case deletion strategy to build compact case bases. The basic idea is to select a subset of cases that perform well and that are well dispersed in the problem space. To achieve this, we evaluate all the cases of the CBR system with respect to some criterion and sort them in decreasing order. Then we create a new case base and we successively add cases, following a decreasing order, that can not be solved by other cases already present in the new case base. This algorithm is presented in Figure 7.

```
function CONSTRUCT_COMPACT_CB (Cases, Criterion), returns a case base
    inputs:  Cases, all the case originally used of the CBR system.
             Criterion, the attribute used to rank cases.
    local variables:
             Sorted_Cases, the cases ranked by some criterion
             New_CB, the result of this function, a subset of the original cases
             SIM_THRESHOLD, a cutoff threshold for forgetting cases.
             Sorted_Cases ← SORT-CB(Cases, Criterion);
             New_CB ← {};
             CHANGES ← true;

    while CHANGES do
        CHANGES ← false;
        For each case C ∈ Sorted_Cases
             if MAX-SIMILARITY (C, New_CB) < SIM_THRESHOLD then
                 CHANGES ← true;
                 Add C to New_CB;
                 Remove C from Sorted_Cases;
        return New_CB
function MAX-SIMILARITY (C, Cases) returns a similarity value
    Sim = 0.0;
    for each case C' ∈ Cases do
        if C.type = C'.type;   // similarity is restricted to pieces of the same type.
        Sim ← MAX(Sim,GET-SIMILARITY(C, C'));
    return Sim;
```

Fig. 7. Algorithm for compacting a case base – Adapted from [13]

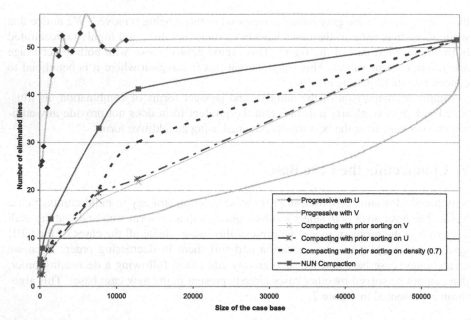

Fig. 8. Compaction of cases using various sorting criteria. Progressive performance profiles refer to the removal of cases without compaction as described in sections 5 and 6 of this paper.

From an intuitive point of view, compaction seems to favor the removal of cases from different regions of the problem space. This approach should provide performance profiles different from those of the progressive forgetting studied in section 5 and 6 of this paper where cases were removed in concentrated areas. By diversifying the regions where cases are removed, we could expect a better preservation of the competence of the CBR system.

Authors in [13] proposed a competence criterion, based on reachability and coverage [12], to determine the extent of cases that can be solved. For our game of Tetris, we consider that a case can solve another if both pertain to the same type of piece and if the configurations of columns are sufficiently similar (i.e. superior to some similarity thresholds). This is a reasonable assumption as, for similar board configurations, a piece can be rotated and translated to produce a reusable solution.

The function CONSTRUCT_COMPACT_CB is sensitive to the ordering of the original cases. To control this factor, we need to sort the cases with respect to some criterion (function SORT-CB). We compared experimental results obtained when cases were sorted based on their usage and reinforcement values. We also considered the possibility, for building a compact case base, to remove cases based on their similarity with other cases. So we estimated for each case the density of its neighborhood (i.e. the average similarity of its nearest neighbors) and we made use of this criterion for our experiments. The resulting performance profiles are presented in Figure 8. To obtain various sizes of case bases, we applied the compaction function for different values of similarity thresholds SIM_THRESHOLD.

We note that the compaction of a case base brings a constant and linear decrease for most of the sorting criterion. While this approach is superior to progressively forgetting cases based on reinforcement values, the various performance profiles obtained using U, V and case density as sorting criteria reveal largely inferior to the progressive approach with case usage.

Finally we also tried a variant of this approach called NUN [13]. While it compares favorably to the other compaction performance profiles, it does not outrank the results obtained by progressive forgetting with case usage.

8 Discussion

We learned from our case study with Tetris that profiles can be built for estimating the performance of a CBR system with various case base sizes. Our results clearly indicate that, for our application, case usage is the best criteria for forgetting cases. Reinforcement values are not necessarily by themselves good indicators for forgetting cases but could contribute if combined with other criteria. Finally a progressive reduction of the case base seems to be more appropriate than compaction for our application.

However this does not mean that reinforcement learning does not contribute to CBR. Our previous work [9] clearly illustrated that reinforcement training of a case base can improve the overall performance of a CBR system.

As mentioned in section 3 of this paper, one of our objectives is to make use of performance profiles to limit the size of a case base when facing time constraints (which we referred to as anytime CBR). This supposes that using fewer cases would imply a degradation of performance. But one of our findings is that using the 55 000 cases that were initially provided to build the CBR system, we could play Tetris at an optimum level by using a subset of approximately 5 000 cases. Hence with such a limited number of cases, retrieval time would never exceed temporal constraints imposed by the game. This is a surprising result as our internal case representation for Tetris has a dimensionality of approximately 70 million different states. But it seems to be a particular situation where the competence of the CBR system is not proportional to the number of cases being used.

We expect that the proposed approach could be applicable to other time-constrained games. For instance, pursuit games could benefit from performance profiles and by dimensioning the size of the case base to meet time-critical situations. For instance, a reactive game like Pacman could be simple and interesting laboratory for conducting such a study. This remains to be done as future work.

References

1. Aha, D., Molineaux, M.: Learning Continuous Action Models in a Real-Time Strategy Environment. In: Proceedings of the Twenthy First International FLAIRS Conference, pp. 257–262. AAAI Press, Menlo Park (2008)
2. Gabel, T., Riedmiller., M.: CBR for State Value Function Approximation in Reinforcement Learning. In: Muñoz-Ávila, H., Ricci, F. (eds.) ICCBR 2005. LNCS (LNAI), vol. 3620, pp. 206–220. Springer, Heidelberg (2005)

3. Gabel, T., Riedmiller., M.: An Analysis of Case-Based Value Function Approximation by Approximating State Transition Graphs. In: Weber, R.O., Richter, M.M. (eds.) ICCBR 2007. LNCS (LNAI), vol. 4626, pp. 344–358. Springer, Heidelberg (2007)
4. Haouchine, K.M.: Chebel-Morello, B., Zerhouni, N.: Méthode de Suppression de Cas pour une Maintenance de Base de Cas, 14e Atelier de Raisonnement à Partir de cas (2006)
5. Kira, Z., Arkin, R.C.: Forgetting Bad Behavior: Memory Management for Case-Based Navigation. In: Proceedings of the 2004 International Conference on Intelligent Robots and Systems, pp. 3145–3152. IEEE, Los Alamitos (2004)
6. Markovitch, S., Scott, P.D.: The Role of Forgetting in Learning. In: Proceedings of The Fifth International Conference on Machine Learning, pp. 459–465. Morgan Kaufmann, San Francisco (1988)
7. Minton, S.: Qualitative Results Concerning the Utility of Explanation-Based Learning. Artificial Intelligence 42, 363–391 (1990)
8. Racine, K., Yang, Q.: Maintaining Unstructured Case Bases. In: Leake, D.B., Plaza, E. (eds.) ICCBR 1997. LNCS, vol. 1266, pp. 25–27. Springer, Heidelberg (1997)
9. Romdhane, H., Lamontagne, L.: Reinforcement of Local Pattern Cases for Tetris. In: Proceedings of Twenthy First International FLAIRS Conference, pp. 263–269. AAAI Press, Menlo Park (2008)
10. Schaff, J.: Fish and Shrink: A Next Step Towards Efficient Case Retrieval in Large Scale Cases-Bases. In: Smith, I., Faltings, B.V. (eds.) EWCBR 1996. LNCS, vol. 1168, pp. 362–376. Springer, Heidelberg (1996)
11. Sharma, M., Holmes, M., Santamaria, J., Irani, A., Isbell, C., Ram, A.: Transfer Learning in Real-Time Strategy Games Using Hybrid CBR/RL. In: Proceedings of IJCAI 2007, pp. 1041–1046 (2007)
12. Smyth, B., Keane, M.: Remembering to Forget: A Competence Preserving Deletion Policy for Case-Based Reasoning Systems. In: Proceedings of IJCAI 1995, pp. 377–382. Morgan Kaufmann, San Francisco (1995)
13. Smyth, B., McKenna, E.: Building Compact Competent Case-Bases. In: Althoff, K.-D., Bergmann, R., Branting, L.K. (eds.) ICCBR 1999. LNCS (LNAI), vol. 1650, pp. 329–342. Springer, Heidelberg (1999)
14. Smyth, B., McKenna, E.: Footprint-Based Retrieval. In: Althoff, K.-D., Bergmann, R., Branting, L.K. (eds.) ICCBR 1999. LNCS (LNAI), vol. 1650, pp. 343–357. Springer, Heidelberg (1999)
15. Sutton, R., Barto, A.: Reinforcement Learning: An Introduction. MIT Press, Cambridge (1998)

iReMedI - Intelligent Retrieval from Medical Information

Saurav Sahay, Bharat Ravisekar, Sundaresan Venkatasubramanian,
Anushree Venkatesh, Priyanka Prabhu, and Ashwin Ram

College of Computing
Georgia Institute of Technology
Atlanta, GA

Abstract. Effective encoding of information is one of the keys to qualitative problem solving. Our aim is to explore Knowledge representation techniques that capture meaningful word associations occurring in documents. We have developed *iReMedI*, a TCBR based problem solving system as a prototype to demonstrate our idea. For representation we have used a combination of NLP and graph based techniques which we call as Shallow Syntactic Triples, Dependency Parses and Semantic Word Chains. To test their effectiveness we have developed retrieval techniques based on PageRank, Shortest Distance and Spreading Activation methods. The various algorithms discussed in the paper and the comparative analysis of their results provides us with useful insight for creating an effective problem solving and reasoning system.

1 Introduction

The knowledge explosion has continued to outpace technological innovation in search engines and knowledge management systems. It is increasingly difficult to find relevant information, not just on the World Wide Web but even in domain specific medium-sized knowledge bases. Despite advances in search and database technology, the average user still spends inordinate amounts of time looking for specific information needed for a given task.

The problem we are addressing in this paper differs from traditional search paradigms in several ways. Unlike traditional web search, the problem requires precise search over medium-sized knowledge bases; it is not acceptable to return hundreds of results matching a few keywords even if one or two of the top ten are relevant. Unlike traditional information retrieval, the problem requires synthesis of information; it is not acceptable to return a laundry list of results for the user to wade through individually but instead the system must analyze the results collectively and create a solution for the user to consider. And unlike traditional database search, the users are both experts who know how to ask the appropriate questions and non-experts who have more difficulty in knowing the exact question to ask or the exact database query to pose. For this reason, existing approaches, such as feature vector based retrieval methods are not sufficient.

K.-D. Althoff et al. (Eds.): ECCBR 2008, LNAI 5239, pp. 487–502, 2008.

Knowledge Representation (KR) has long been considered one of the principal elements of Artificial Intelligence, and a critical part of all problem solving. Many powerful meta models of semantic networks have been developed such as Existential Graphs [1] of Charles S Peirce, Conceptual Graphs [2] of John F Sowa and the Resource Description Framework [3] by the World Wide Web Consortium. This work aims to give an insight into the development of a TCBR system which involves investigating graph based KR formalism as the semantic network model to be used as an indexing mechanism for the system. Different retrieval algorithms are implemented on top of this representation in order to effectively exploit the structure of the representation. As mentioned in [4] commentary paper on TCBR, *"some of the decisions to be made as part of the design and development of CBR systems are how to identify problem solving experiences to populate the case base, what representation for cases to adopt, how to define the indexing vocabulary, which retrieval methods to adopt, and how to extract and represent reusable components."* We have addressed the above problem and explored several design questions in coming up with an effective TCBR system. We argue that there is no universal solution to this design question and the decisions to be made depend on the features of the problem being addressed in such a situation. One of the goals in this paper has been to give the user the option to choose the design he prefers and customize the solutions in his chosen design decision according to his user experience.

The specific problem addressed here is that of domain- specific small corpus precise search for relevant information: helping the user find specific information pertinent to the search problem addressed as a short natural language query. This research falls at the intersection of standard web search systems and question answering systems by trying to bridge the gap between the two systems and providing pertinent results that address the search in a much direct way and learn according to user's preference. We have looked at biomedical articles to research and address this problem.

A typical use case in such context would be trying to find information such as 'symptoms and treatment of prolonged fever during pregnancy' This kind of medical search seeks much targeted information is personal to the user and demands reliability and authenticity of the obtained results Therefore a user cannot rely on typical web search and has to look up information in specific databases. The problem actually lies on the continuum between web search and relational database search. More formally, the problem has the following characteristics:

Diverse users: The user may be an expert user like a doctor searching for specific technical information, a patient searching for disease specific symptoms and treatment options, any layman user with a biomedical information need (such as pain management).

Specialized knowledge bases that are medium-sized, focused, unstructured and reliable: Knowledge bases are not as large or as diverse as the entire World-Wide Web, yet they are unstructured, may contain free text documents, and may not share semantics or ontologies between them.

Precise search: Search queries may be longer than the one or two word queries typical for web search, but they are unlikely to contain all the right keywords. Yet it is not acceptable to return dozens or hundreds of irrelevant results, even if the right answer is amongst them. The aim is to retrieve successive solutions that try to address the search problem precisely.

Knowledge synthesis: The user expects the system to provide an "answer" and not simply a list of documents to read in which the answer may be buried. The system needs to integrate and correlate information from multiple documents, from multiple data sources, and/or from multiple reasoning strategies so as to develop a specific recommendation for the user. The system may need to provide an explanation for the recommendation in terms of supporting cases or documents that were retrieved from the knowledge bases.

2   Related Work

Textual Case Based Reasoning (TCBR) systems are finding applications in areas like Question Answering (Burke et. al), Knowledge Management [5], and Information Retrieval [6]. Traditional approach to indexing and retrieval are based on the Vector Space model where each textual case is represented as a feature vector (bag of words notation). The similarity measure is based on the cosine distance between the feature vectors. This approach, however suffers from problems like synonymy (different words have same meaning) and polysemy (same word has different meanings in different contexts).

Consequently, researchers have explored techniques to overcome the problems of the traditional bag words approach. These involve combining NLP techniques and statistical techniques with ontology to generate a more rich representation for the textual cases. [7] proved that syntax analysis on text can improve the retrieval. [8] used domain specific hand-coded thesaurus to improve the performance of retrieval. The work of [9] proved that inclusion of semantic information from sources like the WordNet [10] can considerably improve the performance of the bag of words technique. [6] describes a hybrid CBR-IR system in which CBR is used to drive IR. Their system uses a standard frame-based representation of a problem and matches it against frame-based representations of cases using a previously developed CBR system called HYPO. Documents stored in those cases are then used to construct keyword queries, which are run against a large document repository using the INQUERY search engine. This approach relies on frame-based symbolic AI representations. Their approach returns a potentially large set of documents for the user to interpret.

With these developments it is sufficiently clear that a knowledge rich representation of text can improve the retrieval efficiency considerably. An extreme case of such a knowledge representation technique, we can foresee is, to represent the text in such rich semantic representation format that the original text is subsumed in the representation itself. Though research is being carried out in this field, there has been little or almost no breakthrough in this regard, We feel that such representations are prohibitively expensive as it would need deep semantic analysis of text and require domain specific ontologies, which would require huge knowledge engineering effort. Also such a system would be well suited for problems involving rule-based inference. For a TCBR system aimed at efficient IR, such representations are not only expensive, but also unnecessary as well.

Recently, researchers have used graph-based technique for such knowledge rich representations. [11] proposes the use of Semantic Graph Model (SGM), while [12] develops a semantic graph based on extraction of triples using deep semantic analysis of text. The advantage of such graph base approach is that we can employ graph based algorithms on them and do interesting things. [13] proposes the use of Spreading Activation for IR, [11] proposes the use of graph structural matching for similarity calculation, while [14] uses Google PageRank [15] based approach for document summarization.

3   System Overview

Our current work attempts to come up with representations that capture pertinent knowledge of the corpus and return documents for queries based on that knowledge and previous query-response episodes containing user's result preferences.

We are particularly interested in a generic TCBR system capable of meaning-ful link based search for diverse users using the knowledge synthesis approach. We strive to improve the quality of retrieval with the use of NLP techniques combined with knowledge from generic ontologies. We see the problem of case representation as a way of having an effective representation scheme that acts as an index into the knowledgebase. Knowledge representation has been dealt with in number of ways by AI researchers that include methods like Frames, Predicate Calculus/Predicate Logic, Production Systems, and Scripts. A technique that is becoming increasingly popular is that of Semantic Networks, where knowledge is represented as a graph, vertices are concepts and edges are the associations between the concepts. Besides, such graph based formalism lends itself naturally to use graph based algorithms and do meaningful statistical and graph based analysis. In this paper, we have explored various techniques for generating such knowledge rich Semantic Networks and evaluated them for their effectiveness in a TCBR system. We have developed a TCBR based IR system that can do precise IR. For our base data, we use a corpus of medical journal abstracts ex-tracted from the Pubmed repository in Nuclear Cardiology domain. Our system retrieves a ranked list of documents from the corpus for a user query. We com-pare the retrieval for different techniques with Pubmed results as a benchmark for evaluation. We use the graph based representation techniques like the one inspired by [14] and compare it with a traditional vector space model. We use spreading activation for similarity calculation, which is similar to the method proposed by Francis et. al. We are using PageRank score and shortest path metrics between graph nodes for ranking documents as opposed to finding im-portant nodes for document summarization (as done by [14]). We create semantic graph using triples, similar to what [12] have done, but we use shallow syntactic analysis and ontology based methods to generate triples as opposed to a deep semantic parse, which we feel is infeasible for our system as it requires domain specific tree banks. In this paper we propose and evaluate the following techniques to generate triples: Syntactic Dependency based representation - Using dependency parser (using the Stanford Parser) to extract dependency triples. Shallow Linguistic Triples based Representation - Using shallow syntactic parse and generating triples based on the Subject Verb Object (SVO) relations. Semantic Triples Representation (UMLS based) - Using existing domain specific ontology to generate triples Semantic chain of closed class words.

4   TCBR System Description

In this section, we explain the various representation techniques and retrieval algorithms implemented to evaluate and compare the outcome of the system. In all our methods, we create link based graph structures where nodes in the graph are fragments of text either associated through relationship links or reified links. Each of the term nodes in the graph has information such as the document ids of the particular abstract, the TFIDF value of the term nodes in each of the abstracts it appears in and the initial activation value stored in it. Our TCBR system makes use of this representation to perform retrieval and adaptation of problem solutions. The case base stores the query and the solution. The knowledge representation acts as an indexing structure where the nodes map on to the documents where the corresponding word appears. A possible enhancement is to enrich the representation sufficiently, such that the document repository can be discarded.

Figure 1 describes the system architecture for *iReMedI*. Figure 2 shows the link structure for our knowledge representation.

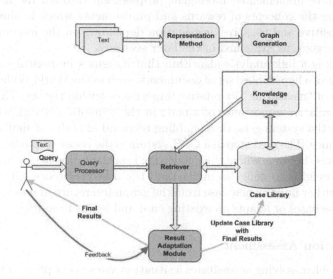

Fig. 1. System Architecture

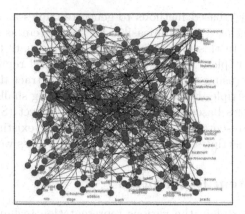

Fig. 2. Knowledge Graph

The Case in the Case Base: A case is a query response episode and stores : -
Set of nodes retrieved from graph - Final ranked retrieved document list

Our current system uses two algorithms for implementing the retrieve stage:

1. Spreading activation
2. PageRank and Shortest distance

Spreading activation is a method for searching associative networks, neural networks or semantic networks. The search process is initiated from a set of source nodes (e.g. concepts in a semantic network) with weights or "activation" and then iteratively propagating or "spreading" that activation out to other nodes linked to the source nodes. Most often these "weights" are real values that decay as activation propagates through the network. In our retrieval mechanism, we have implemented intelligent propagation through the network, i.e, implementing the concepts of rewards and punishments which in simpler terms would be positive and negative propagation depending on the learning that the system undergoes, as explained in the later sections.

PageRank is a link analysis algorithm that assigns a numerical weighting to each element of a hyperlinked set of documents, such as the World Wide Web, with the purpose of "measuring" its relative importance within the set. This is analogous to the relative importance of a node in the semantic network with respect to the input the system gets, thus enabling retrieval of nodes of similar meaning and importance. The next step in a CBR system is the revise step (the adaptation phase). This is the stage where the knowledge representation is modified in terms of assigned weights to nodes to understand the user preference. Given a query, the system either builds a new case from the graph (on return of no similar results from the case base) or adapts an existing case and learns from it by retaining it.

4.1   Situation Assessment

Effective problem-solving necessitates a situation assessment phase. In this phase the system needs to maximize its understanding of the problem. The query is converted from the language of communication to the system-understandable language of representation, depending on the choice of representation structure selected by the user. The query can be any unstructured text in English, for eg., the user may give an abstract to find related abstracts or may just give some keywords to find the relevant abstracts containing them. In the context of textual CBR, the system can improve its understanding of the problem in two ways - 1) by knowing more about different concepts related to the language of communication 2) by knowing more about the concepts related to the query terms in the language of representation. Linguistically,knowing more about the query-related terms helps the system to understand the different ways in which the query terms may be represented in the representation language. This representation is done by applying simple transformations (if any) from the language of communication to that of representation. In our case, the language of communication is English and the representation language is the set of extracted triples. The WordNet ontology is used to find synonyms of the query terms. Thus by using the original query terms and their synonyms which together comprise the expanded query, we can get a better matching when we transform from the problem space to the knowledge representation (concept graph). A more holistic understanding of the problem can be achieved by identifying the concepts that are related to the concepts identified as relevant by the "expanded query and graph" concept matching algorithm. To find such relevant concepts we use a path based approach. Let A and B be two concepts that have been found in the graph after the initial matching. For all such A and B in the expanded query we find the shortest path between them and identify the concepts that we encounter along this path. Given the expanded query, the newly identified concepts which occur most frequently along the shortest paths that we have explored are the most relevant related concepts. This idea is based on the assumption that the shortest path between two concepts will contain the most relevant concepts connecting them. This completes our situation assessment phase. Thus, given a user query in natural language as input to the situation assessment phase, the output is the set of concepts matched with the user query and the concepts related to the query both linguistically and semantically. Retrieval is performed on the documents associated with these concepts.

4.2 Knowledge Representation

In this sub-section we describe in detail the different representation techniques we have tested in our system. All the sample graphs showing the representation have been derived from the sentences : "Pancreatitis may be caused by excessive intake of alcohol. Pancreatitis is the inflammation of the pancreas."

Shallow Syntactic Triples. This representation formalism uses a Part of Speech Tagger (openNLP) to extract the concepts and relations in the form of Subject Verb Object Triples. Stemming and stop word removal is performed to create a rich representation of root terms and relationship links. Common nodes in the triples are merged to create a large forest of connected components

494   S. Sahay et al.

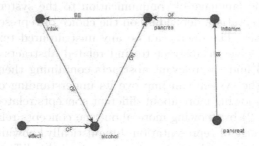

Fig. 3. Shallow syntactic triples representation

that is exploited in the retrieval process. This is a very fast statistical technique and is amenable to web scale data indexing and processing. Figure 3 shows an example graph for shallow syntactic triples.

Typed Dependency Triples. Typed dependencies and phrase structures are other ways of representing the structure of sentences. While a phrase structure parse represents nesting of multi-word constituents, a dependency parse represents governor-dependent dependencies between individual words. A typed dependency parse additionally labels dependencies with grammatical relations, such as subject or indirect object. This is a very rich syntactic representation formalism that captures sentences in the documents as dependency trees. The entire document structure is represented as a graph, hence this method is knowledge-rich and processor intensive but can potentially do away with the need to retain the original document. Figure 4 shows an example graph for typed dependency triples.

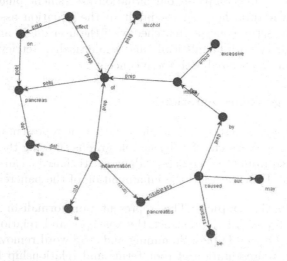

Fig. 4. Typed Dependency triples representation

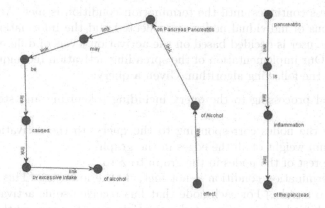

Fig. 5. Semantic Word Chains

Semantic Word Chains. This Knowledge Representation formalism builds a contextual map of related biomedical concepts for the corpus. This representation is constructed using the MedPostSKR Tagger, a POS Tagger trained on biomedical corpus and bundled with NLM's MMTx Mapping System. In this representation, nouns phrases, adjective phrases, verb phrases and preposition phrases are connected as reified chains of terms. The NounPhrases are UMLS concepts in this representation. This method of representation is more akin to knowledge navigation and summarization kind of tasks. We are not extracting triple based relationships, as these semantic relationships are hard to correctly extract and limit the system's retrieval performance. Figure 5 shows an example graph Semantic Word Chains.

4.3   Retrieval Techniques

In this paper, we have focused our efforts on the Knowledge Representation and Retrieval aspect of the TCBR cycle.

Spreading Activation Method. Recall that the graph representation that we have is a weighted graph with edges and nodes having weights (For e.g. In some representation edges hold the frequency of occurrence of that particular relationship. On the other hand the nodes hold the IDF value of that particular concept). Spreading activation in our system intiates the propogation by activating the query nodes, which is then iteratively propagated through the network of nodes . Spreading activation is an iterative process (Pulse-by-pulse process) in which each pulse involves the following operations in each node:

- Gather incoming activation, if any
- Retain activation
- Spread the activation to neighbors
- Termination check

The process continues until the termination condition is met. At this stage, the activations of individual nodes are collected and the information to be returned to the user is decided based on the activation levels of different nodes of the system. Our implementation of the spreading activation technique is briefly described in the following algorithm: Given a query:

1. Do initial processing to the query including tokenizing and stop-word removal.
2. Activate the nodes corresponding to the query, to the activation value = (Maximum weight of all the edges in the graph)
3. Activate rest of the nodes in the graph to zero
4. While termination condition is not met, do the following (This loop corresponds to a pulse) For each node that has received some activation in this pulse and if it has not propagated activation in past pulses, do the following:
   i. Let total edge weight = sum of weights of edges coming out of this node.
   ii. For each neighbor of this node, propagate an activation of value = (weight on edge reaching this neighbor / total edge weight) * Activation of this node
5. Collect activations of each of the individual documents as sum of activations of all its constituent nodes.
6. Return the ranked set of documents based on final activations to the user.

A termination condition is said to be met if either of the following is true:

1. There are no new nodes that have gathered activation in some pulse.
2. The Net activation gained by the entire network reaches a particular threshold. (Net of the network is the sum of activations of the individual nodes in the network)

At the end of the algorithm, the net activations for each of the individual documents is computed as the sum of activation of its associated nodes. A sorted list of documents on the normalized activation levels is returned to the user as the relevant set of documents with relevancy ranking.

PageRank and Shortest Distance Based Method. With this technique, we compute the sum of products of strengths of nodes in the graph along the query node paths to compute the overall strengths of documents. Since our graph nodes capture the associated document information, it is easy to invert the node map to the corresponding document strength maps. The process of retrieval is based on exploration and exploitation of both the structure and the semantics encoded in the knowledge representation. Intuitively the choice of algorithm was guided by the fact that we were dealing with a "link" structure of concepts. Page and Brin's PageRank Algorithm is a link analysis algorithm that assigns a numerical weights, called PageRank values, to each concept of the knowledge link structure, with the purpose of measuring its relative importance within the graph. Applying the idea of PageRank to our context, a concept node which relates to many concepts is considered important. Similarly if many important concepts are relate to a concept node it is considered important. Thus PageRank values give the relevance of each node in the link structure. PageRank gives a structural relevance measure of a concept since it operates on the linkage of the rich knowledge. It also gives a semantic relevance measure since it gives a better rank to the concepts nodes connected to important concepts and a lower rank to the concept nodes connected to less important ones. Once we have identified the most relevant concepts as per the PageRank algorithm, we use TFIDF based measure to rank the documents connected to the nodes. Further, this scheme is also based on the mutual information in all the documents connected to the same concept. This is illustrated mathematically with the formula below:

$$Score_{doc,query} = [\sum_{node_i} (PageRank_{node_i} * \sum_{doc_{ij}} strength_{ij})] * UserRating$$

Here i is the Vertex String Node on the graph and j is the associated documents on nodes i, $strength_{ij}$ is the TFIDF value of Node i in document j. In our implemented scheme, the query nodes are expanded to contain the additional nodes along the shortest paths between pair of recurring nodes in the query. The expanded query is matched with the concept graph to identify the relevant concept nodes. The PageRank values associated with these nodes is taken into account. Then for each document that is connected to a relevant concept node, its TFIDF value for that concept string is calculated. The aggregate sum of the TFIDFs for all documents is calculated. The product of the PageRank and this aggregate gives the score. This is further multiplied by the user rating to boost the documents which are more important from the user's perspective. This user rating is the positive or negative feedback given to the document being shown at the current ranking. Thus we get an overall ranking for the documents based on structure of the knowledge representation, the mutual information of the related concepts, semantics stored in the knowledge representation and the user preference.

4.4 Adaptation

In the adaptation phase, the system modifies the existing solutions to solve a novel but very similar problem. In our case the problem is a query and the solution is the ranked list of documents for that query. The adaptation phase obtains a set of similar cases from the retrieve phase of the CBR, which essentially uses a similarity metric to find the nearest neighbors to the new query. From these retrieved cases, a list of associated weighted documents is retrieved. Once we obtain a list of documents, we re-rank these documents for the new query. The re-ranking is simply sorting the set and presenting the top n to the user. The adaptation phase is multi-pass, where the user can rank the "goodness" of each retrieved document using the UI we provide. We use the user rating to modify the weight of that document and re-sort the documents and present to the user. The adaptation phase ends when the user is satisfied with the solution.

Fig. 6. Adaptation of Results

5   Experiments and Results

5.1   Gold Standard

We used a collection of 50 abstracts taken from Pubmed for testing. 50% of these were related to the topic of diabetes and the rest consisted of abstracts on random topics. We manually created five prototypical queries on diabetes and ranked all the 50 abstracts based on how well they answered the given queries. The following queries were used in our experiments: Q1: What are the medications for type 2 diabetes? Q2: What are the risks of diabetes in adolescents? Q3: Studies on gestational diabetes mellitus. Q4: What are the effects of diet and eating habits on diabetes? Q5: What are the side effects of Thiazolidinediones?

The above queries cover a sufficient range to test our methods as they are the kind of questions a disparate section of people would like to ask. For instance, a medical expert interested in knowing the latest available treatments for type 2 Diabetes would ask such a question as in query 1. The results should suggest specific medication and its effects for the type of disease given. A worried mother asking a question to get a broad overview on risks of diabetes for her adolescent son would ask query 2. The results should give a broad perspective of the risks especially for adolescents. A researcher wanting to know more about a certain topic like gestational diabetes mellitus would ask query 3. The results should be studies conducted on gestational diabetes. A dietician updating her current knowledge would like query 4 answered. The results should give relationships between the eating habits and risk of diabetes. An informed patient analyzing the effects of a particular drug would typically have a query like the query 5. The results should give side effects of the drug mentioned. The manually ranked list of documents was used as the gold standard.

5.2 Baseline

We used the vector space model as the baseline. The abstracts and the queries were represented as vectors based on TFIDF value. Lucene system was used to calculate the cosine distance of each document from a given query and rank the results with respect to the queries. The ranks thus obtained were used as the baseline.

5.3 Evaluation Metrics

Our information retrieval mechanisms output documents in a ranked order. We have used the following metrics to evaluate the performance of the various representation and retrieval methods:

1. Precision and Recall: We used the standard IR evaluation to calculate the precision, recall and the f-score for each method.

- **N:** The number of relevant documents in the corpus. (We used N as 25 in our experiments).
- **Ret:** The number of documents that were retrieved by our system.
- **RR:** The number of documents that were relevant and retrieved by our system.
- **Recall (R)** $R = \frac{RR}{N}$
- **Precision (P)** $P = \frac{RR}{Ret}$
- **F-Score (F)** $F = \frac{2PR}{P+R}$

2. Goodness Score: Since we are dealing with ranking the documents for a given query, it made sense to do a more fine grained analysis on the results rather than a basic precision and recall. We bracketed the ranked results into 4 regions: Highly Relevant (HR): the documents placed among the top 5, Moderately Relevant (MR): the documents placed from 6 to 15, Somewhat Relevant (SR): the documents ranked between 16 and 25, and Irrelevant (I) are the ones below 25. Using the gold standard ranking and the rankings produced by the algorithm, we formed a Table for each query as shown in Figure 9.

The diagonal elements (shaded black) correspond to the perfect classification; we give a score of +4 for each element falling in this region. The entries on either side of the diagonal (cross striped) correspond to a 1 level of discrepancy in the ranking; we give a score of +2 for all such elements. The (checked entries)

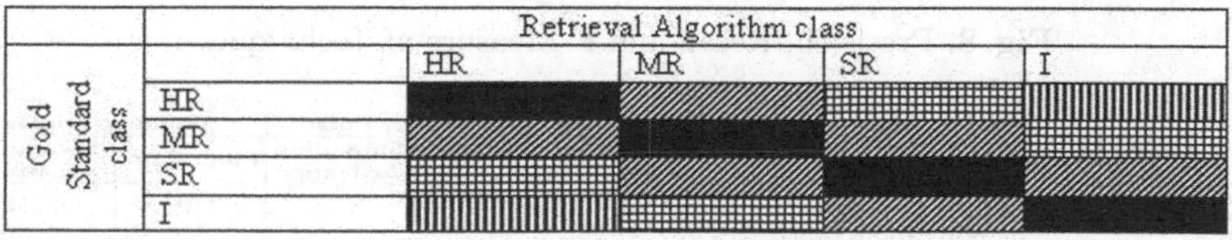

Fig. 7. Fine-grained Goodness Measurement

500   S. Sahay et al.

correspond to a 2 levels of discrepancy in the ranking and we give a penalty of
-2 for each entry in this region. While the two extreme regions (vertical stripes)
correspond to opposite classification and we give a penalty of -4 for such cases.
So the score for each algorithm for a given query is the sum of number in each
entry of the table each multiplied by the score. We normalize the final score to
get the goodness measure.

5.4 Results

Figure 8 shows the Precision (P), Recall (R) and F-Score values of the comparison for different knowledge representation methods using PageRank and Spreading Activation based retrieval techniques. We see that the state of the art Lucene
based VSM method outperforms our other techniques. The typed dependency
triples performs almost at par with the VSM method.

Figure 9 shows the overall goodness score of various techniques.

Here are some observations from our experiments:

- We haven't been able to capture the rich triple relations due to the complexity of the research articles and long sentences.
- The queries we have used are short that do not fully exploit the link based
  rich representations.
- We haven't implemented anaphora and abbreviations resolution that would
  enhance the results of our system.

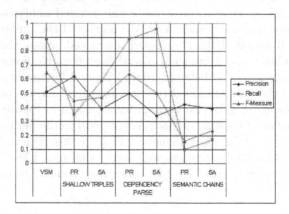

Fig. 8. Precision, Recall and F-Measure of Techniques

	Vector Space Model	Shallow Semantic Triples		Dependency Parse		Semantic Triples	
		Page Rank	Spreading Activation	Page Rank	Spreading Activation	Page Rank	Spreading Activation
Goodness Score	0.67	0.472	0.378	0.584	0.6	0.352	0.254

Fig. 9. Goodness Scores

- The syntactic shallow triples method is very fast and scalable. The other richer representation techniques are viable for a small to medium sized corpus.
- The baseline still performs the best as Lucene system is highly optimized and we have developed an initial prototype system that can be further enhanced in many ways.

6 Conclusion

This paper reports our initial efforts towards the development of a knowledge-rich TCBR infrastructure. We have experimented with different graph based linguistic representation methods and developed some techniques for link based information retrieval. Shallow triples offer fast and effective solution for large scale applications whereas dependency structures provide rich indexed information for advanced reasoning capabilities. The medical ontology based semantic representation requires much enhancements as the semantic word chains are incomplete and hard to exploit effectively. Our ultimate goal is to develop a truly learning adaptive problem solving system that uses planning (Situation Assessment) and TCBR techniques for performing various tasks. We have promising results for our system.

References

1. Peirce, C.S.: The aristotelian syllogistic. In: Hartshorne, C., Weiss, P. (eds.) Collected Papers: Elements of Logic, pp. 273–283. Harvard University Press, Cambridge (1965)
2. Sowa, J.F.: Conceptual graphs for a data base interface. IBM Journal of Research and Development 20(4), 336–357 (1976)
3. Lassila, O., Swick, R.: Resource description framework (RDF) model and syntax specification
4. Weber, R.O., Ashley, K.D., Brüninghaus, S.: Textual case-based reasoning. Knowl. Eng. Rev. 20(3), 255–260 (2005)
5. Weber, R., Aha, D., Sandhu, N., Munoz-Avila, H.: A textual case-based reasoning framework for knowledge management applications (2001)
6. Rissland, E.L., Daniels, J.J.: The synergistic application of CBR to IR. Artif. Intell. Rev. 10(5-6), 441–475 (1996)
7. Mott, B.W., Lester, J.C., Branting, K.: The role of syntactic analysis in textual case retrieval. In: ICCBR Workshops, pp. 120–127 (2005)
8. Brüninghaus, S., Ashley, K.D.: Reasoning with textual cases. In: Muñoz-Ávila, H., Ricci, F. (eds.) ICCBR 2005. LNCS (LNAI), vol. 3620, pp. 137–151. Springer, Heidelberg (2005)
9. Burke, R.D., Hammond, K.J., Kulyukin, V.A., Lytinen, S.L., Tomuro, N., Schoenberg, S.: Question answering from frequently asked question files: Experiences with the FAQ finder system. Technical Report TR-97-05 (1997)
10. Fellbaum: WordNet: An Electronic Lexical Database (Language, Speech, and Communication). MIT Press, Cambridge (May 1998)

11. Shaban, K.B., Basir, O.A., Kamel, M.: Document mining based on semantic un-derstanding of text. In: Martínez-Trinidad, J.F., Carrasco Ochoa, J.A., Kittler, J. (eds.) CIARP 2006. LNCS, vol. 4225, pp. 834–843. Springer, Heidelberg (2006)
12. Leskovec, J., Grobelnik, M., Milic-Frayling, N.: Learning sub-structures of docu-ment semantic graphs for document summarization (2004)
13. Anthony, G., Francis, J., Devaney, M., Santamaria, J.C., Ram, A.: Scaling spread-ing activation for information retrieval. In: Proceedings of IC-AI 2001, July 25 (2001)
14. Jagadeesh, J., Pingali, P., Varma, V.: A relevance-based language modeling ap-proach to DUC 2005 (2005)
15. Brin, S., Page, L.: The anatomy of a large-scale hypertextual web search engine. Comput. Netw. ISDN Syst. 30(1-7), 107–117 (1998)

Adaptation through Planning in Knowledge Intensive CBR*

Antonio Sánchez-Ruiz, Pedro P. Gómez-Martín,
Belén Díaz-Agudo, and Pedro A. González-Calero

Dep. Ingeniería del Software e Inteligencia Artificial
Universidad Complutense de Madrid, Spain
{antonio.sanchez,pedrop}@fdi.ucm.es, {belend,pedro}@sip.ucm.es

Abstract. Adaptation is probably the most difficult task in Case-Based Reasoning (CBR) systems. Most techniques for adaptation propose ad-hoc solutions that require an effort on knowledge acquisition beyond typical CBR standards.

In this paper we demonstrate the applicability of domain-independent planning techniques that exploit the knowledge already acquired in many knowledge-rich approaches to CBR. Those techniques are exemplified in a case-based training system that generates a 3D scenario from a declarative description of the training case.

1 Introduction

In most modern CBR systems, adaptation is not considered at all, or is just delegated to the user. Knowledge acquisition effort and the lack of domain independent adaptation techniques are responsible for this situation.

The motivation behind the work presented here was to determine whether, by authoring a knowledge rich representation of the domain, we could define adaptation procedures that would generate meaningful new cases automatically. The goal was to demonstrate that the additional effort on the representation of the domain would pay off in the long term. By defining an adaptation method which is based on domain-independent planning techniques which are parameterised with a domain ontology, we have given the first steps towards that goal.

We propose a domain-independent algorithm for case adaptation that takes the query as the planner goal and applies operators that transform the most similar retrieved case. This way, case adaptation is the problem of finding a sequence of operators, i.e. a plan, that transform a past solution into a new solution that verifies the constraints of the new query.

The adaptation through planning approach has been tested in a system for case-based training in virtual environments [1,2] where we faced the problem of knowledge acquisition for case authoring. Different elements of a training scenario need to be represented through a time consuming process where every

---

* Supported by the Spanish Ministry of Science and Education (TIN2006-15202-C03-03 and TIN2006-15140-C03-02).

K.-D. Althoff et al. (Eds.): ECCBR 2008, LNAI 5239, pp. 503–517, 2008.

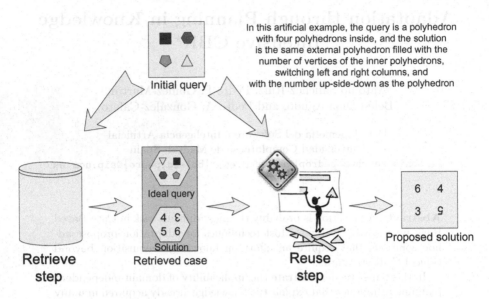

In this artificial example, the query is a polyhedron with four polyhedrons inside, and the solution is the same external polyhedron filled with the number of vertices of the inner polyhedrons, switching left and right columns, and with the number up-side-down as the polyhedron

Initial query

Ideal query

Retrieved case

Proposed solution

Retrieve step   **Reuse step**

Fig. 1. Adaptation working scheme

case is essentially one of a class. We demonstrate that, in that particular domain, case authoring through case adaptation is a feasible and cost-effective solution.

The rest of the paper runs as follows. Section 2 presents the planning approach to adaptation. Section 3 presents the domain that will be used as a test-bed for it, and Section 4 describes the representation of cases within this domain using Description Logics (DLs). Section 5 goes into the details of a running example. Finally Section 6 reviews related work and 7 concludes the paper.

2 Using Planning to Adapt Cases

Literature about CBR adaptation is much smaller than for CBR retrieval. Most of the CBR systems do not provide adaptation at all, or they just use very simple "ad hoc" adaptation rules, that cannot be reused in other systems. Adaptation is a complex task that needs a good understanding of the domain, and even domain experts often have problems to describe what they have learned by experience. However, the more complex adaptations the system is able to do, the less cases are needed in the case base, because the coverage of each case is increased.

Figure 1 shows the general idea. The initial query is used to retrieve a case that does not exactly fit with it. The CBR reuse step manipulates in some way this case in order to adapt the solution.

We propose to use planning for case adaptation in an attempt to define a domain-independent method for the reuse phase in Knowledge-Intensive CBR systems. A planner is a system that gets a formal description of a domain (types of entities, constraints and legal operators to change the state), and a particular problem (initial state and goals), and finds a sequence of operators that

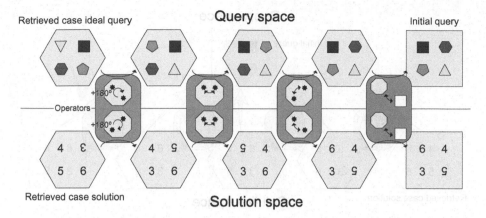

Fig. 2. Adaptation using query-space planning

makes the system evolve from the initial state to another state that holds the goals. Each operator defines the preconditions that the current state must hold to be applicable, and how it will modify the state after being applied. The planning problem is really hard due to the combinatorial explosion that arises from combining operators. In order to deal with this difficulty, different ways of implementing heuristics have been proposed.

To transform the CBR adaptation problem into a planning problem, we use the following rules:

- The retrieved case represents the *initial planning state*.
- The original CBR query is used to set the *planning goals*. Let us remember that we are adapting the retrieved case because it is not an exact match for the query.
- *Planner operators* transform the initial retrieved case, exploring different alternatives while searching a way to satisfy the original CBR query.

Figure 2 shows an example. The *retrieved case query* is shown at the upper-left corner, while the user initial query is in the upper-right one. The planner must change (*applying operators*) the retrieved *query* in order to look for a way to convert it into the user query, while, at the same time transforming the solution accordingly. In the example, operators rotate and swap the internal figures or change the external one. Keep in mind that the planner will test other options that are not shown in the figure. For example, it will try to apply the swap operator to the retrieved query, exploring other paths. Due to the fact that the planner is always manipulating *the query*, we call this approach *query-space planning*.

While changing the query, operators *must also modify the retrieved solution* in a consistent way depending on what they did in the query space. But the important aspect within this model is that the planner never looks at the solution space, that is travelled as a lateral effect of the query manipulation. If operators

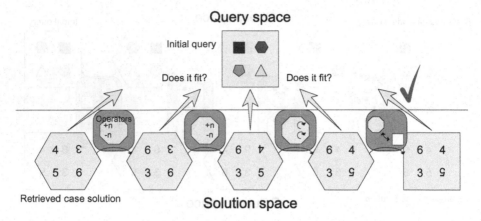

Fig. 3. Adaptation using solution-space planning

can be defined to transform the solution according to every transformation in the query, then when the initial query is reached, a valid solution has been found.

Depending on the domain, defining these operators can be quite difficult if not impossible. A different approach is the *solution-space planning* (figure 3, where operators manipulate only the retrieved case solution and the *planner* explores the solution space. Now the only way for knowing if a goal state (the correct solution) has been reached is to have available a *test function* that checks if a solution is valid for the user query. Depending on the domain, this could be easier than defining the "dual operators" required by the query-space planning. As a drawback, it is more difficult to *optimise* the planner's search because heuristics must deal with a target state that is, in fact, unknown. But due to the expected proximity between initial and final solutions (it is the more similar case, after all), this limitation could not be a big problem in many domains.

When comparing with the *ad hoc* adaptation, the advantages of using planning (over the query or solution space) are:

- *Operators represent atomic changes that are easy to write.* The planner will combine these operators to create complex adaptations, and will manage the dependences between operators.
- *Adaptation knowledge can be represented using a standard logic language,* by means of preconditions and effects. This declarative approach eases the sharing and reutilisation of the adaptation knowledge.
- *Planners are experts solving this type of problems,* and could use complex heuristics to improve the search and to reduce the space of possibilities.

Keep in mind that although this way to proceed is related to Case-Based Planning (CBP) [3], we are not retrieving plans nor trying to adapt them. The retrieved cases are not built using the planning operators. Actually, the operators are only used to *modify* existing cases, and not to create them from scratch. We are using planning to implement the reuse phase of a CBR system, not CBR to solve the planning problem.

One of the strength of CBR systems is that cases may contain implicit knowledge about the domain that we cannot fully model. An interesting concern that may arise is, if during the planning process, after applying several operators, the generated cases are still correct. This general question is beyond the scope of this paper, but obviously, the planning operators must be chosen carefully to protect the cases, and there is a trade off between adaptation and correctness preservation. Later on, in the following section, we describe the safeguards that we use in our domain to deal with this problem.

2.1   Planning with Description Logics

Planners usually work with domain and problem descriptions formalised in some variant of PDDL [4], the standard planning language. PDDL was developed to compare different planners in an international planning competition. During the last few years it has been evolving, letting us to describe more complex problems. However, the language expressivity is kept limited intentionally to be able to check constraints and apply operators fast.

PDDL is used both for writing operators and specifying initial and goal states. Therefore, using PDDL for reuse in CBR, would require using it as *case description language*. Unfortunately, KI-CBR community does not usually represents cases using PDDL. A more convenient alternative are Description Logics (DLs) [5], well-known subsets of First Order Logic whose main strength is that they offer considerable expressivity power, while reasoning is still decidable. This formalism is very useful to represent complex structured domains, and has been chosen as base for OWL-DL[1], the standard language for the Semantic Web.

DLs represent complex domains by means of *concepts*, *properties* and *individuals*. *Concepts* represent *sets* of individuals with common features, and are described by potentially complex logical formulas. *Properties* are binary predicates that relate concepts, and may have additional properties like being symmetric or transitive. The main property is the *is-a* relation that allows to define a hierarchy of concepts. Finally, *Individuals* are simple entities that represent objects in the domain as concept instances.

A Knowledge Base (or Ontology) has two different parts: the TBox, that contains concepts and properties, and represents the domain constraints; and the ABox, that contains individuals and assertions over those individuals, and represents a particular domain instantiation, i.e., knowledge that may change.

DLs allow to represent and reason with complex domains and to compute elaborated similarity metrics, but inferences and reasoning (required for planning) is computationally expensive. Therefore, there are two different options to integrate a planner into a CBR system that uses DLs (such as OWL-DL) as case representation language. The first approach is to translate all the domain knowledge as well as the cases from OWL-DL to PDDL, taking into account the potential loss of semantics during the process. The idea to keep several domain representations with different expressivity has been studied in [6]. The main

---

[1] W3C Recommendation http://www.w3.org/TR/owl-guide/

advantage of this strategy is that the planning process can be done efficiently, and a lot of implemented planners exist. The second approach consists on using a planner that utilises OWL-DL as formal language to describe the domain, i.e., a planner that will keep the original semantics. The main drawback of these planners is the lower performance.

Although the best option would depend on the domain, it should be kept in mind that classical planners are able to solve problems that require the execution of *hundreds of operators*, but in our domain, i.e., case adaptation, we may safely assume that only a few operators are needed to adapt the case. After all, the *initial state* (retrieved case) should be quite near to the *goal state* (initial query) or other case would have been retrieved. Finally, having the knowledge duplicated in different formalisms (DLs and PDDL) carries synchronization problems.

Under these circumstances, planning using DLs is a valuable option. The basic idea behind this planning is to use the TBox as description of the *domain constraints*, and the ABox to represent the *current state*. Operators modify the current state by adding and deleting asserts in the ABox. The technical details of this type of planning can be found in [7,8], but some of its benefits are:

1. *We can solve problems in very complex domains.* DLs reasoners are optimized to work with large ontologies with lots of concepts, constraints and instances. PDDL domains are usually simpler, and the planning complexity is based on the length of the solution plan, not in the domain complexity.
2. *It is easier to write the operators.* We can use all the concepts and properties of the ontology to write the preconditions and effects of the operators, so there is a very rich vocabulary available.
3. *Operator's check.* DLs provide an automatic consistency checking of the knowledge base. Using this feature we can know whether after applying an operator the planner reaches an inconsistent state. That would mean that the operator is not properly written and we should alert the domain scripter. Additionally, some recent research allows to obtain accurate description of the inconsistencies [9] that could be displayed as error messages.
4. *Heuristics based on similarity.* Ontologies can be used to compute similarity metrics that take into account the domain structure [10]. These similarity metrics can be used by the planner to compute a heuristic function that will drive the search.
5. *Reasoning with incomplete knowledge.* Planners usually assume Closed World, but DLs reason with an Open World. Close World means that everything that is not asserted explicitly in the state is false, and the only entities that exist in the state are those which have been defined. On the contrary, Open World assumes that we only have a partial description of the real state, and thus, all the predicates that are not explicitly asserted in the state can be true or false. Moreover, there can exist individuals in the current state that have not been noticed.

(a) User looking for resources   (b) User writing instructions

Fig. 4. JV^{2}M

3   A Domain Example: Case-Based Training

During the last few years we have been working on an educational game where
students learn, in an intuitive way, how to compile Java programs into *object
code*, specifically the *assembler* language of the Java Virtual Machine (JVM).
The system, known as JV^{2}M (figure 4), follows the *learning-by-doing* approach
of teaching. Students confront increasingly complex compilation exercises, and
must figure out the corresponding JVM object code.

The game component comes up as a virtual environment where the student
is immersed. Exercises are embedded in that 3D world, and compiling a Java
code (solving an exercise) consists on looking for *resources* needed to write the
assembly instructions in a terminal. The program incorporates other game components, such as enemies and time limits [11].

The learning process consists on more and more complex exercises, each one
represented in a game level. Therefore, the educational and game components
are merged due to the fusion between a game level and an exercise. In each
learning episode, the system chooses the next exercise to be solved depending
on the user profile. In the first interactions, only simple expressions are put into
practise, but if, while or for structures are presented later on.

The system must also be aware of the student proposed solution, in order to
provide some kind of feedback when errors are committed. In that sense, JV^{2}M
knows the correct solution to the exercise, and is able to compare it with the
alternative proposed by the student. When the user makes a mistake, the system
must decide if she should be interrupted. A balance must be found between the
waste of time while the user is trying bad approaches and the *user freedom*, that
encourage students to browse the environment and explore new ways of solving
exercises (a typical behaviour when playing games).

As said before, JV^{2}M analyses the user model in order to plan the next
learning episode. In that sense, we have divided the taught domain in different

```
public static int euclides(int a, int b) {
  int res;
  if ( (a <= 0) || (b <= 0) )
    res = 0;
  else {
    while (a != b) {
      if (a < b)
        b -= a;
      else
        a -= b;
    }
    res = a;
  }
  return res;
}
```

Fig. 5. Exercise example

concepts (closely related to the Java language structures), such as *StaticMethod*, *AddExpression* or *WhileStatement*. The specific task of the *pedagogical module* consists on selecting which concepts the user must practise in the next exercise. It must also indicate which concepts should *not* be included in the exercise, because they are too difficult for the student.

Once the concepts have been chosen, the system must obtain an exercise that contains them. We are working with a quite structured domain, so it could be possible to automatically create a new Java program from scratch, containing the required source code structures using a bit of randomness. Unfortunately, this process would provide, if done with care, *compilable* exercises, but they would not execute anything interesting. When teaching how to compile source code, the important aspect of the exercise is, actually, that it *compiles*, but semantically useful source code is, obviously, more motivating for students.

That leads us to a case-based approach, where an *exercise base* is manually built by domain experts. A *source code corpus* is made available for the system to look for exercises that match the query proposed by the pedagogical module. Each exercise is indexed using the compilation concepts mentioned previously and they are used in the retrieval process. For example, the Euclidean algorithm shown in figure 5 would be indexed using concepts such as *IfStatement*, *WhileStatement*, *MinusExpression* and some other boolean expression concepts.

Unfortunately, using cases imposes a big work in content creation, something quite annoying in a so structured domain. Furthermore, educational programs need a quite big amount of exercises, in order to create the illusion of a never ending source of alternatives and to avoid repetition and tedium. Therefore, we need a better balance between automatic and manual exercise creation, and knowledge intensive CBR adaptation seems the best alternative.

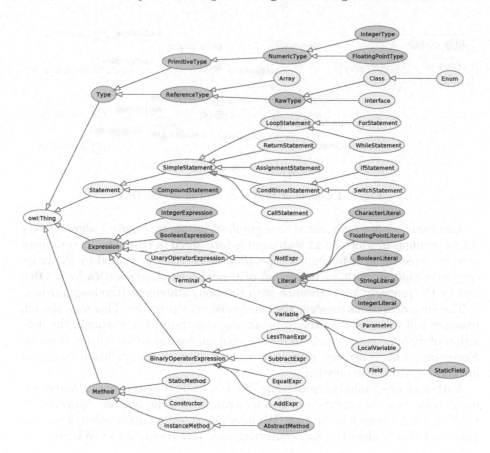

Fig. 6. Partial view of the domain ontology

4   Case Representation in Description Logics

We use DLs to formalise the JV²M domain and to index the case base. DLs
provide us with several benefits. First, we can improve the retrieval phase of the
CBR cycle by means of similarity metrics based on the domain structure. It also
provides a rich vocabulary to index the case base and to make queries. Besides,
DLs can automatically check the consistency of the knowledge base, and so, we
can detect problems during the authoring process. Finally, DLs are a declarative
and standard way to represent knowledge that eases sharing and reusing it.

Figure 6 shows a small part of the ontology that we use to define the domain,
and only the hierarchy due to the *is-a* relation. The actual ontology defines
several more concepts and properties. Light circled concepts represent *primitive
concepts*, i.e., concepts that have been defined using only necessary conditions,
while dark circled concepts represent *defined concepts*, i.e., concepts that are
defined using necessary and sufficient conditions. Instances can be automatic
classified under these defined concepts if they fit the proper conditions.

512   A. Sánchez-Ruiz et al.

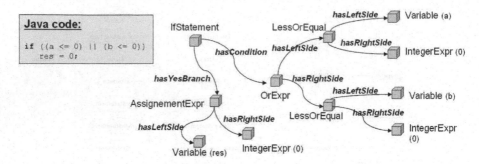

Fig. 7. Example of Java code represented in DLs

Java exercises are represented as a graph of instances. Figure 7 shows a very simple example in which an `if` statement is formalised in DLs. The `if` statement is represented by an individual of type *IfStatement*, that is related by the property *hasCondition* with an individual of type *BooleanExpresion* (a logic OR), and by the property *hasYesBranch* with the body statement (the assignment).

The class definitions preserve the consistency of the model. This way, the DL reasoner will warn us if we try to break any constraint. For example, the definition of *IfStatement* compels to have a relation *hasCondition* with a *Boolean-Expression*. This constraint protect us from writing an `if` condition using, for instance, a numeric expression.

Authoring programming cases using DLs is a really time-consuming and error-prone task. Domain experts are used to write Java code, but not "drawing it" in OWL-DL tools such as Protégé. We have developed an application, known as `java2owl` that bridges this gap converting any Java program to OWL-DL.

5   A Practical Example

Summarising what we have told in this paper, when JV^{2}M has to choose a new exercise for a student, the first step is to decide what type of exercise fits next, using the student profile. The system builds a query containing the statements that the new exercise must have as well as the statements that cannot be part of it. Then, the most similar case in the case base is retrieved using similarity metrics based on the ontology. If the retrieved case fits the query, then we are done, and the case can be used as next exercise. In other case, the retrieved exercise must be adapted using the planner. The planning problem is built using the retrieved exercise as initial state, and the CBR query as goal. Finally, the planner will try do adapt the exercise using the domain operators.

Let us suppose that, using the student profile, the system decides that a good candidate for next exercise must contain `if` and `while` statements, but it cannot contain neither the OR (`||`) nor the NOT (`!`) logical operators. This can be a real situation for a student that still does not know how to compile some logical expressions, but has already practice `if` and `while` statements separately and now must prove that she can manage them combined.

Let us suppose now that, using the previous query, the most similar case in the case base is the Euclidean algorithm that was presented in figure 5. This exercise combines if and while statements; unfortunately, an undesired logical OR appears, that should be avoided. In this situation, the planner must try to adapt this exercise to fit the query but without changing the semantics.

The required operators to solve this problem are introduced next. The vocabulary used to describe the preconditions and effects are the concepts and roles of the ontology. The operator effects are described using two different lists: the *del* list, that contains assertions that must be removed from the current state, and the *add* list with new assertions that will be added. For example, the following operator changes the two branches of an *If-Then-Else*, negating the boolean condition and swapping the statements of the "yes" and "no" branches (the *newIndividual* predicate represents the creation of a new individual, different from the others):

operator swapIfBranches
vars ?if1, ?c1, ?br1, ?br2
pre IfInstruction(?if1), hasCondition(?if1, ?c1), hasIfYesBranch(?if1, ?br1), hasIfNo-
Branch(?if1, ?br2)
del hasCondition(?if1, ?c1), hasYesBranch(?if1, ?br1), hasNoBranch(?if1, ?br2)
add newIndividual(?c2), NotExpr(?c2), hasSubExpr(?c2, ?c1), hasCondition(?if1, ?c2),
hasYesBranch(?if1, ?br2), hasNoBranch(?if1, ?br1)

The second operator simplifies a logical expression as follows: $not(a < b) \Rightarrow a > b$. We can define similar operators to simplify $not(a = b) \Rightarrow a \neq b$, $not(a < b) \Rightarrow a \geq b$, etc.

operator notLessOrEqual
vars ?e1, ?e2, ?le, ?re
pre NotExpr(?e1), hasSubExpr(?e1, ?e2), LessOrEqualThanExpr(?e2), hasSubexpr(?c2,
?le), hasSubexpr2(?e2, ?re)
del NotExpr(?e1), hasSubExpr(?e1, ?e2), hasSubexpr(?e2, ?le), hasSubexpr2(?e2, ?re),
removeIndividual(?e2)
add GreaterThanExpr(?e1), hasSubexpr(?e1, ?le), hasSubexpr2(?c1, ?re)

Finally, we have operators to represent the De Morgan's laws ($not(a \text{ or } b) \Rightarrow not\ a \text{ and } not\ b$, $not(a \text{ and } b) \Rightarrow not\ a \text{ or } not\ b$). Next, we only show the operator for one of them, but the other one is very similar:

operator notOr
vars ?e1, ?e2, ?le, ?re
pre NotExpr(?e1), hasSubExpr(?e1, ?e2), OrExpr(?e2), hasSubexpr(?e2, ?le), has-
Subexpr2(?e2, ?re)
del NotExpr(?e1), hasSubExpr(?e1, ?e2), hasSubexpr(?e2, ?le), hasSubexpr2(?e2, ?re),
removeIndividual(?e2)
add newIndividual(?n1), newIndividual(?n2), AndExpr(?e1), hasSubexpr(?e1,?n1), has-
Subexpr2(?e1,?n2), NotExpr(?n1), NotExpr(?n2), hasSubexpr(?n1,?le), hasSubexpr2(?n2,?re)

We do not need any more operators for this practical example, but several more can be scripted to improve the planner. Next, we describe how, using these

```
int euclides(int a, int b) {
    int res;
    if ( !( (a <= 0) || (b <= 0) ) ) {
        while (a != b) {
            if (a < b)
                b -= a;
            else
                a -= b;
        }
        res = a;
    }
    else
        res = 0;
    return res;
}
```

(a) Euclides 1

```
int euclides(int a, int b) {
    int res;
    if ( !(a <= 0) && !(b <= 0) ) {
        while (a != b) {
            if (a < b)
                b -= a;
            else
                a -= b;
        }
        res = a;
    }
    else
        res = 0;
    return res;
}
```

(b) Euclides 2

Fig. 8. Euclidean algorithm during the adaptation process

operators, the planner will be able to adapt the retrieved Euclidean algorithm, removing the logical OR and completely matching the query

First, the planner uses the *swapIfBranches* operator on the more external if, transforming the code as shown on the left side of figure 8. Then, the planner tries one of the De Morgan operators to remove the negated OR, and the program changes as shown in the same figure on the right. At this point, the planner has removed the OR operator, but has also generated a couple of NOTs. However, this problem can be easily solved using the operators that simplify the logical negation twice. This way, the planner obtains a code that fits the original query (if and while, but no logical OR neither NOT) (figure 9), and the case has been successfully adapted.

6   Related Work

Regarding related work about domain-independent case adaptation, is very relevant the work of Leake [12] and the DIAL system. They use reasoning from scratch to build a library of adaptation cases that are stored for future reuse. The reasoning from scratch process is divided in two different phases. The first one, is a transformation phase based on general rules that define the general strategy for adaptation. Each rule defines the information that needs to be applied, or *knowledge goals*. The second phase uses a planning component to obtain that information using introspective reasoning about memory search strategies. Traces of all this process are stored as cases to enable future adaptation. The system keeps two types of cases: memory search cases encapsulate information about the steps in the memory search process; and, adaptation cases encapsulate information about the adaptation problem as a whole, including both the transformation used and the memory search process followed.

```
int euclides (int a, int b) {
   int res;
   if ( (a > 0) && (b > 0) ) {
      while (a != b) {
         if (a < b)
            b -= a;
         else
            a -= b;
      }
      res = a;
   }
   else
      res = 0;
   return res;
}
```

(a) Euclides 3

Fig. 9. Euclidean algorithm adapted successfully

A difference with our approach is that they use planning to retrieve information from the memory, and thus, their operators describe actions within a "mental" world, rather than within the external world. Our operators describe atomic changes in cases, that will be combined to perform possibly complex and structural changes. Another difference is the lack of general rules to define adaptation strategies in our approach. Although these rules can improve the system performance, the knowledge to define them will not always be available. Finally, the use of DLs in our work, besides the inherent benefits of a knowledge representation technology equipped with a well defined and formal semantic, provides an expressive and standard language for domain descriptions. DL reasoners can take advantage of this semantic information to perform different types of reasoning, and this way, an adaptation process based on DLs becomes more flexible and effective.

Our research group has worked previously in CBR adaptation with DLs [13]. In that work cases are also represented as a net of connected individuals, where each one of them represents a component of the solution. However, that time we chose to represent dependences between individuals explicitly in each case using properties, and adaptation was performed replacing individuals with another similar ones. Similarity was computed using the ontology and when one individual was replaced all its dependences had to be updated. An important limitation of that approach is that cannot change the structure of the solution being adapted. On the other hand, using planning we only need to write planning operators that represent atomic adaptations, but it is the planner responsibility to deal with all the dependences and constraints.

The main drawback of this work is that knowledge about adaptation is needed from the beginning to write the planning operators. An obvious research line is to find different sources of knowledge and learning techniques to relax this assumption. Different alternatives has been proposed, [14] is a framework which focus on what they call knowledge light approaches. This lightness means that they are interested in methods which do not presume a lot of knowledge acquisition work before learning, but, instead, use already acquired knowledge inside the system. Wilke et al present as the first work on this area, the one described in [15], where Hanney and Keane present an inductive learning algorithm to extract adaptation knowledge from the cases in the case base. Craw et al present a more modern work in the same line [16] that achieves more robust learning using different learning algorithms, exemplifying these ideas in a component-based pharmaceutical design system.

7   Conclusions

In this paper we have introduced the idea of using domain-independent planning techniques for CBR adaptation. We use a special kind of planning that makes use of rich ontologies for knowledge representation, but the idea of using a planner for case adaptation is easily extended to other planning paradigms. We have exemplified our approach in JV^2M , a 3D educational game, that teaches how to compile Java code into object code for the JVM. This system uses a CBR subsystem to retrieve appropriate exercises for students, but if there is not a perfect exercise in the case base, we use a planner to implement the exercise adaptation.

An interesting idea for future work is if we can extend the domain ontology with "high level" concepts about algorithms like *final recursive algorithm* or *simple iterative algorithm*. These concepts would allow us to categorise and retrieve cases using not only the vocabulary about Java statements but other more abstract indexes.

It is also interesting the idea of improving the user profile adding more information about what the student knows. This way, we would be able to represent not only if the student knows how to compile a statement, but also in which particular cases (combination of instructions) the student has had problems and needs to improve. Using the planner we will be able to adapt the cases to fit more specific requirements, starting with the general Java exercises from the case base.

References

1. Gómez-Martín, M.A., Gómez-Martín, P.P., González-Calero, P.A.: Aprendizaje activo en simulaciones interactivas. Revista Iberoamericana de Inteligencia Artificial 11(33), 25–36 (2007)
2. Gómez-Martín, P.P., Gómez-Martín, M.A., González-Calero, P.A.: Using metaphors in game-based education. In: Hui, K.-c., Pan, Z., Chung, R.C.-k., Wang, C.C.L., Jin, X., Göbel, S., Li, E.C.-L. (eds.) EDUTAINMENT 2007. LNCS, vol. 4469, pp. 477–488. Springer, Heidelberg (2007)
3. Hammond, K.J.: Case-Based Planning: Viewing Planning as a Memory Task. Academic Press, Boston (1989)

4. Fox, M., Long, D.: Pddl2.1: An extension to pddl for expressing temporal planning domains. Journal of Artificial Intelligence Research 20, 61–124 (2003)
5. Baader, F., Calvanese, D., McGuinness, D.L., Nardi, D., Patel-Schneider, P.F.: The description logic handbook: theory, implementation, and applications. Cambridge University Press, Cambridge (2003)
6. McNeill, F., Bundy, A., Walton, C.: Planning from rich ontologies through translation betweeen representations. In: Proceedings of ICAPS 2005 Workshop on The Role of Ontologies in Planning and Scheduling, Monterey, CA, USA (2005)
7. Sirin, E.: Combining Description Logic reasoning with AI planning for composition of web services. PhD thesis, University of Maryland (2006)
8. Sánchez-Ruiz, A.A., González-Calero, P.A., Díaz-Agudo, B.: Planning with description logics and syntactic updates. In: Salido, M., Fdez-Olivares, J. (eds.): Planning, Scheduling and Constraint Satisfaction (CAEPIA 2007 Workshop), Universidad de Salamanca, pp. 140–150 (2007)
9. Kalyanpur, A.: Debugging and Repair of OWL Ontologies. PhD thesis, 2006 (2006)
10. Díaz-Agudo, B., González-Calero, P.: An Ontological Approach to Develop Knowledge Intensive CBR Systems. In: Ontologies: A Handbook of Principles, Concepts and Applications in Information Systems, pp. 173–214 (2007)
11. Gómez-Martín, M.A., Gómez-Martín, P.P., Palmier-Campos, P., González-Calero, P.A.: Not yet another visualization tool: Learning compilers for fun. In: Panizo-Alonso, L., Sánchez-González, L., Fernández-Manjón, B., Llamas-Nistal, M. (eds.) 8th International Symposium on Computers in Education (SIIE 2006), León, Spain, Universidad de León, October 2006, pp. 264–271 (2006)
12. Leake, D.B., Kinley, A., Wilson, D.C.: Learning to improve case adaption by introspective reasoning and CBR. In: ICCBR, pp. 229–240 (1995)
13. González-Calero, P.A., Gómez-Albarrán, M., Díaz-Agudo, B.: A substitution-based adaptation model. In: ICCBR Workshops, pp. 17–26 (1999)
14. Wilke, W., Vollrath, I., Bergmann, R.: Using knowledge containers to model a framework for learning adaptation knowledge. In: Wettschereck, D., Aha, D.W. (eds.) European Conference on Machine Learning (MLNet) Workshop Notes — Case-Based Learning: Beyond Classification of Feature Vectors, pp. 68–75 (1997)
15. Hanney, K., Keane, M.T.: Learning adaptation rules from a case-base. In: Smith, I., Faltings, B.V. (eds.) EWCBR 1996. LNCS, vol. 1168, pp. 179–192. Springer, Heidelberg (1996)
16. Craw, S., Wiratunga, N., Rowe, R.: Learning adaptation knowledge to improve case-based reasoning. Artif. Intell. 170, 1175–1192 (2006)

Folk Arguments, Numerical Taxonomy and Case-Based Reasoning

Luís A.L. Silva*, John A. Campbell, and Bernard F. Buxton

Department of Computer Science, University College London,
Malet Place, London, WC1E 6BT, UK
{l.silva,j.campbell,b.buxton}@cs.ucl.ac.uk

Abstract. Experts who narrate their knowledge in case-like form often express significant parts of it in folk arguments – considerations for and against alternative recommendations where informal judgment is involved. Such arguments do not fit naturally into common frameworks of case-based reasoning. The knowledge they contain may therefore be overlooked despite its value. The paper indicates a mean of helping knowledge acquisition in such circumstances, proposes numerical taxonomy for structuring case bases where folk arguments are included, and shows how these contributions are used, through an example involving both scientific considerations and subjective expert judgment: allocation of frequencies for shortwave broadcasting.

1 Introduction

In typical case-based reasoning (CBR) applications, cases consist of factual and/or prescriptive information. In stating or justifying the contents of a case, its supplier may use arguments in support of those contents. Explanations which figure in cases when CBR becomes explanation-based reasoning [1] are a form of argument, but they do not capture most of what a supplier would say if asked to reason aloud, for many applications. Our present work has been concerned with recording this more informal variety of argument, which we can call "folk argument" for simplicity, and with representing it for use as an integral part of CBR.

Our starting point was an observation made during acquisition of knowledge that was primarily case-like: apparently significant parts of experts' knowledge which emerged as "folk arguments" – mainly justifications for choices of items that then fitted into standard CBR formats – found no eventual place in the cases themselves. On the assumption that losing any relevant knowledge degrades the quality of later reasoning or computation based on what is captured, we have considered how to exploit reasoning with folk arguments (i.e. arguments that do not have a logical and formal structure as in [2] and do not maintain a logical character in a more informal but detailed representation as in [3]) along with the standard components of cases.

The paper describes this process and the results that it produces in one application: frequency allocation for shortwave radio broadcasting. This application is typical of

---

* This work is supported by CAPES/Brazil (grant number 2224/03-8).

K.-D. Althoff et al. (Eds.): ECCBR 2008, LNAI 5239, pp. 518–532, 2008.

many where folk argument about contents of cases occurs: there is no single strong underlying theory, even implicit, hence no a priori objective criteria for success or failure of a choice. The person/expert who makes the choice therefore rehearses all the arguments for and against each key decision and decides on balance of their apparent weights. We find the same expert behaviour in a second case-based application: authentication of paintings through information about pigments contained in them for which preliminary results are presented in [4].

2 Background to the Work

Argumentation is an active area of research in its own right, both inside Artificial Intelligence (AI) and outside. [2, 5] give a reliable impression of this level of activity. Broadly speaking, the greatest advances and the greatest interest have been concentrated in two overlapping areas: the nature of legal argumentation in legal applications of AI where [6] present a good picture of the state of play in CBR, and the formulation of arguments via some appropriate version of mathematical logic [2].

Whether the initial consideration is systematic in terms of law (e.g. [6]) or reflects the not so systematic nature of human decision-making (e.g. [7]), there has been a strong tendency towards the use of logic to express what a reasoner is doing. This is appropriate for other areas besides law. However, in other areas the domain expert may believe, tacitly at least, that early reference from a consideration or set of considerations to some general "factor", principle or tentative rule is unhelpful or impracticable. This is particularly so when expert behaviour in a subject consists of making recommendations based on considerations for and against intermediate or final conclusions without apparent development of an argument that goes naturally into a logical framework. Imposing any such framework (e.g. as a means of directing an interview of an expert) can then reduce the quality of information given or the expert's degree of cooperation with the interviewer. This is a particular example of a general phenomenon that knowledge engineers in the early days of expert systems discovered and then tried to avoid.

In our experience, it is not difficult to find applications where experts naturally offer "considerations" in support of their conclusions. The same behaviour also occurs frequently in non-expert reasoning towards a conclusion. The term "folk argument" describes the phenomenon rather well, and memorably. A folk argument is a sequence of individual considerations or steps. The most common sequence consists of positive and negative considerations, with item $i+1$ being a supportive or contradictory response to item i. An example is given in section 3. Seeing a case of frequency allocation for shortwave broadcasting with and without its accompanying folk argument F shows immediately that neglecting F loses essential information (and the same is true for use of pigment observations to authenticate paintings). The question is: how can F be used to assist CBR? There is also the subsidiary question of helping to elicit F as fully as possible (addressed in section 4).

2.1 Numerical Taxonomy and Its Role

Suppose that a set of items is given, where each item has various features and where the values of the features can be noted. Suppose also that it is possible to assign or measure directly the relative distances or differences between any pair of values of any one feature. Direct measurement is appropriate, for example, if a feature is a spatial coordinate. Assignment is needed if there is no obvious coordinate in any space, e.g. where a feature is a certain kind of texture or a preferred food. It is required to propose a classification of the specimens in a tree showing their relative closeness to each other. Proceeding upwards from the individuals, the closest are associated first, forming small clusters, and further specimens or clusters are associated into larger clusters, until a single cluster is reached as the root of the tree. Each intermediate node between the leaves and the root represents one association. What is necessary to make this process work?

Historically, the earliest demands for the process came from botany and zoology. Either (usually) there was no strong theory which could be used to make the classification or it was desired to see what would happen and what generalisations the tree (a "dendrogram") could suggest if no theory were assumed. Numerical taxonomy [8] is the response to this demand. In brief, for features 1, 2 ... of specimens x and y, only a distance function D of all the differences x1 − y1, x2 − y2, ... is needed. There are then several clustering algorithms which can use D in generating the dendrogram. For any application there are still questions to be answered in order to define D, e.g. normalisation and scaling of feature values, choice of the functional form of D (a Pythagorean form is a default choice) and - even before these - choice of the attributes to be parameterised in setting up D. [8] treats these issues in detail.

Numerical taxonomy is relevant for the classification or indexing of cases − or, more generally, any items with heterogeneous features. It is particularly useful where the numbers of available items are too small for trustworthy machine learning and where no single set of keys for indexing suggests itself (e.g. when even experts have no preferred framework for the job). The latter consideration holds for folk argumentation characteristics even when it may not be true for the facts of a case.

3 Frequency Allocation for Shortwave Broadcasting

Shortwave broadcasting is an international activity. Even when a station in a given country is intended only for reception by listeners in that country, it has international implications. This is because the short waves (by convention, with frequencies between about 3 and 26 MHz), unlike the 0.5-1.7 MHz medium wave band, are favoured for long-distance reception. It is not unusual for domestic broadcasts, even at the lowest frequencies, to be heard on the other side of the world.

Shortwave stations' choices of frequencies and broadcasting times are registered with the International Telecommunications Union − ITU which makes summary information about the choices available at least annually. In principle this allows stations to plan their allocations to avoid significant instances of interference between different transmitters on the same frequency at the same time. In practice there are several reasons why interference persists. For example, the registration system is too cumbersome to support multi-step negotiation between stations whose choices of allocation risk leading to interference, and some nations (the ITU's informants are national ministries and not stations themselves) have only a hazy impression of what is happening in shortwave broadcasting inside their borders. Therefore, many stations rely on specialist consultants on international allocation to advise them on appropriate choices so that their listeners can hope to hear their broadcasts without interference. Nevertheless, the most accessible and accurate compilations of actual monitored shortwave broadcasting activity, the Passport to World Band Radio - PWBR [9], still show many examples of potential or real interference each year. The graphical content of the "blue pages" there shows also, better than any short explanation in words, why allocation is a complicated exercise.

This is the starting point for our collection of cases of at least potential interference. Each case consists of factual information about broadcasts that may interfere with some given transmission, an expert-level assessment of the quality of the assignment of frequency (including a numerical rating within [0.0, 4.0] in steps of 0.25) and time to that transmission, and the folk arguments relevant to the assessment. The material is taken from the 2003 PWBR. Conclusions drawn by computation on this case base are subject to evaluation by a comparison with what is recorded in the 2004 PWBR, i.e. after the stations had a year of experience and listener feedback concerning the choices, and through the comments of shortwave reception specialists who have a different user perspective from that of an allocation consultant.

We consider the treatment of the folk argument parts of cases in section 4. It may be helpful, first, to appreciate Fig. 1 for several examples of what we mean by a folk argument. This has two purposes. First, it establishes a foundation which makes it easier to understand the more abstract discussion in section 4. Second, it indicates the kinds of terms that occur in radio knowledge, and is evidence for why the argument part of a radio case is too multifaceted and informal for the approaches to argumentation found in publications on legal applications and/or logic. This example refers to the broadcaster "Radio Melodia", a Peruvian station on 5.9975 MHz, with transmitter power of 5 kW, aiming to reach domestic listeners (in principle, a large area around Arequipa, Peru) and transmitting from 11:00 to 14:00 (UTC). A potential interfering station considered is "Voz del Upano", a station in Ecuador on 5.9994 MHz, with transmitter power of 10 kW, domestic listeners and transmitting over the same time interval as "Radio Melodia". Facts regarding target station and potential interfering stations are selected as inputs to the allocation problem. According to the expert analysis of this Peruvian allocation, the rating of this assignment is 3.25 (not perfect, but very acceptable for the transmission purposes).

4 Folk Arguments Revisited

There are several well-developed methods of knowledge elicitation, KADS [10] in particular. Although first devised for acquiring knowledge for use in rule-based expert systems, their foundation in cognitive psychology ensures that such methods are not limited to the recognition of rules. Such methods are not immediately usable for the elicitation of arguments of any kind, but we have adapted the "reasoning template" (the model in which the task and method of reasoning are described in an abstract and reusable way) approach of [10] to this end. A basic template for "radio allocation", the essence of our application, is the central part of Fig. 1. This serves not only as a framework to be filled out by the facts and prescriptions of a case, but also as support for elicitation of pro and con assertions that comprise a folk argument, and eventually as a repository of the knowledge that is expressed in arguments. Examples are shown at the sides of Fig. 1. The complete template can be found in [11].

We began this project by trying to represent expert arguments, folk and otherwise, by using a full structure [3] which covers most of what is presented in argumentation formalisms in the literature [2, 5]. However, our practical experience has shown that the full Toulmin model (which contains data, qualifier, warrant, backing and rebuttal) requires too much information from experts to be an effective knowledge acquisition tool. In practice, as experts' time is valuable, expert arguments can be captured effectively enough as sequences of statements. A statement expresses what we call a consideration in section 2.

The sequences amount to an explanation of the problem-solving process, resembling what is presented as a "fossilised" explanation trace of the decision-making [12] and an anchored narrative [13]. Basically, the representations involve the proposition and qualification of arguments and decisions, in which these two components evolve according to how the expert perceives information in the problem. We also follow a qualitative line of representation [14]. The argument process in our framework, "ArgCases", is expressed as i) *statement,* ii) *Annotated-argument-type* iii) *orientation* and iv) *Inputs* $\Rightarrow_{argument-effect}$ *Outputs.*

A *statement* is a simple textual sentence making an assertion that has some relevance in the problem situation, as at the end of section 3. Once statements like these have been collected from the expert, they are labelled with "argument types". An *argument-type* (AT) summarises the nature of the information exploited by the expert in proposing and testing arguments. In principle, the types summarise what these statements are about. Such a labelling of information comes naturally to experts. Examples of argument types presented in Fig. 1 include: "target station propagation", "features of Braun contour maps" from a set of 25 different argument types, different facets of knowledge, in the shortwave radio application.

The characterisation of statements by using argument types requires a list of types to be obtained in advance. Such a list can be developed by the equivalent of a knowledge engineering analysis of the information contained in any record of arguments available from case problems solved in the past. Then, the list can be refined gradually according to what experts consider to be the most appropriate level of detail. In the radio application, most of these refinements were related to adjusting the wording of argument types and the introduction of new types. In addition to argument types, an argument is characterised by its *orientation*. As exploited in various qualitative methods of decision-making, an orientation states whether the argument is in favour of or against some proposal: *Orientation-type = {in-favour; against; neutral}*. In the current application, for example, arguments are said to be "in favour" (i.e. part of a set of pros) if they give support to the allocation that an expert is evaluating.

Another key aspect of the ArgCases framework is that it records the changes that each statement makes in a running estimate of the quality of an allocation. The symbolic form of this record is *Inputs* $\Rightarrow_{argument-effect}$ *Outputs.* The Inputs and Outputs are each of the form *{<sign$_1$, quality$_1$>, <sign$_2$, quality$_2$>, ...}*. Each quality is a member of a small set of values decided in advance, e.g. {B, U, A, G, E} or {bad, usable, adequate, good, excellent}; {N, Z, S, A, R} or {none, slight, nuisance, problematic, unavoidable}. The adjectives in the last set refer to radio interference. In the earlier set here, they refer to likely overall quality of reception – but they could stand for a

5-stage gradation of a decision estimate on anything in any application. Any quality is accompanied by a sign, drawn from *Signs = {+ +, +, 0, –, – –}* indicating the weight of evidence for or against the value that it qualifies. "0" here denotes "some evidence", while "no evidence" for some quality Q means that Q is absent in the expert' choice. Once the argument information has been collected, the expert is asked to supply an *Inputs ⇒ Outputs* pair for each statement. In a connected sequence of statements, the Input of each will be the Output of the previous statement.

(A1) "Braun maps say the target station propagation is practicable"; *AT01: "Target station propagation"; Pro allocation;* Ø ⇒ {+ +G; +E}

(A2) "For d close to 0, the frequency may be very close to maximum usable frequency - MUF"; *AT23: "Features of Braun contour maps" and AT01: "Target station propagation"; Against allocation;* {+ +G; +E} ⇒ {0A; +G; –E}

(A3) "Shortwave band is traditional over 50+ years for South American domestic broadcasting in mornings / daylight, i.e. the practical evidence is that the propagation will work"; *AT20: "Daytime / night effects"; Pro allocation; {0A; +G; –E} ⇒ {+ +G}*

(A4) "Terrain includes mountainous regions which reduce effectiveness of the basic propagation"; *AT13: "Refinements concerning listeners' locations"; Against allocation;* {+ +G} ⇒ {+A; +G}

(A5) "Most listeners will be in agricultural districts which are relatively open and not hidden in deep mountain valleys"; *AT12: "Location(s) of the most important listeners" and AT13: "Refinements concerning listeners' locations"; Pro allocation;* {+A; +G} ⇒ {–A; +G}

(A6) "Actual target area is much smaller than a country - it's likely to be confined to a small area around Arequipa – hence energy density in the target area is good enough to keep the listeners happy"; *AT05: "Level of energy at target area"; Pro allocation; {–A; +G} ⇒ {+G}*

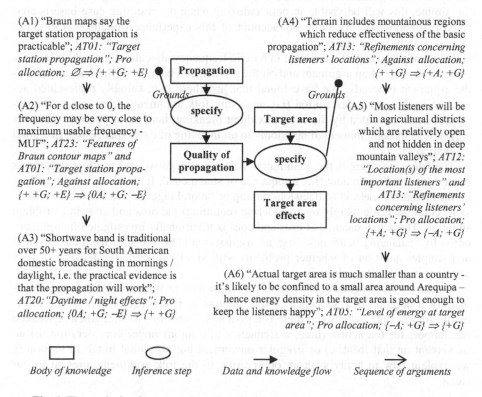

□ Body of knowledge   ○ Inference step   → Data and knowledge flow   → Sequence of arguments

Fig. 1. The analysis of target station allocation (i.e. propagation and target area effects)

Fig. 1 shows what happens when we start to attach the characteristics of the ArgCases argumentation framework to the reasoning template [11] and its representation characteristics [10]. In addition to the list of facts for target and interfering stations as presented near the end of section 3, we used the structure of the template for guiding the elicitation of several pro and con folk arguments and how they were characterised by the expert in terms of "argument types" (ATs). Each folk argument was also represented along with the expert evaluation of possible input and output estimates of an allocation decision. Once not only facts but also folk arguments are available in cases, the next step in the development of a CBR application is the taxonomic analysis of these case characteristics.

5 Numerical Taxonomy Revisited

In order to use numerical taxonomy on folk arguments recorded in cases for CBR, we have to decide what versions or parts of them to parameterise, and then how to parameterise them. The information that an overall folk argument carries has a more immediate effect on the outcome in a case than the details of any individual statement within it. There are many ways to express collective properties by combining local details in folk arguments whose form is indicated in section 4 and Fig. 1. If a choice is too simple, this will be visible in poor indexing when the resulting case base is analysed taxonomically. We omit any account of this experience (touched on in [11]), and go straight to the end-point.

Informally, the expert's estimate in a radio frequency allocation depends at least on the overall trend of an argument and on the pro and con balance of these statements as the argument proceeds. We have found that just these two, suitably represented according to the expert description (i.e. analysing folk arguments according to the degree of detail provided by the expert, without breaking them up in possibly incorrect ways), lead through numerical taxonomy to an indexing of cases that results in a good evaluation.

The *balance feature* is the quantitative balance of negative and positive statements in an overall folk argument (i.e. a sequence of statements). It is at least as old as Benjamin Franklin's method of decision-making or "moral algebra". In his method, decisions could be made merely by considering (counting) the pros and cons in a problem situation. The actual balance of pros and cons is traditionally investigated in argumentation by "balancing heuristics", e.g. as discussed in [15]. We start from the different and simpler question of whether problems with similar quantitative balance of pros and cons have similar solutions.

Separately from balance, a *trend or direction feature* identifying the way an estimate of a decision in a sequence of folk arguments is tending is easy to see informally: for example, whether a) there is a systematic tendency to strengthen or weaken the support for the action (here, a frequency allocation) under consideration, b) no movement on that front, c) or irregular movement but no global trend. In section 6, we explain how to apply such an observation to the folk arguments present in our cases.

5.1 The Observation and Coding of Argumentation Features

The values of balance we use are: *Balance feature* = {"Indecisive", "Positive", "Encouraging", "Negative", "Discouraging"}. The data allow us to distinguish these values reliably, but do not encourage finer distinctions. These values are determined by simple rules involving the number of pros and cons such as IF Pros >= 3 AND Cons = 1 THEN BalanceValue = "Positive". Finally, balance results are recorded in a *Balance Feature Table* (Table 1).

There is a similar simple set of trend values: *Trend feature* = {"Upwards", "Downwards", "Flat", "Irregular"}. "Global trends" in a sequence of folk argument estimates are determined from "local trends" expressed in argument inputs and outputs. Local trends are found via a *Mean Decision Value* (MDV): a simple weighted mean computation between labels of qualities in which the signs of these labels are taken as

Table 1. Balance Feature Table: balance values in each inference in the radio problem

Case name (including the allocation rating)	Balance values of target station arrangements	Balance values of interfering station arrangements	Balance values of listeners' arrangements
s01Rating3.75	"Indecisive"	"Discouraging"	"Encouraging"
s02Rating2.00	"Indecisive"	"Negative"	"Indecisive"
...	...	...	...
s39Rating3.00	"Encouraging"	"Indecisive"	"Positive"

weights. Similar to what happens when symbolic factual features are transformed into numerical features in traditional numerical taxonomy, qualities and signs are connected first to numerical scales: *Numerical qualities* = {"E" = 5.0; "G" = 4.0; ...} and *Numerical signs* = {"+ +" = 1.0; "+" = 0.8; "0" = 0.6; ...}. For instance, the initial qualitative value in A1 in Fig. 1 has an MDV({+ +G; +E}) = 4.44 since "G" = 4.0, "E" = 5.0, "+ +" = 1.0 and "+" = 0.8 (i.e. (((1.0 * 4.0) + (0.8 * 5.0)) / (1.0 + 0.8)) = 4.44). Then, the "local trend" of any individual folk argument can be found from the MDVs of its input and output. For A2 in Fig. 1, {+ +G; +E} ⇒ {0A; +G; −E} is "Downwards" because the MDV({+ +G; +E}) is higher than MDV({0A; +G; −E}). Automatic determination of "Upwards" and "Flat" local trends occurs similarly.

Global trends are determined by computation of the amount by which inputs and outputs change over an individual folk argument: the Degree of Change (DoC). We use a set-theoretic fuzzy approach to calculate DoC (details of fuzzy functions can be found in [16]). Taking {+ +G; +E} ⇒ {0A; +G; −E} as an example, the degree of change is calculated as: Step 1): Take the "E" quality only. The Inputs and Outputs are respectively "+E" and "−E". Apply minimum and maximum functions over the signs of "E", MIN(+E, −E) = "−E" and MAX(+E, −E) = "+E"; Step 2): Repeat (Step 1) for the other Input and Output qualities. The results are MIN(Inputs, Outputs) = {+G; −E} and MAX(Inputs, Outputs) = {0A; + +G; +E}. Then the values of *Numerical signs* from the MIN and MAX elements are substituted in (1), giving DoC({+ +G; +E}, {0A; +G; −E}) = 1.0 − ({+G; −E} / {0A; + +G; +E}) = 1.0 − ((0.8 + 0.4) / (0.6 + 1.0 + 0.8)) = 0.5.

$$DoC(Inputs, Outputs) = 1.0 - \left(\sum_{i=1}^{n} MIN(Inputs_i, Outputs_i) \middle/ \sum_{i=1}^{n} MAX(Inputs_i, Outputs_i) \right) \quad (1)$$

By using information from both local trends and degrees of change when individual folk argument estimates are examined, a pictorial representation for the global trend can be constructed. In this representation, local trend determinations provide the direction of the graph (i.e. up, down and horizontal) and degrees of change provide the points in the graph such that: IF LocalTrendValue(A_n) = "Upwards" THEN LocalTrendPoint(A_n) = LocalTrendPoint(A_{n-1}) + DoC(A_n). Determination of trend points for "Downwards" and "Flat" local trends occur by subtracting a DoC from a previous trend point value and by keeping a trend point value, respectively. The result of the manual annotation of global trends in a sequence of folk argument estimates (e.g. Fig. 2) is recorded in a *Trend Feature Table* (Table 2). Tables 1 and 2 show a simple version of the full folk argumentation information recorded in cases in our

526   L.A.L. Silva, J.A. Campbell, and B.F. Buxton

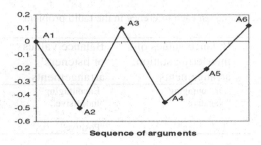

Sequence of arguments

The pictorial representation supports the recognition of "global trends" by the knowledge engineer (and later checking by the expert in the application domain). In the picture here, the overall trend in the sequence of pro and con folk argument estimates presented in Fig. 1 is evidently "Irregular". Note how we represent folk arguments (A_n) on the "x" axis and a) the direction and b) degree of change of "local trends" from each folk argument Input and Output estimates on the "y" axis

Fig. 2. Example of a pictorial representation of trend

Table 2. Trend Feature Table: global trend values in each inference of the radio problem

Case name (including the allocation rating)	Trend values of target station arrangements	Trend values of interfering station arrangements	Trend values of listeners' arrangements
s01Rating3.75	"Irregular"	"Irregular"	"Downwards"
s02Rating2.00	"Downwards"	"Upwards"	"Upwards"
...	...	...	...
s39Rating3.00	"Downwards"	"Upwards"	"Downwards"

case base. Nevertheless, the complete case structure is formed by a) facts, b) folk arguments along with their estimates and c) an allocation conclusion (i.e. a rating).

5.2   The Estimation of Similarity of Argumentation Features

A central aspect in our CBR applications, and also in numerical taxonomy, is the computation of similarity here of not only facts, but also folk argumentation features. The simplest way of computing the similarity between individual balance and/or trend characteristics is to take these features as "strings". Even though matching of strings is simple, the resulting similarities between cases are enough to form case groups containing similar quality of allocation. In more specific detail, useful results follow from the exploitation of what two folk argumentation features in our case base tell us: a) the number of pros and cons in the different balance types and b) the number of different types of local trends within the global trend types.

In exploiting the composition of balance features, for example, the similarity between two balance values (e.g. "Positive" and "Encouraging") is obtained from a table: a *Balance Similarity Table (BST)*. The entries in the BST reflect the similarities of normalised distributions of pros and cons in each different balance feature of the case base (Table 1). For example, the "Positive" balance appears in 33 places in the full Table 1. The composition of one of these "Positive" balances is 3 pros (P) and 1 con (C). This composition is P3 = 1 and C1 = 1. We just count these "Positive" compositions and then normalise them by the number of "Positive" balances in the case base. These normalised distributions are expressed as fuzzy sets of pros and cons (Table 3). The BST records the similarities from the numerical composition sets of

Table 3. Normalised distributions of pros and cons in balance features

Balance feature	Pros fuzzy set	Cons fuzzy set
"Positive"	{P0: 0.00; P1: 0.18; P2: 0.27; P3: 0.36; P4: 0.12; P5: 0.06}	{C0: 0.64; C1: 0.36; C2: 0.00; C3: 0.00; C4: 0.00; C5: 0.00}
"Encouraging"	{P0: 0.00; P1: 0.00; P2: 0.57; P3: 0.22; P4: 0.22; P5: 0.00}	{C0: 0.00; C1: 0.57; C2: 0.39; C3: 0.04; C4: 0.00; C5: 0.00}
...	...	...

Table 3. Applying a geometric fuzzy set similarity function [16] – for a 2-dimensional Euclidean space – to the data in Table 3 for each pair of rows then produces the contents of the BST.

The similarity between two trend values (e.g. "Irregular and "Downwards") is obtained in the same way from a table: the *Trend Similarity Table (TST)*. As for balance distributions, we compute global trend distributions from local trend elements. Normalised by the number of "Irregular" trends in Table 2, its "Irregular" global trend is then: Irregular trend fuzzy set = {Upwards: 1.33; Downwards: 1.55; Flat: 1.28} which leads to a trend feature table analogous of Table 3. The TST is found from this table in the same way as the BST is derived from Table 3.

5.3 Clustering and Determination of Taxonomies for Argumentation Features

Similarities between cases are computed and stored in a similarity matrix which then is used as input in the clustering analysis. We have exploited hierarchical methods of clustering [8, 17], considering both "average" and "complete" linking methods (since they most often give the best hierarchical representation of relationships expressed in a similarity matrix). Fig. 3 presents the hierarchical cluster structure (dendrogram) arising from the similarities of the balance features only in the radio frequency allocation cases (Table 2). These similarities are computed in each of the three subdivisions of the case arguments (target station details, details about interfering station(s) and listeners' arrangements). The balance values in these three areas are the dimensions for a weighted Euclidean distance computation. Fig. 3 shows just the groups that appear when each of the three balance dimensions has the same weight = 1.0. The clusters formed are reasonable in the sense that cases with similar expert ratings for the quality of the frequency allocation tend to occur together. Where low (inadvisable) and high (good) rated cases are present in the same cluster, this may be either because there is some significant consideration in their folk arguments not captured by our simple parameterisation or because the parameters obtained so far have not been scaled appropriately in our distance measure D. To deal with the latter and to improve the clustering results, we experimented with variations in the scales, equivalent to altering the weights.

The procedure starts from an "extreme heuristic" – e.g., using a weight of 20 for each of the three dimensions of Table 1 while the other two weights in these dimensions are unchanged, and examining the changes of cluster membership from Fig. 3. The original weights are then adjusted, subject to expert agreement that they do not distort the relative importance of the dimensions, and values are chosen that maximise the overall agreement between the ratings of cases in the same clusters. This treatment is repeated for the "trend" features of Table 2.

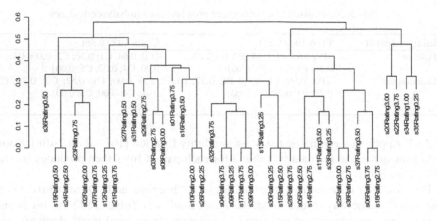

Fig. 3. The analysis of balance features only (weights = 1.0, "average" linking)

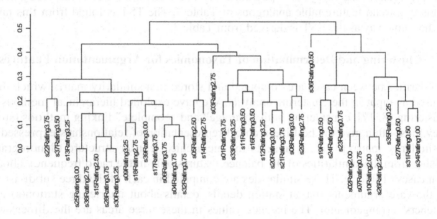

Fig. 4. Weighted and combined balance and trend features ("average" linking)

The process we have described here is typical of applications in numerical taxonomy: a machine-supported process of user-directed learning through construction and examination of different taxonomies. It is appropriate to involve the domain expert in the search for a good taxonomy (and the weights that may lead to it) for the current purposes. The dendrogram structure is clear and simple enough for the expert to make comments about the organisation and relevance of the groups formed. In several situations, the radio expert has started to explain why some groups of cases were formed in the taxonomy according to folk arguments recorded. The information thus elicited was not available before the application of the taxonomic procedures, which shows that even simple folk argumentation characteristics may help to reveal deeper relevant information in the application. In essence, this taxonomic process is a two-way task of both the successive formalisation of the domain by the expert and the improvement of the taxonomic structure by the knowledge engineer. In developing a CBR application, we use folk argumentation information first, for the improvement of similarity assessment and the taxonomic organisation of the cases. In the radio application, the most satisfactory taxonomy from adjusted weights in combined balance and trend features in a six-dimensional Euclidean space is presented in Fig. 4.

6 Evaluation: How the Actual CBR Application Works

The ultimate authorities on the quality of an allocation are the listeners to radio stations. The listeners are amateurs who have gained this intuitive knowledge by long contact with the different kinds of transmission, often in different places via "DXpeditions" (DX = distance, in their argot) to hear exotic stations not audible at home and by exchange of periodicals referring to such experience in other countries. They are best placed to comment on a variety of allocations covering different types of source and target region, broadcasting period and station operator, and to criticise the recommendations of allocation experts.

Fig. 4 is a collection of 39 radio allocation cases indexed to associate most closely the most similar cases. Fig. 4 mimics the behaviour of an allocation expert who focuses on a simple abstract structuring of folk arguments, as discussed in section 3 and Fig. 1, to provide the index for the cases. If the approach were misguided, the resulting index for the case base would make no sense to experienced amateur listeners, who would point out where the similarities it suggested were locally defective and offer counter-suggestions of their own. Substantial correspondence between its structure and their opinions, on the other hand, would amount to a positive evaluation of the means and knowledge used to build it.

The facts and folk arguments of the 39 cases, minus the Inputs and Outputs information and the expert's numerical rating of the quality of each allocation, were provided to two such amateurs together with an explanation of dendrograms and how they were formed. They were asked to construct, as far as possible, dendrograms G showing their view of the similarities of the cases from the perspective of the stations' listeners. After trying, neither one was willing to sketch a full dendrogram. However, they were prepared to group cases into clusters (including clusters of size 1) at some level, and to propose further structure inside some clusters. We contrast these amateurs' clusters with the clusters formed in our numerical taxonomy process. It can be seen from Fig. 4 that the main clustering occurs around 0.25 on the vertical scale. Using this value as a reference, one can draw a horizontal line in the tree and read off the main case families below this line.

After clarification of ambiguities in amateurs' replies but without hints about the detailed memberships of clusters, both respondents offered one large cluster strongly similar to the (s22 ... s32) family in Fig. 4. There were other local differences, none gross, e.g. one gave (s14) (s01 s05 s33) in place of (s05 s14) (s01 s33), and one gave (s08 s11) (s16 s29) in place of (s11 s16) (s08 s29). Informally this indicates a very good agreement between specialist amateur opinions and the set of cases indexed automatically via "balance" plus "trend" folk argumentation characteristics. But more quantitatively, let us suppose a case C and the three most similar cases to it in Fig. 4 as a set S, and look for correspondences between the cluster they form in the figure and the positions of the members of S in a respondent's grouping G. We chose |S| = 4 because we assume that a retrieval of three cases in response to a typical CBR enquiry would be a reasonable user demand. Score 1 for each presence of C and another element of S in the same cluster, or n + 1 if they co-occur n levels down (towards the leaves) in G; add 1 for specificity if the size of the cluster where they are found is no greater than 3; score 0 if they occur in different top-level clusters in G; sum the scores for all Cs, and divide by the size of the case base. High scores indicate a high degree of correspondence between the expected retrieval results and the cases a specialist listener would bring to mind under the same circumstances. For such a G, a dendrogram with perfect agreement would have a score of at least 3 or higher according to how much further structure G has. A random dendrogram score would fall to near 1.

In our analysis, no clear distinction was visible when one of our specimens of G was replaced by the other. If we use the dendrogram formed from "balance" features only with equal weights for the three main parts of the folk arguments as presented in Table 1, the scores for the two specimens of G were 2.64 and 2.66. For a dendrogram like Fig. 3 with the trend rather than the balance information, the quality is lower: 2.43 and 2.45. Finally, for the dendrogram combining trend and balance characteristics as given in Fig. 4, the scores were 2.75 and 2.93.

Actual retrieval of cases during CBR would start using factual information about a current allocation exercise as a probe. Our first evaluation of the quality of retrieval has employed the facts of four new exercises Q present in the 2003 PWBR tables but not in the case base (i.e. new cases proposed by the expert). For each example in Q, the four cases R_{facts} in the case base with the closest match to its facts according to a weighted distance measure for factual items (as described in section 3) were found. R_{facts} is thus the result of this first step of retrieval. For each case in R_{facts}, a second step of retrieval found up to four (depending on a threshold of similarity or distance) of the cases closest to it in Fig. 4. Note we use the most similar cases retrieved by using facts (R_{facts}) as new query cases. Since these new query cases in R_{facts} contain folk arguments, balance and trend characteristics are used to retrieve other cases containing folk argumentation information, which results in $R_{arguments}$. In some situations, some of the retrieved cases may of course occur more than once in the combination of R_{facts} and $R_{arguments}$. Moreover, similarity is computed against all cases in the case base since the case base is small and is likely to remain small. The most similar cases in R_{facts} and $R_{arguments}$ are used to construct a recommendation "template". This is filled out automatically in order to show how the cases in the flat R_{facts} and $R_{arguments}$ retrieval results would be arranged taxonomically as an answer to a query Q. This is possible because both a factual (not shown in this paper) and a folk argumentation taxonomy (Fig. 4) involving cases are used when the CBR application presents the results of the retrieval. Further "filtering" in R_{facts} and $R_{arguments}$ can be applied by considering relevant instances of argument types in the query Q. One such query might be expressed as for example: "Find past allocation cases where the transmitter power is high but one still has concerns regarding their power characteristics". An answer for the query would involve selecting past cases containing high values of power along with folk arguments against the target station allocation that are annotated by the "AT06: Power" argument type.

According to the radio expert, the recommendations and folk arguments for one of the new exercises (Radio Ukraine, 6.02 MHz) were positive about the allocation. For the other three (Radio Polonia, 6.015 MHz; and two Sunday pirate stations with quite low power and with interference from similar unregulated European pirates), the bulk of the retrieved cases (and all the most similar ones) had low ratings. Some of the less similar cases retrieved had high ratings, but their folk arguments contained emphasis on the relatively high power of the transmitters concerned. Someone using the case base for training would thus receive suggestions about a target allocation plus taxonomic information along with argument-based information on what issues to consider further if the suggestions were not uniform.

An independent way of examining the quality of an allocation found in the 2003 PWBR is to compare it with the 2004 tables. If the allocation has disappeared from the later tables, it is at least prima facie evidence that the quality has been unacceptable. All the low-rated test examples Q above were absent from the 2004 PWBR. The high-rated Ukrainian example was still present in 2004. The evaluation above indicates that the use of simple features of folk arguments in cases, assisted by numerical taxonomy, can create a structured case base which reflects what people with specialised knowledge might themselves create.

7 Concluding Remarks

There are subjects where significant information in an expert's stock of case-like knowledge is expressed in "folk arguments" and where this information, even in a simplified or summary form, can be captured and used in the analysis and structuring of case taxonomies. We find that numerical taxonomy is an effective tool that can support this process by the creation of dendrograms, especially where the nature of the knowledge or the small size of a case base excludes other techniques, e.g. from machine learning. We have also developed means of assisting acquisition of folk-argument knowledge: use of a cognitively-inspired reasoning template together with a qualitative notation for the changes in strengths of alternative estimates caused by pro and con folk arguments. We are finding that our framework is equally applicable in a different application area: the use of knowledge about pigments in authentication of paintings. It is thus reasonable to expect that our approach will be relevant and deserving of attention for any problem where knowledge is expressed naturally in cases and where folk arguments are a marked feature of that knowledge.

References

1. Sørmo, F., Cassens, J., Aamodt, A.: Explanation in case-based reasoning–Perspectives and goals. Artificial Intelligence Review 24, 109–143 (2005)
2. Chesñevar, C., Maguitman, A., Loui, R.P.: Logical models of argument. ACM Computing Surveys 32, 337–383 (2000)
3. Toulmin, S.E.: The uses of argument (Updated edition 2003). Cambridge University Press, Cambridge (1958)
4. Silva, L.A.L., Campbell, J.A., Eastaugh, N., Buxton, B.F.: A Case for Numerical Taxonomy in Case-Based Reasoning. In: The 19th Brazilian Symposium on Artificial Intelligence - SBIA 2008, Salvador, Brazil (to appear, 2008)
5. Bench-Capon, T.J.M., Dunne, P.E.: Argumentation in artificial intelligence. Artificial Intelligence 171, 619–641 (2007)

6. Ashley, K.D., Rissland, E.L.: Law, learning and representation. Artificial Intelligence 150, 17–58 (2003)
7. Pennington, N., Hastie, R.: Reasoning in explanation-based decision making. Cognition 49, 123–163 (1993)
8. Sneath, P.H., Sokal, R.R.: Numerical taxonomy - The principles and practice of numerical classification. W. H. Freeman and Company, San Francisco (1973)
9. Magne, L., Jones, T. (eds.): Passport to World Band Radio. Lawrence Magne (2003)
10. Schreiber, A.T.G., Akkermans, H., Anjewierden, A., Hoog, R.d., Shadbolt, N., Velde, W.v.d., Wielinga, B.: Knowledge engineering and management - The Common KADS Methodology. MIT Press, Cambridge (2000)
11. Silva, L.A.L., Buxton, B.F., Campbell, J.A.: Enhanced Case-Based Reasoning through Use of Argumentation and Numerical Taxonomy. In: The 20th Int. Florida Artificial Intelligence Research Society Conference (FLAIRS-20), Key West, Florida, pp. 423–428. AAAI Press, Menlo Park (2007)
12. Schank, R.C.: Explanation Patterns: Understanding Mechanically and Creatively. Lawrence Erlbaum Associates, Inc., Mahwah (1986)
13. Wagenaar, W.A., van Koppen, P.J., Crombag, H.F.M.: Anchored Narratives. The Psychology of Criminal Evidence. St. Martins Press, New York (1993)
14. Forbus, K.S.H.: Qualitative reasoning. In: Tucker, A.B. (ed.) The Computer Science and Engineering Handbook, Ch. 32, pp. 715–733. CRC Press, Boca Raton (1997)
15. Bonnefon, J.-F., Fargier, H.: Comparing Sets of Positive and Negative Arguments: Empirical Assessment of Seven Qualitative Rules. In: Brewka, G., Coradeschi, S., Perini, A., Traverso, P. (eds.) 17th European Conference on Artificial Intelligence (ECAI 2006), Riva del Garda, Italy, pp. 16–20. IOS Press, Amsterdam (2006)
16. Chen, S.-M., Yeh, M.-S., Hsiao, P.-Y.: A comparison of similarity measures of fuzzy values. Fuzzy Sets and Systems 72, 79–89 (1995)
17. Jain, A.K., Murty, M.N., Flym, P.J.: Data clustering: A review. ACM Computing Surveys 31, 264–323 (1999)

Real-Time Plan Adaptation for Case-Based Planning in Real-Time Strategy Games

Neha Sugandh, Santiago Ontañón, and Ashwin Ram

CCL, Cognitive Computing Lab
Georgia Institute of Technology
Atlanta, GA 30332/0280
{nsugandh,santi,ashwin}@cc.gatech.edu

Abstract. Case-based planning (CBP) is based on reusing past success-ful plans for solving new problems. CBP is particularly useful in envi-ronments where the large amount of time required to traverse extensive search spaces makes traditional planning techniques unsuitable. In par-ticular, in real-time domains, past plans need to be retrieved and adapted in real time and efficient plan adaptation techniques are required. We have developed real time adaptation techniques for case based planning and specifically applied them to the domain of real time strategy games. In our framework, when a plan is retrieved, a plan dependency graph is inferred to capture the relations between actions in the plan suggested by that case. The case is then adapted in real-time using its plan de-pendency graph. This allows the system to create and adapt plans in an efficient and effective manner while performing the task. Our techniques have been implemented in the Darmok system (see [8]), designed to play WARGUS, a well-known real-time strategy game. We analyze our ap-proach and prove that the complexity of the plan adaptation stage is polynomial in the size of the plan. We also provide bounds on the final size of the adapted plan under certain assumptions.

1 Introduction

Traditional planning techniques are inapplicable in real-time domains with vast search spaces. Specifically, we are interested in real-time strategy (RTS) games that have huge decision spaces that cannot be dealt with search based AI tech-niques [1]. Case-based planning (CBP) can be useful in such domains since they can potentially reduce the complexity of traditional planning techniques. CBP techniques [10] work by reusing previous stored plans for new situations instead of planning from scratch. However, plans cannot be replayed exactly as they were stored in any non trivial domain. Therefore, CBP techniques require plan adaptation to adapt the information contained in plans. More specifically, CBP techniques for RTS games need adaptation techniques that are suitable for dy-namic and unpredictable domains, and that have a low complexity to be useful for real-time situations. In this paper we present Darmok, a case-based planning

K.-D. Althoff et al. (Eds.): ECCBR 2008, LNAI 5239, pp. 533–547, 2008.
© Springer-Verlag Berlin Heidelberg 2008

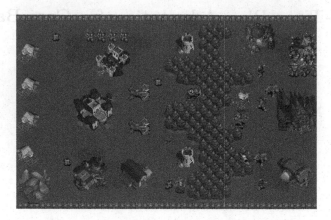

Fig. 1. A screenshot of the WARGUS game

architecture that integrates planning and execution and is capable of dealing with both the vast decision spaces and the real-time component of RTS games. Then, we will focus on the problem of how to adapt plans stored in the knowledge base of our system to suit new situations in real-time. We further analyze the algorithms and establish bounds on their complexity, thus proving that the algorithms presented are suitable for a real-time situation.

It is hard to approach RTS games using traditional planning approaches: RTS games have huge decision spaces [1], they are adversarial domains, they are non-deterministic and non fully-observable, and finally it is difficult to define postconditions for actions (actions don't always succeed, or take a different amount of time, and have complex interactions that are difficult to model using planning representation formalisms). To address these issues, we developed Darmok [8], a case-based planning system that is able to deal with domains such as WARGUS. We apply our plan adaptation techniques to Darmok.

Plan adaptation techniques can be classified in two categories: those adaptation techniques based on domain specific rules (domain specific, but fast) and those based on domain independent search-based techniques (domain independent, but slow). In this paper, we will present a domain independent and search-free structural plan adaptation technique based on two basic ideas: a) removing useless operations from a plan can be done by analyzing a *dependency graph* and b) the insertion of new operations in the plan can be delegated to the case-based planning cycle itself. Thus, the plan adaptation will state that some new operations to achieve a particular goal must be inserted, and the CBP engine will generate a plan for that goal. Our plan adaptation approach has been implemented in the Darmok system with promising results.

In the rest of this paper we introduce the Darmok system in Section 2, and then we focus on plan adaptation in Section 3. Then, we analyze the complexity of the adaptation algorithms in Section 4. After that, we report experimental results in Section 5. The paper closes with related work and conclusions.

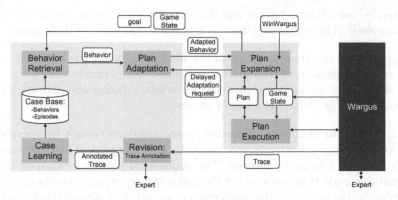

Fig. 2. Overview of the Darmok system

2   Case-Based Planning in WARGUS

Figure 1 shows a screen-shot of WARGUS, a RTS game where each player's goal is to remain alive after destroying the rest of the players. Each player has a series of troops and buildings and gathers resources (gold, wood and oil) in order to produce more troops and buildings. Buildings are required to produce more advanced troops, and troops are required to attack the enemy.

In this section we will briefly describe the Darmok system, in which we have implemented our plan adaptation techniques. In order to play WARGUS Darmok learns behaviors from expert demonstrations, and then uses case-based planning to play the game reusing the learnt behaviors. Figure 2 shows an overview of our case-based planning approach. Basically, we divide the process in two main stages:

- *Plan Learning*: performed by the *Revision* and *Case Learning* modules. Each time a human plays a game, a trace is generated (containing the list of actions performed in the game). During revision, the human annotates that trace stating which goals he was pursuing with each action. This annotated trace is processed by the case learning module that extracts plans in form of cases.
- *Plan Execution*: The execution engine consists of several modules that together maintain a current plan to win the game. The *Plan Execution* module executes the current plan, and updates its state (marking which actions succeeded or failed). The *Plan Expansion* module identifies open goals in the current plan and expands them. In order to do that it relies on the *Behavior Retrieval* module, that retrieves the most appropriate behavior to fulfill an open goal. Finally, the *Plan Adaptation* module adapts the retrieved plans.

Cases in Darmok consist of two parts: *behaviors* and *episodes*. A Behavior contains executable code to achieve a particular goal, and an episode contains information on how successful a behavior was in a particular situation.

A behavior has two main parts: a *declarative* part and a *procedural* part. The declarative part has the purpose of providing information to the system about the intended use of the behavior, and the procedural part contains the executable behavior itself. The declarative part of a behavior consists of three parts:

- A *goal*, that is a representation of the intended goal of the behavior.
- A set of *preconditions* that must be satisfied before execution.
- A set of *alive conditions* that must be satisfied during the execution of the behavior for it to have chances of success.

Unlike classical planning approaches, postconditions cannot be specified for behaviors, since a behavior is not guaranteed to succeed. Thus, we can only specify the goal a behavior pursues. The procedural part of a behavior consists of executable code that can contain the following constructs: *sequence*, *parallel*, *action* (primitive actions in the application domain), and *subgoal* (that need to be further expanded). A goal may have parameters, and must define a set of *success conditions*. For instance, *AbsoluteHaveUnits(TOWER,1)* is a valid goal in our gaming domain that has the following success condition: *UnitExists(TOWER)*.

2.1   Run-Time Plan Expansion and Execution

During execution, the plan expansion, plan execution and plan adaptation modules collaborate to maintain a current *partial plan tree* that the system is executing. A *partial plan tree* in our framework is represented as a tree consisting of *goals* and *behaviors* (similar to HTN planning [6]). Initially, the plan consists of a single goal: "win the game". Then, the plan expansion module asks the behavior retrieval module for a behavior for that goal. That behavior might have several subgoals, for which the plan expansion module will again ask the behavior retrieval module for behaviors, and so on. When a goal still does not have an assigned behavior, we say that the goal is *open*.

Additionally, each behavior in the plan has an associated state that can be: *pending* (when it still has not started execution), *executing*, *succeeded* or *failed*. A goal that has a behavior assigned and where the behavior has failed is also considered to be open. Open goals can be either *ready* or *waiting*. An open goal is ready when all the behaviors that had to be executed before this goal have succeeded, otherwise, it is waiting.

The plan expansion module is constantly querying the current plan to see if there is any ready open goal. When this happens, the open goal is sent to the behavior retrieval module. The retrieved behavior is sent to the behavior adaptation module, and then inserted in the current plan, marked as pending.

The plan execution module has two main functionalities: check for basic actions that can be sent to the game engine and check the status of plans that are in execution:

- Pending behaviors with satisfied preconditions change status to executing.
- Basic actions that are ready and with all their preconditions satisfied are sent to WARGUS to be executed. If the preconditions are not satisfied, the behavior is sent back to the adaptation module to see if the plan can be repaired. If it cannot, then the behavior is marked as failed.

- Whenever a basic action succeeds or fails, the execution module updates the status of the behavior that contained it. When a basic action fails, the behavior is marked as failed, and thus its corresponding goal is open again.
- If the alive conditions of an executing behavior are not satisfied, the behavior is marked as failed.
- If the success conditions of a behavior are satisfied, the behavior is marked as succeeded.
- Finally, if a behavior is about to be executed and the current game state has changed since the time the behavior retrieval module retrieved it, the behavior is handed back to the plan adaptation module.

In the remainder of this paper we will focus on the plan adaptation component. See [8] for a more detailed explanation of the rest of the system.

3   Real-Time Case-Based Plan Adaptation

The plan adaptation module is divided in two submodules: the *parameter adaptation module* and the *structural plan adaptation module*. The first one is in charge of adapting the parameters of the basic actions, i.e. the coordinates and specific units (see [8] for an explanation on how that module works). In this section we will focus on the structural plan adaptation module.

We specifically consider plans which are only composed of actions, sequential constructs and parallel constructs. This implies that we consider only those plans which are completely expanded and do not contain a sub-goal which further needs to be expanded. We generate a *plan dependency graph* using the preconditions and success conditions of the actions. The structural plan adaptation process has two sub-processes: elimination of unnecessary actions, and insertion of required actions. The first one is performed as soon as the plan is retrieved, and the second one is performed on-line as the plan executes.

3.1   Plan Dependency Graph Generation

Figure 3 shows the algorithm for plan dependency graph generation. Each action within a plan has a set of preconditions and a set of success conditions. The plan dependency graph generator analyzes the preconditions of each of these primitive actions. Let p' be an action in the plan which contributes to satisfying the preconditions of another action p. Then, a directed edge from p' to p is formed (function *FindDependencies*, shown in Figure 3). This directed edge can be considered as a dependency between p' and p. Here, we assume that actions in different parts of a parallel plan are independent of each other (a strong assumption, subject to improvement in future work). A pair of actions might have a dependency between them only if their closest common parent is a sequential plan. This is what is effectively done by using the set of actions D, in Figure 3. For any action p' when the function *FindDependencies* is called D contains exactly the set of actions on which p' might be dependent. The set of primitive actions for a subplan p' of p are added to D only if p is a sequential construct. The recursive

```
Function GeneratePlanGraph(p, D)
    G = ∅
    ForEach p′ ∈ p.subPlans
        If p′ is sequential or parallel Then
            G = G ∪ GeneratePlanGraph(p′, D)
        ElseIf p′ is a primitive action Then
            G = G ∪ FindDependencies(p′, D)
        EndIf
        If p is sequential Then D := D ∪ p′.allPrimitiveActions
    EndForEach
    Return G
End-Function

Function FindDependencies(p, D)
    G = ∅
    ForEach p′ ∈ D
        If p′ statisfied any condition of p Then
            G = G ∪ (p′, p)
        EndIf
    EndForEach
    Return G
End-Function
```

Fig. 3. Algorithm for Plan Dependency Graph Generation. Where p is the plan to be adapted, and D is the set of plans on which any sub-plan in p might depend (and it is equal to $\emptyset$ in the first call to the algorithm). $p.subPlans$ refers to the set of sub-plans directly inside p in case p is sequential or parallel. And $p.allPrimitiveActions$ refers to all the primitive actions inside p or in any sub-plan inside p.

call to *GeneratePlanGraph* ensures that nested parallel and sequential constructs can be processed. This process results in the formation of a plan dependency graph G with directed edges between actions that have dependencies.

A challenge in our work is that simple comparison of preconditions of a plan p with success conditions of another plan p' is not sufficient to determine whether p' contributes to achievement of preconditions of p. This is because there isn't necessarily a direct correspondence between preconditions and success conditions. An example is with attacking: the success condition of a goal might specify that a particular enemy unit has to be killed, but the attack actions have no postcondition named "killed", since we cannot guarantee that an attack will succeed (the success condition of the attack action is that a particular unit will be in the "attacking status").

For that purpose, the plan dependency graph generation component needs a precondition-success condition matcher (*ps-matcher*). In our system, we have developed a rule-based ps-matcher that incorporates a collection of rules for the appropriate condition matching. For example, our system has six different conditions which test the existence of units or unit types. Thus the ps-matcher has rules that specify that all those conditions can be matched. In some cases it is not clear whether a relation exists or not. However it is necessary for our system to capture all of the dependencies, even if some non-existing dependencies are included. If a dependency was not detected by our system, a necessary action in the plan might get deleted.

Function RemoveRedundantPlans (p, g)
    $B = \text{GetDirectActions}(p, g)$
    $G = \text{GeneratePlanGraph}(p, \emptyset)$
    $A = \text{BackPropagateActivePlans}(B, G, \emptyset)$
    remove from p all the actions not in A
    Return p
EndFunction

Function BackPropagateActivePlans (B, G, A)
    ForEach $p \in B$
        If p's success conditions are not satisfied Then
            $A = A \cup \{p\}$
            $B' = \text{GetParentPlans}(p, G)$
            $A = \text{BackPropagateActivePlans}(B', G, A)$
        EndIf
    EndForEach
    Return A
EndFunction

Fig. 4. Algorithm for Removal of Unnecessary Actions. Where p is the plan to be adapted, and g is the goal corresponding to p. GetParentPlans(p, G) is a simple function that returns all the plans that have a causal direction with a given plan p, according to a graph G. GetDirectActions(p, g) is a function that returns those primitive actions in p that are *direct actions*.

3.2   Removal of Unnecessary Actions

Figure 4 shows the algorithm for the removal of unnecessary or redundant actions. Every plan p has a root node that is always a goal g. The removal of unnecessary actions begins by taking the success conditions of the goal g and finding out which of the actions in the plan contribute to the achievement of those conditions. This is done by the function call to *GetDirectActions* in Figure 4. These actions are called *direct actions* for the subgoal. Then the plan dependency graph for p is generated using the *GeneratePlanGraph* function in Figure 3. The algorithm works by maintaining a set of *active actions* A. At the end of the algorithm, all the actions not in A will be removed from the plan. The removal of actions proceeds using the plan dependency graph and the set of direct actions, B. The success conditions of each action in B are evaluated for the game state at that point of execution. Each of these actions p with unsatisfied success conditions is added to the list of active actions. The set of actions B' on which the action p has a dependency according to the dependency graph G are recursively checked to see if they have to be activated. Such plans are obtained using the function *GetParentPlans* in the algorithm (that can be easily implemented to have constant time). The result of this process is a set A of actions whose success conditions are not satisfied in the given game state and which

Function AdaptForUnsatisfiedConditions(p)
    C = GetUnsatisfiedPreconditions(p)
    $G = \emptyset$
    ForEach $c \in C$
        $G = G \cup$ GetSatisfyingGoal(c)
    EndForEach
    Initialize q as an empty parallel plan
    ForEach $g \in G$
        add SubGoalPlan(g) to q
    EndForEach
    insert q at the beginning of p
    Return p
End-Function

Fig. 5. Algorithm for Adding Goals for Unsatisfied Preconditions, where p is the primitive action to be adapted. GetUnsatisfiedConditions(p) is a function which returns the set of those preconditions of p which are not satisfied. GetSatisfyingGoal(c) is a function which returns a goal whose success satisfies the condition c. SubGoalPlan(g) is a function which returns a sub-goal plan with goal g.

have a dependency to a direct plan, also with success conditions not satisfied in the given game state. Actions that are not active (not in A) are removed.

3.3   Adaptation for Unsatisfied Preconditions

Figure 5 shows the algorithm for adaptation for unsatisfied preconditions. If the execution of an action fails because one or more of its preconditions are not satisfied, the system needs to act so that the execution of the plan can proceed. To do this, each unsatisfied condition is associated with a corresponding satisfying goal. The satisfying goal is such that when a plan to achieve the goal is retrieved and executed, the success of the plan implies that the failed precondition is satisfied. Initially, all the unsatisfied preconditions of the action p to adapt are computed, resulting in a set C. For each condition $c \in C$, a satisfying goal is obtained, using the function *GetSatisfyingGoal* in Figure 5. This gives a set of goals G which need to be achieved before the action p can be executed. A parallel plan q is generated where each of the goals in G can be achieved in parallel. q is inserted as the first step of plan p.

After the modified plan is handed back to the plan execution module, it is inserted into the current plan. In the next execution cycle the plan expansion module will expand the newly inserted goals in G.

Notice that the plan adaptation module performs two basic operations: delete unnecessary actions (which is performed by an analysis of the plan dependency graph), and insert additional actions needed to satisfy unsatisfied preconditions. This last process is performed as a collaboration between several modules: the plan execution module identifies actions that cannot be executed, the adaptation component identifies the failed preconditions and generates goals for them, and the plan expansion and plan retrieval modules expand the inserted goals.

4   Complexity Analysis

In the following sections we will analyze the complexity of our structural adaptation techniques. We analyze both the removal of redundant actions through plan dependency graph generation as well as the addition of goals to the partial plan to satisfy unsatisfied conditions. In the first case the time complexity of plan dependency graph generation and removal of actions is obtained. In the case of goal additions, the goal addition for a single condition happens in constant time. Here, the time complexity is not as important as the number of goals added during a game play, because the addition of goals has an impact on the size of the plan for winning the game and thereby on the time taken to win the game. We obtain a bound on the number of goals that are added during the plan adaptation stage for satisfying any unsatisfied preconditions.

4.1   Complexity of Removal of Unnecessary Actions through Plan Dependency Graph Generation

Theorem 1. *The time complexity for removal of unnecessary actions through plan dependency graph generation is $O(N(n))$, where $N(n) = kl(n-1)(n-2)/2 + l^2n + (n-1)(n-2)/2$. Where n is the size of the plan, k is the maximum number of pre-conditions and l is the maximum number of success conditions of actions.*

We derive Theorem 1 in the following discussion. A plan dependency graph is generated for a plan which has been expanded to the level of primitive actions. Let the number of pre-conditions in any action be bounded by k and the number of success conditions for any subgoal or action be bounded by l. The maximum number of comparisons that can occur while comparing the preconditions of any action with the success conditions of another action is bounded by $N_c^{max} - kl$.

Now consider a retrieved plan with n actions. If the plan is a sequential plan, to obtain the dependencies we compare the preconditions of each action with the success conditions of the preceding actions. Thus the preconditions of the second action are compared with the success conditions of the first action, the preconditions of third action are compared with the success conditions of the first action and the second action and so on. The total number of comparisons at the level of plans is thus:

$$N_c^P(n) = 1 + 2 + \dots + (n-1) = \frac{(n-1)(n-2)}{2} \tag{1}$$

In case the plan retrieved is a parallel plan we do not try to obtain the dependencies as we assume that the component plans are independent of each other. When the retrieved plan is a combination of sequential plans and parallel plans, some comparisons take place but the number of comparisons will be less than that in the case of a sequential plan. The sequential plan thus provides an upper bound on the number of comparisons. Within each action comparison, there can be N_c^{max} condition comparisons and these condition comparisons take constant time.

When obtaining the direct actions we compare the success conditions of each primitive action with the success conditions for the goal. The maximum number of condition comparisons possible here is l^2 and this is done for each of the n actions. Thus the number of condition level comparisons for obtaining direct plans is bounded by $N_d^{max}(n) = nl^2$.

Once the dependencies between plans have been determined we remove redundant actions. Only those direction actions with unsatisfied success conditions are initially considered active. Then we propagate it to the plans on which the direct plans depend, we also recursively do this for the plans made active. We do the propagation only once for each action. If the total number of actions is n, and the position of an action in a sequential plan is i, the maximum number of actions the action can depend upon is $i - 1$. Thus, the number of links we follow is bound by $N_l^{max}(n)$.

$$N_l^{max}(n) = 1 + 2 + \ldots + (n - 1) = \frac{(n-1)(n-2)}{2} \qquad (2)$$

The complexity of adaptation through plan dependency graph generation is thus $O(N(n) = N_c^{max} * N_c^P(n) + N_d^{max}(n) + N_l^{max}(n))$, proving Theorem 1.

4.2   Analysis of Adaptation for Unsatisfied Preconditions

Considering the maximum number of preconditions for any action to be k and that each precondition when not satisfied leads to the addition of a single goal, the maximum number of goals inserted to satisfy an action's preconditions is also k. Each goal is expanded into a plan. The primitive actions present in this new plan can further have unsatisfied conditions during execution. This may lead to the creation of cycles i.e it is possible that a goal g_1 has a precondition c_1 which leads to goal g_2 and the goal g_2 has a precondition c_2 which leads to the goal g_1, it might lead to the continuous addition of goals. No bound regarding the size of the final partial plan can be obtained if such cycles can occur (Darmok incorporates a simple cycle detection mechanism that prevents these situations).

Theorem 2. *Assuming all plans succeed upon execution and goals do not form cycles, the number of goals added by the adaptation module is $O(M_G^{max})$, where: $M_G^{max} = n_{max}k * (n_{max}^{G-1}k^{G-1} - 1)/(n_{max}k - 1)$. Where n_{max} is the maximum size of any plan in the case base, k is the maximum number of preconditions in any plan and G is the number of different goals possible in the domain.*

If the goals in a real-time planning system cannot form a cycle i.e any plan for a goal g_1 will never lead to a goal g_2 such that the plan for g_2 leads to the goal g_1, a bound can be established on the number of goals added. If the total number of possible different goals in the system is G, the number of possible goals a plan for a top level goal g can lead to is $G - 1$. Let g' be one such goal. The number of goals a plan for this goal can lead to is $G - 2$, and so on. Additionally, the number of goals added for any action is limited by k. Consider the maximum number of actions in any fully expanded plan for a goal to be n_{max}. If the goals added by plan adaptation for the first time are considered level one goals, the goals added within a plan for a first level goal as second goals, and so on, the maximum number of goals that can be added at level l for a level $l - 1$ goal is $n_G^l = min(G - l, k)$. The maximum number of goals added is N_G^{max}:

$$N_G^{max} = \sum_{i=1...G-1} \left((n_{max})^i \prod_{j=1...i} n_G^j \right) \tag{3}$$

If $k < G$ and we replace n_G^l by k we get an upper bound on N_G^{max}, $N_G^{max} < M_G^{max}$:

$$M_G^{max} = \sum_{i=1...G-1} (n_{max})^i k^i = n_{max} k * \frac{((n_{max})^{G-1} k^{G-1} - 1)}{(n_{max} k - 1)} \tag{4}$$

Thus the number of goals added by the adaptation module is bounded by M_G^{max}. This is clearly not a tight upper bound. Better upper bounds can be obtained introducing domain related constraints.

In the case of WARGUS domain, the goals inserted by the plan adaptation module are either to build certain units or buildings or to gather resources. Consider the term *units* to refer to all units other than peasants and the term *buildings* to refer to all buildings other than farms (peasants and farms need to be considered separately). For the further analysis we assume that the opponents have not destroyed any buildings. Let n_0 be the number of primitive actions in the completely expanded plan without adaptation. Let b, f, u and p be the number of buildings, farms, units and peasants inserted by the adaptation module respectively. Farms are required to train peasants and units, each farm allows training of four peasants and units. Considering each of the n_0 actions can produce at most one peasant or unit, the number of units trained is at most $n_0 + u + p$. We know that before executing the plan, the number of farms was enough for the number of units and peasants we had. Thus, the number of farms f that the adaptation component will insert must satisfy the following inequality (because it will not insert more farms than needed): $4f \leq n_0 + u + p$.

Now, consider the peasants inserted by the adaptation module. Peasants are trained to gather resources or build buildings or farms. There are three kinds of resources in WARGUS:wood, gold and oil. Farms require only two of these resources(wood and gold), while a building or unit might require any of the three resources. Farms and buildings also require peasants for building them. Thus, a building can require 4 peasants - one to build it and three to gather the different resources. Similarly, a farm or a unit can require 3 peasants. The maximum number of peasants required by the n_0 primitive actions is $4n_0$. Thus we get the following inequality (because it will not insert more peasants than needed): $p \leq 4n_0 + 4b + 3f + 3u$.

Solving these inequalities gives us: $f \leq (5n_0 + 4b + 4u)$ and $p \leq (19n_0 + 16b + 15u)$. Further, units can only be required by one of the n_0 actions, since they are not required for building or gathering resources. Thus, $u \leq n_0$. The number of goals added is thus $O(N_g)$:

$$N_g = b + u + f + p \leq 24n_0 + 21b + 20u \leq 44n_0 + 21b \tag{5}$$

Thus, the number of extra goals added due to plan adaptation is $O(21b+44n_0)$. Notice also that b is bounded by the number of different buildings (other than farms), because adaptation will never insert duplicate buildings since duplicate buildings are never *required* (although it might be convenient to have them, it is never required). Thus the number of goals added is linearly bounded in the number of building types and the number of actions which were originally present in the plan. The analysis presented, provides a bound on the size of the plan after the adaptation module has finished adapting it, assuming that there are no goal cycles (easily detected in the case of WARGUS).

4.3   Single Cycle Complexity

In order to have a real-time system, it is important that a single execution cycle takes a short time. Each cycle of Darmok involves the expansion of open goals and then execution of actions ready to execute. If the number of open goals is r and the number of actions ready to execute is e, r plans are retrieved and the plan dependency graph is generated for these plans. If n_{max} is the maximum number of actions in any of the retrieved plans, the complexity for the adaptation of retrieved plans is $O(rN(n_{max}))$ (See Theorem 1). While plan execution, adaptation due to failed preconditions of an action can lead to the addition of maximum k goals in a single cycle. Thus the total per cycle complexity of the Darmok planning adaptation module is polynomial, $O(rN(n_{max}) + ke)$.

5   Experimental Results

To evaluate our plan adaptation techniques, we conducted two sets of experiments turning the plan adaptation on and off respectively. The experiments were conducted on 12 maps: 11 different variations of the well known map "Nowhere to run nowhere to hide" (NWTR) and 1 version of "Garden of War" (GoW). NWTR maps have a wall of trees separating the opponents that introduces a highly strategic component in the game (one can attempt ranged attacks over the wall of trees, or prevent the trees to be chopped by building towers, etc.). GoW maps are large maps with an empty area in the middle where a lot of gold mines are located. 10 different expert demonstration were used for evaluation; 8 of the expert traces are on maps from NWTR maps while the other 2 expert traces were for GoW maps. Each one of the expert demonstrations exemplified different techniques with which the game can be played: fighter's rush, knights rush, ranged attacks using ballistas, or blocking the enemy using towers.

We conducted the experiments using different combinations of the traces. We report the results in 12 games (one per map) using all 10 traces. We also report the results in 48 games in nine different scenarios where the system learnt from

Table 1. Effect of Plan Adaptation on Game Statistics

NT	Adaptation						No Adaptation						improvement
	W	D	L	ADS	AOS	WP	W	D	L	ADS	AOS	WP	
1	17	4	27	2158	1514	**35.42%**	9	7	32	1701	1272	**18.75%**	88.75%
2	16	5	27	2798	1828	**33.33%**	15	2	31	1642	1342	**31.25%**	6.66%
3	18	6	24	1998	1400	**37.5%**	10	6	32	1633	1491	**20.83%**	80.00%
4	19	3	26	2343	1745	**39.58%**	8	4	36	1358	1663	**16.67%**	137.40%
5	11	6	31	2141	1842	**22.91%**	7	6	35	1310	1607	**14.58%**	57.13%
6	14	2	32	1709	1695	**29.17%**	3	5	40	1475	1788	**6.25%**	366.72%
7	20	0	28	1941	1448	**41.67%**	9	6	33	1800	1564	**18.75%**	122.24%
8	15	3	30	1887	1465	**31.25%**	6	3	39	1598	1671	**12.50%**	150.00%
9	21	4	23	2110	1217	**43.75%**	7	3	38	1449	1681	**14.58%**	200.07%
10	5	0	7	1533	1405	**41.67%**	2	0	10	1158	1555	**16.67%**	150.00%
	156	33	255	20618	15559	35.14%	76	67	301	15124	15634	17.12%	105.38%

1, 2, 3, 4, 5, 6, 7, 8 and 9 traces respectively. For conducting these experiments, for any number of traces, n, we randomly chose four sets containing n traces and ran our system against the built in AI with each set on all 12 maps.

Table 1 shows the results of the experiments with and without adaptation. NT indicates the number of traces. For each experiment 6 values are shown: W, D and L indicate the number of wins, draws and loses respectively. ADS and AOS indicate the average Darmok score and the average opponent score (where the "score" is a number that WARGUS itself calculates and assigns to each player at the end of each game). Finally, WP shows the win percentage. The right most row presents the improvement in win percentage comparing adaptation with respect to no adaptation. The bottom row shows a summary of the results.

The results show that plan adaptation leads to an improvement of the percentage of wins as well as the player score to opponent score ratio. An improvement occurs in all cases irrespective of the number of traces used. When several traces are used cases belonging to different traces are retrieved and executed, thus, there is a much greater chance of redundant or missing actions being present. Our plan adaptation deals with these problems, improving the performance of Darmok. In some cases the system performs well even without adaptation. This may be because the cases retrieved "tie in" together as they are and do not require adaptation. For instance, in the experiment where the system learnt 10 traces, we can see how the system managed to improve performance from 16.67% wins without adaptation to 41.67% wins with adaptation. Finally, when considering these numbers, we must take into account that our system is attempting to play the whole game of WARGUS at the same granularity as a human would play, and that also results depend on the quality of the demonstration traces provided to the system. Thus, with better demonstrations (by true experts), the performance could greatly improve.

6   Related Work

Case-based planning is the application of CBR to planning, and as such, it is planning as remembering [2]. CBP involves reusing previous plans and adapting them to suit new situations. There are several motivations for case-based planning [10], the main one being that it has the potential to increase the *efficiency* with respect to generative planners (although, in general, reusing plans has the same or even higher complexity than planning from scratch [7]).

One of the first case-based planning systems was CHEF [2], able to build new recipes based on user's request for dishes with particular ingredients and tastes. CHEF contains a memory of past failures to warn about problems and also a memory of succeeded plans from which to retrieve plans. One of the novel capabilities of CHEF with respect to classical planning systems is its ability to learn. Each time CHEF experiences a planning failure, it means that understanding has broken down and something has to be fixed. Thus, planning failures tell the system when it needs to learn. CHEF performs plan adaptation by a set of domain-specific rules called TOPs.

Domain-independent nonlinear planning has been shown to be intractable (NP-hard). PRIAR [4] was designed to address that issue. PRIAR works by annotating generated plans with a *validation structure* that contains an explanation of the internal causal dependencies so that previous plans can be reused by adapting them in the future. Related to PRIAR, the SPA system was presented by Hanks and Weld [3]. The key highlight of SPA is that it is complete and systematic (while PRIAR is not systematic, and CHEF is not either complete nor systematic), but uses a simpler plan representation than PRIAR. Extending SPA, Ram and Francis [9] presented MPA (Multi-Plan Adaptor), that extended SPA with the ability to merge plans. The main issue with all these systems is that they are all based on search-based planning algorithms, and thus are not suitable for real-time domains, where the system has to generate quick responses to changes in the environment. A thorough review on plan adaptation techniques was presented in [5].

7   Conclusions

In this paper we have presented real-time structural plan adaptation techniques for RTS games. Specifically, our technique divides the problem in two steps: removal of unnecessary actions and addition of actions to fill gaps in the sequence of actions. We implemented our algorithm inside the Darmok system that can play the game of WARGUS. The experiments conducted gave promising results for the techniques introduced, however our techniques are domain-independent. Moreover, one of the important aspects of our techniques is that they are efficient at the same time as effective, so they can be applied for real-time domains in which other search-based plan adaptation techniques cannot be applied. The complexity analysis performed shows that the adaptation techniques do not have a significant overhead and are suitable for real time situations.

Our techniques still have several limitations. Currently, our plan adaptation techniques require a plan to be fully instantiated in order to be adapted, thus we cannot adapt plans that are still half expanded. As a consequence, the high level structure of the plan cannot be adapted unless it is fully instantiated. Because of that, plan adaptation as presented in this paper can only work at the lower levels of the plan, where everything is instantiated. This could be addressed by reasoning about interactions between higher level goals, by estimating which are the preconditions and postconditions of such goals by analyzing the stored plans in the case-base to achieve those goals. Another line of further research is to incorporate ideas from MPA [9] in order to be able to merge several plans into a single plan. This can increase the flexibility of the approach since sometimes no single plan in the case base can achieve a goal, but a combination will.

References

1. Aha, D., Molineaux, M., Ponsen, M.: Learning to win: Case-based plan selection in a real-time strategy game. In: Muñoz-Ávila, H., Ricci, F. (eds.) ICCBR 2005. LNCS (LNAI), vol. 3620, pp. 5–20. Springer, Heidelberg (2005)
2. Hammond, K.F.: Case based planning: A framework for planning from experience. Cognitive Science 14(3), 385–443 (1990)
3. Hanks, S., Weld, D.S.: A domain-independednt algorithm for plan adaptation. Journal of Artificial Intelligence Research 2, 319–360 (1995)
4. Kambhampati, S., Hendler, J.A.: A validation-structure-based theory of plan modification and reuse. Artificial Intelligence 55(2), 193–258 (1992)
5. Muñoz-Avila, H., Cox, M.: Case-based plan adaptation: An analysis and review. IEEE Intelligent Systems (2007)
6. Nau, D., Au, T.C., Ilghami, O., Kuter, U., Wu, D., Yaman, F., Muñoz-Avila, H., Murdock, J.W.: Applications of shop and shop2. Intelligent Systems 20(2), 34–41 (2005)
7. Nebel, B., Koehler, J.: Plan modifications versus plan generation: A complexity-theoretic perspective. Technical Report RR-92-48 (1992)
8. Ontañón, S., Mishra, K., Sugandh, N., Ram, A.: Case-based planning and execution for real-time strategy games. In: Weber, R.O., Richter, M.M. (eds.) ICCBR 2007. LNCS (LNAI), vol. 4626, pp. 164–178. Springer, Heidelberg (2007)
9. Ram, A., Francis, A.: Multi-plan retrieval and adaptation in an experience-based agent. In: Leake, D.B. (ed.) Case-Based Reasoning: Experiences, Lessons, and Future Directions. AAAI Press, Menlo Park (1996)
10. Spalazzi, L.: A survey on case-based planning. Artificial Intelligence Review 16(1), 3–36 (2001)

Horizontal Case Representation

Rosina Weber, Sidath Gunawardena, and Craig MacDonald

The iSchool at Drexel, College of Information Science & Technology, Drexel University
{rweber,sidath.gunawardena,craig.macdonald}@ischool.drexel.edu

Abstract. We present a new case representation that seeks to make case-based reasoning (CBR) more suited to real world applications. We propose a horizontal representation that is composed of two features, one to represent the problem and one to represent the solution. We also present a similarity metric tailored to our representation. Rather than parametrizing the distance function with weights, it requires one parameter that recommends the cardinality of values for new problems to be solved by the system. Our representation is less restrictive during case acquisition as it does not constrain how non-experts can populate cases and it requires less knowledge engineering effort than the traditional method. We compare our representation to the traditional case representation and show that it is superior when cases are incomplete. Finally, we illustrate the effectiveness of our representation in a real world application, where the demarcation between problem and solution is blurred.

1 Introduction

In order to increase the widespread adoption of case-based reasoning (CBR) in the real world, we propose an alternative case representation that facilitates the engineering of cases. The proposed representation simplifies knowledge acquisition, making it accessible to users who want to describe experiences, even if they do not understand CBR. Furthermore, it facilitates the engineering of case-based reasoners as it does not require features to be identified in advance or that features be weighted.

Let us consider the goal of building a CBR system to help project managers manage software development projects. Let us also limit this example to a weighted feature-vector representation in a flat memory. The traditional way of designing this system follows a series of steps, e.g., defining the reasoning task, case vocabulary, case problem and solution, features, relative relevance of features, and indexing vocabulary [1]. Most of these steps require knowledge engineering as they refer to multiple knowledge containers [2]. Assuming that cases are to be acquired from project managers, the previously defined case features have to be explained to them and this explanation has to include allowable values. Alternatively, project managers may freely describe their experiences and knowledge engineers can later fit them into the previously defined case features. The latter is prone to incompleteness and misinterpretation. For example, mentioning the morale of the developing team may be interpreted and used as a feature of the problem description when it could have been intended as a feature of the solution.

K.-D. Althoff et al. (Eds.): ECCBR 2008, LNAI 5239, pp. 548–561, 2008.

We propose an alternative way to design such a system, while maintaining the main goal of building a CBR system to help project managers manage a software development project. The steps to be followed to design the system are limited to providing a user interface to project managers who have experiences they wish to describe. This user interface consists of two fields: problem and solution. The guidance given to the project managers, i.e., users who will populate the cases, is to list terms that describe the main features of the problems and then freely describe the solutions they want to convey. We refer to this form as *horizontal case representation*.

Horizontal case representation retains the definition of a case presented in [1], which describes a case as a context and a lesson that teaches something about this context. This definition is sufficiently flexible that it is able to cope with the idiosyncrasies of real world cases. It allows the *context* to be any kind of problem and *something* to be any reasoning task.

Horizontal case representation is less demanding on individual feature-values by reducing the impact of missing feature values on similarity assessment. Furthermore, if new features become relevant to represent a case, they are included with no need to adjust the similarity measure. In a horizontal case representation, terms are grouped in what we call horizontal features (Figure 1). The traditional way of representing cases is more commonly presented as a vertical list.

Vertical Features	Horizontal Features
Problem Feature$_1$: value$_1$ Problem Feature$_2$: value$_2$ Problem Feature$_n$: value$_n$ ... Solution Feature$_1$: value$_1$ Solution Feature$_m$: value$_m$	Problem Feature$_1$:value$_{11}$,value$_{12}$,value$_{13}$,...,value$_{1v}$ ... Solution Feature$_1$: value$_{11}$, value$_{12}$,..., value$_{1s}$

Fig. 1. Vertical and horizontal features

For the purposes of this paper, we will refer to horizontal case bases, ones whose cases use horizontal features only. We will refer to vertical cases bases, ones whose cases use vertical features only. Cases may use one or more horizontal features to represent either problem or solution. In fact, horizontal features may even be weighted. However, for our initial analyses, we will study horizontal cases that are composed of two horizontal features, one to represent the problem and one to represent the solution.

Our experience has demonstrated that users without knowledge of CBR find cases with horizontal features easier to populate than cases with vertical ones. Users can enter any terms they want, with no limits with respect to their quality, specificity, or number. In this paper, we are now concerned with the implications of this simpler way of organizing case knowledge.

In the next section, we describe the background work and motivations that led to this work, and discuss some related work. In Section 3, we propose a method to compute a parameter that is needed to assess similarity in horizontal case bases. This parameter recommends an ideal cardinality for values to be entered in a new problem, which is required due to the varying number of values that cases can have in the case base. In Section 4, we compare horizontal case bases with vertical case bases in the presence and absence of missing values. In Section 5, we discuss additional issues of horizontal cases when used in the real world. We then conclude with final remarks and future work.

2 Background and Related Work

As we explore opportunities for implementing CBR in the real world, we identify challenges that are not usually addressed by theoretical work. In this paper, we are concerned with case acquisition, case representation, case indexing and retrieval, and situation assessment in the context of incomplete cases.

Our experience reveals that populating cases is challenging, whether the source of cases comes either from humans or unstructured sources. When a case base is designed to account for experiences of one reasoning task, design decisions such as the scope of the reasoning task and the indexing vocabulary become additional elements to consider while acquiring cases. The engineered indexing vocabulary–typically represented in cases as feature-value pairs–constitutes a list of required fields when asking users to populate experiences. It requires users to understand the meaning of each feature and to know its allowable values. A rigid indexing vocabulary also limits users who may want to add new values for features, or even new, previously undefined features. From a human-computer interaction perspective, users should not be prevented from communicating aspects of an experience they consider relevant nor should they be limited in how to communicate those experiences. When populating cases in practice, what is required of users is completely different from asking them to describe experiences. However, it is these experiences that need to be captured, and that is what makes CBR unique.

As previously introduced, we envision cases as a problem context and a solution that teaches something about this context [1]. The flexibility stemming from this way of visualizing a case allows a system to perform multiple tasks. As stated in [1], the lessons taught in each case are the means by which the goals of the system are delivered. Thus, the lessons in each case may perform multiple tasks. One of our concerns is that limiting a case base to one single reasoning task places engineered cases and their systems apart from real experiences. Humans live and describe experiences as complete episodes, thus an experience of identifying symptoms of a problem and prescribing a strategy to solve it is always accompanied by some diagnosis. Therefore, it is reasonable to expect that some users would be interested in reusing prescriptions while others would prefer reusing diagnoses.

An alternative to task-oriented reasoners has been previously discussed as community-oriented case-based reasoners [3]. The concept of a community-oriented system would define the scope of a system based on its users rather than on one single reasoning task.

One of the contexts where this notion became popular is in case-based applications for knowledge management [4]. Weber and Aha [5] proposed a case representation for lessons learned that is aligned with Kolodner's definition in [1]. The proposed case representation consists of the case problem (indexing elements) with features called *applicable task* and *preconditions*; and a case solution (reuse elements) with features called *lesson suggestion* and *rationale*.

Another way of utilizing case bases without limiting the need for multiple reasoning tasks is studied by multi CBR, e.g., [6]. Multi CBR is recommended when multiple case bases are already available.

Bergmann and Vollrath [7] have already found situations in which traditional guidelines to build CBR systems and to reuse cases are not the most adequate. For this reason, they proposed the notion of generalized cases, making solutions more accessible to a wider set of problems. These authors have also observed that sometimes the problem and solution distinction is not very clear [7].

One of our main concerns with retrieval performance is the possibility of change in a domain causing changes in features in an indexing vocabulary. As observed by Leake and Wilson, such changes "...may render obsolete prior similarity criteria or cases" [8] pp. 219.

The indexing vocabulary is the basis of a weighing scheme. Weighing schemes are important so that features with different relative relevance are properly represented [9]. The problem with a weighted similarity measure is that it requires revision if features in the domain change, either by changing their importance or because new ones need to be added or existing ones need to be removed.

An important issue arising from a horizontal representation relates to the cardinality of horizontal cases. If we give users one field to describe aspects of an experience, then we should not limit the number of terms they can enter. Even if a limit were required from a practical standpoint, this could not be a small limit. Thus, different users will enter different numbers of terms to describe their experiences. This raises a problem for similarity assessment as one similarity measure should be able to assess similarity and assign a similarity score to any combination of target problem and candidate cases in the case base. However, horizontal case bases will have cases with different number of terms and so will the new target problems entered by the users. Although we choose not to control the varying number of terms in the case base, we should be able to recommend to the user a desirable number of terms to enter to describe a new target problem that is likely to promote retrieval of useful cases. In addition to supporting an accurate retrieval, recommending such a number will also serve the purpose of guiding users on how to best use the system.

The problem of number of search terms has been studied in other search contexts. A study of 1,025,910 user queries in 1999 revealed that on average the web query contains 2.5 terms [10]. This alone discourages the use of case retrieval by the means of traditional vertical cases, given that problem descriptions with 3 features are hardly usual. A way to compute an expected number of terms that are likely to promote retrieval with high levels of accuracy depending on the characteristics of each case base is a promising strategy. Moreover, the resulting accuracy when using such a number should be high. On one hand, it is likely that this number suggests users to enter more than 2.5 terms, going against the status quo. On the other, longer queries do not necessarily improve web search quality [11], so the improved quality has to be evident.

The variations in number of terms have an effect similar to missing data. Incomplete cases have been a concern of many researchers. Some of the work has focused on incompleteness of problem description, others on the performance of CBR when compared to inductive methods. Incompleteness has always been associated with lack of reasoning power [12].

McSherry [13] examines the problem of incompleteness from the perspective of interactive CBR, where data may be incomplete due to the inability of users to provide complete problem descriptions. In this context, he proposes that choices of questions are given to the users. This may increase the chances that a matching case is found but does not address the problem of missing values in the case base. Bogaerts and Leake [14] conduct a comparative study on the use of different methods to retrieve cases based on incomplete problem descriptions. Those methods rely on strategies to assign artificial values for unknown features. The proportion of missing features is low because they only assume missing values in new target problems. Interestingly, given that in conversational CBR incompleteness is usually a problem in the query, query length becomes another issue of concern [15].

Focusing on cases in the case base, Auriol et al. [16] have demonstrated that CBR maintains higher levels of accuracy than inductive methods in the presence of missing values. Furthermore, a study comparing increasing percentages of missing values in conversational case libraries has demonstrated the impact of different forms of inductive retrieval in recall and precision [17].

In conclusion, in order to make CBR systems and case retrieval more widely adopted, it would be useful if some of the existing requirements could be relaxed. Ideally, it would be desirable to keep the same levels of performance in systems that could be reasoning-task independent; where cases could be easily captured directly by humans who live the experiences and/or from experiences as they are available in the real world (e.g., text); that cases were populated with terms only, without feature-value pairs, and in any number; that case terms could be added, could disappear, and change in importance without interfering with system performance; and that CBR systems were equally reliable in the presence or absence of missing values.

3   Retrieving Horizontal Cases: The RCF

No benefits derived from the horizontal representation can justify any loss in accuracy when compared to the vertical representation. The assessment of similarity between a new problem and existing ones in the case base has to produce useful cases. However, a horizontal case base lacks the vertical features that are used to guide users of CBR systems to enter a new problem case. Furthermore, the degree of freedom given to users when populating horizontal cases results in cases that may have different numbers of terms. Consequently, we need to know if there is an ideal number of terms within a horizontal feature to describe a new problem case, such that it can result in the retrieval of useful cases with a level of accuracy comparable to a vertical representation. If this number exists and there is a way to compute it, we can use it to parametrize the similarity measure in order to normalize it and also to guide users on how many values they should enter to describe a new problem. This number is the Recommended Cardinality Factor (RCF).

When RCF is used as a parameter to compute similarity, it bounds the computation of similarity functions between values from the new problem case and existing cases. Each value of the problem case is compared against each value in the existing candidate cases and the results of the functions representing the individual similarities are added until either (a) the number of matches meets or exceeds the RCF or (b) there are no more terms to match in either the target case or the candidate case. In (a), a similarity of 1.0 is assigned; in (b) the similarity is the number of matches divided by the RCF. In other words, the RCF is the number of terms that have to match in order to consider two cases similar.

For example, given an RCF of 3 and a target case with terms *fever, nausea, jaundice* and *vomiting*, a candidate case with terms *dizziness, fever, nausea,* and *jaundice* receives a similarity score of 1 since 3 terms match. Similarly, a candidate case with terms *no fever, nausea,* and *vomiting* receives a similarity score of 0.66 since only 2 terms match (2/3 = 0.66).

3.1 Computing the RCF

One of our goals is to be able to compute the RCF so as to communicate it to the users. This is an important form of guidance for users of the system because it indicates the ideal number of terms to enter given the current state of the case base.

The first step we took was to observe how different potential values of the RCF influence accuracy. For this purpose, we tested average accuracy in 4 horizontal case bases across different percentages of missing values in each (these are described in Table 2 Section 4.1). Our first observation is that as the average number of terms per case decreases, so does the RCF that maximizes accuracy; this observation is confirmed by the correlations in Table 1. The high correlation suggests that an equation derived from these values may be able to predict the optimal RCF value for different datasets.

Table 1. Correlation between average number of terms per case and RCF that maximizes accuracy

Case base 1	Case base 2	Case base 3	Case base 4	Overall
0.977	0.776	0.909	0.99	0.882

To find this prediction equation, a linear regression analysis was performed to determine whether or not there is a linear relationship between the average number of terms per case (TpC) and the optimal RCF, i.e., the value of RCF that maximizes accuracy. Each variable was first transformed with a natural log function (ln) in order to stabilize the variance and maximize the predictive ability of the regression equation. A preliminary analysis suggested that the constant term was not statistically significant and therefore the following model was used:

$$Model: \ln(RCF) = \beta_1 \ln(TpC) .$$ (1)

This regression is significant at the $\alpha = 0.001$ level and has an associated R^2 of 0.984, indicating that 98.4% of the variability of the optimal RCF is explained by this regression. The coefficient (β_1) is also significant at the $\alpha = 0.001$ level, which suggests that $\ln(TpC)$ is a strong predictor of $\ln(RCF)$. Since using the natural log function can be cumbersome, a reverse log transformation was performed and the following equation was generated:

$$RCF = e^{(0.833 \times \ln(TpC))} ,$$ (2)

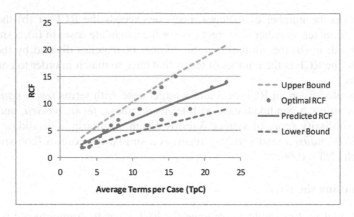

Fig. 2. Comparing optimal RCF to predicted RCF

where RCF is the optimal RCF value and TpC is the average number of terms per case in the case base. This equation can now be used to predict the optimal RCF value for the horizontal representation. Because RCF is a parameter of the case base, it only needs to be computed again if the case base changes.

Based on these results it was then possible to compute a 90% prediction interval for the optimal RCF for different numbers of terms per case. These values were used in the analysis discussed in Section 4. Figure 2 shows the comparison between the optimal (actual) RCF, the RCF predicted by Equation (2), and the upper and lower bounds of the 90% prediction interval as the average number of terms per case increases.

4 Horizontal Versus Vertical Representation

We hypothesize that, in the presence of missing values, case bases that use horizontal representations are at least as accurate as the ones that use vertical cases. The metric we utilize is average accuracy as measured by the leave one out cross validation (LOOCV) method. Average accuracy is computed as the proportion of correct classi-fications proposed by the case retrieved with highest similarity score.

4.1 Methodology and Datasets

Four vertical case bases (Table 2) were converted into horizontal case bases by having their vertical features collapsed into one problem and one solution feature. Each new horizontal problem feature groups all the values assigned to the original vertical fea-tures. We now have 8 case bases: 4 vertical and 4 horizontal.

Each case base is then subject to five iterations of random removal of values, cor-responding to removing approximately 10%, 20%, 30%, 40%, and 50% of the values in each case base. Therefore, from 8 case bases, we generate another 40, resulting in 48 case bases. The vertical case bases were tested with their original similarity meas-ures. The similarity measure used for horizontal case bases is explained in Section 3.

Table 2. Case bases

Case base	Case base 1	Case base 2	Case base 3	Case base 4
# of cases	88	20	24	32
# of vertical features	23 symbolic	4 numeric + 2 symbolic	8 symbolic	16 binary
Ave # allowable values per feature, range	4, [2, 4]	5, [3, 8]	2.9, [2, 3]	2.25
problem	software development projects	air traffic conditions	preferences	software development projects
solution feature	1 indicating success or failure	1 with 10 plans to reroute traffic	1 with 7 vacation destinations	1 with 7 different animals
similarity functions	All binary	3 binary 3 continuous	All binary	All binary
Method to learn weights	Gradient descent	Manually assigned	Manually assigned	Uses no weights
Max weight	0.076	0.381	0.349	0.076
Min weight	0.003	0.048	0.009	0.003

To determine whether or not there is a statistical difference between the accuracy of the horizontal and vertical case bases, a Wilcoxon signed-rank test was performed. We chose this method because it is a non-parametric alternative to the paired sample t-test that is used to compare two related groups of observations without making any assumptions about their underlying distributions [18].

We emphasize that the selection of the RCF is critical to maximizing accuracy. As a result, this comparison was only carried out using the accuracy levels of the horizontal case bases corresponding to the RCF values which fell in a 90% confidence interval for the prediction of the optimal RCF based on Equation (2), derived in Section 3.1.

4.2 Results

Based on the results of the Wilcoxon signed-rank test performed separately for each completeness level over all four case bases, *there is no statistical difference between the traditional vertical representation and the proposed horizontal approach at the levels from 60% to 90% completeness, confirming our hypothesis.* These results show that only as little as 10% incompleteness is needed to render useless all the engineering effort to select an indexing vocabulary and represent the relative importance of features with weights. This also reveals that the proposed method solves the problem of incomplete cases.

The only statistically significant differences between horizontal and vertical representation are at the 50% and 100% levels of completeness. At the 100% level, the horizontal representation is less accurate than the vertical representation (p-value < 0.01). At the 50% level, the horizontal representation is more accurate than the vertical representation (p-value < 0.001).

At the levels from 60% to 90% completeness, despite not having statistically significant difference overall, there do appear to be specific RCF values at which the

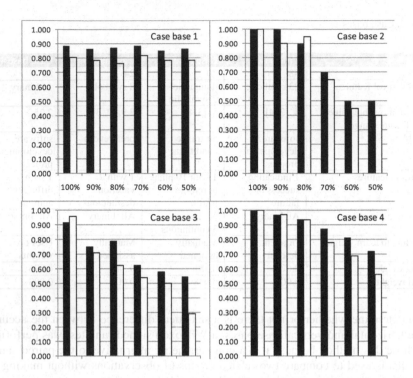

Fig. 3. Horizontal (dark) and vertical (light) accuracy with missing values

accuracy of horizontal representation is superior to that of the vertical (see Figure 3 Case base 1). So it can be said that, assuming again that the proper RCF is calculated, the horizontal representation is at least as accurate as, and sometimes more accurate than, the vertical representation (where features are represented with different weights) for completeness levels between 50% and 90%. *We should emphasize that despite the fact that RCF does not take into account that some features may be more relevant than others, there is no loss of accuracy with the horizontal method.*

5   Horizontal Representation in the Real World

We tested the expected benefits of the horizontal representation by designing a system for a group of users without knowledge of CBR. These users are scientists whose goal is to help each other reuse research methods and solutions. We worked with them to design an interface so they could populate cases on their own.

Figure 4 presents an example of a case populated by a research scientist. The questions in the problem feature and headings in the solution features are there to guide users to populate experiences adopting the notion that each record will discuss a problem and knowledge about it, i.e., a solution.

As previously mentioned, there are two consequences for the fact that what users describe are experiences. First, experiences will not all solve the same reasoning task.

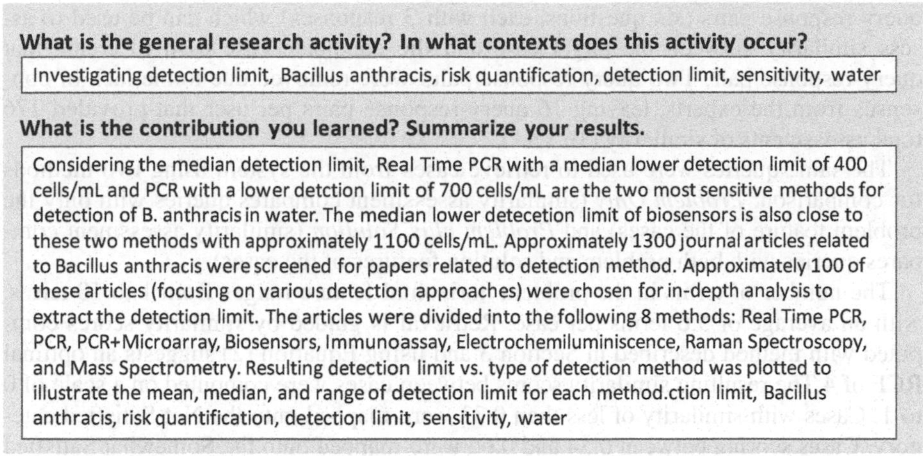

What is the general research activity? In what contexts does this activity occur?

Investigating detection limit, Bacillus anthracis, risk quantification, detection limit, sensitivity, water

What is the contribution you learned? Summarize your results.

Considering the median detection limit, Real Time PCR with a median lower detection limit of 400 cells/mL and PCR with a lower detction limit of 700 cells/mL are the two most sensitive methods for detection of B. anthracis in water. The median lower detecetion limit of biosensors is also close to these two methods with approximately 1100 cells/mL. Approximately 1300 journal articles related to Bacillus anthracis were screened for papers related to detection method. Approximately 100 of these articles (focusing on various detection approaches) were chosen for in-depth analysis to extract the detection limit. The articles were divided into the following 8 methods: Real Time PCR, PCR, PCR+Microarray, Biosensors, Immunoassay, Electrochemiluminiscence, Raman Spectroscopy, and Mass Spectrometry. Resulting detection limit vs. type of detection method was plotted to illustrate the mean, median, and range of detection limit for each method.ction limit, Bacillus anthracis, risk quantification, detection limit, sensitivity, water

Fig. 4. Real-world case populated by a research scientist

In the example, some cases describe a research activity and an experimental design to approach it, whereas others describe a solution obtained through a literature review. Second, experiences may not map into crisply distinct problem-solution pairs. Consequently, we need to learn how to deal with an unclear demarcation between problem and solution description.

5.1 Problem Only vs. Problem Plus Solution

In the previous sections we tested case bases that were originally engineered to use vertical cases. Hence, those cases had crisp boundaries between problem and solution. In this section, we have a case base populated by users who have lived the experiences. Therefore, we use this case base to investigate the suitability of horizontal cases and the similarity measure described in Section 3 for retrieving cases without crisp boundaries between problem and solution.

Methodology. In this study we want to investigate whether it is beneficial to use both problem and solution in the context of retrieving horizontal cases. Because of the unclear distinction between problem and solution, we hypothesize that using both problem and solution features in similarity assessment will be beneficial. We will compare using *Problem Only* with *Problem plus Solution* when retrieving horizontal cases. As reference of retrieval quality, we will use opinions of users. This study utilizes cases populated in a period of one year.

To provide a baseline for comparison, we created queries and asked users to assess retrieval quality. An e-mail survey was distributed to 11 users of the system. The survey consisted of six items. Each item was composed of one hypothetical query, constructed from an existing case, along with three additional cases that were presented as cases retrieved in response to the query. For each retrieved case, the respondents were asked to indicate how satisfied they would be with each if it were given as a result for the given query. The available responses were: Satisfied, Somewhat Satisfied, and Not Satisfied. Thus, each user provided 18 similarity assessments of query-response pairs (six questions, each with 3 responses) which can be used to assess similarity between the target case and the candidate case used to create that query-response pair. Two query-response pairs were removed due to the lack of consensus from the experts, leaving 16 query-response pairs per user that provided 176 total assessments of similarity (16 x 11).

The same queries were used to retrieve cases from the system using two methods for comparison: *Problem Only* (similarity assessment compares queries with only the problem feature of the cases) and *Problem plus Solution* (similarity assessment compares queries with both problem and solution features of the cases).

The number of terms in the problem horizontal feature ranges from 1 to 10 terms, with an average of 5.6 terms per case. Retrieval is guided by similarity scores computed with method described in Section 3 and using Equation (2) suggests an optimal RCF of 4.The resulting similarity scores between cases were computed on a scale of 0 to 1. Cases with similarity of less than 0.33 were mapped onto the Not Satisfied category. Cases scoring between 0.34 and 0.66 were mapped onto the Somewhat Satisfied category and cases with similarities falling in the 0.67 to 1.00 range correspond to the Satisfied category.

Metrics. Because both users and methods being tested produce results in terms of the labels Satisfied, Somewhat Satisfied, and Not Satisfied, we compare them as alternative classifiers. Classifiers are typically compared in a 2x2 matrix that compares 2 true classes with 2 hypothesized classes, true and false. Because we use 3 labels, we adopt a 3x3 confusion matrix to represent 9 possible outcomes (Table 3).

Table 3. Confusion matrix

		True classes		
		Satisfied	Somewhat Satisfied	Not Satisfied
Hypothesized classes	Satisfied	True Satisfied -TP	FP that is true Somewhat-FPS	False Satisfied-FP
	Somewhat Satisfied	False Somewhat that is true Satisfied -FSP	True Somewhat-TS	False Somewhat that is true Not Satisfied-FSN
	Not Satisfied	False Not Satisfied-FN	FN that is true Somewhat-FNS	True Not Satisfied-TN

The 9 outcomes include variations of Satisfied (true) and Not Satisfied (false) considering "somewhat" as an additional intermediary class. We adopt the ROC chart method for discrete classifiers [19] for comparison. We extend the formulas (See equations 3, 4, and 5) for true Satisfied (benefit) rate, false Satisfied (cost) rate, and accuracy from [19]. The formulas for our 3x3 confusion matrix are as follows where P, S, and N respectively correspond to total number of Satisfied, Somewhat, and Not Satisfied.

Benefit rate=TP+TS/(P+S), (3)   Cost rate= FP+FPS+FSN/(N+S), (4)   Accuracy=TP+TS+TN/(P+S+N), (5).

Results. The ROC chart in Figure 5 illustrates the tradeoff between generating True Satisfied and True Somewhat (benefit) and False Not Satisfied (cost) of each method. Any point above the 45° line demonstrates a method that adds value over random guessing. The best possible performance is at the (0, 1) point, i.e., minimum cost and maximum benefit. Figure 5 demonstrates that using *Problem plus Solution* produces a result superior to *Problem Only*. The *Problem plus Solution* method has a benefit rate of 0.867, compared to 0.733 for the *Problem Only*. It also produced greater accuracy: 0.813 compared to 0.688 when using the *Problem Only*. Figure 5 also shows that both methods have the same cost rate of 0.5. Since there is no increased cost of using the solution component as part of the similarity assessment, there is no need to put any restrictions on when to use it.

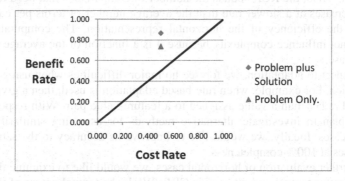

Fig. 5. ROC chart for 2 methods

6 Concluding Remarks and Future Work

The value of this work is in introducing an alternative form to represent cases that, in the presence of missing values, is at least as accurate as or more accurate than the traditional CBR method. This is a very positive result for an approach that does not use weights and where cases can be directly populated by humans who have no knowledge of CBR. The proposed horizontal method includes the benefits listed in Table 4. For these reasons, we believe that it may help expand the adoption of CBR.

Table 4. Benefits of horizontal case bases

1. Reduced engineering effort for design and maintenance.
2. No indexing vocabulary.
3. No list of features to represent cases.
4. Cases can be populated by users without knowledge of CBR.
5. Cases can be populated from sources as they are available.
6. Cases in one case base can describe different reasoning tasks.
7. Values used to populate cases can be new, removed, and change in importance.
8. Horizontal cases can be combined with vertical cases.
9. Perform equally well in the presence or absence of missing features.

The results shown in Section 4 confirm the benefit in accuracy of representing the relative importance of some features. This is reflected at the 100% completeness level where the traditional vertical representation was more accurate than the proposed horizontal form. What we discovered is that by having as little as 10% of missing values in the case base, all the effort of identifying an indexing vocabulary and representing relative relevance with weights would be worthless.

Hence, this work informs a novel design decision for CBR systems. When it is likely that new cases to be populated in a case base will be incomplete, then the designer has the option of selecting horizontal features for case representation.

The horizontal representation does require more comparisons than the vertical. However, increases in the proportion of missing values in cases increases the efficiency in favor of the horizontal representation as comparisons are only made when values exist. Also, the RCF bounds the number of comparisons that need to be made, and this increases at a slower rate than the average number of terms per case, further improving the efficiency of the horizontal representation. The computation of the RCF does not influence complexity because it is a function of the average number of terms per case.

With respect to adaptation, we foresee no major difficulties when using horizontal representation. For example, when rule-based adaptation is used, then a given value is to be found rather than a value assigned to a feature-value pair. With respect to similarity, we plan to investigate alternative methods for assessing similarity between horizontal cases. Ideally, we would like to improve its accuracy to the same level of vertical cases at 100% completeness.

In the further evaluation of horizontal cases, we would like to examine their potential influence for textual and interactive CBR. While the textual nature of the features in the study in Section 5 demonstrates an application of this research in textual CBR, our tests in Section 4 show that horizontal representations are relevant to CBR far beyond textual cases.

Acknowledgements

This work is supported in part by the U.S. EPA-Science to Achieve Results (STAR) Program and the U.S. Department of Homeland Security Programs, Grant # R83236201. Authors thank the members of the CAMRA community, particularly users who answered our survey. The usability testing of the search is being conducted under IRB protocol #16449. Authors also acknowledge use of a dataset from the UCI repository.

References

[1] Kolodner, J.: Case-Based Reasoning. Morgan Kaufmann, San Francisco (1993)
[2] Richter, M.M.: The Knowledge Contained in Similarity Measures. In: Keynote at the 1st International Conference on Case-Based Reasoning, Sesimbra, Portugal (1995)
[3] Weber, R., Kaplan, R.: Knowledge-Based Knowledge Management. In: Jain, R., Abraham, A., Faucher, C., van der Zwaag, B.J. (eds.) Innovations in Knowledge Engineering, vol. 4, pp. 151–172. Advanced Knowledge International Pty Ltd., Adelaide (2003)
[4] Althoff, K.-D., Weber, R.O.: Knowledge Management in Case-Based Reasoning. Knowledge Engineering Review 20(3), 305–310 (2005)
[5] Weber, R., Aha, D.W.: Intelligent Delivery of Military Lessons Learned. Decision Support Systems 34(3), 287–304 (2003)

[6] Leake, D.B., Sooriamurthi, R.: Automatically Selecting Strategies for Multi-Case-Base Reasoning. In: Craw, S., Preece, A.D. (eds.) ECCBR 2002. LNCS (LNAI), vol. 2416, pp. 204–218. Springer, Heidelberg (2002)

[7] Bergmann, R., Vollrath, I.: Generalized Cases: Representation and Steps Towards Efficient Similarity Assessment. In: Burgard, W., Christaller, T., Cremers, A.B. (eds.) KI 1999. LNCS (LNAI), vol. 1701, pp. 195–206. Springer, Heidelberg (1999)

[8] Leake, D., Wilson, D.: When Experience is Wrong: Examining CBR for Changing Tasks and Environments. In: Althoff, K.-D., Bergmann, R., Branting, L.K. (eds.) ICCBR 1999. LNCS (LNAI), vol. 1650, pp. 218–232. Springer, Heidelberg (1999)

[9] Aha, D.: Feature weighting for lazy learning algorithms. In: Liu, H., Motoda, H. (eds.) Feature Extraction, Construction and Selection: A Data Mining Perspective, pp. 13–32. Kluwer, Norwell (1998)

[10] Spink, A., Wolfram, D., Jansen, M., Saracevic, T.: Searching the web: The public and their queries. Journal of the American Society for Information Science and Technology 52, 226–234 (2001)

[11] Boydell, O., Smyth, B.: Enhancing Case-Based, Collaborative Web Search. In: Weber, R.O., Richter, M.M. (eds.) ICCBR 2007. LNCS (LNAI), vol. 4626, pp. 329–343. Springer, Heidelberg (2007)

[12] Sanders, K.E., Kettler, B.P., Hendler, J.A.: The case for graph-structured representations. In: Leake, D.B., Plaza, E. (eds.) ICCBR 1997. LNCS, vol. 1266, pp. 245–254. Springer, Heidelberg (1997)

[13] McSherry, D.: Interactive Case-Based Reasoning in Sequential Diagnosis. Applied Intelligence 14, 65–76 (2001)

[14] Bogaerts, S., Leake, D.: Facilitating CBR for Incompletely-Described Cases: Distance Metrics for Partial Problem Descriptions. In: Funk, P., González Calero, P.A. (eds.) ECCBR 2004. LNCS (LNAI), vol. 3155, pp. 62–76. Springer, Heidelberg (2004)

[15] McSherry, D.: A Generalised Approach to Similarity-Based Retrieval in Recommender Systems. Artificial Intelligence Review 18, 309–341 (2002)

[16] Auriol, E., Manago, M., Althoff, K.-D., Wess, S., Dittrich, S.: Integrating induction and case-based reasoning: Methodological approach and first evaluation. In: Haton, J.-P., Manago, M., Keane, M.A. (eds.) EWCBR 1994. LNCS, vol. 984, pp. 18–32. Springer, Heidelberg (1995)

[17] McSherry, D.: Precision and Recall in Interactive Case-Based Reasoning. In: Aha, D.W., Watson, I. (eds.) ICCBR 2001. LNCS (LNAI), vol. 2080, pp. 392–406. Springer, Heidelberg (2001)

[18] Wilcoxon, F.: Individual comparisons by ranking methods. Biometrics 1, 80–83 (1945)

[19] Fawcett, T.: ROC graphs: Notes and practical considerations for researchers. Tech Report HPL-2003-4, HP Laboratories (2003)

Supporting Fraud Analysis in Mobile* Telecommunications Using Case-Based Reasoning

Pedro Almeida[1], Marco Jorge[1], Luís Cortesão[2], Filipe Martins[3], Marco Vieira[1], and Paulo Gomes[1]

[1] CISUC, Department of Informatics Engineering, FCTUC, University of Coimbra, Coimbra, Portugal
[2] PT Inovação SA, Aveiro, Portugal
[3] Telbit SA, Aveiro, Portugal

Abstract. Fraud in mobile telecommunications is a complex and dynamic problem for Telecom operators. These companies have developed and are exploring new ways of making the fraud detection process more efficient. Most of these attempts are based in fraud management systems, capable of detecting fraudulent communications. In this paper, we present a case-based reasoning system that aids fraud analysts in the classification of potential fraud cases. The system developed, presents to the analyst the most similar past cases, representing suspicious communication episodes that were previously investigated. We also describe an example of how the system is used.

Keywords: case-based reasoning, telecommunication fraud, fraud detection.

1 Introduction

Mobile telecommunications is a very important business with a broad and large customer base. It has become a disputed market with many operators, each one struggling for its market share. For an operator to increase its profit, it is now more effective to reduce costs and losses, than trying to increase the market share. The telecommunications business is a typical target of multiple fraud actions, estimated to affect 3% to 6% of an operator's gross revenue [1]. Fraud Management Systems (FMS) are essential for mobile operators to keep fraud occurrences under control, commonly through a collection of detectors (configured as rules determined by the system administrator) that search the communication space for abnormalities. When an abnormality is found, an alarm is raised and a fraud analyst is assigned to investigate the case and decide if it is indeed fraud or not. However, due to the large customer base and fraud universe, this approach is becoming impractical and a more automated process is needed.

Because the telecomm business is heavily based on computers, there is a huge amount of collected information. This information can be used, in conjunction with machine learning techniques [2], to aid the fraud analysis process.

---

* This work was supported by PT Inovação SA, under program IDEIAS 2007.

K.-D. Althoff et al. (Eds.): ECCBR 2008, LNAI 5239, pp. 562–572, 2008.

In this work, a case-based reasoning (CBR) [3, 4] approach is used to aid in this process. CBR allows for a new, unseen case, to be matched, with a certain similarity, to another case already stored in the case base. The search for similar cases is a powerful tool that can help the analyst, as it aids her/him to infer the fraud status of a given case using as basis relevant information gathered from other cases. This means that, when an analyst is investigating a case, s/he can use the overall system memory to easily and accurately classify the current working case. The main goal of this work is to devise a system that helps the fraud analyst to take faster and more accurate decisions and that is fully integrated in the existing FMS, we named it ECA3RL.

Wheeler and Aitken [6] propose a system within a CBR methodological structure for reducing the number of final-line fraud investigations in the credit approval process. The use of a weighting matrix in contrast to a flat weighting structure for use in case matching is investigated, but due to the already filtered data that they had at there disposal no significant improvement was found. For the retrieval phase they propose an algorithm based on the k nearest-neighbour, but despite the retrieval of a constant number (k) of cases they propose a threshold for the retrieval that only retrieves cases from a specified neighbourhood, with the possibility of a dynamic modification of the threshold. The rest of the paper deals with CBR diagnosis for the analysis of the significance of the cases retrieved. So, a series of algorithms are proposed and tested based on their efficiency. Their final conclusion is that a multi-algorithmic approach to diagnosis proves to be more efficient in the classification of large and noisy data sets.

Other works in the area of fraud detection in mobile telecommunications are based on Data Mining approaches. Burge and colleagues [1] explore fraud detection based on absolute and differential analysis. Absolute analysis, similar to a general fraud profile, uses a set of fixed trigger systems, that if activated, raise an alert status which cumulatively would lead to an investigation. This approach is very effective detecting extreme fraud cases but weak when the fraud does not stand out of the general usage. Differential analysis, similar to user profiles, uses behavioural patterns associated with the mobile telephone comparing its most recent activities with a history of its usage. Triggers can then be determined for each specific client to detect significant usage pattern deviation over a small period of time. Nearly all fraud cases demonstrate a behaviour pattern change over a small period of time. This last approach is specially precise because a behaviour can be considered anomalous for one user but regular for another. For example, thirty high rate international calls can be considered a fraud for an old granny living with her family (who never makes such calls) but a regular day for an international businessman (who regularly makes such calls). With this approach it is possible to determine flexible criteria that allows the detection of subtle frauds only detectable at the customer level.

Weiss [7] focuses the data types when using data mining for fraud detection in mobile telecommunications. There are three main data types: call detail data - every time a call is placed on a telecommunications network, descriptive information about the call is saved as a CDR (call data record); network data - network related data describes the network's software and hardware status; customer data - includes all customer related data. The most important data type for fraud detection is call detail data. CDRs are not used directly for data mining, they represent the individual call level while frauds occur ate the customer level. To transform them, CDRs associated with a customer must be summarised into a record that describes the customer behaviour. The choice of summary features is critical in order to obtain a useful description of the user.

Rosset and colleagues [8] investigate and approach using rules and a modified C4.5 algorithm. The authors stress that call details alone are not enough to establish fraud cases (call details are used to determine a general fraud profile or absolute analysis, described by [1]) and that a user profile or differential analysis like approach is much more effective. In this phase it is important to recognise individual rule's characteristics like: high accuracy in cases - most cases found are really fraud; high coverage of true fraud cases - most fraudulent cases are found; high coverage of true fraud alerts - fraud cases are detected quickly.

The next section provides an introduction to the theme of fraud in mobile telecommunications. Then we discuss the ECA3RL system by presenting its various modules. We also show a typical example of use of the system. This paper then finishes with related work and some final remarks.

2 Fraud in Mobile Telecommunications

Fraud in mobile telecommunications can be classified under the 3M's classification [5]:

- **Motive** - its fundamental objective;
- **Means** - its nature or form;
- **Method** - its overall technique.

From the motive standpoint, fraud is classified by its fundamental objective:

- **Non-revenue fraud** - occurs when a service is used without intent to cover the costs and without intent to profit. It includes providing no-cost services to friends or private usage;
- **Revenue fraud** - occurs when a service is used without intent to cover the costs but with intent to profit or gain financial benefits. It includes call selling or PRS fraud (premium rate service) described below.

From the means point of view, fraud can be classified by the nature or form used to commit it:

- **Call selling** - consists of selling high rate calls, usually international calls, below their market price, without intention to support their real cost;
- **PRS fraud** - consists of placing premium rate service calls to inflate the revenue of that service provider without intention to support the calls real cost;
- **Surfing** - usage of a third person's account without their consent, for example, through card cloning;
- **Ghosting** - refers to obtaining free or cheap rate calls through technical means of deceiving the network, for example, by manipulating the database contents;
- **Sensitive information disclosure** - involves obtaining valuable information (e.g. VIP client details or access codes) and profiting from it. This fraud is usually performed internally to the telecom operator;
- **Content stealing** - consists of obtaining valuable contents (e.g. games, videos, ringtones) for free, by exploiting the non real-time pre-paid billing system (hot-billing) or by avoiding payment of the invoice (post-paid services).

When considering the method, fraud can be classified as:

- **Subscription** - occurs through subscription of services with false credentials that allow debt accumulation by systematic payment avoidance;
- **Technical** - consists of exploiting loopholes found in the operator's platforms;
- **Internal** - when employees of the operator exploit the system for personal gain;
- **Point of sale** - occurs when the dealer manipulates sales figures to increase the compensations paid by the operator.

3 The ECA3RL System

This section describes the system developed and integrated into the FMS used by the telecommunications operator. The main objective of this system is to aid the fraud analyst in the classification process of a potential fraud case. ECA3RL aids the analyst using a Case-Based Reasoning approach, which presents her/him with similar fraud cases to the situation being analyzed.

Next, we present how the proposed approach, regarding the various CBR phases: case representation, indexing, retrieval, ranking, weight learning, and case base maintenance.

3.1 Case Representation

The FMS stores information about analyzed situations. These are cases created by analysts while they perform their job and analyse alarms triggered by the FMS fraud detectors when they encounter abnormalities on a client's account, card or call behaviour. Fraud analysts have to decide if the situation is indeed a potential fraud or not.

For the case representation in our system, we had to identify the various attributes that were located across the FMS. The data used in ECA3RL is mainly demographic, behavioural and financial data. This data is related to two entities:

- **Alerts** – generated when a threshold or detector is triggered by a suspicious event. It comprises features like: the creation date, the process used to identify the alert, the total amount of the call records that originated the alert, the card age, etc.;
- **FMS Cases** – the result of the evaluation of a set of alerts by the fraud analyst. It comprises features like: the creation date, the associated alarms, the detection process, the fraud type, behaviour profile, postal code, amount payed, amount unplaced, and other relevant features.

After the identification of the various attributes, we created the case representation that comprises two parts: a problem description and a solution description. The problem description comprises several types of features:

- **Client's information** – fiscal code, postal code, nationality, etc.
- **Behaviour information** – consumption profile, payment behaviour, etc.
- **Case information** – creation date, the way it was detected, the context that tells if the case relates to a card number or an account number, etc.

- **Related cases** – past cases which are related to this one.
- **Related cards** – cards which are in some way related to this case.
- **Communication Records** (EDRs) – the communication events that originated this case.
- **Alerts** – the alerts that originated this case. These are detected by detection rules, and comprise specific attributes.

The solution description comprises information describing if the case is a fraud situation or not, what was the motivation in case of fraud, the used method, the fraud type and if the case is closed or not.

A Case has a unique identifier represented by the attribute Id Case, which links to the FMS specific situation data. Then, the Problem description represents the various attributes and helps to define the Case description, and linked to that, we have the alert or alerts that originated the case. Finally, associated with the Case, there is the Solution description that defines the classification of the case, that is, if it is a fraud case or not, and other important information.

There is a second type of cases in the system, which are cases representing alerts. These cases are extracted directly from the previous representation and correspond to the Alert representation node. These cases represent specific suspicious events that can be used to be shown to the analyst as an aid. They can show if a specific type of alert is associated with fraud cases or not.

3.2 Case Indexing

For obtaining good performance by the system during the retrieval phase, some attributes were used as indexes for the cases. Domain experts have identified eight attributes that are used as indexes, like the context type (if it is a card or an account), the client's profile and others. These attributes are used as indexes, by creating index structures for each attribute in the database where the classes are stored.

3.3 Case Retrieval

The case retrieval is performed by querying the database. The system then builds a list of cases that are similar to the target case. For the retrieval of the similar cases, we use the following algorithm:

```
RetrievedCases ← ∅
FORALL Attributes DO
   Cases ← Get cases with equal Attribute/Value
   RetrievedCases ← RetrievedCases ∪ Cases
   If(#RetrievedCases == 50)
     break
ENDFORALL
RETURN RetrievedCases
```

The system searches the database for cases matching the attributes chosen for indexes. This insures that the cases retrieved will be the ones that are most relevant because of the importance of the indexed attributes, and performance is made efficient.

3.4 Case Ranking

After the retrieval, the system ranks the cases in descending order by the similarity to the target case. Case similarity is computed using a weighted sum of the attributes similarity (see formula 1).

$$CaseSim(C1, C2) = \sum_{i=1}^{n} \frac{wi \times AtrSim(A(i, C1), A(i, C2))}{n} \cdot \tag{1}$$

Where:

- $C1$ is the target case;
- $C2$ is the retrieved case;
- n is the number of attributes being compared;
- i is the index of an attribute of the case;
- wi is the weight associated with attribute i;
- $CaseSim$ is the similarity metric function between two cases, returning a value in the interval $[0,1]$;
- $AtrSim$ is the similarity metric function between two attributes, returning a value in the interval $[0,1]$;
- A returns the value of the attribute I of the Case C
- Σwi is 1.

The initial weights associated with the attributes, were compiled by asking the analysts about the importance of certain attributes in the classification process. We developed a learning process for adjusting the weights (see section 3.5).

For the $AtrSim$ function different formulas are used depending on the type of attribute. We use logarithmic metrics, similarity matrixes and, in some cases, a simple condition, that when the values are equal, $AtrSim$ returns 1 and in all other cases 0. This metrics were defined in accordance with the domain experts. An example of a logarithmic metric applied to the attribute creation date is:

$$\begin{cases} 1 - \dfrac{\log_3 (|CD1 - CD2| + 1)}{3.5} \Leftarrow 1 - \dfrac{\log_3 (|CD1 - CD2| + 1)}{3.5} > 0 \\ 0 \Leftarrow Otherwise \end{cases} \tag{2}$$

Where CD1 and CD2 are, respectively, the creation date in the target case and in the retrieved case. Other attribute similarity metrics are used, such as, similarity matrixes, Boolean similarities and others, depending on the type of attribute.

3.4.1 Null Attribute Values

One of the most challenging aspects of this work, was the quality of the data that we had at our disposal, as there was a lot of missing values in some of the attributes that defined a Case.

One of the main problems of this lack of data is when the target case has missing values, as it will lead to wrong results during the ranking of the cases. This way, to try to solve this issue, we decided that a *null* value is like an undetermined value. Table 1 presents the action that takes place at the ranking algorithm on the different missing values situations.

In the first row, the rationale is that the similarity metric should ignore this attribute and distribute the weight associated with it among all the other attributes (which are not null). This distribution is performed proportionally to the weights of the other attributes. So if the weight configuration is: attr1 – 20%; attr2 – 40% and attr3 – 40%, and if attr2 is null, then the new weight configuration will be: attr1 – 40%; attr2 – 0% and attr3 – 60%. The same situation happens in the second row, where the reference case is null, and the similarity metric will ignore it.

Row three represents a situation where there is no value for the similar case attribute, so the similarity value should be zero, giving more importance to the reference case attribute. Row four represents a normal situation, where both values exist.

Table 1. Ranking algorithm actions when confronted with missing values

Reference Case	Similar Case	Action
null value on attribute	*null* value on attribute	Proportional distribution of the attribute's weight
null value on attribute	Attribute value different from *null*	Proportional distribution of the attribute's weight
Attribute value different from *null*	*null* value on attribute	*AtrSim* returns 0
Attribute value different from *null*	Attribute value different from *null*	*AtrSim* is calculated normally

3.4.2 Case Presentation

As previous discussed, the system developed in this project had to be integrated into an existing FMS. One important requirement was to present the similar cases information to the analyst in a very simplified way, so that s/he could easily understand the similarities between the target case and the retrieved cases.

So, to clearly show the total similarity value of a case in relation to the target case, colors were used on the cells that display the different values of the attributes of the similar cases. The color should be shown depending of the value returned by *AtrSim* for that attribute.

For *AtrSim* equal to 0, we use red and for a value equal to 1 we use green, values in between have a color that will be close to red or green depending of its proximity. In figure 1 we show a screenshot of the system case retrieval presentation. The alert retrieval is similar to this process.

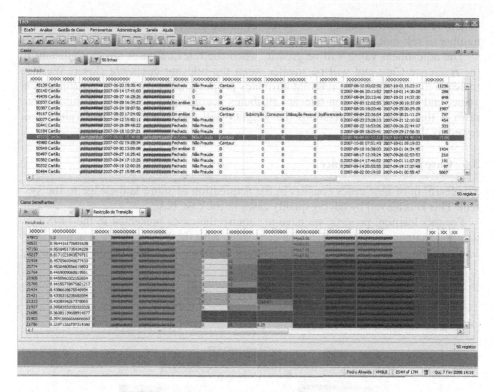

Fig. 1. Similar Cases screenshot. Data masked due to confidentiality issues.

3.5 Weights Readjustment Mechanism

One of the most critical aspects for the suggestion of relevant similar cases is the weights that are associated with each attribute. We decided to implement a mechanism to automatically change the weights based on actions done by the analyst during the operation of the system.

When a list of similar cases is presented to the analyst, we store the cases that were inspected by him, as the premise that these are the cases that helped him during the analysis.

After this, the relevant cases are collected, and a readjustment to the weights is processed. The process used is as follows: for all the relevant cases, we find the attributes that contributed more to the total similarity value, that is, the attributes whose *AtrSim* returned a value greater then zero. Next we list the common relevant attributes from all relevant cases and then compute the adjustment value (Δ) using the following formulas:

$$\Delta = \Omega * \Theta . \tag{3}$$

$$\Omega = \frac{\sum (1 - CaseSim(C0, Cx))}{n} . \tag{4}$$

Where Θ is a growth constant, $C0$ is the reference case, Cx a relevant case, and n the number of relevant cases.

The adjustment value will be greater, when the relevant cases are more distant to the reference Case and will be smaller when the relevant cases are closer. We also increase the weight of the relevant attributes proportionally by adding an adjustment value, and decrease the non-relevant attributes accordingly. The goal of this mechanism is that after some iterations the weights will converge to optimal values preferred by the analysts.

3.6   Case Base Maintenance

The learning of new cases consists in the acquisition of more knowledge to the system. This is achieved by having quality cases in the case base.

For this learning process, we have to acquire the cases presented in the FMS system and maintain our cases database consistent with the FMS. This was achieved by implementing our own database, which stores the cases. The way we do it is by using

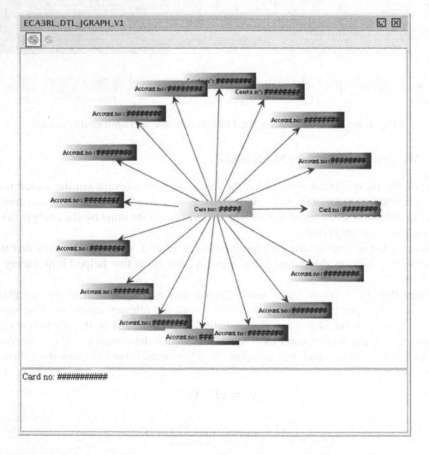

Fig. 2. Context navigation screenshot. Numbers masked due to confidentiality issues.

materialized views of the tables that represent a FMS case. Basically a materialized view is a database engine mechanism that caches a query to the database in the form of a table. This way the query that we use, that fetches data from several places of the FMS is stored in a table and updated from time to time. Then, we only have to refresh our materialized views so that the system will be consistent and updated. Future work includes improving this phase of the process.

3.7 Context Graph Navigation

The last module implemented in ECA3RL was a navigation system between related contexts (see figure 2). This module is not related to CBR but also aids the analyst in determining the classification of a case because it allows him to explore direct relations between different cases by cards and/or accounts.

This means that an analyst can go from a newly classified fraud case to another case with the same account number and to the next with the same phone number and infer if the new case is fraudulent because of the relationship between those fraudulent cases. The information about the cases relations is already presented in the FMS, so we only have to query that information and present it in a graph view to the analyst.

4 Example of Use

The fraud analyst uses her/his past experience to investigate current cases. The problem is when some types of cases have not been investigated by this analyst or when time fades away memories. This means that the analyst has to redo the work previously done.

The context navigation feature (see figure 2) provides navigation between directly linked cases, cards and accounts. This way, the analyst can navigate between related contexts and try to infer, from that relation, the solution of the current case. This means that the analyst does not have to remember/know, for example, that account A has five cards A1, A2, A3, A4 and A5 and that card A5 is related to a fraud case from another account B.

As the context navigation, the similar cases functionality (see figure 1) supports the decision of the analyst by providing related incidents. The cases presented by this functionality are not directly linked to the one in study but are the result of a comparison between that one and the rest. For the analyst to understand that similarity, the system provides the colours seen in the figure. To express differences the system uses the colour red, while to express similarity uses green. With this colour scheme, the analyst can easily verify the similarity between the cases on the given attributes and, if those attributes are significant enough, use the given data to classify the new case.

5 Conclusions

Telecommunications fraud is very dynamic and is becoming very complex to analyze, so it is important to create reliable automatic processes that enhance as much as possible the analyst perception of the fraudulent activity and aid in the decision making. The quality of the data is very critical to this type of study, and even though some algorithms could sustain some missing values, we concluded that some mechanisms should be implemented by the FMS to force the analyst to fully introduce the information related to fraud into the system.

During the project some lessons were learned, namely that the human factor is decisive in making such a project a success. ECA3RL was no exception, one important requirement was for the system to be able to justify case similarity, in a easy and intuitive way. This would be very important for the analysts, because they want to be sure of the decisions that they take. The similarity colouring mechanism is a simple one, but a decisive one for the success of the system. Another aspect related to this, is that the system should provide help, it should not take decision making away from the analysts.

Comparing our approach with the standard Data Mining approach, this is a new way of helping the fraud detection processing, taking into account the human factor, which is not taken by the Data Mining approach, and by making the detection process more efficient. Though we think that both approaches are complementary and can make fraud detection more effective.

The system is going to be adapted and integrated in the operational version of the FMS and will be tested in the real world. Future work with ECA3RL includes getting feedback from the system usage, and analyzing it. This is specially important for the weight learning algorithm, in order to define it's accuracy and learning characteristics. Other issue that can be further explored is the case base maintenance policy, which can and must be improved. With the use of the system, the case base will grow, reaching dimensions that can hinder the system performance.

References

1. Burge, P., Shawe-Taylos, J., Cooke, C., Moreau, Y., Preneel, B., Stoermann, C.: Fraud detection and management in mobile telecommunications networks. In: ECSD (1997)
2. Mitchell, T.M.: Machine Learning. McGraw-Hill, New York (1997)
3. Aamodt, A., Plaza, E.: Case–based reasoning: Foundational issues, methodological variations, and system approaches. AI Communications 7(1), 39–59 (1994)
4. Kolodner, J.: Case-Based Reasoning. Morgan Kaufman, San Francisco (1993)
5. Cortesão, L., Martins, F., Rosa, A., Carvalho, P.: Fraud management systems in telecommunications: a practical approach. In: ICT (2005)
6. Wheeler, R., Aitken, S.: Multiple Algorithms for Fraud Detection. Knowl.-Based Syst. 13(2-3), 93–99 (2000)
7. Weiss, G.: Data mining in telecommunications (2005)
8. Rosset, S., Murad, U., Neumann, E., Idan, Y., Pinkas, G.: Discovery of fraud rules for telecommunications challenges and solutions. In: ACM SIGKDD (1999)

Predicting the Presence of Oil Slicks After an Oil Spill

Juan Manuel Corchado and Aitor Mata

Department of Computing Science and Automatic, University of Salamanca,
Plaza de la Merced, s/n, Salamanca, Spain
corchado@usal.es, aitor@usal.es

Abstract. A new predicting system is presented in which the aim is to forecast the presence or not of oil slicks in a certain area of the open sea after an oil spill. In this case, the CBR methodology has been chosen to solve the problem. The system designed to predict the presence of oil slicks wraps other artificial intelligence techniques such as a Growing Radial Basis Function Networks, Growing Cell Structures and Fast Iterative Kernel Principal Components Analysis in order to develop the different phases of the CBR cycle. The proposed system uses information such as sea salinity, sea temperature, wind, currents, pressure, number and area of the slicks.... obtained from various satellites. The system has been trained using data obtained after the Prestige accident. Oil Spill CBR system (OSCBR) has been able to accurately predict the presence of oil slicks in the north west of the Galician coast, using historical data.

Keywords: Oil spill, Growing Cell Structures, Radial Basis Function, PCA.

1 Introduction

Predicting the behaviour of oceanic elements is a quite difficult task. In this case the prediction is related with external elements (oil slicks), and this makes the prediction even more difficult. Open ocean is a highly complex system that may be modelled by measuring different variables and structuring them together. Some of those variables are essential to predict the behaviour of oil slicks. In order to predict the future presence of oil slicks in an area, it is obviously necessary to know their previous positions. That knowledge is provided by the analysis of satellite images, obtaining the precise position of the slicks.

The solution proposed in this paper generates, for different geographical areas, a probability (between 0 and 1) of finding oil slicks after an oil spill. The proposed system has been constructed using historical data and checked using the data acquired during the Prestige oil spill, from November 2002 to April 2003. Most of the data used to develop the proposed system has been acquired from the ECCO (Estimating the Circulation *and Climate of the Ocean*) consortium [1]. Position and size of the slicks has been obtained by treating SAR (*Synthetic Aperture Radar*) satellite images[2].

The proposed system is a forecasting Case-Based Reasoning system: the Oil Spill CBR (*OSCBR*). A CBR system has the ability to learn from past situations, and to

K.-D. Althoff et al. (Eds.): ECCBR 2008, LNAI 5239, pp. 573–586, 2008.
© Springer-Verlag Berlin Heidelberg 2008

generate solutions to new problems based in the past solutions given to past problems. Past solutions are stored in the system, in the *case base*. In OSCBR the cases contain information about the oil slicks (size and number) as long as atmospheric data (wind, current, salinity, temperature, ocean height and pressure). OSCBR combines the efficiency of the CBR systems with artificial intelligence techniques in order to improve the results and to better generalize from past data.

The results obtained with OSCBR approximate to the real process occurred in near the ninety per cent of the value of the main variables analyzed, which is a quite important approximation.

In this paper, the oil spill problem is first presented, showing its difficulties and the possibilities of finding solutions to the problem. Then, OSCBR is explained, giving special attention to the techniques applied in the different phases of the CBR cycle. Last, the results are shown and also the future developments that can be achieved with the system.

2 Oil Spill Problem

After an oil spill, it is necessary to determine if an area is going to be contaminated or not. To conclude about the presence or not of contamination in an area it is necessary to know how the slicks generated by the spill behave. The most data available; the best solution can be given.

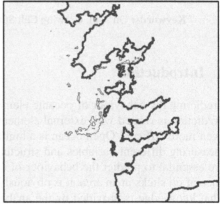

Fig. 1. On the left side, a SAR image is shown. On the right side the interpretation of the left satellite image done by OSCBR.

First, position, shape and size of the oil slicks must be identified. The most precise way to acquire that information is by using satellite images. SAR images are the most commonly used to automatically detect this kind of slicks [3]. The satellite images show certain areas where it seems to be nothing, like zone with no waves; that are the oil slicks. In *figure 1* a SAR image is shown on the left side. There, a portion of the western Galician coast is shown, as long as some black areas, corresponding to the oil slicks. The image on the right side of *figure 1* shows the interpretation of the previous image after treating the data generated by the SAR image. With SAR images it is possible to distinguish between normal sea variability and slicks. It is also important to make a distinction between oil slicks and look-alikes. Oil slicks are quite similar to quiet sea areas, so it is not always easy to discriminate between them. If there is not enough wind, the difference between the calmed sea and the surface of a slick is less evident and so, there may be more mistakes when trying to differentiate between an oil slick and something that it is not a slick. This is a crucial aspect in this problem that can also be automatically done by a series of computational tools.

Once the slicks are identified, it is also crucial to know the atmospheric and maritime situation that is affecting the slick in the moment that is being analysed. Information collected from satellites is used to obtain the atmospheric data needed. That is how different variables such as temperature, sea height and salinity are measured in order to obtain a global model [4] that can explain how slicks evolve.

2.1 Previous Solutions Given to the Oil Spill Problem

There have been different ways to analyze, evaluate and predict situations after an oil spill. One approach is the simulation [5], where a model of a certain area is created, introducing specific parameters (weather, currents and wind) and working along with a forecasting system. Using this methodology, it is easy to obtain a good solution for a certain area, but it is quite difficult to generalize in order to solve the same problem in new zones.

Another way to obtain a trajectory model is to replace the oil spill by drifters [6] comparing the trajectory followed by the drifters with the already known oil slicks trajectories. If the drifters follow a similar trajectory as the one that followed the slicks, then a model can be created and there will be a possibility of creating more models in different areas. Another way of predicting oil slicks trajectories is to study previous cases to obtain a trajectory model for a certain area with different weather situations [7]. Another trajectory model is the created to accomplish the NOAA standards [8], where both the 'best guess' and the 'minimum regret' solutions are generated.

2.2 Models

One step over those solutions previously explained are the systems that, combining a major set of elements, generate response models to solve the oil spill problem.

A different of view is given by complex systems [9] that analyze large data bases (environmental, ecological, geographical and engineering), using expert systems. This way, an implicit relation between problem and solution is obtained, but with no direct connection between past examples and current decisions. Nevertheless arriving at these kind of solutions requires a great deal of data mining effort.

Once the oil spill is produced there should be contingency models that make a fast solution possible [10]. Expert systems has also been used, using the stored information from past cases, as a repository where future applications will find structured information. Some other complete models have been created, to integrate the different variables affecting the spills [11], always trying to get better benefits than the possible costs generated by all the infrastructure needed to response to a problematic generated situation

The final objective of all these systems is to be decision support systems, in order to help to take all the decisions that need to be taken properly organized. To achieve that great objective, different techniques have been used, from fuzzy logic [12] to negotiation with multi-agent systems [13].

3   Oil Spill CBR System – OSCBR

Case-Based reasoning is a methodology [14], and so it has been applied to solve different kind of problems, from health applications [15; 16] to eLearning [17] [18]. CBR has also evolved, being transformed so that it can be used to solve new problems, becoming a methodology to plan [19], or distributed version [20].

Table 1. Variables that define a case

Variable	Definition	Unit
Longitude	Geographical longitude	Degree
Latitude	Geographical latitude	Degree
Date	Day, month and year of the analysis	dd/mm/yyyy
Sea Height	Height of the waves in open sea	m
Bottom pressure	Atmospheric pressure in the open sea	Newton/m^2
Salinity	Sea salinity	ppt (parts per thousand)
Temperature	Celsius temperature in the area	°C
Area of the slicks	Surface covered by the slicks present in the analyzed area	Km^2
MeridionalWind	Meridional direction of the wind	m/s
Zonal Wind	Zonal direction of the wind	m/s
Wind Strenght	Wind strength	m/s
Meridional Current	Meridional direction of the ocean current	m/s
Zonal Current	Zonal direction of the ocean current	m/s
Current Strenght	Ocean current strength	m/s

CBR has already been used to solve maritime problems [21] in which different oceanic variables were involved. In this case, the data collected from different observations from satellites, is pre-processed, and structured in cases. The created cases are the keys to obtain the solutions to future problems, through the CBR system. Oil slicks are detected using SAR images. Those images are processed and transformed to be used by the system.

Figure 2 shows the graphical user interface of the developed system. In that image the different components of the application can be seen (maps, prediction, slicks, studies…) as well as a visualization of an oceanic area with oil slicks and a squared area to be analyzed.

OSCBR determines the probability of finding oil slicks in a certain area. To generate the predictions, the system divides the area to be analyzed in squares of approximately half a degree side. Then the system determines the amount of slicks present in a square. The squares where the slicks are located are coloured with different gradation depending on the quantity of the squared area covered by oil slicks.

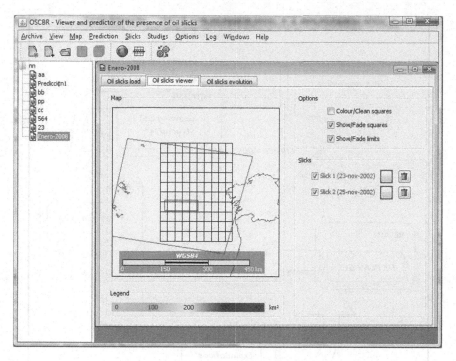

Fig. 2. Graphical user interface of the OSCBR system. The different components of the system can be observed here.

The squared zone determines the area that is going to be analyzed independently. The values of the different variables in a square area in a certain moment as long as the value of the possibility of finding oil slicks in the following day is what is called *a case*, which define the problem and propose the solution.

In *table 1* the structure of a case is shown. The variables present in a case can be geographical (longitude and latitude), temporal (date of the case), atmospheric (wind, current, sea height, bottom pressure, salinity and temperature) and variables directly related with the problem (number and area of the slicks).

Once the data is structured, it is stored in the *case base*. Every case has its temporal situation stored and that relates every case with the next situation in the same position. That temporal relationship is what creates the union between *problem* and *solution*. The problem is the past case, and the solution is the future case, the future state of the square analyzed.

The data used to train the system has been obtained after the Prestige accident, between November 2002 and April 2003, in a specific geographical area to the north west of the Galician coast (longitude between 14 and 6 degrees west and latitude between 42 and 46 degrees north). When all that information is stored in the case base, the system is ready to predict future situations. To generate a prediction, a problem situation must be introduced in the system. Then the most similar cases to the problematic situation are retrieved from the case base. Once a collection of cases are chosen from the case base, they must be used to generate the solution to the current

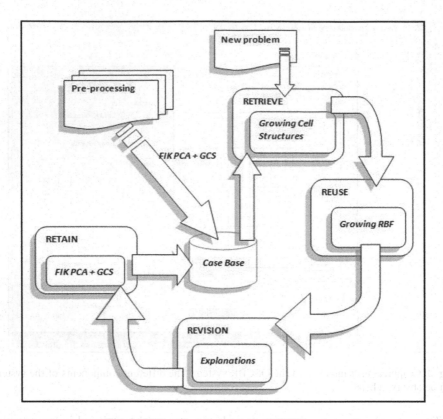

Fig. 3. CBR cycle adapted to the OSCBR system

problem. *Growing Radial Basis Functions Networks* [22] are used to combine the chosen cases in order to obtain the new solution.

OSCBR uses both the capabilities of a standard CBR system and the power of artificial intelligence techniques. As shown in *figure 3*, every CBR phase uses an artificial intelligence technique in order to obtain its solution. In *figure 3* the four main phases of the CBR cycle are shown as long as the AI techniques used in each phase. Those phases with its related techniques are explained next.

3.1 Pre-processing

Historical data collected from November 2002 to april 2003 is used to create the *case base*. As explained before, cases are formed by a series of variables. *Principal Components Analysis* (PCA) [23] can reduce the number of those variables and then, the system stores the value of the principal components, which are related with the original variables that define a case. PCA has been previously used to analyse oceanographic data and it has proved to be a consistent technique when trying to reduce the number of variables.

In this paper *Fast Iterative Kernel PCA*(FIKPCA), an evolution of PCA, has been used [24]. This technique reduces the number of variables in a set by eliminating those that are linearly dependent, and it is quite faster than the traditional PCA. To improve the convergence of the Kernel Hebbian Algorithm used by Kernel PCA, FIK-PCA set η_t proportional to the reciprocal of the estimated eigenvalues. Let $\lambda_t \in \Re^r_+$ denote the vector of eigenvalues associated with the current estimate of the first r eigenvectors. The new KHA algorithm sets de i^{th} component of η_t to the files.

$$[\eta_t]_i = \frac{1}{[\lambda_t]_i} \frac{\tau}{t+\tau} \eta_0 , \qquad (1)$$

The final variables are, obviously, linearly independent and are formed by combination of the previous variables. The values of the original variables can be recovered by doing the inverse calculation to the one produced to obtain the new variables. The variables that are less used in the final stored variables are those whose values suffer less changes during the periods of time analysed (salinity, temperature and pressure do not change from one day to another, then, they can be ignored considering that the final result does not depend on them).

Once applied the FIKPCA, the number of variables is reduced to three, having the following distribution:

```
Variable_1:   -0,560   *   long   -   0,923*lat   +   0,991*s_height   +
0,919*b_pressure      +      0,992*salinity      +      0,990*temp      -
0,125*area_of_slicks   +   0,80*mer_wind   +   0,79*zonal_wind   +
0,123*w_strenght   +   0,980*mer_current   +   0,980*zonal_current   +
0,980*c_strength

Variable_2:   0,292*long   -   0,081*lat   -   0,010*s_height   -
0,099*b_pressure      -      0,011*salinity      -      0,013*temp      -
0,021*area_of_slicks   +   0,993*merl_wind   +   0,993*zonal_wind   +
0,989*w_strenght   -   0,024*mer_current   -   0,024*zonal_current   -
0,024*c_strength

Variable_3:   0*long   -   0,072*lat   +   0,009*s_height   +
0,009*b_pressure      +      0,009*salinity      +      0,009*temp      +
0,992*area_of_slicks   +   0,006*mer_wind   +   0,005*zonal_wind   +
0,005*w_strenght   -   0,007*mer_current   -   0,007*zonal_current   -
0,007*c_strength
```

After applying FIKPCA, the historical data is stored in the case base, and is used to solve future problems using the rest of the CBR cycle. Storing the principal components instead of the original variables implies reducing the amount of memory necessary to store the information in about a sixty per cent which is more important as the case base grows. The reduction of the number of variables considered also implies a faster recovery from the case base.

When introducing the data into the case base, *Growing Cell Structures* [25] are used. GCS can create a model from a situation organizing the different cases by their similarity. If a 2D representation is chosen to explain this technique, the most similar cells (*cases* in OSCBR) are near one of the other. If there is a relationship between the cells, they are grouped together, and this grouping characteristic helps the CBR system to recover the similar cases in the next phase. When a new cell is introduced in the structure, the closest cells move towards the new one, changing the overall structure of the system. The weights of the winning cell, ω_c, and its neighbours, ω_n, are changed. The terms ε_c and ε_n represent the learning rates for the winner and its neighbours, respectively. x represents the value of the input vector.

$$\omega_c(t+1) = \omega_c(t) + \varepsilon_c(x - \omega_c) \tag{2}$$

$$\omega_n(t+1) = \omega_n(t) + \varepsilon_n(x - \omega_n) \tag{3}$$

The pseudocode of the GCS insertion process is shown below:

```
1. The most similar cell to the new one is found.
2. The new cell is introduced in the middle of the connection
   between the most similar cell and the least similar to the
   new one.
3. Direct neighbours of the closest cell change their values by
   approximating to the new cell and specified percentage of
   the distance between them and the new cell.
```

3.2 Retrieve

Once the case base has stored the historical data, and the GCS has learned from the original distribution of the variables, the system is ready to receive a new problem.

When a new problem comes to the system, GCS are used once again. The stored GCS behaves as if the new problem would be stored in the structure, and finds the most similar cells (cases in the CBR system) to the problem introduced in the system. In this case the GCS does not change its structure, because it is being used to obtain the most similar cases to the introduced problem. Only in the retain phase, the GCS changes again, introducing if it is correct, the proposed solution.

The similarity of the new problem to the stored cases is determined by the GCS calculating the distance between them. Every element in the GCS has a series of values (every value corresponds to one of the principal components created after de PCA analysis) and then the distance between elements is a multi-dimensional distance, where all the elements are considered to establish the distance between cells.

Then, after obtaining the most similar cases from the case base, they are used in the next phase. The most similar cases stored in the case base will be used to obtain an accurate prediction according to the previous solutions related with the selected cases.

3.3 Reuse

Once the most similar cases to the problem to be solved are recovered from the case base, they are used to generate the solution. The prediction of the future probability of finding oil slicks in an area is generated using an artificial neural network, with a hybrid learning system. An adaptation of Radial Basis Functions Networks are used to obtain that prediction [26]. The chosen cases are used to train the artificial neural network. Radial Basis Function networks have been chosen because of the reduction of the training time comparing with other artificial neural network systems, such as Multilayer Perceptrons. In this case, in every analysis the network is trained, using only the cases selected from the case base, the most similar to the proposed problem.

Growing RBF networks [27] are used to obtain the predicted future values corresponding to the proposed problem. This adaptation of the RBF networks allows the system to grow during training gradually increasing the number of elements (prototypes) which play the role of the centers of the radial basis functions. In this case the creation of the

Growing RBF must be made automatically, which implies an adaptation of the original GRBF system. The pseudocode of the growing process and the definition of the error for every pattern is shown below:

$$e_i = {}^1/_{p^*} \Sigma_{k=1}^p ||t_{ik} - y_{ik}||,$$ (4)

Where t_{ik} is the desired value of the kth output unit of the ith training pattern, y_{ik} the actual values ot the kth output unit of the ith training pattern.

Growing RBF pseudocode:

```
1. Calculate the error, eᵢ (4) for every new possible prototype.
      a. If the new candidate does not belong to the chosen
         ones and the error calculated is less than a threshold
         error, then the new candidate is added to the set of
         accepted prototypes.
      b. If the new candidate belongs to the accepted ones and
         the error is less than the threshold error, then mod-
         ify the weights of the neurons in order to adapt them
         to the new situation.
2. Select the best prototypes from the candidates
      a. If there are valid candidates, create a new cell cen-
         tered on it.
      b. Else, increase the iteration factor. If the iteration
         factor comes to the 10% of the training population,
         freeze the process.
3. Calculate global error and update the weights.
      a. If the results are satisfactory, end the process. If
         not, go back to step 1.
```

Once the GRBF network is created, it is used to generate the solution to the proposed problem. The solution will be the output of the network using as input data the selected cases from the case base.

3.4 Revise

After generating the prediction, it is shown to the user in a similar way the slicks are interpreted by OSCBR. A set of squared coloured areas appear. The intensity of the colour corresponds with the possibility of finding oil slicks in that area. The areas coloured with a higher intensity are those with the highest probability of finding oil slicks in them.

In this visual approximation, the user can check if the solution is a good one or not. The system also provides an automatic method of revision that must be, anyway, checked by an expert user, confirming the automatic revision.

Explanations are used to check the correction of the proposed solution, to justify the solution. To obtain a justification to the given solution, the cases selected from the case base are used once again. To create an *explanation*, a comparison between different possibilities has been used [28].All the selected cases has its own *future situation* associated. If we consider the case and its solution as two vectors, we can establish a *distance* between them, calculating the evolution of the situation in the considered conditions. If the distance between the proposed problem and the solution given is not greater than the distances obtained from the selected cases, then the solution is a good one, according to the structure of the case base.

Explanation pseudocode:

1. For every selected case in the retrieval phase, the distance between the case and its solution is calculated.
2. The distance between the proposed problem and the proposed solution is also calculated.
3. If the difference between the distance of the proposed solution and those of the selected cases is below a certain threshold value, then the solution is considered as a valid one.
4. If not, the user is informed and the process goes back to the retrieval phase, where new cases are selected from the case base.
5. If, after a series of iterations the system does not produce a good enough solution, then the user is asked to consider the acceptance of the best of the generated solutions.

The distances are calculated considering the sign of the values, not using its absolute value. This decision is easily justified by the fact that is not the same to move to the north than to the south, even if the distance between two points is the same. If the prediction is considered as correct it will be stored in the case base, and it can then be used in next predictions to obtain new solutions.

3.5 Retain

When the proposed prediction is accepted, it is considered as a good solution to the problem and can be stored in the case base in order to serve to solve new problems. It will have the same category as the historical data previously stored in the system.

When inserting a new case in the case base, *Fast Iterative Kernel PCA* is once used to reduce the number of variables used and to adapt the data generated by the system. The adaptation is done by changing the original variables into the principal components previously chosen by the system.

Obviously, when introducing a new case in the case base, the GCS formed by the information stored in the case base, also change, to adapt to the new situation generated. When adapting to the new solution introduced in the case base, the GCS system grows and improves its capability of generating good results as new knowledge is introduced in the system.

4   Results

The historical data used to train the system has been obtained from different satellites. Temperature, salinity, bottom pressure, sea height, wind, currents, number and area of the slicks, as long as the location of the squared area and the date have been used to create a case. All these data define the problem case and also the solution case. The solution to a problem defined by an area and its variables is the same area, but with the values of the variables changed to the prediction obtained from the CBR system.

When the OSCBR system has been used with a subset of the data that has not been previously used to train the system, it has produced encouraging results. The predicted situation was contrasted with the actual future situation. The future situation was known, as long as historical data was used to develop the system and also to test the correction of it. The proposed solution was, in most of the variables, close to 90% of accuracy.

Table 2. Percentage of good predictions obtained with different techniques

Number of cases	RBF	CBR	RBF + CBR	OSCBR
100	45 %	39 %	42 %	43 %
500	48 %	43 %	46 %	46 %
1000	51 %	47 %	58 %	64 %
2000	56 %	55 %	65 %	72 %
3000	59 %	58 %	68 %	81 %
4000	60 %	63 %	69 %	84 %
5000	63 %	64 %	72 %	87 %

For every problem, defined by an area and its variables, the system offers nine solutions: the same area, with its proposed variables and the eight closest neighbours. This way of prediction is used in order to clearly observe the direction of the slicks, what can be useful in order to determine the coastal areas that will be affected by the slicks generated after an oil spill.

In *table 2* a summary of the results obtained is shown. In this table different techniques are compared. The table shows the evolution of the results along with the increase of the number of cases stored in the case base. All the techniques analyzed improve its results when increasing the number of cases stored. Having more cases in the case base, makes easier to find similar cases to the proposed problem and then, the solution can be more accurate. The *"RBF"* column represents a simple Radial Basis Function Network that is trained with all the data available. The network gives an output that is considered a solution to the problem. The *"CBR"* column represents a pure CBR system, with no other techniques included, the cases are stored in the case bases and recovered considering the Euclidean distance. The most similar cases are selected and after applying a weighted mean depending on the similarity, a solution s proposed. The *"RBF + CBR"* column corresponds to the possibility of using a RBF system combined with CBR. The recovery from the CBR is done by the Manhattan distance and the RBF network works in the reuse phase, adapting the selected cases to obtain the new solution. The results of the *"RBF+CBR"* column are, normally, better than those of the *"CBR"*, mainly because of the elimination of useless data to generate the solution. Finally, the *"OSCBR"* column shows the results obtained by the proposed system , obtaining better results that the three previous analyzed solutions.

Table 3 shows a multiple comparison procedure (*Mann-Whitney* test) used to determine which models are significantly different from the others.

The asterisk indicates that these pairs show statistically significant differences at the 99.0% confidence level. It can be seen in *table 3*, that the OSCBR system presents statistically significant differences with the rest of the models.

The proposed solution does not generate a trajectory, but a series of probabilities in different areas, what is far more similar to the real behaviour of the oil slicks.

Once the prediction is generated and approved, it can be exported to various formats. First an html file can be generated with the images that represent the prediction, the solution to the problem. Other output formats are *"Google related"*: the solutions can be exported to *Google Earth* and to *Google Maps*.

Table 3. Multiple comparison procedure among different techniques

	RBF	CBR	RBF + CBR	OSCBR
RBF				
CBR	*			
RBF+CBR	=	=		
OSCBR	*	*	*	

5 Conclusions and Future Work

In this paper, the OSCBR system has been explained. It is a new solution for predicting the presence or not of oil slicks in a certain area after an oil spill.

This system used data acquired from different orbital satellites and with that data the CBR environment was created. The data must be previously classified into the structure required by the CBR system to store it as a case.

OSCBR uses different artificial intelligence techniques in order to obtain a correct prediction. *Fast Iterative Kernel Principal Component Analysis* is used to reduce the number of variables stored in the system, getting about a 60% of reduction in the size of the *case base*. This adaptation of the PCA also implies a faster recovery of cases from the case base (more than 7% faster than storing the original variables).

To obtain a prediction using the cases recovered from the case base, *Growing Radial Basis Function Networks* has been used. This evolution of the RBF networks implies a better adaptation to the structure of the case base, which is organised using *Growing Cell Structures*. The results using Growing RBF networks instead of simple RBF networks are about a 4% more accurate, which is a good improvement.

Evaluations show that the system can predict in the conditions already known, showing better results than previously used techniques. The use of a combination of techniques integrated in the CBR structure makes it possible to obtain better result than using the CBR alone (17% better), and also better than using the techniques isolated, without the integration feature produced by the CBR (11% better).

The next step is generalising the learning, acquiring new data to create a base of cases big enough to have solutions for every season. Another improvement is to create an on-line system that can store the case base in a server and generate the solutions dynamically to different requests. This on-line version will include real time connection to data servers providing weather information of the current situations in order to predict real future situations.

References

1. Menemenlis, D., Hill, C., Adcroft, A., Campin, J.M., et al.: NASA Supercomputer Improves Prospects for Ocean Climate Research. EOS Transactions 86(9), 89–95 (2005)
2. Palenzuela, J.M.T., Vilas, L.G., Cuadrado, M.S.: Use of ASAR images to study the evolution of the Prestige oil spill off the Galician coast. International Journal of Remote Sensing 27(10), 1931–1950 (2006)
3. Solberg, A.H.S., Storvik, G., Solberg, R., Volden, E.: Automatic detection of oil spills in ERS SAR images. IEEE Transactions on Geoscience and Remote Sensing 37(4), 1916–1924 (1999)
4. Stammer, D., Wunsch, C., Giering, R., Eckert, C., et al.: Volume, heat, and freshwater transports of the global ocean circulation 1993–2000, estimated from a general circulation model constrained by World Ocean Circulation Experiment (WOCE) data. Journal of Geophysical Research 108(10.1029) (2003)
5. Brovchenko, I., Kuschan, A., Maderich, V., Zheleznyak, M.: The modelling system for simulation of the oil spills in the Black Sea. In: 3rd EuroGOOS Conference: Building the European capacity in operational oceanography, p. 192 (2002)
6. Price, J.M., Ji, Z.G., Reed, M., Marshall, C.F., et al.: Evaluation of an oil spill trajectory model using satellite-tracked, oil-spill-simulating drifters. In: OCEANS 2003. Proceedings, p. 3 (2003)
7. Vethamony, P., Sudheesh, K., Babu, M.T., Jayakumar, S., et al.: Trajectory of an oil spill off Goa, eastern Arabian Sea: Field observations and simulations, Environmental Pollution (2007)
8. Beegle-Krause, C.J.: GNOME: NOAA's next-generation spill trajectory model. In: OCEANS 1999 MTS/IEEE. Riding the Crest into the 21st Century, vol. 3, pp. 1262–1266 (1999)
9. Douligeris, C., Collins, J., Iakovou, E., Sun, P., et al.: Development ofOSIMS: An oil spill information management system. Spill Science & Technology Bulletin 2(4), 255–263 (1995)
10. Reed, M., Ekrol, N., Rye, H., Turner, L.: Oil Spill Contingency and Response (OSCAR) Analysis in Support of Environmental Impact Assessment Offshore Namibia. Spill Science and Technology Bulletin 5(1), 29–38 (1999)
11. Belore, R.: The SL Ross oil spill fate and behavior model: SLROSM. Spill Science and Technology Bulletin (2005)
12. Liu, X., Wirtz, K.W.: Decision making of oil spill contingency options with fuzzy comprehensive evaluation. Water Resources Management 21(4), 663–676 (2007)
13. Liu, X., Wirtz, K.W.: Sequential negotiation in multiagent systems for oil spill response decision-making. Marine Pollution Bulletin 50(4), 469–474 (2005)
14. Watson, I.: Case-based reasoning is a methodology not a technology. Knowledge-Based Systems 12(5-6), 303–308 (1999)
15. Montani, S., Portinale, L., Leonardi, G., Bellazzi, R.: Case-based retrieval to support the treatment of end stage renal failure patients. Artificial Intelligence in Medicine 37(1), 31–42 (2006)
16. Corchado, J.M., Bajo, J., Abraham, A.: GERAmI: Improving the delivery of health care. IEEE Intelligent Systems. Special Issue on Ambient Intelligence (2008)
17. Decker, B., Rech, J., Althoff, K.D., Klotz, A., et al.: eParticipative Process Learning—process-oriented experience management and conflict solving. Data & Knowledge Engineering 52(1), 5–31 (2005)

18. Althoff, K.D., Mänz, J., Nick, M.: Maintaining Experience to Learn: Case Studies on Case-Based Reasoning and Experience Factory. In: Proc. 6th Workshop Days of the German Computer Science Society (GI) on Learning, Knowledge, and Adaptivity (LWA 2005). Saarland University, Germany (2005)
19. Cox, M.T., MuÑOz-Avila, H., Bergmann, R.: Case-based planning. The Knowledge Engineering Review 20(03), 283–287 (2006)
20. Plaza, E., McGinty, L.: Distributed case-based reasoning. The Knowledge Engineering Review 20(03), 261–265 (2006)
21. Corchado, J.M., Fdez-Riverola, F.: FSfRT: Forecasting System for Red Tides. Applied Intelligence 21, 251–264 (2004)
22. Karayiannis, N.B., Mi, G.W.: Growing radial basis neural networks: merging supervised andunsupervised learning with network growth techniques. IEEE Transactions on Neural Networks 8(6), 1492–1506 (1997)
23. Dunteman, G.H.: Principal Components Analysis. Newbury Park, California (1989)
24. Gunter, S., Schraudolph, N.N., Vishwanathan, S.V.N.: Fast Iterative Kernel Principal Component Analysis. Journal of Machine Learning Research 8, 1893–1918 (2007)
25. Fritzke, B.: Growing cell structures—a self-organizing network for unsupervised and supervised learning. Neural Networks 7(9), 1441–1460 (1994)
26. Haykin, S.: Neural networks. Prentice Hall, Upper Saddle River (1999)
27. Ros, F., Pintore, M., Chrétien, J.R.: Automatic design of growing radial basis function neural networks based on neighboorhood concepts. Chemometrics and Intelligent Laboratory Systems 87(2), 231–240 (2007)
28. Plaza, E., Armengol, E., Ontañón, S.: The Explanatory Power of Symbolic Similarity in Case-Based Reasoning. Artificial Intelligence Review 24(2), 145–161 (2005)

Case Based Interpretation of Soil Chromatograms

Deepak Khemani, Minu Mary Joseph, and Saritha Variganti

Department of Computer Science and Engineering,
Indian Institute of Technology Madras,
Chennai-600036, India
khemani@iitm.ac.in, {minumj,sarithav}@cse.iitm.ac.in

Abstract. This paper focuses on the application of CBR to soil analysis from chromatograms. The shape, size and colour of the chromatogram image are hypothesized to contain important information of the mineral content in the soil. Since chromotogram preparation is cheaper than chemical analysis the goal is to predict the nutrients from the chromatogram image features in the future rather than by direct chemical analysis. The method proposed in this paper will be new, as the current process of chemical analysis of soil is done manually, which is an expensive, time consuming and laborious process. This method of analysis will benefit farmers all across the globe, who are looking for innovative means to obtain their soil characteristics during the process of farming. In this application, the key assumption is that – *similar chromatograms have similar soil properties*. This paper focuses on the definition of similarity measure and determining the weight model for the feature set needed for the application.

1 Introduction

This paper describes an application[1] of case based reasoning (CBR) methodology for the determination of soil properties. A case base of soil properties associated with features of chromatograms is constructed, and similar chromatograms are retrieved to estimate the properties of a new soil sample.

Agricultural productivity is strongly dependant on the choice of the crop that is best suited for the given soil. While traditionally the best crops in different regions have evolved over a period of time, there has also been the influence of new crops being imported from other regions. In addition, the effects of globalization has resulted in certain crops like wheat and rice gaining in prominence due to global popularity, and many crops like cotton are grown because of their increased global demand. Consequently soil testing has become an important step in the agricultural cycle. Not only does this allow the farmer to choose a suitable crop, it also allows him to choose an appropriate fertilizer for growing a specific crop.

Soil testing is usually done in commercial laboratories using sophisticated equipment. The tests are normally carried out to determine the quantities of major nutrients (NPK) like nitrogen (N), phosphorus (P), and potassium (K), along with others like

---

[1] This work is supported by a grant from the Department of Science and Technology, Government of India, and is done in collaboration with the Murugappa Chettiar Research Centre, Chennai.

sulfur, calcium, iron, boron, molybdenum. Other properties that are measured are acidity, electrical conductivity, organic matter and humus. The process of laboratory analysis is typically time consuming and expensive. It is generally advised that many samples should be taken from different locations at each site. In addition the results do not have high accuracy.

Recently an entirely different approach to determining soil properties has emerged. This is based on interpretation of a chromatographic image made from a mixture of the soil solution and a photosensitive chemical like silver nitrate. A sample chromatogram is shown in fig 1. Soil scientists claim that the patterns and the colours in the image contain information about the soil properties [1] & [2]. The circular image has three distinct regions, known as the inner, the middle and the outer region. The inner region is said to contain information about the minerals such as nitrogen, sodium, potassium, and phosphorus; the middle region reveals the presence of organic carbon and organic matter; and the outer regions tells us about humus.

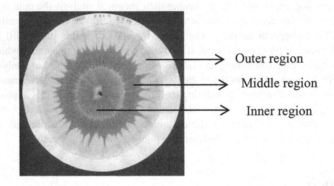

> Outer region

> Middle region

> Inner region

Fig. 1. A sample chromatogram

The difficulty is that interpreting the chromatogram is not a well defined science but more of an art. Furthermore the interpretation by humans is only qualitative in nature, essentially associating colour presences with individual nutrients [1] & [3]. This makes chromatogram interpretation a good candidate for case based reasoning, with the assumption that *similar chromatograms have similar soil properties*.

If one can build a case based interpreter of chromatograms, then the new approach would be an order of magnitude cheaper and much faster than the laboratory analysis process. A large case base will also give us the opportunity of discovering the association between image features and soil properties, and fine tuning the weights to highlight specific properties.

The rest of this paper describes the CBR application. The high level architecture is described in the following section. After scanning, the features of chromatograms are extracted by image processing techniques. A brief discussion on chromatogram features and their extraction is described in section 3. Section 4 describes the set of attributes and the similarity measures used. Section 5 describes the implementation and experimental results, followed by conclusions and discussions in section 6.

2 Architecture of the System

The system described here has been built in collaboration with the Murugappa Chettiar Research Centre (MCRC) in Chennai, an organization doing research in innovative methods in farming. The group in MCRC has collected around ten thousand soil samples from many parts of India. These soil samples have been analyzed by a sister company in the Murugappa group, E.I.D. Parry, working on soil and fertilizers. At the same time the MCRC group has prepared chromatograms for all the soil samples. These chromatograms have been scanned at IIT Madras, where we have also built a CBR system that stores cases as image features along with soil properties, into a system called InfoChrom.

The four major subsystems in this system are: Image Acquisition; Image preprocessor and Feature Extractor; CBR engine; and Soil Nutrient Management System as shown in fig 2.

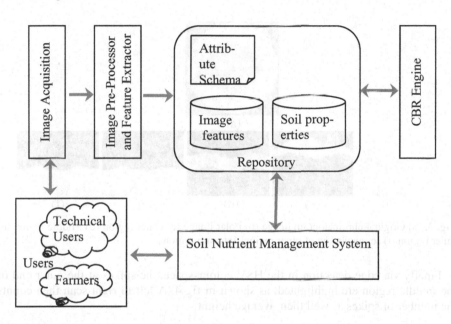

Fig. 2. Architecture of the system

Chromatograms were scanned and features of chromatogram image extracted by image processing algorithms discussed briefly in the next section. This feature set is stored in Image features table. Soil properties of chromatogram provided by MCRC are stored in the corresponding table. The case base is the integration of the two tables. The type and weights of the attributes are stored in the attribute schema. The CBR engine implements the algorithms required for searching the case base and retrieving the most similar cases. The Soil Nutrient Management System integrates the entire system and provides the user interface. It also accesses other data relating soil properties to crops to give crop and fertilizer related advice.

3 Chromatogram Features Extraction

Image pre-processing is an important step before extracting the features of the image. Some of our preliminary work was reported in [4]. The first task is detection of the centre. Once the centre is identified the circular image is converted into a rectangular one by a Cartesian to polar transformation. This means that the x-axis in the polar image corresponds to the center, and the y-axis corresponds to the radial direction. The next stage is the task of segmentation. This is done in stages as reported here. The polar image is transformed from RGB space to HSV colourspace to identify regions of chromatogram. First the outer region is separated by HSV based thresholding. Then the inner and middle regions are separated by *colour based segmentation using HSV colourspace* (see [5]). The inner region often contains various sub regions. These are then separated by a process of colour texture segmentation, adapted from [6]. Fig 3 shows the extracted polar regions from the original circular image.

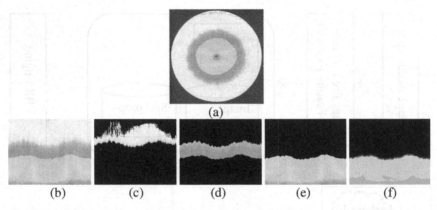

Fig. 3. (a) Original chromatogram image (b) Polar image (c) Outer region (d) Middle region (e) Inner region (f) segmentation of inner regions into sub regions

Finally via edge detection in the HSV colour-space, the spikes at the outer end of the middle region are highlighted, as shown in fig 4. A left to right scan then counts the number of spikes as well their average height.

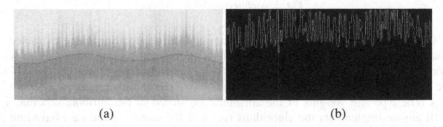

Fig. 4. (a) Spikes of the chromatogram (b) Edge detection to identify spikes

On the polar image, colour quantization is applied to create bands of uniform colour. After the process of colour quantization, we have the dominant colour information. This alone will not be sufficient for accurate similarity computation of images and hence, their spatial locations are also captured vertically i.e., viewed from top to bottom [8]. Dominant colours and their spatial information are referred as ColourMap and ColourSequence in this paper. The former describes the distinct colours and the area they cover, while the latter describes the distinct bands they occur in. Table 1 shows the ColourMap and ColourSequence of chromatogram shown in fig 3.

Table 1. Colour features of the chromatogram shown in fig 3

ColourMap					ColourSequence				
Red	Green	Blue	Distribution		Red	Green	Blue	Width	
158	137	119	8262		229	221	196	7	
178	163	144	16106		224	205	164	14	
229	221	196	82002		194	173	147	11	
224	205	164	51603		178	163	144	12	
194	173	147	16478		170	155	138	79	
170	155	138	72929		229	221	196	119	
					224	205	164	51	
					194	173	147	8	
					170	155	138	7	

4 Case Structure and Similarity

The case structure has five components at the highest level as shown in fig 5. These correspond to the three regions - inner, middle and outer – and the ColourMap and the ColourSequence. The inner region may be divided in up to four sub regions. Each of these is represented by average or quantized colour, width and area. The middle and the outer regions are treated as single regions. The spikes are represented by average height and total number, and are part of the middle region. The ColourMap contains information about the dominant quantized colours, and the area occupied by each. The ColourSequence attribute describes the dominant colours in the order in which they occur. At the low level each colour is represented by RGB values corresponding to the three primary colours – red, green and blue. The total number of low level attributes is 153.

4.1 Similarity Measures

The problem description part of the case can be broken down into outer, middle, inner, ColourMap and ColourSequence attributes by aggregation taxonomy as shown in fig 5. The local similarities for the different attribute types and their aggregation into global similarity are computed as follows.

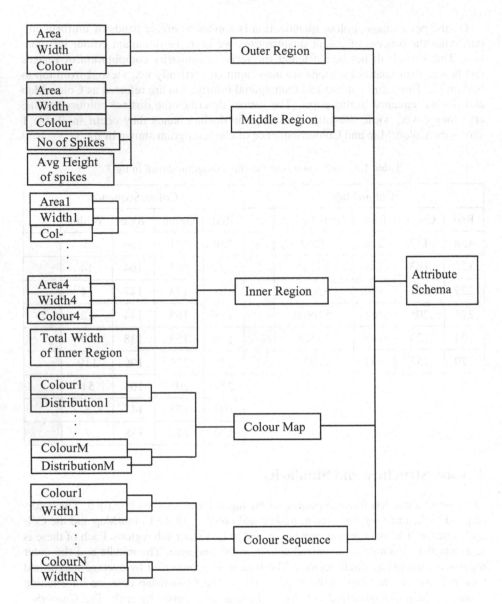

Fig. 5. The image attributes form the problem description which has a hierarchical structure

4.1.1 Simple Attributes

For simple attributes, we define a value range $D_{Ai} = [d_{min}, d_{max}]$ over the domain of attributes within which attributes takes value. We define the similarity measure for these attributes as a linear function, i.e., the similarity decreases linearly in the interval $[0, d_{max}-d_{min}]$ with the increase of difference between the two values. We define a local similarity function for simple attributes as follows which restricts the similarity value within the interval [0, 1].

$$
featureSim_i = 1 - \frac{\delta(q_i, c_i)}{(d_{max} - d_{min})}
$$
$$
where \quad \delta(q_i, c_i) = |q_i - c_i|
$$

(1)

4.1.2 Compound Attributes

In our application, compound attributes are colours of outer, middle and inner regions, and the pattern attributes ColourMap and ColourSequence. A colour is defined by three primary colours – red, green and blue. ColourMap lists the colours that are dominant in the chromatogram and their distribution in terms of pixels. ColourSequence lists the order of occurrence of dominant colours present in the chromatogram when viewed along radial axis from the center. In [8], we have defined the similarity measure for colour and proposed algorithms for matching the ColourMap and ColourSequence of the query and case. Local similarity measure between two ColourMaps can be defined as weighted aggregate of similarity of each colours of ColourMap of query against the ColourMap of case. Local similarity between two ColourSequence is computed by matching corresponding regions in the query and the case image. The algorithm described in [8] is essentially an efficient version of an algorithm that would match the two images pixel by pixel. This is possible because of quantization that leads to bands of pixel with the same RGB values.

4.2 Global Similarity Measure

Global similarity measures are defined by applying an aggregation function to the local similarity value. In this paper, weighted average aggregation function is used to compute global similarity between the query and the case.

$$
Sim(Query, Case) = \frac{\sum\limits_{i=1}^{all\ features} weight_i \times featureSim_i(Query_i, Case_i)}{\sum\limits_{i=1}^{all\ features} weight_i}
$$

(2)

$$
where \quad weight_i \ denotes \ the \ relevance \ of \ the \ features
$$

It might be observed that there is redundancy in the amount of colour information that is present in the case description. The intention is to do experiments with various weight combinations to discover the optimal weights. This could be particularly relevant if different features discriminate different soil properties. Then one may want to build a network of case weights, each combination optimized to retrieve cases with the most similar specific soil property. The goal is to build a system with high cohesion [9]. By this we mean that "similar" chromatograms are also considered similar on the solution side. It might be that for each of the target properties a specialized similarity measure needs to be designed. This is on the future agenda.

4.3 Feature Weighting

Chromatogram features extracted by image processing consists of about 153 attributes. Preliminary experiments were done to determine the feature relevance by selecting

Table 2. Weight sets and their selected feature sets

WeightSets	Feature Sets
Set-I	Features of outer, middle and inner regions
Set-II	Features of outer, middle, inner region and ColourMap
Set-III	Features of outer, middle, inner region and ColourSequence
Set-IV	Features of outer, middle, total width of inner region, ColourMap and ColourSequence

different subset of features from feature set and the results of retrieval were analyzed. We have selected four different weight sets for our experiments which are described in table 2.

4.4 Retrieval

The scenario of using the case base is as follows. A mobile van equipped with a scanner and a computer visits a village and halts for a few days. Farmers desirous of analyzing their soil bring samples over to the van. A chromatogram is made and kept on the scanner. The integrated software system scans the image, calls the image processing for feature extraction, and using the features consults the case base and presents two sets of properties. One is for the best matching case, and the other averaged over the five best matching cases.

Preliminary experiments revealed that with 10000 cases the sequential algorithm would retrieve cases in less than half a minute. Hence the sequential algorithm was used for retrieval. In fact, the complete processing takes about maximum of three minutes, of which the major time is spent on image processing.

5   Experimental Results

Preliminary experiments were done on the different subsets of features over a case-base of 10000 chromatograms to determine their importance by fixing and tuning weights manually. Two hundred test cases with diverse patterns were selected from the case-base to experiment with different weight sets. The retrieved sets for four queries are shown in figure 6 where the first column represents the images of query and the remaining columns represents the images of best matching case and their score for the four weight sets, set-I, set-II, set-III and set-IV.

Table 3 shows the soil properties of query case and best case retrieved with the four different weight sets for query image named KKL0071.

5.1 Analysis of Results

The system was evaluated with one hundred queries using the four different weight sets. Soil properties for the query sample are computed by taking the average of soil

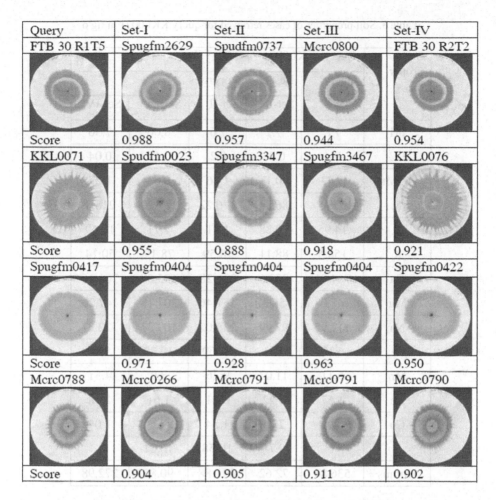

Query FTB 30 R1T5	Set-I Spugfm2629	Set-II Spudfm0737	Set-III Mcrc0800	Set-IV FTB 30 R2T2
Score	0.988	0.957	0.944	0.954
KKL0071	Spudfm0023	Spugfm3347	Spugfm3467	KKL0076
Score	0.955	0.888	0.918	0.921
Spugfm0417	Spugfm0404	Spugfm0404	Spugfm0404	Spugfm0422
Score	0.971	0.928	0.963	0.950
Mcrc0788	Mcrc0266	Mcrc0791	Mcrc0791	Mcrc0790
Score	0.904	0.905	0.911	0.902

Fig. 6. Retrieval results for 4 queries with different weight sets

properties of the five best retrieved cases. The soil properties computed with different weight sets are compared against actual soil properties of queries which are known. The similarity of each retrieved soil property is computed using equation 3. The range of each property has been computed by inspecting the ten thousand cases and has also been corroborated by the soil scientists.

$$Similarity = 1 - \frac{\mid originalvalue - computedvalue \mid}{range} \tag{3}$$

Figure 7 shows the similarity values between computed soil properties and actual soil properties over the one hundred queries for each weight sets. Set-II yields the best results.

Table 3. Soil properties of cases retrieved for query KKL0071 in fig 6

Soil proper- ties	Query- KKL0071				
	Query proper- ties	Best case properties			
		Set-I	Set-II	Set-III	Set-IV
pH	7.8	7.2	7.6	8.06	7.36
EC	0.4	0.23	0.2	0.18	0.04
OrgMtr	1.47	0.1	1.26	0.63	1.57
N	206.5	86.84	176.22	117.29	218.8
P	14.95	10.88	1.81	7.71	12.69
K	158.5	88.11	78.59	78.19	50.14
Ca	764.01	333.6	236.28	135.57	761.16
Mg	147.08	156.37	157.46	207.18	147.26
Na	112.95	97.99	138.02	109.37	122.97
Fe	6.12	7.61	14.69	10.28	5.88
Mn	5.11	11.02	9.26	8.9	4.51
Zn	1.57	0.22	0.11	1.61	1.08
Cu	0.93	2.74	1.54	4.33	1.04
S	1	9.78	10.58	16.21	1
Humus	536.84	72.62	291.88	90.85	272.98

5.2 The User Interface

Fig 8 shows the screen shot of soil composition for a given query, in which best case and average case soil properties were shown. Also shown on the screen are the query and the best matching chromatogram images. The average case are in the section labeled "Composition". One can also observe two buttons on the screen that say "Soil Enrichment" and "Crop Advisor". These initiate the stage of post processing not discussed here. The first one compares soil properties to the properties required by a desired crop and determines the type of fertilizer to be added. The second one is to list the crops that would grow well for the given soil sample. When these procedures are activated they generate the final printouts to be given as reports to farmers.

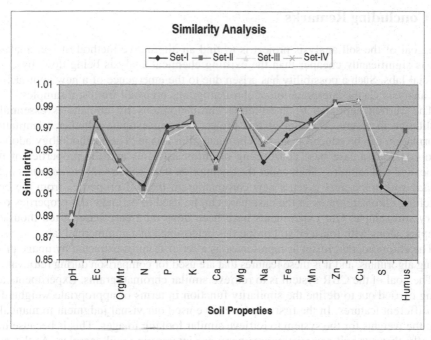

Fig. 7. Similarity analysis of soil properties for different weight sets

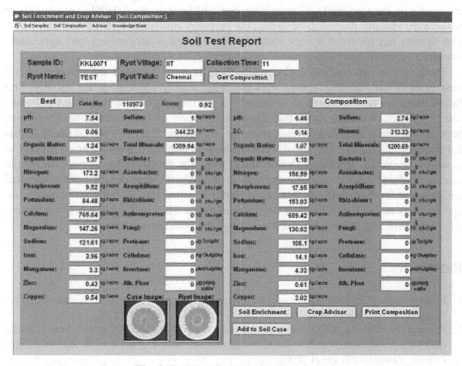

Fig. 8. Soil Test Report of retrieved case

6 Concluding Remarks

The goal of the soil analysis project is to find an alternative method of soil analysis that is significantly cheaper than the existing chemical analysis being done by commercial labs. Such a possibility has arisen due to the emergence of a new approach to soil analysis via the interpretation of chromatograms prepared from soil samples.

The current approach to interpreting chromatograms by humans is essentially qualitative in nature. The aim of this project is to investigate whether quantitative information can be educed from the chromatogram image. The methodology adopted is to construct a case base constituting of chromatograms and the properties of the associated soil samples. Then under the assumption that 'similar chromatograms have similar soil properties' given a new chromatogram the soil properties from the best matching chromatograms in the case base can be used to estimate the properties of a query soil sample. Our experiments have been done on a case base of ten thousand samples, along with fourteen soil properties determined in a commercial lab.

The chromatogram image is represented as a set of features extracted by image processing algorithms, and it is these features that are used for comparison during retrieval.

The goal of the CBR system is to retrieve similar chromatograms. Experiments are being carried out to define the similarity function in terms of appropriate weights for the different features. In the first stage we have used our visual judgment to manually tune the weights for the system to retrieve similar looking images. This is because it is visually that our soil scientist counterparts are interpreting soil samples. At the moment while our visual evaluation of the retrieved chromatograms is very good, the error rates in the retrieved soil properties can still be improved. While the weights in Set-4 were visually judged to be better, the property similarity was better using Set-2. The system has received a very enthusiastic response from farmers and agriculture scientists in recent demonstrations.

There is also the possibility that while there is more accurate information of soil properties in the chromatograms, it is not immediately obvious to us visually. Our future plans are now to tune the weights by a learning algorithm based on the known soil properties. We plan to do this learning for *each* of the different soil nutrients, because they may manifest differently in the soil image. It could then be possible that a different retrieval system (set of weights) may be deployed for each soil property or a set of properties internally, while integrating the results into a common output screen. In doing so we will also be able to identify the features that are associated with each individual nutrient. We could then formalize this association between image features and soil nutrients in the form of rules. This will finally give us knowledge in a form that can be discussed meaningfully with the soil scientists!

References

1. Pfeiffer, E.E.: Chromatography applied to quality testing, Biodynamic Literature, Wyoming, Island, pp. 1–44 (1984)
2. Perumal, K., Vatsala, T.M.: Utilisation of local alternative materials in cow horn manures (BD500): A case study on biodynamic vegetable cultivation. Journal of Biodynamic Agriculture - Australia 52, 16–21 (2002)

3. Bio Dynamic Association of India, http://www.biodynamics.in/chrom.htm
4. Saritha, V., Joseph, M.M., Das, S., Khemani, D.: Chromatogram Image Pre-Processing and Feature Extraction for Automatic Soil Analysis. In: Proceedings of the International Conference on Computing: Theory and Applications ICCTA 2007, Kolkata, India, March 5-7 (2007)
5. A tutorial on Color Based Segmentation using CIELAB Colorspace, http://www.mathwork-s.com/products/demos/image/color_seg_lab/ipexfabric.html
6. Lu, C., Chung, P., Chen, C.: Unsupervised Texture Segmentation Via Wavelet Transform. Pattern Recognition, 729–742 (1997)
7. A tutorial on Color Quantization, http://www.mathworks.com/access/helpdesk_r13/help/too-lbox/images/color5.html
8. Saritha, V., Joseph, M.M., Khemani, D.: Similarity Measures for Colour Patterns, A technical report, http://aidb.cs.iitm.ernet.in/tech-reports.html
9. Lamontagne, L.: Textual CBR Authoring using Case Cohesion, in TCBR 2006 -Reasoning with Text. In: Proceedings of the ECCBR 2006 Workshops, pp. 33–43 (2006)

Case-Based Troubleshooting in the Automotive Context: The SMMART Project

Stefania Bandini[1], Ettore Colombo[1], Giuseppe Frisoni[1], Fabio Sartori[1],
and Joakim Svensson[2]

[1] Research Center on Complex Systems and Artificial Intelligence (CSAI)
Department of Computer Science, Systems and Communication (DISCo)
University of Milan - Bicocca
viale Sarca, 336
20126 - Milan (Italy)
Tel.: +39 02 64487913 - fax +39 02 64487839
bandini@csai.disco.unimib.it,
{ettore.colombo,frisoni,sartori}@disco.unimib.it
[2] Department of Product Support Systems
Volvo Parts
Gothenburg, Sweden
joakim.u.svensson@volvo.com

Abstract. In this paper we present a case–based troubleshooting tool developed in the context of the SMMART project. The application aims at the identification and solution of failures in trucks, exploiting a hybrid approach based on the integration of CBR, model based reasoning and fault trees. The case–based module of the final system allows to identify the most probable part of the truck that is responsible for the failures (e.g. engine, gearbox, and so on): then, model–based reasoning or fault trees can be used to detect the real cause of the problem (e.g. an electric cable in the engine) and to identify the action needed to solve it (e.g. substitute the cable). The project is a collaboration between the University of Milan–Bicocca and Volvo Trucks.

Keywords: Case–Based Reasoning, Automotive Troubleshooting, Industrial Application of CBR.

1 Introduction

In this paper, we present SMMART (System for Mobile Maintenance Accessible in Real Time), a research project funded by the European Community[1]. The SMMART integrated R&D project started in November 2005 and is planned to run for 3 years with an overall budget of around 25 millions, co–funded under the Sixth Framework Programme. Coordinated by TURBOMECA, the project involves 25 companies and institutions from across Europe. The participants includes industry leaders (VOLVO, TURBOMECA, EUROCOPTER, SNECMA

---

[1] Project number NMP2-CT-2005-016726.

K.-D. Althoff et al. (Eds.): ECCBR 2008, LNAI 5239, pp. 600–614, 2008.

SERVICES, THALES), Small & Medium Enterprises who contribute 38% to the project, and 6 research centres. The SMMART project aims at defining a new integrated concept to answer the maintenance challenges of the transport industry – aeronautics, road transport, marine transport:

- to reduce the time and cost for scheduled and unscheduled maintenance inspections of increasingly sophisticated and complex products;
- to remotely provide adequate up–to–date information to assist mobile workers in all their tasks wherever they operate;
- to minimise the cost penalties of unscheduled downtime on large transport fleets;
- to provide new services: advanced troubleshooting tool, global configuration control, resources planning tool.

Fig. 1 shows a sketch of the different Work Packages (WP) composing the project. In particular, this paper focuses on the description of WP 5200 output that consists of a decision support system for experts involved in the truck engine troubleshooting process. In our context, troubleshooting can be defined as the process through which the causes of malfunctions in a product, process or service are detected and managed. In this sense, troubleshooting differs from simple diagnosis, because it concerns not only the identification of a problem emerging from a given set of symptoms, but also the proposal of an opportune way to solve such problem.

To this aim a *Troubleshooting Tool* (TTool) has been designed and implemented in the context of the SMMART project, based on the integration of

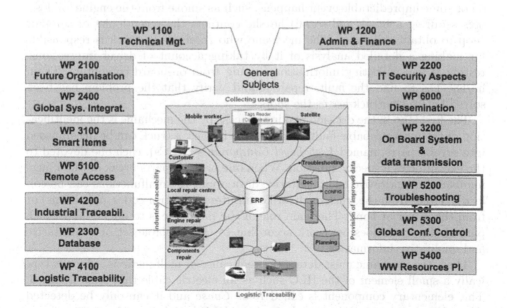

Fig. 1. The SMMART Project

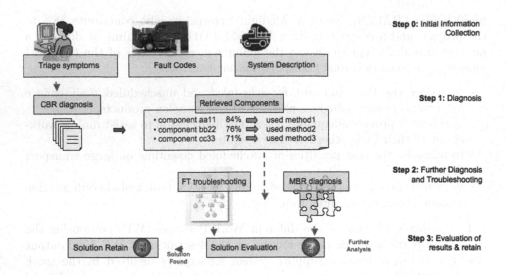

Fig. 2. The approach adopted in the SMMART Troubleshooting Tool

case–based reasoning (CBR) [1], model–based reasoning [2] and fault tree approaches [3]. CBR has been already adopted in the past for building troubleshooting or diagnosis systems (see e.g. [4] [5] [6] [7]).

In the context of SMMART, CBR has been used to guide the troubleshooting tool towards the cause of the truck problem: when a driver recognizes that a problem arises on his/her vehicle (for example, a light of the control panel turns on or some unpredictable event happens, such as smoke from the engine, oil loss, noises during a break and so on) he/she contacts the receptionist of a repair shop to obtain assistance. The mechanic who receives the truck is responsible for making a detailed analysis of it by taking account of driver impressions, testing it and collecting information coming from on-board computers. Then, he/she has to find the fault, repair it and verify that the problem has been solved before the truck leaves the shop.

The first step in the decision making process by the mechanic is the identification of the most probable faulty component. In fact, a truck can be decomposed into several parts, named *High Level Components* (HLCs), each one devoted to the execution of a specific function. When one or more parts break down, a huge number of quantitative and qualitative data about the malfunctions can be collected, either from the truck on–board computers (i.e. error codes and alarms) or from the driver at hand. The main role of the mechanic is to understand which part of the truck does not work according to the available set of quantitative and qualitative information.

Then, the mechanic must detect the real cause of malfunctions, which is typically a small element of the HLC such as an electric cable that is interrupted. This elementary component is called *Root Cause* and it can only be detected through a complete and deep analysis of the HLC based on mechanic experience or troubleshooting methodologies provided by the component manufacturer.

Fig. 2 summarizes a typical troubleshooting session in the SMMART context. The identification of the HLC is performed by the CBR module of the TTool: qualitative and quantitative information about the engine trouble are grouped into an opportune case–structure that is compared with problems solved in the past (Step 1). The faulty HLC is the solution part of the case structure related to the current problem: when it is identified, since no automatic adaptation has been implemented and no further computation is required, the CBR task can be considered finished. The retrieved HLC is then investigated by either the MBR tool (i.e. *Rodon*) or the FT application (i.e. *Grade–X*) in order to help the mechanics in the identification of the root cause (Step 2). Also the suggestion about which method to use is part of the case solution, but the user is free to refuse it and follows his/her own experience. An evaluation of the solution is then provided by the mechanic before retaining the case.

The paper is organized as follows: Section 2 briefly introduces the troubleshooting process at Volvo repair shops, focusing on the actors involved; then, Section 3 describes the CBR application developed in the context of the TTool, with particular emphasis on the case structure and the retrieval algorithm designed and implemented. Section 4 gives a brief overview on the system implementation, describing the TTool from the 4R's cycle [8] point of view as well as some technical details on how the different modules have been integrated. Finally, some conclusions and future work are briefly pointed out in Section 5.

2   The SMMART TTool Domain

In this section we will describe how troubleshooting on a truck is performed now in most official trucks repair shops around Europe and the people involved in this process. Moreover we will show how the adoption of a CBR based troubleshooting tool can support speeding up the diagnostic process and decreasing the warranty costs.

The typical situation starts with a truck driver who goes to the repair shop because a problem arises on his truck. After a detailed interview with the driver, a receptionist of the repair shop registers on a form the type of truck, the declared symptoms and the conditions under which the symptoms occurred. The receptionist is the point of contact between driver and repair shop. The receptionist is a user of the troubleshooting tool and the symptoms' form is the initial source of information that describes the digital case. The symptoms form is sent to the chief mechanic who is the person responsible for diagnosing, repairing and validating the repair on the truck. Sometimes contact between the driver and a mechanic may be necessary, in order to refine the truck symptoms description. Most of the time the chief mechanic himself tests the truck on the road to gain a better understanfding of the symptoms declared by the driver.

The chief mechanic has great experience of problems with trucks, but does not usually have a lot of experience with using computer tools, so only a basic interaction with the troubleshooting tool is required. After a satisfactory definition of the symptoms set, the mechanic makes an automatic inspection of the truck: all main truck producers provide their official repair shops with a tool for collecting the error messages (Fault Codes) generated by the central units (CUs) installed in the truck. On modern trucks there is a number of CUs connected with all the electronic components and with a number of sensors that are able to detect the correct functioning of the controlled parts. When the truck is working the CUs collect and store all the eventual Fault Codes sent by the components or the sensors. The mechanic can then analyze them and have more information on the problems the truck has. The Fault Codes collecting tool will be integrated into the troubleshooting tool.

A precise symptoms list and a number of coherent Fault Codes are often not enough for the mechanic to determine easily the root cause of the failure; in such cases he may erroneously replace components that are not faulty, often increasing down-time, warranty costs and decreasing the clients level of trust. If the mechanic is unable to solve the problem, he can eventually call the mother home helpdesk. The helpdesk technician is an expert on troubleshooting trucks, so he can support the mechanic in his/her problem solving process. The helpdesk technician is a user of the troubleshooting tool that can be started up with data regarding the troubleshooting state defined so far: symptoms description filled by the receptionist and Fault Codes collected by the mechanic. The support given by the helpdesk is not always immediate, since the helpdesk technician may need to contact the expert engineers who have designed the truck to provide an answer to the calling repair shop. Usually there are different responsible engineers for different components or subsystems. The engineer is a user of the troubleshooting tool, since he can browse the information about the case under examination, including the type of the truck, symptoms, conditions and Fault Codes, in order to analyze the problem and suggest a probable root cause.

When the mechanic receives an answer that can be tested as a good working solution to the current case, the process ends, without formal retention of the experience accumulated from this specific case. However, the mechanic will possibly remember about this difficult problem, but the reuse of such experience is left to him and to his ability to find analogies. Moreover no new knowledge is shared with all other repair shops, since the helpdesk technician must wait for a meaningful number of similar calls before raising the flag of "possible frequent fault" to engineers; after the analysis of these cases the company can decide to circulate a technical report to the official repair shops about this frequent fault. This will very likely cause loss of time in the involved repair shops which will undergo an analogous test and fail process before to contact the help desk, causing unnecessary warranty costs for the truck producing company.

A troubleshooting tool that maintains case base of previous problems and their solutions may support helpdesk technicians to immediately find a similar case that was previously solved and provide the solution to the calling mechanic, saving time. Moreover it can support helpdesk technicians and engineers to monitor the occurrence of faults in order to spread out more rapidly the technical information about them to the repair shops, thus saving time and money.

3   SMMART TTool and CBR

The troubleshooting tool allows to exploit and integrate different methods to solve the mechanic's problem that is to identify and remove the cause of a truck engine failure, using a two step–retrieval [9] [10]:

- In the first step, the CBR module is responsible for the identification of the most probable faulty HLC;
- In the second step, the MBR or FT module is used to detect the root cause inside the HLC.

The integration of MBR approaches into CBR systems has been already proposed (see e.g. [11]) as a way to guide the adaptation phase: in the context of the TTool of the SMMART project, MBR of FT methods are used *to refine* the retrieved solution rather than revising it. For this reason, we consider the CBR and MBR and FT paradigms as two distinct entities in the TTool and we focus the rest of this section on the description of the adopted problem representation, in the form of a hierarchical case structure [12], and similarity calculus strategy, based on the *K–Nearest Neighbour* approach [13] (KNN).

3.1   The Troubleshooting Tool Case Structure

In accordance with the traditional literature on case–based reasoning [8], the case structure of TTool module consists of three parts, as shown in Fig. 3:

- *Case description*, containing all the information necessary to characterize the truck problem; that is the symptoms, fault codes, symptoms conditions and general information about the truck (the truck model, the type of on–board computer, and so on);
- *Case solution*, containing the faulty components of the truck together with the suggestion of the approach used in order to analyze the HLC and the root cause;
- *Case outcome*, which is a comment made by mechanic about the solution effectiveness (e.g. *"The tool suggested MBR for identifying the root cause, but I preferred FT"*)

The most important information in the case description are Symptoms and Fault Codes. Symptoms are qualitative information about the truck malfunctions: they are synthetic representations of driver impressions about the problem. Symptoms are represented in a tree structure, in which each subtree is related to a specific HLC (e.g. Engine, Gearbox, ...). Starting from the HLC, different levels of detail can be determined, depending on the available knowledge. For example, as depicted in Fig. 3, three symptoms at Level 1 can be identified for the Engine, i.e. *Engine start, Engine stop* and *Low power*. While further levels of detail can be specified for both Engine start (i.e. *Engine cranks but doesn't start*) and Engine stop (i.e. *Starter motor does not run*), this is not true for Low power because this symptom is the leaf of the subtree it belongs to. This structure is

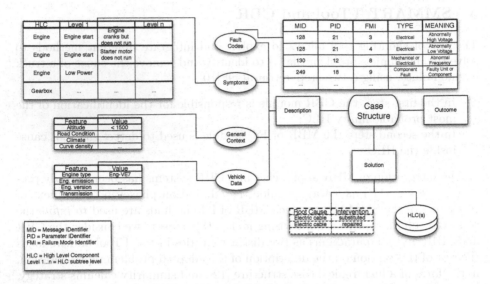

Fig. 3. The case structure adopted by the CBR module of the TTool

extremely flexible and allows the mechanic to represent in a complete way the effects of the problem. Moreover, new levels can be added to the structure when available: at the moment, the maximum number of levels composing a symptom subtree is 5.

Fault Codes are also organized in a tree, and a Fault Code is characterized by three fields, which are:

– MID, the *Message IDentifier*, which specifies the on–board computer generating the error code; for example, the entries with MID 128 in Fig. 3 identify the on–board computer monitoring the engine; for this reason, it can be deduced that the MID indirectly identifies a HLC;
– PID, the *Parameter Identifier*, which specifies which component of the on–board computer has generated the Fault Code; this means that an on–board computer is characterized by the presence of many sensors, each of them dedicated to monitoring a specific part of the HLC under control;
– FMI: the *Failure Mode Identifier*, which specifies the kind of failure detected by the on–board computer (electrical fault, mechanical fault, and so on).

General Context and Vehicle Data contains information about driving conditions and truck characteristics respectively. These two kinds of information are not directly related to fault generation, but they can be useful during the similarity calculus. For this reason, they have been included in the case description.

A case's solution consists of three parts: HLC, the suggestion of the method to adopt to analyze it and the root cause. It is important to highlight that a case can consider more than one HLC in its solution. The reason for this is that the same configuration of case description elements (mainly the set of symptoms and the set of fault codes) could be caused by more than one faulty

HLC. For example, a truck problem could derive from both the Engine and the Gearbox. The other part of the solution is used to suggest which method between Model Based Reasoning and Fault Trees to adopt for further investigation of problem root causes. Thus, the aim of the CBR module is to help the mechanic in discovering which is the most suitable fault tracing method together with the starting point from which to apply it rather than the final troubleshooting solution. In other words, the CBR module supports the mechanic in the correct and quick application of traditional troubleshooting methods.

Finally, the third part of the solution is the root cause. Although the CBR module of the TTool is not able to detect it, the application of the suggested approach between MBR and FT should be. Thus, the result of the MBR or FT application has been included in the solution to be retained. It is important to highlight that the root cause related to a previous case might not be useful for a new one. For example, it could happen that an electric cable substituted in the past could be simply repaired in the current situation. However, a mechanic could decide to save time by the application of the past intervention without any further investigations. In this situation, the indication of the root cause is a very important information.

3.2   The Troubleshooting Tool Similarity Function

Given the current case C_c, for which no solution is given, the goal of the retrieval algorithm is to propose a possible solution (i.e. a HLC together with a method to detect the root cause) by comparing its description with the descriptions of each case C_p solved in the past and included in the case base.

The similarity among cases is calculated with a composition of sub functions, as described by the following formula

$$SIM(C_c, C_p) = \frac{k_1 * SIM_S + k_2 * SIM_{FC} + k_3 * SIM_V + k_4 * SIM_{GC}}{k_1 + k_2 + k_3 + k_4}$$

where:

- k_1, k_2, k_3 and k_4 are configurable weights in $(0.0 \ldots 1.0]$;
- SIM_S, SIM_{FC}, SIM_V and SIM_{GC} are in $[0.0 \ldots 1.0]$.

SIM_S is the similarity between the two sets of symptoms of current case and past case, named S_c and S_p respectively: for each symptom A in the current case, the algorithm finds the closest symptom B (possibly the same as symptom A) in the past case, belonging to the same sub–tree, having the HLC name as its root. For example (see Fig. 4), a symptom *Engine cranks but does not run* has ID = (1) → (1) → (1); its HLC is *Engine* and its sub–tree is the one with root (1); hence only symptoms belonging to Engine subtree will be considered in the past case.

The function *dist(A,B)* gives the minimum number of arcs that separates A and B in the symptoms tree and it is used for calculating the similarity. Similarity between symptom A and symptom B is

$$sim(A, B) = 1 - dist(A, B)/dmax$$

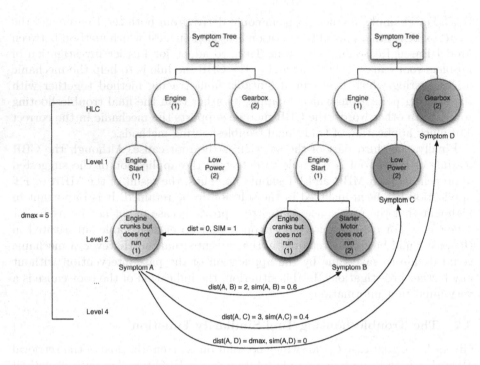

Fig. 4. The calculus of similarity between the symptom A of the current case and the symptoms B, C and D of the past case

where dmax is the constant maximum distance possible between two nodes in the tree (in the current TTool symptom tree dmax = 5). For example, as shown in Fig. 4, given A = (1) → (1) → (1): if B = (1) → (1) → (2), dist(A, B) = 2 and sim(A, B) = 0.6; if C = (1) → (2), dist(A,C) = 3 and sim(A,B) = 0.4; if D = (2) the similarity is 0 because A and D do not belong to the same subtree.

Similarity between symptom A and symptom B is modified by the conditions under which the symptoms occurred; the algorithm evaluates the degree of similarity between the two sets of conditions and modifies the value of sim(A,B) consequently.

The similarity among symptoms SIM_S is the sum of all the sim(A,B) normalized with the number *noc* of couples of symptoms considered and eventually penalized if the two cases are different in number of symptoms; for example, if the current case C_c has two symptoms (sym_1, sym_2), the past case C_p^1 has the same two symptoms (sym_1, sym_2) while the past case C_p^2 has three symptoms (sym_1, sym_2, sym_3), the similarity algorithm gives a higher degree of similarity to C_p^1 than to C_p^2. The final formula is:

$$SIM_S = (SIM_S/noc) * (1 - Penalty)$$

where $Penalty = \frac{(\#S_c + \#S_p - 2*noc)}{\#S_c + \#S_p}$ and $\#S_c$, $\#S_p$ are the cardinalities of S_c and S_p.

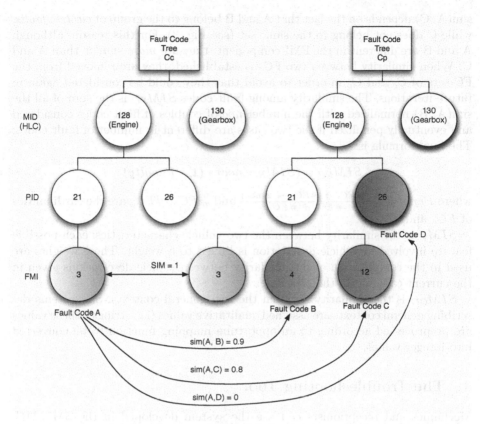

Fig. 5. The calculus of similarity between the Fault Code A of the current case and the Fault Codes B, C and D of the past case

SIM_{FC} is the similarity between the two sets of fault codes (FCs) calculated on each HCL group of FCs (FCs grouped by high level component): the relation between FCs and HLCs is given by mapping the MID of each FC to the HLC name. By doing so, different MIDs (that means FCs coming from different processing units) can be associated to the same HLC. If a FC does not have any MID–HLC mapping entry, the FC will be related to a fictitious HLC, called HLC_0: in this way, Fault Codes which cannot be linked directly to a specific HLC can be compared, with benefits from the final similarity point of view.

When all the Fault Codes of both C_c and C_p have been grouped in the FC_c and FC_p sets respectively, the algorithm compares the information they contain: the similarity sim(A, B) between two Fault Codes belonging to C_c and C_p depends on their PID and FMI values. Fig. 5 shows the different cases considered by the algorithm, given A = (128) → (21) → (3): if B = (128) → (21) → (4), sim(A, B) = 0.9; if C = (128) → (21) → (12), and sim(A, C) = 0.8; if D = (128) → (26) → (any) the similarity is 0 because A and D don't belong to the same processor. The similarity values are fixed and they have been determined with the collaboration of Volvo Truck experts; the difference between sim(A, B) and sim(A, C) depends on the fact that A and B belong to the group of *electric faults*, while C does not belong to the same set (see Fig. 3). For this reason, although A and B are different in the FMI component, they are *more similar* than A and C. When similarity between two FCs is established, they are removed from the FC sets of C_c and C_p in order to avoid that they could be considered again in future iterations. The similarity among fault codes SIM_{FC} is the sum of all the sim(A, B) normalized with the number *noc* of couples of fault codes considered and eventually penalized if the two cases are different in number of fault codes; The final formula is:

$$SIM_{FC} = (SIM_{FC}/noc) * (1 - Penalty)$$

where $Penalty = \frac{(\#FC_c + \#FC_p - 2*noc)}{\#FC_c + \#FC_p}$ and $\#FC_c$, $\#FC_p$ are the cardinalities of FC_c and FC_p.

SIM_V is the similarity between the two vehicle characteristics: each possible feature involved in vehicle description is linked to a weight. These weights are used in the computation of the similarity between vehicle descriptions given in the current case and in the past case.

SIM_{GC} is the similarity between the two general contexts. Since items describing general contexts are assigned qualitative values (i.e. strings), these values are preprocessed according to an opportune mapping function to be converted into integer values.

4 The Troubleshooting Tool

Mechanics and receptionists can use the system developed in the SMMART project to support their troubleshooting activities. TTool provides the users with two possible methods for troubleshooting, which are the fault-tree based and the MBR based. A user can access directly these modules in order to perform troubleshooting directly on a specific high level component. Moreover, in order to speed up the identification of the high level components which cause the misbehaviors of the vehicle, the users can make use of the experiences stored in the system. The use of CBR in the approach means that the solutions (i.e. the high level components) of the most similar cases retrieved from the case base can be proposed as possible and likely solutions of the problem presented in the current troubleshooting session.

TTool uses three different software modules to implement these functionalities and moreover a manager to coordinate the entire software system. Hence, the architecture of the troubleshooting tool, as shown in Fig. 6 is composed by four modules: the TTool manager coordinates the GUIs and sub–modules of the system; Grade-X that manages the fault trees and guides users in finding the root cause that affects an high-level component; Rodon that manages the high-level-component models involved in the MBR methods and suggests the root cause as the fault of one of the sub-components; the CBR engine that is dedicated to the management of the case base and to the retrieval of the past cases.

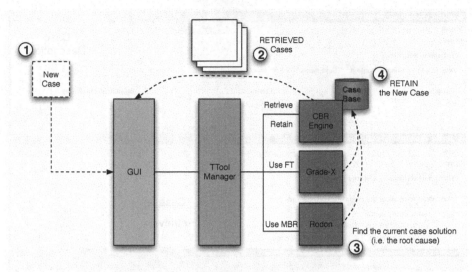

Fig. 6. The TTool CBR Cycle

Fig. 7 shows a typical use case of TTool: through its Graphical User Interface, the CBR engine receives the description of the current problems in terms of triage symptoms, fault codes coming from the on-board computer, general context and vehicle features. Using the similarity function described in the previous section, the CBR engine evaluates the similarity of the past cases and proposes the solution of the most similar case as a possible starting point for further and more detailed troubleshooting analysis by means of the TTool methods.

Whenever during the troubleshooting a root cause is found in a specific high level component, the root cause and the method used to identify are stored. Thus, the description of the solution within the past case contains not only the high level component, but also the root case and how it was found (i.e. the identifier of the fault tree or of the model exploited in the past experience). Actually, only the high level component is used to guide the work of the mechanic. However, the complete solution is given to the user in order to supply all the information for every possible consideration. Further analysis of the system during the test phase should reveal if also the root cause belonging to the past case could likely be the root cause of the current case.

The CBR engine directly manages the case base of the system and its implementation in the database. In fact, the CBR engine has in charge the access to the physical storage device in order to take all the case to be compared with the current case during the retrieval. Moreover, it is the CBR engine that provides the functionality to perform the retain phase of the CBR cycle. When the users find the root causes and add them to the solution description, they can decide to store the experience in the case base.

The CBR engine is developed on the basis of the software framework CReP (Case Retrieval Platform). The latter is a Java-based framework that allows developers to build CBR application in an easy way. In fact, it provides a model

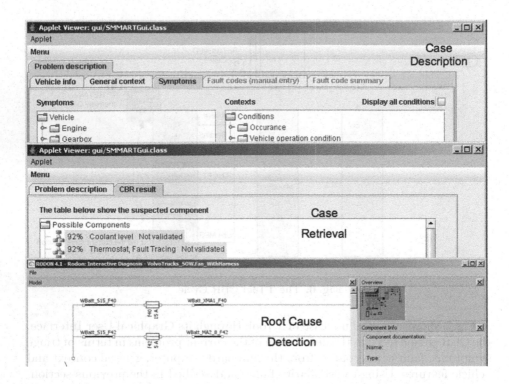

Fig. 7. The TTool Graphical User Interface

and some tools to describe cases, similarity functions on case description parts
and how they must be put together in an aggregation function in order to obtain the global similarity value. CReP is developed by the Artificial Intelligence
Laboratory of the University of Milano–Bicocca.

At the moment, the development phase of the troubleshooting tool is not at
a final stage so that a complete testing of the system would not be useful and
meaninful. However, some parts of the similarity function are fixed and their
analysis and testing has been planned and performed.

The functions designed and implemented for comparing fault codes, symptoms, vehicles and general contexts have been tested with sets of virtual cases
designed for this purpose. The term *virtual* means that they do not come from
real troubleshooting cases but that they have been manually built in order to
stress some specific features of the functions.

For each of the four parts of the case description, a ten–case test set has been
prepared. For instance, the set of cases designed to verify the correct behaviour
of the similarity function for symptoms contain only the part related to the list
of symptoms.

The testing strategy showed that each similarity function gives a value belonging to the interval between 0 and 1. The boundary values of this interval are
given when the compared cases are totally different and completely equal respectively. Moreover, two other cases are significant: when one list of the compared

cases is empty the result of the comparison is 0; when two cases are compared and the corresponding lists are both empty, their similarity is 1.

Once the development of the similarity function is finished, another testing phase will be required in order to test TTool on real cases and verify the actual quality of the results of the retrieval of the past cases and the effectiveness of the entire system.

5 Conclusions

In this paper we have presented a troubleshooting tool for the identification and resolution of failures on trucks. The system is a collaboration between the University of Milan–Bicocca and Volvo Trucks in the context of the SMMART project.

This tool is based on the integration of three different modules: a CBR system to identify the most probable truck component(s) that is (are) responsible for the failure and two applications based on MBR and Fault Trees respectively to detect the root causes of the problem and obtain suggestions about what actions should be taken.

At the moment, the project is in the third and last year of development: a complete prototype has been developed and tested on a small set of data. Indeed, the first impressions of the prototype results are good: the integration of CBR, MBR and FTs allows good coverage of truck failures and the system can be extended quite easily to include new truck components whenever their descriptions in terms of symptoms, fault codes, context and vehicle features become available.

However, an evaluation of the system's ability to support mechanics in their decision making process in real troubleshooting sessions is not possible, since the testing of the system is the main subject of the last year of the project. The evaluation will be conducted together with Volvo experts in the training of mechanics working at the repair shop. In particular, it is planned to connect the case base of the TTool directly to Argus, the training tool adopted by Volvo during training courses. Argus contains hundreds of troubleshooting session descriptions coming from Volvo repair shop that can be stored in the TTool as cases, in order to test the effectiveness of the prototype on real data.

References

1. Kolodner, J.: Case Based Reasoning. Morgan Kaufmann Publisher, San Mateo (CA) (1993)
2. Rayudu, R.K., Samarasinghe, S., Kulasiri, D.: A Comparison of Model–based Reasoning and Learning Approaches to Power Transmission Fault Diagnosis, annes, p. 218. IEEE Computer Society, Los Alamitos (1995)
3. Xiang, J., Futatsugi, K., He, Y.: Fault Tree and Formal Methods in System Safety Analysis. In: Proceedings of 4th International Conference on Computer and information Technology (CIT 2004), pp. 1108–1115. IEEE Computer Society, Los Alamitos (2004)

4. Georgin, E., Bordin, F., Loesel, S., McDonald, J.R.: CBR Applied to Fault Diagnosis on Steam Turbines. In: Watson, I.D. (ed.) Progress in Case-Based Reasoning, First United Kingdom Workshop, Salford, UK, January 12, 1995. LNCS, vol. 1020. Springer, Heidelberg (1995)
5. Lenz, M., Burkhard, H.D., Pirk, P., Auriol, E., Manago, M.: CBR for Diagnosis and Decision Support. AI Commun. 9(3), 138–146 (1996)
6. Ochi-Okorie, A.S.: Disease Diagnosis Validation in TROPIX Using CBR. Artificial Intelligence in Medicine 12(1), 43–60 (1998)
7. Portinale, L., Torasso, P., Ortalda, C., Giardino, A.: Using Case-Based Reasoning to Focus Model-Based Diagnostic Problem Solving. In: Wess, S., Althoff, K.D., Richter, M.M. (eds.) Topics in Case-Based Reasoning, First European Workshop, EWCBR-1993, Kaiserslautern, Germany, November 1-5, 1993. LNCS, vol. 837, pp. 325–337. Springer, Heidelberg (1994)
8. Aamodt, A., Plaza, E.: Case–Based Reasoning: Foundational Issues, Methodological Variations, and System Approaches. AI Communications 7(1), 39–59 (1994)
9. Forbus, K., Gentner, D., Law, K.: MAC/FAC: A model of Similarity–based Retrieval. Cognitive Science 19(2), 141–205 (1995)
10. Bandini, S., Colombo, E., Sartori, F., Vizzari, G.: Case Based Reasoning and Production Process Design: the Case of P-Truck Curing. In: ECCBR – Proceedings. LNCS, vol. 3155, pp. 504–517. Springer, Heidelberg (2004)
11. Portinale, L., Magro, D., Torasso, P.: Multi–Modal Diagnosis Combining Case–Based and Model–Based Reasoning: a Formal and Experimental Analysis. Artif. Intell. 158(2), 109–153 (2004)
12. Bergmann, R., Stahl, A.: Similarity Measures for Object–Oriented Case Representations. In: Smyth, B., Cunningham, P. (eds.) EWCBR 1998. LNCS (LNAI), vol. 1488, pp. 25–36. Springer, Heidelberg (1998)
13. Finnie, G.R., Sun, Z.: Similarity and Metrics in Case-Based Reasoning. International Journal of Intelligent Systems 17(3), 273–287 (2002)

Rapid Prototyping of CBR Applications with the Open Source Tool myCBR

Armin Stahl[1] and Thomas R. Roth-Berghofer[2]

[1] German Research Center for Artificial Intelligence (DFKI) GmbH
Image Understanding and Pattern Recognition Department (IUPR)
Armin.Stahl@dfki.de
[2] German Research Center for Artificial Intelligence (DFKI) GmbH
Knowledge Management Department
Trippstadter Straße 122, 67663 Kaiserslautern, Germany
Thomas.Roth-Berghofer@dfki.de

Abstract. Although Case-Based Reasoning (CBR) claims to reduce the effort required for developing knowledge-based systems substantially compared with more traditional Artificial Intelligence approaches, the implementation of a CBR application from scratch is still a time consuming task. In this paper we present a novel, freely available tool for rapid prototyping of CBR applications that focuses on the similarity-based retrieval step, like for example case-based product recommender systems. By providing easy to use model generation, data import, similarity modeling, explanation, and testing functionality together with comfortable graphical user interfaces, the tool enables even CBR novices to rapidly create their first CBR applications. Nevertheless, at the same time it ensures enough flexibility to enable expert users to implement advanced CBR applications.

1 Introduction

The development of a quite simple Case-Based Reasoning application already involves a number of steps, such as collecting case and background knowledge, modeling a suitable case representation, defining an accurate similarity measure, implementing retrieval functionality, and implementing user interfaces. Compared with other AI approaches, CBR allows to reduce the effort required for knowledge acquisition and representation significantly, which is certainly one of the major reasons for the commercial success of CBR applications. Nevertheless, implementing a CBR application from scratch remains a time consuming software engineering process and requires a lot of specific experience beyond pure programming skills.

Although CBR research has a history of about 20 years now, and in spite of the broad commercial success of CBR applications in recent years, today only few CBR software tools for supporting the development process are available. Software products used for implementing large-scale commercial applications are typically very complex, consist of various modules, and require quite a long time

K.-D. Althoff et al. (Eds.): ECCBR 2008, LNAI 5239, pp. 615–629, 2008.

to get familiar with the various functionalities and configuration possibilities. Another problem are the high licensing costs of these products and also if the vendors provide cheap or even free research licences, it is usually impossible to just download the software without carrying out an annoying registration procedure. This makes these products little attractive for research, teaching, small commercial projects, or first feasibility studies.

For these purposes, more easily available and less complex CBR tools are required. Unfortunately, such solutions are nearly missing today at all. One exception is the Open Source *JColibri*[1] system, which provides a framework for building CBR systems based on state-of-the-art Software Engineering techniques [1]. The key idea of the system is to combine software reuse with the more general AI paradigm of separating the reasoning algorithms from the domain model.

In this paper we present the novel Open Source CBR tool *myCBR*[2] developed at the German Research Center for Artificial Intelligence (DFKI). The key motivation for implementing *myCBR* was the need for a compact and easy-to-use tool for building prototype CBR applications in teaching, research, and small industrial projects with minimal effort. Moreover, the tool should be easily extendable in order to facilitate the experimental evaluation of novel algorithms and research results. Many ideas for the implementation of *myCBR* came from the old *CBR-Works* system[3] [2] but which is not available any more.

The current version of *myCBR* still focuses on the similarity-based retrieval step of the CBR cycle [3], because that is still the core functionality of most CBR applications. A popular example of such retrieval-only systems are case-based product recommender systems [4]. While the first CBR systems were often based on simple distance metrics, today many CBR applications make use of highly sophisticated, knowledge-intensive similarity measures [5]. On the one hand, such extremely domain specific similarity measures enable to improve the retrieval quality substantially. However, on the other hand, they increase the development effort significantly.

The major goal of *myCBR* is to minimize the effort for building CBR applications that require knowledge-intensive similarity measures. Therefore, it provides comfortable graphical user interfaces for modeling various kinds of attribute-specific similarity measures and for evaluating the resulting retrieval quality. In order to reduce also the effort of the preceding step of defining an appropriate case representation, it includes tools for generating the case representation automatically from existing raw data.

In the next Section we give an overview of the basic concept and system architecture of *myCBR*. In Section 3 and 4 we then describe the technical approaches, how rapid prototyping of CBR applications is supported by *myCBR*. In Section 5 we conclude with a summary and an outlook on future plans for improving and extending *myCBR*.

---

[1] http://gaia.fdi.ucm.es/projects/jcolibri
[2] http://www.mycbr-project.net
[3] CBR-Works has been developed at the University of Kaiserslautern in cooperation with empolis knowledge management GmbH, former tecinno GmbH.

2   The myCBR Architecture

From its conception, *myCBR* was designed with improved communication between the system and the user—knowledge engineer and end-user—in mind. The novice as well as the expert knowledge engineer is supported during the development phase of a *myCBR* project through intelligent support approaches and advanced GUI functionality.

The foundation of every CBR system are certain knowledge representation formalisms required to describe the content of the individual CBR knowledge containers, namely the *vocabulary*, the *similarity measure*, the *adaptation knowledge*, and the *case knowledge* [6]. Since knowledge representation is a key issue for most Artificial Intelligence (AI) Systems, various software tools for supporting knowledge engineering tasks are already existing today.

One of the most popular and widely used systems is certainly the Java-based Open Source ontology editor Protégé[4] [7]. A major reason for the success of Protégé is its flexible extensibility by providing a plug-and-play environment that enables users to add and distribute new modules easily. This makes Protégé a flexible base for rapid prototyping and application development in various application domains.

In order to avoid a reinvention of the wheel, we have chosen Protégé as the modeling platform for *myCBR*. In our point of view, the use of Protégé brings two main advantages: First, the effort for implementing data structures and user interfaces for representing the vocabulary and the case knowledge can be saved. Second, it allows to add CBR functionality to existing Protégé applications with minimal effort. Due to the large community of Protégé developers and users, in the long term this may help to spread the use of CBR technology in other AI communities.

The basic architecture of *myCBR* is illustrated in Figure 1. During the development phase of an CBR application, *myCBR* runs as a plug-in within Protégé. This plug-in consists of the following modules:

Modelling tools: These tools extend the existing functionality of Protégé for creating domain models and case instances and add the missing functionality for defining similarity measures.

Retrieval GUI: The retrieval GUI provides powerful features for analyzing the quality of the defined similarity measures. Moreover, it can also serve as the user interface of first prototypical CBR applications.

Retrieval engines: For executing the similarity-based retrieval, different retrieval engines are provided.

Explainer: A dedicated explanation component provides modelling support information as well as explanations of retrieval results for quicker roundtrips of designing and testing (see also Section 4).

After installing and activating the *myCBR* plug-in, the user interface of Protégé is extended with additional tabs to access the *myCBR* modules. Figure 2 shows, for

---

[4] http://protege.stanford.edu/

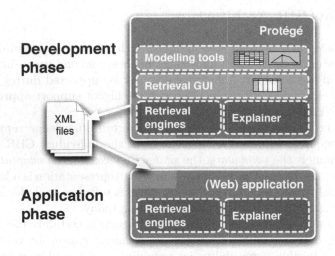

Fig. 1. The system architecture of *myCBR*

example, how the *myCBR* editor for configuring class specific similarity measures integrates into the Protégé environment consisting of class and slot browsers.

As a result of the modeling and development phase, the complete domain and similarity model together with the case base can be exported to XML files.

Although the *myCBR* Protégé plug-in already allows to create a full and running application, in many projects custom-made user interfaces and an integration of the CBR system into existing infrastructure is required. For this purpose, after developing a CBR application using the Protégé plug-in, *myCBR* can also be used as a stand-alone Java module, to be integrated in arbitrary applications, for example, JSP[5]-based web applications. In this application phase, the retrieval engines of *myCBR* just read the XML files generated during the previous development phase and perform the similarity-based retrieval.

End-users of the final *myCBR*-enhanced application can be further supported by providing explanations about the retrieval process.

3   Developing CBR Applications with *myCBR*

In this section we describe in more detail how *myCBR* supports rapid prototyping of CBR applications. This includes the generation of case representations, the definition of similarity measures, the testing of retrieval and use of explanation functionality, and finally the implementation of stand-alone applications.

3.1   CSV Data Import and Automatic Model Generation

The starting point of many CBR projects is the collection of initial case data. The existence of at least some case examples is usually a precondition for modeling an accurate case representation and corresponding similarity measures.

---

[5] Java Server Pages.

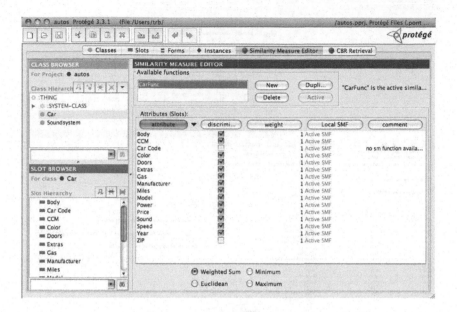

Fig. 2. The *myCBR* Protégé plug-in

myCBR is mainly intended for structural CBR applications that make use of rich attribute-value based or object-oriented case representations. Of course, since attribute values may also contain large parts of pure text, textual CBR applications are also supported by *myCBR*, but are not the main focus of the system. Although Protégé provides powerful graphical user interfaces for modeling attribute-value based and object-oriented representations, their manual definition remains a time consuming task. It includes the definition of classes and attributes (called "slots" in Protégé) and the specification of accurate value ranges required for a meaningful similarity assessment.

In order to facilitate the definition of case representations, *myCBR* provides a powerful CSV[6] data import module (see Figure 3.). CSV files are widely used to store attribute-value based raw data in pure ASCII format. For example, in the Machine Learning community example data sets are usually exchanged by using CSV files[7]. Using the CSV importer, the user has the choice to import data instances into an existing Protégé data model, or to create a new model automatically based on the raw data. In the latter case, *myCBR* generates a Protégé slot for each data column of the CSV file automatically. In order to achieve maximal flexibility, the CSV importer provides the following features:

Slot creation: The importer analyzes the whole CSV data in order to determine accurate value ranges for the slots automatically. For textual data, the user can specify a threshold on the number of unique values, in order to

---

[6] Comma Separated Values.

[7] See, for example, http://archive.ics.uci.edu/ml/

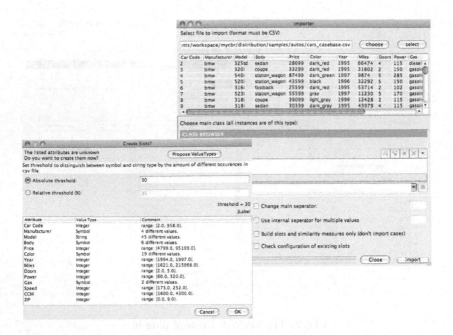

Fig. 3. The CVS data importer

control the generation of symbol and string slots. If a data column contains less unique values than specified, the slot becomes symbolic (with all found values as allowed symbols), otherwise it will be specified as a string slot.

Model Update: If a domain model is already existing, the CSV importer may update the model according to the data in the given CSV file. Then missing slots are created and value ranges of existing slots are updated once the data contains values that do not fit into the predefined ranges. This can also be done in a semi-automatic manner in order to investigate the differences between the data and the existing model in more detail.

Creation of Instances: The user can choose whether he wants to import the data by creating corresponding Protégé data instances or whether he wants to create the domain model only.

Specification of Column Separators: Since the use of column separators (comma, semicolon, etc.) is not standardized in CSV files, the user can specify the used separator prior to the import. By supporting a second level separator, *myCBR* is also able to import set attributes (attributes with multiple values).

After the CSV data has been imported, the user may further modify the generated case model (e.g. extend it to an object-oriented representation) in order to meet the application specific needs. The final case model together with the case base is stored by *myCBR* in XML files.

3.2   Modeling Similarity Measures

After having generated the case representation either by hand or by using the CSV importer, the main task for creating a CBR application with *myCBR* is the definition of an appropriate similarity measure. Here, *myCBR* follows the *local-global approach* which divides the similarity definition into a set of *local similarity measures* for each attribute, a set of *attribute weights*, and a *global similarity measure* for calculating the final similarity value. This means, for an attribute-value based case representation consisting of n attributes, the similarity between a query q and a case c may be calculated as follows:

$$Sim(q, c) = \sum_{i=1}^{n} w_i \cdot sim_i(q_i, c_i)$$

Here, sim_i and w_i denote the local similarity measure and the weight of attribute i, and Sim represents the global similarity measure. *myCBR* is also able to deal with more structured, object-oriented representations and supports suited global similarity measures as described in [8].

The editor for specifying global similarity measures was already shown in Figure 2. Besides the use of a weighted sum, the user can also choose another amalgamation function, i.e. the Euclidean distance. However, the most similarity knowledge is encoded in the attribute specific local similarity measures. For testing purposes and to ensure high flexibility, for both global and local similarity measures the user can define and manage a set of different measures. The measures that are currently marked as active are finally used for the retrieval.

In the following sections we give an overview of the various approaches for modeling local similarity measures depending on the value type of the underlying attribute.

Similarity Editors for Numeric Attributes. For numerical attributes, the similarity computation is typically based on a mapping between the distance of the two values to be compared and the desired similarity value:

$$sim_i(q_i, c_i) = f(d(q_i, c_i))$$

This means, the similarity modeling focuses on the definition of an accurate mapping function f for a given distance function d [5]. For d, *myCBR* provides two alternatives, either the absolute difference $d(q_i, c_i) = c_i - q_i$ or the quotient $d(q_i, c_i) = \frac{c_i}{q_i}$ of the two values. The latter one allows to model similarities depending on a kind of relative distance, however, its application is restricted to strict positive value ranges.

For modeling the mapping function f, *myCBR* provides two editing modes. In the *standard mode*, the user can choose between some typical and adjustable functions (e.g. step or asymptotic decreasing functions). In the *advanced mode*, arbitrary mapping functions can be linearly approximated by specifying a set of sampling points. These sampling points can be easily generated and manipulated by using drag and drop functionality in a graphical editor (see Figure 4).

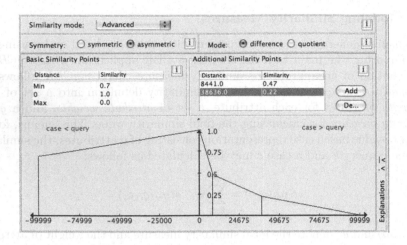

Fig. 4. The advanced similarity editor for numerical attributes

Similarity Editors for Symbolic Attributes. For symbolic attributes, several possibilities to model the similarity are supported. The most general and flexible way is the definition of a *similarity table* where all pairwise value combinations together with their similarities are enumerated explicitly (see Figure 5a). In order to make the editing as comfortable as possible, *myCBR* performs similarity highlighting (similarity values are visualized by different cell colors) and supports multiple cell selection.

However, for larger value sets the definition of similarity tables remains a time consuming and annoying task. Therefore, *myCBR* supports more comfortable approaches for defining similarities on symbolic values. The first one is the definition of a total *order* on symbols which allows to model the similarity like for numerical values by just using their position in the order. The second and more sophisticated approach is the arrangement of symbols in a *taxonomy* by using comfortable drag and drop functionality (see Figure 5b). Once the taxonomy and its application specific meaning is specified, it can be deployed to perform automatic similarity calculations (for details of this approach see [9]).

The user may start with the order or taxonomy approach to obtain a first similarity measure very quickly. In order to ensure maximal flexibility, *myCBR* supports the refinement of the similarity measure by switching to the table mode. Now the user may change some of the precalculated similarity values for considering his application specific needs.

Similarity Editors for String Attributes. Although textual CBR is not the main focus of the *myCBR* system, it provides flexible similarity measures for string processing. First, the user may choose between word or character-based processing modes. Depending on the selected mode, various approaches and configurations to specify the actual similarity calculation are provided, e.g. exact and partial matches, trigram matching, or regular expression based comparisons.

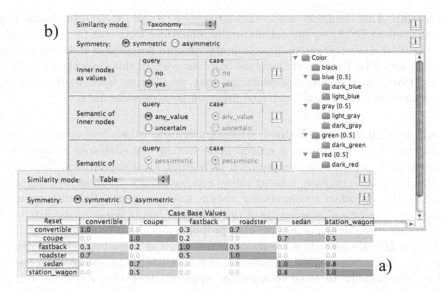

Fig. 5. Similarity editors for symbolic attributes: similarity table (a) and taxonomy editor (b)

Similarity Editors for Set Attributes. Attributes that allow multiple values (either numerical or symbolic) are a powerful concept for representing weakly structured knowledge. However, the similarity calculation for such set attributes is much more complex compared with single values. This concerns the computation complexity as well as conceptional issues. In general, the semantic of the comparison of set values is extremely application specific. For example, a set of values may have a kind of "and" or a kind of "or" semantic. Moreover, the size of the query and case sets may have different influences on the similarity.

myCBR provides various options to configure similarity measures for set attributes. Depending on the chosen settings, the mapping between query values and case values is calculated differently. For example, one might want to match each query value with be best suited case values or vice versa. Moreover, query/case values that could not be matched to a case/query value (e.g. because the query contains more values than the case) may have a different impact on the final similarity. Once the desired mapping is determined, the final similarity computation is based on the basic similarity measures defined for the atomic values of the sets. Depending on the data type, here the previously described editors can be used.

Script-Based and External Similarity Measures. In order to obtain maximal flexibility, for all kind of data types two additional similarity modes are provided:

Script: *myCBR* includes a Jython[8] binding and corresponding editors that allow the user to write own similarity measures in an easy to learn scripting language.

---

[8] Jython is a Java-based scripting language with the same syntax than Python; for details see http://www.jython.org/Project/index.html

External: This similarity mode allows the user to call external programs (e.g. written in C/C++) for calculating similarities. This can be in particular useful, if computation intensive calculations are required or if data types not supported by Protégé are involved (e.g. images). In this case, the underlying attribute in the case representation may provide an URL to the external data source used by the external program to access the data.

Dealing with Missing Values. Missing attribute values (either in the query or in the cases) are always a crucial issue during the similarity computation because they prevent the computation of regular local similarities. Depending on the application domain, missing values can have quite different meanings. For example, in a product recommender system missing query attributes typically represent "don't care" statements of the customer, while missing case attributes correspond to unknown or not existing properties of the products.

In *myCBR* missing values are always represented as *special values*. The default special value is "_undefined_", however, the user is able to specify own special values additionally. In order to cover the application specific requirements, the influence of each special value on the similarity computation can be configured individually.

3.3   Testing of Retrieval Functionality

The definition of an optimal similarity measure is often a difficult and tricky task which requires repeatedly testing and fine tuning. For this purpose, *myCBR* includes a comfortable graphical user interface for performing retrievals and for analyzing the corresponding results in detail (see Figure 6). On the right hand side of the window an overview of the entire retrieval result is shown. In the center part of the GUI the query is opposed to a configurable number of retrieved cases. By providing similarity highlighting and explanation functionality (cf. Section 4), *myCBR* supports the efficient analysis of the outcome of the similarity computation.

The current version of *myCBR* provides two retrieval algorithms, a simple sequential retrieval and a basic case retrieval net [10].

3.4   Building a Stand-Alone Application

After having created and tested the CBR functionality using the *myCBR* Protégé plug-in, one may want to deploy that functionality in the scope of a particular application without relying on the Protégé framework. A typical use case for CBR systems are web-based applications, for example, to implement recommendation functionality in e-Commerce applications.

myCBR provides a Java API which allows easy integration of the retrieval functionality into arbitrary Java applications without requiring a Protégé installation. Using JSP a few lines of code are sufficient to implement a simple web-based CBR application with custom-made user interfaces. An example of such a web-based application is shown in Figure 7.

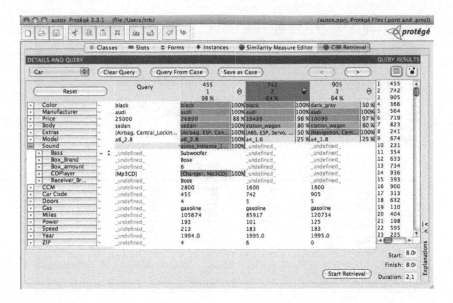

Fig. 6. Retrieval result with attribute values sorted in descending order of similarity values. Note the decreasing highlighting of cells corresponding to local similarity.

During the stand-alone operation of *myCBR* the XML files generated by the Protégé plug-in serve as source for obtaining the similarity model, the configuration options, and the case base. If certain maintenance operations are necessary, the XML files may be updated by using the Protégé plug-in again, or application specific modules may change the XML files directly, for example, to store new or to delete obsolete cases.

4   Explanation Functionality

Ease-of-use as well as approachability of any software system is improved by increasing its understandability, which in turn can be supported by appropriate explanation capabilities [11]. We follow Schank [12] in considering explanations the most common method used by humans to support understanding and their decision making. In everyday human-human interactions explanations are an important vehicle to convey information in order to understand one another. Explanations enhance the knowledge of the communication partners in such a way that they accept certain statements. They understand more, allowing them to make informed decisions.

This communication-oriented view leads to the following explanation scenario comprising three participants (Figure 8). First, the originator that is a system or an agent that provides something to be explained, e.g., the solution to some problem, a technical device, a plan, a decision etc. In our case, the originator comprises the modelling tools and the retrieval engines of *myCBR*. Second, the user who is the addressee of the explanation. Third, the explainer who presents

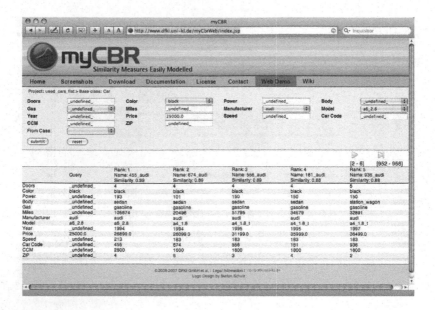

Fig. 7. A *myCBR* web demo application (see also http://www.myCBR-project.net)

the explanation to the user. This agent is interested in transferring the intention of the originator to the user as correct as possible. The explainer chooses the kind of the explanation [13] and is responsible for the computational aspects as well as for organising a dialog if needed. Originator and explainer need to work together rather tightly to improve the communication with the user. The originator needs to provide the appropriate information in order to allow the explainer constructing appropriate explanations.

In order to support the communication scenario described above, *myCBR* provides two general kinds of explanations: forward and backward explanations. *Forward explanations* explain indirectly, presenting different ways of optimizing a given result and opening up possibilities for the exploratory use of a device or application. *Backward explanations* explain the results of a process and how they were generated. Details and technical aspects of how the explanation component works are available in [14].

In order to increase transparency of and trust in the retrieval process [15], *myCBR* creates an explanation object for each case during similarity calculation. This tree-like data structure stores global and local similarity values as comments for each attribute. These retrieval details are presented to the user in the retrieval GUI (Figure 6) either as tool tips or in abbreviated form along with the case's attribute value, e.g., the price of car offer 455 (26,899) is 88% similar to the requested car price (25,000). Another valuable feature is the option to find the most similar cases with respect to a single attribute by simply clicking on the attribute name (row head). In attribute rich cases one might also want to sort the local similarity values of one case in ascending or descending order. This can simply be achieved by clicking on the respective case name (column head).

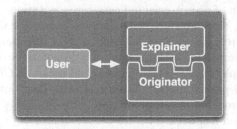

Fig. 8. Participants in explanation scenario

While developing a CBR system an important question is whether a similarity measure leads to the appropriate cases for a given query. Forward explanations (not depicted in the screenshots) help predicting the behavior of the system during modeling time and explain the interdependencies between the similarity measure and the case base. For this, a central explanation component analyzes the case base and gathers statistical information. The distribution of values in the case base can already be quite helpful and may reveal parts of similarity measures that are in fact never used (assuming that the case base covers most of possible queries). Or they reveal missing border cases, which is important for exception treatment.

5   Conclusion and Outlook

In this paper we have presented a novel, freely available CBR tool that supports rapid prototyping of advanced retrieval-based CBR applications. By providing powerful but still easy-to-use model generation, data import, similarity modeling, explanation, and testing functionality, *myCBR* enables even CBR novices to rapidly create their first CBR applications.

Nevertheless, at the same time the support of object-oriented case representations, advanced similarity editors, various configuration options, integration of a scripting language, and the possibility to call custom-made external modules ensures very high flexibility in order to fit also the requirements of expert users and complex application domains.

In focusing on the similarity-based retrieval step, *myCBR* differs from the JColibri system which aims to cover the entire CBR cycle in a flexible way. However, JColibri does not provide comparable graphical user interfaces for defining knowledge-intensive similarity measures but requires to program them by hand. In the future, an integration of both Open Source systems in order to benefit of the advantages of both might be worth to be considered.

myCBR is still an ongoing project and several extensions of the system are already planned or are even already under development. In order to facilitate the work with more structured, object-oriented case representations and to improve the interoperability with existing IT infrastructure, one of the next steps is the implementation of an interface for accessing relational database management systems. This interface will provide an advanced data importer which enables automatic generation of object-oriented case representations similar to the CSV importer. Moreover, this interface will allow to retrieve cases directly from a database instead of relying on XML files for storing case bases.

Another planned extension is the implementation of a rule engine for providing adaptation and completion rules [16]. This would make *myCBR* to a full-fledged CBR system beyond pure similarity-based retrieval. Last but not least, we plan to integrate our approaches to automatically learn similarity measures based on given user/application feedback [17].

We also encourage other researchers to try out *myCBR* in their own research and teaching projects and to contribute to the further development by implementing their own extensions and experimental modules.

Acknowledgements

The authors would like to thank Daniel Bahls, Andreas Rumpf, and Laura Zilles for their great implementation work and all the valuable discussions during the development of the *myCBR* system. This work was partially funded by the federal state Rhineland-Palatinate under the project ADIB (Adaptive Provision of Information).

References

1. Bello-Tomás, J., González-Calero, P.A., Díaz-Agudo, B.: JColibri: An Object-Oriented Framework for Building CBR Systems. In: Proceedings of the 7th European Conference on Case-Based Reasoning. Springer, Heidelberg (2004)
2. Schulz, S.: CBR-Works - A State-of-the-Art Shell for Case-Based Application Building. In: Proceedings of the 7th German Workshop on Case-Based Reasoning (GWCBR 1999) (1999)
3. Aamodt, A., Plaza, E.: Case-based Reasoning: Foundational Issues, Methodological Variations, and System Approaches. AI Communications 7(1), 39–59 (1994)
4. Bridge, D., Göker, M.H., McGinty, L., Smyth, B.: Case-based recommender systems. Knowledge Engineering Review 20(3) (2006)
5. Stahl, A.: Learning of Knowledge-Intensive Similarity Measures in Case-Based Reasoning, Dissertation.de, vol. 986 (2004)
6. Richter, M.M.: The Knowledge Contained in Similarity Measures. In: ICCBR 1995 (1995)
7. Gennari, J.H., Musen, M.A., Fergerson, R.W., Grosso, W.E., Crubézy, M., Eriksson, H., Noy, N.F., Tu, S.W.: The evolution of Protégé an environment for knowledge-based systems development. J. Hum.-Comput. Stud. 58(1), 89–123 (2003)
8. Bergmann, R., Stahl, A.: Similarity Measures for Object-Oriented Case Representations. In: Smyth, B., Cunningham, P. (eds.) EWCBR 1998. LNCS (LNAI), vol. 1488. Springer, Heidelberg (1998)
9. Bergmann, R.: On the Use of Taxonomies for Representing Case Features and Local Similarity Measures. In: Proceedings of the 6th German Workshop on Case-Based Reasoning (GWCBR 1998) (1998)

10. Lenz, M.: Case Retrieval Nets as a Model for Building Flexible Information Systems. Ph.D. Thesis, Humboldt University Berlin (1999)
11. Roth-Berghofer, T.R.: Explanations and Case-Based Reasoning: Foundational issues. In: Funk, P., González-Calero, P.A. (eds.) Advances in Case-Based Reasoning, pp. 389–403. Springer, Heidelberg (2004)
12. Schank, R.C.: Explanation Patterns: Understanding Mechanically and Creatively. Lawrence Erlbaum Associates, Hillsdale (1986)
13. Roth-Berghofer, T., Cassens, J., Sørmo, F.: Goals and kinds of explanations in case-based reasoning. In: Althoff, K.D., Dengel, A., Bergmann, R., Nick, M., Roth-Berghofer, T. (eds.) WM 2005: Professional Knowledge Management, Kaiserslautern, Germany, DFKI GmbH, pp. 264–268 (2005)
14. Bahls, D.: Explanation support for the case-based reasoning tool MYCBR. Project thesis, University of Kaiserslautern (2008)
15. Roth-Berghofer, T.R., Cassens, J.: Mapping goals and kinds of explanations to the knowledge containers of case-based reasoning systems. In: Muñoz-Ávila, H., Ricci, F. (eds.) ICCBR 2005. LNCS (LNAI), vol. 3620, pp. 451–464. Springer, Heidelberg (2005)
16. Bergmann, R., Wilke, W., Vollrath, I., Wess, S.: Integrating General Knowledge with Object-Oriented Case Representation and Reasoning. In: Proceedings of the 4th German Workshop on Case-Based Reasoning (GWCBR 1996) (1996)
17. Stahl, A., Gabel, T.: Using Evolution Programs to Learn Local Similarity Measures. In: Proceedings of the 5th International Conference on CBR. Springer, Heidelberg (2003)

Author Index

Lecture Notes in Artificial Intelligence (LNAI)